The politics of race, class and nationalism in twentieth-century South Africa

Related Longman titles:

Shula Marks and Anthony Atmore (eds)
Economy and Society in pre-industrial South Africa

Shula Marks and Richard Rathbone (eds)
Industrialisation and social change in South Africa: African class formation, culture and consciousness, 1870–1930

The politics of race, class and nationalism in twentieth-century South Africa

EDITED BY
Shula Marks and Stanley Trapido

London and New York

Longman Group UK Limited,
Longman House, Burnt Mill, Harlow,
Essex CM20 2JE, England
Associated Companies throughout the world.

*Published in the United States of America
by Longman Inc., New York*

First published 1987

British Library Cataloguing in Publication Data

The Politics of race, class and nationalism
  in twentieth century South Africa.
  1. Nationalism—South Africa—
  History—20th century   2. South Africa
  —Politics and government—20th
  century.
  I. Marks, Shula   II. Trapido, Stanley
  320.5′4′0968   DT770
  ISBN 0-582-64490-9

Library of Congress Cataloging-in-Publication Data

The Politics of race, class, and nationalism in
  twentieth-century South Africa.

  Bibliography: p.
  Includes index.
  1. Ethnology—South Africa. 2. Ethnicity—
South Africa. 3. South Africa—Ethnic relations.
4. South Africa—Politics and government—20th century.
5. South Africa—Economic conditions. I. Marks, Shula.
II. Trapido, Stanley.
DT763.P72 1987   320.5′4′0968   86–27554
ISBN 0–582–64490–9 (pbk.)

Set in 10 on 12 pt Linotron Garamond
Produced by Longman Singapore Publishers (Pte) Ltd.
Printed in Singapore

Contents

List of Tables

List of Abbreviations

AAC	All African Convention
AB	Administration Board
AFCWU	African Food and Canning Workers' Union
AHI	Afrikaanse Handelsinstituut (Afrikaner Chamber of Commerce)
ALDCWU	African Laundry, Dyers and Cleaning Workers' Union
AMEC	African Methodist Episcopal Church
ANC	African National Congress
AOC	African Orthodox Church
APO	African Peoples' Organisation
ASB	Afrikaanse Studente Bond (Afrikaner Student Association)
ATG	Afrikaanse Taalgenootskap
ATV	Afrikaanse Taalvereeniging
ATWIU	African Textile Workers' Industrial Union
BENSO	Buro Vir Ekonomiese Navorsing, Samewerking en Ontwikkeling (Bureau for Economic Research, Co-operation and Development)
BTI	Board of Trade and Industry
CATA	Cape African Teachers' Association
CBIA	Colonial Born Indian Association
CBSIA	Colonial Born and Settlers Indian Association
CC	Chief Commissioner
CIIR	Catholic Institute for International Relations
CNETU	Council for Non-European Trade Unions
CNO	Christelike Nasionale Onderwys (Christian National Education)

CO	Colonial Office
CPA	Church of the Province Archives, University of the Witwatersrand
CPSA	Communist Party of South Africa
ERPM	East Rand Proprietary Mines
FAK	Federasie van Afrikaanse Kultuurvereenigings
FCWU	Food and Canning Workers' Union
FIOSA	Fourth International of South Africa
FOFATUSA	Federation of Free Trade Unions of South Africa
FSAW	Federation of South African Women
GDP	Gross Domestic Product
GRA	Genootskap van Regte Afrikaners – Fellowship of True Afrikaners
GWU	Garment Workers' Union
GNP	Gesuiwerde Nasionale Party
ICU	Industrial and Commercial Workers' Union
IDC	Industrial Development Corporation
IMF	International Monetary Fund
INC	Indian National Congress
JAH	*Journal of African History*
JSAS	*Journal of Southern African Studies*
LB	Labour Bureau
LDCWU	Laundry, Dyers and Cleaning Workers' Union
NA	Natal Archives
NAD	Native Affairs Department
NEC	Native Economic Commission
NEUF	Non-European United Front
NEUM	Non-European Unity Movement
NGR	Natal Government Railway
NIA	Natal Indian Association
NP	National Party
PAC	Pan-Africanist Congress
PFP	Progressive Federal Party
PRO	Public Record Office
PSA	Pretoria State Archives
SABC	South African Broadcasting Corporation
SABRE	South African Bureau for African Affairs
SACPO	South African Coloured Peoples' Congress (Organisation)
SACTU	South African Congress of Trade Unions
SAGA	South African Government Archives

SAIC	South African Indian Congress
SAIRR	South African Institute of Race Relations
SAJS	*South African Journal of Science*
SANLAM	Suid-Afrikaanse Lewensassuransie Maatskappy (South African National Life Assurance Company)
SANLC	South African Native Labour Contingent
SAP	South African Party
SATLC	South African Trades and Labour Council
SATUC	South Africa Trade Union Council
SOAS	School of Oriental and African Studies
SSRC	Social Science Research Council
TARC	Train Apartheid Resistance Committee
TG	Transvaal Government
TIC	Transvaal Indian Congress
TOB	Transkeian Organised Bodies
TUCSA	Trade Union Council of South Africa
TWIU	Textile Workers' Industrial Union
UCTL	University of Cape Town Library
UG	Union Government
UWL	University of the Witwatersrand Library
WHO	World Health Organisation

Preface

The chapters in this collection address the issues of ethnic boundary-making and the construction of nationalist ideologies and political consciousness against South Africa's changing political economy and class composition since the era of the mineral discoveries in the late nineteenth century.

The volume begins with Saul Dubow's delineation of the evolution of a hegemonic segregationist ideology, and is followed by a chapter by Isabel Hofmeyr which analyses the 'invention' of 'Afrikaner' culture in the early twentieth century. Iris Berger explores the class consciousness of white women workers in the Garment Workers' Union as an alternative to Afrikaner nationalist identification which none the less did not wholly escape the racism institutionalised by the state. Ian Goldin looks at the state's intervention in the definition of 'Coloured' ethnic identity, while Maureen Swan looks at two moments in the radicalisation of Indian political movements in South Africa. These four chapters are followed by a cluster of essays on the making of African nationalist consciousness; Robert Hill and Gregory Pirio examine the role of Garveyism in the creation of an Africanist ideology which permeated all black political organisations in the 1920s; Colin Bundy discusses the relationship of both nationalists and radicals to the agrarian question; William Beinart considers the relationship of migrant workers to rural social and urban political networks; and Tom Lodge uses a case study of urban political conflict to examine the nature of African nationalism in the 1950s. In another case study, Phil Bonner and Rob Lambert analyse ethnicity and class on the East Rand in the 1950s in the light of the Amato textile strike of 1959. The last three chapters by Brian Hackland, Stanley Greenberg and Deborah

Posel deal with the response of capital, the state and the opposition Progressive Party to the increasing economic strains confronting the Republic over the last decade, and the rising tide of black opposition, and its changed geo-political situation.

The editors would like to thank Bryony Mortimer for compiling the index, the American Social Science Research Council and the authors for their patience, and Dr Richard Rathbone for his perceptive comments on the draft introduction.

Acknowledgement

This volume, and the conference upon which it is based, were sponsored by the Joint Committee on African Studies of the American Council of Learned Societies and the Social Science Research Council.

CHAPTER ONE

The politics of race, class and nationalism

Shula Marks and Stanley Trapido

Recent turbulence in South Africa makes the study of its racially divided social order and its national and ethnic heterogeneity an urgent intellectual and political task. For much of the twentieth century, an exclusive form of white Afrikaner nationalism, with its explicit objective the capture of the state by the white Afrikaner 'nation', has confronted its counterpart, a pan-South African black nationalism, which has sought the incorporation of Africans into the body politic. The exclusivism of Afrikaner Christian nationalism with its roots in late-nineteenth-century European nationalism has been confronted by a black nationalism which, despite strong Africanist underpinnings, has in general espoused the nineteenth-century liberal values of multiracialism. Moreover, the salience of 'national' and 'racial' identity for South African state policies and its deliberate manipulation of group differences to prevent interracial class solidarity have shaped the ethnic consciousness of minority groups such as Coloureds or Indians. These groups have in turn constructed their own sense of community, in part by way of response.

Given the complexity of political consciousness and community construction in twentieth-century South Africa, it would be impossible for this collection of essays to provide anything like comprehensive coverage. Nevertheless, the range is considerable. In this introduction we hope to provide the historical and historiographical context of the collected essays, and to show their connections. This is no easy matter in the absence of any satisfactory synthesis of twentieth-century South African history. Nor is it easy to discuss developments in the economy and the state which affected all groups and at the same time to trace their separate trajectories. We have tried to do this through providing a continuous historical account into which we have woven, where appropriate, some of the main insights provided in the essays.

It is not often realised how recent 'national' identifications in South Africa are. In the case of both Afrikaner and African nationalism, Geoffrey Eley's remarks made of European nationalism, are equally appropriate:

> The incidence of 'patriotic activity' in a society first among the intelligentsia and then among the masses 'can most convincingly be related to some complex combination' of economic development, a distinctive social structure, a strong sense of cultural identity, the development of communications, improved literacy and the spread of new levels of socio-political organisation into previously isolated rural communities.[1]

Thus, in South Africa both black and white nationalism can in large measure be seen as responses to late-nineteenth-century industrialisation, imperialism and British 'race patriotism'. Although there is no automatic and immediate relationship, transformations of the economy have led to shifts in the nature of ideologies as the material basis for belief systems have changed. The successive moves of the South African economy from the dominance of merchant capital to mineral exploitation, secondary industrialisation and monopolisation, although regionally varied and uneven, have profoundly affected not only the experience of daily life but also the ways in which men and women have understood their world and their highly differentiated place in it. A multiplicity of strands have constituted the fabric of their understanding, as the more 'structured' ideas of the ruling class and intelligentsia, often shaped by British, European and American ideologies, have interacted with diffuse and heterogeneous popular beliefs.[2]

For all the peoples of South Africa, new ethnic identities emerged around 1910 when the state was being constructed as a single entity out of the British colonies, the conquered Afrikaner republics and African kingdoms in the region. That this unification did not lead to a single pan-South African, pan-ethnic nationalism was the outcome of a history of regional divisions, the racism and social Darwinism of the late nineteenth century and the specific political-cum-class struggles which were being legitimated by the discourse of nationalism. Despite their numerical inferiority in the new Union, it was English-speaking South Africans who dominated the twentieth-century political economy of South Africa, as they had the nineteenth. For them nationalism was an alien and perhaps unnecessary ideology. Continuing ties of language and kinship to Britain reinforced by economic self-interest meant that despite a sporadic South Africanism the sense of English-speaking identity was based on far more diffuse notions of racial and political identity. Confronted with the economic domination of English-speakers, the Afrikaner objective came to be the capture of the state through ethnic mobilisation.

While for Afrikaners the twentieth century has seen the development of a fully-fledged nationalist movement, for other minorities such as the Indians and Coloureds (and even Jews), what was constructed in these years were, in Benedict Anderson's evocative phrase, new 'imagined communities'.[3] Neither they, nor the weak African intelligentsia who constituted the African National Congress (ANC)[4] could have hoped to 'capture' the state. Coloureds and Indians living in the regionally discrete micro-economies of the Western Cape and Natal, could do little beyond mobilising along ethnic networks of loyalty, allegiance and control, unless they could find some way of uniting with other 'blacks', as happened in the 1920s in the Western Cape, or again with the alliances of the 1950s, and with the rise of a black consciousness movement from the late 1960s.

I

In the 1870s at the beginning of the mineral revolution, South Africa was a geographical expression. Precapitalist and capitalist modes of production existed side by side, as did state forms of varying size with their own ruling groups and systems of exploitation. There were two British colonies, two ostensibly politically independent republics and numerous still autonomous African polities. All of these were multi-ethnic and multilingual, although not all languages and ethnicities were equal. Colonists of British and European descent lived side by side in the colonies with large numbers of indigenous peoples, and in Natal with indentured labourers from the Indian subcontinent; African kingdoms were equally heterogeneous entities, composed of people of different origin.

Probably the strongest and most coherent indigenous political entity was the Zulu kingdom, itself a fairly recent creation out of the numerous and linguistically diverse chiefdoms north of the Tugela, with a highly developed sense of political identity and history, sharpened in the conflicts with Boer and Briton in the late nineteenth century. There is also, however, much evidence of an awakening self-consciousness among such people as the Xhosa who had confronted settler expansionism and British troops for almost a century, or the Basotho kingdom which had been established by Moshoeshoe out of peoples fragmented during the wars of the *difaqane*.[5] These elements of resistance were to be drawn on in the construction of both pan-

South African black nationalism and ethnic identities in the twentieth century, although one must be careful of reading fully-fledged ethnic identities back to some primordial 'tribe'. As a number of recent authors on ethnicity in Africa have stressed, by and large ethnicity like nationalism is a modern phenomenon, dependent on the emergence of a new intermediary class, with a vested interest in the local vernacular (often defined in collusion with missionaries) and aware of wider horizons. Their task in forging ethnic consciousness was, however, made far easier when more centralised historical political entities provided the basis of their 'inventions'.[6]

Whatever their political and economic differences in the second half of the nineteenth century, all the peoples of southern Africa existed to a greater or lesser extent under the hegemony of a mainly British merchant capitalism and a British imperialism. The British were willing to give power to local ruling groups, but also prepared to intervene in protecting their economic and strategic interests when these were threatened. The economic basis of settler societies was agricultural production linked to the world economy. The discovery of diamonds in Kimberley in 1868, and gold on the Witwatersrand in 1886, accelerated the pace of change and brought a new form of industrial capitalism to the very heart of the region. This in turn wrought far-reaching political, social and ideological transformations.[7]

Throughout the nineteenth century the omnipresence of the imperial power gave a special position to English-speaking settlers, with their closer ties to a powerful metropole and its economic, technological and ideological resources. Like the economic and technological resources, the ideological resources changed over time. The earlier part of the century saw the dominance of a liberal incorporationist strategy, based on the belief in the ultimate assimilability of indigenous peoples – whether white or black. Political debate in England suggested that incorporation through the extension of the franchise was a cheaper and more effective mode of controlling lower-class militancy than outright coercion.[8]

The mid-nineteenth century was a time of profound rural discontent in the Cape. Rebellion in the Kat River settlement and war on the eastern frontier was paralleled by the threat of insurrection in the Western Cape against the passage of new anti-squatting legislation.[9] In this context, the decision to opt for a low rather than a high non-racial franchise when the Cape was granted representative government in 1853 had much to do with 'a struggle to get particular classes of the lower orders into the meaning of the Act . . .', as the Governor pointed out at the time.[10] William Porter, the Cape Attorney-General was similarly aware of the need to extend political institutions to both black and white. The Coloured people, he said, were like the Dutch-speaking population unschooled in parliamentary practice, yet were capable of exercising the franchise. If Coloureds were a dangerous political group, Porter argued that the best way to disarm them politically would be to give them the franchise. He observed, 'I would rather meet the Hottentot at the hustings voting for his representative than meet the Hottentot in the wilds with his gun upon his shoulder.'[11]

This incorporative strategy, initially intended for the Coloured and Dutch-speaking inhabitants of the Cape was later to include numbers of Bantu-speaking Africans as their territories were annexed by the Colony. The strategy was firmly rooted in the changes which took place in the Cape economy under British rule. Already by the mid-nineteenth century, the creation of a class of indigenous black peasant producers who could supply raw materials for the British merchants and constitute a growing consumer market for their goods provided both the basis and the necessity for such a strategy.[12] By the late nineteenth century it was accepted as much by the Cape Dutch as by English-speakers. Thus, when a delegate to the Afrikaner Bond Conference proposed the removal of Coloured men from the voters' roll, discussion on the subject was brought to a hurried end when J. H. Neethling asked, 'What would be said throughout the world if it were made known that on the 15 March 1890, the Afrikaner Bond had passed such a resolution as this?[13] Belief in the Cape franchise was accompanied by an ideological package which stressed the virtues of free wage labour, secure property rights linked to a free market in land and individual tenure, equality before the law and some notion of 'no taxation without representation'. 'Progress' and 'improvements' were its watchwords.[14]

For white liberals none of this contradicted their belief that the majority of blacks constituted a vast pool of labour available for their exploitation. In this they were at one with the Cape Dutch and Boers of the interior. Unlike the merchants, professional class and English-speaking officials, the latter had little interest in seeing Africans as producers in their own right. While liberals tended to see society in class terms, and to envisage the incorporation of a minority of blacks into the colonial order (at least in theory), the majority of settlers made little distinction between colour and class. The ambiguities were well expressed by J. Angove in an account of the early days in Griqualand West. In a chapter entitled 'The diamond fields as a school in which

Natives are taught the theory of modern civilisation', he argued that in Kimberley, 'we ... see ... just and equal laws are administered, and freedom of labour as well as of capital are elements of prosperity in Africa as well as in Europe'. 'It must be acknowledged', he continued, 'that teaching the Natives the dignity of labour, which is done in the compounds of de Beers Consolidated Mines, prepares the way for the missionary in teaching them all the principles of Christianity'.[15]

Whatever the controlling purpose and ambiguities of the incorporationist strategy, for the emerging black petty bourgeoisie it opened up unintended political opportunity and real material benefits. The expansion of Christianity and mission education in the Eastern Cape from the 1820s (and in Natal in the following decade) had led, by the last quarter of the century, to the emergence of a clearly defined group of Africans who identified themselves with British liberal values and hoped for incorporation in the colonial order. Although the spate of wars in the late 1870s laid strains on their aspirations, and the extent to which they accepted the norms of imperial hegemony has been exaggerated, their response to these tensions was in part to make use of the electoral machinery provided by the Cape colonial government.[16] As early as 1880, they had formed the Native Educational Association and by 1882 an association apparently modelled on and in response to the formation of the Afrikaner Bond,[17] the Ibumba Yama Nyama, had been formed in Port Elizabeth which 'aimed to unite Africans in political matters so they could band together in fighting for national rights'.[18] During the 1880s, after the manifest lack of success of armed struggle, the registration of African voters, 'snowballed'.[19] Cape liberalism continued to provide a powerful counter-ideology for the black intelligentsia, through at least the first half of the twentieth century, long after it had been abandoned by the ruling class.

For the latter, by the late nineteenth century, 'scientific racism', which is addressed by Saul Dubow in Chapter Two, began to undermine the earlier more optimistic assimilationist ideology. It is no coincidence that 'scientific racism', which held that biological differences determined the 'natural capacities and destinies of racial groups', gained an increasing hold as large numbers of 'tribal' Africans were conquered and brought under Cape colonial rule. The liberal incorporationist strategy was always based on the assumption of the superiority of 'Western civilisation' and a somewhat superficial understanding of the processes of individual assimilation. The prospect of being 'swamped' by the 'tribal' African peoples who were manifestly less amenable to the 'civilising mission' eroded any confident belief in the inevitability of human progress.

With the mineral discoveries in the last third of the nineteenth century, moreover, social Darwinism became a powerful legitimating tool.[20] As in Britain and the United States of America, the post-Darwinian conception that the contest of human races entailed a 'struggle for existence' leading to the survival or dominance of 'the fittest' became 'a late Victorian shibboleth', and provided a convenient rationalisation for denying political rights to the allegedly biologically 'inferior' black proletariat.[21] 'Scientific racism' only emerged as a fully-fledged colonial ideology in the early twentieth century, however: in the late nineteenth century it was simply assumed in the everyday discourse of domination. It suffused a developing English-speaking South African identity, which assumed the British 'racial' superiority and imperial mission and which produced a certain ambiguity in the relationship between settlers themselves. As the century wore on there was a growing tendency to see the non-English settlers, who were contemptuously referred to as 'Boers', as members of an 'inferior race'. This was to reach its apogee in the jingoism which accompanied the struggles between the British and Afrikaners in the years before and during the South African War of 1899–1902.[22]

If any one individual epitomised British 'race patriotism' and the racial ideology of social control it was Lord Milner, High Commissioner of South Africa. The quotations are legion; here one, from a speech to the Johannesburg Municipal Congress in 1903, must suffice:

> The white man must rule because he is elevated by many, many steps above the black man . . . which it will take the latter centuries to climb and which it is quite possible that the vast bulk of the black population may never be able to climb at all. . . . One of the strongest arguments why the white man must rule is because that is the only possible means of gradually raising the black man, not to our level of civilisation – which it is doubtful whether he would ever attain – but up to a much higher level than that which he at present occupies.[23]

It was during the Milner reconstruction period that the utility of many earlier practices for an industrialising state were recognised: the allocation of African 'reserves' and their limitation; the control of urban influx through pass laws; the manipulation of chiefs as agents of the colonial state. These were consolidated into a segregationist policy and the guidelines for the future set out. Milner's programme has to be related to material conditions in South Africa at the beginning of the twentieth century. The attempts of the mining industry to wrest vast quantities of unskilled, cheap and coercible labour out of conquered African kingdoms on the one hand, and to find highly skilled workers

on the mining frontiers of the world, on the other, led to the development of an African migrant labour system and a stabilised, relatively
incorporated white working class. African lands which had been successfully defended against settler encroachment in the nineteenth
century could subsidise the welfare costs of the mining industry and
lower wages. Bolstered chiefly authority could help maintain social
control. The system could be justified in terms of the new terminology
of segregation drawn from the United States of America, which also
provided so many of the Rand's senior mining engineers. In South
Africa, unlike the United States, however, 'the language of physical
distance and removal' also disguised a system of labour control and the
exclusion of the mass of the proletariat from political power.[24]

The ideology of segregation did not only speak to the needs of the
mining industry. It addressed a number of different audiences. It
served white farmers demanding additional controls over their tenants
and labourers and white workers seeking protection from cheaper
black labour. It was an attractive solution for the white ruling class in
the face of the rapid urbanisation of poor whites and poor blacks, with
its increased possibilities of competition and conflict as well as miscegenation and a unified class struggle. Its doctrines even provided
opportunities for those Africans concerned to restore 'traditional'
authority, and for those Coloureds anxious to protect themselves
against being reduced to the status of Africans.[25]

That the segregationist solution emerged to solve the problems of
industrialisation was in a sense made possible ideologically through the
development of the ideas of 'scientific racism', social Darwinism and
eugenics. At the same time, it was also seen as a way of mitigating the
harsher effects of domination and the industrial revolution. Increasingly, as Dubow shows, white English-speaking intellectuals
realised that to accept the immutable inferiority of Africans was to
reduce 'native policy' to little more than repression. What was required
was a new synthesis of liberalism and 'scientific racism', which would
hold out the prospect of evolution for individual blacks while avoiding
genetic degeneration. By the 1920s, this synthesis was achieved by
employing the concept of 'culture' which had recently been reconstituted by the new academic discipline of social anthropology. This
provided an escape from both biological determinism and universalist
humanism, and reshaped older ideas of segregation. The revised concept rejected assimilation, yet permitted 'racial upliftment'.[26] Smuts's
1929 Oxford lectures may be seen as the quintessence of this mode of
thought. The African was neither 'essentially inferior', nor was he 'a

man and a brother'. Assimilation, while seeming to advance equality, would destroy 'his African system which was his highest good'. In place of repression or assimilation was 'differential development' or segregation.[27] In this discourse, segregation appeared to be beyond the realm of political dispute, supported by the empirical science of 'Native mentality', social anthropology.

Even while this solution was being offered, it was shown to be irredeemably flawed. Only total separation could hope to avoid domination, yet all the evidence seemed to point to its impracticality. As early as 1926 the Economic and Wage Commission commented on the impossibility of confining Africans to the reserves and excluding them from white-dominated economic activity.[28] Within liberal circles, the debate over segregation finally played itself out at the end of the 1930s when Alfred Hoernlé maintained that if the 'liberal spirit' were to prevail there would have to be a 'sundering or dissociation so complete as to destroy the very possibility of effective domination'. Hoernlé recognised that this had no chance of gaining political support and therefore 'no ultimate hope for the liberal spirit'.[29]

By the time English-speaking liberals recognised these limitations, however, their ideas had been taken up by a far wider group of segregationists, who had no such qualms since their concerns were wholly pragmatic. For them, the notion of African as 'child' deferred any decision about his political participation to a distant future. As J. B. M. Hertzog, the first Afrikaner nationalist Prime Minister remarked:

> As against the European the native stands as an eight-year-old against a man of mature experience. . . . Differences exist in ethnic nature, ethnic custom, ethnic development and civilization and these differences shall long exist. . . . When he achieves his majority in development and civilization, and stands on an equal level with the white man, his adulthood will be acknowledged. Then the time will have come to take his claim to political rights into consideration. . . .[30]

If Hertzog was happy to defer the solution of black–white relationships to an indeterminate future, G. N. Heaton Nicholls, leading spokesman for sugar-planting interests in Natal, perhaps drew the most explicit connections between the contemporary class struggle and segregationist policies. Nicholls, who developed his ideas of what he preferred to call 'adaptation' against the background of the rising black working-class and rural militancy of the 1920s, saw 'Bantu communalism' as the answer to 'Bantu communism'. As he wrote in 1931, an 'adaptionist policy' was necessary if assimilation which 'substituted class for race', and which would 'lead to the evolution of a native proletariat inspired by the usual antagonisms of a class war' were to be prevented.[31]

If Hertzog and Heaton Nicholls shared an instrumental approach to segregation, it is one of the ironies of South African history that by the late 1930s, liberal segregationist ideas were also being espoused by Afrikaner nationalist intellectuals. Drawing on not dissimilar European racist ideological traditions,[32] which they combined with their interpretation of Calvinist theology, they saw themselves as directly countering liberal and English-speaking hegemony. They substituted an Afrikaner 'race patriotism' for Milner's 'British race patriotism', and used it to mobilise a far wider constituency.

II

Modern Afrikaner nationalism, like so many other nationalisms, was constructed out of the older building blocks of language (though, as we shall see, it was only in the twentieth century that the local patois which were to become modern Afrikaans, were welded together), ethnic ties and religious affiliation. It can perhaps best be understood as a response to the social dislocations and problems posed by the uneven development of capitalism in South Africa, the direct outcome of the changes wrought by the mineral discoveries in the political economy of southern Africa and the imperial interventions that ensued. This nationalism evolved further under the impact of urbanisation and secondary industrialisation in the inter-war years. The contemporary development of an advanced Afrikaner capitalism has led to the transformation of its ideology and the fragmentation of a previously coherent nationalist movement.

For much of the nineteenth century in the Cape Colony, the British anticipated the incorporation of the earlier Dutch settler population into the colonial order even if this expectation was always more successful in relation to the urban élite than to the rural population. From the outset of British colonial rule at the Cape, the older Dutch mercantile bourgeoisie were given economic and political opportunities by the new administration. The growth of British-based export houses and banks saw their Anglicisation rather than their displacement. In the mid-century, *De Zuid-Afrikaan*, designed for the literate middle-class published in both Dutch and English. In the middle of the South African War, well after ideas of incorporation had been largely abandoned by the British, and with old allegiances severely strained, a leading Cape Afrikaner, Jacob de Villiers, who was to become acting Governor-General, could reflect:

You know how we have been brought up to love our Queen and admire the English nation and its institutions and that I am incapable of saying or doing anything seditious or disloyal.[33]

Yet even at its height the process of incorporation of the Cape Dutch was far from complete. In the 1850s *De Zuid-Afrikaan* felt compelled to express a sense of resentment against British rule and the arrogance of many of the leading British settlers.[34] For poorer Boers, particularly in the northern and eastern districts, English was an unknown foreign language and the annexation of the Cape was only grudgingly accepted. Although their language, culture, and religious institutions and beliefs were to suffer under British rule, they did not collapse and disappear. They survived at the local level with weak links between districts and regions, so that parochial peculiarities and political associations flourished.[35]

It was, in particular, the presbytery system of Dutch Reformed Church government which provided a forum for local politics, because British institutions and the use of English excluded the majority of Cape Dutch from public life. *Dominee* (minister) and *kerkraad* (church council) came to play a much enhanced role in local politics. It was the church's structure which afforded countrymen the opportunity to articulate and sometimes to press home their political needs, rather than its Calvinist doctrines, which, contrary to the conventional wisdom, were only to be elaborated rather later.[36] No doubt a providential language added conviction to local politics, but the claim to having God on their side was hardly unique. Thus, apart from its religious functions, the church became an arena for the marshalling of political resources in the secular world.

The church offered some of the few professional positions opened to the Cape Dutch. Although the majority of clergymen were still Netherlanders, supplemented more recently by Scotsmen, the church was beginning to offer, for the first time since its establishment at the Cape, a career open to the African-born settler. These clergymen, therefore, saw attempts at Anglicisation as a direct threat to their own place in society. To take communion in English – as became possible in the 1860s in Cape Town – was to threaten both the religious and political authority of the Dutch clergy. Yet, even within the Dutch Reformed Church there were those who advocated the phasing out of Dutch, despite the fact that in the rural areas English spread only slowly. As Hermann Giliomee has remarked, 'In general a majority in the DRC accepted British hegemony as a fact of life which guided their decisions in . . . coming to terms with the political order, although a substantial minority sought to protect the position of Dutch'.[37]

From this it can be seen that the very focus of Afrikaner nationalism and culture, the Afrikaans language, is a very recent phenomenon. As Isabel Hofmeyr shows in Chapter Three, it is very largely a twentieth-century construct, which grew out of a patois which until the late nineteenth century was associated with the labouring poor of town and countryside. Thus, to begin with, Afrikaans was a diverse set of Dutch regional dialects creolised by Khoisan (Hottentot and Bushman) and the Malayo–Portuguese languages spoken by slaves in the seventeenth- and eighteenth-century Cape Colony. Language reflected the inextricable connections between Dutch/Afrikaner settlers and those they called 'Kleurling' ('Coloured'), throughout the expansion of European settlement. The destruction of independent Khoisan bands and their incorporation into the settler economy as ivory hunters, cattle herders and domestic workers transmitted a substantial cultural and linguistic heritage, as did the presence of Asian and African slaves. By the nineteenth century the patois had several local forms in the regions of the Cape and the inland republics, which were not always mutually comprehensible. Everywhere, however, it was the language of exchange between masters and servants, and between the poor themselves, whether settler or 'Coloured'. The upper and middle classes, particularly those living in the Western Cape, spoke 'High Dutch', the language of church and Bible. The Cape Dutch also used English to a considerable extent, since it was the language of commerce, law and administration, as well as, increasingly, high culture.[38]

If English and High Dutch were the languages of the contractual world for men of property, the several variations of 'Afrikaans' provided, even for many of them, the language of daily communication. Nevertheless, there was widespread condescension among the upper classes for whom Afrikaans was a *Hotnotstaal* ('Hottentot' language) and a *kombuistaal* (a kitchen language). It was the achievement of the lower-middle-class intelligentsia that they reconstructed these vernaculars, eliminating those elements reflecting poverty and lower-class origins. Instead they manipulated the language and its literature to suit their cultural-cum-political tasks. In so doing, they not only transformed the language but also attempted to shape the entire cultural identity of the Dutch–Afrikaans population.[39]

The upper-class disdain for Afrikaans as well as the acceptance of English among the Cape Dutch was supported by the prosperity which the imperial connection brought them in the nineteenth century. Yet this prosperity also led to the growth of a new class of educated men for whom there was a less certain niche. Britons dominated in the administration and commerce, and gained the greatest advantage with the discovery of diamonds in 1867. Discriminated against in the more lucrative spheres of employment in commerce, law and government, the growing Cape Dutch intelligentsia took careers in journalism and teaching, and, as we have seen, increasingly in the Dutch Reformed Church ministry. Even in these vocations, however, they found themselves aggrieved. In 1865 Dutch was abolished as a medium of instruction in government schools and this meant that the new revenues from the diamond fields did not go into Dutch-speaking schools with their poorly paid *meesters*, but went instead to support the already well-endowed English-speaking schools. To add insult to injury, in 1874, the predominantly English-speaking Parliament proposed to remove the stipend which all clergymen had previously received. These government actions affected most severely the rural Dutch whose mobilisation had brought responsible government to the colony in 1872. The British annexation of the South African Republic, on top of earlier annexations of Basutoland (1868) and the diamond fields (1871) at the expense of their northern compatriots, further fuelled their sense of grievance.[40]

At the same time, responsible government created new institutions which could be used to further particular interests, and this spurred political organisation among all the Cape's peoples. The Cape Dutch were the first to form organisations beyond simple pressure groups. The story of S. J. du Toit and the Genootskap van Regte Afrikaners (Society of True Afrikaners) is well known, and does not need retelling here. Suffice it to say that this cultural body gave rise to the Afrikaner Bond, the first political organisation with a nationalist programme.[41]

The Bond in du Toit's conception produced a populist programme which advocated the establishment of a national bank and farmers' co-operatives, the boycotting of British commercial institutions and the channelling of state funds to Dutch enterprise and education. In the aftermath of the British annexation and then defeat in the Transvaal, du Toit's following, which was found among the poorer farmers and landless squatters of the Cape, accepted his radical vision. The stable Dutch-speaking landed upper classes of the Western Cape, however, had their own political organisation in the Boeren Beschermings Vereeniging led by J. H. Hofmeyr. They found much that was unacceptable in du Toit's schemes, but needed the electoral support of his following if they were to use the Cape Parliament to ensure themselves imperial markets, credit and troops. The two organisations were therefore merged. As enthusiasm over the Boer victory in the Transvaal waned, Hofmeyr gained the initiative and outmanoeuvred du Toit politically. Under his leadership, the Bond settled down to a parliamentary existence based on pragmatism, patronage and the development of Afrikaner nationalism within the British Empire. The contradictions were well expressed at a meeting to celebrate the Boer victory at Majuba in 1881 at which

> The English flag hung alongside those of the Transvaal and Holland, against a wall that also sported a portrait of the Boer leader at the Majuba Hill battle, General Joubert. T. Louw, MLA for Malmesbury, proposed [a toast to] the Gladstone ministry which had replaced Lord Beaconsfield's annexationist government.[42]

Despite his being superseded, du Toit's long-term contribution to the ideology, culture and political economy of Afrikaner nationalism was substantial. It was du Toit who elaborated a set of Calvinist principles for the nationalism he was offering those he called 'Afrikaners'. Thus, far from being an attribute of the earliest Dutch settlers, 'primitive Calvinism' was, as André du Toit has shown, a mythical construct brought into being in the specific conditions of late-nineteenth-century Cape parochial politics. S. J. du Toit's ideas were directly derived from Dutch neo-Calvinist theologians who formulated the doctrine of Christian Nationalism, which was so important in late-nineteenth-century Dutch politics.[43] From their notion of the absolute sovereignty of God in every sphere of life, to the demand for sovereign independence 'under one's own flag' required no great leap of the imagination. This was a convenient doctrine for du Toit to adapt, and to it he added his own notions of Afrikaner destiny as a Chosen People. This combination was to prove even more potent in the hands of Afrikaner nationalists in the 1930s and 1940s.

While initially du Toit's neo-Calvinism alienated both the church and the wealthier constituency of the Bond, his advocacy of Afrikaner economic institutions was more immediately acceptable. Hermann Giliomee has shown how the Stellenbosch District Bank became a local Cape Dutch institution as the municipality, the divisional council, the Afrikaner Bond and the Stellenbosch Agricultural Show all gave it their accounts. Those who failed to take up shares were accused of lacking in patriotism. Under the auspices of the bank and its major investors, two crucial Afrikaner nationalist projects were set in motion, the University of Stellenbosch and *De Burgher* newspaper.[44] The connections suggest some of the ways in which Cape Afrikaner nationalism and accumulation were to develop in the twentieth century.

Possibly du Toit's most immediate contribution to the political scene was his establishment of a newspaper, *Die Afrikaanse Patriot*. The paper was written in the Paarl dialect of Afrikaans, which du Toit declared was 'die taal van ons volk' (the language of our people). In it, he put forward his vision of white Afrikaners – whom he defined as all those 'who recognise Africa as their Fatherland' – as an 'organic nation'.[45]

The paper sold widely and had the second largest circulation among all Dutch–Afrikaans journals in the 1880s. According to Isabel Hofmeyr in Chapter Three, its readers were very largely the 'genteel poor' of the rural areas. They responded with enthusiasm to the *Patriot's* programme, setting up loosely related sets of cultural and language societies which kept the issue of the Afrikaans language in the foreground.[46]

The Cape language movement provided the model for a second Afrikaner national cultural project in the Transvaal at the turn of the century. White settlers in the interior of South Africa owed their origins to a movement beyond the confines of British rule known as the Great Trek. This movement has been at the heart of much Afrikaner nationalist myth-making. Yet it is important not to confuse the Great Trek with a clearly defined nationalism. Trekkers did not attempt to create a single nation-state in the interior of South Africa on the basis of their undoubted linguistic and ethnic links. Not only did they divide up into separate republican communities, but their once unified church also fragmented.[47] Despite a certain amount of local nationalist sentiment, which emerged at particular moments of heightened imperial intervention in the affairs of the interior, it was only after 1895 that the particularism of the republics gave way to a more sustained pan-South African Afrikaner nationalist movement.[48] Undoubtedly imperial aggression was crucial in this, but equally important was the formation of a new class of dissatisfied intellectuals.[49] Ironically they were given cultural stimulus by Kruger's 'Hollanders', who they felt stood in their way of office in the period before the South African War.

After the South African War, the nationalist movement gained momentum as a result of the Anglicising policies of the British regime which set out to exclude them from educational and administrative positions. The rising intelligentsia of teachers, clerics and journalists set up an alternative educational system, but received little financial or political support from the Boer notables, who were incorporated re-markably quickly into the new colony's political structures. If the intellectuals were to avoid being marginalised, they would have to mobilise wider political support.

Attempts to rally a popular movement, however, very quickly came up against the disruptive effects which capitalism – gold-mining and land alienation – and the war itself had had on Transvaal society. The impact of both was seriously to damage the ties which had bound the underclasses to landowners and clergy and which had sustained the social hierarchy of pre-war Boer society. A new population of workers and landless poor emerged out of the disintegrating old order. The war itself had shown the dangerous class cleavages in Dutch–Afrikaner society.[50] If the dispossessed poor and the new proletariat were to be recaptured for their cause, the social networks so essential to their mobilisation would have to be repaired and replaced. As so often, the need to create a new 'imagined community' arose at the moment of greatest external challenge and internal disintegration.

In some ways, the war and the period of post-war distress created an opportunity for the new intelligentsia. It forced them into proximity with the Afrikaner lower classes, and gave them insights into their plight. This proximity made efforts to alleviate distress natural enough, although the ministering petty bourgeoisie did so within the confines of, and were influenced by, the prevailing imperial ideology of urban welfare. This led them to pursue 'good works' as part of a campaign to 'contain and moralise' the poor.[51]

As in late Victorian England, so in South Africa, philanthropy had its roots in a very real fear of the proletariat. Indeed, as Charles van Onselen has shown, the militant demonstrations of 'angry, unemployed Afrikaners . . . sometimes with, but usually without, the support of their more skilled European counterparts' and the threat they posed during depressions on the Rand led to 'concessions in the form of charity, relief works or white labour experiments from the mine-owners, the municipality and the state' before and after the South African War.[52] The Afrikaner petty bourgeoisie was therefore offering neither radical leadership nor equality, but rather the re-establishment of hierarchy. Not, of course, the old hierarchy, for they had played no part in it, but a new ranking for a newly constructed social order.

If the working class was to be courted and corralled, welfare was to be the material inducement. It was, however, a welfare whose frame of reference was to be suffused by the ideology of a newly created Afrikaner nationalism. Yet this was no easier in the aftermath of the war than it had been before, when working-class consciousness had been 'at least sufficiently developed to present a local challenge to the dominant ideology of nationalism'.[53] Indeed until the 1940s if not the 1950s Afrikaner class consciousness stood as a formidable obstacle to the simple capture of the Afrikaner working class by the apostles of nationalism. As Jon Lewis points out, nationalist ideology 'only succeeded [in penetrating the trade union movement] where it struck resonance with the perceived needs of workers'.[54] It was to take a generation and more of 'ideological labour' and eventually the full onslaught of the state finally to accomplish the task.

Nor was it a foregone conclusion that the new intelligentsia would take the lead in this project. Indeed, in the beginning at least, it was the generals of the South African War who held the initiative. Representing the old – and to some extent the new – landed notables, they had access to the patronage and loyalty which made them more successful restorers of social hierarchy. It was the wartime leadership, at the head of moderate nationalist parties, which successfully brought together Afrikaners to win the first elections in the newly self-governing Transvaal and Orange Free State. Yet the preparedness of the generals to compromise with the forces of mining capital failed to satisfy the aspirations of either the intelligentsia or the poor. In a world in which English was the language of the workplace and English education paved the way for state employment, and where an increasingly unfamiliar Dutch remained the language of the hymn, sermon and Bible, the question of the vernacular was central to the dilemma of journalists, writers, teachers and clerics – and critical if they were to mobilise a new constituency.

Thus, as Isabel Hofmeyr shows, it was in their role as propagators of the Afrikaans language that the new intelligentsia most distinguished themselves from the nationalism of the old notables Botha and Smuts and their organisation, Het Volk. They called for the systematic revision of the vernacular to create a standardised respectable Afrikaans, purged of its lower-class and 'Coloured' associations and capable of holding its own against English. Its Dutch inheritance was to be strengthened to give Afrikaans a modern technical and professional vocabulary and link it with a European language and the Graeco–Roman tradition so important to middle-class white identity in South Africa.[55]

To meet the challenge of cheaply purveyed British culture daily life had to be redefined and an alien world transformed into one in which Afrikaner sensibilities ruled. Hofmeyr suggests that no artefact was too substantial or too small not to have its Afrikaans version, no occupation too eminent or too humble, not to have its Afrikaans mutation. This coincided with the creation and re-creation of Afrikaner history, fiction, the language and cultural institutions, as well as with the increasingly successful economic movement in the Cape, based on the first Afrikaner insurance company, SANLAM.[56] The activities of both cultural and economic nationalists were further developed through the Christian National ideology adopted by the Broederbond, a secret society founded in 1919 and devoted to mobilising Afrikaners for the nationalist programme.[57]

Made up of academics from the Calvinist University of Potchefstroom, clergymen and teachers, the Broederbond was spurred into forming the Federasie van Afrikaanse Kultuurvereenigings (FAK) to give 'clear direction' to Afrikaner cultural life in the face of Hertzog's decision to abandon republicanism. Their sense of urgency was increased by the fusion in 1933–34 of the National Party with its parliamentary rival, Smuts's South African Party as a response to the world depression. Under the leadership of Dr D. F. Malan, the first editor of *Die Burger*, a new party, the Gesuiwerde Nasionale Party (GNP – Purified National Party) was formed, with its greatest strength in the Cape, where it retained most of its parliamentary organisation and grass-roots structure of the old National Party, as well as its press.

In the northern provinces, however, the structure and leadership of the old National Party was taken over by the new United Party. Here the GNP depended on the Broederbond intellectuals and professionals. Acutely aware of the impoverishment of Afrikaners, exacerbated by the depression, and of the continued domination over the economy of imperial mining capital, they determined to go beyond a purely political and cultural programme in order to end the economic dependence of the Afrikaner.

Much of what they wrote was confused and contradictory, but the general directions were clear. Nations and cultures were divine creations, each was sovereign and had its own calling and destiny. Service to the nation was service to God. Not only was the Almighty best served by worshipping Him in the language He had created; without maintaining this language, the culture and nation He had created would not survive. Language, culture and nation were endangered by an alien capitalism and an equally alien communism.[58] As Diederichs wrote in 1937; 'there is a determined struggle underway which is aimed at the working class, the foundation of our people. There are forces at work in the bosom of the People which seek to unite our workers with the Proletariats of other lands. . . . The headquarters of this movement is in Moscow.'[59]

It was not capitalism *per se* which was the enemy of the Afrikaner people, according to the leading Bond member, L. J. du Plessis, but the control of the capitalist system by non-Afrikaners.[60] Afrikaners had to take control of what was their rightful share, through *Volkskapitalisme*, the mobilisation of ethnic resources to foster Afrikaner accumulation. To do this, the northern Broederbond, with its weak financial resources, turned to the Cape-based SANLAM in the calling of the 1939 Ekonomiese Volkskongress (People's Economic Congress). Their alliance was entered into warily. While the Cape entrepreneurs had no hesitation about embracing a project whose objective was profit and whose model was the Johannesburg finance houses, many of the Broederbonders attending the conference had hoped for something more Utopian. They combined a populist anti-capitalism with a desire to redeem 'poor whites' through a 'return to the land' and the establishment of co-operatives. At the Volkskongress, SANLAM launched the first Afrikaner-owned financial house, the Federale Volksbelegging, which by 1981 had become the second-largest single conglomerate in South Africa. The embryonic entrepreneurs of the north were largely excluded from this, and could only look forward to the small business of the one-man firm also advocated by the Kongress. For the Afrikaner poor, the 'solution' offered was employment in the Afrikaner enterprises they were exhorted to patronise. There was a symbiotic relationship between Afrikaner capital and the growing Afrikaner petty bourgeoisie, but it was not a relationship without tension and conflict.[61]

By comparison with its concern to clarify cultural and economic issues, the Broederbond was slow to give priority to 'native policy'. They produced no major policy document on the subject before 1944. By then it had become apparent that a dramatic change had taken place in the South African social and economic system. Secondary industry, with its higher wages, was mechanising extensively and required a larger, more skilled workforce. Increasing numbers of rural Africans were making their way to the urban areas from the white farms and the 'native reserves' which were by now manifestly unable to sustain their population. This not only reduced the labour supply for the farmers, but also increased their perception of the dangers of an African urban proletariat. Their answer was 'the Afrikaner's policy of Apartheid'.[62]

The most comprehensive theoretical statement defining apartheid, which was widely discussed in the Broederbond, was made by the Pretoria sociologist, G. Cronje. Harking back to the debates of the liberal segregationists of the 1920s, Cronje asserted that the dangers of mis-cegenation could be overcome by 'a just separation of the races and not by racial domination'. It was inevitable that a black proletariat would be influenced by communist doctrines of class struggle and liberal teachings of equality. 'The teaching of Bolshevism', Cronje wrote, 'with its emphasis on class struggle, will be attractive to the non-tribal native and other non-whites, because they are in fact the proletariat, which will have to subdue the whites, the ruling class, with force.'[63]

To prevent this, Cronje averred, dependence on black labour had to be eliminated, through white immigration and investment in capital-intensive machinery. Africans and Coloureds should be moved to separate 'homelands', where 'every community should undergo its own socio-economic development and governmental form'. As in the past with the liberal segregationists, the realities of economic integration undermined such Utopian social engineering. While total segregation was desirable, 'it was impossible to do without non-white labour'.[64]

As the journal of the Afrikaanse Handelsinstitut, the *Volkshandel*, observed in June 1948:

> No, a person must be practical. It must be acknowledged that the non-white worker already constitutes an integral part of our economic structure, that he is now so enmeshed in the spheres of our economic life that for the first fifty years/hundred years (if not even longer), total segregation is pure wishful thinking. Any government which disregards this irrefutable fact will soon discover that it is no longer in a position to govern.[65]

Whatever the niceties of the Utopian segregationist debate, the 1948 election campaign was fought with the slogans of the *swart gevaar* (black peril) and the *oorstrooming* (swamping) of the cities. As Dan O'Meara has shown, these racial metaphors successfully articulated and combined the interests of different Afrikaner classes. For the farmers, already aggrieved by wartime measures to control food prices, opposition to *oorstrooming* promised to stem the disastrous flow of African labour from the countryside. For workers, it promised to end the threat posed by black competition for jobs. Finally, Afrikaner commercial and financial interests were attracted by the nationalists' support for white agriculture on which their profits depended.[66]

The legislative programme implemented by the GNP after its 1948 victory contributed to the fulfilment of these promises. In an era in which world commodity prices were high, the nationalists ensured that there was a marked increase in the labour available to farmers, and a significant decline in the wages of urban Africans. The result was a substantial increase in the profits of all capitalist enterprises. Groups which had supported the GNP were rewarded more directly. The financial houses received massive contracts to undertake government business, enabling an expansion which by the 1980s gave them a position of equality with, and the same structural needs as, older foreign and English-owned interests. Restrictions under the Group Areas Act on Asian and Coloured residential and trading rights brought benefits to white property speculators and small-town Afrikaner trading interests. Higher civil servants and officials in the military, police and railway establishments were rewarded for their affiliation at the expense of non-nationalists. The proliferation of the bureaucracy involved in 'native' administration, labour control and racial categorisation, provided employment for large numbers of Afrikaners. Collectively, these measures greatly facilitated Afrikaner accumulation and largely resolved the earlier problem of the 'poor white'.[67] If the material rewards were palpable, there were also ideological rewards. The petty-bourgeois obsession with racial 'purity' and eugenics, was given expression in the passage of the Population Register Act, the Immorality Act and the Mixed Marriages Act.

Crucial to the success of the Afrikaner objective of securing white domination and capitalist accumulation was a set of measures designed to attack the increasingly militant African working-class and nationalist movement. The Communist Party was banned, strikes made illegal and the pass laws tightened up and successfully imposed on women for the first time. With the passage of the Bantu Education Act and the Extension of University Education Act, African education was taken over by the state in an attempt to gain ideological control over the black intelligentsia, who were the product of a mission-based educational system still imbued with assimilationist ideals. Urban networks were destroyed through the use of housing policy and 'slum clearance' schemes and by the late 1950s a concerted attempt was being made to shift the locus of African politics out of the towns. Faced with continued urban unrest, changing world opinion, and the need to streamline labour controls, a new policy of refurbishing 'traditional' authority and reconstructing the 'ethnic identity' of blacks in 'Bantu homelands' in the rural areas emerged. Alternative collaborative structures were established in the reserves where an attempt was made to revitalise 'traditional' chiefly structures of control through the Bantu Authorities Act and the Bantu Self-Government Act. Highly oppressive, these measures simply fuelled the dramatic African rural and urban resistance of the 1950s which we discuss in greater detail below.[68]

From the outset, some Afrikaner intellectuals grouped in the Stellenbosch-based South African Bureau for Racial Affairs (SABRA) and the Afrikaner churches urged that apartheid be given a more positive connotation, by which they meant 'total separation'. Like the earlier liberals they saw this as the only alternative to repression and exploitation. They pressed for the development of the reserves as 'homelands' to which all Africans could be removed and where they could achieve economic self-sufficiency and political autonomy. However, any hopes they may have had were dashed by the government's refusal to undertake the investment to restore economic viability to the 'reserves' advocated by its own Tomlinson Commission. The crushing of African rural resistance by the early 1960s and the banning of the African nationalist organisations in 1961 enabled the extension of the repressive 'Bantustan' policy. As in the past the African reserves continued to function as the basis for the migrant labour system, but this was now refined through the establishment of labour bureaus and 'tribal authorities' to control influx into the urban areas even more rigorously and to cheapen and discipline labour not only for the mines but also for secondary industry, public works and construction.[69]

With decolonisation moving apace in the rest of Africa, state ideologists attempted to legitimate the reserves as potential 'nation-states' which would, in the fullness of time, be granted 'independence'. Thus, willy-nilly, Africans were declared to be members of ten separate 'Bantu homelands' in exchange for losing their citizenship in South Africa. From the 1960s a complex process of ethnic manipulation and constitution-mongering was designed to fragment and diffuse pan-South African black nationalism, and a massive programme of social engineering was implemented. Over the next twenty-five years nearly 4 million people were uprooted, many of them several times over, in pursuit of the policies of apartheid.[70]

Utopian segregationists in SABRA and the churches who joined liberal opinion in attacking the Bantustan programme as a sham in that it failed to provide for the 'separate development' they envisaged, and was simply a continuation of old-style *baasskap*, were marginalised. A handful moved on to accept the logic of their own doctrines and to work, within such bodies as the Christian Institute for a fully integrated South Africa. Sham or not, the Bantustan policies had by the late 1970s created 'new facts'.[71] New political institutions and the deliberate use of welfare to give reconstructed ethnic identities a material reality have created conflicting interests which now have to be taken into account in any struggle for the transformation of South Africa.

III

One of the peculiarities of the literature on nationalism and ethnicity is that it rarely alludes to the position of women. Despite a frequent assertion that national and ethnic identity depend on early socialisation (usually, one assumes, by mothers) and the importance given to notions of 'mothers of the race' by eugenicists and cultural nationalists, very little attention has actually been paid to their role in nationalist movements. Yet through the twentieth century, cultural nationalists among Afrikaners and Africans have sought in their different ways to define a special position for 'mothers of the nation', and have received considerable support from women adherents.[72]

Moreover, while all nationalist organisations have their own 'iconography of women', so women of different classes and ethnic groups have been drawn into political struggles in different ways. As Belinda Bozzoli has pointed out, 'conflicts within the household . . . fought . . . by various urban and rural groups . . . have a clear bearing on the kinds of consciousness which [women] develop. . . . Different experiences of urbanisation, of domestic relationships and different positions in the hierarchy of the proletariat, all of which are connected in complex ways with domestic struggle, have a bearing on their place in urban South Africa' and on their forms of consciousness and modes of struggle.[73] We know even less about the forms of consciousness of rural African women, a matter of some concern in view of the migrant labour system and thus their very different daily experience in the reserves compared to that of their menfolk in the towns. It may well be that women in the reserves in South Africa are the 'chief guardians' of ethnicity as a defence against their urban rivals. In addition, although in the urban areas women have been in the forefront of nationalist struggle – a matter to which we return – in the reserves in the 1970s ethnic identity had been given a new material reality for women through the manipulation of pensions, famine relief, housing and bureaucratic positions for their children.[74]

In this volume we have no contributions which look solely at the problems of black women's consciousness. Both Isabel Hofmeyr and Iris Berger do, however, attempt, almost for the first time, to explore forms of consciousness among Afrikaner women. As Hofmeyr shows, Afrikaner nationalists, concerned with preventing the decay of the family and socialising the young, saw women as a special target for nationalist persuasion. Women's organisations were established for welfare and political purposes. A literature aimed specifically at Afrikaner women was brought into being which emphasised the dangers of urban life (in particular from non-Afrikaner males) to young girls making their way to town from the countryside. Through this literature, the early-twentieth-century idea of femininity and motherhood was given a specifically Afrikaner content.[75] According to this ideal, Afrikaner women should give themselves selflessly, not only to their families but also to the *volk*. The Afrikaner home, so they were urged, should become the bridgehead from which the Afrikaans spirit could be launched.

Afrikaner nationalists addressed women as mothers and wives, but not initially as workers. Yet by the 1920s increased Afrikaner impoverishment meant that large numbers of Afrikaner women were being forced into factory employment, often under highly exploitative conditions.[76] By the 1930s they dominated in industries which were traditionally associated with women's labour in European society and were thus regarded as peculiarly 'suitable for white women'.[77] One of these was the garment industry, which Iris Berger discusses in Chapter Four.[78]

In its early years, this industry relied on skilled European-trained craftsmen. In the late 1920s with the inauguration of mass factory production, Afrikaner women were taken on as semi-skilled operatives, undercutting and deskilling the jobs of white men. In part because, as Berger shows, technological innovation and enlargement of scale afforded only very marginal savings, the industry developed a 'characteristic pattern of continually seeking out new sources of cheap labour and continually breaking up the work process to accommodate the new and ostensibly less-skilled workers'.[79] The state's 'civilised labour policy', promises of tariff protection to employers of white labour, the demands of the mining industry for black male labour and the delayed proletarianisation of black women, all encouraged factory-owners to favour white women over black men or women. In the 1930s, the garment workers' industry became the single largest employer of white female labour, although in the next decade they found themselves ousted from the production line first by Coloured and then by African women.

Berger traces conditions in the garment industry and the ways in which changing social relations at work shaped women's consciousness. Using labour-market segmentation theory, she explores the development of a labour force in South Africa, stratified by gender and by race. The view that a woman's place was in the home, and that women workers were partly supported by male earnings, justified their being paid very low wages. And the ideological emphasis on women's roles as wives and mothers, may have lain behind the difference between the quiescent political attitudes of many garment workers at home and their membership of the apparently radical Garment Workers' Union (GWU).

This union was formed in 1934, following a 'predictable rift' between the skilled male workers and semi-skilled, largely Afrikaner women, and achieved remarkable success in forging a socialist consciousness among the newly proletarianised Afrikaner women. A sense of solidarity resulting from discrimination, common poverty, exploitation, poor wages and working conditions, and 'the union's real successes in mobilising workers to strike and struggle for better wages and working conditions', enabled it to withstand the onslaught of nationalist attacks.[80] Not only did the union render material assistance to the women workers; it was unique also in its 'recognition of the cultural and language aspirations of Afrikaners'.[81] Perhaps the most striking example occurred in 1938 when Afrikaner garment workers dressed in 'traditional' garb appeared at the nationalist Voortrekker Centenary celebrations under the auspices of the union rather than as members of the *volk*.[82] Like the nationalists, the GWU attempted to involve members in a wide-ranging social and cultural network – sporting and musical activities, debates and lectures, outings, didactic literature and dramatic productions portraying working-class struggles.[83] In this way the leaders kept control of the union, and helped diffuse 'the political impact of nationalist ideology'.[84]

For both men and women, withstanding the blandishments of the nationalists did not necessarily mean a colour-blind class consciousness, however. From the nineteenth century, working-class consciousness in South Africa was deeply scarred by the racist ideology more generally prevalent in the industrialised world. Afrikaner workers brought with them a heritage of racist assumptions from the countryside which were frequently sharpened rather than undermined by the competition in town and the deliberate attempts of both capital and the state to manipulate the 'faultlines' of race in an effort to maintain a racially hierarchical division of labour and a divided working class.[85] Bozzoli has argued that because of the ways in which 'gender had shaped the structure of the labour force', Afrikaner women were not as threatened by cheaper black labour in the way 'their male counterparts on the mines certainly were' and that this led to the development of 'a socialist rather than a white-supremacist consciousness'.[86] Some of these propositions are debatable. In fact, workers had multifaceted identities. They could be, and frequently were, simultaneously workers *and* housewives, socialists *and* nationalists, white supremacists *and* internationalists. They saw little reason to grapple with the contradictions. The fact that exploited white women workers were able simultaneously to employ (or aspire to employ) even more lowly-paid black domestic labour may have been a significant element in this.

During and after the Second World War, African and Coloured women were drawn into the clothing industry as it expanded to meet wartime needs and as white women moved into better-paid jobs. Initially, the union tried to extend the benefits it had won for its members, and successfully enrolled black women in the union, and resisted job dilution and the undercutting of white wages. Yet white women workers were shaped by the profoundly racist daily practices of the segregationist and apartheid state, and inevitably this affected relationships between workers on the shop floor.[87] The multiracial leadership of the GWU was forced to implement a 'parallelism' which led not only to separate branches within the union for white, Coloured and African members, but also to the acceptance of the racial status quo, and indeed the advocacy of segregation, at the workplace. Lewis argues that the early non-racialism of the GWU had only survived because it 'was never really put to the test since there was little competition from black labour', and this may be partly true.[88]

In the 1950s the very different nature of production in the industry, the stratification of the workforce and the increased strength of the apartheid state had led to the replacement of its earlier ideology of working-class solidarity by a far more limited and economistic trade-union consciousness. While the leaders of the GWU continued to advocate notions of social justice, many of the white rank and file had become members of the National Party. Its 'non-racialism' was highly circumscribed and ultimately 'weakened the political impact of unionised black labour in the post-war period'.[89]

IV

The contradictory consciousness that contributed to the making of a late-twentieth-century Coloured identity is dependent on the particular history of struggle and adaptation of South Africa's first colonised, conquered and proletarianised people. Although Afrikaner nationalists only began to manipulate Coloured identity in the 1920s, and, in a more significant way, since 1948, the dependence and close connection of Afrikaners and Coloureds has a much longer history. As we have already seen, the making of white Afrikaner identity involved, among other processes, a purging of the Afrikaans patois. In the long run that action also contributed to the making of the twentieth-century political self-consciousness of the discarded people. The creation of a separate Coloured identity also owes much to British 'scientific racism' and imperial policy, and the interests of English-speaking trade unionists and Anglophone businessmen. It would be wrong, however, to see Coloured identity as simply resulting from the definitions of South Africa's ruling class; it also owes much to their resistance and ambiguous collaboration in the specific socio-economic circumstances of the Western Cape.

The Dutch/Afrikaner settlers were inextricably linked to those they called 'Kleurling' – or 'Coloured' – throughout the expansion of European settlement in the Cape Colony. These 'Kleurling' represented many strands in South Africa's past: Late Stone Age hunter-gatherers and herders, collectively known as Khoisan; slaves from the heterogeneous trading networks of the Dutch East India Company in the Indian Ocean; descendants of Indonesian Muslims sent to the Cape as political prisoners or enslaved artisans. The power of the white household led inevitably to a variety of sexual unions which gave all these groups a substantial genetic bonding, although it was control over property rather than ethnic origin which tended to determine who would be deemed white 'Afrikaners', who brown 'Afrikaners', for in the eighteenth century the term 'Afrikaner' was applied to all those who were born in Africa – of whatever hue.

Conversely, in the nineteenth century, the term 'Coloured' was assumed to include *all* peoples of non-European origin, including the Bantu-speaking Xhosa and Mfengu from the Eastern Cape as well as Khoisan and other Cape ex-slave people, as Ian Goldin shows below.[90] Industrialisation, the South African War and shifts in imperial ideology brought this practice to an end early in the twentieth century when for the first time the Cape census made the distinction between 'White', a new category, 'Bantu', and 'Coloured' or 'Mixed'. To be of 'mixed race' was obviously highly pejorative in the racially defined hierarchical society of South Africa. Why those called 'Coloured' deserved the appellation is difficult to explain except in ideological terms, given that all other groups in South Africa are, like the rest of humankind, equally 'mixed'.

Late-nineteenth-century Coloured identity was a product of the changing political economy of the Western Cape. The mineral discoveries and new urban opportunities led large numbers of dissatisfied rural labourers to move from the highly exploitative conditions of the farms into the towns.[91] By the late nineteenth century, the urban 'non-European' poor, particularly those of Cape Town, were perceived as 'a dangerous class', the source of the city's rising tide of crime and violence. Combined with a metropolitan concern with eugenics and 'purity of blood', these perceptions provided a powerful impetus to a middle class anxious to 'moralise' its 'white' poor. Employers and white trade unionists, for their part, as Goldin shows, also found the indigenous working class threatened their interests, and began to substitute African labourers from the Eastern Cape in unskilled, heavy manual work.[92] The consequent exclusion of the Coloured urban poor led to the creation of new forms of 'Coloured' identity.

As had been the case with white Afrikaners, events after the South African War contributed to the shaping of Coloured identity. In the period leading up to the war, British diplomacy denounced the illtreatment of 'Cape boys' in the South African Republic, and proclaimed the rights of British colonial subjects. In response, many Coloureds and Africans gave the imperial forces considerable support at great risk to themselves.[93] Yet when peace was made in 1902, the British conceded the 'Coloured' franchise to the defeated Boer generals. Thus, among many blacks, wartime optimism gave way to the conviction that the unification of the British South African colonies would result in the franchise laws of the Boer republics prevailing in any constitutional settlement.[94]

The anger of Coloured artisans was increased by the restrictive practices of white trade unionists directed against their alleged undercutting during the post-war depression. In this situation, Coloureds reacted with hostility to the treatment meted out to them by governments, employers and even their own ('mixed') trade unions, and for the first time began to form separate political organisations to protect their interests. The most important of these was the African Peoples' (later Political) Organisation (APO), which aimed at securing the franchise rights and employment prospects of its largely artisan and trader membership. Political organisation transformed shared language, religion, history and predicament into ethnic consciousness.

There were other, and at times contrary, factors which contributed to this emerging consciousness. Thus, no sooner had one High Commissioner, Lord Milner, given away the Coloured franchise in the Transvaal, than another, Lord Selborne, tried to ensure that Coloureds would be attached politically to the white population.[95] The leaders of the APO, and in particular Dr Abdurahman, took advantage of 'this strategy of divide and rule' to gain advantages for their constituency.

That Abdurahman could do so owed much to the fact that Coloured voters were influential in at least six Cape Town City Council seats. The incorporationist strand in Afrikaner nationalist thinking about the Coloureds owes at least some of its inspiration to these political and electoral considerations.[96] As late as 1933 Bruchner de Villiers, the National Party member for Stellenbosch, was carried shoulder high from the polling station by Coloured constituents, and considered his subsequent defeat at the polls in 1938 as a direct consequence of the GNP's policy to Coloured voters.[97]

The most paradoxical source of Coloured identity and leverage emerged from the local stirrings of social Darwinism and the eugenics movement. While, as we have seen, racist ideology portrayed Coloureds as a 'mixed race', the illegitimate progeny of 'European civilisation and non-European savagery', their 'European blood' none the less made them hierarchically superior to their 'Bantu' forebears. This indeed lay behind ruling-class fears that 'Coloureds', if they were not placated, would provide leadership for the 'Bantu' masses.[98] As Goldin shows, the ideology of the dominant class in this case, as in others, pervaded the thinking of subordinate Coloured classes and many of them used the language of social Darwinism to defend themselves against white racism. As residential and other controls over Africans increased, so the advantages of a separate identity for Coloureds came to be appreciated by those who benefited. This reached its apotheosis in 1923 with the Urban Areas Act which specifically exempted Coloureds from carrying passes. The APO aimed to show the government that 'an educated class of Coloured people' existed in Cape Town, who should be treated differently from 'uneducated natives'.[99] By the early 1920s it had succeeded.

In 1924, with Hertzog in power, there were renewed attempts to align the Coloured people with the white population, in much the same way as Selborne had attempted two decades before. Thus, Hertzog's proposals to disenfranchise Cape Africans, were accompanied by a formula which would have extended Coloured representation, albeit by removing them from the common voters' roll, in order to avoid disturbing the existing balance of power between the white political parties. In practice little came of Hertzog's proposals. It is significant, however, that while Coloured people found their rights deteriorating in relation to whites, they were nevertheless placed in a relatively advantaged position in relation to Africans. In 1930 they were exempted from influx controls and from legislation governing urban segregation. The divide between those classified as Africans and those classified as Coloureds was growing greater and the racial hierarchy, sustained since the turn of the century, was greatly reinforced.[100]

It is no coincidence that Hertzog's strategy both in its co-optive and its coercive facets came at a time when the state faced a rising tide of black militancy and there were increasing signs of political co-operation between African and Coloured radical leaders. Thus in 1927 the APO and the ANC participated in a non-European unity conference, and Coloured radicals such as Jimmy la Guma became active in both the Industrial and Commercial Workers' Union (ICU) and ANC. This was a rare moment of unity between all the oppositional movements, including the Communist Party. The radical and Garveyite executive of the ANC of the Western Cape encouraged Coloured membership of the organisation. As a result, the APO and the ANC were able to have considerable success in the rural hinterland of the Western Cape, organising Coloured and African support in such districts as Paarl and Worcester.[101]

Yet by the 1930s, for a variety of reasons which we examine below, black political militancy declined dramatically.[102] The adoption of a more exclusively African nationalist position by the conservative leadership of the ANC which came into power in 1930 and promptly suspended the communist and other radical members in the Western Cape led to the exclusion of Coloured members from the ANC in the early 1930s. By this time, too, the ICU, had adopted a more exclusionist policy in relation to Coloured members. Although Coloured intellectuals fell back on ostensibly non-racial organisations, in practice they found themselves either working in organisations composed of Coloured people or required to compete with the ANC, and preoccupied with issues which did not affect Africans. This was exacerbated in the 1940s when opposition to the new Coloured Affairs Department, established to give greater salience to Coloured identity, only served to distance them further from the issues of greatest concern to other blacks.[103]

The attempts of the 1948 nationalist government to consolidate Afrikaner solidarity through a rigid definition of Coloured ethnicity went far beyond anything attempted hitherto. The Population Registration Act, the Prohibition of Mixed Marriages Act, the Immorality Amendment Act, the Group Areas Act and the Separate Representation of Voters Act all contributed to this process of redefinition. Membership of the *volk* was limited to those who were deemed to be *white* Afrikaans-speaking Calvinists, and existing racism was bolstered by legislation in the interests of ethnic consolidation; those who lacked the necessary racist-cum-ideological commitment were to be prevented from drifting into the Coloured population. The Immorality Acts continued the moralising of the Afrikaner poor; the disenfranchisement of Coloured voters was both ideologically satisfying and politically advantageous for the National Party.

Nevertheless, an ideological problem remained. While the lack of political rights for Africans could be justified in terms of the proposed establishment of separate 'Bantu' homelands, no such 'homeland' could be said to exist for Coloured people. The mechanisms for creating some form of representation outside the central state apparatus were therefore more difficult to conjure up. Merely segregating Coloureds from whites was insufficient. The ideologists in SABRA insisted, therefore, that a Coloured 'homeland' should be created, and that the sense of Coloured identity strengthened. As in the 1930s, but with greater determination, the state concentrated on gaining the support of Coloureds through material rewards, and this was embodied in the Coloured Preference Policy. Its major objective was not to provide Coloureds with abundant resources so much as to place them in a position of relative advantage by comparison with Africans. 'Coloured Preference' would, it was hoped, compensate for the disenchantment which state policies created and bolster the paternalism which mediated the relationship between Cape Afrikaners and Cape Coloureds.[104]

A reluctantly accepted sense of identity did indeed follow. Legislative barriers forced Coloured people into a single mould; they uprooted the racially mixed communities in which Coloureds had previously lived, destroyed many of the non-racial trade unions to which they had belonged and put an end to the blurred racial boundaries between ethnic groups which had allowed people to move relatively freely from one racially defined community to another. The world inhabited by people on the Western Cape was fundamentally changed, and a new social entity created, which has been in the forefront of the debates and struggles over the reconstitution of the South African 'nation' in the 1980s.

V

If, in some sense, Coloureds in the Cape benefited from a paternalism which saw them as 'brown Afrikaners', for Indians in Natal, there was no such ideological dispensation. Regarded as aliens in origin, religion, language and race, the main thrust of South African state policy towards Indians in the twentieth century has been to advocate their repatriation, or, failing that, to limit severely their economic and political opportunities in South Africa. As General Smuts put it:

> The whole basis of our particular system in South Africa rests on inequality. . . . It is the bedrock of our constitution. . . . You cannot give political rights to the Indians which you deny to the rest of the colonised citizens in South Africa.[105]

In many respects Indians in Natal occupy the same structural position as Coloureds in the Cape, caught between an African majority and the white ruling class. Compared to the Coloureds, however, they had a far stronger middle class which identified in part with the growing nationalist movement in India and an international leverage which could be used in moments of crisis. This was to give them some protection against a settler regime which denied even the wealthiest Indians equality of status. Nevertheless, while Indians were divided from both the dominant whites and the majority African population by distinct religions, languages and cultures, their own class divisions and heterogeneity meant that any sense of common identity was absent at the beginning of the century. It was thus only on the relatively rare occasions before the mid-twentieth century when Indian politics were radicalised that a sense of community can be said to have existed between the Indian élite and the masses. In her essay in this volume, Maureen Swan is concerned with these moments of radicalisation.[106]

The emigration of indentured labourers from India began in the 1860s in order to create a workforce for Natal's sugar plantations and coal-mines. In 1895 when a £3 tax was imposed upon ex-indentured workers, it was so disproportionately high that more than half of the workers were forced to enter second and even third terms of indenture. When, in 1911, the indentured labour system was brought to an end there were 152,000 Indian workers in Natal, most of them Hindu, the vast majority employed in agriculture. Ruthlessly exploited, they had few mechanisms for expressing resentment or altering their situation.

The indentured labourers were followed by a small number of Indian merchant-traders, largely though not exclusively Gujarati Muslims, whose common commercial interests and regional ties contributed to their sense of being an élite. By the 1890s the wealthiest of their number had begun to form political bodies which claimed to speak on behalf of all 'Indians' in Natal and the Transvaal. This was a claim which the settler regimes were willing to concede initially, perhaps because the cautious and conciliatory merchants accepted colonial class and racial discrimination, provided that they were exempted. Well aware of their vulnerability, the merchants distanced themselves from their indentured compatriots, with whom they had little in common. In the long run their sense of superiority undermined their position as spokesman for any cross-class community alliance.[107]

In the early years of the twentieth century, the merchants' claim to leadership was challenged by a new Indian élite of South African-born clerks, interpreters, teachers and professionals, who emerged from the ex-indentured population. As in the case of the Coloureds, their political perceptions were heightened by political and economic developments after the South African War, and especially by the post-war depression which brought salary cuts and barred them from the Colonial Civil Service. A growing sense of coherence was expressed in the formation of the Colonial Born Indian Association in 1911.

With the emergence of the new organisation, the merchants and new élite came into conflict about how best to defend their interests. Each claimed to represent the underclass. The most notable figure in this conflict was the one man who straddled both the world of the merchants and of the new élite, without being a member of either. This was the renowned M. K. Gandhi, who had played a leading role in merchant politics in the decade before 1906. In that year Gandhi proposed a campaign of passive resistance against Transvaal legislation which required Indians to be registered. It was at this time that Gandhi began to advocate his doctrine of personal honour for which the individual was responsible, and which was later to be elaborated as *satyagraha*. Gandhi combined this ethical doctrine with a political tactic meant to appeal to the immediate self-interest of the merchants.[108]

Successful at first, the movement was undermined in 1908 when registration certificates were linked to the issue of trading licences and Gandhi's merchant support disintegrated. Despite the paucity of his support, however, by this time both the British and the Transvaal government wanted a settlement of the 'Indian Question'. Gandhi, therefore, found himself being treated – with little justification – as the Indian representative. As Swan points out, 'Paradoxically, it was the compromises which Gandhi was required to make in order to retain his legitimacy as principal Indian spokesman which finally led to a dramatic widening of the social base of the movement, and the radical potential of *satyagraha*.'[109]

With the diminution of his merchant support, Gandhi turned to the Colonial Born Indian Association, which had mobilised around opposition to the 1911 Indian Immigration Bill and the £3 tax on ex-indentured labourers, which pressed so heavily on working-class Indians. Thus it was the new élite rather than the merchants who began the process of creating a 'community of culture' in order to channel popular energies behind its separate interests. Both the merchant-based Natal Indian Congress (NIC) and Gandhi promptly advocated the abolition of the £3 tax, and initially, the South African government appeared willing to do so. When it later refused, Gandhi saw this as a breach of faith and was roused to action. Indian workers were called out on strike and it spread 'like a cane fire'. Although the strikers were forced back to work, negotiations followed which gave the passive resisters some of their demands.[110]

In the quarter century after the 1913 strike, the political economy of Natal was transformed, and with it the position of Indians. By the Second World War most South African Indians were part of an urban-based proletariat. Although many were desperately poor, a considerable number had become skilled artisans and were members of recognised unions.[111] A radical political tradition was stimulated by economic change, the nationalist struggle in India, the impact of the war and the spread of education. The urban-based merchant class had also prospered and had come to dominate Indian politics through the NIC once more. In the inter-war years they were prepared to accept some form of racial segregation in return for securing their existing property and to envisage the repatriation of working-class Indians provided their interests remained untouched. Attempts by the intelligentsia to exert an influence on the Congress leadership were largely ineffectual, and this spurred them to work from below.[112]

The 1940s none the less saw the revival of a cross-class alliance. The leadership provided by Gandhi in 1913 was now replaced by a more widely based combination of professional men and trade unionists, some of whom were members of the Communist Party or of the Cape Town-based Non-European United Front (NEUF). During the war years, a combination of Communist Party activists, trade unionists and intelligentsia eroded the power of the merchants within Indian political organisations in both Natal and the Transvaal. The traders fought back, criticising the use of 'foreign ideologies' and attempting to co-opt Indian nationalist ideology. The uncompromising attitude of the radicals to racial segregation, however, together with the poverty and unemployment of many urban Indians, led to the ascendancy of the left-wing alliance over the established political organisations by 1945. In the following year, a passive resistance campaign was launched against the recently introduced Asiatic Land Tenure and

Representation Act, interpreted as an onslaught against the Indian community as a whole. The campaign was not limited to that Act, as organisers proclaimed their opposition to the wider pattern of racial discrimination.

If there was something paradoxical about the Communist Party trying to mobilise 'Indians' in the defence of property rights, and subordinating Indian trade unions and workers to the defence of the Indian petty-bourgeoisie, this reflected the political reality with which they had to deal: 'consciousness' as Swan observes, and this was a view which communists accepted at least implicitly, 'was created by a racial categorisation imposed on them by the state and reinforced by virtually every aspect of their daily lives'; this necessitated cross-class ethnic alliances.[113]

The communists, therefore, set out to radicalise the separate nationalist movements, rather than to establish a cross-ethnic working-class alliance. In Natal David Hemson suggests this resulted in part from the impact of the disastrous strike at the Dunlop Rubber Factory in 1942–43, when employers replaced members of the non-racial Rubber Workers' Union with 'busloads' of Africans from the reserves. This undermined the 'radical leadership in registered trade unions . . . causing distrust and hostility between Indian and African workers', and deepened

> the tendency for political activists in the Indian community to be diverted away from working-class organisation (in particular from the organisation of unregistered trade unions of Indian and African workers) towards political action in defence of the Indian community. . . . The direction of political action was more towards aggressive defence of the trading, investment and residential rights of Indians . . . and an inward looking trade unionism.[114]

The campaign against the Asiatic Land Tenure and Representation Act never achieved Gandhi's level of success, however. The call to defend property rights probably won little support from the Indian working class, while calls for a cross-ethnic struggle for political rights were blocked by the response of the conservative leadership of the ANC in Natal. The fragility of intra-racial ties between workers there was increased by the entrenched form of Zulu ethnic nationalism focused around the Zulu monarchy, exploitative relationships between African workers and the Indian petty bourgeoisie, state-manipulated competition between African entrepreneurs and their Indian counterparts and a continuous stream of white invective against Indians.[115]

The full tragedy of the failure to forge a link between Indian resistance and African oppression was to be revealed in January 1949, when a minor affray set off a violent attack by Africans on the Indian community in Durban which left 142 people dead, 1,087 injured and vast numbers of homes and stores burnt and looted.[116] Although they were widely interpreted in the white press as an example of the 'inevitability' of 'racial strife', and of African 'savagery', and provided justification for government policies of apartheid, the Durban riots show how profoundly structural conditions produce patterns of identity as lived reality, and illustrate the inherent dangers of a rampant ethnicity. The parallels for today are only too frighteningly apparent.

VI

The ferocity of the Durban riots profoundly shocked the leaders of the Indian National Congress and African nationalists. Few were prepared for the surge of popular hatred which the destruction revealed. The earlier institutional history of African nationalism as embodied in the ANC, founded in 1912, and the ICU, founded in 1919, has been relatively clearly charted.[117] Their class composition has been less well understood, although recent contributions have begun to explore this dimension.[118] In this volume, the complex origins and many-faceted and regionally differentiated nature of African political consciousness are illuminated by several contributions, though in the nature of things the story remains incomplete. In their different ways, they all explore the making of African national and class consciousness and its struggles against a particularly vicious form of colonial subordination. This consciousness has drawn not only on indigenous histories and cultures replete with the necessary symbols and myths, but also on a variety of extraneous political ideologies which none the less resonated with local experience, and helped forge 'the historical consciousness of resistance'.[119]

Initially, membership of formal Western-type African political organisations was largely restricted to the Christian intelligentsia, and they continued to dominate well into the twentieth century, with leadership provided by prominent churchmen and women.[120] Mission education and organisation provided the tools, while the contradiction between the universalism preached within the churches and colonial practice has fuelled generations of Christian militants right up to the present. Christian imagery and millenial belief suffused the popular consciousness of even non-Christian Africans, articulating with elements of precolonial cosmologies, while for vast numbers of African men and especially women in both town and countryside it has been the church in its many forms which has provided the strategies of survival in the harsh and heartless conditions of South Africa's towns and an explanation of the universe more powerful than any proffered by the formal political organisations of the time.[121]

The conflict between the Christian intelligentsia and the non-Christian populace has often been overdrawn, although at times mission education acted as a brake on overt popular resistance to colonialism. In the last two decades of the nineteenth century, the wars of resistance constituted a crisis of commitment for Africans throughout the region, and the memories of these struggles permeated twentieth-century African nationalist consciousness. In the Eastern Cape, the contradictions between colonial conquest and the incorporative Cape liberal tradition were only too manifest and led to the first expression in print of nationalist ideas as early as the 1860s. As we have seen, by the 1880s the first Western-type political organisation had been formed. Elsewhere the process came some two decades later, spurred by the hopes inspired by the imperial conquest of the Afrikaner republics, and the disillusion which followed when it became clear that British rule would mean little positive change for blacks.[122]

Thus in the first decade of the century a myriad of organisations sprang up among the African intelligentsia in the different colonies, petitioning for their inclusion in the body politic on the Cape model. For Africans as for Afrikaners, the unification of South Africa led to the consolidation of nationalist organisations, as Africans from all over the region protested against their political exclusion from the forthcoming Union. The result was the founding of the ANC. Although the early ANC is frequently perceived as simply representing the interests of the African petty bourgeoisie, in a colonial situation a group's class position offers no certain guidance to its political affiliation. Despite a powerlessness which predisposed them towards 'moderation' and co-operation with the state, they faced constant rebuff and intensely felt discrimination. In many respects they shared in and identified with the experiences of the masses, and at key moments acted as intellectual catalysts, providing both leadership and a more coherent ideology for peasants and workers.[123]

Despite the formation of the ANC with its protestations of moderation and universality, even the Christian intelligentsia were affected by popular, regionally specific, non-Christian traditions of cultural identity. We know most about this in the Eastern Cape, where these years were marked by a profound separatism, the result both of a

Christian disillusion with the realities of incorporation and the legacy of the Xhosa's bitter struggles against colonial encroachment.[124] In Natal, too, the attempts to destroy the Zulu monarchy as the pivot of national unity had served paradoxically to increase its legitimacy. Here past history and the segregationist ideology of the local state contributed to a strong sense of ethnic identity which could both strengthen local resistance against dispossession and exploitation, but also frequently prevented Natal's full participation in a pan-South African black nationalist struggle.[125] In the Transvaal and Orange Free State, the picture is far less clear, both because of their regional and ethnic diversity and because of the largely Rand-centric nature of research.[126] The Cape seems to have provided particularly fertile ground for the Garveyite ideas discussed by Robert Hill and Greg Pirio in Chapter Seven, Natal the least.

Concerned to examine the force of Garveyite ideas in shaping African political identity in South Africa, Hill and Pirio argue that after the First World War Garveyite ideas developed 'into a potent expression of mass-based African nationalism' which has been greatly underestimated by previous scholars. According to them, 'at the level of popular consciousness', through Garveyite ideas, 'the various phases of African resistance were welded together to express a new sense of common political and racial destiny'.[127] We must be careful to distinguish the panic of white society, always apt to see outside agitators in signs of African unrest, from political reality. Nor should we see 'Garveyism' as a monolithic and coherent body of ideas. Much that was labelled 'Garveyism' in these years represented a form of 'black consciousness' which had long been part of the African response to colonialism, and resonated with it. Moreover, despite the exhortations of McKinley, with which Hill and Pirio open their essay, Garveyite ideas were probably combined by many with a continued belief in the bounty of Queen Victoria, whose portrait adorned the walls of numerous African homesteads well into the twentieth century.[128] As with all popular consciousness, diverse strands were interwoven with little sense of contradiction, as this description of an ICU protest march in 1929 suggests:

> They were an organised body – headed by a brass-band, preceded by Natives in Highland costumes – They had a Union Jack and a Red Flag and a hammer and sickle on it – Many of them were dressed in uniform and carried sticks in military positions.[129]

Combined with these diffuse traditions, the belief in redemption from their brethren in America who would arrive in Garvey's Black Star line, or even more dramatically in aeroplanes, to end colonial rule, provided additional legitimacy and moral support for blacks in their struggles in South Africa. The prevalence and vigour of this belief in the inter-war years is dramatically and convincingly portrayed by Hill and Pirio.

By the time Garveyite ideas spread in South Africa, there had already been a long connection between American blacks and the African intelligentsia. American missionaries, both on the Rand and in Natal, and the visits of Africans studying in the United States had strengthened the links. The 'transatlantic connection' was eclectic.[130] By the beginning of the century, the radical ideas of du Bois and American and other socialists were being circulated by the editor of the Eastern Cape newspaper, *Izwi la Bantu*, A. K. Soga, in direct opposition to those of Booker T. Washington whom he described as 'a menace to Negro freedom in the United States'.[131] Nowhere was Washington's accommodationist message more strenuously emulated than in Natal, where the Rev. John L. Dube, the leading African political figure, explicitly modelled his Christian Industrial School at Ohlange on Washington's Industrial Institute at Tuskegee.[132] For Dube and the more conservative African leaders Garveyism appeared to threaten 'harmonious race relations'.

It was among the younger black intelligentsia and migrant workers in both town and countryside that Garveyite ideas received their most powerful response. Nor is this entirely accidental: in the United States, Garveyism had spread 'like wildfire' among both the black petty bourgeoisie and the 'new and as yet non-integrated Negro proletarians' in the northern industrial cities who bore a certain resemblance perhaps to the migrant workers of South Africa, themselves neither peasant nor proletarian.[133] Black independent churches which originated in the rejection of the white control of mission churches in the late nineteenth century and which proliferated among the dispossessed in the inter-war period, also provided a forum for Garveyite ideas. Some had their own connections with black American churches, such as the African Methodist Episcopal Church. While relatively few were as explicitly Garveyite as the 'Athlican' group in Kimberley, many others drew confidence from its assertion of black integrity.[134]

The turmoil in South Africa's urban areas at the end of the First World War profoundly radicalised a section of the African petty bourgeoisie. Inflation, low wages and appalling housing, as well as the pass laws, affected workers and petty bourgeoisie alike, and led to one of those moments of identity of interest which were to disturb the

South African ruling class sporadically through the twentieth century. Strikes and demonstrations culminated in a major mine-workers strike in 1920, and was met by the familiar dual strategy of coercion and co-option, particularly on the Witwatersrand. The use of armed forces and the law against protesters was paralleled by the establishment of the Joint Councils of Europeans and Natives, which it was hoped would bring together 'moderate' white and black opinion, and the establishment of state channels for the expression of African 'grievances'.[135]

In the context of the successful Russian Revolution, and increased white working-class militancy, politically conscious blacks were inspired on the one hand by the socialist message being preached among white workers on the Rand, on the other by an African nationalism which looked to the redemption of Africans by black Americans, and associated the nationalist cry, 'Africa for the Africans', already current in the 1890s with the name of Marcus Garvey and his Universal Negro Improvement Association (UNIA). Although one must be careful not to collapse all African protest in the inter-war years into 'Garveyism', as Hill and Pirio show, the image of Garvey, as a rather diffuse set of ideas about black Americans as redeemers, pervaded 'all phases of African protest', and resonated powerfully with existing nationalist ideas. On the eve of the 1920 African mine-workers strike, Garvey's Black Star Line was known among Africans on the Rand, while Clements Kadalie, founder of the ICU stated his intention of modelling himself on the 'the great African Marcus Garvey'. The mix of ICU and Garveyism was a particularly potent brew: in many areas, there were organisational and political links between the ICU and Garvey's UNIA, and ICU leaders were seen as 'American Negroes who had come to deliver [the people] from slavery'. In part through the newspaper, the *Black Man*, which Garvey saw as 'the *Negro World* of South Africa', in part through the migrant labour nexus, ICU and UNIA ideas radiated as far afield as Mozambique, South Rhodesia and South West Africa. 'American' notions also influenced members of the ANC. *Abantu-Batho*, the national ANC newspaper, saw the ANC and the UNIA 'as part of a common entity'.[136]

Garveyism was strongest in the Western Cape, which seems to have been a major regional focus of militant political activism in the late 1920s which is only just becoming clear in the literature and which the contributions by Hill and Pirio and by Colin Bundy in this volume both serve to highlight.[137] And within this, a radical black consciousness identified with Garveyism undoubtedly exerted a powerful pull, for both the ICU and the ANC, where it found expression in the local ANC newspaper which was named *The African World* by analogy with UNIA's *The Negro World*. The crucial figure in forging the ANC–UNIA connection in the Western Cape was James Thaele, who had come in contact with the movement while studying in the United States. The presence in the locations of Cape Town of Xhosa from the Eastern Cape, with their traditions of Africanism, and of a number of black Americans and West Indians especially in the docks, where the majority of migrant workers were employed, was important for the diffusion of Garveyite ideas. Significantly, too, through their identification with black Americans, Coloureds could claim their African roots and play a role in local black politics: as we have seen, in Cape Town in the 1920s, both the ANC and ICU opened their doors to Coloured members – a policy which was to be reversed in the following ecade.[138]

Elsewhere, too, while Garveyite ideas seem to have made steady progress in the first half of the 1920s, a period of lull after the turbulence of the immediate post-war years, it was from the mid-1920s, that they shared and perhaps partly shaped the dramatic upsurge of African militancy in the rural areas. Increasingly this period is coming to be seen as a key moment in rural radicalisation, with the mobilisation of rural grievances by the ICU in Natal, the Eastern Cape and the Eastern Transvaal, and in the Western Cape by ANC activists.[139] Deteriorating conditions in the reserves; the massive eviction of tenants following the expansion of 'capitalist farming' and especially wattle plantations and sheep farming in Natal; the intensified exploitation of farm labourers and labour tenants resulting from the fall in world agricultural prices; and further taxation in the Cape and Natal all pressed still further on already hard-pressed rural dwellers. Hertzog's 'civilised labour policy' which increased the pressures on African workers and petty bourgeoisie and prevented their upward mobility; their insecurity in the face of Hertzog's segregation bills in 1926, and the ineffectuality of the co-optive Joint Councils and Urban Advisory Boards led members of the intelligentsia to identify with the rural dispossessed.[140]

Although Hill and Pirio maintain that the spread of the ICU in the countryside was accompanied by 'an almost wholesale embrace of Garveyism',[141] it is difficult to know how far Garveyite ideas contributed to the acknowledgement by the nationalist movements of the significance of the rural class struggles. The agrarian problem has been relatively neglected by scholars, at least until the rural unrest of the 1950s, partly reflecting the preoccupations of urban-based national political organisations. Yet in the later 1920s no national organisation could remain immune to the popular turmoil in the countryside. In the Western Cape, rural campaigning of radical ANC leaders like Bransby Ndobe and Elliot Tonjeni, led to a major upsurge in rural disturbance in the late 1920s. By 1930, the radicals had been expelled from the national organisation. The 'Independent ANC' which they established and which was considerably to the 'left' of the National Congress, demanded 'universal free education, full franchise rights for all and the return of the land to the African people'. As Bundy points out, the 'rupture between the independent ANC and the parent body' highlights 'the gap in class interests and ideology that frequently appeared between the ANC leadership and rural movements during this period.'[142]

In the ICU, also, there was tension between some of the leaders and rural demands.[143] Originally founded among black dock-workers in Cape Town just after the First World War, between 1925 and 1927 the ICU dramatically expanded its membership and began to articulate rural grievances. As Helen Bradford has shown in a brilliant analysis of the movement and its constituencies, the ICU was 'a fluid contradictory movement . . . which encompassed an extraordinary range of struggles'; from a moderate trade union it was transformed after 1924 'into a nationalist movement' and 'briefly channelled and intensified protest of extremely disparate social groups'. In the 1920s, it 'incorporated and transformed elements from a wide range of existing discourses to create a powerful message of resistance'. By 1930 the ICU had 'splintered into innumerable and uncoordinated fragments' – the result of financial mismanagement, internecine battles among the leadership, white liberal intervention, the 'parochial nature of politics in a country which was not yet twenty years old as a unified entity', 'the localised nature of grievances, consciousness and traditions of protest', and perhaps above all the mismatch between the millenarian expectations of its supporters and its organisational and political capacity. Despite widespread disillusion, it nevertheless left a powerful legacy of rural radicalism which was only to resurface in the 1940s and 1950s. Whatever the limitations of the organisation, it encouraged men and women to hope and dream of a better society and future liberation.[144]

In the Eastern Cape, ICU and Garveyite messages were interwoven with millenarian expectations both in the mission of Wellington Butelezi who claimed that Afro–Americans were coming in ships and planes to liberate South Africa, which proved particularly attractive to the increasingly disaffected 'school people' of the Eastern Cape, and in the complex pig-killing movement in southern Natal and Pondoland, which also foretold the end of white rule. A complex intertwining of the Wellingtonites, the ICU and pig-killing took place, and all shared in the popular belief in the coming of the Americans: the result of a desperate people in search of solutions, in the face of the pressures of intensified rural impoverishment, proletarianisation and the migrant labour system.[145]

Garveyite ideas may have in part also influenced the Comintern's attention to rural issues in South Africa and its advocacy of a 'Native Republic'.[146] In 1928 the Comintern's need for anti-imperialist alliances led it to attempt to push the local Communist Party into rural organisation. It maintained that 'the foundation of revolution in South Africa' was the 'national question . . . which is based on the agrarian question. . . . The black peasantry constitutes the basic moving force of the revolution in alliance with and under the leadership of the working class.' Implanted in South Africa, the communist proposal for a 'Native Republic' and Garveyite ideas of an 'African Republic' were mutually reinforcing. Although the 1928 directive from the Comintern was never fully accepted by the South African Communist Party, by this time it was beginning to shed its earlier preoccupation with the white working class and its naïve belief that interracial harmony would grow simply from developing class consciousness. It recognised that the 'main revolutionary task' should be among Africans.[147] The radicalisation of sections of the African petty bourgeoisie in the second half of the 1920s, symbolised in the election of Josiah T. Gumede as President-General of Congress in 1927, encouraged party members in this project. This was after Gumede's visit to Moscow and a meeting in Brussels of the Comintern-sponsored League Against Imperialism, from which he returned not only enthusiastic about the Soviet Union but also espousing Garveyite ideas.[148] At the same time, the communists saw a natural constituency in the rapidly expanding ICU. Although the relationship soon soured, from 1927 the party began to organise African workers on its own account, and within a year, its African membership rose from 200 to 1,600 (out of a total of 1,750).[149]

Rural disturbance fuelled by the potentially powerful combination of black nationalism preaching 'Africa for the Africans' and the revolutionary rhetoric of the communism was sufficient to raise a terrifying spectre before whites in the late 1920s. In the 1929 election 'black peril' and the 'communist menace' became the rallying cry of the Afrikaner nationalists. Although this has generally been treated in liberal texts as the spurious figment of the Afrikaner racist imagination, in fact there were real grounds for alarm in the turbulence of these years, and the state's response was vigorous. Renewed attempts by the Native Affairs Department to 'refurbish traditionalism', through reconstituting the powers of chiefs and headmen were reinforced by the 1927 Native Administration Act which made the Governor-General of South Africa Supreme Chief with drastic executive powers over Africans, and the notorious 1929 Riotous Assemblies (Amendment) Act which made the incitement of racial hatred a criminal offence.[150]

The state coupled these coercive actions with the encouragement of ethnic politics and the consolidation of a variety of co-optive bodies such as Urban Advisory Boards and the Native Representative Council which absorbed much of the energies of the intelligentsia.[151] These strategies, together with the impact of widespread and intense famine between 1931 and 1934 and the world depression, tended to damp down both rural and urban activism, so that the 1930s saw a remarkable diminution in African political militancy. The success of any communist alliance with black nationalism foundered in the face of the onslaught of the state, the expulsion of communist members from the ICU, the regrouping of the conservative wing of the ANC to replace Gumede as President with the right-wing Seme in 1930, further about-turns in Comintern policy and internecine interparty battles. Local, largely white, Communist Party members with their belief that the proletariat was the vanguard of the revolution, and that the white working class had to be 'won over', were bitterly divided from the outset over the 'Native Republic' policy. With the Comintern's Russia-first policies in the early 1930s and then its advocacy of a united front, ideas of a 'Native Republic' and attempts at rural organisation were dropped until after the Second World War.[152]

Nevertheless, sporadic food riots and armed opposition to tax-collectors in rural Natal, a peasant uprising in 1939 in the Northern Transvaal organised by Alpheus Maliba, one of the few Communist Party organisers still operating in the countryside in this period, bitter peasant hostility to government attempts at cattle-culling in the Eastern Cape and the continued operation of localised fragments of the ICU all suggest the continued undercurrent of rural resistance to white rule.[153]

While the millenarian expectations aroused by the Wellington movement and, to a certain extent by both Garveyism and the ICU, could only in the nature of these phenomena be disappointed, it is clear that notions of 'Africa for the Africans' or – as it was translated into the famous Congress slogan *Mayibuye i Afrika* (Come back Africa) –

long outlived any direct links with UNIA and ICU organisation in South Africa. They reinforced the rejection by many peasants of the legitimacy of the white-ruled state and continued to form 'an integral part of the overall ecology of post-war African resistance'.[154] This can only be explained ultimately through the meshing of these ideas with the deeper continuities of African nationalism in the countryside and meant that this nationalist consciousness was able to survive the profound organisational weakness of African political organisations in the 1930s, as well as the 'parochial, disjointed, sporadic and isolated' nature of subsequent rural struggles.[155] When, in the aftermath of the Second World War, political organisations began to regroup, and to reach into the countryside for the first time, they were to draw on older traditions of activism and resistance.

The first to do so, as Colin Bundy (Ch. 8) shows below, was the All African Convention (AAC), a constituent member of the Non-European Unity Movement (NEUM), which had been formed under the patronage of D. D. T. Jabavu in 1936 to fight Hertzog's revised segregationist legislation. By the 1940s, Jabavu and his generation were being ousted by new leaders of the AAC/NEUM, many of them with roots in Marxist, especially Trotskyite, organisations. The Trotskyites in particular had a well-formulated position on the agrarian question as 'the axis, alpha and omega of the revolution'.[156] Although the NEUM's main constituency and organisation was among the urban élite of the Western Cape, between 1945 and 1958, it 'identified the African reserves as areas of potential revolutionary activity' and established links with rural movements. The NEUM/AAC took up the issues which were already arousing intense peasant resentment and resistance in the Transkei and Ciskei and began to link local popular associations and protest into more formidable opposition in the increasingly radicalised Transkeian Organised Bodies (TOB). This was to give the AAC a distinct edge over the ANC in the Eastern Cape in the 1940s and early 1950s when the TOB decided to affiliate with the AAC.[157]

As important to the politicisation of peasant demands was the radicalising of the Cape African Teachers' Association (CATA). From being an essentially 'respectable and moderate body', by 1948 CATA was the leading element of the AAC with many of its militants coming from the Transkei. In the Transkei, teachers played a crucial role as a rural intelligentsia, integrating peasant struggles against land rehabilitation and cattle-culling with resistance to the state's imposition of chiefs and 'Bantu education'. This fusion of the more coherent ideology of the intelligentsia with the ground swell of popular discontent intensified Transkeian resistance during the 1940s and 1950s.

The contrast with what was happening in Natal in this period illuminates the very different roles that can be played by 'organic intellectuals' in different historical circumstances. In that province after the radical fervour of the 1920s the state appears to have had far more success in harnessing latent Zulu nationalism for its own purposes and diverting it into safer channels. Despite the militancy of both the rural and urban proletariat in Natal in the second half of the 1920s, from the early 1930s a considerable section of the Natal intelligentsia was attracted into supporting a 'modernised' Zulu monarchy, a phenomenon which the state was to encourage in the 1930s and 1940s, through its support of the Zulu Cultural Society. For the state, sugar barons, mining interests and African landowners there was a distinct advantage in an alliance with the Zulu Royal Family, with its capacity to appeal across the growing class cleavages among the Zulu.[158] Significantly, the Zulu Society was founded by Chief Albert Luthuli as an offshoot of the Natal Bantu Teachers' Association, and had among its goals the recognition of the Zulu king. Like Inkatha, founded by the Zulu Royal Family and the Natal Christian élite some twelve years earlier and which was seen by the state as a counterweight to the ICU, the Zulu Society had among its chief objectives the restoration of 'traditional' values and the recognition of the Zulu king. Financed directly by the Native Affairs Department until 1946, the Zulu Society was a spent force by 1948. Nevertheless, its activities may partly account for the diminution of militancy among Africans in Natal in these years. The salience of Zulu ethnic identity among the petty bourgeoisie in the 1940s can be glimpsed in the reports of 'tribal hostilities' emanating from Adams, the leading African high school, Natal's equivalent of the Cape's élite black high school, Lovedale. Translated into a different idiom by the frustrated African petty bourgeoisie and impoverished workers in the towns, it gave licence to the anti-Indian feeling which culminated in the tragic riots of 1949.[159]

Elsewhere in South Africa, the urban-based intelligentsia dominated the activities of the ANC through the 1940s. The first signs of the revitalisation of Congress after the war came with the formation of the African Youth League by a number of Africanist-minded members of the organisation. As Gail Gerhart describes the ideas of its leading ideologue, Anton Lembede, Africanism projected 'a new and aggressively positive self-image compounded of pride in the past, confident expectations for the future, and an emotional, burning love for the

African's God-given blackness' and for Africa itself. Initially a somewhat romantic movement of intellectuals concerned with culture, the Youth League none the less picked up the deeper strands of African nationalism and indeed Garveyism with its slogan of 'Africa for the Africans', although there was some ambiguity about how far this meant being 'anti-white', and anti-communist. Some of the tensions this produced were revealed in 1959 when those 'Africanists' who argued that the alliance of the 1950s between the ANC and other racial groups subordinated African national liberation to multiracial co-operation, broke away from the ANC to form the Pan-Africanist Congress. What united the Youth Leaguers in the 1940s, however, and distinguished it from the older generation of Congress was the recognition of the need for mass mobilisation and action. The transformation of South Africa's towns since the depression provided them with their opportunity.[160]

As the South African economy recovered from the depression and the pace of industrialisation quickened, thousands of recently proletarianised workers had made their way to the towns from the impoverished white farms and the increasingly desolate reserves. Appalling living conditions, low wages and inadequate transport coupled with the brutalities of the South African state fuelled the dramatic urban protest movements, the growing trade-union organisation and the sporadic strikes of these years. By the mid-1940s, continued rural impoverishment exacerbated by fierce drought gave a particularly bitter edge to labour disputes and urban politics and lay behind the major black miners' strike of 1946. Called by the African Mine-workers' Union, the internal organisation of the strike seems to have depended to a considerable extent on ethnic, regional and even criminal networks, as Beinart suggests in this volume.[161] Despite the rapid crushing of the strike, it did show the possibilities of mobilising workers, and it was after the strike that the nationalist intelligentsia in the ANC Youth League turned to this new and highly volatile constituency. In the course of the 1950s, as it attempted to incorporate ever-growing rural and urban protest, the once 'moderate' ANC was profoundly transformed, and its leadership radicalised.[162]

Congress's campaigns in the urban areas and the mass mobilisation of the 1950s in the Defiance Campaign, the Congress of the People and the protests against the Bantu Education Act, the extension of the pass laws to women, and the western townships removals are relatively well known and need no elaboration here.[163] Given the significance of the new proletariat, the urgent social problems of the urban areas and the extent of the grass-roots protest these engendered, it is perhaps not surprising that Congress leaders were more immediately responsive to the demands of this constituency. In this volume, four contributions look at the events of the 1950s through a rather different lens, in an attempt to get behind the institutional and ideological bias of much of the existing literature. Thus Colin Bundy looks at rural protest, William Beinart explores the consciousness of an individual activist, while both Tom Lodge and Philip Bonner and Robert Lambert are concerned with the local expression of nationalist and class politics.

Despite the endeavours of Govan Mbeki, General Secretary of the TOB and a member of the ANC, to convince Congress leaders of the radical potential of the rural areas, it was only in 1952 that a revitalised ANC began to pay some attention to rural issues. Thus in the Defiance Campaign of that year, it included the Stock Limitation (cattle-culling) Act of 1949 among the six unjust laws to be defied. This may in part have been behind the 1952 Defiance Campaign's success in the towns of the Eastern Cape, especially East London, where the local populace was intensely aware of the acute rural poverty of its Ciskeian hinterland and the bitter unpopularity of state 'betterment' schemes.[164] Significantly, the AAC/NEUM decision to boycott the Defiance Campaign marked the beginnings of its decline into squabbling factions. Like the 1920s, so the 1950s saw widespread urban protest followed by an upsurge of rural resistance which forced itself on the consciousness of Congress. With the Mpondo revolt of 1960, the ANC leadership finally recognised the radical potential of the countryside, although even then it 'followed rather than initiated the action'.[165]

It is the Mpondo revolt which provides the starting-point for Beinart's concern with the life and political role of M, whose story he records in this volume. Through M's life and ideas, his involvement in youth subculture and migrant associations, as well as his later involvement in both working-class and nationalist organisations, Beinart explores the intertwined concepts of worker consciousness, ethnicity and nationalism, and shows how ethnic identity and radicalisation are not necessarily mutually exclusive.

The great value of this chapter is the insight it offers into migrant subculture. Revealing, also, is his allusion to M's membership of a criminal 'gang', a reminder of the importance of gang and criminal culture in the making of the South African working class, which recurs also in Chapters Ten and Eleven by Lodge, Bonner and Lambert, and which is only just beginning to be recognised in the wider literature.[166] Through a study of the 'ethnic' associations to which M belonged,

Beinart examines the very diverse nature of migrant consciousness shaped by the urban workplace, rural loyalties and beliefs and the changing forms of ethnic identification. Contrary to much of the South African literature on ethnicity which stresses the ways in which it has been manipulated by both the state and capital in order to divide and control the workforce, Beinart concludes:

> particularist associations in the workforce did not preclude the possibility of united working-class action. They may even have made such action possible. . . . M's shift to broader nationalist and class-conscious positions in the 1950s was clearly a response to his changing position . . . as a worker. But . . . he took with him some of the ideas values and networks that had been central to his previous experience; these were overlaid with, or meshed with his newly developing political ideas. Nationalism was not an exclusive position for him. . . . Indeed, it was the very complexity of the layers of his ideas which proved most useful to the Congress movement.[167]

Beinart's interest in the nature of political consciousness is paralleled by Tom Lodge's chapter on 'the sociology . . . aims, ideology and . . . extent' of early post-war African resistance and political organisation (Ch. 10). Specifically focusing on developments in East London, he is concerned with the 'eclectic range of intellectual influences, the social complexity of both leadership and rank and file, and the regional variations in the popular impact' of African political organisations. He probes the rather simplistic notion of class consciousness in some of the available literature, and looks at the way in which much protest occurred outside the formal political organisations, which then attempted to bring it – not always successfully – under their control.[168]

Lodge explores these themes through an analysis of the history of the ANC and its offshoot, the Pan-Africanist Congress, in Duncan Village, an appallingly impoverished and grotesquely overcrowded African township on the outskirts of East London, which was one of the most successful centres of the 1952 Defiance Campaign. Although it was subject to constant new influxes of population from the even more intensely impoverished Transkei and Ciskei, the insecurity of its inhabitants, as well as their 'continuing involvement with rural society', slowed the development of any straightforward working-class politics or political consciousness; within the community, 'populism reigned'. In the 1950s 'the most vigorous political group' in the township was 'an Africanist-inspired branch of the Congress Youth League', founded in 1949 by three high-school graduates, influenced by their contacts with student activists at Fort Hare who looked to the peasantry as a revolutionary force.[169]

Whatever their successes, ultimately they were unable to control the violence and bloodshed which brought the Defiance Campaign in East London to an abrupt and disillusioning end. The recourse once again to violence by East London ANC activists in the early 1960s, despite the condemnation of bloodshed by the national leadership, suggests the difficulties umbrella organisations have in controlling their local constituents.[170] While Congress was prone to claim the credit for local political protest, on occasion local activists used the organisation's name to sanction the furtherance of what may have been local vendettas.

Violence and lawlessness then as now was at the heart of the daily experience of township life for millions of people.[171] For Africans in the 1950s, as in the 1980s, the daily arrests for purely statutory offences were a ready reminder of the coercive omnipresence of the white state. Yet then, as now, the police frequently turned a blind eye to the high number of robberies, rapes and murders among blacks, themselves a reflection of the massive dislocations of social life. Confronted by the insecurities of township life, for many of the newly urbanised the answer has been in vigilante groups, 'protecting' their property and their women, and in organised crime, the two very often being associated.[172] That this should have permeated political organisations is, under the circumstances, hardly surprising. Lodge concludes that in East London, the weakness of the petty bourgeoisie and working-class identity 'produced a politics shaped not so much by sectional interests but rather the feelings of anger, fear and weakness which pervaded the whole community'. And these structural conditions and the politics they bred may in turn partly explain the outbursts of political violence both in East London and elsewhere, then and since.[173]

Certainly gangsterism and crime were a feature also of the politics of Benoni as described in Chapter Eleven by Bonner and Lambert. There, the heterogeneous African proletariat grew from some 12,000 in 1939 to over 77,000 less than twenty years later. As elsewhere, '. . . instability and insecurity were compounded by pressure on virtually every kind of urban service and resource'. Conflict was internally directed and the working class fractured along lines of origin, ethnicity and differential access to jobs and housing, which hampered working-class and popular organisation. Desperate competition for the barest necessities led to an ethnically informed gang warfare. Thus, in the 1950s, the Rand townships, and Benoni in particular, were the scene of warfare between gangs who styled themselves 'Russians', 'Berliners', 'Americans', 'Gestapo', using labels drawn from the newspaper headlines of the day to signal the ethnic divisions of the Rand's hard-pressed African populace. As in East London, 'a diffuse Africanism was the most likely and available rallying cry' against whites and, in the case of Benoni, as in Durban, also against Indians.[174]

Organisation at the workplace was equally inhibited by the small scale of industrial manufacture and the unskilled nature of the workforce: industrial workers still only represented about half the urban employed in Benoni, and of whom about a quarter were the approximately 4,400 workers at Amato Textiles, organised in a union which 'became a symbol of working-class militancy throughout the Rand',[175] and which provides the focus of Bonner and Lambert's chapter. The Amato hessian factory, like the rest of the textile industry in the 1950s, was in the vanguard of technological innovation, which had enabled the construction of larger factories using more substantial quantities of machinery. This in turn gave these male textile workers a stronger bargaining position than their unskilled compatriots employed in the still undercapitalised and small-scale industries elsewhere in South Africa. Drawn from the more permanently urbanised working class, their wages were higher although conditions were far from satisfactory, and workers were forced to meet 'extremely tight production deadlines'. In these circumstances, working-class organisations were able to establish themselves more successfully than elsewhere.[176]

At Amato, constant work stoppages and the employers' need to resolve them led by 1951 to full recognition of the African Textile Workers' Union, which organised a number of successful strike actions through the 1950s: 'Particular conditions . . . provided both the incentive and the space for a strong union presence.' In the period of economic growth, the union had had a measure of success in opposing attacks on workers' living standards, and through the 1950s the relatively well-organised Amato workers represented a substantial proportion of the workers in the South African Congress of Trade Unions (SACTU) – the confederation of nineteen unions associated with the ANC, which grew from some 20,000 members in 1956 to 55,000 in 1962 after the ANC had been banned.[177]

By the late 1950s, however, as the economy contracted, even advanced sections of the industrial working class were vulnerable to the assault which was mounted on 'popular and working-class organisations' by both the state and employers. The second half of the 1950s saw a decided increase in the tempo of industrial turbulence, with an increasing recognition by Congress leaders of the importance of the organised working class (through the alliance with SACTU), the call for a £1 a day wage by SACTU activists, the Alexandra bus boycott and an unprecedented number of industrial strikes.[178] For Amato workers, too, discontent mounted, as living costs soared and the employers were unable to meet the demand for increased wages. On 12 February 1958, when they came out on strike, the workers were met with massive state repression. Large numbers were injured, some of them seriously, the workers were dismissed, many of them banished to the reserves and the union was destroyed. It was a further phase of the repression which had characterised the state response to the increasing worker protest of the late 1950s.

The changing technology of the textile industry and the continued vulnerability of workers also affected the increasing number of African women in the textile industry who are the subject of the final section of Iris Berger's chapter on the GWU (Ch. 4), already discussed on pp. 24–6. Initially the GWU had been able to incorporate black members and to hold out for the registration of African women workers, but this possibility was removed by the Native Labour (Settlement of Disputes) Act of 1953, which prevented any African from belonging to a registered union. Behind the government's concerted effort to bring women under the control of industrial legislation and the pass laws for the first time was the escalation in their numbers in industry – by 142 per cent between 1947 and 1952.[179]

According to Berger, as the government introduced new controls over black women, garment workers supported resistance on racial/national as well as class grounds. Leading members of the African section of the GWU played a major role in radical and nationalist organisations, such as the ANC, Women's League and the Federation of South African Women. Despite some participation in the non-racial SACTU, however, in 1956 the Executive Committee of the African GWU disaffiliated from SACTU, perhaps because of the latter's decision to affiliate with the ANC. By this time there was a major ideological gap between different groups of women workers, whatever the more ambiguous traditions of the union, with both black and white women workers identifying with very different nationalist/racial goals.

VII

The state's attacks on Africans culminated in the killings at Sharpeville on 19 March 1960. The immediate international response was a massive outflow of capital with gold reserves falling by half by May 1961, and there were now calls for reform from big business. After some initial uncertainty, however, the state responded forcefully, by banning Congress organisations and crushing working-class opposition. The Bantustans were restructured to increase control over the labour force and to serve as dumping grounds for the unemployed, the very old and the very young.

At the same time, a political ideology which was designed to legitimate the Bantustans as nation-states and to co-opt a new collaborative class of 'tribal chiefs', became hegemonic, both within the state apparatus itself and among a majority of whites. Drawing selectively on historic forms of identity and authority, the state deliberately encouraged ethnic awareness and gave it a new material reality. This was never *simply* invented by Verwoerdian ideologues, however. Throughout the twentieth century, the migrant labour system trapped women in rural areas and led workers to foster their links with rural authority, particularly where the latter still controlled access to land. Faced with their exclusion from the white state, there were always those who favoured forms of African separatism. These forces were now given tremendous impetus. New politically conservative bureaucracies were created with a vested interest in their balkanised statelets; some opportunities were provided for the frustrated African petty bourgeoisie; and the fact that welfare payments were made dependent on Bantustan officials compelled claimants to accept the existence of these socially engineered institutions. In the Bantustans, ethnic identity could now be used to exclude 'outsiders' from employment and housing, despite decades of peaceful coexistence, and opened up possibilities of oppression and corruption. History was invented to sustain these reconstructed ethnic identities.[180]

After the flight of capital at the time of Sharpeville, the government placed curbs on foreign exchange dealings, imports and the outflow of gold. In the event, this served the interests of the Anglo-American Group which stepped in to stabilise capital markets and greatly increased its hold over the South African economy. By 1980 it had diversified into every sector of the economy and controlled something like 27 per cent of the Gross Domestic Product (GDP). Together with the state interventions, this laid the basis for a ten-year boom, especially in manufacturing, which was increasingly dominated by monopoly capital. By the early 1970s, however, in part as a result of the massive import of machinery and equipment over the previous decade, South Africa once again faced a serious balance of payments deficit. The concentration and interpenetration of capital contributed to high unemployment rates, inflation climbed steeply, and the GDP dropped dramatically from the levels achieved in the 1960s.[181]

Larger factories, new technology and the total inability of the Bantustans to subsidise welfare costs transformed the position of the black working class in this decade. The early 1970s saw a formidable growth in African working-class militancy, with 98,000 workers involved in strikes in 1973; this was followed by the Soweto uprising of 1976, the culmination of seven years of African regrouping and student activism in the Black Consciousness movement, which bore a similar relationship to the Black Power movement in the United States as older forms of Africanism had to the Garveyism of the 1920s.[182]

Despite attempts to foist independence on the Bantustans and greatly increased state expenditure within them, the 'homeland' strategy could not address the problems of the urban intelligentsia and proletariat. Nor were all 'homeland' leaders prepared to accept a white-imposed 'independence'. In Kwazulu, Chief Gatsha Buthelezi rejected the state's terms, while using its institutions to propagate his ostensibly cultural movement, the revived Inkatha, using a complex and contradictory discourse of ethnic nationalism. For its members, large numbers of whom are women, Inkatha provides security both materially and psychologically. Notwithstanding Buthelezi's denunciation of tribalism and violence, however, and his claim to represent the true tradition of the ANC, his organisation has become increasingly coercive and chauvinist, opposed by students and radicals, both Indian and African, in Natal. At the same time it has received the support of the parliamentary opposition party, the Progressive Federal Party (PFP), and increasingly even of sections of the ruling party.[183]

The reorganisation and growth of African trade unions after the strikes of 1972–73 was perhaps the most significant development over the next decade. Work stoppages combined with the flight of capital to disrupt the economy which also came to reflect the growing world recession. The upsurge in gold prices disguised the serious nature of the 'economic malaise' between 1978 and 1980, but with the fall in the gold price in 1981, the country has experienced economic stagnation with a shortfall in foreign investment, record inflation and unemployment rates and a massive drop in the value of the rand. By the mid-1980s the severe economic recession was exacerbated by the campaign advocating economic sanctions in the United States. Economic difficulties were paralleled by an unprecedented public breast-beating, with the Prime Minister warning white South Africans in 1978 to 'adapt or die' and the Minister for Co-operation and

Development declaring in Washington, in June 1979, that 'apartheid is dead'. In July 1985 a State of Emergency was declared and some 2,000 dissidents arrested.[184]

These economic changes and political developments form the background to the last three chapters in this collection by Brian Hackland, Stanley Greenberg and Deborah Posel, which deal with changing ideological strategies of the state, capitalists and the parliamentary opposition. All three authors in this final section look at how elements in the ruling class attempt to cope with the state's absence of 'legitimacy' among Africans as a product of National Party strategies of the 1950s and 1960s, though all were written before the wave of protest which erupted in the wake of the constitutional 're-forms', in September 1984.

We open the section with Brian Hackland's chapter on the Progressive Party, both because his is the most extensive discussion of the structural changes which have necessitated ideological shifts, and perhaps because paradoxically in the new dispensation the state has stolen some of the ideological clothing of its erstwhile political enemies. Hackland discusses the formation of the Progressive Party and its ideology of incorporation, beginning with its constitutional commissions under Donald Molteno between 1960 and 1962, and Frederik van Zyl Slabbert between 1974 and 1980. Both commissions were set up and reported at a time of heightened instability; the differences between their proposals are a measure of the changes in South Africa in the twenty-year interval between their respective reports. In both cases, the party was 'responding to political change and pressures in South Africa and . . . the needs of its class constituency'. Most prominent among its members from the outset was Harry Oppenheimer, head of the Anglo-American Group. Significantly, too, by the time of the Slabbert Report, the PFP had become South Africa's official parliamentary opposition.[185]

While the Progressive Party hoped to gain support from all sectors of the white electorate, after 1966 it geared its efforts specifically at 'businessmen', basing its appeal on the need for political concessions in order to prevent the revolutionary overthrow of the system. It attacked the government's economic policies, and in particular its restriction on the training and use of skilled black labour. By the 1970s, the arguments had changed even more markedly. Progressives now asserted that the use of low-wage, unskilled labour was limiting productivity and earnings for all South Africa's people, an argument which reflected the growing need of capital-intensive manufacturing industry for an educated, skilled and politically neutralised working class. At the same time, party leaders came to appreciate the disenchantment among increasingly militant young blacks with 'old-time capitalism' and called for 'a new deal for black people'.

As the revived black organisations, such as the Black Consciousness movement of the late 1960s and the trade unions of the 1970s, came to introduce concepts of class into their analyses of South African society, so too did the Progressives: 'The question of colour was no longer seen as fundamental, but as a divide which disguised far more dangerous class divisions. The threat of revolution was no longer primarily a threat to white power, or to "Western Civilisation", but to capitalism itself.' If capital accumulation was to continue, a more incorporative political and ideological system seemed imperative. It is this recognition which led to the historic meeting in Lusaka in September 1985, between members of the exiled ANC and leading businessmen, including the Anglo–American Corporation's Chairman, Gavin Relly.[186]

Apart from matters of representation, in many ways by the 1980s the solutions proposed by the Progressives to South Africa's problems no longer appeared so different from those which were being propagated within Afrikaner ranks, as Stanley Greenberg shows. By the late 1970s, many Afrikaner intellectuals had begun to doubt openly the efficacy of a system built on racial discrimination and state intervention in the economy. These doubts reached a climax in the publication in mid-1985 of a Human Sciences Research Council Report, based on extensive 'scientific research' by essentially Afrikaner academics, showing that apartheid policies had led to a deterioration in black–white relations. In part this back-tracking from the orthodoxies of the past involved a substantial rewriting of history, in part the construction of a system rationalised by an affirmation of the primacy of market principles as a counter to both racist and socialist counter-ideologies.[187]

Despite the role which an earlier generation of Afrikaner entrepreneurs had played in the construction of the apartheid state, by the middle and late 1970s Afrikaner businessmen also began questioning Bantustan policies, influx control measures and efforts to deny African proletarianisation. Like the intellectuals, the Afrikaner business community elevated the private sector, attacked the extensive public corporations which had proliferated over the previous decade and argued that free enterprise could solve the problems of black poverty. Together with the Urban Foundation, which had been founded by the

Progressives to address problems of African welfare, the Afrikaanse Handelsinstituut has attempted to come to terms with African urbanisation, and to express concern at the extent of African poverty and discontent. Aware perhaps of the need for a more skilled workforce and an internal consumer market, businessmen have stressed the poor living conditions and unemployment of urban Africans, and have urged a rethink of influx control. They saw these 'reforms' as essential to the winning over of 'stable' and 'middle-class' elements in the black population from the threat of communism.[188]

For officials within the state's administration, market mechanisms seem far less immediately obvious a solution to the problems of control. Generally hostile to 'free market principles', few officials are prepared to jettison their 'core tenet', the need for state control over labour markets. Indeed they envisage 'a growing rather than a diminished role for the state in the regulation of African labour'. They justify continued influx control in terms of the need to 'protect' the local urban African population, part of an official acceptance that Africans have been permanently urbanised.

The result, as Greenberg shows, is an intense political struggle within the state bureaucracy over how to respond to the intellectuals, the newly assertive Afrikaner bourgeoisie and spreading African discontent. While at lower levels of the bureaucracy, officials see little problem with the existing order, at the top officials are concerned with African disaffection and find themselves in the contradictory position of both defending state control and identifying with Afrikaner business demands.

Whatever the divisions among the bureaucracy, the dominant political leadership affirms free market principles rather than state intervention as the basis of policy. Yet Greenberg concludes that their views lack clarity about the nature of the 'free enterprise system'. Nor is this entirely surprising: for National Party leaders 'free enterprise' is largely a strategic political resource to mobilise support, yet it leaves them 'exposed – dependent on the fragments of a new ideology they barely understand'.[189]

Deborah Posel, drawing on Habermas's analysis of the late capitalism, extends this discussion of the nature of the ideological transformation in South Africa over the past decade with her examination of the emergence of a new language of legitimation and its role as a form of state control since 1978. In place of apartheid orthodoxy have come the catchwords 'realism', 'pragmatism', 'reform' and 'effective government': the 'apolitical' language of technocratic rationality. The destructive consequences of National Party policies are increasingly explained as the inevitable results of economic growth and industrialisation, to which experts can find solutions which are technical, non-ideological and therefore non-contestable. Closely connected is what is termed the 'total strategy' designed to overcome the 'total onslaught' which South Africa is said to be facing: this too is justified in view of the 'objective facts' as a 'rational necessity'.[190]

The 'total onslaught' also allows for changes in the *form* of state. Since 1980, constitutional reforms have greatly increased the power both of the head of the state and of cabinet committees which are no longer necessarily drawn from Parliament. As Posel points out, given the anticipated opposition to the State President's programme, 'it is not surprising . . . that the commitment to reform should have been accompanied by the centralisation of decision-making and withdrawal from the arena of party and parliamentary discussion'. As significantly, the power of the military has also been greatly increased, with military men playing an important role as 'experts' on the cabinet committees and in interdepartmental meetings, and through the enlarged powers of the Department of Military Intelligence and the National Security Council which 'is now the main advisory and planning body' of the state's 'total strategy'. '"Total strategy" is defined sufficiently widely to cover anything which the government or military experts deem a matter of "national security"', whether military or civilian.[191]

As we have already seen, there have also been important consultations between the government and businessmen, and this has included members of the opposition Progressive Party. Businessmen have been drawn into cabinet committees as 'experts' on economic matters and their recommendations have not infrequently found their way into state policy. As in the case of the military, the language of technocratic rationality enables their collaboration to be depicted as politically neutral. By labelling an issue 'political', the government can exclude capitalist participation and reserve any such issue for its own decision-making.[192]

Given the multiple challenges to the state, the language of legitimation has to win over several audiences simultaneously: the National Party's existing, largely Afrikaner, constituency, the disaffected black population, and big business. All these set constraints on the nature of the language adopted. Whites have to be placated in the face of threats to their privileges, blacks given some hope of 'reform', 'big business' offered 'more "rational" ways of organising the country's economy and polity'. The language of technocratic rationality is intended to address all audiences simultaneously.

Not surprisingly, this language is not without its contradictions, some of which are being bloodily demonstrated in the townships of South Africa as this introduction is being written. Elements of the old apartheid ideology with its moral imperatives and its connections to Afrikaner nationalism have continued to be adumbrated, especially before National Party audiences. *Kragdadigheid* has to be demonstrated, the party's Programme of Principles to be presented as unchanging and the unity of the *volk* to be revered at the very moment that a premium is placed on the need for change and 'teamwork' between English- and Afrikaans-speakers.

As Posel explains it, the old ideological language has persevered precisely because the new language of legitimation eschews 'ideology' and morality, and cannot provide answers to 'issues concerning the ethics of apartheid and status of the *volk*'. It is around these that the conflicts within Afrikaner ranks have revolved since 1978. The Herstigte Nasionale Party which broke away from the National Party in 1969 was given new political momentum as the latter moved away from Verwoerdian policies, and was joined by the Conservative Party which further fractured the ruling party as a result of opposition to the new dispensation. The bitterness of the splits within the National Party, the vehemence of their Afrikaner opponents, and their electoral potential as economic recession threatens not inconsiderable numbers of white workers, civil servants, farmers and small-scale businessmen, have forced the 'reformists' on to the defensive, making them reiterate the principles of nationalism and 'separate development'.[193]

Racist and segregationist ideologies which have been so internalised by whites cannot be easily discarded. Whereas the Verwoerdian discourse of apartheid gave value and meaning to individual subjectivity, and legitimated white rule, the new language of legitimation cannot. Posel suggests that where ideologies can, through sets of symbols and practices, enter and transform individual consciousness, languages of legitimation have a narrower role. Prophetically, she concludes, 'To this extent therefore, the ideological potential of the state's new legitimatory discourse seems inherently limited. Hence too the limits of the alternatives to coercive or repressive control in the maintenance of "organised domination" by the present "reformist" state.'[194]

VIII

Constitutional developments in South Africa in the early 1980s underlined once more the pervasiveness of ethnic thinking in its ruling-class strategies, and the complexity of its ethnic order. The 'reformed' constitution, which has a tricameral but racially divided legislature with a related franchise, is part of a set of stratagems devised by the ruling Afrikaner National Party (NP) to cope with a number of wide-ranging challenges to existing social, economic and political relationships. The reformist strategy is perceived by its creators as a far more radical departure than any other made by Afrikaner nationalists. The purpose of the constitutional reforms is to win the collaboration of Coloureds and Indians, ethnic groups that have previously been excluded explicitly from even the trappings of legislative power.

The new constitution, however, was not unanimously welcomed in South Africa. Although it received the support of the majority of white electors as well as the endorsement of much of big business, it failed to win the approval of either the PFP or dissident Afrikaner nationalists. The PFP maintained that the new constitution fell far short of the reforms necessary to ensure stability, because it made no provision for the majority black population. Although the constitutional arrangements were unlikely to lead to the defeat of the dominant Afrikaner party in the new Parliament, the Afrikaner opposition parties perceived the constitution as the thin edge of the wedge, the first step on a political path that would lead ultimately to majority rule.

More importantly, those for whom the new constitution was ostensibly devised, the minority Indian and Coloured populations, clearly rejected this institutional creation by refusing to make use of the racially and ethnically defined franchise which was presented to them. Despite widespread attempts to persuade would-be electors to the polls, the turn-out at the racially separated elections was extremely low. In the political space created by the state's need to legitimate the constitutional changes, new political organisations arose, which para-doxically led the call for the successful boycott of the new South African Parliament. Most prominent of these was the United Demo-cratic Front (UDF), a new 'umbrella' organisation of Africans, Col-oureds and Indians, which claimed the Congress tradition and its Freedom Charter as their own, and brought together many of the contradictory legacies of African political consciousness we have ex-plored in this volume.

These radical opponents boycotted the election on the grounds that the new constitution denied representation of the majority black population and was designed to co-opt the Indian and Coloured populations – and particularly their middle classes – in the struggle to maintain power over the largely proletarian African population. The effect on the excluded African populace has been catalytic: they have seen the constitutional proposals as an outright affront to their legitimate political aspirations and the elections precipitated a new phase of protest and violent insurrection.

Even among NP followers, support for the new legislature has been lukewarm. And, indeed, there is very little in this constitutional manipulation that can be used to arouse enthusiasm. On the contrary, unable to proclaim that their grand design paves the way for a great moral crusade that will transform South Africa into a new and just society, the 'reformers' have been forced to assert, as we have seen, that they are concerned with no more than a series of technical exercises in the interests of 'good government'. Yet the requirements of the new state programme, however inadequate from the vantage-point of the ruled, of necessity flies in the face of previous policy and ideology. The new situation demands that fundamental aspects of the ideology and institutions of apartheid should be jettisoned. To do this is to ask the ruling political party not merely to change its spots, but to create a new beast. Not surprisingly, therefore, the party has chosen to bypass the dilemma by claiming that it would do no more than cope with the technical problems common to all modern industrialising societies. To do this has meant presenting South Africa's ethnic divisions and apartheid structures as somehow 'natural' and immutable for the black population, while at the same time telling Afrikaners that their own nationalist identity is outmoded in some particulars.

There is nothing new about this process. Despite the rhetoric, ethnic categories in South Africa are neither natural or immutable. The boundaries of ethnic identity are fluid, and have constantly shifted in response to political, social and economic circumstance. For much of this century, the state has actively intervened to shape this ethnic identification. The new constitution itself is but one of a host of examples of the way in which this has been done. Paradoxically, however, this attempt to create institutions based upon ethnic identities, which the NP has largely defined, has undermined a crucial element of Afrikaner self-identification. It has provoked unprecedented African protest by way of response, and an unprecedented threat to the apartheid state.

Yet if the boundaries of ethnicity are mutable, the current phase of protest has also followed the contours of earlier resistance to the South African state. The continuities of Eastern Cape radicalism and the traditions of African nationalism have been symbolised by the banners of the banned ANC and the Communist Party of South Africa flying at the funerals of Matthew Goniwe and his associates in Cradock, an old nationalist centre; the strength of working-class consciousness on the East Rand, and also its ethnic division and violence have been equally demonstrated in recent events; while once again Natal after a period of relative quiescence has seen the backlash of conservative forces against vulnerable groups, in part a product of the politics of cultural nationalism. Deep-rooted political traditions have been reworked to meet the demands of a dramatically changing present.

Notes and references

1 'State formation, nationalism and political culture in nineteenth-century Germany', in Raphael Samuel and Gareth Stedman Jones (eds), *Culture, Ideology and Politics. Essays for Eric Hobsbawm* (London 1982) p. 278.

2 For a discussion of the difference between 'inherent', and disparate, popular ideology and 'structured' ideology, and the relationship between the two, see George Rudé, *Ideology and Popular Consciousness* (London 1980) Ch. 2.

3 Benedict Anderson, *Imagined Communities* (London 1983).

4 Originally the South African Native National Congress, founded in 1912.

5 The wars on the highveld which accompanied the rise of the Zulu kingdom in the second and third decade of the nineteenth century.

6 The literature on the construction of ethnicity is considerable and growing; for specific Southern African applications, see the contributions to Leroy Vail (ed.), *The Political Economy of Ethnicity in Southern and Central Africa* (forthcoming). More generally for the ways in which identities are constantly reconstructed, E. Hobsbawm and T. Ranger, *The Invention of Tradition* (Cambridge 1983).

7 For a general overview of the changes in the nineteenth century, see the introductions to S. Marks and A. Atmore (eds), *Economy and Society in Pre-industrial South Africa* (London 1980) and S. Marks and R. Rathbone, *Industrialisation and Social Change* (London 1983).

8 S. Trapido, '"The friends of the natives": merchants, peasants and the political ideological structure of liberalism in the Cape, 1854–53', in Marks and Atmore (eds), *Economy and Society*, p. 248.

9 J. Marincowitz, 'Rural production and labour in the Western Cape, 1838 to 1888, with special reference to the wheat-producing districts', Ph.D thesis (London 1985) pp. 87–105.

10 Cited in S. Trapido, 'The origins of the Cape franchise qualifications of 1853', *Journal of African History*, (hereafter *JAH*), V, 1, 1964, p. 51.

11 *Ibid.*, p. 53.

12 Trapido, '"The friends of the natives"', pp. 248–51.

13 *Ibid.*, p. 268.

14 Brian Willan, 'An African in Kimberley: Sol T. Plaatje, 1894–1898', in Marks and Rathbone (eds) *Industrialisation and Social Change*, pp. 241–5.

15 John Angove in his *In the Early Days: Pioneer Life on the South African Diamond Fields* (London 1910) p. xxviii.

16 André Odendaal, 'African political movements in the Eastern Cape, 1880–1910', D.Phil. thesis, (Cambridge 1983) pp. 32, 43.

17 See pp. 13–14 below.

18 Odendaal, 'African political movements', pp. 57–9.
19 *Ibid.*, p. 48.
20 See Ch. 2 below.
21 G. M. Frederickson, *White Supremacy: A comparative study in American and South African history* (New York and Oxford 1981) p. 188.
22 See Marks and Rathbone, *Industrialisation and Social Change*, p. 5.
23 'Watchtower speech', 18 May 1903, in C. Headlam (ed.) *The Milner Papers, 1899–1905*, vol. 2 (London 1931) p. 466.
24 Cf. John Cell, *Segregation. The Highest Stage of White Supremacy. The origins of segregation in South Africa and the American South* (Cambridge 1982) p. 48; S. Marks and S. Trapido, 'Lord Milner and the South African State', *History Workshop*, 8, 1979; for Coloureds, see Ch. 5 below.
25 Cell, *Segregation*; M. Lacey, *Working for Boroko* (Johannesburg 1981); Ch. 5 below.
26 See Ch. 2 below.
27 Cited in Ch. 2 below.
28 *Report of the Economic and Wage Commission* (1925) UG 14–1926, para. 275, cited in R. Buell, *The Native Problem in Africa* (New York 1928) vol. 1, p. 135.
29 Paul B. Rich, *White Power and the Liberal Conscience. Racial segregation and South African liberalism, 1920–60* (Manchester 1984) pp. 68–9.
30 D. Moodie, *The Rise of Afrikanerdom* (Berkeley 1980) p. 261, citing Hertzog's *Gedenkboek*, p. 238. It is fascinating that President Botha made use of this speech in August 1985.
31 Heaton Nichols Papers, Killie Campbell Library, Durban, MS. Nich. 2.08 Folder 3, nd KCM 3323, cited in S. Marks, 'Natal, the Zulu Royal Family, and the ideology of segregation', *Journal of Southern African Studies* (hereafter *JSAS*), 4 (2) 1978, 180.
32 Cf. George L. Mosse, *Towards the Final Solution. A history of European racism* (London, Melbourne and Toronto 1978).
33 E. A. Walker, *Lord de Villiers and His Times: South Africa 1842–1914* (London 1925) p. 5.
34 31 Aug. 1857.
35 *De Zuid Afrikaan*, 31 Aug. 1857 cited in S. Trapido, 'White conflict and non-white participation in the politics of the Cape of Good Hope, 1853–1910', Ph.D. thesis (London 1970) p. 50; J. du P. Scholtz, *Die Afrikaner en sy Taal* (Cape Town 1939) p. 111.
36 André du Toit, 'Puritans in Africa? Afrikaner "Calvinism" and Kuyperian neo-Calvinism in late nineteenth-century in South Africa', in *Comparative Studies History and Society* 27, 3, April 1985, pp. 209–240, see also his 'No chosen people: the myth of the Calvinist origins of Afrikaner nationalism and its history', *American Historical Review*, 88, 1983; 'Captive to the nationalist paradigm: Prof. F. A. Van Jaarsveld and the historical evidence for the Afrikaner's ideas on his calling and mission', *South African Historical Journal*, 16, 1984.
37 H. Giliomee, 'Constructing Afrikaner nationalism, 1850–1915', in Vail (ed.), *The Political Economy of Ethnicity*.
38 See Ch. 3 below.
39 See Ch. 3 below.
40 For these well-known episodes, see, for example, C. W. de Kiewiet, *The Imperial Factor in South Africa* (Cambridge 1937).

41 See T. R. H. Davenport, *The Afrikaner Bond. The history of a South African political party, 1880–1911* (Cape Town, London and New York 1966).
42 Marincowitz, 'Rural production and labour', p. 244.
43 Du Toit, 'No chosen people', p. 951.
44 H. Giliomee, *JSAS*, (forthcoming).
45 Initially *Di Patriot*; Giliomee, 'Constructing Afrikaner nationalism'.
46 See Ch. 3 below.
47 See F. A. Van Jaarsveld, *The Awakening of Afrikaner Nationalism, 1868–1881* (Cape Town 1961) pp. 19, 53–57.
48 As late as 1895, there was a real danger of civil war between Afrikaners in the Cape and the Transvaal, as the famous 'drifts crisis' of that year revealed.
49 On the importance of the intelligentsia to nationalist movements, see Anthony D. Smith, *The Ethnic Revival* (Cambridge 1981) Ch. 6; Anderson, *Imagined Communities*, Ch. 5.
50 A. M. Grundlingh, *Die 'Hensoppers' en 'Joiners'. Die Rasionaal en Verskynsel van Verraad* (Pretoria and Cape Town 1979).
51 See Ch. 3 below.
52 Charles van Onselen, *Studies in the Social and Economic History of the Witwatersrand 1886–1914, 2 New Nineveh* (Johannesburg and London 1982) pp. 112, 159.
53 *Ibid.*, pp. 112–13.
54 Jon Lewis, *Industrialisation and Trade Union Organisation in South Africa, 1924–55* (Cambridge 1984) p. 79.
55 See Ch. 3 below.
56 See Ch. 3 below.
57 Dan O'Meara, *Volkskapitalisme. Class, capital, and ideology in the development of Afrikaner nationalism, 1934–1948* (Cambridge 1983) pp. 59–66.
58 Moodie, *The Rise of Afrikanerdom*, is by far the best account of the ideology of this period.
59 *Die Oosterlig*, 8 Nov. 1937, cited in Moodie, *The Rise of Afrikanerdom*, p. 168.
60 Moodie, *The Rise of Afrikanerdom*, p. 203.
61 O'Meara, *Volkskapitalisme*, pp. 110ff.
62 E. G. Jansen before the FAK *Volkskongress*, 1944, cited in O'Meara, *Volkskapitalisme*, p. 173.
63 G. Cronje, *'n Tuiste vir die Nageslag* (A home for posterity) (Johannesburg 1945) p. 40, cited in H. Simson, *The Social Origins of Afrikaner Fascism and its Apartheid Policy* (Uppsala Studies in Economic History, vol. 21) 1980, p. 184.
64 G. Cronje, *Voogdyskap en Apartheid* (Trusteeship and Apartheid) (Pretoria 1948) pp. 60–1; see also, G. Cronje, W. Nichol and E. P. Groenewald, *Regverdige Rasse-Apartheid*, (Just Racial Apartheid) (Stellenbosch 1947).
65 *Volkshandel*, Feb. 1947, cited in O'Meara, *Volkskapitalisme*, p. 175.
66 O'Meara, *Volkskapitalisme*, pp. 242–7. On Afrikaner nationalism in the 1950's we benefitted from discussions with John Lazar who has since

gone on to produce a number of papers which greatly add to the understanding of this subject.

67 See H. Adam and H. Giliomee, *Ethnic Power Mobilised. Can South Africa Change?* (New Haven and London 1979) pp. 160–76.

68 See pp. 47–52 below.

69 M. Legassick, 'Legislation, ideology and economy in post-1948 South Africa, *JSAS*, I (1) 1974, 5–35.

70 The literature on uprooting is considerable. For a synthesis based on the five volumes of data collected by the Surplus People's Project, see Laurine Platzky and Cherryl Walker (for the SPP) *The Surplus People. Forced Removals in South Africa* (Johannesburg 1985).

71 The 'Bantustans' may have no international recognition, but for the people living within their boundaries, the dictates of their so-called 'homeland' governments have very material effects on daily life. See for example, B. Streak, *Render Unto Kaizer* (Johannesburg 1981).

72 There is remarkably little even in the European literature on nationalism on the role of women, despite their significance, for example, in Nazi ideology, and the reliance on the explanation of 'early socialisation' as a crucial in the fostering of a sense of national or ethnic identity. For some reflections on the problem in twentieth-century Natal, see S. Marks, 'Patriotism, patriarchy and purity: Natal and the politics of cultural nationalism: in Vail (ed.), *The Political Economy of Ethnicity*.

73 Belinda Bozzoli, 'Marxism, feminism and South African Studies', *JSAS*, 9 (2) 1983, 161.

74 There is very little literature on this, but see C. Murray, 'Ethnic nationalism and structural unemployment: refugees in the Orange Free State', in *The Societies of Southern Africa in the Nineteenth and Twentieth Centuries*, vol. 12 (Collected Seminar Papers, Institute of Commonwealth Studies, London 1982) pp. 108–16. For suggestive insights into the manipulation of ethnicity by a Bantustan bureaucracy. Murray does not deal specifically with women – the majority of Bantustan residents.

75 For imperial ideas on the subject, see A. Davin, 'Imperialism and motherhood', *History Workshop*, 5 (Spring) 1978, 9–66.

76 For a pioneering account, see Hansi Pollack, 'Women in Witwatersrand industries', MA. thesis (University of Witwatersrand 1932).

77 Lewis, *Industrialisation and Trade Union Organisation*, p. 144, citing the Industrial Tribunal of 1957.

78 See pp. 124–55 below.

79 See Ch. 4 below.

80 See Ch. 4 below.

81 Lewis, *Industrialisation and Trade Union Organisation*, p. 74.

82 Elsabe Brink, 'Plays, poetry and production: the literature of garment workers', *South African Labour Bulletin*, 9 (8) 1984, 34.

83 *Ibid.*, pp. 39–44.

84 Lewis, *Industrialisation and Trade Union Organisation*, p. 74.

85 For an account which focuses on the manipulations of the state, see R. H. Davies, *Capital, State and White Labour in South Africa, 1900–1960* (Brighton 1979).

86 Bozzoli, 'Marxism, feminism and South African Studies', p. 162.

87 See Ch. 4 below.

88 Lewis *Industrialisation and Trade Union Organisation*, p. 150.
89 *Ibid.*, p. 60.
90 See Ch. 5 below.
91 See Marincowitz, 'Rural production and labour', p. 238 and ff.
92 See Ch. 5 below.
93 For black participation in the South African War, see especially, P. Warwick, *Black People and the South African War, 1899–1902* (Cambridge 1983) and specifically on the Cape, W. R. Nasson, 'Black society in the Cape Colony and the South African War of 1899–1902: A social history', Ph.D. thesis (Cambridge 1983).
94 André Odendaal, *Vukani Bantu! The beginnings of black protest politics in South Africa to 1912* (Cape Town 1984) discusses this at great length.
95 See Ch. 5 below.
96 Ian Goldin, 'Coloured Preference Politics and the Making of Coloured Political Identity in the Western Cape Region of South Africa, with particular reference to the period 1948–1984', D. Phil. Oxford, p. 77
97 Goldin, *Ibid.*, p. 177
98 This is the theme behind John Buchan's best-selling novel, *Prester John* (London 1910), but it was also expressed by Lord Selborne, for example, in 1907. See Ch. 5 below.
99 Cited in Ch. 5 below.
100 In Ch. 5 below.
101 See W. Hofmeyr, 'African politics in the Western Cape', M.A. thesis (Cape Town 1984).
102 See p. 44.
103 Ian Goldin, 'Coloured preference Politics'.
104 See Ch. 5 below.
105 Cited in F. Ginwala, *Indian South Africans* (Minority Rights Group Report, London 1977) p. 7.
106 See pp. 182–208 below.
107 See Ch. 6 below.
108 See Swan, Ch. 6 below. Also her *Gandhi. The South African Experience, 1890–1914* (Johannesburg 1985).
109 See p. 198 below.
110 See p. 199 below.
111 Dave Hemson, 'Dockworkers, labour circulation and class struggles in Durban, 1940–1959', *JSAS*, 4 (1) 1977, 100–2.
112 See Ch. 6 below.
113 See Ch. 6 below.
114 Hemson, 'Dockworkers, labour circulation and class struggles', p. 102.
115 J. F. J. Matthias, 'The 1949 Durban Riots', M.A. thesis (London 1978) pp. 20–21; Marks, 'Patriotism, patriarchy and purity'.
116 J. F. J. Matthias, 'The 1949 Durban Riots', p. 30.
117 See Odendaal, *Vukani Bantu*; P. Walshe, *The Rise of African Nationalism in South Africa* (London 1970); H. J. Simons and R. E. Simons, *Class and Colour in South Africa, 1850–1950* (Harmondsworth 1969); E. Roux, *Time Longer than Rope* (Madison, 1964); Mary Benson, *Struggle for a Birthright* (Harmondsworth 1963); P. Wickens *The Industrial and Commercial Workers' Union of Africa* (Cape Town 1978).
118 Most notably by Brian Willan, *Sol T. Plaatje African Nationalist*

1876–1932 (London 1984); Tom Lodge, *Black Politics in South Africa since 1945* (Johannesburg and London, 1983); Shula Marks, *The Ambiguities of Dependence in South Africa. State, class and nationalism in early twentieth century Natal* (Baltimore and Johannesburg 1986); Helen Bradford, 'The African Industrial and Commercial Workers' Union in the South African countryside', Ph.D. thesis (University of Witwatersrand 1985); P. Bonner, 'The Transvaal Native Congress, 1917–1920: the radicalisation of the black petty bourgeoisie on the Rand', in Marks and Rathbone, *Industrialisation and Social Change*, pp. 270–313.

119 See Ch. 7 below.

120 The first President of the ANC was a prominent churchman, the Rev. John Dube, and Presidents Magkatho and Luthuli were devout Christians; the leadership of the United Democratic Front in South Africa today also contains a number of outstanding churchmen – notably Bishop Tutu and the Rev. Alan Boezak.

121 Bengt G. M. Sundkler's pioneering studies, *Bantu Prophets in South Africa* (London, New York and Toronto 1961) and *Zulu Zion* (Uppsala 1976) were perhaps the first to make this clear. By 1960 there were some 2,000 separate independent churches in South Africa, by the 1980s many more. Their adherents have always outnumbered the membership of the more formal political organisations.

122 Odendaal, 'African political movements in the Eastern Cape', p. 43.

123 Bonner, 'The Transvaal Native Congress' discusses one of these moments, and the potential of the African petty bourgeoisie to swing in different directions; Helen Bradford, 'Mass Movements and the Petty Bourgeoisie: social origins of ICU leadership, 1924–1929', *JAH*, **25** (3) 1984, 295–310, discusses the downward pressures on the petty bourgeoisie in the late 1920s and the radicalising effects this had. See also Ch. 8 below. Similar radicalising pressures for class combination appears to be operating at present in South Africa.

124 See Odendaal, 'African political movements'; also Donovan Williams, *Umfundisi. A Biography of Tiyo Soga* (Lovedale 1979). But see also the work of P. Mayer and, in particular 'The origins and decline of two rural revolutionary ideologies', in P. Mayer (ed). *Black Villagers in an Industrial Society* (OUP Cape Town 1980) pp. 1–80.

125 See Marks, 'Patriotism, patriarchy and purity'.

126 Bradford, 'The Industrial and Commercial Workers' Union' is the outstanding exception to this generalisation.

127 See Ch. 7 below.

128 See Ch. 7 below.

129 Pretoria Archives, K22, vol. 4, Evidence to the Native Riots Commission (Durban) (the de Waal Commission). Evidence C. W. Lewis, 29 July 1929, p. 24.

130 The phrase is Tim Couzens's. See '"Moralizing leisure time": the transatlantic connection and black Johannesburg', in Marks and Rathbone, *Industrialisation and Social Change*, pp. 314–38.

131 Cited in Trapido, 'White politics and non-White participation', pp. 365–70; the quotation is on p. 367.

132 For Dube and Booker T. Washington, see R. Hunt Davies, 'John L. Dube: A South African exponent of Booker T. Washington', *'Journal of African Studies*, 2 (4) (Winter) 1975–76, 497–528; W. Manning Marable, 'African nationalist: the life of John Langalibalele Dube', Ph.D. thesis (Maryland 1976).

133 Harry Hayward, *Negro Liberation*, 2nd edn (Chicago 1976) pp. 198–9.

134 See Ch. 7 below.

135 For the role of the Joint Councils in 'moderating African opinion, see B. Hirson, 'Tuskegee, the Joint Councils, and the All African Convention', in *The Societies of Southern Africa in the Nineteenth and Twentieth Centuries*, vol. 11, (Collected Seminar Papers, Institute of Commonwealth Studies, London 1981); Couzens, "Moralizing leisure time".

136 See Ch. 7 below.

137 For the radicalism and activism of black politics in the Western Cape, see especially Hofmeyr, 'African politics in the Western Cape'.

138 See Ch. 5 below.

139 Bradford, 'The Industrial and Commerical Workers' Union'; Hofmeyr, 'African politics in the Western Cape'.

140 See Ch. 8 below.

141 See Ch. 7 below.

142 See Ch. 8 below.

143 Bradford, 'The Industrial and Commercial Workers' Union'.

144 *Ibid.*, pp. 418ff.

145 *Ibid.* This is dealt with at some length in Chapter 7, entitled 'Pigs, Mpondulu, Americans and the millenium: the ICU in the Transkeian territories, 1927–32'.

146 For the Native Republic see M. Legassick, 'Class and nationalism in South African protest. The South African Communist Party and the "Native Republic", 1928–1934' (ocasional paper, Syracuse 1973); Legassick also suggests that most black members of the Communist Party in the United States were ex-members of UNIA (*ibid*).

147 See Ch. 8 below.

148 For an account of Gumede in Moscow, see Harry Hayward, *Black Bolshevik* (Chicago 1978) pp. 214–41.

149 See p. 261 below.

150 See Lacey, *Working for Boroko*; for a detailed discussion of the Native Administration Act, see S. Dubow, 'Holding "a just balance between white and black": the Native Affairs Department in South Africa, c1920–33', *JSAS*, 12(2), April 1986.

151 For the role of these co-optive bodies and of state-manipulated ethnic associations, see Marks, 'Patriotism, patriarchy and purity'; see also P. Harries, 'Capital, class, and internal colonialism: the emergence of ethnicity among the Tsonga speakers of South Africa', in Vail, *Political Economy of Ethnicity*.

152 See Ch. 8 below.

153 B. Hirson, 'Rural revolt in South Africa, 1937–1951' *The Societies of Southern Africa in the Nineteenth and Twentieth Centuries* vol. 8 (Collected Seminar Papers, Institute of Commonwealth Relations, London 1977) pp. 115–32; Bradford, 'The Industrial and Commercial Workers' Union', 420–4. For urban developments, see pp. 47–52 below.

154 See Ch. 7 below.
155 See Ch. 8 below.
156 Cited in B. Hirson, 'Land, labour and the 'Black Republic', paper presented to the SSRC Conference on 'South Africa in the comparative study of race, class and nationalism' (New York, Sept. 1982) p. 23.
157 See Ch. 8 below.
158 See Marks, 'Natal, the Zulu Royal Family and the ideology of segregation', 172–94; S. Marks, *The Ambiguities of Dependence in South Africa*, Ch. 2.
159 See above, p. 36. For the Zulu Society, see S. Marks, 'Patriotism, patriarchy and purity'; for 'tribalism' at Adams in the 1930s and 1940s, see E. Mphahlele, quoted N. C. Manganyi, *Looking Through the Keyhole. Dissenting essays on the black experience* (Johannesburg 1981) pp. 16–17. See also his *Down Second Avenue* (London 1959) pp. 145–56; cf. also Killie Campbell Library, Minute Books, General Purposes Committee, Adams, Report No. 2, 24 June 1949.
160 G. Gerhart, *Black Power in South Africa. The evolution of an ideology* (Berkeley, Los Angeles, London 1978) pp. 54–65.
161 See Ch. 9 below. More generally on the mine-workers strike, see D. O'Meara, 'The 1946 African Mine Workers' Strike and the Political Economy of South Africa; *Jnl of Commonwealth and Comparative Politics*, 13, 2, 1975; and D. Moodie, 'The Moral Economy of the Mine and the African Mine Workers' Union: 1940s mine disturbances', *JSAS* 1986 (forthcoming).
162 Tom Lodge, *Black Politics in South Africa since 1945* (London and New York 1983) Ch. 1.
163 The most recent account is in Lodge, *Black Politics*.
164 For the Defiance Campaign in East London and its hinterland, see Lodge, *Black Politics*, pp. 56–7.
165 See Ch. 9 below.
166 Apart from this example provided by Beinart, there seem to have been some attempts in the 1950s by local ANC activists to enlist criminal gangs, and equivalent attempts by the state and capitalist interests, as happened during the Evaton bus boycott and the Newclare evictions. For the latter, see Jeff Guy and Motlatsi Thabane, 'The *Ma-Rashea*: a participants perspective', paper presented to the Witwatersrand History Workshop, '*Class, community and conflict: local perspectives*', Jan. 1984; and Lodge, *Black Politics*, pp. 176–7.
167 See Ch. 9 below.
168 See Ch. 9 below.
169 See Ch. 10 below.
170 The parallels with occurrences in South Africa's urban and rural locations today, carried out ostensibly under the umbrella organisations, whether of the Left, like the UDF, or the Right, like Inkatha, are frightening.
171 For a brief examination of the contemporary meaning of violence, see WHO, *Health and Apartheid* (Geneva 1983) pp. 165–6, 175–7. Despite its historical and contemporary significance, the nature of violence in South Africa has been relatively little explored, whether at the state level or internally directed. For a pioneering attempt to look at rural violence, translated into so-called 'faction-fights', see J. Clegg, '*Ukubuyisa*

Isidumba – "Bringing back the body": an examination into the ideology of vengeance in the Msinga and Mpofana rural locations (1882–1944)', unpublished paper to African Studies Seminar (University of Witwatersrand, May 1979).

172 Guy and Thabane, 'The *Ma-Rashea*'.

173 Lodge, *Black Politics*, p. 193.

174 See Ch. 11 below.

175 K. Luckhardt and B. Wall, *Organise or Starve, The History of the South African Congress of trade Unions* (London 1980) p. 217.

176 See Ch. 11 below.

177 Lodge, *Black Politics*, pp. 190, 193.

178 *Ibid.*, Ch. 8.

179 See Ch. 4 below.

180 For the processes involved, see the essays in Vail, *The Political Economy of Ethnicity*.

181 See Ch. 12 below.

182 For the black consciousness movement, see Gerhart, *Black power*; its relationship to the Black Power movement in the USA is discussed on pp. 270–81. See also C. H. D. Halisi, 'Black Consciousness: ideological and political realignment: notes towards an interpretation', paper presented to the SSRC Conference 'South Africa in the comparative study of race, class and nationalism' (New York Sept. 1982).

183 For a discussion of some of the contradictions, see John Brewer, 'The membership of Inkatha in Kwamashu', *African Affairs*, **84** (334) Jan. 1985, 111–35; Marks, *Ambiguities*, Ch. 4; for the relationship with the PFP, see Ch. 12 below.

184 For some of the factors leading up to the State of Emergency, see John Saul and Stephen Gelb, 'The Crisis in South Africa. Class defence, class revolution', special issue of *Monthly Review*, **33** (3) 1981. For the implications of the State of Emergency, see *The Weekly Mail*, vol. 1, no. 7, 26 July–1 Aug. 1985, 'Activists on the run as police dragnet spreads' p. 1, and 'From a state of lawlessness to a state beyond law: The state of emergency explained: The powers of the police, the rights of detainees', pp. 10–11.

185 See Ch. 12 below.

186 *The Weekly Mail*, vol. 1, no. 14, 13–19 Sept. 1985, 'What Relly will tell the ANC' p. 1. For the views of young Africans on capitalism., see 'Most blacks want sanctions, poll shows', p. 6, and 'White capitalism and black rage', p. 9.

187 See Ch. 13 below.

188 See Ch. 13 below.

189 See Ch. 13 below.

190 See Ch. 14 below.

191 See Ch. 14 below. See also CIIR, *South Africa in the 1980s* (London 1985).

192 See Ch. 14 below.

193 Posel's prescience has been illustrated by recent events, and especially Botha's much-heralded and in the end disastrous speech to the National Party Conference in Natal in Aug. 1985.

194 See Ch. 14 below.

CHAPTER TWO

Race, civilisation and culture: the elaboration of segregationist discourse in the inter-war years*

Saul Dubow

Victorian pessimism, evolutionary thought and scientific racism

The core principles of classical liberalism, as exemplified by Benthamite utilitarianism and the *laissez-faire* political economy of Smith and Ricardo, reached their prime by the mid-nineteenth century. Thereafter, confidence in the inevitability of human progress, which strongly informed the imperial mission, began to lose its force.

Economic depression in Britain during the 1880s was accompanied by serious unemployment and an increase in working-class radicalism. This crisis provoked a reassessment of traditional social objectives. There was a growing consciousness of the need to preserve social order and an awareness that the problems of poverty and social welfare could not be solved by *laissez-faire* policies alone. Thus social reformers began to embrace measures which were by nature collectivist rather than individualist.[1]

The demise of cherished liberal ideals – such as the equality of man and the doctrine of inevitable progress – found expression in a number of ways. One important measure of this change is the spectacular explosion of biologically based racial science in the second half of the nineteenth century.[2] The development of racist thinking is an enormously complex (and developing) subject. Whatever its origins, there appears to be consensus among scholars that the second half of the nineteenth century experienced a marked

---

* An earlier version of this chapter (with a stronger emphasis on anthropology) was given to the Witwatersrand University 1984 History Workshop, and in a revised form to the University of Cape Town Africa Seminar. This chapter has been rewritten to take account of criticisms and includes a new section on racial biology. It was presented to an Oxford seminar in 1985. The present version has been read and commented on by Stanley Trapido and Willian Beinart, to whom thanks are due.

increase in racist discourse. In England, concludes Nancy Stepan, 'the nineteenth century closed with racism firmly established in popular opinion and in science'.[3] In the United States too, the preoccupation of European racists with evolution and eugenics had come to dominate American racist thought by the turn of the century.[4]

The bizarre (if vigorous) debates within racist science are exceedingly intricate. But despite their differences, social Darwinists, Spencerians, Lamarckians, craniologists and physical anthropologists all set themselves the task of classifying the world's races according to a natural hierarchy. The biological sciences in particular were of great importance in this process. Deeply embedded evolutionist assumptions together with the doctrine of the 'survival of the fittest' came to be applied to the human situation. Biology, writes Greta Jones, helped to 'create the kind of moral universe in which nature reflected society and vice versa'.[5] Racial thought also drew heavily on the metaphor of the family, an 'area where subordination was legitimised'.[6] Imagery derived from the biological sciences and the family gave rise to ubiquitous notions of the 'dependent' or 'child races'. In the imperial context this was later transformed into conceptions of 'separate development' and 'trusteeship'.

Stepan argues that the mid nineteenth-century mood of social optimism had, by the turn of that century, conceded to a profoundly pessimistic outlook which was 'perfectly expressed' by the advent of Francis Galton's eugenics movement.[7] Eugenics was the so-called science of 'racial stocks'. It was founded on the idea that social ends could be efficiently achieved by the deliberate manipulation of genetic pools. As such, eugenics was deliberately intended as a practical guide to the administration of society and the formulation of social legislation.

Eugenics drew strongly on the late nineteenth-century fear of working-class discontent and was infused with an 'air of catastrophism'.[8] It was deeply influenced by both Darwinian and Malthusian thought and effectively served to set the doctrine of evolutionary progress on its head. According to Galton, Western civilisation was on the decline. It could only be saved through the adoption of radical measures of social and biological engineering.

The influence of the eugenics movement, and of racial biology more generally, was deeply pervasive in Britain and the United States by the early decades of the twentieth century. Eugenics was by no means the exclusive preserve of intellectual cranks. Its powerful potential as a force of social engineering attracted widespread interest among influential radical and socialist thinkers. J. M. Keynes, Sidney Webb,

H. G. Wells, Bernard Shaw and H. J. Laski are just some of the prominent thinkers who (in varying degrees) expressed an interest in eugenics as a means of effecting fundamental societal reforms.[9]

Within Britain eugenics was primarily addressed to questions of class and was viewed as a mechanism to deal with problems of poverty and the physical and moral 'degeneration' of the urban proletariat. Its language and applications were, however, readily transferred to the colonial domain, where it was applied to questions of race. In the form of social imperialism (a turn-of-the-century political programme designed to ameliorate domestic class conflict by incorporating the working classes into support of the imperial mission) eugenists and social Darwinists were prominent in proclaiming the breeding of an 'imperial race'.[10]

Eugenics, incidentally, has an interesting association with southern Africa. The ideas of Francis Galton, its inventor, were strongly influenced by his experiences in South West Africa (Namibia) during 1850–51, where he was a pioneer explorer among the Damara.[11] Eugenist ideas were powerfully reinforced when the initial setbacks of the Boer War and the poor physical condition of the working-class recruits became a cause for imperial 'panic'.[12] It is noteworthy too, that Lancelot Hogben, the most effective and consistent scientific critic of eugenics, was deeply influenced through his direct exposure to racism in South Africa, having served as professor of zoology at the University of Cape Town from 1927–30. Hogben referred to South Africa as a 'chromatocracy' and ridiculed the bigotry of his academic colleagues there.[13]

Social Darwinism, eugenics and social imperialism are all reflective of the growing pessimism and collectivism of late nineteenth-century British thought. The development of these movements was in part a response to the depression of the 1880s and the growing radicalism of the working classes. George Mosse notes a 'new tone of urgency' informing racial biology at the beginning of the twentieth century, and he associates this with 'accelerated urbanism and population growth' in western and central Europe.[14] Abroad, major events like the 1857 Indian Mutiny, the Governor Eyre controversy of 1865–66 in the West Indies, and the Boer War of 1899–1902, together served to cast doubt upon the viability of the imperial mission. These setbacks provided fertile ground for the pessimism implicit in social Darwinism and encouraged the use of social engineering to reverse the decline.

In South Africa itself, similar processes are discernible. A number of writers have remarked on a distinct ideological shift in the late nineteenth-century Cape. Parry, for example, has demonstrated the manner by which the 'amalgamationist' policies of Sir George Grey had been gradually undermined by the close of the nineteenth century. Although the rhetoric of 'civilising the backward races' persisted, the combination of administrative difficulties and the new conditions occasioned by the mineral revolution, combined to rob the classical liberal vision of its practical force. Thus Parry regards Rhodes's Glen Grey Act of 1894 as a key moment in the replacement of the assimilationist strategy by one of segregation.[15]

Russell Martin's analysis of the Transkeian administration in the late nineteenth century traces the transition in social evolutionary theory which so strongly informed the world-view of the administrators. He shows how, particularly after the wars of 1877–78 and the rebellions of 1880–81, administrators became ever more sceptical of the potential for success of the Victorian civilising mission. By slow degrees 'the orthodoxy of Grey who had sought to promote "civilisation by mingling" became the heterodoxy of the Transkeian magistrates who set their face against what they called "amalgamation"'.[16] This change in perspective appears to have been true of the British Colonial Office as a whole. Thus Hyam, writing of the Liberal government of 1905–08, claims that by this time 'the mid-Victorian objective of turning Africans into black Europeans had long been given up, and the question of educating them towards self-government of the European type relegated to the distant future ... the tendency was towards segregation rather than assimilation'.[17] Hyam ascribes this change to the historical experience of colonialism, as well as to the teachings of 'pseudo Darwinian science'.[18]

As a theory, segregation was strongly associated with the demise of mid-Victorian liberalism and the ascendancy of racial science, in particular eugenics. Segregation was most often presented as a compromise between the discredited policies of 'assimilation' and 'repression', or as Edgar Brookes put it, 'between the Scylla of identity and the Charbydis of subordination'.[19] This implied a rejection both of classic liberalism *and* of overt forms of racism. The rejection of these polar opposites did not, however, constitute a total break with its central assumptions. Born out of compromise, segregation was not a new philosophy. It was essentially a synthesis of divergent political traditions of political thought and practice. The discourse of segregation therefore continued to carry within its terms resonances of those very elements which it professed to reject.

Racist thought in South Africa

The lived relations of paternalism which bound black and white together in South Africa presented white supremacy as part of the natural order of things in its (im)moral universe. To an extent, this obviated the need for the elaboration of explicit theories of racial superiority as evidenced in Britain or the United States. It is nevertheless anomalous that so little attention has been given to the development of racist thought in South Africa. Aside from maverick individuals like Fred Bell, it is true that there is a relative absence of virulent scientific racism in early twentieth-century South Africa.

This point has recently been made by Paul Rich.[20] In making it, however, Rich has underrated the extent to which scientific racism was an implicit component of the political discourse of the time. Indeed, it is perhaps in virtue of the fact that racist assumptions were *so* prevalent in the common-sense thinking of early-twentieth-century South Africa that the relative absence of eugenist or social Darwinist theories is to be explained. In the pre-Nazi era, theories of racial superiority derived from the biological sciences were widely prevalent in South Africa. If we return with John Coetzee to 'the discourse of racism before 1945, what strikes us first about it, is its nakedness, its shamelessness'.[21]

The imagery of social Darwinism is clearly discernible in three important areas of political debate: speculation about the relative intelligence of blacks and whites; the almost universally expressed horror of 'miscegenation'; and fear of racial 'degeneration' following upon the uncontrolled development of a black and white proletariat in the cities.

With respect to urban legislation, the language of biological racism is especially clear. Maynard Swanson, writing of the 'sanitation syndrome' in the early-twentieth-century Cape, examines the 'imagery of infectious disease as a societal metaphor', and demonstrates its role in the evolution of the ideology and institutions of urban segregation.[22]

In the view of many, Africans were 'naturally' part of the land. Cities were portrayed as an 'alien environment' for which Africans were supposedly not yet ready. To the new migrant the city was seen as the site of vice and immorality, 'influences far too potent for his [the African's] powers of resistance'.[23] The phenomenon of 'poor whiteism' was frequently held up as a warning of what would occur should unrestrained African proletarianisation be allowed to continue. For many biological determinists 'poor whiteism' was a perfect illustration of the inevitable tendency of civilisation to decline.

Concern was expressed for the physical and moral 'degeneration' of Africans in the foreign environment of the cities. In the 1920s urban social welfare became an important area of liberal concern, as liberals attempted to arrest physical and moral 'decay' and to defuse the potential for social and industrial conflict.[24] Notably, the ideological presentation of the 1923 Urban Areas Act stressed the measure as a 'protective' measure which would assist Africans in their confrontation with 'industrialism'.

The language of eugenics is strongly evident in the obsession with 'race fusion' or 'miscegenation'.[25] Eugenics added fuel to the prevalent fear of racial mixing, since it warned against the dilution of 'pure racial stocks' and the 'decline of white civilisation'. Miscegenation, particularly among the working classes, was held to sap the fibre of white civilisation at its most vulnerable point. 'Race fusion' was portrayed in the most apocalyptic terms by such eugenist-inspired catastrophists as Ernest Stubbs and George Heaton Nicholls.[26] Maurice Evans, associated himself (as did most white liberal thinkers) with the opinion of the 'average white South African' that the 'admixture in blood of the races is the worst that can happen, at least for the white race, and perhaps for both'.[27] So strong was feeling on this point that African politicians took care to distinguish their political claims from the implication that they desired 'social equality' – often as not, a euphemism for miscegenation.

The dangers of miscegenation were powerfully exploited at the hustings. In his speeches on segregation Hertzog invariably warned of the vulnerability of white civilisation in the face of the numerical preponderance of Africans, and he frequently equated political rights for Africans with 'swamping'.[28] The full force of these warnings escape us today – as they have eluded those liberal historians who naïvely attempt to show by means of figures that Hertzog's fears of the rapid expansion in the African franchise were unfounded.[29] The impact of 'swamping' or of the 'rising tide of colour' is rendered more comprehensible when set in the prevailing mood of the time, with its paranoia about civilisation's retrogressive tendencies and its vulnerability in the face of a 'vigorous' and 'virile' mass of 'barbarians' who were 'flooding' into the cities.

This point was observed by the liberal philosopher Alfred Hoernlé who noted that 'the fear of race mixture is at the root of the "anti native" attitude of many White South Africans'. He explained that those who were 'primarily afraid of the native's economic competition or of being swamped by the native vote' were 'easily strengthened in their opposition' when it was put to them that economic and political integration would 'inevitably lead to a breaking down of social barriers and thus of the racial integrity of the white group'.[30]

The writings of Heaton Nicholls and Sarah Gertrude Millin are suffused with the language and imagery of biological degeneration. Some of these themes are brilliantly analysed by John Coetzee in his essay, 'Blood, flaw, taint, degeneration: the case of Sarah Gertrude Millin'.[31] It was in fact another writer of the period, William Plomer, who turned the threat of miscegenation on its head in his controversial novel *Turbott Wolfe*.[32] The book's fanciful solution to South Africa's racial problems amounted to a form of positive eugenics; the main protagonists of *Turbott Wolfe* propose the establishment of a Young Africa Society, whose function it would be to eradicate race itself through the adoption of a deliberate policy of miscegenation.

The widely debated question of the relative intelligence of blacks and whites, is a further area in which the impact of social Darwinism is evident. The question of the capacity of the African races to rise in the scale of civilisation became an integral part of any discussion on segregation. 'The direction which native policy should take' was, as Rheinallt Jones explained, 'dependent upon the view we take of the place which the primitive races are destined, by reason of their inherent capacities, to have in modern civilisation'.[33] He therefore called upon scientists, psychologists and anthropologists to establish the data upon which a sound social policy could be formulated.

Peter Nielsen, an administrator in Rhodesia, devoted an entire study to answering the question 'Is the African Native equal to the European in mental and moral capacity or is he not?' This, he considered, was the 'crux of the Native Question in South Africa . . .' and the issue on which Africans' 'proper place in the general scheme of our civilisation' would depend. After an exhaustive discussion of contemporary theories of racial biology, he concluded that there was 'good reason for accepting the Bantu as the equals of Europeans in every respect save past achievement . . .'[34]

The problem of genetic inheritance provoked three major problems with respect to Africans; their innate as opposed to their potential mental capacities; whether their intellect was 'originative' as well as 'imitative'; and whether their mental development was 'arrested' after adolescence.[35] The results of intelligence testing, derived from Amercian models then in vogue, was frequently invoked in support of arguments for or against segregation.[36]

Speculation about the relative mental capacity of the different races was by no means confined to those who may obviously be considered to be racists. Prominent liberal thinkers like Maurice Evans, Rheinallt Jones, C. T. Loram and Alfred Hoernlé, all addressed themselves to the question of innate intelligence at one time or another.[37] A. R. Radcliffe-Brown, then professor of social anthropology at the University of Cape Town, was equivocal on the matter. He thought it likely that there were some physiological differences between whites and blacks, but supposed it would not make a vast amount of difference.[38] As regards this form of speculation, the general consensus was expressed by S. M. Molema who said that 'neither capacity nor incapacity have been shown conclusively to be characteristic of the backward races, or more plainly, of the African race'.[39] Notably, a similar conclusion on the indeterminacy of intelligence testing was reached by Werner Eiselen in 1929, later to become a key ideologist and implementor of apartheid.[40]

If most writers were agreed that the matter of biological differences between the races was in doubt, this did not prevent them, however, from making inferences based on their own prejudices and suspicions. For some, innate racial differences were manifestly obvious; the only question which remained was the extent to which Africans could be expected to bridge the intelligence gap. In the case of others, the inconclusive results of scientific research offered hope for the ultimate achievement of liberal ideals. In general, however, to pose the question of biological differentiation in itself presupposed an acceptance of some form of segregation; a policy of benign differentiation, it seemed clear, was the best social laboratory in which the true capacity of Africans could be tested.

The decline of the Victorian 'civilising mission'

If forms of social Darwinist thought informed one aspect of segregationist thought, liberalism constituted another. Mention has been made of the decline of mid-Victorian liberalism, both abroad and in South Africa. In Britain the pessimism and collectivism which replaced earlier confidence in industrial progress, did so against a background of economic and social crisis. In the Cape, the decline of mid-Victorian liberalism occurred in the context of industrialisation, frontier wars and the tenacious resistance of African social systems to their dissolution and incorporation into colonial society.

D. M. Schreuder's study of the British 'civilising mission' is an excellent – if perhaps overstated – interpretation of Victorian imperialism in its late heyday.[41] Schreuder's novel thesis is that the sombre 'official mind' of the British Colonial Office obscures a more purposeful and belligerent form of cultural imperialism in the colonial periphery. Schreuder examines the ideology of 'progress', 'individualism' and 'assimilation' or 'identity', and considers its zealous application by Cape 'native administrators' between the 1860s and 1880s. He indicates how colonial officials devoted themselves to rooting out the 'triad' of traditional cultural and political forms constituted by polygamy, *lobola* and above all, chieftainship.[42] Schreuder displays sensitivity to the material context in which this ideology flourished, and deals with such issues as the desire to establish a limited African peasantry, to secure a force of individual wage labourers and to develop political alliances with an acculturated African 'improving' class.[43]

Although Schreuder does point to a demise in the coherence of the imperial mission by the 1880s, it appears that he exaggerates the belligerence and confidence of the mid-Victorian Cape administrator. He provides us with an ideal image of Victorian cultural imperialism which was never realised in practice. The question of historical reality is not, however, at issue, for I am chiefly concerned here with an analysis of the structure of ideas from which the framework of segregationist ideology was constructed. Notably, a conception of nineteenth-century Cape liberalism as a force for 'assimilation' (very similar to the one outlined by Schreuder) *was* used as a foil by thinkers in the 1920s in their attempt to develop a theory of liberal segregation.

South Africa's transition from a mercantile to an industrial economy in the late nineteenth century was the material context in which the assumptions of classic liberalism were called into question. It was, however, only during the Milnerite reconstruction period, and especially during the decade following the conclusion of the First World War, that the full implications of industrialistion became clear. The declining agricultural capacity of the reserves, the rapid dis-solution of the tribal system, nascent working-class radicalism and the growth of urban slums, were the chief social consequences of South Africa's rapid process of industrialisation. It was in this context that social theorists began to draw on the brand of liberal reformism and collectivism which had been gathering strength overseas. The new liberalism which developed after the Boer War and coalesced on the Witwatersrand during the early 1920s, was born in explicit opposition to its Cape forebears.

By the 1920s Cape liberalism was widely seen as being somewhat archaic, its legacy surviving through ageing patricians like Merriman, Burton and James Rose-Innes. Important African figures like Jabavu, Thema and Plaatje also derived their political world view from this powerfully symbolic tradition. By contrast, the newly constructed liberalism of individuals such as Edgar Brookes, Howard Pim, C. T. Loram and J. D. Rheinallt Jones was strong on pragmatism but rather weaker on principle.

Although in many senses the inheritors of the Cape tradition, the new establishment liberalism eschewed essential tenets of the mid-Victorian project. The writings of Evans, Loram and Brookes rejected the policies of 'identity' and 'assimilation'. In the hands of the liberal segregationists 'civilisation' was replaced by 'culture', 'progress' became synonymous with 'differentiation', while 'individualism' was subsumed into the collective interests of 'racial groups'.

If scientific racism was equated with 'repression' and mid-Victorian liberalism with 'identity', segregation was seen as the synthesis of these polar opposites. An intellectual organising principle was required to validate this synthesis or compromise. The development of an anthropological notion of 'culture' came to serve this purpose admirably.

Anthropology and Bantu studies

The study of anthropology in South Africa was institutionalised during the decade after the First World War.[44] South Africa was a pioneer in this respect. In 1921 A. R. Radcliffe-Brown, one of the acknowledged founders of modern social anthropology, was appointed to the newly established chair of social anthropology at the University of Cape Town. Within a few years all four teaching universities in the country had departments offering courses in Bantu studies and anthropology, or their equivalents.

From the outset, anthropology was looked to as a source of applied knowledge. Influential individuals like C. T. Loram, J. D. Rheinallt Jones, James Duerden and Jan Smuts were instrumental in establishing and promoting anthropology in South Africa. All of them stressed the role that anthropology could play in providing a solution to the so-called 'native question'.[45] In the words of Radcliffe-Brown social anthropology was 'not merely of scientific or academic interest, but of immense practical importance . . .'. Given a situation where the economic, social and cultural situation of the 'native tribes' was being 'altered daily', Radcliffe-Brown extolled the value of anthropological knowledge in 'finding some social and political system in which the natives and the whites may live together without conflict . . .'.[46]

The extravagant claims made as regards anthropology's utilitarian value to native administration, echoed the professed intentions of the International Institute of African Languages and Cultures which was established in 1926 under the patronage of Lord Lugard. In its journal *Africa*, Bronislaw Malinowski articulated the need for a modern 'functional school of anthropology' to be conducted under the aegis of the institute. Its purpose would be to bridge 'the gap between theoretical anthropology and its practical applications' and to provide analytical data on such questions as education, taxation, labour and direct versus indirect rule.[47]

Whether or not the institute and the developing school of functional anthropology fulfilled their intentions in British colonial Africa, is not of immediate concern.[48] In South Africa consistent attempts were made to harness the developing schools of anthropology to the interests of the state.

The universities soon devised diploma courses in Bantu studies which were specially tailored to the perceived needs of native administrators. They also held annual vacation courses with a distinct anthropological bent, for the benefit of missionaries and administrators. In 1925 the Native Affairs Department (NAD) appointed G. P. Lestrade as head of its newly created ethnological section.[49] By and large the attempts by anthropologists to forge links with the state amounted to little more than special pleading by a fledgling discipline anxious to attract funding. Ultimately, the efforts of anthropologists, self-appointed 'experts' and liberal activists to aid in the formulation of a modern 'native policy', were largely ignored by the state.

If the instrumental effects of anthropology on state policy were limited, its contributions to the development of an ideology of segregation was, however, significant. Prominent liberal thinkers with segregationist tendencies, especially those involved in the Joint Council nexus, were strongly influenced by anthropological thought. J. D. Rheinallt Jones was a part-time lecturer in the Bantu studies department of the University of the Witwatersrand as well as editor of its journal *Bantu Studies*. The philosopher Alfred Hoernlé, doyen of liberal intellectuals in the 1930s, also served for a time as head of the Bantu studies department. His wife, Winifred Hoernlé, trained a number of important South African anthropologists and taught in the department. C. T. Loram, together with Rheinallt Jones and Hoernlé, sat on the Inter-University Committee for African Studies which funded and controlled anthropological research in South Africa. Edgar Brookes, in his capacity as professor of public administration at the Transvaal University College (Pretoria) was instrumental in offering courses on 'native administration' to officials of the NAD.[50]

For these members of the liberal establishment, anthropology and the new theory of 'culture contact' offered new and valuable insights into the 'changing native'. Its recognition of the complexity of African society and of the distinctive nature of African 'culture', informed their efforts to provide for the differential development of Africans. As an empirical science of a distinctive 'native mentality', anthropology was eagerly seized upon by positivistically oriented experts seeking a 'solution to the native question'.[51]

Common to both the civilising mission and scientific racism were the ingrained assumptions of nineteenth-century evolutionism. The universalism of classical liberal thought held to the doctrine of inevitable progress culminating in the perfection of Western civilisation. Scientific racism, too, viewed the world within the parameters of evolutionism, governed by the extremities of 'barbarity' and 'civilisation'. But scientific racism differed from classical liberal thought in two respects. First, it contended that civilisation was as likely to retrogress as to progress. Second, the biological determinists thought that the relative position of 'pure races' along the evolutionary scale was immutable.

It was the pluralism and relativism characteristic of anthropological thought which offered a way out of the evolutionist constraints of biological determinism, as well as those inherent in classical liberalism. It provided those seeking a synthesis between 'identity' and 'repression' with a powerful intellectual justification. The key concept was 'culture'.

George Stocking, the American historian of anthropology, has convincingly demonstrated how the work of Franz Boas and his students in the period 1900–30 served to 'free the concept of culture from its heritage of evolutionary and racial assumptions, so that it could subseqently become the cornerstone of social scientific disciplines completely independent of biological determinism'.[52] This view is supported by Newby's observation that the impact in the United States of Boasian thought had caused a precipitous decline by 1930 in the 'amount of scientific literature purporting to prove the Negro's alleged inferiority'.[53]

The influence of the Boasian school, explains Stocking, generated a specifically anthropological concept of culture which became current in the Anglo–American tradition. This notion of culture, as formulated by Boas's students, Kroeber and Kluckhohn, was distinctively relativistic. It was contrasted to the humanist sense of culture 'which was absolutistic and knew perfection'. Thus

> anthropological 'culture' is homeostatic, while humanist 'culture' is singular. Traditional humanist usage distinguishes between degrees of 'culture'; for the anthropologist, all men are equally 'cultured'.[54]

The attractiveness of the anthropological sense of culture to segregationists seeking a way out of the evolutionist constraints of biological determinism and universalist humanism, should be apparent. As disseminated through Malinowski and possibly through Boas, a popular notion of 'culture' came to serve as a credible linguistic peg upon which the segregationist compromise was hung. It did so by incorporating the evolutionist assumptions of both liberal assimilationists (who believed in the capacity of the black man 'to rise') and of racist 'repressionists' (who maintained the inability of Africans to ascend the evolutionary scale). This proposition may be illustrated with reference to contemporary usage of the term 'culture'.

Culture and adaptation

The first use of 'culture' to be examined is that which functioned as a synonym for 'civilisation'.[55] Consider Howard Rogers's description of NAD ethnological research into the '. . . relationships of the tribes, their languages and *state of culture*'[56]; the *Friend*'s report of a 'mass meeting of over 500 natives of *all stages of culture* [which] was held yesterday near Middeldrift'[57]; J. B. M. Hertzog's assertion that 'Kadalie had been a very active agitator and one of *no mean culture* . . .'[58] and *Imvo*'s complaint in the wake of his 1926 speech that 'General Hertzog, far from being magnanimous and generous with his *superior culture* is this week engaged in pushing through Parliament the Colour Bar Bill with its designs to arrest Bantu industrial progress in advance.'[59]

In the first two examples the customary formulation 'state of civilisation' is directly transposed as 'state of culture', while in the last two examples 'culture' is strongly associated with progress along the barbarian/civilisation continuum. All four examples are similar to the extent that 'culture' is portrayed as a dynamic quality located within the idiom of orthodox Victorian developmentalist thought.

The direct obverse of this use of 'culture' assumes a congruence between distinct, biologically defined human 'races' or 'stocks', and inherently 'inferior' or 'superior' civilisations. 'In short the basis of culture is biological: it varies with the innate qualities of human stocks. Culture is a function of race.'[60]

A revealing example of this racist sense of 'culture' is evident in George Heaton Nicholls's novel *Bayete!* which was written as an explicit manifesto for racial segregation and bears the strong imprint of eugenist ideas. At one point the chief protagonist (and prophetically named?) Nelson gazes at his future wife Olive with Lamarckian adoration:

> His mind was filled with her beauty, and he found himself weighing the value of heredity. Many generations of culture had gone to her making, as indeed, many generations of grave Arabs had gone to his.[61]

Out of these two opposing uses of 'culture' there emerged a third anthropologically influenced notion of culture. While implicitly racist and openly hostile to nineteenth-century ideas about assimilation, this sense of the word carried within its web of associations room for a gradual process of racial 'upliftment'. It was this notion of culture that was to become part of the legitimising ideology of segregation.

A paradigm example of this mode of thought is evident in General Smuts's celebrated 1929 Oxford lectures.[62] In his historical account of 'native policy', Smuts rejected the view which saw the 'African as essentially inferior or subhuman, as having no soul, and as being only fit to be a slave'. He also rejected the converse, whereby the 'African now became a man and a brother'.[63] Although this view had given Africans a semblance of equality with whites, it involved the ruthless destruction of 'the basis of his African system which was his highest good'.[64] For Smuts both these policies had been equally harmful.

The solution was to be found in a policy of differential development or segregation. 'The new policy', he explained, 'is to foster an indigenous native culture or system of cultures, and to cease to force the African into alien European moulds.'[65]

The idea that the culturally assimilated and missionary-educated native was somehow fraudulent ('about as original as a glass of skimmed milk') and that one would have instead to 'build up a good Bantu future' on the basis of their own culture, was consistently argued by the government ethnologist G. P. Lestrade.[66] In 1931 Lestrade informed the Native Economic Commission (NEC)

> . . . there is a middle way between tying him [the native] down or trying to make of him a black European, between *repressionist* and *assimilationist* schools . . . it

is possible to adopt an *adaptationist* attitude which would take out of the Bantu past what was good, and even what was merely neutral, and together with what is good of European culture for the Bantu, build up a Bantu future. To this latter school I would take this opportunity of declaring my adherence.[67]

Lestrade's doctrine of cultural adaptationism was to become a crucial organising principle for the proponents of segregation. J. E. Holloway, the chair of the monumental NEC, commented that witnesses had fallen into 'two diametrically opposite' positions; one group representing the adaptationist view of Lestrade, the other holding to a policy of assimilation.[68] A year later the influential report of the NEC 'unhesitatingly affirm[ed]' its adherence to Lestrade's formulation of adaptationism which it considered 'not only the most reasonable but also the most economical approach to the native question'.[69]

The diffusion of 'culture'

Although it derived from anthropology, the politicised notion of 'culture' or of 'cultural adaptation' should not be too closely associated with the discipline of social anthropology itself. Isaac Schapera, for example, was strongly critical of Lestrade's theory of cultural adaptation as adopted by the NEC. Schapera derived his understanding of culture contact from Malinowski, and laid stress on its dynamic qualities.

For Schapera, the penetration of Western civilisation in the form of 'the missionary, the teacher, the trader, the labour recruiter, and the farmer' was irreversible. It was therefore impossible to 'bolster up the chieftainship and Native legal institutions . . .'. He noted perceptively that 'a thorough-going policy of adaptation thus calls for a complete segregation of the Native under absolute administrative control extending to every aspect of life'.[70] That, he wrongly thought, was inconceivable.

Schapera's understanding of the integral relationship between European and African cultures suggests the absorption of Macmillan's historical insights into his anthropology. In passing, it is worth noting that Macmillan himself was bitterly contemptuous of the 'rather doubtful doctrines' of anthropology from as early as 1923.[71] He attacked the liberal establishment for its involvement in anthropological studies, complaining angrily of the 'paralysing conservatism' of their approach.[72] In Macmillan's view rural poverty and tribal disintegration had 'already gone too far'. It was therefore 'more urgent that we see he [the African] is provided with bread, even without butter, than to embark on the long quest to "understand the Native mind"'.[73]

The concept of 'culture' and of 'cultural adaptation' was widely appropriated in the political domain. In the hands of Heaton Nicholls, one of the foremost ideologues of segregation, it was imperative to re-create a tribally based culture or 'ethos' as the only alternative to class warfare. In his view

> An adaptationist policy demands as its primary concept the maintenance of chieftaindom without which tribal society cannot exist. . . . It assumes some measure of territorial segregation. It assumes what is in effect the growth of a national consciousness among the Bantu themselves which will either become inimical to the interests of the Europeans or form a harmonious part of our complex society. The opposite policy of assimilation substitutes class for race, and if continued on its present basis, must lead to the evolution of a native proletariat inspired by the usual antagonisms of a class war.[74]

Werner Eiselen, lecturer in ethnography and Bantu languages at Stellenbosch University, also emphasised the need to recognise and en-courage 'Bantu culture' in order to promote a policy of differentiation. 'The duty of the native', he explained, was 'not to become a black European, but to become a better native, with ideals and a culture of his own.'[75] Eiselen later became Secretary of Native Affairs under Hendrik Verwoerd and was a central figure in the implementation of apartheid.[76]

In introducing the 1937 Native Laws Amendment Bill to Parliament, Minister Grobler explained that 'the effect of the influx of young natives into surroundings foreign to their mental outlook and culture is one of the most serious problems we have to face'.[77] In this situation 'culture' became associated with white fears of African proletarianisation and it echoed eugenist arguments about the 'degeneration' of Africans in the urban environment.

These examples serve to indicate the wide dissemination of 'culture', an ideological concept originally generated by anthropology and sub-sequently absorbed and utilised for political ends. In the 1920s and 1930s the notion of Africans as the 'child races' lowest down on the 'scale of civilisation', was still ubiquitous. The usefulness of this concept was its essential ambiguity; as 'children' it could be expected that Africans would in time attain the maturity of white civilisation. On the other hand, however, it could also be implied that on account of their essential differences, Africans would remain children, perhaps for ever.[78]

The assumptions behind this metaphor were strictly evolutionist, its imagery deriving from biology and the family. The concept of culture gradually came to replace this formulation, rendering it increasingly obscure. In drawing upon a wide range of racist assumptions, while at the same time avoiding the strong associations of biological determinism, 'culture' came to function as a more subtle form of 'race'. Its relativism and pluralism was ideally suited to the propagation of policies of differential development or segregation.

The language of cultural adaptation was of distinct advantage in the attempt to link South African segregation to the wider imperial policies of indirect rule and trusteeship. This linkage constitutes a major theme of Smuts's 1929 Oxford lectures in which he outlined a policy of segregation based on the preservation of 'native culture' and social institutions. Smuts sought to demonstrate that the South African policy of differentiation was enshrined in the trusteeship clauses of the League of Nations' Covenant.[79]

In his keynote statement on the draft Native Bills in 1935 Heaton Nicholls reinforced this connection. He claimed that the essence of the bills 'differ in no way in principle from the new conception of native government which is embraced in the word 'trusteeship' and translated into administrative action through a policy of 'adaptation' in all British states.[80] The policy of adaptation, he added, was not new to South Africa 'where the people have learned their anthropology at first hand from actual contact with native life'.[81]

In Britain, Lugard's doctrine of indirect rule was lent theoretical coherence through its association with social anthropology and, in particular, the Malinowskian concept of 'culture contact'. For both the advocates of segregation and of indirect rule, the vocabulary of 'culture', 'adaptation' and 'parallelism' constituted a strikingly similar ideological discourse. This fact was a source of considerable embarrassment to British social anthropologists and commentators for whom South Africa was increasingly seen as a retrogressive or aberrant member of the Empire.

The attempt to distinguish indirect rule from segregation was awkwardly accomplished. Margery Perham, in her elaboration and defence of indirect rule, claimed that it was 'strange that segregation and indirect rule should have been confused'.[82] She argued that whereas segregation was characteristic of the 'mixed territories', indirect rule had only been applied in the 'purely native territories'. In contrast to segregation which was essentially 'a selfish and negative plan', indirect rule was a benign and flexible mode of administration.[83]

Perham's arguments were elaborated on at greater length by Lucy Mair.

For Mair, as for Perham, indirect rule was not a magic formula whose essence could be deduced theoretically. In the final analysis, the distinction between Nigeria and Tanganyika (where the finest attributes of indirect rule were apparently exemplified) and South Africa (which was based on the selfish preservation of white 'supremacy') could only be judged empirically.[84] Perham and Mair were undoubtedly correct in their concern to distance indirect rule from segregation. Their manifest difficulty in doing so, however, is testament to the power of the language of cultural adaptation in South Africa as a justificatory ideology of segregation.

Conclusion

The declining confidence in the efficacy of the Victorian civilising mission, and a marked rise in the propagation of scientific racism, was characteristic of the development of collectivist thought in the British metropole. This phenomenon was markedly reinforced by the effects of economic depression and the growth of working-class radicalism.

In South Africa similar processes were at work. Social conflict attendant upon its rapid process of industrialisation was accentuated in the period following the First World War. The policy of segregation which was elaborated by liberal theorists in the first decade of the twentieth century was essentially conceived as a conservative policy of social containment. It was portrayed as a compromise between the extremes of 'assimilation' and 'repression'. 'Assimilation' or 'identity' was associated with the discredited brand of nineteenth-century liberalism and its 'civilising mission'. Repression referred to those political policies (often associated with the Boer republics) which entrenched the subordination of Africans.

The emerging discipline of anthropology, and the notions of 'culture' and of 'adaptation', came to serve as a vital organising principle for the ideology of segregation. Although many anthropologists flaunted the utilitarian value of their research in dealing with problems of native administration, it would be misleading to overestimate the direct influence of anthropology on the conception and implementation of segregation.

The indirect influence of the conception of 'cultural adaptation' (which was drawn from and associated with anthropology) was, however, of great importance in the elaboration of a discourse of segregation. The dissemination of these ideas into the popular domain was seized upon by advocates of segregation. Brookes came to argue that the older anthropological school had 'supplied the segregationists with a badly needed philosophy'[85]; Lancelot Hogben commented that 'some of our anthropologists... have upholstered Hertzog's segregation policy for starving out the Bantu with a pedantically sentimental plea for the right of the native to evolve along his own peculiar line of self-expression.'[86] Even Heaton Nicholls, who was dismissive of academe, credited anthropology to some degree in promoting the 'change of view' by which segregation and trusteeship had gained acceptance.[87]

The ideological force of cultural adaptation lay in its capacity to feed upon a wide range of racist assumptions without being pinned down to a patently untenable theory of biological racism. At the same time it avoided the discredited assimilationist project which was associated with classical liberalism. Thus the pluralism and relativism inherent in 'culture' transcended the legacy of nineteenth-century evolutionist thought, whose unyielding logic lay at the heart of both Victorian individualism and of scientific racism.

Notes and references

1 G. Jones, *Social Darwinism and English Thought* (Sussex & New Jersey 1980) Ch. IV. See also E. J. Hobsbawm, *Industry and Empire* (London 1968) pp. 201–2.

2 See for example N. Stepan, *The Idea of Race in Science: Great Britain 1800–1960* (London 1982); D. A. Lorimar, *Colour, Class and the Victorians* (Leicester 1978); I. A. Newby, *Jim Crow's Defense, Anti-Negro Thought in America 1900–1930* (Louisiana 1965); Jones, *Social Darwinism*.

3 Stepan, *The Idea*, p. 111.

4 Newby, *Jim Crow's Defense*, pp. 8–9.

5 Jones, *Social Darwinism*, p. 147.

6 *Ibid.*, p. 144.

7 Stepan, *The Idea*, p. 117. For a discussion of eugenics see G. R. Searle's *Eugenics and Politics in Britain 1900–1914* (Leyden 1976); M. Banton, *The Idea of Race* (London 1977); also Jones, *Social Darwinism*, Ch. VI.

8 Jones, *Social Darwinism*, p. 103.

9 *Ibid.*, pp. 110–17. Searle, *Eugenics and Politics*, pp. 10–14, describes the 'intellectual calibre and social prestige' associated with the membership of the Eugenics Education Society.

10 See Bernard Semmel's remarkable *Imperialism and Social Reform. English Social–Imperial Thought 1895–1914* (London 1960).

11 F. G. Galton, *The Narrative of an Explorer in Tropical South Africa*, (London 1891) 4th edn. The introduction by G. T. Bettany claims that 'This book occupies a relation to Mr Galton's career similar to that which

Darwin's celebrated *Journal of the Beagle* occupied in his lifework' (p. ix.) Galton was a cousin of Charles Darwin.

12 Searle, *Eugenics and Politics*, pp. 9, 20.

13 L. Hogben, *Dangerous Thoughts* (London 1939) pp. 47–8. Hogben describes a typical academic conversation like this:

'*Almost any South African graduate:* If you have to live in this country as long as I have, you would know that a native can't be taught to read or write.

'*Myself*: Have you ever visited Fort Hare Missionary College?

'*Almost any SAG*: Don't talk to me about missionaries.

'*Myself*: Well, I have. I have seen a class of pure blood Bantu students from the Cis-kei working out differential equations.

'*Almost any S.A.G.*: What would you do if a black man raped your sister:'

This conversation is also cited in Gary Werskey's account of left-wing science in Britain, *The Visible College* (London 1978) p. 106.

14 G. L. Mosse, *Toward the Final Solution. A History of European Racism* (London 1978) p. 78.

15 R. Parry, '"In a sense citizens, but not altogether citizens . . ." Rhodes, race and the ideology of segregation at the Cape in the late nineteenth century', *Canadian Journal of African Studies*, **17** (3) 1983, 384–8.

16 S. J. R. Martin, 'Political and social theories of Transkeian administrators in the late nineteenth century', unpublished Masters thesis (University of Cape Town 1978) p. 82.

17 R. Hyam, *Elgin and Churchill at the Colonial Office 1905–8* (London 1968) p. 539.

18 *Ibid.*

19 E. H. Brookes, *The History of Native Policy in South Africa from 1870 to the Present Day* (Cape Town 1924) p. 501.

20 P. B. Rich, *White Power and the Liberal Conscience* (Johannesburg and Manchester 1984) p. 5.

21 J. M. Coetzee, 'Blood, flaw, taint, degeneration: the case of Sarah Gertrude Millin', *English Studies in Africa*, **23** (1) 1980, 41.

22 M. Swanson, 'The sanitation syndrome: bubonic plague and urban native policy in the Cape Colony 1900–09', *JAH*, **XVIII** (3) 1977, 387.

23 C. T. Loram, *The Education of the South African Native* (London 1917) pp. 9, 11. See also Brookes, *History*, Ch. XVIII. On p. 403 Brookes states that 'The native . . . is not naturally a town-dweller or an industrialist.'

24 Rich, *White Power*, pp. 10–17. Rev. Ray Phillips's *The Bantu are Coming* (London 1930) is a revealing manifesto for the role of the 'modern' missionary in urban welfare work.

25 The fear of miscegenation was so widespread that it is futile to attempt to document it. An interesting critical survey of the phenomenon is a pamphlet by G. Findlay, *Miscegenation* (Pretoria 1936); Stubbs papers A954 Ea (Church of the Province of South Africa Archives, University of the Witwatersrand– hereafter CPSA).

26 E. Stubbs, *Tightening Coils. An Essay on Segregation* (Pretoria 1925); G. H. Nicholls, *Bayete!* (London 1923).

27 M. Evans, *Black and White in South East Africa. A Study in Sociology* (London 1911) p. 223.

28 See for example Hertzog's Smithfield and Malmesbury speeches in *The Segregation Problem. General Hertzog's Solution* (Cape Town n.d.).

29 C. M. Tatz, *Shadow and Substance in South Africa. A Study in Land and Franchise Policies Affecting Africans 1910–60* (Pietermaritzburg 1962). On pp. 41–5 Tatz isolates and evaluates the validity of twelve arguments advanced by Hertzog for the removal of the Cape African franchise.

30 R. F. A. Hoernlé, 'Race mixture and native policy in South Africa', in I. Schapera (ed.) *Western Civilisation and the Natives of South Africa. Studies in Culture Contact* (London 1934) p. 265.

31 Coetzee, 'Blood, flaw, taint'.

32 W. Plomer, *Turbott Wolfe* (London 1926).

33 J. D. Rheinallt Jones, 'The need for a scientific basis for South African native policy', *SAJS*, **XXIII**, 1926, 91.

34 P. Nielsen, *The Black Man's Place in South Africa* (Cape Town 1922) pp. 3–4, 148. Somewhat out of tune with his findings, Nielsen concluded that territorial separation was necessary for 'peace and happiness in South Africa, though on account of "unalterable physical disparity, and not because of any mental inequality"', p. 148.

35 See for example J. E. Duerden, 'Genetics and eugenics in South Africa: heredity and environment', *SAJS*, **XXII**, 1925.

36 See for example M. L. Fick, 'Intelligence test results of poor white, native (Zulu), Coloured and Indian school children and the educational and social implications', *SAJS* **XXVI**, 1929; Loram, *The Education.*

37 Evans, *Black and White*, pp. 36–7; Rheinallt Jones, 'The Need'; Loram, *The Education;* Evidence of Prof. and Mrs Hoernlé to NEC, K26 Box 9, pp. 9183–5 (Pretoria State Archives – hereafter PSA).

38 Union Government (UG) 14–'26, *Economic and Wage Commission* (1925) pp. 326–7.

39 S. M. Molema, *The Bantu – Past and Present* (Edinburgh 1920), p. 328.

40 W. Eiselen, *Die Naturelle Vraagstuk* (Cape Town 1929) pp. 3–4.

41 D. M. Schreuder, 'The cultural factor in Victorian imperialism: a case study of the British "civilising mission"', *Journal of Imperial and Commonwealth History*, **IV** (3) 1976.

42 *Ibid.*, pp. 292–4.

43 On the material basis of Cape liberalism, see Stanley Trapido's pioneering essay '"The friends of the natives": merchants, peasants and the political and ideological structure of liberalism in the Cape, 1854–1910', in S. Marks and A. Atmore (eds), *Economy and Society in pre-industrial South Africa* (London 1980).

44 On the institutionalisation of anthropological studies in South Africa and its relationship to segregation see my '"Understanding the native mind": anthropology, cultural adaptation and the elaboration of a segregationist discourse in South Africa, *c.* 1920–36', unpublished seminar paper (UCT 1984). For a discussion of the impact of anthropology on liberal thought in the 1920s and 1930s, see Rich, *White Power*, Ch. 3.

45 Loram, *The Education*, pp. vii–viii; J. D. Rheinallt Jones, 'Editorial' in *Bantu Studies*, 1 (1) 1921, 1; J. E. Duerden, 'Social anthropology in South Africa: problems of nationality', *SAJS*, **xviii**, 1921 4–5. According to Adam Kuper, *Anthropologists and Anthropology* (London 1973) p. 62, Smuts, in

consultation with Haddon of Cambridge, was personally responsible for inviting Radcliffe-Brown to UCT.

46 A. R. Radcliffe-Brown, 'Some problems of Bantu sociology', *Bantu Studies*, **1** (3) 1922, 5.

47 B. Malinowski, 'Practical anthropology', *Africa*, **II** (1) 1929, 37–8. See also Lord Lugard, 'The International Institute of African Languages and Cultures', *Africa*, **I** (1) 1928; E. W. Smith, 'The story of the institute. A survey of seven years', *Africa*, **VII** (1) 1934.

48 The relationship between anthropology and colonialism is a subject of considerable debate. See T. Asad, *Anthropology and the Colonial Encounter* (London 1973); G. Huizer and B. Mannheim (eds) *The Politics of Anthropology* (The Hague 1979).

49 Dubow, '"Understanding the native mind"', pp. 6–14.

50 Of these individuals only Winifred Hoernlé can really be considered to be part of the modern discipline of social anthropology. The above-mentioned were not consistent segregationists. After his break with segregation, Brookes, for example, offered a critical evaluation of the teachings of anthropology in his 1933 Phelps–Stokes lectures. See his *The Colour Problems of South Africa* (Lovedale 1934) Ch. VI.

51 See Rich, *White Power*, Ch. 3, esp. pp. 54–63.

52 G. W. Stocking, *Race, Culture and Evolution. Essays in the History of Anthropology* (New York 1968). For an assessment of the impact of Boasian thought see also M. Harris, *The Rise of Anthropological Theory* (London 1968) Chs IX, X.

53 Newby, *Jim Crow's Defense*, p. 51.

54 Stocking, *Race, Culture and Evolution*, pp. 199–200.

55 See the entry on 'culture' in R. Williams, *Keywords. A Vocabulary of Culture and Society* (London 1976) pp. 78–9. Williams describes how 'culture', understood as a unilinear concept, became separated from 'civilisation' through a 'decisive change of use in Herder', and how this plural sense became common in twentieth-century anthropology. The following analysis is indebted to Williams.

56 H. Rogers, *Native Administration in the Union of South Africa* (Johannesburg 1933) p. 251. The emphasized words in this and the following three quotations are my own.

57 *The Friend*, 7 July 1927.

58 *The Star*, 11 May 1926.

59 *Imvo*, 4 May 1926. See also Evans, *Black and White*, p. 7, where Africans are referred to as a conservative race 'at a lower stage of culture'.

60 Hoernlé, 'Race mixture', p. 270.

61 Nicholls, *Bayete!*, p. 236.

62 J. C. Smuts, *Africa and Some World Problems* (Oxford 1930).

63 *Ibid.*, p. 77.

64 *Ibid.*, p. 77.

65 *Ibid.*, p. 84.

66 AD1438 Box 9, p. 8787, evidence of G. P. Lestrade to NEC, Pretoria, 5 June 1931 (CPSA).

67 Lestrade papers, BC255 K1.11, 'Statements in answer to general questionnaire issued by the NEC' (Manuscripts Division, Jagger Library, University of Cape Town).

68 K26 Box 9, pp. 9198–9, evidence of Prof. and Mrs Hoernlé to NEC, 13 June 1931 (PSA).
69 UG 22–'31, *Report of the Native Economic Commission, 1930–32*, p. 31, para. 200. Note that Dr Roberts of the Native Affairs Commission and NEC, dissented from this view, adding. '. . . the way of progress for the Native lies along the path of the Native assimilating as rapidly as possible the European civilisation and culture', p. 31, para. 201.
70 Schapera, *Western Civilisation*, pp. xi–xii. See also his 'Changing life in the native reserves', *Race Relations*, 1 (1) 1933. See Max Gluckman's paper 'Anthropology and apartheid: the work of South African anthropologists', in M. Fortes and S. Patterson (eds) *Studies in African Social Anthropology* (London & New York 1975) p. 36. Gluckman credits Schapera as the dominant figure in reorientating British anthropology towards the idea that Africans and whites were 'integral parts of a single social system, so that all had to be studied in the same way'.
71 W. M. Macmillan, *My South African Years. An Autobiography* (Cape Town 1975) p. 194.
72 *Ibid.*, pp. 214–19. Macmillan criticised Rheinallt Jones, the Hoernlés and especially Loram for their involvement in anthropological research. For details of his failed attempt to subvert Jones's course on native law and administration, see University of Witwatersrand Arts Faculty Minutes, vol. VIII pp. 38–40b (University of Witwatersrand archives).
73 W. M. Macmillan, *Complex South Africa. An Economic Footnote to History* (London 1930) preface, p. 8.
74 Heaton Nicholls papers, KCM 3323, file 3. Handwritten memo. on native policy, n.d., p. 1 (Killie Campbell library, University of Natal).
75 Records of the South African Institute of Race Relations (hereafter SAIRR) AD843 1372.1. Unmarked newspaper clipping, 10 May 1929 (CPSA). For the full Afrikaans version see Eiselen, *Die Naturelle Vraagstuk*.
76 On Eiselen's retirement the Bantu Affairs Department official journal *BaNtu*, VII (8) 1960 devoted an entire issue to him. A lengthy eulogy to Eiselen quoted extensively from the 1929 address cited above. It was represented as a direct antecedent to his views on apartheid.
77 *House of Assembly Debates*, vol. 29, 1937, col. 4219.
78 For examples of the child metaphor used to justify segregation, see Hertzog, *The Segregation Problem*, p. 13, 'The native stands in relation to the European as a child of eight years to a man of mature experience'; Smuts, *Africa*, p. 75, 'It [the "Bantu"] has largely remained a child type with a child psychology and outlook.' On the other hand see Molema, *The Bantu*, p. 335, where the child metaphor is employed to sustain the idea that 'human progress and human perfectibility' is 'an axiom and a law of philosophic history'.
79 Smuts, *Africa*, pp. 88–9.
80 SAIRR papers, AD843 B53.1, *Natal Advertiser*, 15 May 1935 (CPSA).

81 *Ibid.*
82 M. Perham, 'A restatement of indirect rule', *Africa*, **VII** (3) 1934, 326.
83 *Ibid.*, 326–7.
84 L. Mair, *Native Policies in Africa* (London 1936) pp. 261–9.
85 Brookes, *The Colour Problems*, p. 145. Brookes was more welcoming of the 'newer' school of social anthropology which considered problems relating to 'contact'. His distinction is not entirely clear.
86 Hogben, *Dangerous Thoughts*, p. 45.
87 SAIRR papers, AD843 B53.1.3, *Natal Advertiser*, 15 May 1935 Nicholls was apt to cite the authority of 'anthropology' in his advocacy of segregation. See for example *House of Assembly Debates*, vol. 19, 1932, col 4319.

CHAPTER THREE

Building a nation from words: Afrikaans language, literature and ethnic identity, 1902–1924

Isabel Hofmeyr

Introduction

Any student of South African history with even a passing interest in Afrikaner nationalism would probably read the following comments by Nairn with some envy:

> We have all studied the phenomena so consistently accompanying [nationalism]: the 'rediscovery' or invention of national history, urban intellectuals invoking peasant virtues which they have experienced only through train windows on their summer holiday, schoolmasters painfully acquiring 'national' tongues spoken only in remote valleys . . . and so on.[1]

In South African history we have not studied these phenomena consistently, despite the legion of books on Afrikaner nationalism. Very few of these texts have asked the type of questions implicit in Nairn's paragraph. This essay will attempt to raise some of these questions by examining aspects of the 'invention' of Afrikaner nationalism between 1902 and 1924. The major focus of this piece will be the manufacture of an Afrikaans literary culture which was an important terrain in which nationalist ideologies were elaborated. In the pages that follow, I will attempt to trace the trail of this literary development through the contours of a broader political, economic and social geography.

The story of Afrikaans literature during these years has been told many times before in books of meticulous scholarship.[2] But, like so many texts on Afrikaner history, they package these developments into a tight nationalism. This set of ideas is generally predicated on a deeply rooted organic 'Afrikaner identity' which rumbles through South African history and mysteriously unites all Afrikaners into a monolithic *volk*. However, much recent theorising on nationalism has shown that nations are almost invariably artificial and manufactured categories which can be unmasked as historically contingent.[3] This contingency has to do with the sprawling and skewed development of capitalism, as Nairn has shown, and nationalist ideologies have their genesis in the social relations precipitated by industrialisation.[4]

In the pages that follow, I will attempt to locate the fabrication of an Afrikaans language and literature in the changing social relationships surrounding the spread of capitalism in South Africa. I will begin in the Cape of the late nineteenth century, as it was here that the first attempt emerged to systematise Afrikaans as a language and social category which could draw together certain people who traditionally constituted themselves in provincially and regionally diverse ways.

The linguistic background

By the nineteenth century the language Dutch–Afrikaans was extremely diverse by region, dialect and social class. This diversity of dialect had partly to do with the historical trajectory of the lowland Dutch dialects spoken by the seventeenth-century settlers. In confronting the language of the slaves – Malay and Portuguese creole – along with Khoisan speech, this Dutch linguistic cluster had partly creolised. In later years it picked up shards of German, French and Southern Nguni languages and a goodly layer of English after 1806.[5]

This linguistic interaction led to loosely related dialects which spread out with master and servant into the regional economies that migrant farmers set up in the Cape and subsequently the two republics. By the late 1800s the Cape could be divided into a dialect map whose boundaries approximated provincial divisions.[6] In addition, dialect tended to modulate according to social class. The poorer the community, the more their language varied from that of the 'civilised' Western Cape.

This social and regional variation of language increased with the rapid stratification brought about by the proletarianisation which occurred both before the mineral discoveries and, at an accelerating rate, thereafter. Linguistically this social differentiation expressed itself in an upper and middle class who spoke English. Included in their number were wealthy Dutch families who manipulated a variety of linguistic registers. These stretched from what passed for High Dutch, through more informal discourse to a language for servants, workers and farm labourers. These workers, along with 'the poor', were rapidly accumulating in jumbled racial communities, in which the language 'Afrikaans' was emerging quite clearly.[7] The variety of terms by which

Afrikaans was known all pointed to a strong association with poorness and 'colouredness'. Some of these terms included 'hotnotstaal' (Hottentot language), 'griekwataal' (Griqua language), 'kombuistaal' (kitchen language), 'plattaal' (vulgar language) and 'brabbeltaal' (patois/lingo). In the 1870s another term was to be added to this list: 'patriots' or, as it was pronounced in the Cape, 'patterjots'.[8]

This name came from the newspaper *Die Afrikaanse Patriot* which began in 1876 and was the first publication to use 'Afrikaans' systematically. The publication was the organ of Die Genootskap van Regte Afrikaners (GRA) (Fellowship of True Afrikaners) and we must look briefly at the background of this movement for the developments of the early twentieth century were to draw on its work.

Groping towards a definition of Afrikaners

The organisation arose in the 1870s from a closely knit group of teachers and clerics from wine farming backgrounds in and around Paarl.[9] This concentration, even 'overproduction', of educated men was a common feature of Cape social life where commerce and government were British dominated. The Dutch intelligentsia tended to congregate in those professions – church, school, journalism – which cushioned them from the more irritating aspects of discrimination. Increasing British investment in the diamond fields seemed only to aggravate this discrimination. Enlarged state revenue flowed more towards wealthy urban English schools than to poorer rural Dutch schools. Also in the air was talk of a scheme to remove state stipends to church ministers.[10] To certain Dutch-speakers, British imperialism appeared to be more of a hindrance than a help.

Other people in the Cape, however, were doing extremely well out of British imperialism. Dutch and English farmers, merchant interests and an emerging class of mining capitalists looked to the British imperial economy as the basis for their existence.[11] But politically the constitutional changes bringing responsible government activated these various groups to new possibilities and alliances. The GRA or Pêrelspan (Paarl bunch) as they were known, were quick to respond to these political opportunities. The GRA group under S. J. du Toit floated the Afrikaner Bond and its initial programme called for the establishment of small banks, boycotts of 'foreign' traders and more funds for Dutch education.[12] At the same time, the *Patriot* gave this populist vision some cultural and historical substance. Written in a

Paarl dialect of 'Afrikaans', the magazine attempted to define white Afrikaners in terms of a cultural, organic nation.[13]

Initially these men hatched their schemes under the carapace of wealthy Dutch farming interest. Hofmeyr, for example, gave them support in his newspaper *De Zuid Afrikaan*, which was in the process of defining its own more minimalist nationalism. But when du Toit and his men hesitantly moved out into the open, Hofmeyr and his following easily outmanoeuvred them and took over the Bond. This grouping had little taste for du Toit's vision of an organic nation, and they scoffed at his schemes to promote the 'brabbeltaal' of the disreputable populace above the glories of Dutch.

But what surprised many was that this populace bought the *Patriot* in numbers sufficient to make it the second highest selling 'Dutch' paper in the Cape.[14] Who were these buyers? The question is difficult to answer except in the broadest speculative terms. Firstly, the people involved were probably not terribly sure themselves. They knew who were *not* reading the paper: people whom they characterised as 'urban Afrikaners' or, in other words, a propertied 'Dutch' middle class who stood behind Hofmeyr and probably read the *Illustrated London News*.[15] This group had nothing but scathing cosmopolitan contempt for the *Patriot* filled with sturdy popular wisdom.

In defining the people who did read the paper, the Pêrelspan categorised them as rural, Afrikaans and *minderbevoorreg* (underprivileged).[16] But by underprivileged they could not have meant the very poor, since in the Cape throughout the years of the *Patriot*'s publication, a third of white children of school-going age never saw the inside of a classroom.[17] Of this third, a high number must have been Dutch–Afrikaners. Rather, and arguably, by *minderbevoorreg*, they meant something in the sense of 'genteel poor'.[18] One thinks, for example, of the legion of dubiously certificated teachers, the clerics in poor parishes, faced with having their state stipends removed and small shopkeepers and traders. These people, leading a precarious life, would have responded positively to the populist programme of the early Bond.

There were also enough of these people to continue the work started by the *Patriot*. They set up a loosely related set of cultural organisations, debating societies and a language conference, to give the issue of Afrikaans some institutional visibility. All of this activity was subsequently to be called the First Language movement, a term which, however, implies an organisational unity and smoothness which never existed in reality.

It was in the space opened up by the *Patriot* that the Second Language movement was to begin. Again this movement was to be loose and uneven, and it was to be started by a small group of men in the north who found themselves in conditions broadly analogous but more extreme than their Paarl counterparts.

The lay of the land in the North

The social geography of the north, as others have described, fell into three broad groupings: the landed notables, those with tenuous land rights and the entirely landless. The processes underlying this stratification have also been outlined elsewhere and involved a combination of rising land prices, inheritance law and natural disaster. Land prices had risen sharply after the intrusion of the mines into the Transvaal and the notables made good these speculative opportunities because of their hold on key government posts. Through this concentration of land, wealthy farmers swallowed up numerous 'dwarf-proprietors of oft-divided land', who then became bywoners, a term which covered a multitude of social relationships.[19]

Whatever their precise form, these landlord/tenant ties involved humiliating relationships of subordination, whose friction was diffused through ideological mechanisms of *familie* (kinship), *huisgesin* (the household) and the church. Landlords were, after all, wealthy relations, church officials or in close association with religious authority, and they used these positions to ransom the acquiescence of their tenants.[20]

Standing between the landed and the landless was a group of small farmers who stood to gain from these kinship/authority networks. By manipulating their ties to wealthier landed notables, these small farmers could glean the smaller pickings of government office. They could also, in turn, extract rent from their smaller number of tenants.[21]

It was with changes and divisions like these that the two republics went to war in 1899. The crisis and chaos of the war fused the emerging differences and prised these divisions open even further. Some bywoners followed their landlords into war and supported them throughout.[22] But others, and often the most numerous group, made use of the war to express their feelings. Thirteen per cent refused to heed commando call-ups. Others laid down arms and declared their neutrality while, on average, one in five actively joined the British.[23]

After the war these divisions were to sharpen as the landowners moved quickly and decisively to reconstitute themselves often at the direct expense of the landless bywoners whom many landlords refused to take back.[24] What specifically concerns us here is the way in which the social web of authority in Boer communities was beginning to wear thin. In general terms these changes expressed themselves as a hardening interface between bywoners and landlord. In 1906 one of an increasing number of indigency commissions noted: 'The bywoners are no longer on the old terms of familiarity with the landowners but are becoming a separate and inferior class of society'.[25] Kinship ties which had previously bound the two groups together were shrivelling. Within the *huisgesin* itself, authority began to crumble along lines of age and sex as it so often does in a 'proto-industrial' situation.[26] The logical strategy for some families was to send their young women to the cities from whence they could remit part of their wage to the household economy. Other families no doubt moved together, first to a small town and then to a city, where initially there might have been some opportunity to utilise their skills. But the city's employment profile had very little room for unskilled white male adults, and even less for old men.[27] Teenagers, often by virtue of their greater physical strength, stood a better chance of employment, no matter how mean or temporary, than their parents.[28]

In the towns and cities young people and particularly young women, were in a position to question the authority of their fathers. This many people began to do by deserting the Dutch Reformed Churches in large numbers to join the growing number of apostolic sects. The disparaging referred to these church meetings as *lawaaigedoentes* (noisy affairs), but many must have discovered there an emotional satisfaction which they had failed to find in the joylessness of Calvinism.[29] Others sought solace in a working-class culture of sport, liquor and popular entertainment which provided some compensation for the harshness of industrial life.[30] Within this working-class environment, non-Afrikaner white men greatly outnumbered white women, and at least some Afrikaner women must have married non-Afrikaners.[31]

All of these changes and realignments began to alarm a large section of the urban and rural community. Some of these people belonged to that legion of middle-class moral brokers who took it upon themselves to spread the imperial gospel of the family which appeared to be disintegrating under the impact of industrialisation.[32] Within this ensemble were various Dutch-Afrikaners who had greater cause for alarm. Not only was the family under stress, but the Afrikaner community itself appeared to be falling apart. One does not wish to overemphasise this disintegration. In places like Johannesburg, ordinary Afrikaners congregated in a reasonably defined community that filled the western suburbs. The church, one of the few Afrikaner institutions to survive the war intact, also remained a strong force which could shore up some of the cracks in the community. After the war, the church's position was enhanced when it played an important part in reconstructing poor Afrikaners – a class which neither the notables nor the British had any overriding desire to rehabilitate. Yet to many clerics the situation still appeared dire. For many years they had depended for their livelihood on the smooth functioning of kinship and religious patterns of authority in the community. By the early 1900s, these patterns seemed to be crumbling.[33]

Another group who felt some anxiety about the changing texture of the Boer community was the small farmers. This group regarded the chasm that was growing between landlord and tenant with economic and social apprehension. In 1905 one of these small farmers spoke for many when he lashed out against the rich landowners. 'These rich farmers', he wrote, 'these selfish, self-righteous bloodsuckers! . . . Even our great generals who make such nice speeches, oppress the poor in private and enrich themselves from the impoverished.' If these developments went unchecked, there would remain a social world of 'the rich and the desperately poor: the bosses and the white kaffirs. God forbid!'[34]

All of these processes can be illustrated with a vignette of Ugie, a small hamlet which, although in the Cape, was probably similar to others further north. Between 1903 and 1918 this community had driven away six ministers. When the seventh, the Rev. Smit arrived, he did not find the welcoming party he had expected, but was met instead by an exhausted and brow-beaten deacon. The Rev. Smit then set off on horseback to meet his parishioners who quite clearly had no interest in meeting him since many of them 'took flight to the hills' on glimpsing their new minister. His first sermon attracted only ten people, who could just muster 1s. 9d. for the collection box. When the Rev. Smit finally got to meet more of his flock, he found 'illiterate men of sixty who had never been baptised', and women taking off by themselves for East London and Johannesburg. He found, as well, people living in mixed racial communities.[35]

The Rev. Smit was to find some support for his problems in the pages of *Die Brandwag* (The Sentinel), a magazine started in 1910 by another group of men who did not like the way things were going.

These men included journalists, clerks and the like, and even before the war this group were occupationally insecure, displaced as they were from middle-range state posts by a *Hollanderskliek* of Dutch officials imported by Kruger. Many of these marginal men had already chafed against Kruger's regime. Some, like Marais, had taken up Afrikaans as a language issue, both to expand their constituency and to make certain points to the Dutch middle class about the linguistic propinquity of the 'landzoonen' (sons of the soil).[36]

Included among these 'sons of the soil' was a collection of indigenous teachers who felt no great love for the *Hollanderskliek*. After the war their situation deteriorated rapidly as Milner's educational schemes of Anglicisation affected them most directly. To try and defend themselves, some of these teachers had grouped together in the Christelike Nasionale Onderwys (CNO) schools, which tapped funds from Holland and drew on Kuyperian theology. This theocratic thinking with its emphasis on schools independent of state, no doubt made a great deal of sense to embattled Dutch–Afrikaans teachers.[37]

All of these groups – journalists, clerks, clerics, small farmers and teachers – hoped for a better dispensation after the war. The generals had, after all, drawn most Afrikaners together in Het Volk, which could initially mute the contradictions in a broadly based programme of nationalism which was made to sound different in different quarters. But Het Volk, dominated by wealthy Transvaal farmers, had little time for the disaffected intelligentsia. Not surprisingly, the generals soon began to slough off the irritating petty bourgeoisie by refusing funds to the CNO movement, whose Dutch money had dried up. Secondly, the Het Volk leadership played down the whole issue of Dutch in government and school. Some Afrikaners had hoped for favourable legislation on Dutch which could have given them some protection in a world that was brutally British.

Slighted in this way, the Afrikaner petty bourgeoisie had to look elsewhere for support. And their only possible constituency lay in a populist direction.[38] But the populace themselves were experiencing all manner of changes, which as we have seen, were upsetting the traditional links which had held the Boer community together. Ordinary Afrikaners were consequently not immediately available to be mobilised through old established ties of allegiance and authority. The Afrikaner petty bourgeoisie, wishing to enlist popular support, had then to embark on a programme of rediscovering and reconsolidating their old congregations and constituencies. Part of this rediscovery was to be done for the Afrikaner intelligentsia who had the poor thrown up against them both in the wake of the war and in the broader movement of containing and moralising the poor in the cities. But part of this search for a popular base was to involve hard ideological labour. As good middle-class citizens, educated Afrikaners involved themselves actively and often humanely in this welfare work of ministering to the poor and fashioning them into workers. But this educated class had an overriding interest to create *Afrikaner* workers who would refill Afrikaner churches, attend Afrikaner schools and buy Afrikaans books.[39]

The simultaneity of middle-class philanthropic 'intervention' and nationalist innovation is crucial to grasp since many other commentators have attributed to Afrikaners a particular propensity for being more religious (*kerkvas*) and moral than the rest of society.[40] Afrikaner nationalist discourse *was* deeply moralistic and religious, but this vocabulary was shared by other sections of the South African middle classes, both black and white.[41] Equally, these educated Afrikaner men and women were not calling for a radical realignment of social relationships in which all Afrikaners would be equal. The intelligentsia wanted an ordered and hierarchical world. But it was not quite the world which Afrikaner workers wanted, and they resisted its strictures in the workplace, on the streets and at times by rejecting Afrikaner middle-class authority of church and charity. However, workers are seldom left alone to create their own consciousness, and many accept or have thrust upon them some elements of 'middle-class morality'. And for some this morality was to be coloured with an Afrikaner hue. In short, class formation and nationalist ideology were in the process of being formed and they scarred each other deeply.

The Second Language movement was shaped by these heteroclite processes.[42] In broad outline, the movement involved a petty bourgeoisie in search of a wider audience that could turn language and educational broking into a new professional avenue for a group of people who feared marginalisation. Their endeavours were to pay off handsomely in the end, and the Afrikaans and literary industry were to expand remarkably during the first two decades of this century. But our story starts in the early 1900s and then the prospects seemed much bleaker.

Taking Afrikaans seriously

By 1905 journalists in various centres throughout the four colonies had started using 'Afrikaans' in their papers, many, like Marais to expand their circulation.[43] These various developments were first systematically drawn together by Gustav Preller in his by now famous series of articles: 'Laat 'T

Ons Toch Ernst Wezen' (Let's take this matter seriously).[44] In these pieces he pointed to the gap which separated the spoken and written language of Dutch Afrikaners. The latter was a type of High Dutch, the former, according to Preller, was 'Afrikaans' and he argued strongly for its adoption as a professional, written discourse. His ideas have generally been construed as an act of nationalist altruism, an acute feeling for *land, volk* and *taal*, and this was part of the story, particularly in the wake of the Anglo–Boer War. But Preller in his articles was also pleading for the professionalisation of Afrikaans and for its adoption in newspapers, books and schools. However, editors and publishers who could realise such developments prefer hard facts and figures to the warm sentiments of *volksgevoel*. These figures Preller provided. He alluded first to the poor circulation records of papers printed in Dutch, and claimed that no such paper had exceeded sales of about 1,000. He then referred to the *Patriot*'s high readership figures, and finally pointed to the tantalising possibilities in terms of markets and circulation. 'We have a white adult population of at least 300,000 of whom a good 200,000 speak Afrikaans'.[45] The figures might have been misfounded, but the essential point remained. Out there somewhere was an audience waiting to be captured by the enterprising, the imaginative and the adventurous. To give his argument more depth, Preller also pointed to those who had already glimpsed the business opportunities that went with Afrikaans.

> One of them is the practical businessman. If he wishes to reach the buying and commercial public, he tells the publishers of his adverts, 'In Boer-language, otherwise people won't understand.' And, good heavens, what linguistic abominations result. Quite enough to make one ill. But, my trusted reader, these are the commercial Boers, they are the voice of a dumb nation.[46]

Preller, then, was trying to motivate Afrikaans as a professional industry in which many could find occupational mobility on the basis of their linguistic and cultural skills. But to professionalise Afrikaans was no small task. Before this goal could be attained, a number of preliminary battles had to be fought on various fronts. The first of these was to make Afrikaans respectable, to reinvent it as a standard language, *'n algemeen beskaafde taal* (a standard language). To accomplish this aim one had to shake off the very strong associations of poverty and particularly 'colouredness' which clung to the language. The second task entailed giving the language some substance by creating books and written material in Afrikaans. These, in turn, required markets, publishers, printers and distributors. The two sections that follow will trace these developments in some detail, first between the years 1905 and 1914 and then from 1914 to 1924.

Redefining Afrikaners: some initial attempts, 1905–1914

The columns of Preller's paper *De Volkstem* soon began to carry innumerable articles which began the long task of making Afrikaans respectable. Some of these spoke about 'Taal en Self-Respek'. Others attempted to legitimate an Afrikaans language struggle by referring to similar developments in other parts of the world, most notably Flanders but also Quebec, Wales and Ireland.[47] Subsequent articles began to emphasise the links between Dutch and Afrikaans, which made the latter a 'white man's language', and gave it an entree via Dutch into that font of civilisation, the Graeco–Roman tradition.[48]

Through these debates carried out in various journals, the people involved refined their objectives. The first was to try and standardise a middle-class variant of Afrikaans. The point was made in many ways,[49] but nowhere more clearly than in the following sentences:

> Language unity is the natural outcome of national unity, the necessary precondition for a national culture. In a situation where there are a variety of dialects, language unity can only be achieved when one of these dialects becomes hegemonic. (*Hegemonie oor die ander verkry*.)[50]

To achieve such a 'civilised' discourse, Preller and others realised that Afrikaans needed massive injections of Dutch to save it from the English and 'Coloured' structures which permeated it.[51]

This insistence on cleaning up Afrikaans with Dutch was not only an attempt to make it more civilised and middle class, it also reflected the extent to which these early Afrikaans initiatives had to shelter under the more powerful lobby which wanted Dutch recognised as the official language. The Afrikaans grouping had tried to give themselves an independent identity by congregating together in the north in the Afrikaanse Taalgenootskap (Afrikaans Language Society) (ATG), set up in 1905. The southerners joined together in the Afrikaanse Taalvereeniging (Afrikaans Language Union) (ATV), the following year. The response in the north was disastrous as nobody wanted to touch an organisation dominated by Preller, an upstart clerk of dubious peasant background and his rather peculiar *outré* friend, Marais. The response in the south was better where ATV members could reactivate allegiances and structures of the First Language movement.

The whole issue of Afrikaans had to wait until Union before it could make any significant advances. Firstly, in the negotiations preceding Union, people interested in Dutch grouped together in the Academy for Language, Literature and Art. In this powerful body with access to resources, the Afrikaans lobby could make its voice heard. But secondly, and more importantly, the massive ideological labours around Union with its emphasis on white unity, citizenship, national symbols and generally its growing infrastructure of press, common taxation, education and postal system, created an atmosphere propitious for the advancement of Afrikaans. For, as other historians have pointed out, it is at moments like these that nationalisms can find a broader popular resonance by entering their claims into a communication network which unites previously divided communities and promotes a sense of commonality amongst citizens.[52] Given these factors, it is not surprising that Preller and his ATG, despite almost insuperable financial problems, scrambled desperately to get their magazine *Die Brandwag* off the ground in 1910. The project had first been mooted five years previously.[53]

The post-1910 situation looked far more optimistic. The ATV and ATG spawned a series of related organisations which united their constituency of teachers, clerics and small farmers on a consistent basis while the columns of *Die Brandwag* put these people in touch with each other. In 1911 Dutch–Afrikaans student bodies formally added their support to Afrikaans and through it they must have glimpsed a partial solution to their clogged careerist mobility. In 1914 the provincial councils promulgated a ruling allowing Afrikaans to be taught up to Standard IV. This, in turn, required materials production for schools; linguistic engineers to produce a standard language; printers, publishers and distributors.

Afrikaans, too, found a fertile base amongst the many Afrikaner women's organisations which had arisen both during and after the Anglo-Boer War. Middle-class women grouped together in these associations to try and right the particular disabilities and discrimination which they experienced as a sex. They took as their constituency the poor and specifically poor Afrikaner women. These eminent *volksmoeders* worked in an atmosphere where poverty was increasingly being ethnicised. These welfare initiatives along ethnic lines must, in turn, have influenced sections of the poor who derived benefits from identifying and presenting themselves as 'white Afrikaners'.[54]

Post-Union political development also aided the cause of the language lobby. The unity of Union was short-lived. The ruling South African Party (SAP) seemed increasingly to be at the beck and call of the mine magnates. The wealthy Transvaal farmers in the SAP gained from lucrative maize agreements with the mines – agreements which excluded the Free State Farmers.[55] In addition, wealthy landowners continued to swallow up small farmers. On the Rand, Afrikaner workers competed with unskilled black labour, and when white workers struck to protect their relative privilege, they came up against the full force of the state. When, in 1914 General J. B. M. Hertzog broke away to form the National Party (NP) he drew all these disaffected groups behind him.

The language lobby flocked to join the new party. Hertzog had courted the language men thoroughout and in the NP they found something of a political home from whence they could continue with their work of forging a language and a literature.

The outbreak of the First World War also fuelled the language issue. When the SAP took South Africa into the war on the British side, certain sections of Afrikaner society rebelled. For many rural poor whites who supported the rebellion, it took on the character of a messianic movement. But instead of the promised kingdom on earth, they found themselves and their leaders in prison or facing fines.[56] In this atmosphere there was an increasingly sharpening definition of an Afrikaner – a development that happened on several organisational levels. One thinks, for example, of the opening of Die Vrouemonument in 1913. There was also the Helpmekaar (Co-operation) movement which paid the rebels' fines ensuring that many received concrete benefits for having behaved as 'Afrikaners'. The movement reputedly raised £180,000 in two months, and some of this money went 'to endow certain Afrikaner cultural organisations'.[57] The pattern of competitive donation used in this campaign was copied during the First World War to help set up Nasionale Pers, the publishing house for the NP. In addition, the canonisation of Jopie Fourie, the executed rebel, led to a spate of orally circulated poetry.[58] Within the organisational shelter afforded by these institutions, it became immeasurably easier for the Afrikaner petty bourgeoisie to press their claims for a language and literature. Their successes soon assumed the shape of a rapidly rising graph as dictionaries and books appeared in great numbers. In 1918 Afrikaans became a subject in two universities. In the same year Afrikaans achieved legal recognition as a type of third language when legislation was passed to the effect that the word 'Dutch' in Article 137 of the constitution included Afrikaans for all state and official purposes outside, but not inside, the House. This legislation represented a small legal victory, but its effects on the ground were limited. The Civil Service continued to be English dominated despite 1912 legislation which stipulated Dutch–English bilingualism after five years in the service.[59] The Nationalist coalition victory in 1924 improved the prospects of Afrikaans considerably. Dr Malan steered through legislation which conferred full official status on Afrikaans and on 8 May 1925 the motion was carried unanimously by both Houses in an atmosphere of goodwill and *toenadering*.[60]

However, this incrementalism has been made to appear much smoother in retrospect than it did at the time, and the Afrikaans language lobby continued to face opposition from various quarters. English-speakers dominated state positions and commerce and the final Supreme Court judgment in Afrikaans was delivered only in 1932.[61] Certain Dutch-speaking members of the middle class continued to scorn what they saw as an upstart language and its protagonists. In church circles Dutch opposition to Afrikaans remained fierce and helped to delay the translation of the Bible which eventually appeared in 1933.[62] The project had first been mooted in the 1870s by GRA members in order to proselytise more successfully among 'coloureds'.[63]

In this atmosphere the manufacture of a literary culture was no simple task and the section that follows addresses itself to the hard struggle of the literary and language entrepreneurs to build a literature.

Sharpening the outlines: 1913–1924

The whole issue of fostering a literature was crucial largely to ensconce the linguistic hegemony of the language that was being hammered out by specialists in various bodies.[64] The point was stressed in many places and in many ways. Celliers put it in this form: 'It must surely be apparent to every Afrikaner that we can only reach our goal through our own literature, nurtured in Afrikaans soil, permeated by an Afrikaans spirit and thoroughly accessible to Afrikaners in language and content.'[65]

To create such a literature, the Second Language institutions used a variety of techniques. They assiduously cultivated any emerging or established writers not already involved.[66] They instituted innumerable literary competitions and prizes which overtly or subtly encouraged people to write about 'Afrikaans' subjects.[67] The general idea seemed to be to build as broad a base as possible which could then attract a wide spectrum of readers. And it is this diversity of Afrikaans literature which needs to be stressed, for all too often literary historians see this writing as expressing a narrow straight-jacketed nationalism.[68] One is not denying that much of this literary discourse operated within a boundary of nationalism. But the variety of interpretation given to the meaning of nation reflected the debates on precisely that issue which filled the wider political arena.

The diversity of Afrikaans literature arose from the variety of region, intellectual tradition and even social class from which its authors came.[69] Many writers had been exposed to different European literatures and they mobilised this knowledge in their work.

One does not wish, of course, to reduce such profusion to individual idiosyncrasy. The point about the diversity was that it constituted the building blocks from which a more common sense of identity could be constructed. *Die Brandwag*, in introducing a piece by de Roubaix who documented life in Namaqualand, made the point in this way: 'His work teaches us about a part of our country and especially our volk about whom most of us know desperately little.'[70] Furthermore, to popularise all of this work, magazines like *Brandwag* and *Die Huisgenoot* (The Family Companion) fabricated a tremendous cult of personality around certain literary figures whom they depicted in personalised articles and full-page pictures.[71] Many historians who speak of these writers, refer to them as *volksdigters* spontaneously adopted by an adoring populace, which was partly the case.[72] But what needs stressing is not the spontaneity but the artifice.

Much of this fiction was historical. A good deal of it dealt with the Anglo-Boer War, which was hardly surprising. Every war spawns a literature of its own since it has a ready-made market.[73] Within this atmosphere of heightened historical interest, certain people set to work to stitch together an 'Afrikaner' history which could become a myth of national origin. In creating this history, writers could draw on the work of the First Language movement but its products were sparse.[74] The serious elaboration of an Afrikaner past was started by that ubiquitous linguist, Preller, and his work on Retief which he soon turned into a full-scale Voortrekker industry. The Trek is now so massively institutionalised that it is hard to imagine a time when every schoolchild did not learn about the Trekkers every year. But at the turn of the century the word itself was relatively new and had only entered the vocabulary in the 1880s. As late as the 1910s people still used the word by which the migrant farmers had always been known – *emigrante* or *landverhuisers* (emigrants).[75] Preller, however, changed all of this. He started his series on Retief in 1905, a few days before

Dingaan's Day and linked his writing to the preparations leading up to that event. The first article opened by regretting the fact that people knew too little about Retief, and Preller declared his intention to right this absence. But he did so in a demotic fashion and set out to create a cult of personality around Retief and other 'Trekker' leaders.[76] Preller's articles were to be serialised in a host of other papers and subsequently appeared in book form which went into ten editions and some 15,000 copies. The book itself was unabashedly emotional, affective and colourful, and probably made most readers feel that Retief was a member of their family. The success of Preller's venture soon attracted a group of imitators who applied the personality principle to an abundance of Afrikaner heroes from the past.[77] Together these works established a semiotics of Afrikaner history involving key events of 'black barbarism' and 'British perfidy', personified in great, strong men whose names could be invoked like talismans.[78]

But it was not enough to tell readers that they had their own history and literature. For this literary production to catch on, people needed a strong sense of themselves as Afrikaners, and such an assumption could not be safely made. The 'traditional' Afrikaner community was crumbling while Afrikaners of all classes seemed to be adopting the trappings of an 'English' culture:

> A foreign culture is ensconced in powerful fortresses and citadels. With every new delivery by sea thousands of cheap English books are distributed throughout the country.... Our biggest daily papers, the cinemas, the school system, the language of our courts, the shops with their fashions and merchandise, the furniture in our houses are all bastions and agents of a foreign culture which claims for itself the right to overrun and conquer the world.[79]

Another language man was to dub these conditions a *bioskoopbeskawing* (bioscope/flick culture) and Afrikaner cultural organisations devoted considerable energy to devise ways of supplanting this movie mania with something more moral and something more Afrikaans. Preller, for example, tried to beat the *bioskoopbeskawing* at its own game by making a film on the Trekkers. But most people had to settle for less ambitious media which could work towards a crisper definition of 'Afrikaner' on a number of levels. Part of this work was done in literature and historical writing, but most of it was carried out in debating societies, drama associations, reading circles, coffee houses, some schools and the columns of Afrikaans magazines.[80] All of this endeavour amounted, in effect, to a redefinition of everyday life. The pages of *Die Brandwag* and *Die Huisgenoot*, for example, carried articles, advertisements, pictures and stories which took every imaginable phenomena of people's worlds and then repackaged these as 'Afrikaans'. A brief list would include food, architecture, interior decoration, dress, etiquette, health, humour, landscape, monuments, the plastic arts, music, handicrafts, transport, agriculture, nature study and so on.[81] For the readers of these articles, what had previously been furniture became 'Afrikaans' furniture and what had been a house became an 'Afrikaans' house built in an *Afrikaanse bouwstijl* (Afrikaans architecture).

All of this redefinition formed part of a broader intellectual movement known as *volkskunde* (folklore studies). It was first picked up by academics studying in the Netherlands and Germany at the turn of the century. Under their influence many others began collecting songs, antiques, oral history and folklore.[82] These *volkskundiges* soon developed a love of tradition common to those who live off it. In addition, much of this ideological innovation was taken over by small entrepreneurs who marketed Afrikaner artefacts like pictures of leaders, furniture and records.[83] As one of their number put it:

> Much attention is being devoted these days to Afrikaans art, not only in architecture, but also in interior decoration, and whoever wants to furnish their house in an 'up to date' style shows their friends at least half a dozen chairs and a chesterfield made of (wood) and other materials used in olden times by Afrikaner carpenters and wagonmakers.[84]

But to describe all of these cultural forms and ideological innovations is not to explain their effects or the markets and readership which they found. Part of that readership was predictable and came from the Afrikaner petty bourgeoisie which produced the cultural products and 'consumed' them. But the literary intelligentsia could not survive off itself; it had to broaden its audience.

Popular responses

The metaphor most frequently used with regard to audiences for Afrikaans literary materials was that of capture. And an appropriate word it was too, since the language lobby faced the odds of a splintering community who seemed to *verengels* (Anglicise) every day. To counter these tendencies, writers and journalists knew they had to try and lay their hands on every available Afrikaner. Celliers phrased the issue like this:

The (Afrikaans) writer in our country faces a particularly difficult task. He has the problem that the rural population requires different reading material from their urban counterparts. The writer cannot leave the rural population to its own devices by saying, 'I only concern myself with city dwellers', because Afrikaners are too few compared with the immigrants from outside, and because every Afrikaner is an essential element in the struggle for our language and *volk*. The national writer must . . . ferret out every single Afrikaner, find him a school, a teacher, a book that he can understand and which uplifts and educates him.[85]

Already in 1905 the far-sighted Preller knew from whence the bulk of an Afrikaans audience was to come: 'Our nation is deteriorating to the level of an ignorant proletariat – and it is to these people that we wish to speak through books, newspapers and magazines.'[86] To reach these people, the language purveyors and their magazines expanded the concept *leeslus* (love of reading) which had first been elaborated in the pages of the *Patriot*. No issue of *Die Brandwag* or *Die Huisgenoot* went by without extensive discussion on 'hoe om leeslus op te wek' (how to arouse a love of reading).[87] The most obvious strategy was to keep things simple and write in a tone and register accessible to those of uncertain education. Articles also discussed how to encourage a book-buying habit amongst people, while more generally these magazines tried to educate people into the values of a literary culture with its rules about originality, copyright and plagiarism.[88]

What effects did all of this exhortation have? Again one can only speculate in broad terms since figures are hard to come by. But it would appear that certain literary ventures met with considerable success. *Die Huisgenoot*, for example, was set up in 1916 to bale out a financially ailing *Burger* and since this magazine was closely modelled on *Die Brandwag* one can only assume that the latter was reasonably successful. *Die Brandwag* faltered and folded in 1922. But *Die Huisgenoot* went from strength to strength. Always prodigiously illustrated, it turned this feature into its main selling point in 1923 when it dropped its literary orientation to become a weekly modelled on the American *Saturday Evening Post*. By the mid-1920s it was said to be the most popular magazine in South Africa.[89] Publishers, too, did well from Afrikaans books. Burger (later Nasionale) Boekhandel was set up in 1917 and during the next 23 years it produced 1,100 books which sold 3,274,581 copies.[90] One does not know what the graph of sales looked like over the years. Neither does one know what type of books they were selling and quite possibly many were school texts. But the point remains that publishing Afrikaans texts was a lucrative business. Certain writers like Preller consistently sold well, while newspapers and publishers would go to unprecedented and sometimes un-scrupulous lengths to procure Marais's work.[91]

All of these statistics do not, of course, imply that *die onkundige proletariaat* (the uncultured proletariat) was rushing out to buy books. However, it would seem clear that at least some of this welter of printed matter made its way into ordinary Afrikaner homes. Some people perhaps read it for reasons of personal enjoyment. Many women, particularly rural dwellers, bought magazines to alleviate their boredom.[92] *Die Huisgenoot* carried a lot of educational material and was known as 'the poor man's university' and in an age when education was becoming the key to advancement, many people would go to considerable lengths to 'improve' themselves.

But the success of magazines like *Die Huisgenoot* can also be ex-plained in broader more structural terms and these have largely to do with the family and women's position within it. Throughout the 1910s and 1920s there was to be a steadily mounting barrage of material addressing itself to these two related groups. To understand this con-cern, one has to try and untangle a complex confluence of factors which were in essence 'overdetermining' these two 'structures' in the Afrikaner community.

Firstly, and most obviously, these years saw a heightened imperial concern for the decay of the family under industrialisation and a concomitant focus on women as the means of holding the family together.[93] But for the Afrikaans language grouping it was even more crucial to 'capture' these two terrains. Women were after all the ones who were going to socialise children as Afrikaners, and it was not for nothing that Afrikaans was so frequently called 'the mother tongue'. The writer of an article might well have put these questions to other mothers: 'Does the child know that he is an Afrikaans child and because he is Afrikaans that he must speak his own language, know the history of his *volk*, be familiar with his Bible. . . . By the seventh year the child must know what the word Afrikaner is.'[94] This task of 'saving' Afrikaans women for the *volk* was taken up by women's organisations, books, fiction, and then in an Afrikaner women's magazine *Die Boerevrouw*, set up in 1918. Together these media created a series of interlocking stereotypes which partly drew on dominant ideals of womanliness but filled this broad category with a particularist content. Afrikaner women consequently were like all others, 'selfless', but this altruism was not only for family but *volk* too.[95] Afrikaner women were also unaffected; they did not rise above themselves.[96] Those that did were 'verengelsing' (becoming Anglicised) and they married Englishmen. In fiction these women came to sticky ends.[97] Furthermore, Afrikaner women stayed in nice families, not in boarding-houses.[98]

But these women's media did not only provide negative images of what Afrikaner women should not do and be. Magazines like *Die Boerevrouw* also focused on the domestic sphere which it tried to dignify and professionalise. In doing this, articles drew on a 'domestic science ideology' which attempted to permeate housework with a modern, 'scientific' ethos.[99]

In their toils to try and make women live in nice Afrikaner families who spoke Afrikaans and bought *Die Brandwag*, these women were aided by the language men themselves, who had an overriding interest in making the Afrikaans family a solid reality. This concern was understandable since almost the only place where Afrikaans or some form of it was consistently spoken was in the household. At work most people spoke English. In church until 1918 and 1919 (officially but often actually much later) they heard Dutch sermons and sang Dutch hymns, while in school many parents opted for English education since English language skills were a crucial passport to jobs in a 'British' urban economy.[100] *Die Brandwag* put the point as follows:

> We have chosen to concentrate on a point where the land lies unprotected: the Afrikaans family. . . . With the help of well-intentioned Afrikaners, the *Brandwag* is determined to steal the place in the Afrikaans family which is at present empty or is filled with foreign nonsense like *Home Notes, Home Chat* and *Home Journal*.[101]

Die Huisgenoot always carried a cosy family scene on its cover.

This barrage on the family must have had some effect, particularly when one remembers that a lot of the information going into the home was refracted in very personal ways. Language itself is personal enough, but Afrikaans was associated with the intimate terrain of the household. Women's magazines gave advice on sex education and marital problems which were then indirectly linked to the broader issue of 'Afrikaner identity' which filled the remaining pages.[102] Many housewives, in any event the ones most bound to an ethnic community, probably internalised bits of this 'Afrikaner' ideology. Their husbands in the workplace mostly subscribed to an 'English' Labour Party political culture which the NP did very little to alter, dominated as it was by a rural ideology and back-to-the-land schemes.[103] But these men returned to a household with at least a few 'Afrikaner' trappings. Some of these, like Preller's book on Retief, presented a world view of struggling Afrikaners pinioned between 'black hordes' and English overlords – a structure which resonated with the worker's own experience in the economy.[104]

But no 'ethnic identity' is all encompassing and the Afrikaner women and men, like everybody else, had a conception of the world which, in Gramsci's words, was 'disjointed and episodic [they belonged] simultaneously to a multiplicity of mass human groups'.[105] These people no doubt continued to see themselves as Jo'burgers, Kapenaars (Capetonians), lovers, workers, mothers and so on. However, below all of this was a sediment of 'Afrikanerness' which had settled in many households.

In the 1930s and 1940s, as O'Meara has shown, Afrikaner workers were to be intensively mobilised behind an Afrikaner nationalism that represented a new ensemble of class forces. But these workers did not march mindlessly to the beat of this new nationalism. Instead, their response was influenced by their economic position in a changing labour process which disposed certain Afrikaner workers to throw in their lot with the new NP. And the disjointed fragments of 'Afrikanerness' that some people and particularly women had internalised during the first twenty years of the century must have made the work of the new nationalists considerably easier.

Conclusion

In bringing this essay to a close I would like briefly to move beyond literature, and make some tentative generalisations about Afrikaner nationalist ideologies during this period.

By the end of the nineteenth century, Boer societies were undergoing processes which both cleaved them apart and yoked them together in new situations. These new situations were in fact the massive social movements which went into reconstruction after the Anglo-Boer War. Part of this complex set of social developments had to do with the reconstruction of poor Afrikaners, either proletarianised in the city or headed in that direction after the devastation of the war. This group were there thrown up against their educated kinsmen who assumed, sometimes by default, the task of containing, moralising and fashioning these fractious bywoners into a working class which could then be interpolated into a burgeoning capitalist economy. As upstanding members of their community this work came easily to this group of moral agents and their moral labour was aided by borrowing from imperial thinking on social engineering of various types.

At the same time this group was very aware of itself as a middle class *manqué*, aspiring to occupations and life styles from which various British agents seemed to exclude them. And to right this wrong, sections of this aspiring middle class began elaborating nationalist notions often through the medium of literature. Their toils of socialising the poor consequently began to assume a particularist content. For in the very moment that these educated Afrikaners were beginning to explore the category of 'their nation' through which they hoped to wrest some of capitalism's benefits for themselves, they were discovering the support which could give their nationalist vision some substance and clout. The process then of becoming a worker – or a worker's wife who was socialised in a gender specific way – was, for some, the process of being made into an Afrikaner. Class formation was, in other words, deeply inscribed with the fabrication or restructuring of ethnicity.

This contradictory and unstable process lies at the very heart of nationalist ideologies during the first two decades of this century. Furthermore, in locating the genesis of nationalist thinking in this unstable process, one can hopefully resuscitate some of its complexities which have for too long been muffled under the deadening weight of organic and idealist interpretations. These analyses tend to reduce nationalisms to inert categories of language and religion which somehow suggest themselves from below. The object of this chapter, however, has been to show that these relationships are perhaps less predictable and more arbitrary than traditional wisdom has lead us to believe.

Notes and references

1 T. Nairn, *The Breakup of Britain* (London 1981) p. 340.
2 For details see note 42 below.
3 See Nairn, *The Breakup*, and G. Eley, 'Nationalism and social history', in *Social History*, **6**, 1981, 83–107 and his 'State formation, nationalism and political culture in nineteenth-century Germany' in R. Samuel and G. Stedman Jones (eds), *Culture, Ideology and Politics* (London, 1982) pp. 277–301, in which he uses such theories. See also J. Sheehan, 'What is German history? Reflection on the role of the nation in German history and historiography', *Journal of Modern History*, **53**, 1–23. This article deploys theories of invention and manufacture. See too E. Hobsbawn and T. Ranger (eds) *The Invention of Tradition* (Cambridge 1983).
4 Nairn, *The Breakup*, Ch. 9.
5 Paragraph drawn from M. F. Valkhoff, *New Light on Afrikaans and 'Malayo-Portuguese'* (Louvain 1972); J. Combrink, 'Afrikaans: its origins and development', in L. W. Lanham and K. P. Prinsloo (eds) *Language and Communication Studies in South Africa* (Cape Town 1978) pp. 69–95; and Anon.

'Afrikaans', in J. Reinecke *et al.* (eds) *A Bibliography of Pidgin and Creole* (Honolulu 1975) pp. 322–3.

6 G. R. von Wielligh, article in *Die Brandwag*, Jan. 1918, pp. 276–9. The divisions he mentioned were: the Western Cape, the lower north-western provinces, Namaqualand, the Midlands and Karroo, the south-western areas and the eastern provinces.

7 For details of poverty in the Cape see Colin Bundy, 'Vagabond Hollanders and runaway Englishmen: white poverty in the Cape before poor whiteism', in *The Societies of Southern Africa in the 19th and 20th Centuries*, vol. 13 (Collected Seminar Papers, Institute of Commonwealth Studies, London, 1984).

8 Terms drawn from G. R. von Wielligh, *Eerste Skrijwers* (Pretoria 1918) pp. 99–100. The translations are my own as are all subsequent quotations.

9 This section is based on T. R. H. Davenport, *The Afrikaner Bond* (Cape Town 1966) Chs 3 and 4; H. Giliomee, 'Reinterpreting Afrikaner nationalism', in *Societies of Southern Africa*, vol. 13, op. cit.; J. Kannemeyer, *Afrikaanse Letterkunde en Bewegings voor 1900* (Johannesburg 1975); von Wielligh, *Eerste Skrijwers*; Dan O'Meara, *Volkskapitalisme. Class, capital, and ideology in the development of Afrikaner nationalism* (Cambridge 1983) pp. 21–43.

10 J. C. Moll (ed.), *F. W. Reitz – Outobiografie* (Cape Town 1978) pp. 22–3, gives details of this *vrywillige stelsel* (voluntary system).

11 O'Meara, *Volkskapitalisme*, p. 23.

12 Davenport, *The Afrikaner Bond*, pp. 35–6.

13 See, for example, *Die Afrikaanse Patriot 1876* (a facsimile edition of the first volume) (Cape Town 1974), which carried poems and articles defining a nation in terms of language, country, religion and history.

14 The *Patriot* started with fifty subscribers in 1876 and by 1881 its sales had reached 3,700. Figures from Davenport, *The Afrikaner Bond*, p. 34.

15 Von Wielligh, *Eerste Skrijwers*, p. 11. Details of *Illustrated London News* from W. de Klerk, *The Puritans in Africa* (Harmondsworth 1976) pp. 96–7.

16 von Wielligh, *Eerste Skrijwers*, p. 11.

17 Figures from E. G. Malherbe, *Education in South Africa* vol. 1 (Cape Town 1925) p. 100.

18 Phrase from L. Rousseau, *The Dark Stream: The story of Eugène N. Marais* (Johannesburg 1982) p. 7. It was used in connection with Marais's father, originally from the Cape, who lived on uncertain means in the Free State and then Pretoria.

19 See, for example, S. Trapido, 'Landlord and tenant in a colonial economy: 1880–1910', *Journal of Southern African Studies*, 5 (1) 1978, 26–56, and S. Trapido, 'Reflections on land, office and wealth in the South African Republic, 1850–1900', in S. Marks and A. Atmore (eds), *Economy and Society* (London 1980) pp. 350–68; L. Salomon, 'The economic revival of Afrikaner nationalism', in J. Butler (ed.), *Boston University Papers in African History* (Boston 1964) pp. 219–42 and D. Denoon, *A Grand Illusion* (London 1974) pp. 59–63.

20 Paragraph based on G. Cronjé, 'Die Patriargale Familie in die Afrikaanse kultuurontwikkeling' in P. Pienaar (ed.) *Kultuurgeskiedenis van die Afrikaner* (Cape Town 1968) pp. 99–110, and J. van Bruggen, *Op Velde en Rande* (Pretoria 1920), a collection of short stories on bywoners. Despite their

fictionality and their later setting, these realistic stories give a good feeling for the social universe of landlord and tenant.

21 This point has been extrapolated from D. Blackburn, *Prinsloo of Prinsloosdorp* (London n.d.). Again this is a novel, but Blackburn was an acute sociological observer. See, for example, his *Secret Service in South Africa* (London 1911). His fiction is noted for its satirisation of recognisable social types.

22 Trapido, 'Landlord and tenant', p. 367, fn. 40.

23 A. Grundlingh, 'Collaborators in Boer society', in P. Warwick (ed.) *The South African War* (London 1980) pp. 258–78.

24 Paragraph drawn from Denoon, *A Grand Illusion*, pp. 63–95.

25 *Report of the Transvaal Indigency Commission 1906–1908* (Pretoria, TG 13-'08) p. 74.

26 See, for example, J. Scott and L. Tilly, 'Women's work and the family in 19th century Europe' in *Comparative Studies in Society and History*, **XVII**, 1975, 36–64, and M. Anderson, *Approaches to the History of the Western Family* (London 1980).

27 See Charles van Onselen, 'The main reef road into the working class . . .', in *Studies in the Social and Economic History of the Witwatersrand 1886– 1914*, vol. 2, *New Nineveh* (London 1983) pp. 113–21 for details of artisanal and self- employment opportunities for Afrikaners in Johannesburg, pp. 121–5 for patterns of Afrikaner unemployment.

28 On the issue of employment for the young, see Rev. Theron's evidence in the *Report of the Transvaal Indigency Commission 1906–1908*, p. 116. The Reverend said that from his experience daughters could get jobs in laundries and sons could sell newspapers. But parents could not get employment 'having no trade or education and not being able to speak English'. See also R. Krut, 'Working class "youth" and "delinquency" in Johannesburg, 1890–1913', paper presented to the Education Department Seminar, University of the Witwatersrand, 9 June 1982 in which she discusses informal sector employment for the young.

29 Phrase from van Bruggen, *Op Velde en Rande*, p. 28. For details of apostolic churches and Afrikaners see: B. Sundkler, *Zulu Zion* (London 1976) pp. 13–67 on multiracial Zionist churches in Johannesburg at the turn of the century and D. Gaitskell, 'Women, religion and medicine in Johannesburg between the wars', paper presented to the African History Seminar (SOAS, London 18 May 1983) in which she mentions Afrikaner involvement in faith healing apostolic movements, p. 4.

30 For details of popular entertainment in Johannesburg, see N. Lazarus *et al.*, 'Hamlet through a haze of alcohol: entertainment in white Johannesburg 1910–1913', unpublished Honours dissertation (University of the Witwatersrand 1976).

31 *The Report of the Transvaal Indigency Commission 1906–1908*, p. 115 estimated that in the Transvaal as a whole white women over 15 outnumbered men by between two and three to one.

32 For a fuller discussion of this imperial family ideology see R. Krut, 'Maria Botha and her sons: the making of a white South African Family' (mimeo 1983).

33 As an index of the Afrikaner intelligentsia's alarm, see the attitudes expressed to falling church attendance in urban and rural areas: Grundlingh, 'Collaborators', p. 275, and J. J. Fourie, *Die Afrikaners in die Goudstad, Deel I*,

1886–1924 (Pretoria 1978) p. 148. For the world of Afrikaner workers on the other hand, see van Onselen, *New Nineveh*, pp. 111–70.

34 *De Volkstem*, 1 Nov. 1905.

35 *Die Brandwag*, editorial, April 1918.

36 Paragraph drawn from Rousseau, *The Dark Stream*, pp. 46–55.

37 Information from Denoon, *A Grand Illusion*, pp. 87–92 and I. Hexham, *The Irony of Apartheid* (New York 1981) Ch. VII, and Fourie, *Afrikaners in die Goudstad*, pp. 131–3.

38 For more details of this search for a popular base, see p. 111–15 below. See also a statement made in connection with finding a constituency for Afrikaans: 'Church and school are not the only or the most important terrains in which we can struggle and toil for our language. . . . There is a wide and fertile field which lies empty: our volk, our entire willing volk.' 'Afrikaans', in *De Volkstem* 6 Sept. 1905.

39 This point is elaborated on pp. 108–15 below.

40 This interpretation comes across strongly in Hexham, *The Irony*, who sees Afrikaner nationalism as being engineered by a small group of Calvinists. This Calvinist thought was, of course, present, but it was one among many strands. Much nationalist discourse was secular in tone and style. Preller, very much a leading light of the movement, and his friend Marais apparently never went to church, except for weddings and funerals.

41 If one looks at any novels on urbanisation and its effects from this time, their language is all shot through with a profound moralism. See, for example, the later sections of W. Scully, *Daniel Vananda* (Johannesburg 1923), and R. R. R. Dhlomo, *An African Tragedy* (Lovedale n.d.).

42. The developments of the Second Language Movement have been documented in numerous books. For matters of fact I have relied mainly on R. Antonissen, *Die Afrikaanse Letterkunde van Aanvang tot Hede* (Johannesburg n. d.), E. C. Pienaar, *Taal en Poësie van die Twede Afrikaanse Taalbeweging* (Cape Town 1926), P. C. Schoonees, *Die Prosa van die Twede Afrikaanse Beweging* (Pretoria 1922), J.C. Steyn, *Tuiste in eie Taal* (Cape Town 1980) and E. C. Pienaar, *Die Triomf van Afrikaans* (Cape Town 1943).

43 For details see E. C. Pienaar, *Taal en Poësie*, p. 15.

44 Gustav Preller, 'Laat 't Ons Toch Ernst Wezen', reprinted in D. J. C. Geldenhuys, *Pannevis en Preller* (Johannesburg 1967) pp. 54–89.

45 *Ibid.*, pp. 78–79.

46 *Ibid.*, pp. 80–1.

47 'Taal en Self-Respek', in *De Volkstem*, 11 Nov. 1905; 'Vlaanderens Strijders', in *ibid.*, 1 April 1905; 'Fraanse Kanadesen', in *ibid.*, 1 Nov. 1905; 'Die taalkwessie in Ierland', in *ibid.*, 28 Oct. 1905, and 'Die Onderwys-kwessie in Wales', in *ibid.*, 8 July 1905.

48 See the statement made by one, van Rijn, in 1914: 'Afrikaans is no *bastard tongue*. . . . It is a true *white man's language*, Dutch to the core.' (Emphasis original.) Quoted in Reinecke *et al.*, *A Bibliography*, p. 322. By about 1910 D. F. Malan was linking Afrikaans to Dutch, German and French, 'the natural inheritors of the civilisation and art of the old Greeks and Romans'. Quoted in Schoonees, *Die Prosa*, p. 13.

49 See, for example, Preller's comment: 'We must make a distinction between civilised Afrikaans and the language of the street, playground and servants.' Quoted in Pienaar, *Taal en Poësie*, p. 44.
50 Quoted in *ibid.*, p. 142.
51 Preller, 'Inleiding tot Jan Celliers: Die Vlakte en ander Gedigte', in Geldenhuys, pp. 40–1. For attempts to exorcise the 'coloured' nature of Afrikaans, see 'Is Afrikaans plat?' *Die Huisgenoot*, Aug. 1919 and then the debate on this article in *ibid.*, Nov. 1919.
52 The point was made in G. Eley, 'Nationalism and social history', *Social History*, 6, 1981.
53 For more details see Pienaar, *Taal en Poësie*, pp. 61–3.
54 For a comparative perspective see Mary P. Ryan, 'The power of women's networks', in J. Newton *et al.*, *Sex and Class in Women's History* (London 1983) pp. 167–86. See also R. Krut, 'Saving the children and policing the parents', (*mimeo* 1983) and her 'Maria Botha', for models of women's welfare work and the ethnicisation of poverty. This latter point is raised in Bundy, and J. Butler, 'Afrikaner women, social welfare and education in a small South African town, 1920–1939', paper presented to the International Conference on the History of Ethnic Awareness in Southern Africa, Charlottesville, 7–10 April 1983. I am deeply indebted to Riva Krut for her help and knowledge on women's history.
55 Trapido, 'Reflections on land, office and wealth', p. 363.
56 T. R. H. Davenport, 'The South African Rebellion, 1914' *English Historical Review*, 78, 1963, 73–94. He mentions that the poverty-stricken western Transvalers entered the rebellion behind their 'prophet' van Rensburg.
57 *Ibid.*, 93.
58 Paragraph drawn from Davenport, 'The South African rebellion', pp. 90–3 and R. van Reenen, 'Ontvangenis van *Die Burger*', in J. P. Scannell (ed.) *Keeromstraat 30* (Cape Town 1965) pp. 2–3.
59 Information drawn from Pienaar, *Die Triomf* pp. 361–2 and Steyn, *Tuiste en eie Taal*, pp. 202–3.
60 See Pienaar, *Die Triomf* pp. 362–8.
61 Steyn, *Tuiste in eie Taal*, p. 203.
62 See Pienaar, *Die Triomf*, pp. 388–411. Other factors delaying the translation included debates about whether to translate from the Dutch Bible or the Greek; a lack of literary as opposed to translation skills on the part of certain translators and an underestimation of the task which was initially tackled in the late 1910s by a group of men trying to do the work part- time.
63 From H. Giliomee, 'Class, community and conflict: mobilizing the Cape Dutch and the Boers in the nineteenth century', paper presented to The History Workshop, University of the Witwatersrand, 31 Jan.–4 Feb. 1984, 39–40.
64 A similar point had been made but from a slightly different perspective by Tony Davies, 'Education, ideology and literature', in Tony Bennett *et al.* (eds) *Culture, Ideology and Social Process*, (London 1983) pp. 251–60.
65 Schoonees, *Die Prosa*, p. 31.
66 Celliers was apparently invited to return from his self-imposed exile in Europe. *Die Huisgenoot*, Aug. 1918, p. 440.
67 See, for example, *De Volkstem*, 14 June 1905, which announced a short-

story competition. Preference would be given to Afrikaans rather than Dutch entries and to stories based on 'Afrikaanse leven'. To indicate the type of story required, the paper gave an example: 'The story of a nickname'. Its first sentence was 'We have a custom – a good old Afrikaans custom . . .'

68 See particularly, Jack Cope, *The Adversary Within: Dissident writers in Afrikaans* (Cape Town 1982) p. vii.

69 Most writers were overseas graduates from good families: Marais, Leipoldt, Totius, Celliers. Others like Preller, van den Heever and de Roubaix came from small farming backgrounds and had a South African secondary education. Many Afrikaans writers, de Roubaix, Totius, A. G. Visser, D. F. Malherbe, were educated at Paarl schools which were to the Afrikaans petty bourgeoisie what places like St Peters were to the black literary petty bourgeoisie.

70 *Die Brandwag*, Dec. 1918, p. 227.

71 See, for example, *Die Huisgenoot*, Aug. 1918 for such a piece on Celliers which was followed with this poem:
Don't disturb the poet . . .
He inhabits a separate world
Which you cannot enter. Its beauty
You cannot fathom.
It's too deep, sublime for you . . .

72 See T. Dunbar Moodie, *The Rise of Afrikanerdom* (Berkeley 1975). He tends toward such an interpretation in his discussion of the early poets, pp. 41–6.

73 For an extensive discussion of the poetry of the Anglo-Boer War, see M. van Wyk Smith, *Drummer Hodge* (Oxford 1978).

74 By 1905 there were very few Afrikaans (rather than Dutch) history books. The two major works were S. J. du Toit's *Geskiedenis van ons Land* and *'n Eeu van Onreg* (A Century of Wrong).

75 F. A. van Jaarsveld, *Die Tydgenootlike Beoordeling van die Groot Trek* (Pretoria 1962) pp. 5–7.

76 *De Volkstem*, 9 Dec. 1905.

77 Those who explicitly acknowledged Preller's influence were H. H. Joubert who wrote *Verse Oor Piet Retief* (1911) and C. J. Langenhoven who dedicated his anthology *Die Pad van Suid Afrika* to Preller, 'the writer who first gave me an insight into the greatness and meaning of the Trek'. Details from Pienaar, *Taal en Poësie*.

78 For an overview of this work see F. A. van Jaarsveld, *Ou en Nuwe Weë van die Suid Afrikaanse Geskiedskrywing* (Pretoria 1961) pp. 17–19.

79 Insert into *Die Huisgenoot*, July 1919, advertising *Die Burger Leeskring*.

80 For details see Schoonees, *Die Prosa*, pp. 1–28. The National Party set up the Eendracht Koffiehuis in 1917 to try and bridge the social gaps in the Afrikaner community; 'die koffiehuise hou alles wat Afrikaans is in eer; afrikaanse kookkuns en afrikaanse lekkernije speel 'n groot rol', Fourie, *Afrikaners in die Goudstad*, p. 160. (The coffee-house honours all things Afrikaans; Afrikaans cuisine and Afrikaans sweetmeats play an important part.)

81 To list all of these articles would be to list a great deal of the contents of the two magazines. But see particularly 'Die Afrikaanse Bouwstijl', *Die*

Huisgenoot, Nov. 1918 and Feb. 1919; 'Die Prente aan ons Mure', *ibid.*, April 1919; 'Volksgesondheid', *ibid.*, Feb. 1919 and 'Ons Veldmiddels', *ibid.*, Dec. 1918; 'Korsies van Pasteie' (Bits and Pieces), a monthly column devoted to Afrikaans humour, *ibid.*; 'Afrikaansetiepes in ons kuns', *ibid.*, July 1920, and 'Afrikaanse Houtsneekuns', *ibid.*, Oct. 1920; 'Die Kakebeenwaentjie', *ibid.*, Jan. 1920; 'Die Ou Boerploeg 'n Kultuur-historiese opstel', *ibid.*, May 1920, and 'Afrikaanse Soogdiere', *ibid.*, Aug. 1918. *Die Brandwag* carried similar pieces but specialised in monuments and no issue went by without at least one picture of an 'Afrikaans' monument. These two magazines also carried pictures of 'Afrikaanse mense', 'Voortrekker mense' and scenes of 'Afrikaans landscape'.

82 Abel Coetzee, 'Die Afrikaner se Volkskunde', in Pienaar, *Kultuurges-kiedenis*, p. 112 and F. Schonken, *De oorsprong de Kaaps-Hollands Volksoverleveringen* (Amsterdam 1914). Schonken was one of the earliest folklorists, and his books did much to popularise the discipline. By 1918 *Die Huisgenoot* was carrying articles urging people to collect memorabilia and oral history. 'Ou Mense' *Die Huisgenoot*, Jan. 1920 and 'Die Skakel of Bande van die Verlede,' *ibid.*, Aug. 1918.

83 See for example the advert for a wagon-maker in *Brandwag*, Jan. 1918; adverts for poems set to music and sold as sheet music, 'Onze Moeders', *Die Huisgenoot*, 1918, and 'Winternag', *Die Boerevrouw*, June 1919. Reitz's popular poem 'Klaas Geswint en sijn pert' was made into a record. Moll, *F. W. Reitz*, pp. 104–5.

84 *De Volkstem* 2 Dec. 1905.

85 Schoonees, *Die Prosa*, p. 51.

86 Quoted in Pienaar, *Taal en Poësie*, p. 53.

87 Again these discussions were numerous but see particularly, 'Afrikaans bij die hoër onderwijs', *Die Huisgenoot*, Nov. 1918; Review of *Nationale en Afrikaanse Gedigte* by Melt Brink, *Die Huisgenoot*, and an article by Celliers, 'Die Roman', *ibid.*, Aug. 1919.

88 Editors frequently exhorted people not to plagiarise and reminded their readers that postcards did not qualify for photo competitions. See 'Letterdiewerij', *Die Huisgenoot*, Sept. 1918 and the editorial, *Die Boerevrouw*, July 1919.

89 Details from the entry *Huisgenoot* in the *Standard Encyclopaedia of Southern Africa* (Cape Town 1972).

90 *Standard Encyclopaedia of Southern Africa*, entry on *Nasionale Pers*.

91. Van Schaik, a publisher in Pretoria, reputedly manipulated Marais's morphine addiction in order to extort contracts from him. Rousseau, *The Dark Stream*, pp. 484–5.

92 'Korrespondensie', *Die Boerevrouw*, Aug. 1919.

93 See Krut, 'Maria Botha'.

94 'Ons Kinders', *Die Huisgenoot*, Feb. 1919.

95 See for example editorial, *Die Boerevrouw*, March 1919, and the short story 'Die Verraaier' which deals with the theme of 'opofferende liefde' (selfless love) for husband and country, *Die Huisgenoot*, Aug. 1918 and subsequent editions.

96 See for example the story 'Groot Fant en sy vrou Tant Annie'. Tant Annie is not 'one of these fictional heroines who faints at any excuse', *Die Huisgenoot*, March 1919.

97 This was a favourite theme for stories. See 'Elke hond kriji sij dag' in which an Afrikaans woman takes to calling herself Mary and speaking English. She marries a perfidious British man who deserts her, *Die Huisgenoot*, Sept. 1918; 'En Volgden andere Goden na' in which Helen (from a wealthy family) starts to develop fancy English notions. But she comes right when she marries Hennie from a lowly but honest family of 'unaffected Afrikaners – hospitable, homely, pleasant and patriotic', *ibid.*, Feb. 1919; and on a slightly different tack, 'Die Muurkassie' in which Andries marries an Englishwoman under whose influence he 'wanders from traditional morality' and ends up as a 'poor white'. Review of this book in *Die Huisgenoot*, Nov. 1919.

98 'Van Moeder aan Dogter', *Die Boerevrouw*, March 1919, and editorial, *ibid.*, June 1920. *Die Boerevrouw* tried to capture the image of all this 'Afrikaner womanliness' in the picture on its cover; a photograph of a van Wouw statuette of what we today recognise as a *voortrekkermeisie* with a *kappie*. However, the image was initially unrecognisable to many Afrikaner women who wrote in to say that the *kappie* was ugly or atypical while the *meisie* was too slight and too young. See 'Korrespondensie', *ibid.*, May 1919, Aug., Oct. and Dec. 1920. The magazine responded by carrying articles by historians and museum curators vouching for the *kappie's* authenticity, *ibid.*, May 1919 and Dec. 1922.

99 See for example the editorial which launched *Die Boerevrouw*. It said *inter alia*: 'If a woman runs her house with skill and knowledge – knowledge of hygiene and domestic science . . . and if she leaves nothing to chance, then her children will go far and achieve greater things for country and *volk*. If Afrikaans women read and pick up ideas from this magazine, and then apply this knowledge to the household, then a better future awaits her children,' *ibid.*, March 1919. Later editorials and articles developed these themes.

100 See Abel Coetzee, *Die Opkoms van die Afrikaansekultuurgedagte aan die Rand* (Johannesburg 1938) p. 201.

101 Quoted in Pienaar, *Taal en Poësie*, pp. 61–2.

102 See for example *Die Boerevrouw*, May 1919, whose editorial advocated a book called *Witte Rosen* intended for girls of 'about 13' and 'to aid parents in their discussions with children'. The magazine also carried an 'agony column' called 'Om die Koffietafel'.

103 See O'Meara, *Volkskapitalisme*, pp. 21–34.

104 This point is and can only be speculative. But Preller's history of the Trek and Trekker republics casts all black/white relations as competitive and confrontational, whereas the relationships between black and white polities in the nineteenth-century Transvaal involved elements of conflict and co-operation in a delicate balance of power.

105 Quoted in Bennet *et al.*, *Culture, Ideology and Social Process*, p. 201.

CHAPTER FOUR

Solidarity fragmented: garment workers of the Transvaal, 1930–1960*

Iris Berger

The garment industry provides particularly rich material for examining the relationships between class, race, nationalism and gender in recent South African history. During the thirty-year period between 1930 and 1960, the industry offered employment to new groups of recently proletarianised workers, predominantly women, from all of South Africa's major racial groups. Not only did the prevailing contemporary ideologies hold out both class and a racially defined nationalism as possible bases for identification and political activism, but groups espousing these alternative ideological positions actively competed for garment-worker support. Yet, understanding why and how women were drawn to identify with particular viewpoints at given historical moments is complex and cannot be explained by any simple correlation either between race and ideology or between objective membership in the working-class and proletarian-class consciousness.

Several different theoretical perspectives inform this discussion. Recent work on trade unionism in stratified societies helps to clarify the political strategy of the Garment Workers' Union (GWU) by suggesting that such unions, unlike craft unions, cannot create job monopolies based on skill scarcity; they must therefore protect themselves from labour substitution and undercutting either by joining all workers together on a multiracial basis (whether in a single union or in parallel unions) or by erecting barriers that artifically limit competition from subordinate workers.[1] Many aspects of the history of the Transvaal garment workers explain their preference for the first strategy,

* I am grateful to the National Endowment for the Humanities and the Social Science Research Council for providing the funding that supported this research. They, of course, bear no responsibility for any of my conclusions. I also wish to thank Baruch Hirson for generously sharing his ideas on an earlier draft of this paper.

although the organisational forms for implementing this policy varied over time in relation to changing state mandates, shifts in the composition of the labour force and changes in the organisation of work.

The external factors affecting workers' ideology during this period, and particularly the strength of Afrikaner nationalism, are well known. But the impact of developments within capitalism and of changes in the organisation of work have been less clearly delineated. Labour-market segmentation theory provides a framework for understanding this process that highlights, in particular, the way in which the growth of capitalism leads to a shift from a more homogenised workforce to a more stratified one. By encouraging the division of the labour market into distinct submarkets on the basis of race, sex and ethnicity, workers are increasingly separated along status lines, and class solidarity is directed to an identification with one's subgroup in society.[2]

This theory is important in illuminating the material basis for what appears to be a heightened racism among white garment workers in the 1950s. Yet, by treating sex as simply another variable that operates in precisely the same way as class and race, it may mask some of the distinctive features of gender. In an effort to explain the relation of gender divisions to capitalism, Marxist–feminist writing has demonstrated convincingly the benefits to capitalism of maintaining women's unpaid labour in the home and of reinforcing their primary identification as wives and mothers.[3] This ideological emphasis on women's household roles, bolstered by both secular and religious traditions of patriarchy, may partially explain the contradiction apparent among many garment workers between their political attitudes at home and those they expressed in the workplace. The belief that women belonged at home also affected the class position of working women by justifying their relegation to low-status, low-paying jobs. As a result, married working women belonging to the dominant group in a racially stratified society may experience a disjuncture between their class status at work and the class position of their families. This contradiction would be accentuated in times of prosperity for male workers from the ruling group. During the period under consideration, ideological tensions between home and work and between ethnicity and class were important aspects of the history of Transvaal garment workers.

Although clothing manufacture in South Africa began on a small scale during the early years of the twentieth century, mass factory production dates only to the late 1920s, coinciding with the general growth of secondary industry at that time. Relying heavily in its early years on skilled, European-trained craftsmen, the industry expanded during a period when poverty was forcing large numbers of young, Afrikaans-speaking women into the cities to seek work and when the state's 'civilised labour policy', backed up by promises of tariff protection, encouraged employers to favour white over black workers. Popular acceptance of a wide male-female wage differential and the easily justified notion of sewing as 'women's work' made these newly proletarianised women ideal candidates for the large number of jobs as semi-skilled operatives that opened up in the garment industry.

Amidst charges of undercutting and work dilution from the highly paid male craftsmen, the industry developed its characteristic pattern of continually seeking out new sources of cheap labour and continually breaking up the work process to accommodate the new and ostensibly less-skilled workers. The source of this pattern lay partly in the structure of the industry, particularly in the fact that for manufacturers of quality women's and children's wear, technological improvements and enlargement in the scale of production yielded only minimal savings. Thus, some changes in these areas notwithstanding, reduction in the cost of labour and deskilling have remained the major means of lowering costs and increasing surplus value for capital.[4] In the 1930s the predictable rift between the skilled male workers and the increasing numbers of semi-skilled, predominantly Afrikaans-speaking women led in 1934 to a split between the Witwatersrand Tailors' Association and the newly formed GWU of South Africa. Male African workers, prohibited from belonging to officially 'registered' unions, had several years earlier formed the South African Clothing Workers' Union.

Most recent writers on the garment industry agree that the strength of the Transvaal-based GWU lay in the ability of its leaders, especially Solly Sachs who headed it until his banning in 1952, to gain material advantages for its members by stressing the primacy of 'bread-and-butter' issues. The union also built up solidarity and a tight-knit organisation by assisting the young, newly urbanised women in practical ways such as finding accommodation, and by sponsoring dances, picnics and other social activities that encouraged informal contacts among union members. The GWU also gained support by campaigning actively on issues of concern to women, such as confinement allowances and crèches.[5] As black women began to enter the industry in the Transvaal in greater numbers in the 1940s, the union made every effort to include them in the benefits it had won for its members.

Through the success of their class-based, increasingly multiracial position, the GWU earned a reputation throughout South Africa as somehow 'different' from other initially white trade unions. Explanations of this distinctiveness have varied. Although 'openness' has been a successful strategy among industrial unions, other unions in the same position took more popular exclusive stances, so that this explanation alone is insufficient. Sachs attributed this political and ideological difference to the subordinate position of Afrikaans-speaking women which, he argued, made them less prone to feel a sense of racial superiority.[6] However attractive this notion might be from a feminist perspective, the life histories of many of the women who became active fighters for a multiracial union indicate that they once shared the racist attitudes of their families. Johanna Cornelius, an important union member, offered a more materialist explanation grounded in the low pay and hard work endured by garment workers, combined with the industry's long international tradition of working-class organisation and struggle.[7]

Yet, by the mid-1950s, belief in the union's non-racialism was so severely strained that at least one member, Ray Adler, castigated Solly Sachs and his followers for not promoting the equality of black workers and for appeasing racialism. Rather than entering this heated debate directly, this paper will analyse the GWU and its members in the 1940s and 1950s in order to clarify the relationship of structure to ideology. While recognising the crucial impact of national economic and political policies on women's feelings about class, gender, race and nationalism, my concern is primarily to demonstrate the way in which social relations at work may in themselves have enhanced and even generated certain attitudes and ideologies.

As previously noted, working conditions during the 1930s fostered a certain class unity among members that was reinforced by ethnicity and gender as well as by the intensely exploitative conditions in which the vast majority of women worked. In a study of 540 women industrial workers on the Witwatersrand conducted between 1930 and 1932, Hansi Pollak found that most were young and Afrikaans-speaking. Clothing factories were often located in 'wholly unsuited, congested, poorly constructed buildings' that were ill-lit, badly ventilated and unheated. In a few clothing and boot factories, Pollak concluded that 'the accumulated dirt and debris defies description'. Fewer than 10 per cent of the 1,323 clothing workers she visited were provided with adjustable chairs; others sat all day at their machines on backless stools. The same dirty, untidy space usually doubled as restroom and lunchroom, so that most women preferred to eat at their machines or standing in the street.[8]

Wages in virtually all of the industries that employed women at this time were extremely low, predicated on the fallacious notion that these young women (the median age in the clothing industry in Pollak's sample was 20; 71 per cent were under 25)[9] were partly supported by husbands and families. In fact, slightly over one-third belonged to a family group with no male wage-earner, while nearly one-fifth were the sole breadwinners in families that averaged 4.5 members. All of the single women living away from home assumed total responsibility for their own support, while 15 per cent in addition still supported dependants in their former homes.[10] Not only were the legally determined wages extremely low to begin with, but employers found countless ways to evade full payment, rarely granted raises when they were due and frequently laid off workers as a result of seasonal fluctuations. During the time of Pollak's research, changing jobs seemed to be among the main strategies of resistance against employers who refused to comply with wage agreements, although this sometimes meant accepting a new position at reduced pay.[11] Women also complained of the task work system, of routine dismissals of workers who had become qualified and entitled to higher wages, of frequent sexual harrassment, of rudeness on the part of supervisors and of mandatory overtime.[12] Considering the living standards of these young women, Pollak wrote:

> It is impossible to go into any detail on whether £2 a week is a truly 'civilised wage', but on the Witwatersrand it is well nigh impossible for any respectable girl to live on less. . . . The managing on £2 a week implies a careful distribution of resources and a familiarity with prices, far in excess of that usually found among women industrial workers.[13]

Interviews with women who lived through this period verify the sense of struggle and difficulty. Most, by the time of the depression, earned less than the £2 a week average that Pollak describes.[14]

In addition to the shared experience of gender, ethnicity and exploitative working conditions, hiring practices may have contributed to a sense of common experience, as some employers found it useful to respect the preferences of the women to work alongside those they already knew.[15]

Many features of the labour process also would have contributed to a consciousness of shared experience, for the vast majority of young white women had begun to work only recently and were engaged in very low-paying, semi-skilled operative work. Confined to machining, trimming and finishing, they received their only training while on the job and were clearly separated by wages and function from the small number of skilled white men.[16] These men, who marked, laid out and sometimes cut patterns, received £4–£5 a week. African men worked as cutters, pressers and cleaners at wages more comparable to those of the women, although somewhat lower. Control and enforcement of industrial discipline was a function of the skilled male workers.[17]

In order to absorb this new female labour force, sufficient deskilling had occurred so that only on the cheapest clothing did a worker make the entire item (except for buttons and buttonholes); other clothing was made by sets or teams that varied from two to ten people, depending on the type of item. Each worker, therefore, gained skill only in making a particular type of garment.[18] Yet the labour process had not undergone sufficient subdivision to introduce any degree of stratification among machinists, apart from that separating learners from qualified workers.

The family circumstances of these women probably influenced their ideological orientation. As predominantly young and single and from impoverished families, the majority did not face the constraints of the 'double day' or the psychological commitments to a dependent family that some have argued may inhibit women's class consciousness. But those garment workers who were married (roughly 25 per cent in Pollak's sample) worked out of economic necessity, because of their husbands' inadequate wages.[19]

Blatantly discriminatory attitudes towards women workers also may have helped to shape a sense of solidarity. In industries with male and female workers, where apprenticeship committees had been formed, apprenticeship applied exclusively to juvenile (white) males.[20] Furthermore, government policy firmly supported the principle of a male–female wage differential. The Industrial Legislation Commission recommended paying women two-thirds of what men earned, while Pollak found that female wages were roughly 50–60 per cent of those of men. Reporting on its own study of the question in 1935, the commission found a variety of reasons for continuing to advocate lower wages for women than for men, some of them resting on probably accurate projections concerning labour supply, others founded on no more than stereotyped visions of women, and fear. For example, concluding that it was 'doubtful whether the adoption of the principle of equal pay for equal work is in the interest of the women themselves', it suggested that if women were paid more, they 'would not want to get married, since the higher the wage a woman receives, the less the economic urge to induce her to enter the married state'. From this perspective, low wages became an outright means of social control. The *Report* also referred, rather discreetly, to the need of many industries to keep women's labour cheap, noting the opinion expressed in testimony that equal wages 'would inflict unbearable hardships on industries which have been established primarily on female labour, especially where such industries are in competition with similarly organised industries in other parts of the world.'[21]

This context of poverty, exploitation, a relatively great uniformity of wages and working conditions and differential treatment of women workers created fruitful ground for the emergence of a class-conscious ideology, born of both this objective situation and of the real successes of the union in mobilising workers to strike and to struggle for better wages and working conditions.[22] By 1935 the *Wage Board Report* on the industry observed: 'It is interesting to note that on the Rand women workers in the clothing trade, most of whom are Afrikaans speaking and therefore with no industrial tradition, have organised into what is quite a strong union.'[23]

This organisational strength resulted from an energetic policy of recruitment fuelled by large-scale strikes in 1931 and 1932 and by the impetus given to the emergence of rank-and-file women leaders after the male craft-oriented tailoring workers seceded from the GWU in 1934. Following the general strike of 1931, elections of factory committees and shop stewards occurred, and a generation of strong, dedicated, Afrikaans-speaking young women arose as trade-union leaders. The ruthless repression of strikes during 1932 further helped to galvanise support for the union. By the end of 1933, as South Africa emerged from the depression, workers became more independent. Union bargaining success in that year, combined with an intensive organising effort, boosted GWU membership to over 3,000 in a period of six months. From 1934 onward, a new era of co-operation began between the GWU, the employers and the Industrial Council for the Clothing Industry,[24] although not without protracted and often bitter and difficult negotiations each time an agreement expired. Yet even the union's growing strength did not destroy the prevalent belief that women's wages need not be excessively high; nor did the living conditions of women workers change overnight. In a discussion of the need for hostels to house some of the nearly 2,000 women factory workers in Germiston (most of whom were clothing workers), the city was depicted as fast becoming 'a glorified slum in which live poor factory workers, poor railwaymen in conditions approaching that of a Native location'.[25] The GWU made enormous gains during the early years, but further struggles clearly remained necessary.

In the judgement of Jon Lewis, the union's most important

achievement during the 1930s lay in promoting a strong degree of class consciousness among a group of women with little or no tradition of working-class organisation or solidarity and a strong sense of Afrikaner exclusiveness. As Johanna Cornelius, the long-time GWU President, later admitted:

> It took me years to get used to the notion that even the English – let alone the natives – were human beings.[26]

Sachs summed up the union's policies and strategies in a report on his organising trip to Durban and Cape Town in 1935. In describing the work there as only beginning, he elaborated:

> We have the recruits, and we must now turn them into class-conscious, loyal and disciplined soldiers, by propaganda and agitation; by building up a cadre of leaders, shop stewards, voluntary helpers, a properly functioning Central Committee, and, above all, by protecting the interests of the workers.[27]

As he noted in his speech, the union's main strength lay in its practical and successful advocacy of workers' interests. But it also helped to mould a sense of both national and international working-class unity among its members by encouraging participation in annual May Day demonstrations, sending prominent GWU members on trips to Russia sponsored by the Friends of the Soviet Union and by articles in the union newspaper, the *Garment Worker*, that expressed a pro-Soviet, anti-fascist stance.[28] In addition, women from the GWU organised mass rallies against fascism and Nazism, put enormous time and energy into organising unions among the workers in other low-paying industries and worked actively to build branches of their union among garment workers in coastal areas. All of the activities of the period exuded a strong conviction of the inseparability of trade unionism and politics.

Nationalist attacks on the union from the late 1930s onward repeatedly tested the degree of this commitment to principles of working-class unity. Yet whenever the leaders faced internal criticism, they received the overwhelming support of the membership and soon became as skillful as their opponents at manipulating the symbols of Afrikaner nationalism.[29] Their approach was to favour 'healthy nationalist aspirations' as opposed to those associated with exploitative capitalist interests. Addressing a mass meeting in the mid-1930s, for example, Johanna Cornelius urged:

> As workers we must fight against all capitalists whatever their nationality may be, and we must not allow our ranks to be broken by the filthy racial propaganda of Greyshirts.[30]

Many years later union leaders expressed the same sentiment:

We have no quarrel with the decent, honest Nationalists. Our quarrel is only with the rich landowners, financiers, estate agents, etc. who are exploiting the noble Afrikaner traditions for their own selfish ends.[31]

Appeals to its members as women formed another critical aspect of union ideology during the 1930s. The content of these appeals was intended to further solidify women's consciousness as workers by attacking the class bias of middle-class women's organisations rather than to foster an independent feminist solidarity. A 1936 article by Sachs articulated the union's position. While prefacing his remarks with a strong statement of support for women's rights – 'Every gain made by women towards complete equality, is a step along the road of progress and a break in the chain of slavery'[32] – he went on to attack bourgeois women's organisations for concentrating on the rights of wealthy and middle-class women and for ignoring such concerns as low wages, substandard housing, government callousness towards expectant mothers and the absence of unemployment and health insurance for working women. Unlike associations of privileged women, the GWU fought specifically for the needs of women workers through its organisational efforts and advocacy work. It helped to organise trade unions in the millinery, confectionery and tobacco industries where many of the workers were women and played a major role in forming the Federation of Women Workers, an organisation dedicated to attacking the problems that other women's groups had ignored.[33]

Another aspect of the effort to mobilise women focused on changing their self-image as factory workers and encouraging greater public respect for them. Pollak related a conversation with 'an experienced trade unionist' who had explained that one argument against paying equal rates to men and women was the fact that women did not expect it. She also reported a number of comments by women workers that pointed to the connection between their low self-esteem and their low economic expectations.

Ach, I'm only a woman, my work isn't worth more to the boss.
I'm getting as much as a woman can expect to get.
He's a man and ought to get more than me.[34]

Although workers probably varied in the extent to which they shared the political orientation of Sachs and the union leaders and shop stewards, their support was sufficiently strong to enable the Transvaal GWU to build up a successful industrial union. In it a sense of unity and struggle on the basis of class was reinforced by the union's respect for separate ethnic traditions, its active attention to the specific needs of female workers, the relatively uniform situation in the labour process of the vast majority of women workers and the extreme poverty in which they lived and laboured – at wages little higher than those of African men during the same period. It responded to the problem of undercutting by aggressively trying to organise branches in the coastal areas whose workers received wages far lower than those in the Transvaal. But sufficient geographical specialisation prevailed within the industry so that the coastal standards did not pose a dire threat to workers in Johannesburg and Germiston.

By the late 1930s and early 1940s this situation was changing in ways that tested the extent to which the commitment to class solidarity extended across racial boundaries. From the mid-1930s, small numbers of Coloured women began to work in garment factories, entering in much larger numbers by 1940. During the Second World War, the opening up of higher-paying opportunities for white women, combined with the expansion of the clothing industry to meet wartime needs, also drew African women into the industry. In the Transvaal, while the number of white women employees continued to rise – from 5,923 in 1937 to 6,322 in 1943 and to 6,979 in 1947, the number of Coloured women in the same years rose from 250 to 1,850 to 3,078 and the number of Africans from 8 to 454 to 873. In effect, the number of whites among the female labour force decreased from 96 per cent to 64 per cent between 1937 and 1947, while the percentage of Coloured women rose from 4 per cent to 28 per cent. By 1947 African women comprised only 8 per cent of women garment workers in the Transvaal.[35]

Yet during this period a critical trend began that would completely transform women's labour-force participation – the tendency of larger numbers of positions to open up for white women in white- collar and clerical positions, as increasing numbers of proletarianised black women sought jobs that were less demeaning than domestic service, and even higher paying than the professional opportunities open to them.[36] Although the large-scale movement of white women out of industrial production became most pronounced after the Second World War, it was apparent as early as the mid-1930s when Labour Department employees began to note a refusal on the part of young women to accept factory employment, preferring jobs in shops, offices and restaurants, and began to complain of labour scarcity in Transvaal clothing factories.[37] By the Second World War, when thousands of garment workers left the industry to work in munitions plants or to volunteer for the armed forces, there were few young Afrikaans-speaking women entering the clothing factories; most young women from the towns preferred office or shop work. Even after munitions work ceased, many unemployed women preferred returning to their homes rather than to industrial employment, leaving the Department of Labour to lament the shortage of the 'right type of worker', especially in clothing factories.[38]

For black women, on the other hand, work in the clothing industry appeared attractive by comparison with other possibilities. In an article discussing the need for an African Housewives' League in 1938, *Umsebenzi* had criticised the fact that African women were 'debarred from the right of working in factories', and were therefore forced into doing washing at the unspeakably meagre wages of 7s. 6d. a month.[39] As work in the garment factories opened up, one indication of its greater relative appeal to them than to whites lies in the figures on turnover in the industry. In 1946, 37 per cent of white women left before working for three months, as compared with 11.4 per cent of black women.[40]

Within a very short period of time factory work came to be seen as a principal economic activity for African women, despite the small numbers involved. By 1941, 'working in factories at 15s. a week' had entered the depictions of the hopeless and ill-paying possibilities open to them, alongside 'domestic drudgery' and beer-brewing.[41] Two years later, during protests over increased bus fares, a statement entitled 'Specially presenting the women's case' gave high priority to the needs of factory workers.[42]

The entry of black women into garment factories was not simply a function of labour supply, however, but also a part of the industry's continuous process of seeking new and cheaper sources of workers. By 1947, the industry had made little effort to rationalise production or to implement the techniques of scientific management favoured by their overseas counterparts and by the Board of Trade and Industry. Lowering labour costs thus remained a primary means of saving money.

In theory, the addition of new groups of labour into an industry still lacking great sophistication in rationalising the labour process favoured the continuation of a class-conscious cohesion among the workers. To some extent this was true. When employers first began to engage African women their numbers jumped very rapidly in a brief period because they received lower pay than other workers based on a completely out-of-date wage determination. Manufacturers justified their action by claiming that African women were not covered by the Industrial Council agreement. The union and the employers' association contested the issue and finally resolved that the Industrial Council should take the matter to the Supreme Court. The GWU maintained that African women were employees in terms of the Industrial Conciliation Act, while the employers flatly refused to accept the union's interpretation. Finally, on 9 November 1944, the court ruled in favour of the union, agreeing that, as women were not required to carry passes, they were exempt from the provisions of the Industrial Conciliation Act that prevented 'pass-bearing' Africans from belonging to registered trade unions and sharing in the benefits of Industrial Council Agreements. Immediately after the judgment the union, now able to prevent capital from hiring African women at reduced wages, demanded that the Industrial Council claim back pay for all the African women who had been underpaid. It also began to recruit African women as members, appointing a black shop steward, Lucy Mvubelo, as organiser.[43]

Despite the very real and important benefits this decision granted to African women in the industry, it did not completely obviate some of the more divisive conditions under which these groups of women laboured. The Board of Trade and Industry, in its general report on manufacturing, strongly pushed not only greater rationalisation of production, but also the idea of stimulating the development of manufacturing by deskilling, stressing in particular that the optimum utilisation of labour resources involved not simply the formal classification of categories of work but, more crucially, the wage rate granted to each category. The Board strongly favoured breaking down categories 'so as to derive the full benefit of the large resources of comparatively low-paid, non-European labour'.[44]

During the 1940s the fragmentation that the Board advocated had not yet occurred in the Transvaal clothing industry and new workers continued to be incorporated at existing pay scales into established categories of work. Women were classified either as 'learners', with weekly wages rising every three months, or as 'qualified', after a period of thirty months. One of the few major changes from the 1930s lay in the industry's attitude towards skilled workers; whereas during the previous decade the union had had to force capital to retain a ratio of one qualified worker to every three learners, the problem now was to try to retain the qualified workers.

Despite the lack of change in the labour process, the GWU was alert to the threat of deskilling and argued cogently that, although wages had improved over the years, they remained far too low. In 1946 learners' pay began at £1 11s. 0d. per week and rose to £3 12s. 6d. by the end of the qualifying period. The union estimated, however, that a 'self-supporting female employee without dependants' living in

Johannesburg required £7 a week to live 'in frugal decency (not in comfort)'.[45] In order to prevent any further debasement of workers' living standards, the GWU strongly condemned the extreme subdivision of work in the coastal areas as leading to 'disgracefully low wages', thereby hampering efficiency and the workers' possibility of learning the trade. A memorandum to the Wage Board notes:

> In the Transvaal where all female workers excluding cutters (who need special application and education) receive the same wage irrespective of the operation they are engaged on, it is found that they are given more opportunity to become first-class tradesmen. Not only do some workers get a chance to learn how to make every part of a garment but through experience it is proved that workers change their employment so as to enable them to make all types of garments in the Industry, and it is common for an experienced woman machinist to be able to complete all classes of men's and women's garments in the Transvaal.[46]

While the leadership of the GWU continued its efforts to forge a self-conscious body of working-class women during the 1940s, the tone of its pronouncements shifted in a number of important respects, particularly after 1945. Such changes in emphasis reflect the greater conservatism of the post-war period, as growing white prosperity and heightened anti-communist sentiment made class analysis increasingly less appealing. Although the *Garment Worker* continued to attack racial prejudice and to support the struggle for trade-union rights in South Africa and abroad, the highlighting of selected modern factories and the brief introduction of 'women's pages' discussing dress, appearance, recipes and knitting suggest that an effort was being made to acknowledge both the altered political climate and the changing age and marital status of many of the workers.

Despite the union's continued theoretical commitment to non-racialism, the attitudes of some members forced the GWU leaders to make policy decisions that, by their own admission, violated these principles. In 1940, as increasing numbers of Coloured women entered the industry, they were incorporated into the union as a separate No. 2 branch. Thus, while the union always worked vigorously to organise all garment workers, the question of the relationship of black women to the parent body seemed to pose difficulties. In the light of much later arguments advocating black separatism, some of the defences of the decision to create a separate Coloured branch may appear plausible. But, considering the ideological context of the 1940s, and the fact that the organisational initiative came from the registered union rather than from the Coloured workers, these arguments cannot help but seem a rationalisation for steps the union felt compelled to take.

Moreover, once introduced, segregation gradually spread, until it included separate entrances, lifts and offices for black and white garment workers.[47]

On 26 September 1940 the *Guardian* reported that the Coloured garment workers in Johannesburg had decided to form a special section to cater for their particular needs. The workers had elected a committee to look after their interests and to advise the Central Executive Committee on matters concerning them. Although a number of workers had objected to the section's formation as a kind of segregation, a union official called this a misunderstanding, explaining that the new members would retain all the rights of main branch membership, including the right to attend general meetings, and would have the opportunity to attend to their own interests and train their own leaders. In an argument that became common later, the spokesperson continued:

> It has been felt that the Coloured workers always remained in the background at general members' meetings, that they hardly ever express their views on questions affecting them, etc. Therefore, the formation of the section serves a need which must be satisfied.[48]

According to Sachs the union began to organise Coloured workers in the mid-1930s and, soon after, began to solicit the opinions of the membership and the shop stewards on how to structure their participation. About 10 per cent favoured complete equality without racial discrimination, while over 80 per cent preferred a parallel organisation with separate black and white branches; the overwhelming majority were against mixed meetings, but only an 'insignificant number' completely opposed Coloured entry into the union. The prevailing sentiment favoured a parallel branch whose members were entitled to the unqualified right to manage their own affairs and finances, to elect their own officials and to have an equal say in determining union policy and in making industrial agreements. He reported explaining to the Coloured workers that, while the union leadership favoured complete equality, the majority of members did not share this view. The No. 2 branch was then established along the parallel lines suggested above, although 'by unanimous decision' its members decided to leave the administration of finances to the Central Executive Committee. Sachs continued that, although such a racially defined structure was 'against all trade union principles, . . . in practice it worked well.'[49]

This response to coloured membership clearly suggests that workers did not support a policy of complete non-racialism. Officials expressed a clear awareness of the benefits to capital of such divisive sentiments, but explained them by reference to racially biased Afrikaner traditions maintained by workers' families and husbands. In the words of Johanna Cornelius:

> We have been brought up on the platteland where we are taught to hate the Africans and coloured people, as also Jews. The majority of the people on the platteland still have these views. We very often go to the factories, but the trouble is that the workers are married to men who work on the mines, or who come from families who live on farms, where they treat the Africans like dirt.[50]

Although the union had succeeded in reshaping some of these attitudes, extensive work remained essential.

During the 1940s the union was called upon not only to formulate an organisational strategy for incorporating new workers that was both workable and principled, and to continue the ever-present struggle against threats of undercutting – both in the Transvaal and by the coastal manufacturers – but also to formulate policies to confront any racial conflicts that arose on the shop floor.[51] In the most celebrated case of the decade involving shop-floor relationships among workers, two women in Germiston, Mrs Nell and Mrs Moll, were expelled from the union (which, under the closed-shop agreement, meant loss of employment), for having incited a strike to protest against the hiring of two Coloured women as machinists. The union, in this case, worked strongly in favour of ensuring everyone's right to earn a livelihood. None the less, it was not powerful enough locally to avert the outcome of the protest – an informal agreement by Germiston employers not to hire black machinists that lasted into the following decade.

During the 1940s, then, as new groups of workers entered the industry, the GWU was successful at preventing undercutting and at resisting changes in the labour process that might have subverted the intention of incorporating black women at equal pay by multiplying and diluting the work classifications. But the political climate within the union had led to the creation of two separate branches. And this segregation also had its own consequences. In combination with the spatial segregation of workplace facilities mandated by the Factories Act, it probably made it more difficult for women in the industry to develop the friendships and informal networks that might have helped to extend the sense of working-class consciousness on a non-racial basis. The Nationalist victory in 1948, leading to the elaboration of new forms of racial domination, further reinforced the existing tendencies towards separation. A pattern emerged during the 1940s that solidified further during the 1950s: the union engaged in strong and militant action to prevent newcomers from receiving lower wages than those already established, but compromised when necessary on questions involving union organisation. The GWU never was successful, however, in preventing geographically based undercutting from lower-paid workers in other areas, white or black. This failure assumed major significance later.

The 1950s saw the ever-increasing incorporation of black women into the labour force and the greater power of employers, supported by the state, to enforce work fragmentation that allowed their inclusion at lower wages. By this time, capital was determined to lower costs, and did so partially by investing in unregulated 'border industry' factories in which wages were so low that they threatened the standards of even the low-wage coastal areas. Further exacerbating the fears and divisions that these developments fostered came new state policies. Determined to prevent the formation of a trans-racial unity that included the massive numbers of proletarianised blacks who were joining the industrial labour force in the 1940s and 1950s, the government finally prohibited all Africans, women included, from belonging to registered trade unions.

Following the rapid development of the war and post-war years, by the 1950s the clothing industry had become the fourth most important secondary industry in South Africa, surpassed only by iron and steel, metal products and construction. By 1951–52, nearly half of all black women (47 per cent) and over one-quarter of all white women in secondary industry manufactured clothing. Just as women had begun to replace men in the late 1920s and 1930s during the transition from craft production by skilled tailors to mass production by lower-paid, semi-skilled machinists, there were similar shifts in the 1950s that eventually allowed the incorporation of large numbers of new groups of workers. Between 1947 and 1952, the number of women workers in the clothing industry in the Transvaal rose from 10,930 to 15,061, an increase of 38 per cent. During this five-year period, black women predominated in meeting the demand for new sources of labour; 2,029 Coloured women joined the industry, an increase of 66 per cent, while the number of African women increased by 1,243, a rise of 142 per cent. By 1960 the number of white women garment workers had decreased dramatically from 52 per cent in 1952 to 25 per cent of female employees. The percentage of Coloureds rose from 34 per cent to 44 per cent, although with a very small increase in absolute numbers (from 5,107 to 5,612), and the percentage of Africans rose from 14 per cent to 31 per cent.[52]

This dramatic shift in the composition of the labour force in the post-war years reflected the increased proletarianisation of black women, driven into cities by rural impoverishment and a desire to keep their families together, and perhaps drawn by the increased possibility of employment in the factories. These women, like their counterparts in the 1930s, whom a generation of Labour Department bureaucrats had sought to turn into household workers, found factory work more attractive than domestic labour. Furthermore, the class struggle of the earlier trade unionists had improved conditions in the majority of urban factories.

Yet the white workers were not simply pushed out of the industry as National Party propaganda maintained. As noted earlier, once the most devastating effects of the depression had begun to subside, young white women opted for white-collar jobs and, as the economy expanded after the Second World War, new sources of wage employment in the clerical and distributive sectors began to open up to them. According to the *Wage Board Report* on the clothing industry in 1947:

> Owing to the shortage of European labour during the war and post-war years, girls have been finding work in spheres of employment more congenial to them than industry, and especially in the service trades. The result has been an almost complete absence of new European entrants into the trade, and the consequent aging of the European labour force.[53]

The 1957 *Report of the Industrial Tribunal* added:

> Factors such as the raising of the school-leaving age, the more agreeable nature of the work, the higher status and better rates of remuneration, especially in regard to the commencing wages, the freer atmosphere and the less exacting discipline, attracts girls to the service trades generally rather than to secondary industry.[54]

This change in employment patterns caused a drastic change in the age composition of white garment workers compared with the 1930s. Whereas then the majority of women were under 25 and single, by 1957 only 9 per cent of white women in the clothing industry were in the 16–24 age group; 65 per cent were 35 and over. Their median age was now 39.2.[55]

While it would be imprudent to assume any simple correlation between advancing age and conservatism, this drastic change in age structure meant the vast majority of white women probably were married and possibly less independent politically than they had been as young, single women. Furthermore, even if their salaries were still extremely low, the greater prosperity and social mobility of large numbers of Afrikaans-speaking male workers during the years since the depression made married women far more comfortable than they had been a generation earlier. Indeed, union officials in the post-war years referred frequently to the workers' rising social aspirations.[56] Yet despite these aspirations, which were reflected in the occupations of their children, the lack of mobility within the industry may have shaped a consciousness among white women that was distinct from that of their husbands.

The Transvaal GWU was concerned at the changing composition of the working population since, in the context of a highly segmented labour force, it threatened the union's previous gains. Thus, in March 1957, the GWU distributed a questionnaire to its members entitled, 'Why is your daughter not a garment worker?' The responses were virtually unanimous on two points – the work was too hard and the pay too low. Some of the respondents also referred to their uncertain future in the industry and to the difficulty of achieving better wages and working conditions. Of those whose daughters were already working, most were engaged in office work, often in banks or post offices. The intended jobs of those whose daughters were not yet employed were similar, although slightly more varied; they were concentrated in typing, general office work and nursing.[57]

But the sources of working-class disunity lay not in the transformation of the labour force alone, but also in the way in which capital and the state chose to manipulate these changes. By 1950, manufacturers clearly expressed their unwillingness to continue to absorb new groups of workers without pressing for tangible benefits to themselves. In a letter to the General Secretary of the GWU in that year, E. Reyneke of the Transvaal Clothing Manufacturers' Association proposed that a new wage category be added to those already prescribed to cover certain classes of female workers: cleaners, folders, stampers, markers and sorters. He expressed his belief that making special provisions in the agreement for workers in less skilled tasks would stabilise what was, in effect, the current practice. He wrote:

> Today, learners are engaged on these types of work and when they reach a scale where it is no longer economic to employ them, they are dismissed and replaced by new workers.[58]

A 'realistic' wage scale, he argued, would avert the need to resort to such dismissals.

A new state policy put into effect shortly thereafter came to the rescue of manufacturers concerned about 'excessive' wages in the industry; the Native Labour (Settlement of Disputes) Act of 1953 forbade any Africans from belonging to a registered trade union. From the standpoint of the government and capital, the legal anomaly that had kept the wages of African women 'unnaturally' elevated was laid to rest. As soon as the new law was passed the GWU established a separate branch for African women. At the request of the Minister of Labour, the union then asked the Industrial Council to consider extending the agreement to all African workers. The employers' representatives reportedly were amenable on the question of African women, but they were unwilling to include African men, although Johanna Cornelius reported in a letter to Solly Sachs that 'it appears as if they (employers) were pre-pared to consider the matter favourably provided we can find a solution maybe through different grading and classification'.[59]

This apparent honeymoon with capital was short-lived, however. By March 1954, the union was reporting cases of drastic wage reductions for African women already employed, and of efforts to replace higher-paid women with Africans. Cuts at the Star Shirt and Clothing Co., for example, affected thirty African women as beginners' wages were reduced from £2 15s. 6d. to £1 10s. 9d. and the pay of experienced workers from £6 14s. 2d. to just over £4. Within a week, over 1,000 African women held a protest meeting in Johannesburg pledging 'to be in readiness for any action which our union or the GWU of South Africa may call on us to take'. They also demanded the reinstatement of wages at the level of the Industrial Council Agreement and the payment of back wages to all those women whose pay had been reduced. By early April, four more factories had lowered the wages of African women. The union immediately sent a telegram to the Minister of Labour urging his prompt intervention and reporting on the high degree of unrest among the workers. Yet, by the end of April, not only were increasing numbers of employers reducing the pay of African women, but some also had begun to replace white and Coloured workers with Africans.[60]

Throughout this period, the workers remained united in their attitudes towards these cuts. In a letter to E. S. Sachs, Johanna Cornelius reported:

> The workers in our industry, European as well as non-European were up in arms immediately and they are prepared to take part in a struggle even if it would mean strike-action to protect their present wages and working condi-tions. This fortunately is not only the opinion of the European and Col-oured workers who have a great deal to lose, but the African women are 100 per cent united with us on this issue.[61]

By April she observed: 'The position at the present moment looks explosive. I doubt whether we will be able to avoid strikes from breaking out in the various firms.'[62] Finally, in early June, just after the 31 May expiration of the old agreement, the employers agreed to extend coverage to all workers in the industry, in exchange for union acceptance of the further subdivision of certain categories of work, extension of the learnership period for some categories and reduced wages for certain groups of qualified workers. The resulting fragmentation was dramatic – an increase in the number of work classifications from six to seventeen; many of the new areas covered those in which Africans were employed.[63]

The issue of competition from cheaper labour did not end with this wage agreement, however. During 1955 and 1956 one employer began switching from all white to all black labour, thereby replacing a largely experienced workforce with one primarily composed of learners, while another, employing African men, applied for an exemption from the wage agreement.[64] By 1956, the GWU was finally forced to agree to the introduction of two sets of wages for each category of work, effectively lowering wages for the new groups of black workers in the industry still further, since the reorganised work categories had already reduced the pay of many black workers. The new category B pay scale applied to all new employees and to workers of certain classifications who had less than a specific minimum of experience or who were receiving less than specified minimum wages by 30 November 1956. Barker sees this new set of wage categories as 'not based on any racial discrimination', but rather as part of an ongoing struggle between labour and capital – the outcome of a 'determined stand' by the Transvaal employers to arrest the steep rise in wages of the preceding twenty years that was undermining their competitive position and as the employers' first successful attempt to rationalise the wage structure.[65] The new wage agreement represented a triumph for the employers and a defeat for the workers, a sign that under changing economic and political conditions the union would have difficulty maintaining a strong bargaining position.[66]

As a result of these structural changes, the division of labour in the industry assumed a new and more complex shape. A skilled labour shortage broke down some of the gender barriers among white workers while black women replaced white women in the lower levels of the hierarchy. By contrast with the 1930s, 86 per cent of the supervisory employees (foremen/women, supervisors) were now women, overwhelmingly white, although most women remained machinists and table hands. None the less, the work of white women was defined more rigidly than that of black women. For, in addition to doing the stereotypically female work of the industry, black women also worked as pressers and general workers alongside African men who formed over half the workers in each of these categories.[67]

Ultimately more threatening to the living standards of Transvaal garment workers than any local structural and labour-force changes was the widespread development of unregulated garment factories in the areas bordering on the African reserves. The GWU, since its inception, had expressed continual concern over the challenge to workers' wages resulting from the lower-paying clothing factories in the coastal areas; its concern was reflected in endless unsuccessful efforts to form a single national union that would raise all wages to the level of those of the Transvaal. But now capital began turning to sources of labour that were more difficult to organise and whose unions, if organised, could not receive official recognition. Indeed, the government-sponsored Tomlinson Commission specifically encouraged the development of a rural clothing industry with lower wages and longer working hours than those in the urban centres. The Wage Board contributed to further reductions in labour costs in the uncontrolled areas by its decision not to establish any ratio of qualified workers to learners, effectively sanctioning the dismissal of workers who had passed through the learnership period, and by allowing longer working hours and less annual and sick leave.[68] Before the Wage Board investigation, the GWU had estimated the wages in the rural factories at approximately one-third of those prescribed in the Transvaal agreement. The new ruling gave clothing establishments additional incentives to withdraw from the urban areas.[69]

This continual pressure on the wages of women created a great deal of anxiety. In a letter to the Minister of Labour the GWU protested:

> Needless to say our members are in a state of unrest. The majority of them are older workers who are not in a position today to successfully adapt themselves to new posts. Their contention, therefore, that in no other industry will they secure employment for the same wage they have been receiving is quite logic [*sic*] and justifiable. The six thousand garment workers will, in the event of them not being prepared to offer their services for a wage that will suit the pockets of the hard-minded employer of cheap labour, have no alternative but to face unemployment.[70]

Yet at the same time as official policy encouraged developments that threatened their livelihood, other aspects of policy aimed at undermining any degree of class consciousness or non-racial organisation among women garment workers and at placing workers in a situation in which their fears of displacement by cheaper labour would be translated into racial terms. These policies sometimes backfired, however, as in 1952 when the banning of E. S. Sachs, the long-time General Secretary of the GWU, led to a massive multiracial demonstration of some 15,000 women that could only have served the interests of working-class solidarity. Similarly, the development of rural garment factories affected all workers in the urban centres and, in theory, provided an issue around which they might unite.

Two state measures of the later 1950s, however, – the Industrial Conciliation Act and job reservation – served to keep the racial division of the working class in the forefront of people's consciousness and attempted to split workers on political as well as on racial lines. The Industrial Conciliation Act of 1956 forced the No. 1 and No. 2 branches to divide even further into two completely separate unions, a move that progressive members of the union were only persuaded to accept because nationalist supporters were threatening to form breakaway all-white unions. Under the new provisions, the government would recognise mixed unions only if members supported them unanimously. An article in the *Garment Worker* pronounced the decision to divide the two branches 'absolutely contrary to the principles of trade unionism'.[71] Yet, during the ensuing months, the issue of maintaining the union's strength came to be seen in racial terms as three competing white unions sought ways to unite. In its invitation to the executive members of all the No. 1 branches to hold a joint meeting, the GWU Central Executive Committee argued that unity among white garment workers was the only way for them to maintain employment in the clothing industry:

> With the danger which is on our doorstep of the clothing industry going into the hands of cheap Native Labour – which has already made its entrance at places such as Charlestown Location, Standerton, Ladysmith, the Transkei and Vryburg in the Cape, . . . we in the Transvaal cannot afford to fight among ourselves.[72]

By the middle of 1955, two racially based unions were in the process of forming and seeking registration – a new GWU of European workers and the GWU of South Africa (Coloured, Malay and Asiatic), with members in the Transvaal, the Eastern and Northern Cape and the Orange Free State.

In addition to mandating racially separate trade unions, the Industrial Conciliation Act also granted the Minister of Labour the power to reserve certain categories of work in any industry on a racial basis. Thus, while the white union was still attempting, less and less successfully, to protect its members through inclusive strategies, the government made an effort to erect artificial, and ultimately unworkable, barriers to limit competition from subordinate urban workers. On 27 October 1957, the *Government Gazette* announced that in the clothing industry, as of 4 November, the work of machinists, super-visors, choppers-out and table hands would be reserved for whites, although the enforcement of the measure was to be postponed until the various Industrial Council agreements had expired. Of about 40,000 employees in these categories, only 4,500 were white. On 4 November, at the call of the GWU, most of the 22,000 black workers doing 'reserved' jobs in Johannesburg, Kimberley, Port Elizabeth and Germiston stayed away from work to demonstrate the impracticality of the proposal; 300 factories throughout the country were forced to close down.

The measure was so totally unworkable – as the government tacitly admitted by immediately granting exemptions from it – that by the end of the decade it was modified yet again. This time a complicated plan was devised to prevent the percentages of whites from falling below a certain level (different for each region) and to check the employment of Africans in urban factories. In view of the disruption and uncertainty that these policies caused to both capital and labour, one can only conclude that their ultimate intent was to promote the growth of the rural clothing industry, under a smokescreen of 'protecting' white workers.

The intense pressures that the Transvaal garment industry faced in the 1950s, the relentless efforts of the state to blame the difficulties on competition from black workers and the general political antagonism accompanying the implementation of apartheid, led to a number of ideological changes during the decade. Yet it would be a mistake to ascribe these changes solely to white racism. For the increased work-place stratification had, in itself, created new divisions among workers through the multiplication of job categories, the creation of A and B wage scales and the relatively high wages paid to some women, partly because of their lengthy employment in the industry. Figures relating hourly wages to the retail price index make this point starkly. Whereas in 1946 the index of hourly wages ranged from 163 to 189, in 1958, it ranged between 81 and 331.[73] Although these divisions did not necess-arily fall along racial lines, whites tended to earn considerably more than the minimum for their job category, while blacks always earned close to the minimum.[74]

Other developments of the decade, like the enforced separation of trade unions, also helped focus these status distinctions on race, as did the pattern of extensive workplace segregation. Not only did factory facilities have to be segregated, but this mandatory separation meant that the vast majority of garment workers during the 1950s laboured in factories that employed only a single racial group. By requiring separate facilities, the Factories Act gave employees a financial incentive to seek out a homogeneous workforce.

The GWU received extensive criticism from the left during the 1950s for its ostensible ideological changes. Oscar Mpetha of the African Food and Canning Workers' Union, discussing the Industrial Conciliation Act of 1956, charged, 'Even the GWU, left inclined formerly, had turned practically right and decided to persuade all non-Europeans to accept the present Act.'[75] Ray Adler chided the GWU leaders for acting with 'indecent haste' as the first union to accept the principle of separate black and white unions and for remaining obsessed with complying with legal formalities in order to maintain their registration, rather than embracing all sections of the population 'in united and democratic trade union organisations'.[76] Some of these criticisms are valid.

In the context of a more highly stratified working class, now divided much more starkly on economic as well as racial grounds, GWU ideology reduced its emphasis on class struggle and working-class internationalism, and stressed instead a pragmatically based unity that might, if necessary, operate in a multiracial rather than a non-racial fashion. The main purpose of this unity remained, now as before, to prevent undercutting and the destruction of the gains that the workers had built up through struggle. Reluctantly accepting this reality, Johanna Cornelius expressed a typical sentiment of the period when she depicted the time as 'a tragic stage' in the South African trade union movement, but added:

> . . . we must never forget that the main object of a Trade Union is to get the highest wages and best working conditions for their members. The Trade Unions are being forced, by the introduction of the Bill, to reorganise themselves differently to what has always been believed was proper, but we libe [*sic*] in a different time and may have to change our methods to suit the circumstances.[77]

Despite the GWU's pragmatism on questions of union organisation, it did not drop its adherence to social justice. In a speech to the 1958 Conference of the Trade Union Council, for example, Johanna Cornelius condemned job reservation for the suffering it would cause workers of all races[78] and in its memorandum to the Industrial Tribunal on the reservation of work, the union insisted on the tribunal's responsibility to consider the interests of all groups of employees rather than recommending measures that would favour one group over another.[79]

The membership seemed to approve of this moderate position, which may have accurately reflected its ambivalence. In 1951, Johanna Cornelius had told the English journalist Basil Davidson that the union had about 600 shop stewards who took a progressive attitude on the colour question within the union, although many of the same women also voted for the National Party.[80] Shortly thereafter, however, Cornelius, wrote that 'the Nationalists did make quite a bit of progress among our European Garment Workers with their outrageous attack on the Trade Union Movement under the cloak of communism'.[81] A few months later, discussing union efforts to politicise the workers, she lamented, 'Unfortunately they do not wish to take our advice and somehow the Nationalist Party with their vile propaganda seem to have a better hold on them than we can muster.'[82] Yet on the next page she expresses greater optimism. After describing the union as advocating the closest co-operation with Africans but, if necessary, organising on parallel lines, she added that this policy was working perfectly. 'I do not think that our members were ever as united as they are at the present moment.' Though opposition supporters continued to make trouble, their strength in Johannesburg had 'dwindled down to nearly nothing'. This sense that most members outside of the Nationalist stronghold of Germiston agreed with the leadership was borne out in the election following the creation of the European union; Anna Scheepers received 83 per cent of the vote for President and Johanna Cornelius 85 per cent of the vote for General Secretary against the two male opponents put up by the Nationalists. After extracting the Germiston vote from these totals, the support for these women was nearly unanimous.

Despite the violation of trade-union principles implied in the division of the unions along racial lines, both before and after 1950, this separation did afford black women some opportunity to develop their own leaders and their own political positions. Their further support of non-union organisations involved in fighting primarily against the exploitation and oppression of blacks, or of black women, point to the impact of state policy as well as industrial policy on workers' consciousness. As the Nationalist government continued to intensify the control and exploitation of black labour and to introduce controls over black women that had been absent previously (through an extension of the pass laws), garment workers readily supported resistance on racial as well as class grounds. As labour-force segmentation increased during the 1950s, so did the ideological gap between different groups of workers, although their dependence on the white GWU undoubtedly shaped the choices of the black leadership. In the late 1940s, the No. 2 branch initiated donations to the Passive Resistance Movement, to the leftist newspaper, the *Guardian*, to the South African Institute of Race Relations and to the First People's Assembly,[83] and black garment workers took an active part in progressive groups of the period that organised around both women's and working-class issues.

Individual white workers also may have participated in some of these groups, but the union leaders were not among them. Hetty du Preez, organiser of the No. 2 branch, was involved in 1947 in an effort to form a left-wing non-racial women's organisation and she, along with Lucy Mvubelo, Sybil Hedley and Betty Flusk were among the convenors of the first national conference of the Federation of South African Women (FSAW), the multiracial women's organisation that spearheaded the decade's massive anti-pass demonstrations. Hetty du Preez also became a member of the first National Executive Committee of the FSAW.[84] The organisation's Vice-President, Lillian Ngoyi, who at one time served on the Executive Committee of the GWU of African Women, also served on the National Executive Committee of the African National Congress (ANC) and as Transvaal President of the Women's League. Having worked as a garment worker from 1945 to 1966, she recalled marching with thousands of other garment workers during the demonstration after Solly Sachs's banning as one of her formative political experiences.[85] There is no indication, however, that the GWU of African Women ever formally affiliated with the FSAW, as did the Food and Canning Worker's Union, a radical non-racial union with a large female membership.

The left-wing, non-racial South African Congress of Trade Unions (SACTU) also attracted some of the same leading militant young black women in the GWU of African Women. The main branch of the GWU, by contrast, continued its involvement in the South African Trade Union Council (SATUC), which excluded Africans, although GWU leaders presssed repeatedly for a liberalisation of SATUC's racial policies. Lucy Mvubelo, the most prominent SACTU activist among garment workers, was elected as a vice-president of the organisation in 1955 and then unanimously re-elected in 1956; in that year twenty members of the GWU of African Women attended the SACTU conference in Cape Town. Mvubelo also was selected as the SACTU representative to the FSAW conference in Johannesburg in May 1955. On 26 November 1956, under circumstances that still remain unclear, the Executive Committee of her union unanimously decided to disaffiliate from SACTU. According to the SACTU minutes, the decision resulted from the formation of a liaison committee with SATUC that would serve 'the interests of all garment workers, irrespective of their colour or creed'. In a later interview, however, Mvubelo attributed the action to SACTU's decision to affiliate with the ANC; her union voted against the motion because 'politics was a death-knell to us'.

The alternative trade-union federation, the Federation of Free African Trade Unions (FOFATUSA), which garment workers were instrumental in forming in 1959, was ostensibly aimed at keeping 'trade-union activities within the bounds of worker grievances'.[86] Whatever the politics involved, Mvubelo did not remain totally silent on the political struggles of the decade after her break with SACTU. In 1958, for example, on the occasion of a large-scale protest, she took a strong public stand 'on behalf of all the African women in my organisation who are opposed to the passes'.[87]

During the 1930s, then, when the GWU developed its strength and support from among a relatively homogeneous working-class population composed of large numbers of newly proletarianised Afrikaans-speaking young women, its success lay not only in the organising skill of the leadership and its ability to gain substantial improvements in wages, benefits and working conditions, but also in the fact that the vast majority of women were semi-skilled operatives who stood in roughly the same position in the labour process. During this period the phrase 'poor white women', combining a joint appeal to class, ethnicity and gender, applied to the overwhelming majority of workers.

By the 1950s a more stratified workforce had developed. Despite the continued gender uniformity, rapid job fragmentation was producing substantial inequalities among different groups of workers. These status divisions, combined with increased racial diversity and pressure from new state policies, made class-based unity more tenuous. At a time when both capital and the state were deliberately manipulating fears of racial competition, the GWU was forced into great defensiveness. Without wholly abandoning its earlier inclusive industrial trade unionism or its theoretical commitment to workers' equality, the drastically altered material situation of the industry and the growing strength of the apartheid state mitigated against a primary emphasis on a non-racial, class-conscious ideology. In place of the working-class consciousness of the 1930s, the GWU emphasised a more narrowly based trade-union consciousness. And, in the face of government pressure, it abandoned its earlier belief in the inseparability of politics and trade unionism, fashioning instead an ideology of apolitical 'bread-and-butter' unionism which it passed on to its African counterpart. The areas of compromise remained selective, however. While the GWU continued to fight vigorously and militantly to prevent undercutting, it was willing, as it had been in the 1940s, to make concessions in areas relating to union organisation. Thus, opponents of the GWU were correct in noting a shift in ideological emphasis during the 1950s. But the change was not as total as they portrayed it and resulted as much from changes within the industry as from a deliberate policy of 'appeasement to racialism'.

The experience of the Transvaal garment workers seems to verify the theory that workers' ideologies diverge increasingly as the labour force becomes more stratified. Yet, this divergence cannot be separated from state policies that reinforced, and sometimes mandated, these divisions. Furthermore, the relationship between class consciousness and other ideological tendencies is not entirely clear-cut. Working-class women, for example, seem to concentrate on women's issues with a class-based or a nationalist orientation. Similarly, where there is a high correlation between poverty and national identity – whether Afrikaner or African – the dividing line between class issues and nationalist issues is often indistinct. Thus, despite the theoretical conflict between these two ideologies, the women workers of the Transvaal have drawn on both simultaneously without perceiving any contradiction. While this convergence gave strength to a working-class identity in the 1930s, the union's failure to acknowledge the contradiction worked to undermine a class-conscious ideology in later years. For black women in the industry, the correlation between class and nationalism is still high; the outcome of this conjuncture remains uncertain.

Notes and references

1 Stanley B. Greenberg, *Race and State in Capitalist Development* (New Haven and London 1980) pp. 284–5.
2 Howard M. Wachtel, 'Class consciousness and stratification in the labor process', in Richard C. Edwards, Michael Reich, David M. Gordon (eds) *Labor Market Segmentation* (Lexington Mass 1973) pp. 104–7. See also the articles by Edna Bonachich in *Insurgent Sociologist*, X (2) Fall 1980, and *American Sociological Review*, XXXVII, 1972.
3 Natalie J. Sokoloff, *Between Money and Love: The dialectics of women's home and market work* (New York 1980) provides an important statement of this perspective.

4 H. A. F. Barker, *The Economics of the Wholesale Clothing Industry of South Africa* (Johannesburg 1962) pp. 192–3. These were the main products of the clothing industry in the Transvaal.
5 Jon Lewis, 'Solly Sachs and the Garment Workers' Union', *South African Labour Bulletin*, III (3) Oct. 1976, 70–2.
6 E. S. (Solly) Sachs, *Rebels Daughters* (London 1957) p. 36.
7 Interview. I am indebted to Stanley Greenberg for providing me with a transcript of this interview.
8 Hansi P. Pollak, 'Women in Witwatersrand industries', MA thesis (University of the Witwatersrand 1932) pp. 65, 71, 101–2, 112, 171.
9 Pollak, 'Women', p. 259.
10 Pollak, 'Women', p. 67. See also her article, 'An analysis of the contributions to family support of women industrial workers on the Witwatersrand', *SAJS*, XXVIII, Nov. 1931, 572–82.
11 Pollak, 'Women', pp. 230–1.
12 'Facts about the present strike in the clothing industry, Witwatersrand', 1 Sept. 1932, GWU, Bch. 72; 'Dispute at clothing and shirt manufacturers, Johannesburg', 1931, GWU Bch. 1.50.
13 Pollak, 'Women', p. 193.
14 Sachs, *Rebels Daughters*, pp. 40–57.
15 Pollak, 'Women', p. 143.
16 In 1932 there were 200 men compared with 2,200 women in the Witwatersrand garment industry.
17 'Facts', p. 4; Pollack, 'Women', p. 77.
18 Pollak, 'Women', p. 77.
19 See for example Confinement Allowance, Factory Act Section 18, 'Applications Refused During 1932.' Apart from one man who was in jail, job information on the others was unavailable; *Report to the Honourable Minister of Labour by the Wage Board, Garment Making Trades*, 12 April 1935, p. 23, shows the loss of qualified married workers as their husbands' wages improved.
20 Pollak, 'Women', p. 57.
21 Union of South Africa, *Report of the Industrial Legislation Commission*, (Pretoria 1935) UG 37, 1935, pp. 23–7.
22 Pollak, 'Women', p. 48.
23 *Wage Board Report*, 1935, p. 19.
24 Sachs, *Rebels Daughters*, pp. 87–8, 91–2, 98, 101–3.
25 *Umsebenzi*, 12 Dec. 1936.
26 Basil Davidson, *Report from South Africa* (London 1952) p. 197.
27 'Report of the General Secretary, E. S. Sachs, on his visit to Durban and Cape Town', May 1935, GWU, Reel 5.
28 *Umsebenzi*, 11 May 1935.
29 An often-cited instance was their participation in the Voortrekker Centenary Celebration of 1938 as a union group. See Lewis, 'Solly Sachs', p. 72 for additional details.
30 *Umsebenzi*, 30 March 1935.
31 From a leaflet by A. Scheepers and Maria Beggs (Johannesburg n.d., but probably 1952).
32 *Garment Worker*, Nov. 1936.

33 *Garment Worker*, Oct. 1938. The lack of information on this organisation after its initial meeting raises the question of whether it was ever a functioning group.
34 Pollak, 'Women', p. 49.
35 These figures come from the Industrial Council for the clothing industry, Transvaal, GWU, Bch. 1.
36 Lucy Mvubelo, for example, turned from teaching to working in the garment industry because wages were better.
37 *Cape Times*, 30 June 1936; *Industrial Legislation Commission Report*, (Pretoria 22 July 1935) pp. 127–8, 130–1; *Report of the Department of Labour for the Year Ended 31st December, 1939*, (Pretoria 1940) UG 36, 1940; *Umsebenzi*, 27 March 1937.
38 Sachs, *Rebels Daughters*, p. 122; *Report of the Department of Labour for the Year Ended 31st December 1945* (Pretoria 1947), UG 9, 1947; 'Problems of the Clothing Industry of South Africa', memorandum submitted by E. S. Sachs to the Arbitration Tribunal, Clothing Industry, Transvaal, Aug. 1948, SATLC Dc 8.73. (University of Witwatersrand library).
39 *Umsebenzi*, 12 March 1938.
40 Union of South Africa, *Report No. 303 of the Board of Trade and Industries on the Clothing Industry* (Pretoria 9 Dec. 1947).
41 *Guardian*, 27 Feb. 1941.
42 Alexandra Women's League, 'Features of the grievances regarding the transport operating between Alexandra Township and the city of Johannesburg', 11 July 1943, A. B. Xuma Papers, 430711b. I am indebted to Alf Stadler for referring me to this source.
43 Anna Scheepers, 'Trade unions face challenge', address delivered at the Third Research Workshop of the Abe Bailey Institute of Interracial Studies, University of Cape Town, Jan. 1973, pp. 11–12. A simultaneous case on behalf of an African man exempt from carrying a pass failed.
44 Union of South Africa, Board of Trade and Industries, 'Investigation into manufacturing in the Union of South Africa', *Report No. 282* (Cape Town 1945) p. 45.
45 'Memorandum submitted by the Garment Workers' Union to the Wage Board investigating into the clothing industry of South Africa', Aug. 1946, pp. 7–8.
46 'Memorandum to the Wage Board', pp. 15.
47 H. J. and R. E. Simons, *Class and Colour in South Africa 1850–1950* (Harmondsworth 1969) p. 535. Gana Makabeni, head of the black male Clothing Workers' Union, felt that separate unions gave blacks increased opportunity to assume responsible positions. See Leslie Witz's recent University of the Witwatersrand MA thesis on the limits of Sachs's vision of class unity.
48 *Guardian*, 26 Sept. 1940.
49 Sachs, *Rebels Daughters*, pp. 118–9.
50 'Minutes of the First National Conference, Garment Making Trade Unions', Johannesburg, 23 Aug. 1942, reprinted in *Garment Worker*, Sept./Oct. 1942, 10–14.
51 'Report on Organisation', 2 March 1943–10 Oct. 1943; 'Report on Activities of No. 2 Branch', 14 July 1943–20 Oct. 1943, GWU, Bba 23.26.

52 Industrial Council for the Clothing Industry (Tvl), 'Number of employees all factories – Transvaal', GWU, Bch. 1.
53 Quoted in *Report of the Industrial Tribunal to the Honourable Minister of Labour on the Reservation of Work in the Clothing Industry* (Pretoria 2 Oct. 1957) p. 12.
54 *Report on the Reservation of Work*, p. 12.
55 Calculated from statistics in *Report on the Reservation of Work*, p. 22.
56 References to single women in this period usually were to widows.
57 Garment Workers' Union of South Africa, 'Why is your daughter not a garment worker?' (Johannesburg March 1957).
58 Letter to the General Secretary, Garment Workers' Union, from E. Reyneke, Transvaal Clothing Manufacturers' Association, 28 February 1950. SATLC, Dc 8.87.
59 Letter from [J. Cornelius] to E. S. Sachs, 10 Dec. 1953, GWU, Bce 2.1.
60 *Garment Worker*, 12 March, 19 March, 30 April 1954.
61 Letter from [J. Cornelius] to Solly Sachs, 18 March 1954, GWU, Bce 2.1.
62 Letter from [J. Cornelius] to Solly Sachs, 3 April 1954, GWU, Bce 2.1.
63 *Garment Worker*, 4 June and 11 June 1954; Scheepers, 'Trade Unions', p. 15.
64 Correspondence between the Garment Workers' Union of South Africa and the Department of Labour, 30 Aug. 1955–13 March 1956, TUCSA, Memoranda.
65 Barker, *Wholesale Clothing Industry*, p. 387.
66 It is interesting to note that, despite the employers' claim that wages had become too high from a competitive standpoint, workers no longer were as uniformly well off as they had been in 1946. In that year the hourly wage rates of all workers were well above the retail price index, whereas by 1958 the wages of many fell substantially below it.
67 Considerably more African women than Coloured women worked as pressers, 29.5 and 13 per cent respectively, whereas the percentages as general workers were more even, 24 and 21 per cent. Of the general workers, 3.5 per cent were white women. See also Clothing Industry, Transvaal, 'Analysis of employees by occupation, race and sex on reserved jobs as at August 1957', and 'Analysis of employees by occupation, race and sex on unreserved jobs as at August 1957', GWU, Bba. 2.3.15.
68 Barker, *Wholesale Clothing Industry*, pp. 150–2. The rates for the main classes of work were about 56 per cent lower for men and 49 per cent lower for women than those in Natal District No. 2 (Pietermaritzburg and Lower Tugela), the lowest-paying areas covered by an Industrial Council agreement.
69 Between 1952 and 1956, at least 182 clothing establishments withdrew from the Transvaal.
70 Letter to the Honourable Senator J. de Klerk, Minister of Labour, from E. F. Else and H. Cornelius, 11 October, 1956, GWU, Bba. 5.1.3.4.
71 *Garment Worker*, 20 April 1956.
72 *Garment Worker*, 22 June 1956.
73 Barker, *Wholesale Clothing Industry*, p. 387.
74 *Report on the Reservation of Work*, p. 15.
75 'Second Annual Conference of the South African Congress of Trade

Unions held at No. 3 Trades Hall' (Johannesburg 12–14 April 1957). Carter–Karis Collection, 2:LS2:30/7. (CAMP Microfilm)

76 Ray Adler, 'The Garment Workers', *Liberation*, **XXVII**, 26 Sept. 1957, 26.

77 'Extracts from 105th meeting of the Central Executive Committee', 16 April 1956, GWU, Bba. 1.

78 Ray Alexander and H. J. Simons, *Job Reservation and the Trade Unions* (Cape Town 1959) p. 32.

79 *Report and Recommendation by the Industrial Tribunal to the Honourable Minister of Labour on Reservation of Work in the Clothing Industry*', 11 Feb. 1960, p. 7.

80 *New Statesman and Nation*, 4 Aug. 1951.

81 Letter from [J. Cornelius] to Solly Sachs, 10 Dec. 1953, GWU, Bce 2.1.

82 Letter from [J. Cornelius] to Solly Sachs, 18 March 1954, GWU, Bce 2.1.

83 Industrial Legislation Commission of Enquiry, Pretoria, 28 July 1950, 'Minutes of Proceedings', pp. 13462–3.

84 Cherryl Walker, *Women and Resistance in South Africa* (London 1982) pp. 139 and 155; 'Conference to promote women's rights', to be held in the Trades Hall, Johannesburg, Saturday 17 April 1954, Carter–Karis Collection, 2:WF1:47/3.

85 Helen Joseph, *If This Be Treason* (London 1963) p. 165.

86 South African Congress of Trade Unions, 'Annual report and balance sheet for the year ended March 1957', presented to the Second Annual National Conference, Johannesburg, 12–14 April 1957, Carter–Karis Collection, 2:LS2:30/8.

87 *Golden City Post*, Nov. 23, 1958; Leo Kuper Papers, Ser. 4, Box 20, 'Status of women' (CAMP microfilm). See also, 'Interview with Lucy Mvubelo by G. M. G.', Nov. 1973, Carter–Karis Collection, 2:XM1:70, 'The National Union of Clothing Workers: interview with Mrs Lucy Mvubelo General Secretary', *South African Labour Bulletin*, **V** (3) Oct. 1979, 97–100. Both interviews refer to her negative views on the close relationship of FOFATUSA and the Pan-Africanist Congress.

CHAPTER FIVE

The reconstitution of Coloured identity in the Western Cape*

Ian Goldin

Introduction

This chapter focuses on the reconstitution over time of the racial category 'Coloured' in South Africa.[1] For over eighty years, Coloured identity has been a locus of ideological and political conflict in South Africa, and in the 1980s the intense debate concerning Coloured identity has come to the forefront of the struggles being waged against the South African regime. As this chapter shows, however, the notion of Coloured identity has changed over time and the development of the racial categorisation of 'Coloured' has been closely related to the objectives of ruling-class ideologists. At the same time racial ideologies have not simply been imposed on subordinate classes in the form of 'false consciousness'. Coloured identity has in part been forged from within the working class and petty bourgeoisie. The survival of Coloured identity, however muted, has depended on the continued support of sections of the working class and petty bourgeoisie.

The Western Cape region of South Africa is currently witnessing two major programmes of social engineering; the first is that associated with the introduction of a tricameral parliamentary system in which Coloureds elect representatives responsible for the administration of Coloured affairs. The second is that connected with the renewed onslaught on Africans in the Western Cape and the brutal enforcement of influx control there.

Resistance to the restructuring process has been widespread. However, the links between the two prongs of the state's attack have not been investigated, although, as will be seen, the restriction of African employment and residence is intimately connected with attempts to

---

* I am most grateful to Shula Marks and Stanley Trapido for their helpful comments on earlier drafts of this paper.

reconstitute Coloured political identity. The restructuring process is rooted in a legacy of divide and rule which spans three centuries of South African history. Here it is only possible to touch on three periods of critical importance: the turn of the century, the 1920s and the 1950s. The first section, by way of introduction, is concerned to show how current conceptions of Coloured identity were forged around the turn of the century and are therefore a relatively recent phenomenon. Coloured identity was in part a product of ethnic mobilisation to maintain or improve relative social positions. Changes in the material conditions provided the unique circumstances associated with the assertion of Coloured identity by sections of the petty bourgeoisie and skilled members of the working class.

In the 1920s, the second part of this chapter shows, Coloured identity was entrenched. Part of the explanation for this, we suggest, lies in the fact that although the position of Coloureds deteriorated sharply, the position of Africans was eroded even more rapidly. At the same time, except for brief periods in the history of the Industrial and Commercial Workers Union (ICU) and the African National Congress (ANC), Coloureds were in the 1920s isolated from the mainstream of African resistance. The exclusion of Coloureds from these mass organisations furthered the division between Coloured and African workers and isolated Coloured intellectuals from the main resistance organisations. In the 1950s, we note in part three of this chapter, the impact of the exclusion of a generation of Coloureds from the mainstream of African resistance continued to be reflected in the existence of separate organisations, many of which reproduced the racial divisions of apartheid.

Parts three and four of this chapter focus on the first decade of National Party (NP) rule. It shows that in the 1950s, the maintenance of Coloured identity was associated with a greater degree of state intervention than that of previous governments. The NP, by means of the Coloured labour preference policy and a host of other legislative measures, attempted to restructure and segregate the world that people defined as Coloured inhabit. In so doing, the ruling party set out deliberately to manipulate and reconstitute Coloured identity.

The legacy of divide and rule[2]

By 1853, a complex racial hierarchy was firmly established in the Cape.[3] But this had not yet been articulated in the exclusion of all

Bantu-speaking people from the franchise. Nor had racial ideologies crystallised around the distinction between Bantu-speaking and other colonised people. Class allegiances and to a lesser extent religious criteria continued to provide the principal symbols for political and ideological mobilisation. A critical distinction was between 'heathen' and uneducated 'blanket Kaffirs' and the minority of missionary-educated Africans. 'Blanket Kaffirs' were mainly confined to the eastern frontier. The 1865 census recorded that 674 'Kaffirs' resided in the Western Cape. Many of these Africans were educated and eligible for the vote. The fact that they constituted a small minority and that a large proportion were 'civilised' facilitated the inclusion of Africans in the Western Cape into the category of people defined as Coloured. In 1865, approximately 14,000 'Coloured' people resided in the Western Cape.[4]

The term 'Coloured', until the turn of the twentieth century, generally referred to all non-European people. The use of the term was thus not unlike that in current use in North America. The official Cape census of 1875 included in the category 'Coloured' all "non-European" people, including 'Kafir proper'.[5] The 1891 census maintained the same distinctions, declaring that the Cape population 'falls naturally into two main classes, the European or White and the Coloured'.[6] Private employers tended to perceive similar distinctions. So, for example, in 1890 A. R. McKenzie, the principal labour contractor in the Cape Town docks, referred to the fact that he employed 'principally Kaffirs; all our labourers are Coloured, and are of different nationalities and tribes'.[7]

In the latter half of the nineteenth century the term 'Coloured' referred chiefly to 'all non-European people'. Yet, by 1904 this wide definition was no longer acceptable. In marked contrast to the census of 1890, the Cape census of 1904 distinguished between three 'clearly defined race groups in this colony: White, Bantu and Coloured'.[8] Included in the last category were 'all intermediate shades between the first two'.[9]

Clearly, a decisive shift in colonial discourse took place at the turn of the century. The reconstitution of the term 'Coloured' and the identification of the Coloureds as a group distinct from other non-European people was not, however, only associated with changes within the colonial administration and ruling class; the crystallisation of a distinct Coloured identity also reflected a reorientation of allegiances and ideas within the subordinate society.

It is no accident that the period which saw the evolution of a distinct

Coloured identity also saw a dramatic transformation of productive relations. The series of economic depressions which had begun in the 1860s marked a major step in the proletarianisation of rural Coloured, many of whom migrated to the towns of the Cape Colony, including Kimberley, and after 1866 to the Rand. Despite an insatiable thirst for labour on the Cape farms in this period, many Coloureds migrated to Cape Town where they joined a growing army of the unemployed. Farmers, responding to what they in 1880 regarded as a 'serious want of labour' increasingly recruited African workers.[10] Urban employers of unskilled labour began to display similar preferences. In 1880 a strike in the Cape Town docks had been foiled by the recruitment of 230 African workers.[11] Within ten years Africans had virtually replaced 'Cape Boys' in heavy manual jobs in the docks, quarries and municipal services. By 1899 it was estimated that over 9,500 Africans resided in the Western Cape.[12]

The number of people defined to be 'Hottentot', 'mixed race' and 'Malay', in industrial and commercial occupations rose from 9 per cent in 1891 to 20 per cent in 1904.[13] The educated and skilled strata did particularly well; the number of Coloured clerks, storekeepers and hawkers more than tripled in the period 1894–1904 and the number of masons more than doubled.[14] But the majority of Coloured people were unskilled and employed as servants or industrial labourers. This strata was vulnerable to wage undercutting by African work-seekers and to competition from the continual stream of refugees which drifted into Cape Town. Already by 1899, a local clergyman observed that Cape Town had become 'the city of unemployed'.[15] In that year, the problem was compounded by the arrival in the Cape of over 5,000 'Cape Boys' who had been deported from the South African Republic.[16]

The South African War brought a brief period of prosperity to the Western Cape. The uneven impact of the boom, however, tended to undermine rather than foster class unity. Employment at the docks increased rapidly and in part accounts for the dramatic increase in African employment in the war years. Coloured artisans engaged in the manufacture of carts and other essential items also prospered. But the largest group of Coloured artisans were engaged in construction which suffered a period of slow growth during the war years. It was in this sector that skilled and artisan workers increasingly began to assert a distinct racial identity. In 1900 white stonemasons, many of whom were immigrant workers with an experience of craft unionism, instituted a closed shop.[17] Coloured stonemasons were excluded from work on public buildings. The following year the Plasterers' Union barred Coloured labour and forebade its members to work 'on a scaffold with a Coloured or a Malay under pain of a fine'.[18] The end of hostilities, however, brought little comfort to Coloured artisans. From 1903 until 1909 a severe depression again ravaged the Cape Colony. At the same time, Cape Town was flooded by demobilised British soldiers, some of whom were skilled artisans. For Coloured artisans in the construction industry the position deteriorated even further. By 1904 Coloured bricklayers had been discriminated against and John Tobin, a founder member of the first Coloured political organisation, could accuse the Cape unions of being 'rotten with colour prejudice'.[19]

The effect of the colour prejudice which arose from within the working class was to promote a defensive response from artisans who were discriminated against. The overwhelming majority of the Coloured artisans were people of mixed Khoisan and European descent and descendants of slaves. Bantu-speaking people constituted a small minority of the artisan class in the Western Cape. Thus the exclusion of Coloureds from the artisan crafts led non-Bantu-speaking people to distinguish themselves from the Bantu-speaking people who previously had also been labelled as Coloured. In addition to their shared experience of exclusion and their shared class position (artisan) many also spoke a common language (proto-Afrikaans) and shared a common religion (Islam). Spurred by the threat of the deskilling of their jobs and impoverishment it is not surprising that the wealth of shared experience was mobilised in support of a reconstituted ethnic identity which bound the aggrieved individuals in defence of their embattled position.

The development of a distinct Coloured identity among the skilled and educated class of Coloureds was given further impetus at the turn of the century by circumstances associated with the South African War. The British had made Coloured rights a feature of their war propaganda; discrimination against the Coloureds was presented by Milner as a justification for intervention in the interior.[20] Not surprisingly, Coloureds looked forward to a British victory which Chamberlain had promised would bring 'equal laws, equal liberty' to all South Africans.[21] The Coloureds, Marais noted, 'gave the British cause their enthusiastic support'.[22] It therefore came as a bitter disappointment to Coloureds to discover that the Vereeniging treaty served only to perpetuate their indeterminate position. Increasingly Coloured men and women came to fear that with the proposed Union the practices of the interior republics would be extended to the Cape and that Coloured rights would be sacrificed in the process of re-conciliation.

The increased attacks on the Coloureds by white trade unionists, together with the ambiguity towards Coloureds of British High Commissioners, like Milner and Selborne, promoted within the petty bourgeoisie and skilled class of Coloureds a growing self-awareness. The assertion of a distinct Coloured identity became a means by which to mobilise in defence of the erosion of franchise, trade-union and residence rights. The assertion of Coloured identity specifically excluded Africans, and therefore marked the reconstitution of Coloured identity. Skilled and intellectual Coloureds saw in the assertion of a distinct Coloured identity a possible escape from the attacks being directed at non-European people in general.

The fears of Coloured intellectuals were fuelled in the late nineteenth century by the mounting racism being levelled against all non-Europeans. Late Victorian ideology had been associated with major changes in ruling-class perceptions about the nature of poverty. Transmitted to South Africa, this reorientation was associated with calls for greater state intervention to alleviate the 'poor white problem'. In this process, according to Bundy, 'assumptions of (white) ethnic solidarity replaced the older forms of ideological distance and hostility along class lines'.[23] In the poorer areas of Cape Town there had been, Bundy notes, 'a very real blurring of ethnic identity'.[24]

At the turn of the century, late Victorian notions of social Darwinism had a decisive impact on the Cape colony. The pseudo-scientific writing of Benjamin Kidd and Karl Pearson and his associate Francis Galton, the father of 'eugenics', informed the prejudices of the English ruling class and the activities of the British High Commission in South Africa.[25] In South Africa, these notions were popularised in the writing of John Buchan and in later years by Sarah Gertrude Millin.[26] Imported to South Africa, social Darwinism and eugenics provided a source of leverage for poor whites and a legitimation for racist politicians who were eager to maintain white dominance. Miscegenation was regarded as a peril to the survival of white supremacy and the 'mixed race' people branded as the physically and mentally mutant offspring of an illegitimate mixing of European civilisation and African savagery. At the same time the 'mixed race' people, due to their claim on European blood were regarded as hierarchically above the African people. Their skills and leadership abilities, it was argued, were testimony to this superiority.

The impact of late Victorian ideologies was not confined to the

European population. In the growing climate of racism, it is not surprising that elements of social Darwinism were taken up by sections of the skilled and educated stratum of Coloured men and women. This group used the language of social Darwinism to defend itself from the mounting racial prejudice. It was argued that 'respectable Coloured men' should not be classed with the 'barbarous native'.[27]

The High Commission from the turn of the century was committed to a racial ranking of the South African population in which Coloureds increasingly were differentiated from Africans. Africans bore the full brunt of the housing and other ordinances. For Coloureds there was little to be gained from an identification with African people. The distinction in the 1904 census between Coloured and African people marked the triumph of social Darwinism and embodied an implicit racial ranking. Many Coloured people had no desire to slip further in the hierarchy and sought to distance themselves from Africans.

In the 1890s a stream of reports in the principal Cape papers, the *Cape Times* and the *Cape Argus*, branded Coloureds as the dangerous elements of the impoverished class. These served to fuel the prejudices of the whites and fears of the Coloureds. The attacks on people defined as Coloured at this time were not narrowly directed towards the category of people who later were to be distinguished from Africans. Nevertheless, the attacks did have the effect of alienating the educated and wealthier Coloureds who wished to distance themselves from the social stigma of the increasing ethnic identification of all Coloured classes. These concerns came to a head when in 1901 a Plague epidemic provided the excuse for residential segregation of the Cape Town population. Although the plague was by no means confined to Africans, racial stereotyping by 1901 was reflected in the local authority's racial diagnosis of the problem. Over 7,000 Africans were hounded out of the inner city and forced to move to the hastily erected Uitvlugt compound.[28]

The assertion of a distinct Coloured identity provided an escape route from the prison-like location. Educated and enfranchised non-Europeans in the Western Cape formed the core of the reconstituted Coloured group. This stratum still exercised a not inconsiderable influence in the Cape Town Council and those who could swing the vote in at least six seats were spared the full brunt of the local authority's attack. But the media campaign waged against all non-Europeans forced the reconstituted Coloureds to mobilise in resistance to urban segregation. The organisation of this resistance was entrusted to the emerging Coloured organsiations. The most prominent of these was the African Peoples' Organisation (APO).

Despite its name, the APO effectively excluded Africans. In the main, it sought to advance the interests of the Malay artisan stratum and the petty-bourgeois Coloured men and women in the commercial sector. The APO aimed to show the government that 'an educated class of Coloured people in Cape Town' existed.[29] For the reconstituted Coloured group, the APO provided the channel through which to articulate their pleas for the differential treatment of non-European people. The formation of the APO in 1902 marked a watershed in the development of a reconstituted Coloured identity. As Mr W. Collins, the first President, told the assembled delegates at the founding conference: 'This is the first time in history that we are meeting together to discuss our affairs.'[30] One of the first tasks of the executive was to gain from the City Council of Cape Town an assurance that the segregative measures being imposed on Africans would not be extended to Coloureds.

By 1905, a Coloured identity had been established which stood in marked contrast to that which had existed only ten years previously. The process of reconstitution resulted from a particular constellation of forces, many of which were indigenous to the subordinate classes. Coloured identity, in the form which exists today was forged in the white heat of the years surrounding the South African War. In that period the artisan and petty-bourgeoisie class of non-European people found in the ethnic identification of their position in isolation from the rest of the non-European people a protection against their further disenfranchisement and impoverishment. Of course, the mobilisation of this identity was premised on the pre-existence of symbolic and material points of identification. These included elements of the Malay and Cape Afrikaner traditions combined with petty-bourgeois and artisan identifications. An 'imagined community', to use Benedict Anderson's suggestive phrase, was established as a unique outcome of a peculiar historic configuration of circumstances.[31]

The identity is entrenched

The reconstitution of Coloured identity at the turn of the century provided the bedrock from which future generations would mould and reshape the evolving Coloured identity. The APO was committed to the defence of Coloured rights 'as distinguished from the native races'.[32] This was not unrelated to the turn-of-the-century pursuit by the High Commissioners of a strategy of 'divide and rule'. Selborne, High Commissioner of South Africa during the formative stage of the development of a distinct Coloured identity warned that:

Our objective should be to teach the Coloured people to give their loyalty to the White population. It seems to me sheer folly to classify them with the Natives, and by treating them as Natives to force them away from their natural allegiance to the Whites and making common cause with the Natives.[33]

The strategy of divide and rule provided a lever with which the leader of the APO, Dr A. Abdurahman, was able to extract concessions rom successive governments. The APO attempted to arrest the decline of the Coloured artisans and petty bourgeoisie and spare them the fate being suffered by African people of a similar class. As the residential and other controls endured by Africans increased, the advantages of an identification as Coloured became more keenly appreciated. So, for example, Coloureds were relieved to note that the Urban Areas Act of 1923 reiterated that:

any existing law or regulation, which makes compulsory the carrying, or possession of a pass, shall be deemed to be repealed in so far as it affects Coloured persons[34]

The rearguard defence by the APO of the declining position of the Coloureds played into the hands of white politicians eager to fragment the dangerous alliance of Coloured and African people. This alliance provided a particularly strong challenge to the regime in the period 1919–21; at that time the mushrooming Industrial and Commercial Workers' Union (ICU) in the Western Cape embraced Coloured and African workers. The ICU was not, however, immune to pressures of racism and by 1925 had reversed its previous commitment to overcome the divisions between African and Coloured workers. (This change in direction may in part be attributed to the impact of Garveyism on the African members of the ICU leadership, the antagonism of Africans to the campaign by the APO for the replacement of African dock and railway workers by Coloureds and the divisive effect of government policies which appeared to favour Coloureds relative to Africans.) By 1926, the Coloured leadership had been expelled from the ICU. Although the ICU in its formative years provided a potent organisational base for the overcoming of the divide between Coloureds and Africans, in the second half of the 1920s, the exclusion of Coloureds from the organisation served to isolate Coloureds from the mainstream of African resistance.

By 1929, many of the Coloured radicals who had been excluded from the ICU had found a temporary home in the Western Cape branch of the African National Congress (ANC). From 1929 to 1930 the ANC in the Western Cape went from strength to strength, and in

1930 protest campaigns involving African and Coloured workers took place throughout the region. The government, in an attempt to quell the resistance, resorted to the arrest of its leadership and the banning of further meetings. With the silencing of the radical Western Cape leadership, the ANC in the region became dominated by a more conservative leadership. The new leadership reorientated the organisation away from the forging of a common alliance with Coloured men and women, and Coloured radicals once again found themselves excluded from African mass organisations.

The marginalisation of Coloured radicals from the ANC isolated this group politically and placed Coloured radicals on a separate political trajectory to the ANC. The isolation of Coloured resistance from the mainstream of African resistance had the effect of reproducing in the politics of resistance the racial divisions which Hertzog was intent on developing.

In 1924, the coming to power of Hertzog had a marked impact on the political development of Coloured identity. Hertzog believed that 'without a solution to the Coloured problem there will be no solution to the Native problem'.[35] His aim was to engineer an alliance of Coloured and whites, as advocated by Selborne, but never vigorously applied by him. Hertzog berated the failure of previous governments in this regard and announced that 'There can be no question of segregation. Economically, industrially and politically the Coloured man must be incorporated with us.'[36] Strategically, he insisted:

> It would be foolish to drive the Coloured people to the enemies of the Europeans – and that will happen if we expel him; to eventually come to rest in the arms of the native.[37]

To effect his strategy, Hertzog proposed a comprehensive segregation programme, which he later incorporated in four bills. The bills proposed on the one hand to enfranchise Coloured men and gradually incorporate them into the dominant political structure, while on the other to totally disenfranchise and segregate Africans.

Hertzog's programme never progressed beyond the committee stage and his Coloured Persons' Rights Bill failed to secure the required two-thirds majority in Parliament. In fact, the position of the Coloureds was made worse; the passage of the Women's Enfranchisement Act for whites drastically reduced the effectiveness of the Coloured votes from 19.8 per cent of the Cape electorate in 1929 to 9.9 per cent in 1931.[38] Hertzog's programme served to increase the alienation of the Coloureds. The more educated, wealthy and enfranchised Coloureds were particularly aggrieved. While on the political front their rights had been eroded by the enfranchisement of white women, on the economic front their access to skilled jobs had been severely curtailed by the passage of the Apprenticeship Act of 1922. The Act set an educational standard (Standard VI) on apprenticeship which the overwhelming majority of Coloured people were unable to meet. According to Abdurahman the Act was 'the most potent weapon ever forged for the purpose of carrying on a callous and brutal one-sided war against the Coloured youth'.[39] The position of Coloureds in the labour market was undermined further in the process of restructuring which accompanied the civilised labour policy and the great depression. The civilised labour policy was not directed at Coloureds, but, as Sheila van der Horst observed, 'many employers believed that the civilised labour policy was designed to substitute White for Coloured labour'.[40] With the onset of the great depression the substitution process, with government backing, gathered momentum. However, although the position of Coloureds declined sharply, the position of Africans deteriorated even more rapidly.

By the 1930s the exemption of Coloureds from influx controls and from the legislation governing urban segregation had in the Western Cape increased the material divide between people defined as African and those classified as Coloured. A clear racial hierarchy had been established in which Coloured people were given preference over people defined as African. But, although Hertzog had flirted with the idea of reconstituting Coloured identity, the form of racial discourse broadly followed the patterns established at the turn of the century. Hertzog's rule was associated with the vigorous enforcement of strategies of segregation which were developed by previous governments. The inter-war period was not associated with a coherent attempt fundamentally to alter the pattern of racial discourse.

The National Party and the reconstitution of Coloured identity

The coming to power of the NP signalled an unprecedented drive to reconstitute racial categories in South Africa. The NP was committed to a restructuring of Coloured identity. The central design of the NP scheme, apartheid, had been evolved in the run-up to the 1948 election. It reflected the balance of forces between the various conflicting tendencies within the NP. The aim was not to reject the existing system out of hand but to remould it in terms of an ideology rooted in Afrikaner Christian Nationalism.

The victory of the NP owed much to the successful mobilisation of disparate economic classes around a common cause. Under a petty-bourgeois political leadership the resources of Afrikaner agricultural capital were combined with the pooled contributions of Afrikaner workers to provide the financial reserves and the numerical muscle necessary to win the election. In this process, class differences were subsumed in the new-found unity of the Afrikaner *volk*. The unity of the *volk*, as O'Meara has elaborated, was the vehicle for the success and prosperity for all categories within it.[41]

The notion of *volk* wove together various strands of Afrikaner history and language, rearticulating popular culture in order to mobilise the Afrikaners politically and economically. At the same time the rearrangement of the webbing binding Afrikaners served to exclude from the *volk* many who might previously have considered themselves Afrikaners. Afrikaans has been the mother tongue of most people categorised as Coloureds. Yet, the ideological kernel of the new *volk* proclaimed that its purpose was to preserve the purity of the all-white nation. Admission to the *volk* was restricted to white, Afrikaans-speaking Christians.

The notion of *volk* had provided the organisational basis from which the NP was able to assert its political supremacy. At the same time, it provided the philosophical foundation for apartheid; Afrikaners had found their salvation through the coming together of a *volk*; the establishment of separate nations for all South Africans was to be the divine mission of Christian Nationalism.[42]

The most urgent task facing the Nationalists was to resolve the 'native problem'. The South African Bureau of Racial Affairs (SABRA), an academic institution closely associated with the Transvaal NP, and the Broederbond, a secret organisation of NP members whose leadership provided the ideological and organisational foundations of the NP, were entrusted with the reformulation of state policy. The solution to the 'native problem', they insisted, lay in the segregation of Africans into a multitude of 'nations' each forcibly relocated in fragmented 'homelands'.[43] The SABRA academics, suggested that the same policy be applied to the resolution of the 'Coloured' problem. But, whereas the support of the NP for the African 'homeland' policy was unequivocal, the party was divided on issues affecting Coloured people. Differences concerning the political and social position of Coloured people from the outset provided a major source of friction between antagonistic tendencies within the NP.

The ambiguity of the Nationalist administration's conception of Coloured identity was reflected in the imprecision of the definition of Coloureds in the Population Registration Act of 1950. The Act was regarded as a 'foundation-stone to the whole apartheid structure'.[44] Yet, this pivotal measure could provide no more than a residual definition of Coloureds, declaring them to be all those who were not defined as 'white' or 'native'. The Cape Coloured group was defined to comprise one subgroup of the broader Coloured category. The Cape Coloured group, the Population Registration Act defined:

> shall consist of persons who are, or who are generally accepted as members of a race or class known as Cape Coloured.[45]

The Cape Coloureds (henceforth Coloureds), posed a dilemma for the Nationalists; they shared a common language (Afrikaans) and historical homeland (the rural areas of the Western Cape). Many, although this was never publicly admitted, shared a common ancestry. In addition, due to the close involvement of Coloureds in Cape politics and to the language bond, many Cape Nationalists were well disposed to Coloured intellectuals and considered Coloureds to be 'brown Afrikaners', 'a part of Western civilisation' and deserving a closer association with the whites.[46]

The symmetry of apartheid, other prominent Nationalists claimed, demanded the forging of a Coloured 'nation'. And yet, it was widely recognised that a national identity did not exist among the Coloured. The task, as H. J. Erasmus, a Nationalist ideologist, argued in Parliament, was for the nurture of 'new ideas and ideologies in the minds of the Coloureds'.[47] Paul Sauer, the Minister of Transport who, as a self-appointed nation-builder was one of the few Cape Nationalists to favour the rapid segregation of Coloured men and women, noted that:

> There has been a tendency among the Coloured people of late for one section to do its best to become White, while another section has been engaged in taking up with the Natives. A sense of national awareness . . . has not been developed among them . . . and if one wants to stop him from splitting up one can only hope to succeed if one develops that sense of national awareness and that sense of pride in himself and his people *sic*.[48]

National Party ideologists talked at length about their ambitions to develop a sense of pride and achievement among Coloureds which would herald the birth of a Coloured nation. But, in the end, their strategy rested on a cruder, but nevertheless effective, two-pronged attack. Recognising that identification is firmly rooted in material experience, the NP set about restructuring the social, political and economic world of the people they defined as Coloureds. Interlocking legislation was introduced which served to segregate Coloureds and break their links with people defined as white, native or Indian.

Allied to the realisation that the establishment of a 'whites only' *volk* demanded the forceful extraction of the Coloured components was a clear desire to restrict the absorption into the white population of the Coloured middle class. Until the turn of the century, as Trapido and Watson have shown, it was relatively easy for wealthy and skilled Coloureds to 'pass for White'.[49] Findlay has estimated that by 1936 38 per cent of the people classified as white in the Cape Province were of 'mixed descent'.[50] Although obviously limited by the lightness or otherwise of the skin pigmentation of the people concerned, the passing process had provided a mechanism for the siphoning off of the Coloured élite into the ruling bloc, thereby incorporating many of the potential leaders. Until 1950, 'passing for white' remained an escape route for many Coloureds. In that year, the passage of the Population Registration Act, the Immorality Amendment Act and the Group Areas Act set out to block many of the remaining avenues for passing.

Legislation governing the interaction of whites and Coloured was designed both to prevent whites from becoming part of the Coloured society and to prevent the movement of people in the opposite direction. By cutting off all escape for the Coloured middle class, the Nationalists hoped to promote its development. This class, it was envisaged, would provide the intellectual and economic core for the new Coloured nation. Without the inspiration of a successful Coloured élite, it was stated, the Coloured working class would have no ambition to work for an improvement within the apartheid system. The logic of the government's position was outlined by H. J. Erasmus:

> What it will do will be to arouse a sense of national pride in the Coloureds. In the past . . . their chief aim has been to filter into the ranks of the Europeans. . . . By means of the different laws we have enacted, for example, the Prohibition of Mixed Marriages Act, the door is being closed to them and they are given the opportunity, in their own ranks to aspire to a higher status for themselves. . . . They will now attain a separate status.[51]

It was not long before Coloureds felt the full brunt of apartheid. In 1949, despite a campaign of opposition mounted by the Train Apartheid Resistance Committee (TARC), apartheid was introduced on trains in the Cape Peninsula. A few months later, by the Prohibition of Mixed Marriages Act, marriage across the colour line was declared illegal. The Population Registration Act and the Group Areas

Act of 1950 continued the process of segregation. The aim, the Minister of the Interior, T. E. Donges, roundly declared, was 'to remove the points of contact' between people defined to be members of different racial groups.[52]

Miscegenation was an anathema to apartheid. The survival of the white race, Nationalists insisted, was threatened by the merest trace of non-white blood. Coloureds were singled out for particular attention. Poor whites, it was widely recognised, had for years resided alongside Coloureds in District Six and other areas of Cape Town. The assertion of apartheid identity demanded that these communities be destroyed and that legislation be enforced which would prevent miscegenation and residential mixing of races. According to Nationalist parliamentarians, the mixed residential areas of Cape Town were the 'death-beds of the European race' in which poor whites stood 'in danger of being absorbed by the Coloured community' and where there is 'the inevitable miscegenation'.[53] Urban segregation, Nationalists explained, would prevent the 'colour feelings of the Europeans becoming dulled' and thereby guarantee the 'White man's protection'.[54]

The NP victory at the 1948 polls was secured with a slim majority of five seats. The role of the 50,000 Coloureds eligible to vote was regarded by the NP as a serious threat to the survival of the government as the Coloured vote was considered to be decisive in seven constituencies.[55] The removal of the remaining Coloured common roll representation, it was argued within the NP, would bring several seats within the grasp of the party.[56] The Separate Representation of Voters Act of 1951, at least in part, may be understood as a means to further this objective. But it has a deeper significance; the disenfrachisement of the Coloureds, together with their complete segregation in terms of the Population Registration Act, the Group Areas Act and other legislation, was a focal point of NP ideology.

In 1951 the Separate Representation of Voters Bill was introduced. Five years later, after steamrollering through constitutional and extra-parliamentary resistance, the Act was implemented. The Act removed the remaining direct representation of Coloureds in Parliament and provided for the representation of Coloureds on a separate voters' role. The legislation, the Minister of Interior argued, was designed to 'place the Coloured vote beyond the zone of fear'.[57] In so doing the Nationalists were able to disenfrachise a source of vocal opposition which, Paul Sauer explained, many whites saw 'as a threat to the survival of the white race'.[58]

By 1956, political and social discourse in the Western Cape had been realigned by a state obsessed with racial purity. The severing of 'points of contact' between people defined to be members of different 'race groups', was integral to the NP's national building plans.[59] The segregation and isolation of people defined as Coloureds, Nationalists explained, was necessary in order to foster the development of a distinct Coloured identity. But, the Nationalists soon discovered, the process of segregation was doomed to failure; disenfranchisement and social segregation spurred a mass campaign of resistance and the growing identification of people defined as Coloured with people defined as Africans.

The Coloured labour preference policy

The SABRA ideologists insisted that the construction of a distinct Coloured nation could be achieved only through the rearranging of the material circumstances in which Coloureds found themselves. It was essential, they argued, that Coloureds regard themselves as distinct from Africans.[60] The undermining of non-European unity became a strategic priority. A range of measures was adopted which sought to reinforce the existing distinctions between Coloureds and Africans. A legacy of divide and rule had already given Coloureds advantages over Africans. Coloureds were not compelled to carry passes and were not governed by influx control legislation. They also had not borne the brunt of measures designed to undermine trade unions and prevent squatting. However, the NP was committed to the segregation of all aspects of Coloured life. The position of Coloureds deteriorated as they fell victim to legislation designed to institute residential segregation, disenfranchisement and job reservation. At the same time, their position was improved relative to Africans. This attempt to incorporate Coloureds was achieved through an unprecedented attack on the African population of the Western Cape.

The Western Cape was regarded by SABRA as the 'national homeland' of the Coloureds and it was in this region that the regime planned to nurture a Coloured nation.[61] In 1951 it was estimated that 980,000 of the 1,100,000 people defined as Coloured lived in the Cape.[62] The majority resided in the Western Cape. Clearly, any resolution of the thorny question of Coloured identity would have to take into account the fact that the Western Cape was the home of the majority of Coloureds. The reluctant recognition of this fact fuelled the concern of many Nationalists who saw in the Western Cape a final refuge for white South Africans – a white homeland. In the apartheid model, the destiny of the whites was not intertwined with that of the Africans. But the division between the Coloureds and the whites was less clear-cut, and led to calls for the upliftment of the Coloureds. As J. Albertyn, a prominent Cape Nationalist explained:

> We and the coloureds are here together and we have to live together. That's why we have to get the low class of coloured uplifted; so that he becomes a better neighbour.[63]

The disenfranchisement of the Coloureds and the enforcement of the Group Areas Act had not paved the way for an amicable relationship. The disaffection of the Coloureds threatened to disrupt the apartheid plans as growing numbers of Coloureds joined the resistance to the regime. Embarking on a damage-limitation exercise, the SABRA strategists hoped to defend their apartheid scheme by incorporating Coloureds through a Coloured labour preference policy. In 1953 Dr Malan, the Prime Minister and Dr Verwoerd, the Minister of Native Affairs, outlined the terms of the bargain when they told a delegation of Coloured notables that:

> If you agree to be removed from the common voters' roll, then we would be prepared to talk to our people to provide the means for your development.[64]

The intention of the Department of Native Affairs was to phase Africans out of the Western Cape and replace African with Coloured labour. The department in one stroke intended to achieve two objectives: enforce apartheid through the denial of African residence and employment rights in the Western Cape, and incorporate Coloureds through giving them labour preference. The fortunes of Coloureds were thus inversely related to the predicament of Africans.

The employment preference policy of the NP was implemented first among the government's own employees. Within a year of coming to power 1,696 Africans had been replaced by 1,290 whites and 406 Coloureds.[65] Building on the existing legislation the party immediately set about extending the controls over the employment, residence and movement of Africans. In May 1949 African work-seekers were prevented from remaining in the Cape Peninsula for more than fourteen days a year. In 1952 the Native Laws Amendment Act streamlined the controls over the residence of Africans in the prescribed (urban) areas. At the same time the movement of Africans out of the reserves was curtailed. In 1953 this and other legislation provided the means to implement a strict control over all Africans in the Western Cape.

Women in the Western Cape first bore the full brunt of the apartheid attack. By December 1954 20,000 women had been registered and their employment and residence predicated on the production of an official permit.[66] The Institute of Race Relations noted in 1954 that 'influx control is operated even more strictly in the Western Cape than elsewhere in the Union'.[67] The attack on Africans in the Western Cape signalled the initiation of the Coloured labour preference policy.

W. W. Eiselen, Verwoerd's Secretary of Native Affairs and first lieutenant explained that:

> Briefly and concisely put, our Native policy regarding the Western Province aims at the ultimate elimination of Natives from this region.[68]

The policy aimed to provide substance to the attempts by SABRA to construct a Coloured nation. Eiselen elaborated at length that the policy was involved with the

> weal and the woe of the Coloured people and the question of whether they are to be offered the opportunity of progressive development . . . the influx and residence for long periods of Natives in the Western Province may well lead to the moral decline and economic impoverishment of the Coloured community. . . . Even the use of Native migrant workers, which is perfectly permissible in ordinary European areas, can only be permitted in this part of the country, with its permanent Coloured population, as a temporary expedient.[69]

By 1956 the scheme had left a trail of destruction and despair and 5,000 women had been endorsed out of the Western Cape.[70] The regime from 1956 turned their attention to the rest of the African population. By 1962 over 30,000 Africans had been endorsed out of the region.[71] Permission to remain rested on the continued employment of the remaining Africans in jobs which Coloureds were unwilling or unable to occupy. The unprecedented attacks on Africans in the Western Cape, as was hoped, did lead to the assertion of Coloured identity by people desperate to escape the full force of the Coloured preference policy. Passing for Coloured in the 1950s became as important to working-class people as passing for white had been to petty-bourgeois people in the past. Draconian legislation attempted to raise impenetrable barriers to passing for white or passing for Coloured. Nevertheless, passing for Coloured in the 1950s took place on a large scale.

The Coloured labour preference policy was intimately linked with attempts to reconstitute a distinct Coloured 'nation' in South Africa. The implementation of the policy was associated with the ascendancy of the Transvaal NP and the SABRA ideologues under the leadership of Verwoerd. These people regarded Coloureds as 'a nation in their own right' and aimed to construct a separate political structure for the Coloureds.[72] Arguing that 'we definitely do not accept that there will be intermingling of the political structure for the Coloured and for the white man',[73] Verwoerd and his allies demanded the disenfranchisement of the Coloureds on the grounds that 'they are a race which has completely different racial characteristics'.[74] Political equality, the SABRA ideologues argued, was the antithesis of their nation-building plans. For, as a prominent Transvaal Nationalist declared:

> If we have political equality, why cannot we also have social equality? . . . this is the root of the dangerous attitude of the Coloured people today. . . .[75] The Coloured people are after all, a subordinate non-European race.[76]

The aim of the restructuring process, Paul Sauer insisted, was to develop a national consciousness among the Coloured people.[77]

The apartheid programme towards Coloureds was initially expressed in terms of the principles of Nationalist racial egocentrism. In this the strategic concerns of the administration remained hidden within the philosophical cocoon of apartheid. By 1960, however, the strength of resistance to the restructuring process forced the regime to emphasise the strategic imperatives of their plans for the Western Cape. The campaign of defiance waged against the regime peaked in 1960 bringing a renewed vigour to the attempts by the cabinet to foster a client Coloured group. The Minister of Finance, Dr Donges, drew attention to the urgency of the situation declaring that:

> The disturbances have taught us another lesson to which the Government has also directed attention previously. The lesson is that in those areas where the Coloured community forms the natural source of labour, it is wrong to import Bantu in large numbers, and eventually to create two unprosperous communities.[78]

The call by the Minister of Finance for stricter controls over Africans was endorsed by the Minster of the Interior and by all the Boland MPs who, according to *Die Burger*, felt that

> work must be done on a dramatic scale to implement the policy of removing Africans systematically from the Boland.[79]

According to another MP given prominence in *Die Burger*, every 'self-respecting White' should make an 'obsession' of getting rid of Africans from the Western Cape.[80] 'The carrying through of the plan in the Western Cape,' the MP declared, 'is of the greatest importance, and has been given priority by the government.'[81]

From 1960 the administration began to implement even more strictly its Coloured labour preference policy. The position of Africans deteriorated further as they were subjected to increased harassment and control. Between January 1959 and March 1962 over 23,000 Africans were deported from the Cape Peninsula.[82] Included in this number were many people classified as 'idle and undesirable', a clause widely interpreted to include militant unionists and other 'trouble-makers'. At the same time, following 'an overwhelming debate' within the ruling party the cabinet gave approval to what the Cape NP mouthpiece termed a 'new vision' for the Coloured people.[83] Verwoerd, despite objections from the Cape NP, refused to consider direct parliamentary representation for Coloureds. Instead he proposed 'Coloured self-government within a White state' accepting at the same time that the establishment of a separate Coloured homeland was 'not practical politics'.[84] His concern was to place Coloureds in a position of preference to Africans. For, as he later explained:

> If the minority group becomes the tail that wags the dog . . . surely it is much better to give such a minority limited powers and opportunities . . . ensuring at the same time by means of an entrenched section in the constitution that the white man retains absolute supremacy.[85]

Conclusion

The Coloured labour preference policy was a strategy devised to fragment the disenfranchised and subordinate classes in the Western Cape. Increasingly, access to jobs, residence and housing in the Western Cape became predicated on the assertion of Coloured identity. By restructuring the world that the working class and petty bourgeoisie inhabit, the regime laid the material base for the continued ethnic fragmentation of opposition to the ruling class.

Significantly, resistance to the restructuring process in the 1950s was supported by the petty bourgeoisie and skilled stratum of Coloureds. This stratum at the turn of the century had actively participated in the forging of a distinct Coloured identity. But, whereas the assertion of a distinct Coloured identity at the turn of the century had been associated with the defence of skills and the franchise and the desire on the part of the petty bourgeoisie and craftsmen to distance themselves from Africans, the attacks on the franchise and the rapid deterioration in the position of Africans in the 1950s led to a different response. In the 1950s the political mobilisation of Coloureds under the leadership of the Non-European Unity Movement (NEUM) and the South African Coloured People's Congress (SACPO) attempted to prevent the reassertion of Coloured identity by people anxious to escape the plight of Africans. At the same time, the failure of the NEUM to attract a mass following within the African communities of the Western Cape, and the racial exclusiveness of SACPO, meant that the main organisations of resistance institutionally reproduced the racial divisions against which were committed to fight. Furthermore, we have noted that, although attempts by the regime to create and co-opt a Coloured nation met with the virtually unanimous condemnation of the Coloured petty bourgeoisie, the assertion of a Coloured identity provided for many people an escape from the full brunt of the state's restructuring process.

In the 1950s attempts by the NP to reconstitute Coloured identity may have failed to foster the development of a distinct Coloured political identity or a Coloured nation. But the effect of the re-structuring process went much deeper and its impact continues to be felt today. The destruction of racially mixed communities, the segregation of racially mixed trade unions, the enforcement of job reservations and other apartheid measures altered fundamentally the world which every member of the Western Cape population inhabited. Possibilities for non-racial organisation and action were stifled and the daily lives of the Western Cape working class regimented along racial lines. Under these conditions increasing numbers of ordinary people came to see their lives in terms of the ethnic horizons set by the increasingly authoritarian regime.

Attempts by the NP to deepen racial divisions were challenged from the outset by organisations committed to a non-racial society. In the 1980s, progressive trade unions and community and student organisations have strengthened this challenge and forced the NP to reconsider its strategies designed to develop a distinct but docile Coloured identity. The introduction by the NP of the tricameral parliamentary system has, however, failed to achieve its aim of incorporating Coloured and Indian men and women. On the contrary, the exclusion of Africans from the tricameral system has acted as a stimulus for the organisation of fresh campaigns of resistance. Organisations in the Western Cape have been at the forefront of this resistance, thereby offering a direct challenge to the attempt by the NP, by means of the Coloured labour preference policy and other measures, to incorporate Coloureds in the region. Coloured men and women, and particularly the younger generation of Coloureds, have taken the lead in the development of student and community organisations which are committed to overcoming racial divisions between Africans and Coloureds. And, just as the Coloured labour preference policy has failed to neutralise Coloured resistance, it has also been unable to break the spirit of African resistance in the region; the protracted struggles against the destruction of squatter communities and the determination of Africans to resist resettlement in the barren wastelands of the Eastern Cape have forced the government to accept the permanence of Africans in the Western Cape. In 1984, the final recognition of the failure of the Coloured labour preference policy was marked by the scrapping of the policy. Although the ending of the policy was a political victory over the NP, the significance of this has been eroded by the failure of this policy shift to result in any positive change for Africans in the region; legislative measures which control all aspects of African employment and residence have meant that since 1980 the policy has ceased to have more than a political significance.

The decision of the cabinet to abolish the legislation prohibiting inter-racial sex and marriage represents another major concession on the part of the beleagured NP leadership. But the significance of this well-timed attempt to distract attention away from the chilling evidence of the inquiry into the massacre at Uitenhage should not be exaggerated; although the restrictions on marriage and sex will be lifted, related legislation which prohibits the co-residence of different 'race groups' in any residential area, and the continued commitment of the cabinet to segregation of virtually every other aspect of everyday existence undermines much of the impact of the government's 'reforms'.

The introduction of the tricameral parliamentary system, the scrapping of the Colour labour preference policy and the revision of the statutes governing inter-racial sex and marriage, are part of the latest attempt on the part of the NP leadership to meet the growing challenge to its authority. Separate political representation, the Coloured labour preference policy and the Immorality and Mixed Marriages Acts were foundation-stones of the NP's attempt in the 1950s to construct a distinct Coloured identity. Three decades later, the party has been compelled to drop its commitment to all three of these attempts to entrench racial divisions. But in its retreat the government has developed alternative mechanisms by which it intends to hold off the challenge to its authority. The desire to promote a distinct Coloured identity and to incorporate Coloured men and women politically and economically is at the core of the 1980s 'total strategy' of the NP leadership, just as it was in the 1950s and in the 1920s. In the 1920s and in the 1950s, as we have shown, the development of new strategies for promoting Coloured identity were the outcome of fresh challenges to the state. The reform of the system failed to achieve its objectives and resistance against the discriminatory measures has grown to the extent to which the NP has again been forced – at the cost of alienating many of its traditional supporters – to devise fresh methods of coping with the growing challenge of non-racial organisation.

Notes and references

1 The racial classification of the population of South Africa will follow the official classification outlined in the Population Registration Act, No. 30 of 1950. For definitions of the statutory race categories see M. Horrell, *Legislation and Race Relations* (Johannesburg 1971). The term 'Coloured' is that used in the twentieth-century census classifications. Coloured identity does not necessarily correspond with the official classification and many people reject the official race designations.
2 This section draws on my essay in L. Vail, ed. *The Political Economy of Ethnicity in Southern and Central Africa* (forthcoming).
3 See, for example, G. Frederickson, *White Supremacy: A comparative study American and South African history* (Oxford 1981) pp. 131–3.
4 S. Trapido 'The friends of the natives; merchants, peasants and the political and ideological structure of liberalism in the Cape, 1845–1910', in S. Marks and A. Atmore (eds) *Economy and Society in Pre-Industrial South Africa* (London 1980) *passim.*
5 *Census of the Cape of Good Hope*, 1891, G6–1892, xvii, paras. 98–100.
6 *Ibid.*, para. 98.
7 Select Committee Report of the Cape Colony, A12–1890, 40, cited in V. Bickford-Smith 'Black labour in the docks at the beginning of the twentieth century', in C. Saunders and H. Phillips (eds) *Studies in the History of Cape Town*, Vol. 2 (Cape Town 1980) p. 87.
8 *Census of the Cape of Good Hope*, 1904, G19–1905, 10.4, para. 102.
9 *Ibid.*
10 Cited in S. Greenberg, *Race and State in Capitalist Development: Comparative perspectives* (New Haven 1980) pp. 151–2.
11 D. Budlender, 'A History of Stevedores in the Cape Town Docks', unpublished M. A., University of Cape Town, 1976, p. 2.
12 C. Saunders 'The creation of Ndabeni', in C. Saunders (ed.) *Studies in the History of Cape Town*, Vol. 1 (Cape Town 1979) p. 135.
13 *Cape Census, 1891*, 97–100, Tables I–IV; *Cape Census, 1904*, paras. 160–77, Tables VIII–X.
14 *Ibid.*

15 E. van Heyningen 'Refugees and relief in Cape Town 1899–1902', in C. Saunders *et al.* (eds) *Studies in the History of Cape Town*, Vol. 3 (Cape Town 1980) p. 70, citing Rev. J. McLure.

16 *Ibid.*, p. 82.

17 H. Simons and R. Simons, *Class and Colour in South Africa, 1850–1950* (Harmondsworth 1969) p. 74.

18 *South African Spectator*, 23 March 1901, cited in S. Trapido 'White conflict and non-white participation in the politics of the Cape of Good Hope, 1853–1910', Ph.D. thesis (University of London 1970) p. 399.

19 Simons and Simons, *Class in South Africa*, pp. 74–6.

20 J. Marais, *The Cape Coloured People, 1652–1937* (Johannesburg 1957) pp. 275–6.

21 Chamberlain cited in G. Lewis 'Your votes are your guns: the emergence of Coloured political organisation at the Cape', Cape Town University Seminar Paper, Sept. 1983, p. 21.

22 Marais, *The Cape Coloured People*, p. 276; see also B. Nassan 'These natives think the war to be their own', in *The Societies of Southern Africa in the Nineteenth and Twentieth Centuries* (Collected Seminar Papers, Institute of Commonwealth Studies, London, vol II, 1981) pp. 4–8.

23 C. Bundy, 'Vagabond Hollanders and Runaway Englishmen: white poverty in the Cape before poor whiteism', in *The Societies of Southern Africa*, op. cit., vol. 13 (London, 1984).

24 *Ibid.*, p. 8.

25 See B. Semmel, *Imperialism and Social Reform* (London 1960) pp. 29–52, 176–87.

26 See, for example J. Buchan, *Prester John* (London 1910); S. G. Millin, *God's Stepchildren* (London 1924) and, for an analysis, V. February, *Mind Your Colour: The 'Coloured' stereotype in South African literature* (London 1982) pp. 52–70.

27 Abdurahman in R. van der Ross, *The Founding of the African Peoples' Organisation* (Pasadena 1975) pp. 21–3.

28 Saunders 'The creation of Ndabeni', p. 143; see also M. Swanson, 'The sanitation syndrome', *JAH*, **18** (3) 1977, *passim*; V. Bickford-Smith 'Dangerous Cape Town: middle-class attitudes to poverty in the late nineteenth century', in C. Saunders *et. al.* (eds) *Studies in the History of Cape Town*, Vol. 4 (Cape Town 1981) *passim*.

29 Lewis, 'Your votes are your guns', p. 37.

30 Van der Ross, *The founding of the APO*, p. 12.

31 B. Anderson, *Imagined Communities; reflections on the origins and spread of nationalism* (London 1983) *passim*.

32 *APO*, 9 April 1910.

33 Cited in B. Magubane, *The Political Economy of Race and Class in South Africa* (London 1970) pp. 10–11.

34 Native (Urban Areas) Act, No. 21 of 1923, Section 28.

35 Cited in C. Tatz, *Shadow and Substance in South Africa: A study of land and franchise policies affecting Africans* (Pietermaritzburg 1962) p. 63.

36 Cited in S. Patterson, *Colour and Culture in South Africa: A study of the Cape Coloured people within the social structure of the Union of South Africa* (London 1953) p. 14.

37 *Hansard*, Joint Sitting, 12–15 Feb. 1929, p. 169.
38 L. Thompson, *The Cape Coloured Franchise* (Johannesburg 1949) Appendix.
39 A. Abdurahman Family Papers, Box 3, Folder 7, Presidential Address to the 1939 APO Conference.
40 S. van der Horst, *Native Labour in South Africa* (London 1971) p. 250.
41 D. O'Meara, *Volkskapitalisme – Class, Capital and Ideology in the Development of Afrikaner Nationalism, 1934–1948* (Johannesburg 1983) p. 164.
42 *Ibid.*, pp. 68, 175.
43 See, for example, W. Eiselen, 'The meaning of apartheid', *Race Relations*, XV (3) 1948, 69–86.
44 *Hansard*, 1950, p. 71, col. 2651, D. J. van der Heever.
45 Population Registration Act, No. 30 of 1950, Section 5.
46 See, for example, *Die Burger*, 2 Dec. 1970 and 24 April 1971; *Woord en Daard*, May 1974, p. 4.
47 *Hansard*, 1951, p. 71, col. 2703, H. J. Erasmus.
48 *Hansard*, 1951, p. 75, col. 5426, P. Sauer.
49 S. Trapido 'The origins and development of the African Peoples' Organisation', *The Societies of Southern Africa in the Nineteenth and Twentieth Centuries*, vol. 1 (Collected Seminar Papers, Institute of Commonwealth Studies, London 1970) pp. 90–1; G. Watson, *Passing for White* (London 1970) p. 120.
50 G. Findlay, *Miscegenation* (Pretoria 1936) p. 44.
51 *Hansard*, 1950, p. 71, col. 2703, H. J. Erasmus.
52 *Hansard*, 1951, p. 68, col. 5387, T. E. Donges.
53 Cited in M. November 'The origins of the Group Areas Act', University of London MA thesis, 1981, p. 16.
54 *Ibid.*, p. 17.
55 L. Marquard, *The Peoples and Politics of South Africa* (Oxford 1962), p. 80.
56 Prof. E. Theron, Interview, Stellenbosch, 23 Sept. 1981.
57 *Hansard*, 1951, p. 68, col. 5388, T. E. Donges.
58 *Hansard*, 1951, p. 68, col. 5429, P. Sauer.
59 *Hansard*, 1951, p. 68, col. 5387, T. E. Donges.
60 See, for example, 'Gesigpunte in verband met die kleurling en sy plek in die samelewing', *Journal of Racial Affairs*, V (3) 1954.
61 E. Eiselen, 'The Coloured people and the natives', *Journal of Racial Affairs*, VI (3) 1955.
62 *Union Statistics for Fifty Years* (Pretoria 1960) A–4.
63 J. Albertyn, MP, Interview, Cape Town, 22 Jan. 1982.
64 Cited in D. Woods (ed) *Conference at Bulugha: South Africa's first all-race assembly* (East London 1973) p. 5.
65 M. Horrell (comp.) *Survey of Race Relations, 1950–1951* Johannesburg 1951) p. 50.
66 M. Horrell (comp.) *Survey of Race Relations, 1956–1957* (Johannesburg 1957) p. 71.
67 M. Horrell (comp.) *Survey of Race Relations, 1953–1954* (Johannesburg 1954) p. 41.
68 Eiselen, 'The Coloured people and the natives', p. 32.

69 *Ibid.*
70 Horrell, *Survey 1956–1957* p. 71.
71 *Hansard*, 1962, p. 108, col. 1542.
72 *Hansard*, 1961, p. 107, col. 4192–3 H. F. Verwoerd; *Hansard*, 1968, p. 10, col. 3737, C. P. Mulder.
73 *The Cape Times* 13 Dec. 1980.
74 *Hansard*, 1951, p. 68, col. 5588, J. E. Potgieter.
75 *Ibid.*, col. 5593.
76 *Ibid.*, col. 5587.
77 *Hansard*, 1951, p. 75, col. 5426, P. Sauer.
78 *Hansard*, 1960, p. 106, col. 8342, T. E. Donges.
79 *Die Burger*, 2 Dec. 1961.
80 *Die Burger*, 5 Dec. 1961.
81 *Die Burger*, 24 Sept. 1962, F. S. Steyn.
82 *Hansard*, 1962, p. 108, col. 1542.
83 *Die Burger*, 17 Nov. 1960.
84 *Hansard*, 1961, p. 107, col. 4191, H. F. Verwoerd.
85 *South African Digest*, **XII** (17) 1965, 5.

CHAPTER SIX

Ideology in organised Indian politics, 1891–1948

Maureen Swan

The history of organised Indian politics from the 1890s to the 1940s is mainly the history of trader politics – an almost unbroken line of accommodation to the demands of the ruling white minority, or, at most, selective reformism. Only on two occasions has this line been breached. Between 1907 and 1913, and again in the 1940s, a new leadership emerged in the Transvaal and Natal which attempted to transform Indian politics by mobilising the under-classes for direct confrontation with state policies. The process began at the level of ideology. These two periods of 'radicalism'[1] are therefore useful focal points for any study of the ideologies which have helped shape South African Indian politics: they demand an examination of not only the new ideologies but also the old.

No attempt is made here to discuss the passive resistance movements which were the end result of Indian radicalism, except in so far as is necessary to explore some of the issues which this chapter has sought to address: the articulation of trader and radical ideologies; the potential of radical ideologies to forge cross-class or, indeed, cross-race alliances; the extent to which that potential was realised, and the role of the Indian lower middle classes in its realisation.

The notion of community among South African Indians implied in the title of this chapter will come as some surprise to anyone even remotely familiar with the history of the Indian nationalist movement. In India itself, the first stirrings of national consciousness began among the Western-educated intelligentsia only in the 1880s. The Indian National Congress (INC) which was decades later to become the backbone of a mass nationalist movement, was inaugurated only in 1885. Thus most emigrants from the Indian subcontinent reached South Africa long before the INC had moved beyond the rarefied atmosphere of the intelligentsia in its attempt to build an overarching sense of national identity in a vast society shaped by enormously varied historical experiences and riven by the most fundamental cultural differences. These differences were well represented among the emigrants to South Africa. The only reason, therefore, that one can speak of 'Indian' politics or an 'Indian community' in South Africa as early as 1890 is the fact that both colonial and republican states in South Africa classified all emigrants from the subcontinent – and their descendants, even if South African born – as Indians. The tensions which this created in a population divided not only along cultural lines with deep historical roots, but also along class lines, are a good part of what this chapter is about.

The chapter begins with a discussion of Indian social stratification at the turn of the century and in the 1940s. This is meant, first of all, to provide the background to an understanding of the essentially conservative entrenched political parties which the radicals attempted to transform. The discussion also illuminates the conditions under which radicalism emerged. Finally, it sketches the social and economic conditions of the Indian under-classes in order to identify their specific interests. The varying extent to which, and the way in which, those interests were represented by Indian politics at different times is in itself a significant commentary on changes in the content of their ideological underpinning.

Indian social stratification

By the turn of the century three broad strata were discernible within the Indian population. Dominating the social and economic hierarchy was a trader élite. Some 1,800 in total, they were based mainly in Natal – home of the vast majority of South African Indians – but there were several hundreds in the Transvaal. Most of them had emigrated on their own initiative in the decades between the 1870s and the 1890s; most of them were from western India (mainly Gujarat), and many of them were members of the heterodox Muslim sects.[2]

The élite created and nurtured many social and religious organisations which celebrated narrow cultural distinctions imported from India. In Natal these included the Anjuman Islam, the Memon Committee, the Brahman Mandal and the Kathiawar Arya Mandal. In the Transvaal, identifiable subgroupings, though some were perhaps less formally constituted, included the Gujarati Kunbis, the Konkanis, the Gujarati Hindu Society, the Sanatan Veda Dharma Sabha, the

Hamidia Islamic Society and the Hamdarde Islamic Society. But these narrow loyalties were in part counterbalanced by the fact that Muslims in both areas supported the international Red Crescent Society and, for a time between 1905 and 1908, committees which were established in Johannesburg and Durban to collect funds for a 'Holy Railway' from Damascus to Medina. Even the far more fundamental distinction between Hindus and Muslims was counterbalanced by an élite consciousness, however ill defined, of themselves as an Indian élite – or, more precisely perhaps, as a Gujarati élite. There is an abundance of evidence to suggest that by the 1890s their most extravagant secular social activities were attended by all of the group; and, though they may occasionally have included guests of honour of other races, these were essentially Indian celebrations.[3]

But although these ascriptive similarities and differences were important in moulding the traders' social life, it was, above all, their shared economic interests which as early as the 1880s bound them together as a self-conscious élite. Their interests in Natal and the Transvaal were closely intertwined through a network of partnerships (often involving family members), through credit networks which linked the petty traders to big traders, and through the fact that in Natal the more affluent often owned the property where smaller traders rented shops.[4]

By the turn of the century a new Indian élite was beginning to emerge as an objectively definable group in Natal. By 1910 its perimeters were clearly distinguishable, though its members were still groping towards a self-conscious sense of identity. In the main, they were 'colonials' – the materially more successful of the young, Natal-born offspring of indentured or ex-indentured labourers. They numbered around 300 in 1904.

Part of what prevented them from coalescing earlier was the fact that in terms of ethnicity and religious affiliation they were somewhat less homogenous than the established commercial élite. Although the overwhelming majority were Tamil-speaking Hindus from Madras, important members of the group were Tamil Christians (whose first language was English) while others were Telegu Hindus or Christians, or Hindi speakers from northern India. Their early social organisations were attempts to retrieve some of this diverse cultural legacy from the shattering experience of indenture: the most important were the Hindu Young Men's Association (whose language of business was Tamil, and which was founded not by the new élite themselves but by a visiting Hindu missionary in 1905), and the Young Men's Catholic Society.

Unlike the traders, this emerging élite lacked any overarching association before 1909.

But, if the absence of a clear-cut cultural legacy hampered the development of a unifying ideology, it also opened the way for the new élite to perceive their new world in ways more appropriate to coping with it. What they did have in common was a Western education and a superior position in the occupational structure relative to the Indian underclasses from which they had risen. The most successful were a few highly trained professionals: lawyers, civil servants, accountants and a lone newspaper publisher. Lower down the occupational ladder were teachers, bookkeepers, clerks, interpreters, petty entrepreneurs and small farmers, whose holdings on the outskirts of Durban allowed close communication with town-dwellers. Most of the emerging élite, however, were salaried white-collar workers dependent for a livelihood on the colonial administration. Their salaries obviously varied, but it seems accurate to suggest that until around 1905–06 most were economically comfortable, if not wealthy.

It is not surprising, then, to find that the new élite began to cohere as a distinct, self-conscious group during the post-war depression in Natal, when widespread salary cuts, the imposition of a new form of taxation and an attempt by the state to debar 'Indians' from the Civil Service made it increasingly difficult for the Western educated to maintain existing standards, far less to aspire to anything higher. At the same time, social organisations, sporting, proto-political and, finally, political organisations all played a part in generating a sense of community among the emerging élite. Their activities were reported in the Anglo-Tamil weekly, *African Chronicle*, whose coverage of this community in the making was in itself a significant contributing factor to identity formation. Although the paper carried other news as well, the bulk of its reporting dealt with the affairs of, or matters of interest to, upwardly mobile young South Africans of Tamil descent, thus defining both by inclusion and exclusion the perimeters of the group.[5] What is of particular interest here is not so much this familiar process as its end result. The ideological form which the new élite found to express their sense of common identity – South Africanism – permitted them to link themselves downwards to the underclasses, and, as we shall see, produced the crucial challenge to both trader and radical ideology which changed the shape of the first passive resistance movement.

The final broad stratum in the Indian population, referred to thus far rather unhelpfully as the underclasses, needs to be disaggregated, even for a brief sketch of their social and economic conditions. The most crucial distinction here was between indentured workers and others.

The vast majority of the South African Indian population resulted from the flow of indentured labour which began in 1860. By 1911, when the importation of Indian workers ceased, 152,184 had been shipped to Natal – approximately one-third out of Calcutta and the rest out of Madras. The sugar industry in Natal was built on their cheap labour. Indian contract workers were also the mainstay of up-country farms and wattle plantations. After the 1890s they were used in industry as well, principally on the Natal Government Railway (NGR) and the northern cornfields. In addition, they were valued as domestic servants in private residences, and as service workers in hotels, restaurants, boarding-schools and hospitals. However, they were primarily agricultural workers. Agriculture rarely absorbed less than 75 per cent of the total Indian contract workforce, which numbered 30,000 towards the end of the first decade of the century.[6]

Some 52 per cent of these migrant labourers stayed on in Natal after their term of indenture had expired. From there, several thousands drifted north to the Transvaal before the South African War; but most of them remained in Natal.[7] Initially, they and their descendants enjoyed modest material success. There were numerous opportunities for involvement in petty enterprises in the rural areas which required little or no capital investment.[8] During the economic depression in Natal after the South African War, however, they began to experience severe economic pressure. Apart from the impact of the depressed economy, they bore the burden of an annual £3 tax to which those who had entered indenture after 1895, and their offspring, were subject. Heavy indebtedness and widespread unemployment and destitution are reported in a variety of sources between 1905 and 1908. The NGR and the sugar plantations lowered their wage levels for free Indian labour, so that even those who were employed experienced unusual pressures.[9] One possible avenue of escape – the Rand gold mines which had attracted Indian wage workers before the war – was blocked off after the British administration in the Transvaal started clamping down on Indian immigration in 1903 and 1904. The pre-war opportunities for Indian hawkers in the Transvaal were, of course, similarly restricted. Increasingly, then, the ex-indentured were driven back into contract work, where payment of the £3 tax was suspended as long as a worker remained under contract. A measure of how hard this community was hit by the cumulative pressures of the tax and the depressed economy is the fact that in 1913, some four years after the beginning of economic recovery, 65.25 per cent of the entire indentured workforce was under second or subsequent terms of indenture. Most of these were on the sugar plantations.[10]

Conditions for the indentured workforce obviously varied from employer to employer.[11] But a close reading of the files of the Protector of Indian Immigrants suggests a number of persuasive generalisations. In theory, the workers' conditions were dictated by the terms of their contracts, which conformed to Government of India regulations and which offered an adequate, if very meagre, level of subsistence. The terms of contract were, however, all too often abused, particularly on the sugar plantations, where only savage cost-cutting could make Natal sugar competitive on the world market. Overwork (as much as a seventeen- or eighteen-hour day in the overlapping crushing and planting seasons), malnutrition and squalid, degrading living conditions formed the pattern of daily life for most plantation workers.

Although the material conditions of industrial indentured workers were slightly less oppressive, the vast majority of contract labourers clearly suffered extreme privation. Elaborate controls were necessary to keep them on the job. These varied with the harshness of conditions, ranging from employer and official encouragement or sanctioning of palliatives (drugs and alcohol abuse, gambling and money-lending, for instance) to sjambok-wielding gang bosses and a legal system that was heavily stacked in favour of employers. 'Leaving the estate in a body' was illegal and punishable by fines or gaol sentences, even if workers had left to complain about a breach of contract and even if that complaint was upheld by the magistrate or the Protector. No indentured Indian could move more than two miles beyond his place of work without a written ticket of leave. Thus the workforce was atomised by law. Any politically active worker who tried to organise others in his compound, or even his workgang, was immediately transferred elsewhere – the final divisive mechanism.

These conditions, the constraints on workers' actions, and the fact that the workers were at most only a few years removed from the preindustrial Indian countryside, produced patterns of resistance consistent with George Rudé's characterisation of 'pre-industrial protest' informed by a 'traditional' or 'inherent' ideology.[12] Protest was usually individualistic and often of a type which required little or no prior organisation – malingering, absenteeism, petty larceny, destruction of employers' property and desertion, for instance. As the numbers of reindentured workers rose sharply after 1906, bringing into the contract workforce the new set of grievances that stemmed from their inability to remain free, resistance increased. Although their protests were still mainly individualistic and incapable of producing any significant change, indentured workers clearly had a profound sense of grievance about their living and working conditions.

What is particularly important for present purposes is simply to underscore both the more pressing grievances of indentured and ex- indentured workers and their inability to represent, far less redress, these grievances effectively. Nor, contrary to the rhetoric of trader politics – and, indeed, the existing literature[13] – were their grievances represented by the commercial élite, unless representing them could be seen to serve élite interests in some way.[14] Indeed, the only real linkages between the commercial élite and the under-classes were the essentially exploitative patron–client relationships formed by money-lenders, shopkeepers and the owner-operators of the Durban produce market. Thus, as the emerging new élite in Natal began to develop a unifying ideology, and to create a separate political identity, the field was clear for them to claim this vast potential worker constituency.

Whatever attempts were made to mobilise the Indian underclasses for political action in the early years of the century proved to be short-lived. By the 1940s they were still poorly served by organised Indian politics, and they still suffered oppressive social and economic conditions. Recruitment for indentured labour in India had stopped in 1911: the last contracts were being worked out by 1916. The £3 annual tax on ex-indentured workers had been abolished in 1914. But opportunities for the ex-indentured and their descendants to earn an independent livelihood in the countryside had steadily declined between the wars, particularly during and after the 1929–32 depression. Evictions by landowners, extending their own operations in the rural areas, and by the Durban City Council as industrialisation advanced through the peri-urban areas, pushed others off the land. The 1936 Sugar Agreement, meant to protect small white cane farmers from the growing monopoly of large plantations, eliminated numbers of petty Indian cultivators who could not meet the quotas set by the agreement. By the census year 1946 only 15.4 per cent (12,008) of the total male Indian working population remained in the countryside – virtually all of these, as at the turn of the century, in Natal. Nearly half of this number were wage workers, mainly in the sugar-mills, which were noted by contemporary observers as among the lowest-paying employers of Indian labour. Of the rest, only a small proportion owned their land, most of them holding monthly or yearly leases with no security of tenure. Contemporary studies describe their life style as hand to mouth at best. Families were large, and largely illiterate; they lived in shanties which lacked sanitation, lighting and adequate water supplies. Intestinal diseases were rife.[15]

Part cause and part effect of the shrinking rural Indian community was the rapid growth of the Indian urban wage-labour force.[16] Between 1936 and 1946 it soared from approximately 30 per cent to 53 per cent of the total male Indian working population. Some 88 per cent of these (around 36,000) were in Natal, mainly Durban.[17] It is difficult to assess to what extent these newly urbanised workers developed a sense of worker consciousness, and to what extent they might have maintained their links with, and continued to identify with, the rural areas which they had so recently left. In general, rather than complete families it was the young males, whom family smallholdings could no longer support and who clearly could not afford to buy their own land, who moved to the towns. In earlier decades the strength of the Hindu joint family system would have ensured close links between town and countryside. But, at least within the urban areas, the joint family rapidly disintegrated during the Second World War, partly as a result of the separate accommodation offered to many married male workers by employers and partly due to rebellion by the young – particularly young women. Although a residual sense of obligation may have kept the newly urbanised in touch with the rural areas, the linkages were probably insufficiently strong for them to continue to identify closely with them.[18]

The rapid growth of Indian trade unionism in the 1930s and 1940s also suggests that old loyalties and old forms of consciousness were being replaced by new, however tentatively the replacements might initially have been formulated. Indian unions which, like African unions in secondary industry, began to flourish after 1928 in the wake of the Industrial Conciliation Act (1924) and the Wage Act (1925), claimed 22,000 members by 1948.[19] In the early years of the Second World War the unions were instrumental in helping to improve wage-rates for Indian workers, securing Wage Board investigations and attempting to ensure that Wage Board Determinations were actually implemented. Indeed, at first sight the success of organised labour appears quite striking: in many industries Indian wage-rates doubled or even trebled between 1937 and 1946. But this is a measure mainly of the rate of inflation and of how low Indian wages were in the mid-1930s. In any event, hemmed in by the 'civilised labour' policy,[20] and by grossly inadequate educational facilities, the majority of Indian workers remained semi- or unskilled at the lower levels of the wage spectrum. Real improvements – if, indeed, there were any – during this decade were minimal.[21]

A number of surveys conducted in the 1940s reached the same basic conclusion: 'not only is malnutrition serious among the Indian community in Durban, but also . . . for large numbers the quantity of food is insufficient'. This was despite the fact that between 65 and 70 per cent of income was spent on food.[22] The sudden upsurge in the urban population, relatively low wages and high expenditure on food resulted in housing conditions which were consistently condemned by contemporary reports.[23] In 1940 one of these noted *inter alia* that:

> A large proportion of the Durban Indian community is housed in shacks and other poorly constructed dwellings which are scattered over the undeveloped agricultural lands along the western boundaries of the City. Some of these are actually cultivators, but by far the larger number have leased a patch of land, usually about half an acre in extent, and have erected on it one of the poorest types of dwelling imaginable. Old tar drums, relics of corrugated iron, and old pieces of wood are pressed into the construction, which with its earth floor and smoke grimed walls offers more suitable accommodation for the cockroaches and other vermin who share the uneasy symbiosis. The water supply for these shacks is drawn from springs and streams which are frequently highly polluted, and commonly nothing but the most primitive methods of stercus disposal are attempted.[24]

By the mid-1940s these problems were exacerbated by severe overcrowding and escalating rents which will be discussed more fully shortly.

The extensive surveys conducted by the University of Natal Department of Economics, and by others, are lacking for the Transvaal. But the files of the Johannesburg Indian Social Welfare Association are rich with detail which leaves no doubt that the conditions of existence of the small Transvaal Indian wage-labour force were little different than those of the Natal Indians. They suffered the same low wage-rates. They lived in urban slums which, like those in Natal, were consistently condemned by contemporary investigators.[25]

Wartime inflation and the tightening of restrictive legislation had also made its impact on the Indian élites by the 1940s. The more successful among the commercial élite in both Natal and the Transvaal (still mainly descendants of the Gujarati immigrants of the late nineteenth century) had continued to flourish economically. Much of their wealth they invested in property in Natal and the Transvaal, as they had been doing for decades. Between 1932 and 1946 millions of pounds' worth of property was bought by Indians in the Transvaal.

Between 1927 and 1940 the rateable value of Indian properties in the Old Borough of Durban increased from £1,441,210 to £3,448,230, while the 'added areas' of Durban – site of the urban slums described above – it increased from £1,736,910 in 1934 to £2,394,300 in 1940. Purchasing, particularly in the more affluent hitherto 'European' suburbs (as they were called at the time) of the Old Borough, reflected the wealthy Indians' dissatisfaction with slum or near-slum conditions in the predominantly Indian areas of Durban. At least 70 per cent of these new properties, however, seem to have been acquired strictly for investment purposes: though owned by Indians they were not occupied by them. The 1942 and 1943 Broome Commissions noted that Indians had only two investment outlets – commerce and immovable property. But the expansion of trade was restricted by the licensing laws in both provinces (particularly rigorously in the Transvaal after 1939), and the Indian occupation of land or immovable property they had not previously occupied was temporarily prohibited in the Transvaal in 1939. In the face of these cumulative threats the Natal property market was an increasingly important investment outlet for the commercial élite of both provinces after 1939.[26]

But Natal was not slow to follow the Transvaal. The 1943 'Pegging Act'[27] closed off the élite's only remaining major avenue of investment by prohibiting the transfer of property from whites to Indians in the Durban municipality for the next three years. As a result of these new restrictions, property prices and rents soared in the predominantly Indian areas of Johannesburg and Durban. Already crowded slums and near-slums swiftly became severely overcrowded under the combined impact of natural population increase, the impossibility of movement elsewhere and, in the case of Natal, continued migration from the countryside. Landlords charged exorbitant 'key money' or 'goodwill' for the right to rent a single dilapidated room. Workers' conditions under these circumstances have already been described. To a certain extent these conditions were also suffered by petty traders and white-collar workers who, though they numbered among the Indian notables for social and political purposes, did not have the economic resources which had enabled the more affluent members of the élites to buy their way into more congenial surroundings. Indeed, Indian white-collar workers had been hard hit by the 'civilised labour' policy, while petty traders suffered the insecurity of knowing that their small businesses would be the first to collapse if segregation were permanently enforced. In the meantime they found themselves trapped with the wage workers in the rapidly deteriorating predominantly

Indian areas of Johannesburg or Durban. Though they were not confined to the makeshift shanties of the workers, their surroundings were overcrowded and squalid.[28]

By the mid-1940s, then, the single most pressing problem for the majority of the Natal and Transvaal Indians was the new legislation which confined them to specific areas of Durban and Johannesburg. This legislation was ostensibly temporary, but laws were being worked out which promised to be at least as restrictive, threatening not only to confine Indians to specific areas but also to expropriate their holdings in others. Yet these restrictions weighed on different strata of the community in different ways. For the wealthier members of the élites the proposed legislation threatened loss of their major investment outlets – choice urban property either as an investment in itself or for commercial expansion – and, crucially, possible loss of existing investments. For the less affluent members of the élites, urban segregation meant almost certain loss of livelihood for some; or, at best, sharing the increasing squalor of increasingly working-class neighbourhoods – a privation which they felt keenly. For the underclasses segregation was two-edged: while some would be rendered homeless because of escalating rents, or through slum clearance, for others it held the possibility of rehousing in new municipal housing schemes.

Indian politics

From the first formal Indian political campaign in 1891, until the 1940s, Indian politics were dominated by the Natal and Transvaal commercial élite. Their major political organisations – the Durban-based Indian Committee (founded c. 1890), the Natal Indian Congress (1894), the Transvaal British Indian Association (1904 – later changed to Transvaal Indian Congress in 1926) and the South African Indian Congress (1919) – were founded to protect vested commercial interests and were controlled by the wealthiest merchants.[29]

Given the colonial and republican definition of all emigrants from the Indian subcontinent as 'Indians', these parties claimed to be the representatives of the entire 'Indian community', and were recognised as such by successive South African, British and Indian governments. However, party membership consisted overwhelmingly of the commercial élite. Despite elaborate organisational structures and procedures, the political parties only functioned intermittently and usually without regard to their own rules and regulations. Mobilisation for political action was successful only when new or proposed legislation was perceived to pose a threat to trader interests. Indeed, it was only attempted under these circumstances. Political action, except in the periods of radicalism which will be discussed shortly, consisted of constitutional protest: letters, petitions and deputations to key officials in South Africa, Britain or India. These forms of protest were generally extra-parliamentary since South Africa Indians were not enfranchised.

The ideology which informed trader politics changed little during this half-century. Although formal ideological statements from the traders were rare, clearly definable ideological assumptions are implicit as well as explicit in the pattern of their politics and political discourse. In so far as they had a secular ideology it was fairly typical of any merchant class, and certainly typical of the Gujarati trading communities (whether Hindu or Muslim) from which they had migrated. Maximum emphasis was placed on protecting their privileged economic position. Socially and politically they were conservative. They worked within the framework of the existing social order, and although they protested against white discrimination against Indians (hence their claim to represent the entire 'community') they protested from a class rather than a national or racial position. Indeed, in the first few decades, their political rhetoric is shot through with references to the distinction between themselves and the Indian underclasses. They not only accepted the inequalities between traders and indentured or ex-indentured workers, but legitimised them by offsetting the commercial élite as the 'respectable' members of the 'community'.

There is no doubt that this strand in the merchants' ideology was brought from India: caste/class prejudices were an integral part of nineteenth-century Indian cultural baggage, whether Hindu or Muslim. The notion of a South African 'Indian community' remained at the level of political rhetoric for the merchants in large part because these distinctions of caste and class had been shaped by, and had helped shape, the most fundamental cultural differences in India over many centuries. In India, as in South Africa, the underclasses in the late nineteenth and early twentieth century – particularly in Madras – were, in the main, descendants of indigenous peoples of wholly different origin and language to the Aryan and Arab invaders who were the forefathers of the Gujarati commercial classes. The dominant ethos in élite culture, reflected in their social organisations, was Islam for most, and the Hinduism of the northern higher castes for a few, while the social life and world view of the underclasses was crucially moulded by the variant of Hinduism practised in South India. If distinctive regional cultures had emerged in India by the late nineteenth century, a national culture had not. Thus the class cohesion of the traders was reinforced by their common cultural background, just as their distance from the underclasses was reinforced by profound cultural differences.

These imported distinctions were further reinforced in South Africa. This was particularly so in nineteenth-century Natal where the traders felt threatened by being identified as members of a race which was placed low in the colonial racial hierarchy, and for whose vast majority restrictive legislation already existed. But at the same time as they opposed racial discrimination which affected – or might affect – themselves, they shared the whites' prejudices against blacks. These prejudices were also, almost certainly, brought with them from India where hereditary hierarchical social divisions were largely congruent with skin colour (indeed, this in itself must have constituted part of the barrier between the commercial classes and the generally much darker-skinned Madrasi underclasses). This prejudice, too, was strongly reinforced in South Africa. In the late-nineteenth-century Transvaal, in particular, the traders feared that discriminatory legislation would be justified by their identification with 'non-whites' (*kleurlings*).

The ideology which informed the traders' politics, then, was drawn from a complex web of class and race prejudices, rooted both in the Indian traditions of their communities, and in the specific circumstances of their existence in late nineteenth and early twentieth-century Natal and Transvaal. Perhaps the best indication of how little the traders' consciousness changed in South Africa is that when they did look beyond their own ranks for long-term support, they looked not to the Indian underclasses in Natal and the Transvaal, but rather to their peers in India. The end result of this was the appointment of an Agent of the Government of India in South Africa. The first Agent took up his post in June 1927. He, like his successors, worked closely with, and for the interests of, the established Indian political organisations.[30]

Indian radicalism

The merchants' political tactics and ideology were first challenged by Mohandas Gandhi. Gandhi had been hired as a legal representative and political organiser by some of the wealthiest Natal-based Indian merchants in 1894. For more than a decade, operating first from

Durban then from Johannesburg, Gandhi planned and co-ordinated the activities of the Natal Indian Congress and the Transvaal British Indian Association which he had helped found. The political patterns and ideology which had been established by the pre- Gandhian Indian Committee remained unchanged during this time. In September 1906 Gandhi attempted to radicalise Indian politics by calling for passive resistance against the Transvaal government. This was the beginning of a crisis-ridden campaign that lasted off and on (more the former than the latter) for over seven years.[31]

The developments in Gandhi's personal philosophy which underpinned this attempt to impose radicalism from above need not be discussed. What is of interest here is the ideology of the movement; its potential; the extent to which that potential was realised and the subtle changes of ideological flavour which accompanied tactical shifts to accommodate planned and unplanned changes in the movement's social base.

At its most pure and basic level Gandhian passive resistance, or *satyagraha* as it came to be called, was a set of beliefs which contained within it both a simple existential truth and a command for private and public action. *Satyagraha* presupposed moral autonomy. It rested on the assumption that man must be a free and independent moral agent, master of his own destiny rather than the passive object of someone else's will. But at the same time Gandhi accepted the legitimacy of the state and of the broad outlines of the existing patterns of social relations, and the need for an external structure of authority. Indeed, implicit within his writings and activity of this period is the belief that social oppression – or its opposite – derived simply from the will of the government. Thus the revolutionary potential of one strand of his ideology was held in check by a liberal, reformist strand which demanded only that men of conscience should challenge manifest injustices in an otherwise acceptable body of law.

Whatever its limitations, *satyagraha*, by implying cross-class solidarity within the Indian community, clearly held enormous radical potential for Indian politics. Yet, despite the universalist and humanist tone of his philosophy, Gandhi's notion of community had yet to transcend that of his peers, the commercial élite. He thus chose initially to work within, and for, existing Indian political structures. The obvious political advantages to be derived from this were outweighed by equally obvious disadvantages: nothing in the history of trader ideology or politics suggested that the élite would respond to a moral call to action. Indeed Gandhi's philosophy had been worked out in the context of his despair at what he saw as the moral degradation of the Indian élite. The radical potential of *satyagraha* was thus further whittled down to fit it to the needs and interests of the traders.

These compromises produced a movement whose initial goal was the repeal of a law which demanded that all Transvaal Indians submit to registration by the government. The traders were moved to action by Gandhi's suggestion that the legislation admitted the principle of racial discrimination against Indians, which would then be used to enforce urban segregation at the expense of their commercial interests. Given the Transvaal's history of attempts to confine Indians to designated locations (and Natal's occasional stabs in the same direction), and given the Milner administration's recent survey of proposed urban sites for Indians, the connection between these two propositions was far less tenuous than it might seem at first sight. This logic allowed Gandhi to tap the very core of trader fears, and the one issue which had mobilised them in the past: protection of their vested interests. The two dominant themes in the movement's ideology were thus a moral one – articulated as a confused conception of Indian national honour and individual honour – and a simple economic rationale.

Passive resistance began in mid-1907 when Indians refused to take out registration certificates by the specified date. The initial response was overwhelming. The Transvaal notables used their credit, client, ethnic and religious networks to enforce solidarity. The Natal notables were generous with both moral and financial support. The first arrests caused a flutter of panic in the movement, but more rigorous manipulation of social and business linkages within the community steadied it again. In early 1908, however, the movement's fatal weakness was exposed when the government linked registration certificates to the renewal of trading licences. Suddenly the campaign violated the cardinal principle of trader politics. This immediately broke the back of trader support.

Loss of trader support allowed Gandhi to impose his personal ethical preoccupations on the movement. They dominated its philosophy from 1908 onwards, replacing 'self-interest' with 'self-sacrifice'. The economic imperative was dropped from the ideology, and it was shifted to a more purely ethical footing. The confused conception of honour which had comprised the initial moral content of the ideology was clarified. The movement now rested mainly on the pursuit of 'truth' (right action against injustice by a fearless man of action); but the nationalist overtones of the first stage of the campaign continued to flavour the ideology. Two new goals were added to the original: the preservation of the theoretical right of educated Indians to immigrate to the Transvaal, and the protection of the residence rights of all pre-war Indian residents. These goals were in keeping with Gandhi's personal ethics, but since they were of no direct relevance to his notional constituents they added nothing to the movement's appeal. On the contrary, they obviously made the original goal of the campaign harder to achieve since it was now linked to two others.

Throughout 1908 and 1909 Gandhi and a handful of committed supporters (one or two of them big traders) turned from one stratum to another of the Transvaal Indian community in an effort to keep the movement going. Ideology, goals and tactics remained the same, but the focal point of recruitment efforts changed. Attention was focused, increasingly unsuccessfully, on hawkers, petty traders, hawkers again, and finally the big traders with whom the movement had been started. Gandhi also visited Durban in an unsuccessful attempt to open a second front in Natal. But the movement offered no tangible benefits. By the end of 1909 it had completely collapsed, except for Gandhi and his handful of committed supporters, who continued to seek arrest throughout 1910.

From late 1910 to late 1913 the 'movement' existed only at the level of negotiations between Gandhi and the Union government. The fact that it existed at all is in part a testament to Gandhi's commitment to his newly developed ethics: attainment of the movement's goals had become a personal moral war for him. As important was his ability to command the attention of the government. The barrage of carefully planned publicity which the early stages of the campaign had received in India and Britain, and the sensitive political situation in India, ensured continuing imperial government interest in a peaceful settlement. Indeed, it had been discussed with Smuts (who dealt with the movement first as Transvaal Colonial Secretary, then as Union Minister of the Interior) during the final round of Union negotiations in London in mid-1909. Smuts's interest in a peaceful settlement far exceeded sensitivity to the political situation in India, however. The price he exacted from the imperial government for keeping open negotiations with the passive resisters was an end to the flow of indentured Indians to Natal, which he had sought since 1908. Once this bargain was struck, the goals of the movement were included in the deliberations for the first Union-wide Immigration Bill which began early in 1911.

Smuts attempted to simplify and minimise the South African 'Indian question' by treating Gandhi as the national spokesman on Indian immigration, thus formally extending his influence to an all-South-Africa level. But this assumed a degree of control over Indian politics which Gandhi had never had. Paradoxically it was the compromises Gandhi was now required to make in order to retain his legitimacy as principal Indian spokesman which led to a dramatic widening of the social base of the movement, and the realisation of the radical potential of *satyagraha*.

In March 1911, as the negotiations for the Immigration Bill began, the new Natal élite formed a political party called the Colonial Born Indian Association (CBIA). Hitherto, in the classic pattern of an upwardly mobile group, their ambitions had been expressed in an alliance with those above them in their social hierarchy – the traders from the Indian subcontinent with whom the state identified them. During the post-war depression, however, when the upward mobility of the Western educated received its first serious check, it became clear that trader politics did not adequately represent their interests and were opposed to them in some instances. The process of differentiation which gave birth to the new élite, and culminated in the emergence of the CBIA was largely a response to these pressures. The party marked the creation of a unifying ideology by the new élite. The basis of their perceived unity, expressed in the name which they chose for their organisation, was their local origins. They saw themselves as South Africans who, though they happened to be of Indian descent, could legitimately claim those rights and privileges of South African citizenship which were denied to them as 'Indians'. More importantly, the party confirmed the new élite's realignment of loyalties away from the foreign-born commercial class, and downwards to the underclasses from which they had risen. The first meeting of the party made it clear that its leaders included at least the upper levels of the underclasses in their perception of themselves as South Africans. The chairman's opening speech singled out the iniquity of the £3 tax on ex-indentured workers, noting that their future constituents would increasingly include Natal-born Indians who were subject to the tax. Thus it was the new élite rather than the merchants who began to frame a '"community of culture" in order to channel popular energies behind its separate interest'.[32]

The possibility that the CBIA might mobilise the underclasses, transforming Indian politics and endangering the uneasy coexistence which the traders had established with the Natal government, was sufficient for the NIC hastily to include the abolition of the tax in their own political platform. Gandhi, struggling to maintain his credibility in the role of national spokesman for the South African Indians, equally swiftly included it in his. More forceful representations against the tax by a new élite pressure group in late 1911 and early 1912 saw the tax question elevated to the top of the Gandhi–NIC list of South African Indian grievances. But the tax was not adopted as a goal of the passive resistance movement whose original goals now seemed capable of being met by negotiation. However, when a revered elder member of the INC (G. K. Gokhale) toured South Africa at Gandhi's invitation later that year, the tax was among the South African Indian problems that he discussed with Union cabinet ministers. Gokhale carried away the impression that they had promised to repeal the tax. Their refusal to do so was perceived by Gandhi as a morally unacceptable breach of faith, satisfying both his ethical preoccupations and political needs of the moment – the idiosyncratic blend that had already become the hallmark of Gandhian politics. This allowed him to adopt the tax as a goal of the movement in mid-1913 when the long-drawn-out negotiations on the Immigration Bill had reached an apparently final impasse.

On 16 October 1913 Gandhi and his committed supporters started a strike of Indian workers on the Natal coalfields for the repeal of the £3 tax. The immediate success of the strike call was a testament not only to the workers' awareness of the burden imposed by the tax in a low-wage economy, but to the multiplicity of grievances in the daily lives of indentured labourers. But the real success for Gandhi came when the strike – unexpectedly and unintentionally – spread like a cane fire through the vast brutally oppressed workforce on the coastal sugar plantations, and from there to coastal Indian workers in general. By the end of November when lack of resources and state repression had driven most of the strikers back to work the strike had, at one time or another, paralysed the Durban and Pietermaritzburg produce markets, closed down some of the sugar-mills, stripped many coastal hotels, restaurants and private residences of their domestics, resulted in some 150 acres of cane being illegally burned, and inconvenienced the coal industry, the NGR and other smaller industries in coastal Natal. Not surprisingly, the negotiated settlement for the seven-year-old re-sistance campaign came soon after this.

The road to radicalism in the 1940s, though similar in some key respects, was in the main rather different. Although Yusuf Dadoo emerged as a commanding figure, likened to Gandhi by some, he was only one among numbers of South African Indians – mainly in Natal – who began to challenge the politics of accommodation in the mid- or late 1930s. Their backgrounds differed. Some were well-qualified professionals, sons of wealthy traders, who had been educated abroad. Others were workers with little formal education. Many of them entered Indian politics via organisations with a wider perspective. They were trade-union officials and/or members of the Communist Party of South Africa (CPSA) or the Non-European United Front (NEUF) which was established in Cape Town in March 1938. The NEUF was the product of growing militancy among the Coloured and black lower middle classes, one of several abortive attempts in the 1930s to create a broad-based movement capable of mobilising mass support from the blacks. These initiatives were assisted and encouraged by the CPSA which, with international communism in general, underwent a strategic reorientation towards united front politics during this period. At NEUF's first annual conference in April 1939 Dadoo and H. A. Naidoo – both of them CPSA officials – were elected to the National Council, Dadoo representing Johannesburg and Naidoo, Durban.[33]

The ideology which informed these politics was all encompassing, calling for cross-class and cross-racial alliance in the formation of the broadest possible united front against white minority rule in general and racial segregation in particular. The tactics which were agreed on in 1939 were boycotts, active and passive resistance, strikes and demonstrations. Dadoo, however, entered South African Indian politics with an additional ideological frame of reference. As a child in Krugersdorp he had attended discussion groups held by former associates of Gandhi's which focused both on the South African Indian resistance movement of 1907–13, and on the swelling tide of nationalism in India in the 1920s. As a youth at college in northern India, and a young man studying medicine in London and Edinburgh, he had become involved in local and overseas Indian nationalist politics.[34] At least in the popular perception, these politics were personified by the increasingly charismatic folk-hero figure of Gandhi in the 1920s and 1930s.

Both of these ideological strands underpinned Dadoo's attempts to radicalise Transvaal Indian politics in 1939. The issue which he chose to address was the Asiatic (Transvaal) Land and Trading Act which prohibited the transfer of property from whites to Indians for the next two years pending the passage of more permanent legislation. Dadoo called for passive resistance not only against the Act, but against 'any legislative or other measures' whose objective was segregation.[35]

As Gandhi had done, Dadoo tried to work through the established political parties. Former associates of Gandhi's and others, who like Dadoo had an active interest in the Indian nationalist movement, responded to the mainly nationalist appeal in the ideology of the proposed campaign. The petty traders whose low profit margins rendered them most vulnerable to segregation also pledged support. However, the big traders who controlled the Transvaal Indian Congress (TIC) remained unresponsive to this mixed appeal to the national honour of India and non-European unity in South Africa. Taking their lead from the Transvaal, the Natal and South African Indian Congresses also refused to support a campaign. Radicalism had run foul of the central principle of trader ideology and politics once more. Although the traders obviously did not welcome segregation they were prepared to accept it since they seemed likely to gain, in exchange, security of tenure for the millions of pounds' worth of property they had acquired in recent years. In the event, however, Dadoo called off the proposed campaign in July, on the advice of Gandhi who urged further negotiations with the government. The evidence does not suggest, in any case, that response to the campaign would have been widespread.[36]

This abortive attempt to impose radicalism from above was followed by a slow-moving and more cautious attempt to transform the existing political parties from below.[37] In the Transvaal Dadoo met big trader opposition by establishing a splinter group of the TIC which he named the nationalist bloc. In Natal the initial attempt to erode trader power in organised politics took the form of a handful of Indian CPSA members encouraging the creation of a new party, the Natal Indian Association (NIA). The NIA emerged from the amalgamation of the Natal Indian Congress and the Colonial Born and Settlers Indian Association (CBSIA). The CBSIA, like its predecessor the CBIA, had the capacity to incorporate the underclasses. The party had been formed in 1933 by the Natal white-collar élite during a moment of perceived crisis when it seemed that trader politics were inimical to their interests. Indeed many of its officials had posed their first ephemeral challenge to trader politics under similar circumstances as officials of the CBIA a quarter of a century earlier. In 1933, as in 1911, the party's manifesto claimed the rights and privileges of citizenship for its members on the basis of their being South African born. The manifesto also looked to the Indian underclasses for the party's constituency.[38] However, the presence of a handful of CPSA and NEUF members on the executive of the newly created NIA in 1939 marked the first concerted attempt to realise this radical potential.[39]

The increasing interpenetration of the CPSA, organised Indian labour and the Indian political parties during the next six years simultaneously eroded big trader power in the political parties and began to widen their social bases. The traders, however, struggled to retain control of organised politics. The cross-class, cross-race orientation of the new Indian radicalism was thrown sharply into relief as Indian CPSA and NEUF members engaged in anti-war work before the German invasion of the Soveit Union. Indeed, Dadoo was gaoled in September 1940 for publishing an anti-war 'appeal to all non-European people of South Africa', which listed both general and particular instances of their oppression.[40] The traders fought back by accusing the radicals of using 'foreign ideologies' which endangered the 'Indian cause', and by co-opting the Gandhian and Indian nationalist ideology which Dadoo had used in 1939, but which they had then rejected.[41] These ideological differences were translated into political reality at the level of complete rejection of segregation by the radicals, and conditional acceptance by the big traders who were still prepared to negotiate with the state in the hope of securing at least their vested interests.[42] At the same time both sides sought to mobilise worker support (or, at least, deny it to the other side) by representing the full range of workers' grievances.[43] This struggle is most clearly demonstrated in the continuous process of amalgamation, dissolution and reamalgamation that Natal Indian politics underwent between August 1939 and October 1945. The radicals, and their allies among the petty traders and white-collar workers who were already suffering the bite of segregation and other forms of discrimination, formed political splinter groups when they were not able effectively to influence policy-making, and moved back into mainstream politics when they were.[44]

A similar though less attenuated process occurred in the Transvaal. By late 1945 the old-established political parties were dominated by radicals.[45] In mid-1946 they began a passive resistance campaign which lasted until 1948. The campaign demanded the repeal of the Asiatic Land Tenure and Representation Act – the Ghetto Act as it became known – which made permanent, and extended, the segregationist legislation of the preceding seven years. However, the Act was portrayed simply as an instance of the wider pattern of racial discrimination in South Africa, and it was this that the campaign was directed against. There are thus striking parallels with Gandhi's passive resistance movement. The ideology of the post-war movement was also not dissimilar to Gandhi's, despite continuing trader accusations about the use of dysfunctional imported ideas. Gandhi's ethical preoccupations were missing in 1946, but the new movement rested, like his, on a basically liberal reformist ideology which called for the elimination of unjust laws. Gandhi's watchwords had been 'truth' and 'conscience'; in 1946 these were replaced by 'equality' and 'democracy'.[46]

But there were also crucial differences between the two campaigns. Passive resistance in 1946 was inspired and backed by the CPSA. The seeming paradox of CPSA support for a movement with a reformist ideology which sought only to mobilise Indians is a reflection of the political reality with which they had to deal – deeply rooted separate racial organisations and potential constituencies for whose members a significant level of consciousness was the racial categorisation imposed on them by the state and reinforced by virtually every aspect of their daily lives. The CPSA response to this dispensation in the 1940s was to attempt to build up and radicalise the separate 'nationalist' movements as a prelude to a united cross-race struggle.[47] Thus although the 1946–48 passive resistance campaign sought only to mobilise Indians, the wider potential of the ideology was never ignored. The *Passive Resister*, published weekly in Johannesburg during the campaign, makes frequent reference to *herrenvolkism* directed against blacks and Coloureds, as well as Indians. Just as frequently readers were also urged to read *Inkululeko* which was described as a progressive paper which advocated co-operation between all the races for a democratic South Africa. In June 1947, on the first anniversary of the campaign, Dadoo noted that 'we have entered into a period of active co-operation between the oppressed peoples for basic human rights'.[48] The other crucial difference between the two campaigns is that despite the potential for inter-class solidarity implicit in the ideology of both, recruitment efforts were focused largely on the traders in the earlier movement (until, of course, its final stage), and largely on the workers in the 1940s. It is worth noting finally, however, that the 1946–48 campaign never achieved Gandhi's belated, but nevertheless magnificent, level of mass mobilisation: only an estimated 2,000 people sought arrest, just over half of whom were workers. Although my research on the 1940s is not yet complete, a tentative explanation for this is offered in the conclusion.

The ideologies which have shaped South African Indian politics run the gamut from class and racial exclusivity to inter-class and inter-race solidarity. Indians have been politically mobilised by perceiving themselves as an élite, as workers, as Indians, as South Africans or as non-Europeans (to use the terminology of the time). One of the most interesting aspects of this history is the way in which self-perceptions are capable of change, sometimes with breathtaking rapidity. But the more things have changed the more they have stayed the same. New forms of consciousness, like those they replaced, almost invariably served the perceived interests of those who underwent the change: ideologies were accepted, rejected or tentatively toyed with on the basis of their seeming compatibility with those interests.

This history also demonstrates the pivotal role of the Indian lower middle classes – the new élite, or the white-collar/petty-trader élite, as I have called them – in the process of Indian radicalisation. Both at the turn of the century, and in the 1930s and 1940s, their temporary realignment of loyalties away from the big traders and towards the Indian underclasses proved to be the crucial intervention which made possible the at least partial realisation of the potential of radical ideology.

One final point is worth addressing, if somewhat tentatively: the limited success of the 1946–48 campaign in achieving widespread mobilisation. I would like to suggest that this did not derive from any intrinsic limitation in the ideology (nor, indeed, in the organisational infrastructure of the movement),[49] but rather from the programme of action which the radicals chose to adopt. It is clear that the Transvaal Indian working class welcomed the escape from Johannesburg's over-priced slums to the Indian township which was to be established under the provisions of the Ghetto Act.[50] Thus their most pressing needs were put before any wider or longer-term consideration of the implications of segregation (as, of course, were the traders'). Whether these calculations were also made by Natal workers in 1946 is somewhat less certain.[51] The fact that the passive resistance movement, despite strong links with organised labour, and despite the manifest grievances of Indian workers, mobilised only around 1,000 of the 22,000 Indian trade-union members, in itself suggests that they might have been. From this, I would like to suggest that ideologies with a generalised overarching appeal, which are capable of utilisation by different social strata, and which, indeed, are capable of ideologically linking different strata, are nevertheless capable of effecting widespread sustained political mobilisation only by being addressed to the specific fundamental grievances of those strata. Both the 1907–13 and the 1946–48 passive resistance movements would seem to support this proposition.

Notes and references

A series of interviews (twenty-four, approximately an hour each in length) conducted in London and Durban during 1983 and 1984 provided valuable insights for the latter part of this chapter. The informants range from former officials of district committees of the CPSA to rank and file members and trade-union organisers and retired workers. For reasons which are obvious it seems best that they should remain anonymous. Tape recordings of these interviews are housed in the African Studies Institute, University of the Witwatersrand, under restricted access. They are numbered 1–24. Where direct reference has been made to a particular interview I have used that number and the date of the interview. The archives of the South African Institute of Race Relations (SAIRR) and the Rheinallt Jones and Ballinger collections are in the University of the Witwatersrand manuscript library.

1 I use this term as a convenient shorthand. The extent to which it is relative is made clear in the discussions on radicalism.

2 NA, Gov. 1599/374/1908; TABA, Gov. 823/PS, 15/9; *Indian Opinion*, 4 May 1907, 11 May 1907, 18 Jan. 1908, 3 Feb. 1912.

3 Occasional mention of all these societies is scattered throughout the press. In particular see *Indian Opinion*, 16 Nov. 1912, 18 Jan. 1913; *African Chronicle*, 24 July 1909; *Rand Daily Mail*, 17 Feb. 1914.

4 *Indian Opinion*, 9 Feb. 1906, 4 May 1907, 11 May 1907, 18 Jan. 1908, 22 Aug. 1908, 26 June 1909, 3 July 1909, 3 Feb. 1912.

5 For more detail on these processes see M. J. Swan, *Gandhi: The South African experience* (Johannesburg 1985) Chs 1, 5.

6 See my article, M. J. Tayal, 'Indian indentured labour in Natal, 1890–1911', *Indian Economic and Social History Review*, **XIV** (4) 1978; 'Report of the Protector of Indian Immigrants', *Natal Departmental Reports* (annual).

7 CO 551/27/19319; NA II 1/77/66/95; NA II 1/77/209/95; NA II 1/77/380/95; NA II 1/79/1147/95; NA II, 1/80/1799/95.

8 'Report of the Protector of Indian Immigrants', *Natal Departmental Reports*, 1890, p.A42; *ibid.*, 1899–1900, pp. A16, A42; *Natal Official Handbook*, 1886, p. 90.

9 *The Natalian*, 6 Sept. 1907; *African Chronicle*, 5 Dec. 1908; *Report of the Indian Immigrants Commission* (Pietermaritzburg 1909), p. 7; 'Report of the General Manager of Railways', p. 20, *Natal Departmental Reports*, 1908; 'Report of the Protector of Indian Immigrants', *ibid.*, 1905, p. 13.

10 CO 551/56/12682.

11 See Tayal, 'Indian indentured labour' for a fuller discussion of the material summarised on the following two pages.

12 G. Rudé, *Protest and Punishment* (Oxford 1978) pp. 52–4.

13 For example, L. Fischer, *The Life of Mahatma Gandhi* (London 1951); R. Rolland, *Mahatma Gandhi* (Zurich 1925); and, especially, R. Huttenback, *Gandhi in South Africa. British imperialism and the Indian question, 1860–1914* (Ithaca and London 1971).

14 Swan, *Gandhi*, Ch. 2.

15 Department of Economics, Natal Univ. College, 'Indian land and agriculture in South Africa' (n.d., *c.* 1946) pp. 6–8, 11, 18; R. Burrows, *Indian Life and Labour in Natal* (SAIRR 1952) pp. 12, 13, 15, 63; Union of South Africa, *1946 Census*, vol. 5, p. 152; *Guardian*, 17 June 1938, 22 Dec. 1939, 26 Sept. 1940, 24 July 1941.

16 Contemporary sources while sensitive to the obvious 'push' factors behind rapid urbanisation also suggest that higher urban wages acted in part as a 'pull' factor.

17 Union of South Africa, *1936 Census*, vol. 7, **XVII**; *ibid.*, 1946, vol. 5, pp. 152–62.

18 Department of Economics, Natal Univ. College, 'Indian land and agriculture', p. 16; SAIRR, Rheinallt Jones (hereafter RJ) Collection, AD 843/B90.6.2, Memo submitted to Natal Indian Judicial Commission by Soc. Services of South Africa (Durban branch), 15 June 1944, p. 5; SAIRR, RJ, AD 843/Indian Affairs 1933–1943/B.82, f. 31, Report of Natal Regional Conference organised by SAIRR, 31 July 1943, p. 3; interview 3, 3 May 1983.

19 J. Lewis, 'The new unionism: industrialisation and industrial unionism in South Africa, 1925–1930', *South African Labour Bulletin*, 3 (5) 1977, pp. 25–49; H. G. Ringrose, *Trade Unions in Natal (Cape Town 1951) p. 47;* H. J. and R. E. Simons, *Class and Colour in South Africa* (Penguin edn, Harmondsworth 1969) pp. 371–2; Burrows, *Indian Life and Labour*, p. 18.

20 The 'civilised labour' policy was meant to create employment opportunities for unskilled whites (by substituting whites for 'non-whites' in a variety of occupations), and to protect those in semi-skilled positions.

21 Burrows, *Indian Life and Labour*, pp. 18, 22–4, 38; SAIRR, RJ, AD 843/Ind. Affairs 1943–44/Ind. Ed. and Ind. Affairs, Memo. on Univ. and Tech. Ed. for Indians in Natal by Indo-European Council (*c.* Aug. 1942), p. 2; SAIRR, RJ, AD 843/B77.1.4, Acting Chair, Coloured and Indian JA Board to Div. Inspect. of Labour, Durban, 8 Aug. 1942; Table IX, showing number of employees according to skill, race, sex and age 1937–48 in *Department of Labour Annual Report*, 1948.

22 Burrows, *Indian Life and Labour*, pp. 32–7 (which draws on a number of contemporary surveys). See also SAIRR, RJ, AD 843/B.78.5, Memo. on Natal Indian Health Services, with particular ref. to Child Welfare Socs., Jan. 1945, p. 1; V. S. Naidoo, 'Survey of the income and expenditure of Indian employees of the Durban Corporation, living at the Magazine Barracks, Durban', *South African Journal of Economics*, **XIV–XV**, 1946–47, pp. 40–62; *Guardian*, 10 July 1941.

23 Naidoo, 'Survey'; Burrows, *Indian Life and Labour*, pp. 52–3; SAIRR, RJ, AD 843/Ind. Affairs 1933–1943/1943 B.82, f. 31, Report of Natal Regional Conference organised by SAIRR, 31 July 1943, p. 6.

24 SAIRR, RJ AD 843/Ind. Affairs 1933–1943/1942 B. 182, f. 76, A Preliminary Report on the Housing of the Indian Community in the City of Durban, Oct. 1940, p. 1.

25 For example, SAIRR, RJ AD 843/JISW 1939, 1940, 1947/JISWA 1947, Pres. 1939, 1941, 1948, Application for grant from Central School Board: statement by Katz, *c.* April 1940; and see SAIRR, JISWA minutes 1940s.

26 SAIRR, RJ, AD 843/Indian Affairs/ Indians 1948–1950, Memo. on Ownership, Occupation and Trading by Indians in the Transvaal, *c.* 1949, p. 4 (in 1949 the estimated value of the property in the Transvaal was between £8 million and £10 million. One of my informants pointed out that many Indian capitalists 'made fortunes' during the war, partly through black marketeering. For obvious reasons they preferred to put this into property rather than a bank. Interview 2, 4 May 1983); *Report of the Indian Penetration Commission* (Pretoria 1942) pp. 65, 69, 71, 74; *Report of the Second Indian Penetration (Durban) Commission* (Pretoria 1943) p. 5; Indians were prevented from significant investment in industry by strict control of manufacturing licences. SAIRR, RJ, AD 843/B77.1.4, Memo. by NIC for Indian Tech. and Univ.

Enquiry Commission, 11 Aug. 1942, p. 14; *Report of the Asiatic Land Laws Commission* (Pretoria 1939) pp. 64–5.

27 The formal title of the Act is the Trading and Occupation of Land (Transvaal and Natal) Restriction Act.

28 For example Burrows, *Indian Life and Labour*, pp. 55–6, 64; Dept. of Econ., Natal Univ. College, 'Indian land and agriculture', p. 21; *Star*, 19 March 1940; SAIRR, RJ ibid,, AD 843/JISW, 1939, 1940, 1947/JISWA 1947, JISWA to Sec. Nat. Health Services Commission, March 1943; *ibid.*, JISW 1939, 1941, 1948/Rand Aid, statement by Katz (*c.* April 1940) on Diagonal St slums; SAIRR, RJ, Indian Affairs 1948–1950/Indians 1948–1950, Rheinallt Jones to Mgr. Municip. Non-Eur. Affairs Dept, Johannesburg, 8 Nov. 1949; SAIRR, RJ, B77.1.4, Memo. submitted by NIC to Indian Tech. and Univ. Enquiry Committee, 11 Aug. 1942; *Daily Express*, 13 Jan. 1939 for similar conditions in Germiston and Boksburg.

29 For trader politics to 1914 see Swan, *Ghandi*; for the later period see F. Ginwala, 'Class, consciousness and control: Indian South Africans, 1860–1946', unpub. D.Phil. thesis (Oxford 1975), and E. Pahad, 'The development of Indian political movements in South Africa, 1924–1946', unpub. Ph.D. thesis (Sussex 1972).

30 Pahad, 'The development', pp. 225–33.

31 Swan, *Gandhi*, Chs 2–4, 6, for elaboration of following summary of passive resistance and documentation.

32 To Nairn, *The Breakup of Britain* (London 1977) p. 123.

33 Simons, *Class*, Ch. 21; E. Roux, *Time Longer than Rope* (Madison, Wisconsin 1966) pp. 357–8.

34 Simons, *Class*, pp. 501, 503–4; Ginwala, 'Class, consciousness and control', pp. 409–10 (extracts from interviews with Dadoo).

35 *Sunday Times*, 14 May 1939.

36 The proposed campaign was widely reported in the press. See, for example, *Rand Daily Mail*, 2 March, 20 April, 15 June, 10 July, 8 Aug. 1939; *Mercury*, 18 April, 24 July 1939; *Sunday Times*, 14 May, 4 June 1939; *Star*, 12 Jan., 30 March, 4 July 1939; *Guardian*, 7, 14 July 1939; see also Ginwala, 'Class consciousness and control', pp. 408–10, abstracting from interviews with Dadoo, for support from petty traders and Gandhian nationalists; see SAIRR, RJ, AD 843/B.77.5.5, TIC to Min. Interior, 15 Feb. 1939 and *ibid.*, B.77.5.6, SAIC to Min. Interior, 21 Feb. 1939 for response of big traders.

37 This was part of a wider CPSA decision to start working for a non- European united front by building up grass-roots for the national organisations, Interviews 2, 3, 3, 4 May 1983.

38 SAIRR, RJ, AD 843/B.77.6.1, Ag. Gen. to Rheinallt Jones, 22 Dec. 1933, encl. CBSIA manifesto, constitution and rules.

39 *Daily News*, 28 Aug. 1939; *Natal Witness*, 30 Dec. 1939; Pahad, 'The development', p. 160.

40 *Rand Daily Mail*, 28 Aug., 7 Sept. 1940; *Guardian*, 12 Sept. 1940.

41 A particularly elaborate statement of this is in M. Ballinger papers, correspondence: Indian Affairs (Gen.), A 410/B.27/1946–1947, Chairman's speech delivered by A. S. Kajee at the Natal Indian Provincial Conference, 4 May 1947. But see also *Leader*, 30 Jan. 1943, 24 Feb. 1945, for earlier examples.

42 Indian representatives, for example, co-operated with the first and second Broome Commissions of Enquiry. The apogee of the politics of accommodation was the short-lived 'Pretoria Agreement' of 18 April 1944. A reconstituted, trader-dominated Natal Congress claiming to represent the Indian community of Natal agreed to voluntary segregation regulated by a five- man board, in exchange for repeal of the Pegging Act. M. Ballinger papers, Correspondence: Indian Affairs (Gen.), A 410/B.27/1926–1945, Memo. submitted by the Natal Indian Congress, as representing the Indian community of Natal, to the Rt Hon. Field Marshal J. C. Smuts, 18 April 1944.

43 For example, *Natal Mercury*, 14 Nov. 1944. But see, in particular, election platforms for the 1945 Natal Congress elections, *Guardian*, 15 Feb., 25 Oct. 1945; Pahad, 'The Development', pp. 194–9.

44 *Guardian*, 21 June, 19 July 1940, 2 Sept. 1943, 4 May 1944, 18 Oct. 1945; *Call*, July 1940; Pahad, 'The Development', pp. 158–200.

45 *Guardian*, 21 Dec. 1944, 13 Dec., 20 Dec. 1945. See also Pahad, 'The Development', pp. 158–200. His explanation for these processes is limited. He does, however, note the course of events.

46 The weekly issues of the *Passive Resister* are a good source for the ideology of the movement. For example, 13 Dec. 1946, 16 May, 12 June, 11 Sept. 1947. On trader accusations see, in particular, 25 April 1947. On ideological expositions see also Cape Passive Resistance Council, *Resist . . . Indian Ghetto Act* (Cape Town 1946); G. Singh, *The Asiatic Act* (Durban *c.* 1946); Joint Passive Resistance Council of Natal and the Transvaal, *How We Live* (Durban *c.* 1946); Y. M. Dadoo, *Facts About the Ghetto Act* (Johannesburg 1946).

47 Interviews 1, 2, 3, 15 April, 3, 4 May 1983.

48 *Passive Resister*, 12 June 1947.

49 On which see D. Carter, 'Organised non-violent rejection of the law for political ends: the experience of blacks in South Africa', unpub. Ph.D. thesis (Durham 1978), pp. 130–91.

50 SAIRR, RJ, AD 843/1948–1950/Indians 1948–1950, Memo. presented to the Hon. Min. of Interior by Johannesburg Tamil Benefit Society, Feb. 1946; SAIRR, RJ *ibid.*, Johannesburg Tamil Benefit Society to Sec. Inst. of Race Relations, Southern Transvaal Branch, 18 July 1949; SAIRR, RJ *ibid.*, same to same, 8 Nov. 1949. See also *Rand Daily Mail* 15 June 1939 for opinion of Rev. B. L. E. Sigamoney who was in close touch with working-class Indians on the Rand, and *Star*, 26 July 1949 for an individual opinion. Also, interview 6, 7 Aug. 1983.

51 But see interview 2, 4 May 1983, confirming these views for the early 1950s; and interview 14, 7 May 1984, interviews 15, 16, 17, 8 May 1984, interview 23, 10 May 1984, in which, although enthusiasm or admiration may have been displayed for the passive resistance movement, these retired workers recalled that they had had no time for resistance, or that they were not interested, or that resistance to government policies was ineffectual. See also correspondence in the Natal *Mercury*, 14, 17, 19, 22, 30 July 1943 confirming these views for the early 1940s.

CHAPTER SEVEN

'Africa for the Africans': the Garvey movement in South Africa, 1920–1940

'After all is said and done, Africans have the same confidence in Marcus Garvey which the Israelites had in Moses.'
Enock Mazilinko, Johannesburg, South Africa, **Negro World**, 9 February 1929

Robert A. Hill and Gregory A. Pirio

At a meeting called by the African National Congress (ANC) at the Parade in Cape Town in May 1930, 'an American Negro' was said to have amused the crowd when, in his address, he urged that they 'substitute for the pictures of "English royalty and lords" hanging in their homes the likenesses of Kadalie, Thaele and, among others, Marcus Garvey, who, he predicted, would one day "sit in the chair of your South African Parliament which Hertzog occupies today".'[1] The speaker was Arthur McKinley whom Edward Roux would later describe in *Time Longer Than Rope* as having been one of Garvey's 'most vociferous followers in South Africa'.[2] McKinley's pronouncements that afternoon may well have sounded slightly comic in the attenuated political circumstances of 1930, at a time when the post-war mobilisation of African protest had already exhausted itself. Yet, as we propose to show in this paper, such declarations flowed logically from the radical nationalist perspective that the Garvey movement had advanced, starting in 1920 on the question of the South African state. Furthermore, the documentary record confirms, in our view, the historical accuracy of McKinley's conception of Kadalie, Thaele and Garvey as a political triad.

Variously known as the 'Africa for the Africans' movement, a motto which signified its historic link with the antecedent phenomenon of Ethiopianism,[3] the Garvey movement developed in South Africa after the First World War into a potent expression of mass-based African nationalism. Under its ideological stimulus, moreover, the old liberal ideology that had provided the chief political rationale of the African petit-bourgeois leadership, namely, the impartiality and supremacy of Britain as the ultimate protector of African interests, was undermined. Its displacement was to be aptly summed up by 'a native female from

Benoni' who, in recommending to the annual meeting of the ANC in April 1925 that Africans boycott the visit of the Prince of Wales, let it be known – 'The Dutch had been given the right to rule by the English in this country and it was therefore immaterial whether the Dutch or English ruled in this country.' In place of what had become a debilitating political illusion, there arose after the First World War a new emancipatory vision under the general aegis of the revitalised cry, 'Africa for the Africans'. At the level of popular consciousness, the various phases of African resistance were welded together to express a new sense of common political and racial destiny. It was this fusion of political sensibility that ultimately validates McKinley's tribute to the emblematic qualities of Kadalie, Thaele and Garvey. Likewise, James Stehazu, another Cape Town Garveyite, was to express the same awareness when, in 1932, he asserted that 'Marcus Garvey is now admitted as a great African leader'.[4]

For the most part, however, South African historiography has tended to downplay the significance of the Garvey phenomenon, when it has not simply ignored it. Those few commentators who have discussed the movement have tended to view it as almost completely derivative or else as a kind of local aberration from the political norm.[5] By obscuring the pervasive link that Garveyism established with all phases of African protest in the inter-war years, the scholarly record has failed to account for the potency and appeal of the 'Africa for the Africans' ideal or to record its class determinants in the South African racial economy.

Garveyism and the 'American Negro' paradigm

If the Garvey phenomenon had a large hand in undermining the myth of a safeguarding England that had prevailed from the time before Union, it is also essential to recognise that the extraordinary vigour with which the 'Africa for the Africans' movement erupted on the post-war South African scene resulted from another countervailing myth. There had been some faint warning before it made its full-scale appearance in the aftermath of the First World War: in Sekukuniland, in 1905, it was reported that 'Senamela' of the African Methodist Episcopal Church was 'informing into the Native mind the feeling that some day with the help of their Ethiopian brothers in America [the natives] will become the possessors of South Africa' and in the aftermath of the 1906 Bambatha uprising in Natal there were similar rumours of redemption from America.[6]

Although this belief remained an undercurrent in African perceptions, at the end of the First World War 'the moral and military power of America came into prominence' once more. According to the African historian W. D. Cingo writing in 1927:

> Large numbers of uneducated Africans now came to regard the voice of America as that of a mighty race of black people overseas, dreaded by all European nations. These people, our unfortunate friends, imagine in their confusion, manufacture for their own purposes, engines, locomotives, ships, motor cars, aeroplanes, and mighty weapons of war. The mad dreams and literature of Marcus Garvey, a black American Negro, were broadcast on the winds. Hopes for political and economical emancipation were revived and to-day the word America (*i Melika*) is a household word symbolic of nothing else but Bantu National Freedom and liberty.[7]

It should be stressed here that Africans were not alone in this apocalyptic transformation of political consciousness: 'Let us go possess South Africa', Rosetta Stenson, a Garvey movement supporter in Muskogee, Oklahoma, wrote to tell the *Negro World*, the official organ of Garvey's Universal Negro Improvement Association (UNIA). 'Tell the Kaffirs to awake, awake, put on the whole armor and prepare for Armageddon.'[8]

The recurrent myth of imminent black liberation from America was clearly an active feature in the South African arena of struggle, on the eve of the black mine-workers' strike of 1920. A native identified only as 'Mgoja of Johannesburg' took the floor at a meeting of the Transvaal Native Congress, at Boksburg, on 8 February, a few days before the strike began, and stated that 'he had come there to strengthen the purpose of the Congress'. He finished what he had to say by assuring his listeners that 'the Congress members who were sent to Europe are on their way to America and that they will get satisfaction there, America said they will free all natives, and they will help. *That America had a black fleet and it is coming*'[9] [emphasis added].

The mention of a 'black fleet' supposedly on its way from America was a sign that word of Marcus Garvey's 'Black Star Line', promoted as the means whereby the course of the redemption of Africa was to be effected, had been picked up by Africans on the Witwatersrand. How, at this early stage it penetrated there, we still cannot say. However, once it reached there, it passed around quickly. One form in which we know it came was described by the South African police who reported the following occurrence at a meeting of the Natal Native Congress in Durban in October 1920, at which it was said approximately 1,000 Africans (chiefs, headmen, and delegates from various parts of Natal) were present:

At the evening meeting an American Negro named Moses arrived and was introduced to the meeting as being a man who had arrived from New York and who wished to say a few words to them. Moses then stated that he had arrived at the right time when they were holding their meeting, and that they were doing precisely the same as the American Negroes were doing in the United States. He stated that he was one of the Negro organisers who had been sent to South Africa on behalf of the Negroes, and that in America, he stated, they as Negroes had found out they must free Africa, as they were under the impression that the natives here had been ill treated by the Europeans, that they had had their meetings and come to the conclusion that they were bound to free Africa sooner or later, that they had built their own fleets and had their own ammunition, and that they had their own flag, which was red, white [sic] and green, and that this flag would be hoisted whenever Africa was free; that their leader Magascavo [Marcus Garvey] was the man they relied upon, and who would free Africa; that the first vessel of the fleet was named 'Frederick Douglas[s]', and this vessel had been sailing to different places, and he assured the meeting that they could rely upon the fact that Africa would be freed, and by Magascavo [Marcus Garvey]. . . .[10]

Following his intervention, Moses proceeded to respond to questions put to him by one whom the police report referred to as, simply, 'native: "Dube"', whose questions showed a keen awareness of the problems that the 'black fleet' had been experiencing in America. Perhaps it was significant that a short time after the Durban meeting, one of its participants, Nikiniki Tshezi, refused to dip his cattle, and then advised natives in Mngayi Valley, who were reportedly experiencing 'a certain amount of unrest' at the time, that the land was theirs and they should refuse to pay taxes.[11]

We believe that Garvey's propaganda achieved its most important breakthrough, however, when news of his speech before the historic opening of the UNIA's First International Convention of Negro Peoples of the World, in August 1920, was disseminated in South Africa. 'The bloodiest of all wars is yet to come,' intoned Garvey, 'when Europe will match her strength against Asia, and that will be the Negroes' opportunity to draw the sword for Africa's redemption.' This bold declaration so agitated *Umteteli wa Bantu*, the vernacular newspaper of the Chamber of Mines, that it felt compelled to run a lengthy editorial dismissing the 'perfervid utterances of Mr Marcus Harvey [sic]' and warning Africans that it was 'as wise to work in harmony with the Europeans in our midst as it is lunatic to be influenced by the impossible ideal of an "All-Black Africa"'. Then, early the following month reports appeared in the white South African press making known the fact that the UNIA convention 'after a debate lasting a month, passed a resolution in favour of proclaiming the whole of Africa a Republic, administered and exploited by Negroes'. It was also reported that '[t]he Conference appointed Mr Marcus Harvey [*sic*] provisional President of Africa'. White opinion-makers at this juncture treated this 'ideal of a black republic which is ultimately to take possession of Africa' mostly as an occasion for comic relief. Thus, so far as the *Diamond Fields Advertiser* could tell, the news 'excited little interest and no comment in this country'. At the same time, it claimed to be able to find 'no appreciable signs that the scheme has taken root in the native areas of South Africa'. 'Nevertheless,' it declared, 'the question is not one lightly to be ignored or passed by, for the measure of success of the movement in America is bound sooner or later to open the door to the propagandist in South Africa and with our native policy, benign as it is, still leaving something to be desired, the propagandist would find his seed fall on fruitful soil.'[12]

The African soil was obviously ready for the Garvey seed since it responded immediately. The *Umteteli wa Bantu* editorial, rather than dampening African interest, instead roused Africans to hope. Gilbert Matshoba, a law clerk in Queenstown and the nephew of Enoch Mgijima, leader of the Israelite sect, read the editorial and exactly two days after it was published wrote to inform his prophet-uncle, who had placed him, in Matshoba's own words, 'on the outskirts of the wood':

> Regarding the world, Father of the 14th Ab [August]. It says: A meeting of Negroes in America was held on this Ab [August] 1920, in New York. In the chair was Mr Marcus Harvey [sic], President of the Conference of Negroes, an association which looks for the rights of the Negroes (the blacks). Speaking concerning Africa, he said: We will not ask England, France, Italy or Belgium, or in other words we will not ask from them why are you (the countries mentioned) in this place. We will only direct them to get out. We will only formulate a Bill of Rights embracing all the black natives and also law to administrate their welfare. The blood of all wars is about to arrive (its compensation is due). When Europe puts her might against Asia! then it will be the time for the Negroes to lift up the sword of the liberty of the Africans. Father, that is the news of our black countrymen. It is published in the newspapers.[13]

Whether or not the message conveyed in Garvey's historic speech helped in any way convince Mgijima that the old order was collapsing, whence he may have found additional justification for his tragic and intransigent stand that issued in the Bulhoek massacre, we shall probably never know. But before the massacre of the Israelites took place, a report in *Imvo Zabantsundu*, the King William's Town Xhosa newspaper, disclosed that 'the story of Garvey's Americans coming to assist them' had been circulating among the members of the sect.[14] Perhaps this was what led the former South African Prime Minister and Cape liberal patriarch, John X. Merriman, speaking in support of the police's use of force against the Israelites, to state that he 'regretted that the "Africa for the Africans" movement had not been stamped out years ago'.[15]

Elsewhere in the Eastern Cape, the same volatile mixture of millenarian religion and political myth was also brewing. It involved an African prophetess, 'Nonteto', who was said to belong to the tribe of Chief Ngangelizwe, Ngabassa Location. By late 1922, Nonteto (more correctly Nonteta) had reportedly developed a quite substantial following in the King William's Town area. The police report regarding her activities – she was arrested and later placed in a mental institution – revealed that

> she advised the natives not to go to the mines, or plough their lands, as judgment day is coming. She encourages, however, the slaughter of stock and all her meetings are attended by the killing of sheep and goats, which, of course, has provided food for her followers and at the same time enhanced her popularity. Nonteto condemns Churches of the European denominations and advocates that the natives keep to themselves in matters of this nature. The religious aspect of Nonteto's activities are regarded as cloaking a more serious objective, for information has been received that her followers discuss the overthrowing of the Europeans by a combination of the black races and the coming of the American Negroes.[16]

In view of the by now widespread belief in 'the coming of the American Negroes', it can be understood why *Umteteli wa Bantu* should have expressed the view, in an editorial on 12 March 1921, that '[t]he American Negro is a force to reckon with, – a force which may well affect the destiny of South Africa through its effect upon South Africa's black population'.

Garveyism and the ICU in the Cape

It was in Cape Town, however, that the appeal of Garvey's message found the most sustained organisational response. The Superintendent of Locations in Bloemfontein reported on this in November 1920, when he disclosed having been told by a Rev. Tantsi of the AME Church ('a very well affected Native Wesleyan parson and teacher'), shortly after the latter's return from America on church business, that 'very few of our people here (in Bloemfontein) were interested, but the people in Cape Town expected big things from the movement'.[17]

'My essential object is to be the great African Marcus Garvey and I don't mind of how much I shall pay for that education' – these words were written by none other than Clements Kadalie, the guiding light of the Industrial and Commercial Workers' Union of South Africa (ICU), in a letter, on 20 May 1920, to his colleague and cofounder of the ICU, S. M. Bennett Ncwana. Alluding to what can plausibly be interpreted as a reference to the UNIA's renowned *Constitution and Book of Laws*, Kadalie closed his letter to Ncwana with a fervent request:

> Kindly, be good to forward the Constitution by post before next Friday meeting 21st. inst., for there is great work to be performed out of the Constitution. . . . Hoping you will do this without failure.[18]

The similarities between Kadalie and Garvey were striking: both were charismatic political leaders, sharing the same style of personal leadership as well as being powerful platform orators. George Shepperson long ago correctly noted that 'Kadalie, like Garvey, often saw himself in the role of a dark Moses, the legendary "Black Man from the North" who was ordained to save black people of the South from their white oppressors.' It is appropriate to point out in this connection that ICU leaders were often looked upon as ambassadors of Marcus Garvey; it was said at the time that 'people who joined [the ICU] are under the impression that the ICU leaders are deputising for Marcus Garvey'. This was merely the particular expression of a much broader phenomenon. Thus, at the time that the ICU penetrated rural Natal in 1927, Gilbert Coka recalled how 'Many country people thought that the ICU leaders were American Negroes who had come to deliver them from slavery.' Again, in the Eastern Transvaal in 1926–27, after leading a successful campaign that saw blacks for the first time able to share the pavements with whites, the ICU's Thomas Mbeki became 'perceived by many rural Africans as so different from ordinary South African blacks that they nicknamed him "America"'. The symbolism had also had the more inter-personal counterpart which was expressed in the ICU's *Workers' Herald*, when it published in its issue of 15 November 1927 a letter from a black boatswain, C. Levy, who was then bound for New York on the SS *Kabinga*. Writing to H. D. Tyamzashe, the Provincial Secretary of the Transvaal ICU, Levy informed him:

> I have visited three divisions in South Africa, viz., Capetown, East London and Durban, and it gives me great pleasure to take the news to America, so as to let them know [how] our brothers and sisters are trying their best in

Africa. . . . I am leaving for Capetown, and from thence to New York, where the headquarters of our Association is, of which I am a full member.

The modishly dressed Kadalie was himself also frequently mistaken for an American Negro, an impression, we suspect, that he may even have tried to foster by affecting 'a slight American accent', as noted by a *Sunday Times* reporter, in his style of speaking English. Throughout the Cape, the simple truth is that identification with American Negroes was a generalized phenomenon, although the term did not apply exclusively to American blacks: West Indians were usually confused with American Negroes, as was the case with Arthur McKinley who was West Indian but who was referred to in 1930 by the *Cape Times*, as we saw, as 'an American Negro'. Thus, in an article entitled 'Poisoning the native mind', the *Cape Argus* counted 'about 200 American Negroes in Cape Town alone'. In all likelihood, the great majority of these persons were actually West Indians, as, for example, when the President of the ICU, a West Indian by the name of Johnson, became known as 'a Negro from America'.[19]

Popular identification with the 'American Negro' archetype found greatest expression among the new breed of radical petit-bourgeois leaders – chiefly teachers and clerks – who joined the ranks of the emergent ICU. These new leaders politically rejected the tenets of the old Cape liberal tradition, particularly the loyalty to Britain that amounted almost to a religion among the older African leaders. Instead, the adoption by the new leaders of 'American' accoutrements served to set them off from the elders of their class who remained faithful to the alliance with white liberals. It also served to legitimise them in the eyes of the aroused working class, particularly the militant dock-workers who formed the bedrock of ICU support in Cape Town and among whom the idea of Garvey's 'black fleet' garnered considerable popular support.

In all, therefore, the image of the 'American Negro' had come to symbolise a radical black consciousness which rested on a multitude of organisational and political linkages between the ICU and UNIA and their respective leaders in Cape Town. Kadalie, for example, speaking before a meeting of the Parow Division (the UNIA in Cape Town actually took in several divisions – Goodwood, Parow, Claremont, Woodstock, West London and Cape Town proper) made known his position: 'This is a movement', he said, 'which assures every man and woman of his or her salvation. We must therefore unite with racial pride that at least Africans will be redeemed and all her sons returned where nature first put them.[20] Joining Kadalie on the platform was his friend from Zonnebloem College and fellow ICU organiser, S. M. Bennett Ncwana, who began his remarks by declaring: 'We would show our cordial appreciation of the very first step taken by the Hon. Marcus Garvey to show his solidarity with us.' Unfortunately, we have not succeeded in determining the substance of Garvey's gesture of solidarity toward the ICU at this juncture, but whatever its nature, it caused Ncwana to stress the reciprocal ties binding the UNIA and ICU:

> We should ourselves set a great example by acknowledging the community of interest, and, above all, that community of sacrifice on which alone the Negro movement can permanently rest. It will therefore depend upon how we treat this movement. It is not a movement inaugurated by us, but one that comes to us from our children abroad. Our faith and determination is being weighed in the scale. Liberty and freedom calls upon you Africans to respond.[21]

Ncwana's publication, *The Black Man*, for which Kadalie was the business manager, was also responsible for spreading the message of Garveyism. In a report published in the *Negro World*, Ncwana recounted how the staff of the *Black Man* was first approached by 'a most enthusiastic member' of the UNIA in Cape Town who 'unfolded a tale of surpassing interest'. After this initial meeting, Ncwana informed his own readership: 'We are making the closest inquiries into this great movement, and in later issues will deal with its influence upon our movement in South Africa.'[22] By March 1921, Garvey actually referring to Ncwana's *Black Man* newspaper as 'the *Negro World* of South Africa'; moreover, Garvey laboured under the misconception that the *Black Man* was 'edited by the president of the Cape Town division of the UNIA'. Furthermore, it seems that the name of Ncwana's newspaper exerted a strong attraction for Garvey, since he proceeded to use it in naming his proposed *Blackman* journal in 1922, the daily *Blackman* newspaper that he published in Jamaica in 1929–31 and, finally, his *Black Man* magazine that he published from 1933 to 1939.

The editorial statement carried in the inaugural August 1920 issue of the *Black Man* contained the following acknowledgement: 'We have been moved by that tender touch of brotherly feeling which inspired the Hon. Marcus Garvey to appeal to the men and women of [the] Negro race to save the freedom and liberty of their future generation.' It is hardly surprising, therefore, that *Umteteli wa Bantu* should have seen the paper as working 'for the propagation and development of Garveydom in Africa' and should have criticised it for being 'pathetically vehement in its declaration of the reality of the Negro 'Back to Africa' movement'. African readers of the *Black Man*, conversely, wasted no time in using it to exhort others: thus a Port Elizabeth subscriber, V. A. Pillay, in the *Black Man*'s 20 August 1920 issue, referring to Garvey's 'Negro Conference [held] recently', concluded: 'Let us realise we are under the banner of Black entirely . . . and [it is] our mutual duty to honour such a tradition in alluding to a Commonwealth of Black Nations in the Union of South Africa so as to link with these brave souls across the great Atlantic.' The fact that a Pretoria subscriber to the *Negro World* could also conclude a letter by extending his 'best wishes to the Blackman [sic] and its staff' should also give some indication of the degree of assimilation that existed in readers' minds between the two papers.[23]

At the same time, Ncwana was also only one of several ex-members of the South African Native Labour Contingent (SANLC), which had served in France in the First World War, who were affiliated with divisions of the Cape Town UNIA. Ncwana had held the position of sergeant in SANLC's Third Battalion and he was also the veterans' leader in Cape Town. African veterans brought back with them to South Africa from their experiences in the First World War – indeed, it may have been from them that the notion of black American liberators was originally spread – a heightened sense of black nationalism, an important fact which D. D. T. Jabavu took pains to point out.[24] Jabavu, described by Walshe as 'a colossus in the African intellectual world', was also the one to point up the connection that he believed existed between 'the riots and threatened riots for a living wage, as seen at Port Elizabeth, Durban, East London, Cape Town, King William's Town and elsewhere in all the provinces' and the further spread of this 'native unrest' in the form of Garveyism:

> The lack of consideration on the part of employers in this matter (unjust wages obtaining at a time of severe stress in the cost of living) has rendered the Natives, in their disturbed state, easy victims to the belief in Marcus Garvey, whose Black Republic propaganda promises such great things. It promises among other things: the expulsion of the white man and his yoke of misrule from their midst; Negro autonomy ('I Afrika mayi buye' – Let Africa be restored to us) with Garvey himself as Lord High Potentate; a black star fleet with powerful black armies bringing salvation and bags of grain to relieve Africans from the economic pinch. This because of its attractiveness has made a deep impression on our illiterate people. . . .[25]

The importance of Cape Town as one of the principal radiating points from whence the Garvey movement spread was confirmed by the *Cape Argus* on 29 January 1923. After observing that Garvey's propaganda had produced 'an unsettling effect (among the natives), and is beginning to cause anxiety among the white people who have worked for the good of the natives, and among the educated natives, who foresee danger in the present situation', the newspaper revealed that it based its assessment on 'some letters [brought] to the *Argus* office today which threw light on the unsettled mental state of the natives'. The person providing the letters was 'an educated native', it said, with connections to the African press. The extracts of letters published were 'just as they appear in the original letters'. One of the letters was 'written from a town within easy reach of Cape Town', and the paper reported that it said: '"They (the natives) are looking day after day when the 400,000,000 Negro Americans will arrive here. They are very proud to hear such a thing."' The paper also quoted from a letter written by 'a native teacher', who declared in it – 'we pray day and night that the Africans in America may come, as we have no doubt they will come'. There was also 'a letter from Pondoland [that] requests that an enclosed letter should be forwarded to "the agent, Negro World"'. Finally, the report mentioned that 'the great charter' of the movement (a reference to the 'Declaration of rights of the Negro peoples of the world' passed at the August 1920 UNIA convention in New York) was being circulated 'among the educated and the semi-educated natives of South Africa'. After presenting the paper's readership with excerpts of a couple of the declaration's clauses, it concluded that 'sufficient has been reproduced to show the insidious propaganda that has emanated from America'.[26]

Carried from Cape Town the UNIA message also reached beyond the borders of the Union. On 10 November 1922, His Britannic Majesty's Consul-General at Lourenço Marques in Mozambique wrote to the Governor-General of South Africa to inform him that 'a Portuguese native, lately believed to have been resident at Muizenberg for about two years where he was employed as a hotel servant', and 'one Zuze Anderson Lewis', had been detained by the Beira police. Found in their possession was a certificate – 'a somewhat ornate affair, well printed on tough paper with a heavy scroll border' – certifying that 'Mr Jeffrey Matthew Edward of Muizenberg, is a duly registered member' of the UNIA and bearing the signatures of the officers of the Cape Town Division – William O. Jackson (President), J. Caesar Allen (General Secretary), and William B. Chaswell (Treasurer). The consular official went on to note:

These two natives are from the Tete district of this Province, which is near the district of the Barue, where a serious insurrection occurred in 1918. The

Beira police have detained these men as they are suspicious of the nature of the Association to which they belong and are not anxious that they should be allowed to return to their homes, possibly to stir up further dissatisfaction by spreading Pan-Ethiopian propaganda.[27]

This irradiating tendency of the UNIA and its contacts also came to the attention of the colonial authorities in Southern Rhodesia (Zimbabwe). The Superintendent of Natives, Stanley W. S. Jackson, on 7 July 1923 wrote to advise the Chief Native Commissioner in Salisbury:

I understand that there is an East African Benefit Society, with headquarters in Cape Town. That this Society works in conjunction with the American Improvement Society and the Industrial Commercial Union at Cape Town. The Society is for natives from north of the Union who are working in the Union.[28]

The 'East African Benefit Society' was in actuality the African Universal Benefit Society (the presence of the word 'Universal' in the title was a give-away of UNIA influence). The secretary was E. Sinenke of Chilimanzi district, who reportedly was employed by Hepworths Ltd of Cape Town. In 1925, Sinenke would turn to the *African World* of the Garveyite James S. Thaele for publication of his letter asking the Prime Minister of Southern Rhodesia, who was about to visit Cape Town, for the opportunity to interview him.[29]

Namibia was another area outside the Union where a link was forged with the Cape Town Garvey movement. In June 1921, S. M. Bennett Ncwana made an initial visit, and even though he was not allowed to stay more than fourteen days, since he was without a residence permit, none the less within that short space of time he helped to get the Luderitz Division of the UNIA started. In July of the following year, however, using the assumed name of 'W. O. Jackson' (the name of the Cape Town UNIA President), Ncwana returned to Luderitz. Ncwana informed the immigration officer at the dock that 'he had travelled to Luderitz to start up a bootmaking business, but when the officer searched for stocks in trade, he found only "books which had something to do about labour"'. (The person who met Ncwana at the dockside was 'a Mr Johnstone who told the official that he and Jackson had served together in the Labour Corps in France'.) However, it came out in the testimony presented at his trial, in August 1922, that Ncwana had confided to a 'Kroo-boy' who travelled on the ship from Cape Town with him that the true reason for his visit was to meet with two individuals, Fitz Headly and J. de Clue, on 'UNI [*sic*] business'.[30] Headly was the President of the Luderitz UNIA Division and de Clue, in addition to being a prominent member, was also an active figure in the Luderitz ICU. Both Headly and de Clue were West Indians.

Outside the ICU, the Garvey movement also forged links with independent black churches. This came out in 1925, during Garvey's incarceration following his conviction on mail fraud, when three religious groups submitted joint petitions to President Coolidge asking that Garvey be granted a pardon. The groups were the Universal African Bible Students Association (the name suggests that it was a spin-off from the Watchtower movement), the Universal Temple of Africa and the Universal African Missionary Convention'[31] At the head of the petitioning letters was written the motto, 'One God! One Servant! One Church! One Jesus!', which was an echo of UNIA's well-known motto 'One God, One Aim, One Destiny'. The same was true of the use by the three groups of the word 'Universal' in their names emulating the UNIA name.

Further afield, in the Northern Cape, the House of Athlyi sect (otherwise known as the Afro-Athlican Constructive Gaathly, which propounded a doctrine based on teachings from *The Holy Piby* or 'Black Man's Bible') was reported by the Kimberley police, in November 1928, to have had ties with an office

> at Woodstock, Cape, where all books, newspapers, etc., are received and from there distributed. 'The Negro World' is supplied from there, direct to subscribers. Important messages contained in 'The Negro World' are read by ministers to all members.

Joseph Masogha, the leader of the Athlican group, had been formerly trained as a disciple of 'Bible Watch Tower' in Cape Town for two years. After leaving school in Standard III in Kimberley, he was employed variously as a postman and as a constable in the municipal sanitary department. The divisional police inspector of the Eastern Cape Division reported, however, that around 1920 Masogha became known as 'a notorious agitator at Barkly West', afterwards moving back to Kimberley where he rose to become 'a very prominent member of the Native National Congress and whilst a member of the Congress he received American newspapers in bulk and subsequently distributed them to other centres in the Union'. It was Masogha who, in 1924, provided the Rev. Daniel W. Alexander of the Ethiopian Church with the copy of the *Negro World* (9 August 1924) containing the convention sermon of the UNIA's Bishop George A. McGuire ('What Is That in Thine Hand?'). Three years before, at the time that he was Chaplain-General of the UNIA, McGuire had established the African Orthodox Church (AOC) under his leadership. Now, after reading his 1924 sermon before the UNIA, Alexander felt so moved that he decided to apply immediately for membership in the AOC, which eventually became established in South Africa with Alexander as its first African bishop.[32]

Looking to duplicate this success elsewhere, Masogha was untiring in his efforts, as he recounted in a letter to the *Negro World* published on 27 September 1924:

> May I let you know that I have spread the propaganda in Bechoanaland to the chief thereof, to whom I, Joseph Lechwenyo, so-called Joseph Masagha by marriage, am a royal blood relative – Chief Botlhasitse and Mothibi, children of the great Chief Mankuroana. They wish you a blessing, that God may be with the United Negro Improvement Association for the redemption of Africa.
>
> I am known in the whole of Bechoanaland as their own son. I am only doing the little I can do. If I had education I would play my game. I lack a good education. All I could do is to spread the opinion of the United Negro Improvement Association and get books of its photos to spread this spirit of the new Negro. I have given my heart as an offering for this land of ours. I quite follow that there must be a sacrifice. I hope the United Negro Improvement Association will guide me.

A correspondent signing himself 'Z.M.', in a letter confirming Masogha's dedication to the cause, wrote to the *Negro World* (13 September 1924) to inform it that 'Mr Masogha got a slap in the face as a matter of compliment and called a d--d nigger in the post office for getting *The Negro World*, from New York, actually 8,000 miles away, to awaken and enlighten Negroes here.'

Opposition to the Garvey movement

Writing in 1921–22, D. D. T. Jabavu acknowledged that Garvey's impact on Africans had been extensive, so that 'even from the backwood hamlets', he said, 'rings the magic motto "Ama Melika ayeza" (the Americans are coming)'. Nathanial Ntengo of Cape Town also observed that 'Even the deaf, dumb and half dead have caught the vision of Mr Garvey that Africa must be freed from the hands of the exploiters.'[33]

In the face of this wide appeal, the opposition that arose to the Garvey movement faced difficult odds. However, it was helped by the fact that the principal opposing force did not come from within South Africa itself but, ironically, emanated from America. Morever, the opposition that was based in South Africa was borne primarily by

AME missionaries whose antecedents were in the preceding 'Africa for the Africans' phenomenon of the early part of the century. Now allied more firmly than ever before to the South African state, these Afro-American churchmen waged a determined rearguard struggle to preserve their freedom of operation. By the same process of opposition, it must be noted, the perspective opened up by the overall Garvey phenomenon was cast into ever greater relief – 'What can be said of a people who conspire for the overthrow of a government to which they constantly declare their loyalty and submission?' asked *Umteteli wa Bantu* in consternation on 9 July 1921, believing as it did that Marcus Garvey was the convenor of the Pan-African Congress to which delegates from South Africa had been invited.

The first warning about Garvey reached South African officialdom at the start of 1920. It took the form of a lengthy letter from Samuel Augustus Duncan, an early UNIA leader who had split with Garvey, addressed to the Governor-General of South Africa. In fact, the letter was very similar to those that Duncan also circulated to colonial governors in the West Indies and to the Colonial Office in England. Without exhibiting the least trace of any of the racially patriotic spirit of the 'New Negro', Duncan claimed that Garvey's movement was 'engaged in the most destructive and pernicious propaganda to create disturbances between White and Colored people in the British Possessions'. His letter advised the Governor-General:

> I venture to suggest that your Excellency would be serving well the cause of the Empire and contributing in no small way to the promotion of Peace and good-feeling between the White and Colored people in the British Empire, should you cause to be carefully scrutinized and precautionary measures taken in the cases of all Colored persons coming into the Union of South Africa, from the United States and the Panama Canal with the view of ascertaining whether such persons are members of the Universal Negro Improvement Association and African Communities League, subscribers to and readers of the Negro World, Stockholders of or in any way connected with the Black Star Line. And upon affirmatively establishing any of these facts to exercise your official discretion as to their admission into the Union of South Africa.[34]

The official reaction upon receipt of this bombshell of a letter was immediate alarm. All immigration officers were 'warned to be on the watch' for 'persons from the United States of America engaged in propaganda work on behalf of certain Negro organisations'. They were told to watch 'especially ships' crews' and to do everything to prevent entry into the Union of such persons. British passport officers were instructed to refuse 'applications from persons who are not unquestionably of European descent'. Finally, shipping companies were alerted to the establishment of an 'embargo on any person with a touch of "colour"'.[35]

This exclusionary policy had an ironic twist. It fell hardest upon those AME missionaries who were precisely the ones that could have been most depended upon to oppose the spread of Garveyism in South Africa. Thus, for example, Rev. H. A. Payne, an American Negro missionary who had been stationed at Buchanan Mission, Middle Drift, 'though rejected', in November 1920 wrote to let the Secretary of the Interior know about 'clippings in the "East London Despatch" concerning a movement in America by the Negroes to take Africa'. Moreover, Rev. Payne made a special point of stressing that the Garvey organisation was 'not fostered by true American Negroes, but what are called West Indians'. And, as if to confirm Duncan's earlier warning, he averred as to how

> this organization has been sending literature to this country which, if not stopped[,] may prove disasterous [*sic*] by disturbing the peace of the Native population. The reason I say this is because the leaders speak of impossibilities concerning the taking of Africa. From what I have heard the Native people are prone to misinterpret and overjudge the value of this organization.[36]

In the month before this information was presented, the South African delegates to the General Conference of the AME Church meeting in the United States (at which Rev. Tantsi of Bloemfontein was a delegate) issued a sharp denunciation of the 'Negro movement' that had arisen in South Africa. The statement, which was published in the South African press, caused the editor of the *Black Man* to be 'extremely shaken', since, according to Ncwana, 'Though not wholly wedded with some of the objects of this movement, yet we must candidly confess that we are wholly wrapped up with the new Negro movement.' The AME delegates from South Africa were led by the American Negro missionary who had served for almost thirty years with the AME in the Cape, Rev. Francis M. Gow. Their denunciation confirmed the wide gulf that separated the earlier Ethopianism and the newer 'Africa for the Africans' movement. Said Ncwana:

> No sane leader of any nation will ever allow himself to be the useful instrument of the enemies of his race, like Rev. Gow and Co., only those who have made it a practice to court the favour of the White man at the expense of their poor people. We would like to know how many of the members of this denomination are in favour of Africa, our only hope, being made a White man's country? If not, why then allow those divine gentlemen, who purport to represent you and who, 35 years ago,

championed the cause of severing relations with the White man's Church, to publish in the White man's paper such low and disgraceful statements to the detriment of the general welfare of our race here and abroad? We say the leadership of such men must come to an end. They are not at all fit to guide the sentiments and aspirations of the new Black man. . . .[37]

The South African state, however, was slow in recognising and exploiting this conflict. The reason was that it viewed all Afro-Americans as agents of racial consciousness who were bent on contaminating the African natives with visionary and disruptive ideas. We can see the lack of a discriminating official sense in the interview of the Superintendent of Locations in Bloemfontein with Rev. Tantsi, for example, since, as he said, '(Rev. Tantsi) having just returned from America[,] I was anxious to know if he had brought back any of the Garvey literature. Fortunately, he has not.' As late as 1923, the Governor-General of South Africa, in reporting to the Colonial Secretary in England regarding the 'deputation of natives' who met with Smuts to discuss the Native Urban Areas Bill, advanced the view that '[m]any of these native agitators are American Negro ministers who imagine that they have been selected by Providence to bring about the emancipation of the African native'. He also claimed that they preached to the Africans that 'they will liberate by imparting the knowledge they have acquired in America to their brethren in this Continent'. This was the spectre raised by the Ethiopianism of yore but one that officialdom was clearly not about to part with, as the newly elected head of the AME Church in South Africa, Bishop William T. Vernon, discovered when he arrived there in 1920. According to Oswin Bull, General Secretary of the YMCA in Cape Town, Bishop Vernon 'suffered a great deal of inconvenience and delay before he could get into the country'. 'There is pretty strong prejudice in most quarters', Bull observed, 'against the American Coloured man', Bull continued, citing as one of the chief factors the fact that 'recently the newspapers have given a good deal of prominence to the egregious antics of Martin [sic] Garvey and Co. and that has not tended to weaken the prejudice.'[38]

Gradually, however, some officials seem to have come around to a greater political discrimination, so that by the time of Bull's writing in February 1921, the South African Police Commissioner was able to inform the Secretary of Justice that 'Touch has been maintained with the American (Negro) Bishop Vernon, of whom mention has been previously made.' The Commissioner's report went on:

It would seem his views are that the natives of this country are being wrongly led into political rather than Christian paths, and his objective is to correct this. In his speeches, he has laid great emphasis on the necessity for natives to loyally obey the laws of the Government, and it is believed that his influence will be all to the good in sobering the minds of those who regard the European only in the light of an oppressor.[39]

This was, indeed, true. On 6 May 1921, Bishop Vernon himself wrote to retired AME Bishop C. S. Smith to complain that '[t]he agitation now in America among some, if well meaning, certainly mistaken[,] elements who are preaching the doctrine of Africa for the Africans is making for a false and misleading hope among the credulous, suffering Natives, and rendering less easy the task of those from abroad who seek to elevate the Natives'.[40] Vernon's accommodationist position was entirely consonant with that which Bishop Smith had himself adopted shortly after taking up his position in 1904 as AME Bishop in Cape Town. At that time, Smith had declared that it was his desire 'to have the cooperation of the Government so as to enable me to get rid of "undesirables" referred to by the South African Native Affairs Commission'.[41]

The record reveals only a single instance during this post-war period of any black missionary who stood even momentarily outside the accommodationist and anti-Garvey current. The Rev. Kenneth E. M. Spooner, who was West Indian, came out to South Africa as a missionary of the Pentecostal Holiness Church in January 1915 and in time he established a thriving missionary station at Rustenburg in the Transvaal. In October 1920, he was reported to have addressed a meeting of the Transvaal Native Congress, and according to the police account of his speech, Rev. Spooner 'told the meeting that he had always been in constant communication with the South African Native National Congress delegates whilst they were overseas, and that he was also in constant communication with his people in America, and that although he, the speaker, was born in America, he was an African, and he urged the natives to do all in their power to obtain their rights; he stated that some of his people were now on the seas coming to South Africa with a view to beating the European people here, and that in about six months changes would be observed'.[42] It is impossible to imagine any AME missionary in South Africa at this time ever uttering such words.

The standard of opposition to Garvey's 'Africa for the Africans' movement, however, was borne by James E. Kwegyir Aggrey who arrived from America in March 1921 with the Phelps–Stokes African Education Commission. Aggrey's chosen vehicle for countering the Garvey movement was the system of joint councils of Europeans and

Africans which he inaugurated in Johannesburg.[43] That his central concern was the spread of the Garvey phenomenon in South Africa was confirmed by D. D. T. Jabavu who commented:

> His [Aggrey's] origin was a real advantage to him for it gave him the ear of whites who otherwise, on account of their dread of Ethiopian doctrines, are always suspicious of American Negroes; whilst it secured him the attention of the indigenous Africans who, ever since the reports of Marcus Garvey's Black Star Fleet, have had their eyes turned to overseas Negroes for succour from the prevailing economic depression as well as for liberation from the injustice of the white man in whom they are tending to lose faith.[44]

In the event, Aggrey would come close to being 'mobbed for this "political trickery"' and he was denounced by S. M. Bennett Ncwana's *Black Man* as 'a slipper tongued liar'. Thaele characterised Aggrey as 'that theologian whom, in the American terminology, we simply dismiss as "a me-too-boss-hat-in-hand nigger", [who] was trying to hold "Garveyism" in ridicule to the tune of the other fellow'.[45] An observer who attended an Aggrey meeting in the Eastern Cape later recalled: '[Aggrey] addressed a great gathering of Natives among whom there were a considerable number who expected that the eloquent Negro had come to inaugurate an era of freedom from taxation and from the role of the white man. What they described as the pro-white sentiments of the speaker filled them with disappointment.' In the Transkei, where a 'fervid reception' was accorded him, Aggrey's biographer reveals that 'Aggrey was supposed by some to be the herald of an invading band of Negroes – they thought all Americans were Negroes – who would drive the whites of South Africa into the sea.'[46] When the inevitable collision between Aggrey and supporters of 'Africa for the Africans' came, it was dramatic, as in the following graphic report published in the African World (28 May 1921, p. xi):

> Speaking at Johannesburg about the dream of an African Republic which he called 'a fine, beautiful dream – a mid-summer night's dream', Dr Aggrey said to a native interrupter he had a message for them 'because I am African and love Africans . . .'. The native interrupter: 'We want a republic because we are not civilised now but we will be.' In the course of his remarks, Aggrey announced that he 'hoped to have another meeting with them later, and wished to meet all the most advanced radicals among them' in order that 'he could tell the natives about the African Republic'. After saying that 'as for the others (meaning the Afro-Americans), they are not coming', he was again interrupted by a voice that said: 'Speak something decent.'

Above the din of such public confrontation it was still possible to hear the truly important message that Aggrey wished to get across to his African listeners, one which also takes us to the heart of his opposition to Garvey and the 'Africa for the Africans' idea. It provides the key, in our view, that explains why, in Aggrey's words, 'this African Republic has caused us a lot of trouble'; why, in other words, as one African commentator put it at the time, his 'touring the large centres in the Union [was] for the purpose of blotting out of the heads of the natives the idea that if the Negroes set their feet on this country the Bantu races would enjoy the freedom and salvation as citizens of the country'. D. D. T. Jabavu described Aggrey's rhetoric about inter-racial co-operation, self-improvement, Christian ethics, etc. as 'an edifying message of self-help based on Booker Washington's principles and on Christian ethics'. For Garvey, all this was just an instrument that served Aggrey's overriding political goal, which was to restore the greatly diminished confidence of Africans in British overlordship. Until the Garvey movement's onslaught against it, the rhetoric had never seriously been challenged. Examples showing how it had pre-vailed in pre-war African political discourse are not only plentiful but demonstrate its effectiveness in blocking any radical perspective on the South African state. The Rev. John L. Dube, in his acceptance letter as first President of the ANC, laid stress on the fact he would be guided by a 'hopeful reliance in the sense of common justice and love of freedom so innate in the British character'. In 1909, Booker T. Washington, who was the 'guiding star' of the ANC at the time of its founding, informed the Transvaal Commissioner of Education, E. B. Sargent, that 'since blacks are to live under the English government, they should be taught to love and revere that government better than any other institution'. Likewise, D. D. T. Javabu's father, Tengo Jabavu, made it known, in 1881, that his mission was to educate 'the people to attain their rights under the Queen's sway'. In contemporary terms, Garvey's Sotho critic in the United States, M. Mokete Manoedi, the son of an old headman in the Leribe district, explained that what Garvey's 'destructive work' consisted in was 'impressing the American people with the idea that the British African is dissatisfied with British rule'.[47] Thus the battle against Garvey transcended South Africa to encompass British rule in Africa as a whole.

For Africans to be turned away from Garvey – 'Do not have anything to do with Marcus Garvie [*sic*]. . . . If you love your race tell it all round that Marcus Garvie [*sic*] is their greatest enemy' were the words Aggrey used in his final address at Lovedale, venerable site of the co-optation of the largest section of educated Africans prior to the establishment of the University College of Fort Hare in 1915 – the imperative was to re-establish the hegemonic 'sway' of the British ideal among Africans. The goal was one of political restoration, though it was couched in rather apocalyptic terms, perhaps because it was so far removed from reality. Declared Aggrey:

> In this year of 1921, the spirit of union, of British justice, is in this land; it is being felt now as never before because of the war and because of the restlessness. What we need is some great messiah of the Anglo-Saxon race to rise up and give fair play and reciprocity. I have dedicated my life to see that we work for co-operation. I pray that before long South Africa will be the best place on earth for white and black; so that Great Britain may lead the whole world; that the lion and the lamb shall lie down together, and a little child may lead them.[48]

If we may be permitted to extend the metaphor, it might be said that Aggrey wished to lead the 'lamb' back to the 'lion'. The Garvey movement's influence, by contrast, might be said to represent the African attaining to the status of a 'lion' so that it might defend its rights in its own right.

The difference between the two positions was starkly posed at the beginning of 1923, when Garvey announced his intention of making a world tour that included a projected visit to Africa. The speed with which news of the announcement reached South Africa was amazing: Garvey first mentioned it in a speech reported in the *Negro World* on 20 January 1923 and nine days later the *Cape Argus* was able to report: 'One of the many absurd stories that are being circulated among the natives is that the notorious Marcus Garvey, of Black Star Line fame, will soon arrive in South Africa with a large force of black soldiers to drive the white man out of the country.'[49] And a few months later, at a meeting of the Transvaal Coloured Labour Union in Johannesburg, on 25 April 1923, it was reported that one de Beer, in addressing the gathering, 'mentioned the holding of a conference during the year when *Marcus Garvey* might possibly be present'.[50]

Garvey never explicitly indicated which countries in Africa he proposed to visit, yet the news that his tour plan included Africa was sufficient to cause the South African government to make a dramatic shift in assessing Garvey and his movement. It went from one basically of scepticism to one that suggested genuine alarm. The former attitude was expressed by Prime Minister Smuts in his response to a request made to him for providing a financial contribution towards the propaganda campaign being waged against Garvey in the United States by the Sotho M. Mokote Manoedi. Smuts declined the request on the ground that the Garvey movement had 'attempted propaganda work in the Union, chiefly in Cape Town and Johannesburg, but', he stated, 'not with very conspicuous success'. Smuts went on to reassure the Governor-General:

> No repressive action has been taken against the agents of this organisation although its activities are being carefully watched. No immediate trouble is anticipated, the organisation being without moral or financial stability.
>
> That a certain amount of mischief is being done by misleading ignorant and credulous persons is beyond doubt and to this extent Ministers regard the organisation with disfavour.[51]

That was where things stood in February 1923, prior to the government learning about Garvey's projected tour. Once word of his intention was passed to it by the Governor of Nyasaland, the reaction became quite a different one. On 2 June 1923, the Minister of Native Affairs was informed by his acting secretary: 'The language of the "Negro World" is not such as we could wish to see enforced in this country by the oratory of Garvey himself and it is considered that it would be wise policy to use all means at our disposal to prevent his visit.' Likewise, the Commissioner of Police advised the Secretary of the Interior: 'His [Garvey's] presence, or that of his supporters is most undesirable in South Africa, and neither he nor any of his supporters should be allowed to land in this country.'

The result of all this advisement was that Garvey was declared a prohibited immigrant under Section 4(1)(d) of the Immigrants Regulation Act of 1913. In addition, the South African High Commissioner in London was notified that he should refuse any application made by Garvey for a visa to travel to the Union. Moreover, principal immigration officers in all of South Africa's ports were notified of the prohibition. The Secretary for Native Affairs also recommended that the Union government's prohibition 'be communicated to the Governments of the other African States and Dependencies with a view to their cooperation in preventing Garvey's influence reaching the Union overland'.[52]

Such drastic precautionary measures arose out of a clear understanding of the political potential that a visit from the *soi-disant* Provisional President of Africa entailed. The response could well have precipitated a crisis between the African population and the state. Certainly, the response of Africans to Garvey's presence would have dwarfed the welcome that Aggrey met on his visit to the Union.

The Garveyism of James S. Thaele and the ANC

On December 4, 1922, G. Boyes, a Cape Town magistrate, wrote to E. Barrett, Secretary of Native Affairs: 'The evolution, amalgamation of native black races and the various changes and movements are, in my opinion, rapidly arriving at a crisis.'[53] Thus, by early 1922, the Lovedale establishment was articulating the concern it felt in light of the impression that Garvey's ideas had been making on members of the African educated élite: 'Marcus Garvey carries away some of our Native friends', an editorial in the *South African Outlook* lamented. The Garvey movement, the editorial went on, 'seduced not a few earnest workers for the wellbeing of Bantu South Africa away from paths of practical service, into dubious and sterile relationships', causing 'their attitude towards the Europeans with whom before they were co-operating [to become] embittered.'[54] At about the same time as this editorial was published, the Native Affairs Department reported an almost identical concern but on a much broader scale: 'The race consciousness of the South African Native is steadily growing', it declared, warning that 'The danger lies in the probable tendencies of the development of race consciousness to become anti-European and to seek expression in action subversive of law and order.'[55]

In face of this mounting pressure from an aroused African racial consciousness consequent upon the 'Africa for the Africans' movement, 'Professor' James S. Thaele, BA, BSc., former Lovedale student, arrived back in South Africa after being away in the United States for ten years, during which time he graduated from Lincoln University and the University of Pennsylvania. But Thaele was also, in an important sense, a graduate of the Ethiopian movement, since he had been among the twenty-two South African students who attended Lincoln University, one of the major Afro-Americn centres of higher education in the United States, between 1896 and 1924. Moreover, Thaele's subsequent plan for an 'African land settlement' scheme (Thaele was general secretary and S. M. Bennet Ncwana was president), whose aim was 'inducing Natives living in towns to settle on the land', would appear to have connected him to that phase of the earlier Ethiopian phenomenon which involved land purchases. Thaele's plan, in fact, bore a certain resemblance to the AME's land syndicate scheme organised by the AME's Rev. Allen Henry Attaway, principal of Bethel Institute, which consisted of a 10,000-acre farm at Croen River, the later site of the AME's Chatsworth Industrial High School.

Described by commentators as flamboyant and eccentric in terms of both rhetoric and dress – 'spasms of twisted eloquence and weird posturings' was *Umteteli wa Bantu's* contemporary description – Thaele, in fact, personified the 'American Negro' style of post-war Cape Town radicals. Thaele, upon his return from the United States, quickly moved the Western Cape Congress of the ANC into a radical Garveyite direction, in the process becoming simultaneously the driving force of Cape Town Garveyism. The same overlapping quality was to be repeated when the ICU moved its headquarters from Cape Town to Johannesburg in 1925, at which time the Cape Town ICU members turned to Thaele and the Western Cape Congress for leadership. All three groups – Western Cape Congress, UNIA, ICU – were virtually synonymous under Thaele's leadership.[56]

The South African police described Thaele as 'intensely anti-white in sentiment, an active member of UNIA, and a devoted follower of Marcus Garvey, whose slogan is "Africa for the Africans"'. The police recognised that his racial sensibility made for a problematical relationship with the formal ICU leadership: 'While greatly interested in the ICU, Thaele himself has refused point blank to co-operate with European Communists, stating quite openly that he does not trust or wish to associate with any white man.' But Thaele's hostility becomes somewhat more understandable when viewed in the specific South African racial context. Thus, white socialists of the International Socialist League, forerunner of the Communist Party of South Africa (CPSA), had passed a resolution at their January 1921 conference denouncing the 'Africa for the Africans' idea on the grounds that it was reactionary in South Africa – 'for here the whites had come to stay' – at the same time that it criticised 'nationalist native organisations [as] instruments of the ruling class – safety valves'. For his part, Thaele in a speech to a meeting of the Cape Town UNIA, on 23 August 1922, was reported to have 'dealt with the salvation of our race, at the same time bringing home to the audience that the salvation of the Negro races throughout the world does not depend upon the white man. But solely depends upon the Negroes themselves.'[57]

The following year, in an article in the *African Voice* entitled 'Garvey and Garveyism' (one of the earliest if not the first occasion on which this historic formulation was used), Thaele announced that '[t]he Garvey program must be studied by the Bantu politicals in season and out of season'. It was Thaele's opinion that 'in its platform lies the solution of the "black problem"'. The same issue of the *African Voice* contained, we are told, the accusation against Kadalie by opponents of his 'being in the pay of Moscow'.[58] On another occasion, Thaele counselled Africans along traditional Ethiopianist lines: 'Keep out of white churches as much as you can.'[59]

But it would be incorrect to view Thaele, as Walshe does, as the person 'who brought Garveyism into the ranks of Congress'. The truth is that 'the American notions among Natives' (*Imvo Zabantsundu*, 11 July 1921) resonated among members of Congress hardly less strongly than among other Africans; indeed, at the time of Bishop Vernon's arrival, Enoch Mgijima's nephew, Gilbert Matshoba, felt so repulsed by the utterances that came from the black American divine that he claims to have 'sent word to the President of the Congress that liberty will not come from America'. It would not have been necessary for Mathshoba to resort to this if he did not think that there was sympathy for such a view among Congress's leaders. *Abantu Batho* (official ANC organ) had published correspondence sent to it by Garvey from as early as 1920. Then, following the news of Garvey's spectacular August 1920 convention, *Abantu Batho* featured a lengthy analytical article enquiring into the '"Back to Africa Movement"', which, it suggested, had had the effect of making many Africans 'rather elated over the fantastic idea of a Black Republic'. The article went on to assimilate Garvey's UNIA convention to South African political terminology – 'About three months ago, the Negroes in the United States of America have held their *National Congress* . . . to establish a Black Republic that will rule the whole of Africa under a President and a *National Congress*' [emphasis added]. After exhorting readers to follow the American Negro example, the article declared: 'Let us strengthen our political weapon – the *National Congress*' [emphasis added]. In this fashion, Garvey's UNIA and the South African Congress were presented as parts of a common entity. *Abantu Batho* also reproduced in full Garvey's 'Proclamation to the Negroes of the world' in its editorial of 27 January 1921. W. O. Jackson, President of the Cape Town UNIA Division, also was in attendance at the supposedly 'secret conclave' called to hear the report of the ANC deputation (one of whom was S. M. Bennet Ncwana) that interviewed Prime Minister Smuts in June 1923 regarding the Native Urban Areas Bill. According to the confidential report of the meeting, Jackson addressed the meeting at the end and said: 'The message of the American Negroes' movement to you is this: 'We, not only in Africa but also the 15,000,000 Negroes abroad, collaborate with you in your undertakings, viz: "Africa for the African only"'.[60]

What Thaele did, and it was important, was to expand upon this base of political discourse that had gone on for some time between the two organisations. His distinctive contribtuion was to infuse the activities of the Western Cape Congress with the symbols and rituals of Garveyism. Thus, the official organ of the Cape ANC was named *The African World* to identify it, no doubt, with Garvey's popular *Negro*

World. The slogan of the journal – 'Africa for the Africans and Europe for the Europeans' – was also transparently Garveyite in its provenance. Its inaugural issue of 23 May 1925 opened with a statement on 'The African Empire', which was one of Garvey's favourite political phrases, saying that 'The Universal Negro Improvement Association and African Communities League is the biggest thing to-day in Negro modern organisations. Its programme must be scrutinised, imbibed and assimilated by us.' Garvey's canonical 'African fundamentalism' statement, which he wrote in the Atlanta federal penitentiary in June 1925, was translated into southern Sotho and published in the *African World* accompanied by the following introduction:

> When you look at the review in last week's paper, you will find a letter in the third page that was written by the most Hon. Marcus Garvey requesting that this letter ['African Fundamentalism'] should appear in full and in all its details, and that it should be translated into all 800 languages of the [African] world. This important news comes from the far regions of Georgia in the United States of America. This letter is a guideline of the principles of government that shall be ours. This shall be the primary Code underlining all the fundamental practices that shall guide all future rule in Africa.

The translation was carried out by Bransby Ndobe, the radical Provincial Secretary of the Western Cape ANC, who later, in 1929–30, spearheaded the vigorous rural campaign for improved wages. When he was charged with incitement to public violence under the 'hostility' clause of the 1927 Native Administration Act (he was later banned from the areas of rural agitation under the draconian Riotous Assemblies (Amendment) Act of 1930), Ndobe explained to the court that his use of the 'Africa for the Africans' slogan was, as Walshe described it, 'simply an assertion that black people did not have sufficient freedom in South Africa'.[61] The Cape ANC headquarters was also named 'Liberty Hall', the name of the general assembly hall that was the spiritual centre of the UNIA in New York. A picture of the building was published in the *Negro World* accompanied by an editorial, 'A Liberty Hall for the African Congress', which said;

> The African [C]ongress stands for the principle, 'Africa for the Africans', which the Universal Negro Improvement Association stands for, and they give Hon. Marcus Garvey the credit due him as the pioneer and chief spokesman of all Negroes who are fighting for African redemption and repatriation. . . . The editor of the *African World* understands this fact just as well as does the editor of *The Negro World*. The African Congress in Africa and the UNIA in the new world are working by the same sign and by it they cannot but succeed in arousing and unifying the Negro people. It is a great and glorious work.[62]

The *African World*, in turn, recommended to readers 'the daily reading of the Negro World, to imbibe the Gandhian philosophy [of non- cooperation]'. The idea of employing the Gandhian tactic of non-cooperation was one that Thaele had viewed 'as the most effective weapon for the Natives' use'. 'We will approach the Chiefs', he is reported to have told a meeting on the Grand Parade in Cape Town in early October 1924, 'to withdraw our people from the Johannesburg mines and other industrial centres as much as they can. . . . The only way to make the white man listen to you is to withdraw your industrial and other support.'[63] This was an attempt to convert the general sentiments of Garveyism into a programme of concrete political action, though it appears that the attempt failed to get launched.

Thaele also took the lead in keeping before the South African public the plight of Garvey in prison in the United States. Two months after his incarceration in Atlanta, Thaele spoke at the meeting of the Transvaal Native Congress in Johannesburg in April 1925, where he tried to have the following resolution approved, namely, that 'this Native Congress requests the President of the United States of America to show clemency towards Marcus Garvey (an exponent of race freedom [who] had suffered in the cause of race freedom) in regard to the term of five years imprisonment imposed upon him'. Branches of the Cape ANC were likewise urged to honour 7 June 1925 as 'Garvey's day' and to attend a big meeting that was to be held on that day at the Parade in Cape Town to pay honour to the 'man who offered himself as a sacrifice for the Black nation'.[64]

At this juncture, the ANC leadership began to adopt towards Garvey an attitude that was explicitly supportive, so it can be said that Thaele's efforts had paid off politically. In December 1925, for example, Rev. Zaccheus R. Mahabane, President-General of the ANC, referred to Garvey as being 'President General Moses of [the] African Republic'. In his call for the Bloemfontein convention of the following year ('which will make us to go to Parliament with "Black eyes"'), Mahabane explicitly included 'the Negroes in the United States of America . . . and his excellency Marcus Garvey in Georgia, Atlanta Penetentiary [*sic*] Institution'. Ironically, at the time of Aggrey's visit to the Union in 1921, Mahabane was one of the most enthusiastic proponents of the anti-Garvey joint council idea.[65]

The following year a leading member of the Transvaal Native Congress, Johannesburg branch, David Hlakudi, was stopped at Benoni by a police detective who confiscated his month-old edition of the *Negro World*.[66] Shortly after this, J. Barnard Belman wrote to inform the *Negro World* in October 1925:

The general opinion of the black people in the Transvaal is that the Hon. Marcus Garvey is the great king. They simply swear by him. I am sure that they would go through fire and water for him and with him.

My sale of the [*Negro World*] papers is exceptionally good considering the fact I have not handled them long. I am looking forward to the time when I may sell many thousands a week. There are more than 185,000 Negroes in the Transvaal alone and our papers should have an exceptionally large sale here considering the interest the people have in the work.[67]

This was the same year that the *Negro World* also spoke of the UNIA's Evaton Division having achieved an extremely lively membership: 'The attendance [at a mass meeting on 14 June]', the report stated, 'was unusually large; nearly four hundred were present. Seventy new members were added to the roll.'[68] What this signified, in our view, was a renewal of popular support on the Witwatersrand for the principles of the UNIA from the mid-1920s onward.

It was in this context that the new infusion of race consciousness in statements by ANC leaders must also be viewed. The publication of Hertzog's segregation bills in July of that year was undoubtedly an important contributing factor as well. At the same time, the shift in attitudes would also have been reinforced by the dramatic transformation that the ICU underwent during 1927–28 throughout the Eastern Transvaal countryside, while the Western Cape was also becoming the site of a major rural agitation campaign conducted the radical wing of the Western Cape Congress.[69] As a result of this radicalisation of the ANC in the period after 1925, there was an almost wholesale embrace of Garveyism. *Abantu Batho*, the Johannesburg ANC newspaper, in 1926 came out strongly endorsing the second volume of *The Philosophy and Opinions of Marcus Garvey*, which had been compiled by Garvey's second wife, Amy Jacques Garvey, and published earlier in that year. 'The Black Race owes its gratitude for this service', the paper announced in its lengthy appreciation, 'which has aroused and electrified race consciousness to the articles and orations of Hon. Marcus Garvey.' It then went on:

But above all else, both the compiler and her husband have exposed more than anyone before them the hypocrisy, color-prejudice, injustice and discrimination of the white race against the black men. More important still is the warning of the Negro Leader that the only avenue through and by which the Negro will win the respect of the world is by self-exertion and contribution in the founding of a Black Government by black men for black men in Africa, the home of the black man.[70]

The following year the official ANC letter-head was glossed with a map of Africa inside of which was printed the motto, 'One God One Aim One Destiny', the official UNIA motto![71] Further evidence of this turn towards

Garvey and the UNIA was provided, in August 1929, in a report by the South African police which claimed that the African Orthodox Church's Bishop Daniel Alexander had 'attended secret meetings held by Josiah T. Gumede at Kimberley in November 1928'. Gumede, who was elected President-General of the ANC in June 1927, was described by the police report as 'one of the most dangerous agitators in this country, who not only works for the Communist party but also corresponds with Marcus Garvey, President General of the Universal Negro Improvement Association (UNIA) the slogan of which is "Africa for the Africans"'. Once again, however, we witness a dramatic shift in position relative to the early 1920s. According to the published report of Gumede's speech before the Ethiopian Church in Queenstown, in July 1921, bearing on the question of Aggrey's visit to the Union, he had stated

> that it was true that there prevailed the Back to Africa American Negro Movement, which in the long run would prove futile, and it was a mere dream. Hence, the Bantu races would do well not to pay heed to that childish and silly movement, as the American Negroes would not treat them better than the white man, because those people in America had never stretched out their hand to help them in anything, and how could we expect them to come and deliver us here from oppression by the white man.[72]

How different this was from his presidential address to the founding conference of the communist-organised League of African Rights in 1929, at which time, borrowing one of the favourite rhetorical devices used by Garvey, Gumede let it be known at the very outset of his speech that '[t]he four hundred millions of Negroes to be found all over the world claim Africa to be their only home'. That same year Gumede assumed the proprietorship of *Abantu Batho* and the following May editorials appeared lauding Garvey as 'a dangerous man for all the great powers that are exploiting Africa' and defending Garvey's slogan of 'Africa for the Africans'. Additionally, the paper also ran a statement by Garvey under the caption, 'Marcus Garvey urges Negroes to build for racial uplift'.[73]

As a strong sympathiser of the CPSA and someone who had travelled to Moscow in 1927 as an invited guest to the tenth anniversary celebrations of the Russian Revolution, Gumede was doubtlessly now acting in accord with the position articulated in 1928 by the Sixth Congress of the Communist International which proclaimed the slogan of the South African 'Native Republic'. But apart from being convenient as a means of conveying the new CPSA line, the adoption of Garvey's rhetoric and programme also would have proved useful in isolating the conservative wing of the ANC leadership. Edwin A. T. Mofutsanyana, one of the leading African militants of the CPSA, in an interview with Robert Edgar, recalls that 'Marcus Garvey at one time in the African Congress became the hope of the black man'.[74] The mediating role of the CPSA was also evident in the comment made by Robert A. Dumah, a former ICU organizer in the Orange Free State, in an article that appeared in the *Negro Worker*, the communist organ of the International Trade Union Committee of Negro Workers published out of Hamburg. 'Garveyism teaches self-consciousness,' asserted Dumah, 'and the RILU [Red International of Labour Unions] teaches the workers the values of revolutionary determination and achievement.'[75]

The struggle for self-definition that this imposed on South African Garveyites became plainly audible. By late 1928, resistance was sounded in a meeting of the Pretoria UNIA held in the Marabastad location. L. R. Sabata spoke as follows:

> We have nothing to do with the Red Russians. . . . We don't know that movement at all. We are going to get Africa for the Africans by ourselves, and not with the aid of Communism. We are going to work along peaceful lines.[76]

But the truth was that the 'Native Republic' slogan of the CPSA was difficult to distinguish from the Garveyite demand for 'a black republic'. The result was that as the strenuous decade of the 1920s was drawing to a close, the traditional Garvey movement found itself forced on to the defensive. But this was also the period characterised by the political exhaustion of not only the UNIA but also the ICU and ANC as well, in fact all organised bodies of African protest, a consequence in part of the rapidly increased level of state repression during 1929–30 resulting from passage of the Riotous Assemblies (Amendment) Act in the latter year. The ICU had already collapsed by 1928, while by the spring of 1930 the ANC entered upon a state that has been described as 'almost total moribundancy', sinking to its nadir point by the middle of the depression decade. Perhaps it was this general state of political impotence that explains why, upon hearing of the plans Garvey was making for the holding of the Sixth International Convention of the UNIA, Alexander Njaba, a Garvey supporter in William King's Town, lamented forlornly: 'We South African Natives are the only people who seem to be "marking time", while our brothers in consanguinity elsewhere on the globe show remarkable progress and initiative'.[77]

Garveyism's refuge in the Transkei

As Robert Edgar has shown, the phenomenon known as the 'Wellington movement' was the local Transkeian manifestation of the conjoined myth of the American Negro liberator and the Garvey UNIA. The Transkei in time became the scene of several flourishing divisions of the UNIA – Tsolo, Umtata Engcobo, Gcaleka and Qumbu. In the make-up of the Wellington movement, however, it is possible to see the coming together, in a concentrated fashion, of the systemic elements that laid the basis for Garveyism within the Union.

At the most general level, Wellington Butelezi, the leader of the movement in the Transkei, represents the mimetic 'American Negro' phenomenon taken to its furthest extreme. According to Edgar, Wellington's identity as an 'American' became so complete that in court he refused to admit his African parentage, in spite of the fact that his actual father was brought to the court. Indeed, Wellington went so far in his American indentification that he even tried to have his name changed officially.[78] Moreover, in professing to be a medical doctor, he became identified with another protégé of the American phenomenon: thus both Wellington and 'Professor' Thaele, his fellow Lovedale alumnus who wrote letters on his behalf in his unsuccessful attempt in 1924 to obtain a passport, were disparaged as 'Native "doctors" and "professors" who came over from America' and who together 'posed with a multitude of titles after their names'.[79]

It is believed that Wellington's conversion to the Garvey movement came at the hands of the West Indian, Ernest Wallace, in Durban. Wallace had formerly been a resident of Cape Town for some twenty years; as it turns out, Wallace was one of the two so-called 'American Negroes' whose landing in Durban in 1920 caused the authorities such consternation and led to the stiffening of exclusionary immigration regulations. Wellington was then living in Durban; afterwards, he moved his headquarters to Edendale near Pietermaritzburg in Natal.

The Transkei, according to Aggrey's biographer, was where 'a number of the inhabitants were looking to America for redemption from their troubles', and where also 'people had expected an earthly deliverer who was coming to wage war, not against wrongdoing, but against their conquerors and rulers'. The Transkeian peasantry was engulfed throughout this period in a deepening crisis. Among the results of Wellington's movement, we are told that it had the effect of 'disorganising the work of the Churches and Schools', two of the key supports of the stratification system that reflected the deepening social inequality among Africans. The movement also promised 'Freedom from taxation and from the rule of the white man to those who destroyed their pigs and dash away paraffin, needles, cups and saucers and certain other articles introduced into Africa by the white man.'[80] This injunction to destroy 'articles introduced into Africa by the white man' undoubtedly bore witness to the crushing debt system enforced by European traders upon the Transkei's peasants.

However, if the original stimulus for Wellington's conversion emanated from Cape Town, the fact remains that the consciousness of Wellington's constituents was to a large extent shaped by the experience of exploitation on the Rand. The Transkeian Territories, the area possessing the most concentrated African settlement in the Union, was the largest reservoir of migrant mine-labour for the gold mines of the Witwatersrand. Indicative of this consciousness of the migrant- labour system was the belief widespread among Wellington's followers that 'on the day set apart [5 November 1927] for the destruction of all white men and their native followers . . . [t]hose women found in possession of the handkerchief bearing the design of the Native Recruiting Corporation and give[n] as a gift to the wives of those recruited for the mines, would not escape destruction'. At the same time, it is significant that in rural Pondoland the Wellington movement became known by the name 'ICU'; according to William Beinart, 'the ICU name and the spirit of the movement were absorbed and welded into an ideology dominated by Buthelezi's millenial thinking'.[81] Here we see the welding together of both the UNIA and ICU within the Transkeian epiphenomenon.

In formal terms, the Wellington movement functioned as a benefit society in the mould of the traditional UNIA. In January 1929 the Butterworth police handed in to the Solicitor-General an active member's dues card of Stephen Mxesibe of the Gcaleka UNIA Division showing that he had paid 1s. (dues) and 6d. (death tax). In return for paid-up dues, each member was said to be entitled to receive a '75 dollars death grant'. But like Congress's membership dues card in the Eastern Transvaal, where many claimed that it 'entitled them to plough where they liked and gave them the right to refuse to pay rent as well as the right to farms', or the red ICU membership card, possession of which helped to transform consciousness, the UNIA's membership card carried with it in the Transkei definite political overtones. This led the Secretary for Native Affairs to write to the Secretary of Finance stating that he 'would be glad if all possible advantage could be taken of existing legal provision to suppress the activities of what are really political movements operating under the guise of bogus benefit societies'. This political ascription was to some extent borne out in 1939, in the area of Tsolo, described as 'once a Wellington stronghold', when Meshak Bobi Mgidlana, a visiting member of the Ethiopian Church of Africa, wrote to inform the magistrate that he was 'trying to transfer [the]

Universal Negro Improvement Association into [the] African National Congress'. Mgidlana also informed 'To all it may concern' that he had been appointed 'Organiser of the ANC in the Transkeian territories.'[82]

The continuing political vitality of the Transkeian UNIA through the 1930s and even up to the early years of the First World War was manifested in two important instances. The first was the trial in the Mount Frere Circuit, in 1939, of Lutoli Semekazi, President of the Qumbu branch of the UNIA, along with James Gazu, President of the Cape Town UNIA division. According to the report of the trial published in *Imvo Zabantsundu* (3 June 1939), 'The two men were first charged with high treason [alternatively sedition, alternatively conspiring to public violence] in that during the period January 1935 to July 1938 they conspired to foster the ideas of Marcus Garvey, which [promises] the restoration of Africa to the black peoples, couched in the motto: "Africa for the Africans".' From correspondence between the accused that was presented in court, it was adduced that 'the intention was to take advantage of the unsettled state of world affairs and launch a sudden attack on Europeans with assistance from Negroes in America'. In summing up, Mr Justice Gore was reported to have referred to 'Marcus Garvey's scheme [as] the most preposterous and visionary ever propounded'.[83] Both Semekazi and Lutoli were sentenced to four months' imprisonment with hard labour, suspended for three years on condition of good behaviour.

A second indicator of continued political vitality was provided by Saul Mbulwa of Tsolo district who was reported, in June 1940, to have been attempting to revive the UNIA. The districts that were affected were Mount Fletcher, Matatiele, Umzimkulu, Mount Frere, Mount Ayliff, Qumbu, Tsolo and the whole of Eastern Pondoland. Police investigation disclosed that large numbers of people had become members in these areas and that the 'certificate of membership was exactly similar to those signed by Dr Wellington as President'. Magistrate F. C. Pinkerton of Engcobo the following month sentenced three people to terms of imprisonment, ranging from three to eight months' hard labour, for declaiming to persons attending a UNIA meeting in Qumanco, Engcobo:

> Why should we pay for our water? Why should we pay for our wood when God has planted it there for us? This is now the right time that Africa should be returned to the Blacks and the Lord has given a sign that the time for redemption is at hand.

This was a particularly worrisome sign for the authorities. That same month, the Secretary for Native Affairs, D. L. Smit, brought to the attention of the Chief Control Officer in Pretoria the fact that, although most natives were loyal and law-abiding, 'To the raw Native, however, there is little distinction between pro-Nazi propaganda and American negro propaganda. Both allege that the present rulers of the country will be driven out and that the new regime will confer multifarious advantages on the Natives.' Based on this assessment, Smit and the Department of Native Affairs recommended the internment of UNIA 'agitators', which they said 'would have a most salutary effect'. (Shortly after this, on 10 August 1940, Smit informed the Chief Magistrate for the Transkeian Territories that Garvey's pamphlet, *The Tragedy of White Injustice*, had been declared objectionable by the Board of Censors.) The proposal for establishing an internment camp for Garveyites during the Second World War failed to win approval; in place of it, however, the South African Minister of the Interior advised, in October 1940, that 'any subversive movements and statements by members of the [UNIA] League should be dealt with under the Emergency Regulations and the culprits brought before the criminal courts'.[84]

Conclusion

Contrary to what has hitherto been written, South Africans – with help from resident West Indians and assorted American Negroes in the Union – 'engineered' the Garvey phenomenon into a general national movement. The legacy of these years would play an active role, moreover, in shaping the historical consciousness of resistance. Echoes of it reverberated in the ANC Youth League's 1948 manifesto, 'Basic policy of Congress Youth League', wherein 'two streams of African Nationalism' were postulated. 'One centres round Marcus Garvey's slogan – "Africa for the Africans",' the document stated. 'It is based on the "Quit Africa" slogan and on the cry "Hurl the Whiteman to the sea".' Although the Youth League took the position that '[t]his brand of African Nationalism is extreme and ultra revolutionary', it is significant that it none the less adopted the Garvey movement's slogan, 'Africa for the Africans', as its own slogan.[85] The Youth League's attempt in the late 1940s at formulating a philosophy of 'Africanism' would not have been possible without the South African Garvey movement that preceded it.

This post-Second World War ideological legacy, however, was built upon the idea of 'Ama Melika ayeza' (the Americans are coming) that exploded throughout South Africa in the aftermath of the First World

War and that heralded the coming of liberation – 'I Afrika mayi buye' (let Africa be restored to us). From them came the motor-force of the Garvey movement. At the same time, the publication of material and correspondence back and forth between Garvey's *Negro World* and the South African black press was proof of a high degree of political reciprocity between the two spheres. The radical post-war effulgence of 'Africa for the Africans' was also characterised by both links of continuity as well as cleavages of discontinuity with the earlier phenomenon of Ethiopianism. Radiating outward from Cape Town and Johannesburg, and to a lesser extent Durban, the Garvey movement penetrated the respective political hinterlands of these urban centres and became in the process an integral part of the overall ecology of post-war African resistance. In undermining the hold among the popular classes and the African petit bourgeoisie of the idea of imperial Britain as the real political overlord of South Africa, an idea that had circumscribed African political protest since well before the turn of the century, the Garvey movement scored an important achievement that led to the liberation of African political consciousness in the inter-war period. The same imbricated texture suffused the multiple inter- connections between, on the one hand, the Garveyite idea and the 'American Negro' paradigm, and, on the other hand, the leadership and rank and file of the ICU and ANC. One major difference between them, however, was that long after the ICU and ANC had collapsed, the Garveyite idea, secure in its refuge in the Transkeian Territories, continued to mobilize African support.

The depth and complexity of the myriad of these relations are what, in our view, constitute the inner dynamic of African nationalism as it unfolded in the period between the two world wars. Although the initial influence may have originated from outside, the Garvey movement fast developed into a truly broad-based South African phenomenon. It is one that should be studied for what it reveals, not only about the nexus between African nationalism and Afro-American ideology. It also reveals importantly some of the ways of popular consciousness and its relation to the evolution of the South African state.

Note and References

1 *Cape Times*, 12 May 1930, quoted in A. P. Walshe, *The Rise of African Nationalism in South Africa: The African National Congress, 1912–1952* (Berkeley 1972) p. 167.
2 Edward Roux, *Time Longer Than Rope: A history of the black man's struggle for freedom in South Africa* (2nd edn), (Madison, 1964) p. 112. For Garvey's obituary of McKinley, see *Black Man* (London) 4 June 1939, 19.

3 George Shepperson and Thomas Price, *Independent African: John Chilembwe and the origins, setting and significance of the Nyasaland rising of 1915* (Edinburgh 1958) p. 504; George Shepperson, 'Ethiopianism: past and present', in C. G. Baeta (ed.) *Christianity in Tropical Africa* (London 1968) pp. 249–68, 'Notes on American Negro influences on the emergence of African nationalism', *Journal of African History*, I 1960, 299–312; Paul Rich, 'Black peasants and Ethiopianism in South Africa, 1896–1915', in *Conference on the History of Opposition in Southern Africa* (Development Studies Group, University of the Witwatersrand, Johannesburg 1978) pp. 119–140; Alexander Ball, 'American Negro influence on black nationalist and proto-nationalist movements in South Africa, 1898–1930', BA (Hons.) thesis (University of the Witwatersrand 1979); Carol Page, 'Black America in white South Africa: church and state reaction to the African Methodist Episcopal Church in Cape Colony and Transvaal, 1896–1910', unpublished Ph.D. thesis (University of Edinburgh 1977).

4 South African Government Archives (hereafter SAGA), Pretoria, Interior Department, File 3/1064/18 Part 3, Reports on Bolshevism in South Africa, 25 April 1925; 'An African letter,' *Negro World*, 16 July 1932. The South African journalist, Gilbert Coka, reveals that in the ICU tea-room in Johannesburg 'Fine pictures of distinguished black men, like Marcus Garvey and others, decorated the wall.' ('The story of Gilbert Coka of the Zulu tribe of Natal, South Africa, written by himself', in Margery Perham (ed.) *Ten Africans: A collection of life stories* (London 1963) p. 306. Coka, the editor of the short-lived *African Liberator*, asserts that his early political development was 'largely influenced by Garveyism' (Perham, *Ten Africans*, p. 313).

5 See Monica Hunter, *Reaction to Conquest* (London 1936); Roux, *Time Longer Than Rope*; Mary Benson, *The African Patriots* (London 1963); Walshe, *The Rise of African Nationalism*; P. L. Wickins, *The Industrial and Commercial Workers' Union of South Africa* (Cape Town 1978). The notable exception to this long-standing pattern of intellectual closure is Robert Edgar, 'Garveyism in Africa: Dr Wellington and the "American" movement in the Transkei', *Ufahamu*, 6, 1976, 31–57. An imaginative re-creation of Garveyite 'Ethiopianism' in South Africa is to be found in the novel *Wild Deer* (London 1933) by R. Hernekin Baptist (pseud.). We would like to thank the Jamaican journalist and historian, H. P. Jacobs, for bringing the latter work to our attention.

6 Quoted in Rich, 'Black peasants', p. 132.

7 W. D. Cingo, 'Native unrest', *Kokstad Advertiser*, 30 Sept. 1927; see also T. O. Ranger, *The African Voice in Southern Rhodesia, 1898–1930* (London 1970) *passim*.

8 Rosetta Stenson (UNIA Division 412, Muskogee, Oklahoma), *Negro World*, 1 Oct. 1921.

9 SAGA, Justice Department, Detective Head Constable H. St P. P. Brandon to the District Commandant, South African Police, Boksburg, 9 Feb. 1920; see Philip Bonner, 'The Transvaal Native Congress, 1917–1920: the radicalisation of the black petty bourgeoisie on the Rand', in Shula Marks and Richard Rathbone (eds) *Industrialisation and Social Change in South Africa* (London 1982) p. 305, and 'The 1920 black mineworkers'

strike: a preliminary account', in Belinda Bozzoli (comp.) *Labour Townships and Protest* (Johannesburg 1979) pp. 273–97. The only member of the 1919 Congress delegation to visit the United States was Sol Plaatje (see Brian Willan, *Sol Plaatje, South African Nationalist, 1876–1932* (Berkeley 1984) pp. 259–82, for an account of his North American tour).

10 SAGA, Interior Department, File 168/74B, vol. 2, A. E. Trigger, Inspector in Charge, CID Transvaal, Johannesburg, to Deputy Commissioner CID for the Union, Pretoria, 11 Oct. 1920 (No. 8/168/7). In the opinion of the South African Commissioner of Police, Moses gave 'expression to views which are dangerous to the peace of this country and calculated to cause serious unrest amongst our native population . . . his speedy departure from Durban has not lessened the possible harm done by him during his brief visit, and I feel strongly that Government should issue instructions to the Immigration Department to prevent the landing of any and all American Negroes at Union ports who are likely to busy themselves in mischievous propaganda amongst the native people' (SAGA, Office of the Governor-General, File 36/171, Immigration, contained in Secretary for Justice to the Secretary for the Interior, 8 Dec. 1920 (no. 13/168/74). On 15 Dec. 1920, the attempt at exclusion proved insufficient after two more 'American Negroes' landed in Durban, with the result that the Department of the Interior declared that 'all such Negroes are to be absolutely barred from landing and must remain on their ships whilst in port. Land borders are also to be carefully watched to prevent entry and, with the aid of the Police, a look out should be kept for the presence of such Negroes about the towns, both at the Coast and inland, and enquiry made as to their rights of domicile, deportation following if that right is not established' (SAGA, Asiatic Department, File M257, Marcus Garvey (Negro Organization), Under-secretary for the Interior to the Principal Immigration Officer, Pretoria, 15 Dec. 1920 (no. 13/168/74).

11 SAGA, NTS (Department of Native Affairs) 1681, File 2/276, vol. 1, Sergeant W. Mulholland, Savuti Post, to District Officer, South African Police, Umzinto, 8 Nov. 1920; G. Walker Wilson, Magistrate, Umzinto, to Chief Native Commissioner, Pietermaritzburg. We would like to express our appreciation to Dr Tim Couzens, University of the Witwatersrand, for abstracting the contents of the above file for us.

12 *Umteteli wa Bantu*, 14 Aug. 1920; 'Negroes convention – Africa proclaimed a republic', *Diamond Fields' Advertiser*, 6 Sept. 1920; 'A black republic', *ibid.*, 8 Oct. 1920.

13 Cape Archives Depot, Cape Town, *Rex* v. *Israelites*, Queenstown, Oct.–Nov. 1921, quoted in part in Robert Russell Edgar, 'The fifth seal: Enoch Mgijima, the Israelites and the Bulhoek massacre, 1921', unpublished Ph.D. dissertation (University of California, Los Angeles 1977) p. 58. We are grateful to Dr Edgar for providing us with a copy of his transcription of the original letter.

14 *Imvo Zabantsundu*, 17 May 1921, quoted in Edgar, 'The fifth seal', p. 121.

15 Quoted in H. J. and R. E. Simons, *Class and Colour in South Africa, 1850–1950* (Harmondsworth 1969) p. 254.

16 SAGA, Interior Department, Reports on Bolshevism in South Africa, File 3/1064/182 Part 3, Confidential, Commissioner, South African Police, to the Secretary for Justice, Pretoria, 7 June 1923.

17 SAGA, NTS 1681, File 2/276. Town Clerk, Bloemfontein, to Secretary for Native Affairs, quoting report delivered by Superintendent of Locations to meeting of the Native Affairs Committee of the Town Council, 9 Nov. 1920.

18 Killie Campbell Africana Library, Unversity of Natal, J. S. Marwick Papers, Clements Kadalie to S. M. Bennett Ncwana, Zonnebloem College, Cape Town, 20 May 1920, no. 74, KCM 8315. For the text of the UNIA's *Constitution and Book of Laws*, see Robert A. Hill (ed.) *The Marcus Garvey and Universal Negro Improvement Association Papers*, vol. I (Berkeley 1983) pp. 256–77.

19 George Shepperson, 'External factors in the development of African nationalism with particular reference to British Central Africa', *Phylon*, **22**, Fall 1961, 195–6; 'Congress and ICU', *Umteteli wa Bantu*, 15 Nov. 1924; 'The story of Gilbert Coka', in Perham, *Ten Africans*, p. 295; *Cape Argus*, 29 Jan. 1923; *A Chief is a Chief by the People: The autobiography of Stimela Jason Jingoes*, John and Cassandra Perry (comps) (London 1975) p. 100; Rand *Daily Mail*, 5 May 1928, quoted in Helen Bradford, '"A taste of freedom": capitalist development and response to the ICU in the Transvaal countryside', in Belinda Bozzoli, (ed.) *Town and Countryside in the Transvaal* (Johannesburg 1983) p. 137; Clements Kadalie, *My Life and the ICU: The autobiography of a black trade unionist in South Africa*, edited, with an introduction, by Stanley Trapido (New York, 1970) p. 66. We would like to express our appreciation to B. M. Motau, Institute of African Studies, University of the Witwatersrand, for translation of the *Umteteli wa Bantu* article, and to Prof. Charles van Onselen, Director, for arranging it.

20 *Negro World*, 23 Oct. 1920.

21 *Ibid*. Ncwana shortly afterwards was invited by Kadalie to join the *ad hoc* negotiating committee of three to negotiate in the ICU's first face-to-face meeting with employers (Kadalie, *My Life*, p. 45, and Wickins, *Industrial and Commercial Workers' Union*, p. 34). The third member was J. G. Gumbs, West Indian Vice-President of the ICU and one of the leaders of the UNIA in Cape Town.

22 'UNIA attracting attention in South Africa', *Negro World*, **21**, Aug. 1920.

23 *Negro World*, 3 March 1921; 23 Oct. 1920; *Umteteli wa Bantu*, 30 July 1921; *Black Man*, Sept. 1920; H. L. Thumbran, 'A voice from South Africa', *Negro World*, 26 May 1923.

24 *The Black Problem* (Lovedale 1920) p. 17; Brian P. Willian, 'The South African Native Labour Contingent, 1916–18', *JAH* **XIX**, 1978, 83.

25 Walshe, *The Rise of African Nationalism*, p. 115; D. D. T. Jabavu, 'Native unrest in South Africa', *International Review of Missions*, **2**, April 1922, 249–59, and 'Unrest among South African natives', *Negro World*, 2 July 1921. James S. Thaele subsequently castigated the 'Me-too-boss' attitude of Professor Javabu of Fort Hare to under-railroad the other 'natives' by advising them in his infamous article, 'The native unrest', 'to continue worshipping at the shrine of Whiteaucracy.' ('The chicanery of Negrophobist publications', *Negro World*, 14 April 1923.)

26 'Poisoning the native mind', *Cape Argus*, 29 Jan. 1923. It seems probable that the 'educated native' referred to was S. M. Bennet Ncwana, who was also a Mpondo. In an interview with the representative of the *Cape Argus* in Namibia the previous September, it was stated: 'Ncwana, who edited the native paper called "The Black Man", has ability, and he is emphatic in his professions of being desirous to work in harmony with the authorities. "I have been a moving spirit", he said, "in the native movement, but never an agitator. I did adopt an aggressive policy in my paper and tried to start afresh on the lines of educating European opinion."' ('S. W. Natives organisation', reprinted in the *Windhoek Advertiser*, undated fragment.) Ncwana informed Prime Minister Smuts that he had also presented the CID in Cape Town with a memo warning against the 'Africa for the Africans' movement. 'Through the organ with which I have been connected for the last two and a half years "The Black Man"', Ncwana wrote, 'I propose to antagonise this movement in the Sub Continent and to enlighten our people on the danger of supporting foreign movements.' At the time he was interviewed by Acting Prime Minister Malan, Ncwana declared: 'I am continuing the publishing of "The Black Man" with the headquarters at Kimberley and here I will make it my business to work in harmony with the local authorities.' What he asked for was 'the sympathy of the government' in the form of financial support (SAGA, NTS 1681, File 2/276.) The first indication that we have found of Ncwana's defection from the Garvey ranks was a letter published in the United States in the *Crusader* (Jan.–Feb. 1922), the official organ of the African Blood Brotherhood, which was one of the chief antagonists of the Garvey movement at the time.

27 SAGA, Office of the Governor-General, File 50/1026. Timothy L. Robertson, President of the UNIA Parow Division, declared in 1920: 'Some of our brethren think that this movement is being confined to the bushes. It is not true; we must first lay a foundation before we can begin to build.' (*Negro World*, 23 Oct. 1920.)

28 National Archives of Zimbabwe, Office of the High Commissioner, File A 3/18/11.

29 *The African World*, 10 Oct. 1925.

30 South-West African Government Archives, File A.68/1, W. Evans to Divisional Officer, Criminal Investigation, 30 July 1922; Trial of Bennet Ncwana, 1 Aug. 1922; File A 312, vol. 20, no. 77, H.G.R., Administrator (Windhoek) to J. C. Smuts, 18 June 1923. There were two UNIA divisions in operation at Windhoek and Luderitz respectively, with rural branches established at Swakopmund, Usakos, Karibib, Okahandja, Rehoboth and Maltahohe.

31 National Archives and Records Service, Washington, DC, Record Group 204, File 42–793. Replies from the United States Pardon Attorney were dated 21 July 1925 and 11 Jan. 1926.

32 SAGA, Native Affairs, File 128/214, The Afro-Athlican Constructive Gaathly; Emory University Library, Atlanta, Papers of Daniel W. Alexander and the African Orthodox Church of South Africa, Minutes of the Preliminary Meeting held for the purpose of forming the African Orthodox Church, Beaconsfield, 6 Oct. 1924; Bengt Sundkler, *Bantu*

Prophets in South Africa, 2nd. edn. (London 1961) pp. 58, 278; Richard Newman, 'Archbishop Daniel William Alexander and the African Orthodox Church', *International Journal of African Historical Studies*, 16, 1983, 615–30, and Introduction to *The Negro Churchman* (official organ of the African Orthodox Church) (Kraus Reprint, Millwood, NY 1976). For Rev. McGuire's sermon, see Randall K. Burkett (ed.) *Black Redemption: Churchmen speak for the Garvey movement* (Philadelphia 1978) pp. 157–80.

33 Jabavu, 'Native unrest in South Africa', pp. 249–59; *Negro World*, 23 Aug. 1924.

34 SAGA, Office of the Governor-General, File 36/171, Immigration; NTS 1681, File 2/276; Transvaal Archives Depot, Pretoria, Justice, File 269, no. 3/1064/18.

35 SAGA, Interior Department, File 168/74B, Under-secretary for the Interior to the Principal Immigration Officer, Pretoria, 23 April 1920 (no. 1/168)74); Office of the Governor-General, File 50/1064, Secretary of the High Commissioner for the Union of South Africa, London, to the Secretary for the Interior, Pretoria, 9 July 1923 (no. 26/168/74). After meeting with the members of the South African 'Native Deputation', British Prime Minister Lloyd George wrote to inform J. C. Smuts: 'It is clear the dark age of Africa is commencing to pass away. The negro population is beginning to stir into conscious life. It has developed many leaders of force and ability as you will realise if you have followed recent movements among the negroes of America. The negro-question, therefore, is one which affects us all, for what is done in South Africa immediately reacts outside, and what happens outside similarly has its effect in South Africa.' (Public Record Office (hereafter PRO), Kew, Surrey, Colonial Office (hereafter CO) 537/1197, 3 March 1920, no. 1486). In an earlier letter (7 Jan. 1920), Lloyd George had enclosed for Smuts a clipping of Garvey's speech at Madison Square Garden that appeared in *The Times*, 7 Jan. 1920. We are specially grateful to Dr Brian Willan for bringing these records to our attention.

36 SAGA, Interior Department, File 168/74B (no. 12/168/74).

37 'A.M.E. Church and Negro movement', *Black Man* (Oct. 1920); cf. Walshe, *The Rise of African Nationalism*, p. 163; see n. 17 above.

38 PRO, CO 537/1046, Arthur Frederick, Governor-General, to Duke of Devonshire, CO, London, 8 June 1923; YMCA Historical Library, John Mott Papers, Oswin Bull to John Mott, 18 Feb. 1921, Box 67.

39 SAGA, Interior Department, Reports on Bolshevism in South Africa, vol. 289, Confidential Cabinet 33, no. 3/1064/18 Part 2, 21 Feb. 1921. Cf. Gilbert Matshoba to Enoch Mgijima, 15 Oct. 1920: 'A certain man hailing from America has arrived. He is in Johannesburg. Now this black man who had recently arrived does not advocate the cause of the black people. He is on the side of the Europeans. It appears that our nations to-day are altogether at a loss. I even sent a word to the President of the Congress that liberty will not come from America.' (Cape Archives Depot, *Rex* v. *Israelites*.)

40 Quoted in C. S. Smith, 'The Pan-African Congress', *New York Age*, 18 June 1921, reprinted in *Umteteli wa Bantu*, 30 July 1921. Smith also remarked: 'Sunday, June 5, 1921, I had the pleasure of listening to an illuminating and exceedingly interesting address by Rev. M. Q. Cele, a

Zulu from Natal, South Africa, who had been educated at Hampton Institute, in which he stressed the conviction that Garvey's African Empire and Dr Du Bois's Pan-African Congress are not only impracticable, but calculated to work to the detriment of the Natives in South Africa.'

41 Quoted in Rich, 'Black peasants', p. 132.

42 SAGA, Interior Department, File 168/74B, Secretary of Justice to the Secretary of the Interior, 18 Oct. 1920 (no. 7/168/74). The Pentecostal Holiness Church was the result of a merger in 1911 of the Fire-Baptized Holiness Church of Georgia and the uplands areas of the Carolinas, and the Holiness Church of North Carolina (Vinson Synan, *The Holiness-Pentecostal Movement in the United States* (Grand Rapids, Michigan, 1971) *passim*). For a graphic account of Rev. Spooner and the Rustenburg mission station, see Naboth Mokgatle, *The Autobiography of An Unknown African* (Berkeley 1971). Compare Naboth Mokgatle to Robert A. Hill, personal communication, Jan. 1978: 'Marcus Garvey inspired me greatly in his time in my youth in South Africa, in the thirties (30s). I became a member of a group, we called ourselves the Garveyites and I was one of the sellers of his magazine "The Blackman".'

43 *African World*, 30 July 1921.

44 D. D. T. Jabavu, 'Dr J. E. Kwegyir Aggrey in South Africa', *Imvo Zabantsundu*, 14 June 1921; see also Kenneth King, 'James E. K. Aggrey: collaborator, nationalist, Pan-Africanist', *Canadian Journal of African Studies*, 3, 1970, 511–30. Addressing an audience in Aliwal North on the subject of 'The black man's place in South Africa', in which he dealt with 'the various shades of Native African thoughts', Jabavu was reported to have discussed the respective merits of Booker T. Washington, Marcus Garvey, and W. E. B. Du Bois, but according to the report, 'Marcus Garvey, the negro Bolshevist was . . . dismissed in a sentence or two as a wild impracticable extremist. His claims to unite the African people in an aggressive policy were both absurd and impracticable and would bring no good but only loss to the world. Not by fighting but by education would the African win redemption.' ('A Lecture Tour', *Imvo Zabantsundu*, 9 Jan. 1923.) Compare James S. Thaele: 'Mr Jabavu has (unfortunately) received his education in England, not in America, where in the words of De Waal, Boer administrator of the Cape education, "natives come back with dangerous ideas".' ('The chicanery of Negrophobist publications', *Negro World*, 14 April 1923)

45 *Umteteli wa Bantu*, 30 July 1921.

46 *Imvo Zabantsundu*, 23 Oct. 1928; Edwin W. Smith, *Aggrey of South Africa: A study in black and white* (London 1929) pp. 180–1.

47 *African World*, 28 May 1921; 'CPN Congress', *Queenstown Free Press*, 12 July 1921; *Imvo Zabantsundu*, 23 Oct. 1928; Louis R. Harlan, 'Booker T. Washington and the white man's burden', *American Historical Review*, LXXI, Jan. 1966, 449; Walshe, *The Rise of African Nationalism*, pp. 3, 38; SAGA, NTS 1681, File 2/276, M. M. Manoedi to Rt Hon. Winston Spencer Churchill, Secretary of State for the Colonies, 30 Sept. 1922.

48 'Dr Aggrey's closing address at Lovedale', *Christian Express*, 1 June 1921; *ibid.*, 2 May 1921; see also 'The Anglo-Saxon and justice', *African World*, Supplement, 30 July 1922; *Church Chronicle*, 26 Jan. 1922. In his earlier

address at Lovedale, Aggrey was reported to have inveighed: 'There has never been a war between America and the English people. Get your history right. It was between America and German kings – the Georges.' (*Christian Express*, 2 May 1921.)

49 *Cape Argus*, 29 Jan. 1923. The formal announcement of Garvey's projected tour, which never materialised, was published in the *Negro World*, 23 Jan. 1923.

50 SAGA, Interior Department, File 3/1064/182 Part 3, Reports on Bolshevism in South Africa, 7 June 1923. It was reported that a letter from the ICU was read at the meeting of the Transvaal Coloured Labour Union 'inviting affiliation'.

51 SAGA, Office of the Governor-General, File 50/1036, J. C. Smuts, Minute No. 129, 28 Feb. 1923. The UNIA divisions on the Rand were New Clare, Sophiatown, Evaton, Pretoria and Waterpan. Compare J. D. Ngubane to the *Negro World*, 2 Aug. 1924; 'I am not well educated, but I can read and write a little. I am a worker here in Johannesburg. I've read newspapers of both black and white since I started to work, but I was not interested in either of them, till 1922, when for the first time I set my eyes on *The Negro World*.'

52 SAGA, Office of the Governor-General, File 50/1052, R. Rankine, Acting Governor of Nyasaland, to Governor-General and High Commissioner, Cape Town, 15 May 1923; Acting Secretary for Native Affairs to Minister of Native Affairs, 2 June 1923; File 50/1064, 6 June 1923 (no. 20/168/74); Under-secretary for the Interior to the Commissioner of Police, Confidential, 13 June 1923.

53 SAGA, NTS 1681, File 2/276. Referring to the UNIA, Boyes declared: 'A Black Republic and Socialism appear to be the bedrock of this Association'.

54 *South African Outlook*, 1 March 1922, p. 51.

55 *Report of the Native Affairs Department for the Years 1919 to 1921* (UG 34–1922) p. 1.

56 Gail M. Gerhart and Thomas Karis, *Political Profiles, 1882–1964* (Stanford 1977) pp 154–5; Walshe, *The Rise of African Nationalism*, p. 166; 'The African land settlement,' *APO*, 8 April 1922, and Wickins, *Industrial and Commercial Workers' Union*, p. 66; Josephus Coan, 'The expansion of missions and the African Methodist Episcopal Church in South Africa, 1896–1908', unpublished Ph.D. dissertation (Hartford Seminary Foundation 1961), cited in Rich, 'Black peasants', p. 138, fn. 33. According to Helen Bradford, the idea of land schemes was also popular among ICU branches in the Eastern Transvaal countryside in the period 1926–28 '"A taste of freedom"', p. 141.) Compare 'Congress and ICU', *Umteteli wa Bantu*, 15 Nov. 1924: 'It is time we know exactly what our standpoint is as a nation. If the ICU is under congress, we must know how they are affiliated and what the conditions are. And I would also like to know, if the two organizations are one thing, why is it that the ICU and Congress have got separate offices? I would also like to know if Mr Clements Kadalie is working at his office at Fox Street with the [Steering] Committee which is alleged to have been chosen by Congress.'

57 'Non-Cooperation', *Umteteli wa Bantu*, 18 Oct. 1924; Walshe, *The Rise of African Nationalism*, p. 225; SAGA, Interior Department, File 3/1064/18,

Part 3, Reports on Bolshevism in South Africa, 5 Feb. 1926; Simons and Simons, *Class and Colour*, p. 260; 'Successful meeting of Cape Town Div., UNIA & ACL', *Negro World*, 4 Nov. 1922.

58 'Garvey and Garveyism', *African Voice*, 22 Sept. 1923, reprinted *Negro World*, 17 Nov. 1923; Wickins, *Industrial and Commercial Workers' Union*, p. 67. Toward the end of 1921, a split in the ICU occurred – Ncwana split from Kadalie and joined Impey Ben Nyombol and the rival ICWU (Wickins, *Industrial and Commercial Workers' Union* pp. 66); thereafter, Ncwana's *Black Man* became the organ of the ICWU, though shortly afterwards it was superseded by the *African Voice*. Thaele was a member of the ICU executive (*Umteteli wa Bantu*, 18 Oct. 1924).

59 *Umteteli wa Bantu*, 18 Oct. 1924.

60 Walshe, *The Rise of African Nationalism*, p. 166; *Abantu Batho*, 27 Jan. 1921, referred to in SAGA, Justice Department, vol. 289, Bolshevism in the Union of South Africa, 21 Feb. 1921 (No. 3/1064/18); 'Back to Africa movement', *Abantu Batho*, 11 Nov. 1920; PRO, CO 537/11046, Arthur Frederick, Governor-General, to Duke of Devonshire, CO, 8 June 1923. The Deputy Commissioner, CID, wrote on 12 July 1922 to inform the Secretary for Native Affairs that while he did not think that Garvey's *Negro World* had 'any appreciable circulation among the native people in South Africa', nevertheless, 'There is no question, however, but that the doctrine enunciated by the paper is re-echoed in the South African Native press and there is little doubt that its importation into the Union is mischievous.' (SAGA, NTS 1681, File 2/276.)

61 *Negro World*, 12 Sept. 1925; Walshe, *The Rise of African Nationalism*, pp. 166, 180–3; *Cape Times*, 8 Feb. 1930; Tom Lodge, *Black Politics in South Africa since 1945* (London 1983) p. 8. We are indebted to Prof. Mazisi Kunene, Department of Linguistics, University of California, Los Angeles, for providing the English translation.

62 *Negro World*, 10 Oct. 1925. The *African World* was described as 'our young esteemed contemporary of Cape Town, South Africa' (*Negro World*, 8 Aug. 1925.)

63 'What history to read: a lesson to "Ilanga Lase" Natal', *African World*, 2 Sept. 1925; 'Non-co-operation', *Umteteli wa Bantu*, 11 Oct. 1924; *Rand Daily Mail*, 7 Oct. 1924.

64 SAGA, Interior Department, Reports on Bolshevism in South Africa, File 3/1064/18 Part 3, 25 April 1925; 'The Garvey day,' *African World*, 13 June 1925.

65 'A call by Rev. Z. R. Mahabane, President-General of African Congress', *African World*, 5 Dec. 1925; Walshe, *The Rise of African Nationalism*, p. 99.

66 'Ringing message to Negro: boy and suspicious literature, native detained in Benoni', *Rand Daily Mail*, 30 April 1926. Moses Mphahlele, District Branch Secretary of the Transvaal African Congress, had earlier had selections published from his book of poems, *The Dark Musician of the Northern Transvaal*, in John E. Bruce's weekly column in the *Negro World* (29 April 1922); at this time Mphahlele was working as an interpreter on the staff of the Pietersburg Native Commissioner (for biographical information, see T. D. Mweli Skota, *The African Yearly Register* (Johannesburg 1930).

67 *Negro World*, 25 Oct. 1925. Joseph Masogha confirmed the paper's popularity on the Rand: 'The Negro World does not sell well in Kimberley. Native African mine workers in Johannesburg buy the Negro World, but Kimberley mine workers are practically prisoners.' (*Negro World*, 14 Aug. 1926.)

68 *Negro World*, 22 Aug. 1925. Evaton township near Vereeniging was the site of the AME's Wilberforce Industrial Institute; after it was relocated there from the Northern Transvaal in 1908, it was, according to Rich, to play 'an important part in the growth of African political consciousness in the following forty years' (Rich, 'Black peasants' p. 134; see also Heather Hughes, 'Black mission in South Africa', BA (Hons.) thesis (University of the Witwatersrand 1976).

69 Walshe, *The Rise of African Nationalism*, pp. 111–13; Richard Haines, 'The opposition to General Hertzog's Segregation Bills: 1929–1934', pp. 149–82, in *Conference on the History of Opposition in Southern Africa*, Bradford, '"A taste of freedom"'; Peter Wickins, 'The Industrial and Commercial Workers' Union', Ph.D. thesis (University of Cape Town 1973) chapter dealing with the ICU in Natal.

70 Reprinted in the *Negro World*, 7 Aug. 1926. A full-page advertisement of Garvey's *Philosophy and Opinions* appeared in the ICU's *Workers' Herald*, 22 March 1926. In Johannesburg, the books were distributed through Jack Barnard's Bookshop (*Workers' Herald*, 15 Dec. 1927.)

71 Gwendolen M. Carter and Thomas Karis, Microfilm Collection of South African Political Materials, Melville J. Herskovits Africana Collection, Northwestern University Library, Evanston, Illinois, Item 13b.

72 National Archives of Zimbabwe, File S1542 M8c, Missions, African Orthodox Church, 1927–36, South African Police Commissioner, Pretoria, to the Superintendent CI Department, British South Africa Police, Bulawayo, Confidential, 22 Aug. 1929; 'CPN Congress', *Queenstown Free Press*, 12 July 1921.

73 *South African Worker*, 31 Dec. 1929; *Abantu Batho*, 1 and 15 May 1930, quoted in Walshe, *The Rise of African Nationalism*, p. 168.

74 Interview by Robert Edgar with Edwin Mofutsanyana, Roma, Lesotho, July 1981; see also Mofutsanyana, 'South Africa', *Negro World*, 3 June 1933. We are grateful to Dr Robert Edgar for granting us permission to quote from this interview.

75 *The Negro Worker*, 1, April–May 1931, 11; see also n. 19, *A Chief is a Chief*, p. 103.

76 *Johannesburg Star*, 23 Nov. 1928. After reading the reprint of the article in the *Negro World* (26 Jan. 1929), Dr Theodore M. Kakaza, South African-born President of the Buffalo division of the UNIA in the United States, wrote a series of lengthy articles entitled, 'A cry to the native South African tribes', which appeared in the *Negro World*, 11, 18, 25 June, 9 and 16 July 1929. Dr Kakaza, who was from the Eastern Cape, was a member of the group of South African students who entered Wilberforce University in the United States in 1894–96.

77 Walshe, *The Rise of African Nationalism*, pp. 220–22, 254; Bradford, '"A taste of freedom"', p. 145; Lodge, *Black Politics*, p. 9; 'Garveyism', *Imvo Zabantsundu*, 12 Feb. 1929. Garvey's letter of invitation to the Rev. C.

Nyombolo of Burghersdorp, Cape Province, was published in *Imvo Zabantsundu*, 5 Feb. 1929. A similar letter of invitation was sent, on 15 Oct. 1928, to one 'Mobraw', described as 'an ex-secretary, S.A. National Congress' (SAGA, File J 269, League Against Imperialism, Commissioner of Police to the Secretary of Justice, 15 Jan. 1929 (No. 3/1064/18)). R. V. Selope-Thema of the ANC was elected to attend the UNIA conclave in Jamaica, but no funds were available for his expenses (SAGA, NTS 1681, File 2/276, Deputy Commissioner, Witwatersrand CID, *c*. 10 July 1929, concerning delegates to the Sixth Convention of Negro Peoples).

78 Robert Edgar, 'Dr Wellington and the American Movement in South Africa, 1920–1940', unpublished seminar paper, Colloquium on Pan-African Biography (African Studies Center, University of California, Los Angeles, May 1982).

79 'Worthless Degrees', *Unteteli wa Bantu*, 16 August 1924; SAGA, Justice Department, file 26/327, Thaele to Superintendent of Native Affairs, 15 August 1924. We are grateful to Dr Robert Edgar for providing us with the reference to Thaele's letter.

80 Rev. J. G. Locke, 'The Wellington movement', *Imvo Zabantsundu*, 20 Nov. 1928.

81 W. Beinart, *The Political Economy of Pondoland, 1860–1930* (Cambridge 1982), p. 158. The quotation is from Locke, 'The Wellington movement'.

82 SAGA, NTS 1681, file 2/276, E. W. Baxter, Solicitor–General, to the Secretary of the Treasury, 25 January 1929; Secretary for Native Affairs to Secretary for Finance, 19 March 1929; Bradford, op. cit., p. 133.

83 *Imvo Zabantsundu*, 3 June, 1939.

84 SAGA, NTS 1681, file 2/276.

85 Gerhard, *Black Power in South Africa*, chapter 3, 'Lembede and the ANC Youth League, 1943–9', pp. 45–83; also Karis and Carter, *From Protest to Challenge*, vol. 2, pp. 98–106.

CHAPTER EIGHT

Land and liberation: popular rural protest and the national liberation movements in South Africa, 1920–1960 *

Colin Bundy

Introduction

The starting-point of this essay was an attempt to reconstruct and to understand certain features of the rural struggle in the Transkei during the late 1940s and 1950s. The salient elements of the episode (discussed more fully on pp. 266–75 below) may be very briefly summarised. From 1945 onwards, the South African state sought to restructure aspects of life in the 'reserves' and 'played an increasingly interventionist role in the countryside' for some twenty years.[1] Policies of 'reclamation', 'rehabilitation', stock-culling and resettlement attempted to increase food production and to regulate labour migrancy; the introduction of Bantu (Tribal) Authorities aimed at Balkanisation along ethnic lines (in opposition to nationalist movements and loyalties) and the exercise of more effective political control in rural areas. Throughout South Africa these efforts affected the lives of reserve-dwellers and – at different times and places – provoked unrest and resistance. Lodge has characterised the period 1945–65 as having witnessed 'a succession of bitter localised conflicts between peasants and authority in the African reserves of South Africa', and he locates individual instances of rural revolt 'in the context of a generalised background of unrest which affected almost all African rural communities'.[2]

Resistance movements in the Transkei, between 1945 and about 1958 – before, that is, the larger-scale 'peasants revolt' in Pondoland of 1960

---

* An earlier version of this chapter was published in *The Review of African Political Economy*, No. 29, 1984.

and the 'Thembu revolt' of 1962–63[3] – displayed many of the characteristics of rural protest anywhere. They were small-scale, sporadic and
dispersed incidents of social action; they were frequently limited in
their resources and organisation and could be contained or crushed
with relative ease by the state. Local and particularist 'traditional' or
'inherent' ideological currents flowed with – and sometimes flowed
against – broader, more 'structured' or 'derived' beliefs and aims.[4] The
struggles in the Transkei were not, of course, waged by 'pure' peasant
movements: there was a significant interplay between rural grievances
shaping local resistance and the efforts of political organisations
centred elsewhere to articulate, link and broaden these struggles. Indeed, in the late 1940s there was a considerable measure of competition
between the African National Congress (ANC) and the All African
Convention (AAC) in reaching and directing rurally based movements
in the Transkei. The ANC, the oldest nationalist movement in South
Africa, had never – since its formation in 1912 – established an effective
presence in the Transkei; in the 1940s, however, it began more
persuasively than before to mobilise certain groups and individuals.
Much of the new impetus came from the efforts of the energetic
political organiser, Govan Mbeki. Through his links with the national
leadership of the ANC the task of organising resistance in the Transkei
was at least placed on the agenda of the Congress. Mbeki's main
organisational base, the Transkeian Organised Bodies (TOB), swung
away from the ANC and affiliated instead to the AAC.

The AAC was a constituent body of the Non-European Unity
Movement (NEUM). The NEUM was a numerically unimpressive
wing of the movement for national liberation; it was then and has
subsequently usually been characterised as Trotskyist; it was bitterly
critical of the Communist Party of South Africa (CPSA): and it dis-
puted with the ANC that body's claim to be *the* African national
party. The NEUM's theoretical claims to being a nation-wide
movement were considerably more developed than its actual
organisational strength, which was largely located in the urban
Western Cape. It effectively failed to survive its opposition to the 1952
Defiance Campaign, and as the Congress Alliance gained in
membership during the 1950s *in pari passu* did the NEUM lose ground
and credibility. In 1958 an already depleted movement spent much
passion and energy on an internal feud that split its ranks into a
number of warring camps.[5]

Nevertheless, between 1945 and 1958 the AAC/NEUM not only
identified the African reserves as areas of potential revolutionary

activity, but also acted on this premise, establishing political links with a number of disparate and localised rural movements. A relatively small number of AAC activists enjoyed a striking degree of success in joining, strengthening and even leading local popular movements. Both in its theoretical stand and in its practical involvement in the rural struggle the NEUM/AAC stood apart from other nationalist and revolutionary movements, until in the 1950s an awareness of and commitment to a rurally based struggle manifested itself more broadly in the national liberation movements.

As indicated, the research on which this essay is based was initially concerned almost exclusively with the details of the popular resistance in the Transkei, with the involvement of the AAC and ANC, and with the interplay between local and national political movements then and there. Gradually, then insistently, a number of other questions imposed themselves on the original more limited framework of enquiry. Why did the AAC decide to work within the peasantry? What barriers – social, organisational and ideological – operated to preclude or delay similar decisions within other nationally organised political movements? Is it realistic to ask whether other movements *might* have accorded a higher political importance to rural mobilisation than they did; and, if so, with what possible consequences? To what extent does the history of struggle in South Africa's rural areas suggest that with political alliances or leadership from other social groupings peasant grievances and 'primitive rebellions' might have played a weightier role than they did in the struggle against domination and exploitation? Equally, what structural constraints inhibited or blocked successful linkage between the leadership of nationally organised movements (whether revolutionary or reformist) and the parochial rural social movements?

It is in pursuit of tentative answers to these questions that this chapter has taken shape. Although it depicts in some detail the Transkeian resistance which instigated the enquiry, it also makes some preliminary sketches on a broader canvas. It surveys the entire period from the 1920s to the 1960s, indicating on the one hand what was actually happening in the South African countryside and also examining, on the other hand, the responses (or lack of response) to those events by political organisations. It asks how the nationally organised movements viewed rural issues over a period of more than forty years; what attention they devoted to rural mobilisation; and how those perceptions and efforts altered over time. Implicit in the approach here is the premise – which William Beinart and I have argued more fully elsewhere[6] – that the extent and potential significance of rural struggle in the period has not been fully recognised. This is due in part to the obvious problems of evidence and the difficulties in the historical reconstruction of small-scale, short-lived and unsuccessful instances of rural class conflict; but it is also a reflection of the relatively low priority given to rural issues (until the 1950s: see pp. 275–8 below) by most of the nationally organised political bodies. These were pre-dominantly urban in geographical location and social composition; their ideological momentum tended to come from what Rudé calls 'structured' or 'derived' beliefs – whether nationalist-democratic or socialist revolutionary – which were universalist, 'modernising' and sought full entry into the wider South African society. This meant that the movements could be insensitive at times to rural grievances, or even hostile to what they saw as 'backward' or 'tribal' peasant protests.

Viewing the period 1920 to the 1960s as a whole, it is suggested that (given a society which saw wars of conquest and territorial dispos-session in the nineteenth century, given the Land Acts of 1913 and 1936 and given the different forms of expropriation and exploitation historically visited upon peasants, labour tenants, farm-workers and migrant workers) the agrarian question has not been accorded the practical or theoretical attention one might have anticipated.

The agrarian question in theory and practice, 1920–1945

There are two reasons for commencing this survey in the 1920s. In that decade the first attempts were made to theorise the nature of class struggle in the South African countryside and, secondly, there existed during the latter half of the decade a state of generalised class conflict and resistance in the South African countryside – a phenomenon that has recently attracted scholarly attention. This conflict, and the politi-cal forms it took, was in several senses analogous to the wave of urban protest of 1918–24. Between about 1926 and 1930 there was not only an increased level of resistance among farm-workers, labour tenants, reserve peasants and peasant migrants, but also a search for new and appropriate forms of resistance. The reasons for this heightened con-flict are complex, but they appear to include the following: acute and explicit pressures on labour tenants and squatter-peasants; dislike of the 1925 legislation which (for Natal and the Cape) raised taxation; alarm generated by Hertzog's 'Native Bills' of 1926; economic privations due to drought and rising consumer prices; and possibly a relocation of radicalism from urban into rural areas consequent upon the entrenchment by 1924 of a conservative petty-bourgeois leadership in African urban areas.[7]

The ICU and the countryside

The late 1920s saw the Industrial and Commercial Workers' Union (ICU), the ANC and the CPSA increase their involvement in rural areas; the CPSA and ANC adopted policies denoting a considerable shift to the left. The first organisation to expand its membership and to dramatise rural grievances in the 1920s was the ICU. In 1925, twenty of its twenty-seven branches were in the Cape Province. Even then, the ICU was not exclusively urban; small town Eastern Cape branches had a strong, even predominantly, agricultural membership, but its activities were very largely confined to the cities and larger towns. In evidence to a 1925 Commission, the ICU stated that most of its members were 'drawn from urban and detribalised natives and also from the coloured workers'.[8] But by mid-1927, the composition and orientation of the movement had been transformed. The major element in the massive growth of the ICU in Natal, the Orange Free State and the Transvaal was new rural support. Of about 100 branches, fully two-thirds were in small towns.

Natal was the area of the most dynamic growth – and the reasons are clear. In northern Natal and the midlands the extension of capitalist agriculture (especially with the wattle and sheep booms) meant that 'rural relationships were now radically restructured for the first time'.[9] Crucially, acute pressures were applied to squatters and labour tenants in the form of mass evictions, prosecutions for dipping and rent arrears, tougher tenancy terms and maltreatment. One way in which resistance from those thus affected expressed itself was in the mushrooming sales of the ICU's red tickets. A young Zulu teaching in Vryheid left a graphic account of an ICU recruiting meeting there. Rumours of deliverance and the stir of discontent fused to bring a vast crowd of would-be members; veterans of the Zulu War, young and old men from the farms, middle-aged men from the mines, workers from the town – 'all marching, column upon column, towards the venue of assembly'. Speeches were made and membership cards issued ('I wrote till my arm ached') – 'And those people flocked to the ICU as to the ark which would convey them to safety.'[10]

Although at one point Wickins asserts that the ICU 'became a rural protest movement' and elsewhere that the 'movement became a peasants' revolt' neither he nor Sheridan Johns gives any indication of precisely how rural membership grew so fast.[11] Did ICU leaders, nationally or locally, identify farm-workers or labour tenants as the targets for a membership drive? Or did the demand for membership stem from disaffected rural dwellers, who as it were 'called in' the ICU, already the most visible and potentially the most potent organ of the subordinate classes? Henry Slater has suggested that in Natal the ICU served as 'a channel for existing discontent which had already produced unrest and thrown up its own local institutionalised forms. The ICU can be seen as capturing what was already something approaching a popular movement.'[12] It was definitely among labour tenants and farm-workers that the movement gained most support – and analysis of those ICU recruiting speeches that have survived does not support Ballinger's sneer that 'farms were promised to all and sundry' for 3d. a week. Rather, as Helen Bradford has argued,

> an important ideological element in the ICU's discourse was a nationalist agrarian element . . . present in its radical form only in the initial stages. This element represented the lived relations of the African peasantry in the transition to capitalism in the countryside . . ., through the articulation of grievances concerning land, concerning the oppressive nature of the state and farmers in the countryside and through promises that land and national autonomy would be restored.[13]

In the Transvaal and Orange Free State too, ICU activists held mass meetings, set up new branches, distributed literature and sought redress over specific grievances.[14]

In addition to the struggle of farm-workers and labour tenants, the 1920s also witnessed unrest and a rash of localised peasant movements in the reserve areas. In the Transvaal, a number of chiefs joined the ICU, bringing their followers with them; but in Zululand, the Transkei and Ciskei, and the Northern Transvaal reserves the ICU's gains were limited, piecemeal and unsustained. The ICU did not – indeed probably could not – become an effective vehicle of reserve peasant discontent. At the union's special conference of December 1927, the Eastern Cape delegate Theo Lujiza insisted that the land question was crucial to the future of the ICU, and he called for something to be done. Nothing constructive was. Kadalie's hubristic scheme for mass land purchases was only one of the casualties of the next two years, as the ICU fell apart at the seams.

The CPSA, the Native Republic and the agrarian question

The rural tensions and developments described above formed part of the background against which the CPSA arrived at its 'Native

Republic' policy in 1928. The party adopted the slogan of 'An independent South African Native Republic as a stage towards the Workers and Peasants Republic, guaranteeing protection and complete equality to all national minorities'. The debates which led to this new departure have been extensively reviewed elsewhere[15] and will be summarised very baldly here – except that the analysis here emphasises a feature largely overlooked in the existing literature: how the national and agrarian questions intersected, the major role envisaged for the peasantry and the emphasis placed on rural mobilisation.

The sources of the new policy were twofold: on the one hand, they stemmed from local experience in the 1920s and the growth in the black membership of the CPSA; on the other hand, they were a local reflection of changing policy within the Communist International movement. To take the first of these: by 1928, of a total party membership of 1,750 about 1,600 were African members. They came (Eddie Roux told the Comintern Congress) 'largely from the smaller semi-rural locations'. The 1928 Comintern Congress was that at which the relationship between Communist Parties and nationalist/anti-imperialist movements was reviewed for the first time since the adoption of the Lenin/Roy theses in 1920.

In 1920, Lenin had urged communists to seek close alliances with national and colonial movements engaged in struggles against imperialism; whether the alliance would be proletarian/communist or bourgeois/democratic would be determined by objective conditions in the country concerned. In backward countries, communists must be prepared to aid bourgeois–democratic liberation movements, and especially to support the peasantry against large landholders and 'all relics of feudalism'. Roy distinguished sharply between bourgeois – democratic nationalist movements (led by the national bourgeoisie or petty bourgeoisie) and 'struggles of landless peasants against every form of exploitation', and insisted that the communist movement must support the latter rather than the former. Lenin's theses became the accepted basis of theory; Roy's supplementary theses were largely forgotten. The ambiguity in Lenin's theses – that the allies of today were the class enemies of tomorrow – remains an ineluctable dilemma for theorists of a revolution in stages.

At the 1928 Congress the desirability of alliances with anti-imperialist movements was urged even more emphatically; and the logic of this position was extended to the South African case. In its resolution on 'The South African question', the Executive Committee of the Comintern stressed that South Africa was a society of 'a colonial type'; that this meant that the crucial forms of expropriation were those affecting 'the Negro population'; that it was a 'correct principle' that South Africa 'belongs to the native population'; and that therefore the CPSA's main task was to 'influence the embryonic and crystallising national movements among the natives in order to develop these movements into *national agrarian revolutionary movements*' (emphasis added). This call for agrarian revolution is buttressed elsewhere in the same resolution:

> The bulk of the South African population is the black peasantry, whose land has been expropriated by the white minority. Seven-eighths of the land is owned by whites. Hence the national question in South Africa, which is based on the agrarian question lies at the foundation of the revolution in South Africa. The black peasantry constitutes the basic moving force of the revolution in alliance with and under the leadership of the working class.[16]

Similarly, the Executive Committee called on the CPSA to

> work out concrete partial demands which indicate that the basic question in the agrarian situation in South Africa is the land hunger of the blacks and that their interest is of prior importance in the solution of the agrarian question. Efforts should be made immediately to develop plans to organise the native peasants into peasant unions, while attention to the poor agrarian whites must in no way be minimised.[17]

After the Moscow Congress, the CPSA was thus committed to participation in embryonic nationalist movements like the ANC and to its new objective of a 'Native Republic'. At the same time (as the quotations above have indicated) the party was also adjured to a wholly new policy on agrarian issues. The party newspaper heralded the new direction in an editorial calling for 'the mobilisation of the agrarian masses, who constitute the great bulk and potentially, owing to land hunger, perhaps the most revolutionary section of the oppressed race'.[18] In 1930, a directive from the Executive Committee of the Comintern spelled out exactly what the new policy called for, in practical terms. The proletariat must organise the peasantry and agricultural workers; in 'white areas' the party must 'immediately organise the poor peasants, sharecroppers, [and] labour tenants and establish separate Trade Unions for farm workers'. All organisations thus created were 'to be based on the immediate demands of the respective sections of the population in the various districts'. The CPSA should form organisations in the Transkei and see to it that landless peasants played a leading role; their need to migrate for wages should be used as a way of extending activities among mine-workers.[19] The party's responses to these policy changes and directives was to undertake more work than previously in the rural areas – but still not very much. It established links with the League of the Poor in Lesotho; it launched the League of African Rights in some rural areas as well as in the cities; it supported the left wing of the ANC in the Western Cape (see below); and Bunting ran for Parliament in 1929 in the Transkei seat of Tembuland. Yet a number of mutually reinforcing tendencies blunted or deflected the CPSA's involvement in rural areas immediately following the adoption of the 'Native Republic' policy. The party's founders had accepted unconditionally the proletariat as the only revolutionary class; most industrial workers in the 1920s and the overwhelming majority of urban trade unionists were white; and many CPSA members found it difficult or impossible to accept the 'Native Republic' policy – which they considered overemphasised racial matters at the expense of class-based analysis and action. The tenets of orthodox Marxism, the involvement of leading members of the party in trade union work, and their prior conviction that the white working class had to be 'won over' all combined to emphasise the centrality of urban areas in the class struggle, and to rule out any re- examination of this assumption.

It thus seems doubtful that, even in more favourable circumstances, the CPSA would have moved more effectively into rural organisations during the 1930s. In the event, the party hove to at the end of 1930 on a left-wing tack at the direct behest of the Comintern. The 'Bolshevisation' of the party – with its concomitant dogmatising, wrangling, resignations and explusions – may have left it ideologically purer, but certainly rendered it immeasurably weakened as a potential radicaliser of a national liberation movement. Estimates of its total membership by 1935 vary from 150 to 300. The only two country branches (according to Roux) that remained active were Cradock and Tarkastad (and these, as he did not mention, were primarily the creation of the Independent ANC). In the mid-1930s, the policy of the CPSA swung sharply again, this time to the politics of the united front. It was not until after the Second World War that further analysis of the national question and agrarian question was resumed in CPSA publications. Although it could not avert the policy changes which did take place, there is a fascinating letter written by Moses Kotane in February 1934 advocating 'that the Party become more Africanised . . . study the conditions in this country and concretise the demands of the toiling masses from first hand information'. The letter was written while Kotane was in the small town of Cradock and sent to a party committee in Johannesburg; in it, he recounts his experiences in Queenstown and Cradock and argues that the 'non-intellectual section' of the African population were the most significant element: 'They are revolutionary, but have not yet learnt the weapon of organisation'; he paid tribute to the political success of the Independent ANC in Cradock and Tarkastad and commented wryly of some of its followers that he 'would be very pleased to see such serious people among our so-called Party members'.[20] This letter may fairly be regarded as a final echo of the 1928 policy prescription for nationalist mobilisation around rural issues and in rural arenas.

The ANC and the land question

The internal history of the ANC has been fairly extensively chronicled, and is very briefly reviewed here. Brought into being as a response to the Act of Union, significantly broader in its membership than the many African political associations which preceded it, it represented in 1912 the interests, hopes and fears of 'several hundred of South Africa's most prominent African citizens: professional men, chieftains, ministers, teachers, clerks, interpreters, landholders, businessmen, journalists, estate agents, building contractors, and labour agents'.[21] Its tone and tactics derived from its professional and petty-bourgeois character. In the first few years of its existence the Congress was at pains to establish its dignity, decorum and standing as the 'responsible' voice of African opinion. Then, in the immediate post-First World War years there was a brief phase of more radical and militant political involvement by Congress convincingly illustrated in the case of the Transvaal by Bonner.[22] Without entering into the debate as to whether this phase can accurately be termed a class alliance between working-class and petty-bourgeois blacks[23] it is clear that considerable influence was exerted by popular radical forces in these years. Equally, it is apparent that this radicalism was undercut in the early 1920s by a combination of factors. These included competition from the ICU and CPSA; the opening of incorporationist channels to the educated black petty bourgeoisie; and actual concessions offered by the Smuts government between 1920 and 1924 to 'those who were educated and civilised'[24] – and who perceived themselves in such terms.

In the late 1920s, however, there was a second phase of more radical rhetoric and activity within the ANC. Spurred by the example of the ICU, stimulated (after 1928) by CPSA work within ANC branches, stung by the policies of the Pact government, swayed by Garveyite ideas, and disillusioned with the wordy caution of joint councils and urban advisory boards, a number of ANC leaders moved leftwards.

The election of Gumede to the presidency in 1927 saw the organisation committed, in theory, to becoming a mass movement. The tensions between Gumede (whose own politics were tinged both with Garveyism and by his links with the communists) and the conservatives who served with him on the ANC national executive finally led in April 1930 to Gumede's ousting, his replacement by Seme and a lurch by the ANC towards right-wing 'moderation' and organisational disarray. For the next five years, the ANC was 'unsuccessful in reconstituting its unity even to the extent of meeting regularly' and during the 1930s it 'functioned almost exclusively as a disorganised organ of petty-bourgeois protest'.[25]

What, during these years, was the ANC policy on the land question? A great deal of its attention in its earliest years was directed towards the terms and the effects of the 1913 Natives Land Act – and there is ample evidence of the urgency with which the Congress responded to the discriminatory and punitive aspects of the Act. At the same time – as Walshe clearly establishes – once the Act became law, the position of Congress was somewhat ambiguous. The Congress leadership continued to draw heavily on 'Christianity, the Cape tradition and a vision of racial co-operation within one economy and one body politic'; but once the *fact* of territorial segregation had been established, they sought to amend the terms of land allocation rather than dispute the principle:

> To congressmen . . . segregation meant land segregation only, and more specifically rural land segregation. In this way they were ultimately prepared to acquiesce, provided the actual division of the land was not characterised by the quite unacceptable allocations of the 1913 Act, and provided that racial discrimination was not to be applied as the basic principle underlying all Native policy. . . . In short, rural land segregation safeguarding and extending the tribal areas was not seen as an obstacle to equal opportunity for educated Africans in the wider South Africa.[26]

During the 1920s, ANC hostility to the Land Act remained constant, but continued to be expressed in terms of a critique of the inadequacy of the Act's provisions. This somewhat abstract commitment to an ultimately satisfactory allocation of land was not easily translated into support for rural movements concerned with the immediate burdens of stock dipping, evictions, higher rents, declining market opportunities and the like.

A more radical approach to agrarian issues was evinced by a group of younger activists in the Western Cape ANC in 1929 and 1930. They mounted a rural campaign attacking the 'tot' system and calling for higher wages for farm-workers. Bransby Ndobe and Elliot Tonjeni were expelled from the ANC, and set up the Independent ANC, calling for agitation, mass demonstrations and civil disobedience. Their programme was well to the left of the ANC on three counts: a demand for universal free education; full franchise rights for all; and the return of the land to the African people. The Independent ANC continued to win a following in the Western and Eastern Cape, especially in Cradock and Tarkastad (whither Tonjeni had been banished by Pirow).[27]

The rupture between the Independent ANC and the parent body serves to highlight a broader issue: the gap in class interests and ideology that frequently appeared between the ANC leadership and rural movements during this period. The ANC leadership was preponderantly involved in a struggle to extend political and civil rights, to win better social and educational facilities and to provide scope for incorporation within a common multiracial society. Rural resistance movements, however, possessed their own logic and their own dynamics. They cannot be viewed merely as a less sophisticated variant of African nationalism. Indeed, they commonly contained features which were at odds with the liberal or incorporationist thrust of the educated nationalist leaders. The Wellington movement, for example, which affected the Transkei and portions of Natal and the Eastern Cape in the late 1920s, was shot through with millenial, anti-white and separatist tones. Peasant resistance (as Coquery-Vidrovitch has suggested) aspires 'not to *change* power but to *reject* it'[28]: such a retreat from incorporationist ideology, taken together with the fiercely local idiom of rural solidarity, made it extremely difficult for the ANC leadership of this period to represent demands emerging either from peasant/migrant communities or from tenants and workers on white-owned farms.[29]

During the 1920s – this section has argued and tried to illustrate – there was a considerable increase in rural conflict in South Africa. None of the political movements discussed so far was entirely insensitive to this: all sought more effectively than previously to give voice to rural grievances, to win rural support and to provide some political leadership in the countryside. The ICU, spectacularly if briefly, came closest to attracting large-scale support from rural popular classes and to providing a bridge between urban and rural struggles. The CPSA arrived (although it soon departed) at a policy which identified landlessness as a central issue and rural political work as a priority.

The 1930s, however, saw the ICU, the CPSA and the ANC in decline. None was organisationally capable of enlarging its membership, let alone of extending the area of its activity into rural areas. There was little public discussion of rural issues, except in the agitation centring on the 1936 Land Act – which again was largely concerned with legal and political rights. The 'left-wing groups in the country were unable to intervene effectively in the clamour over these issues'.[30] Baruch Hirson has documented the recrudescence of rural unrest in the aftermath of the 1936 legislation – especially in the Northern Transvaal, as the anti-squatting measures were applied. With the doughty exception of the CPSA activist Alpheus Maliba, no effective links appear to have been established with any of the local movements thrown up by the local agitation against the Act. The impetus within the political movements towards rural mobilisation was dissipated; protest and struggle in rural areas remained parochial, disjointed, sporadic and isolated.

The AAC, the ANC, and the Transkei

There was, during the 1930s, one exception to the overall lack of enthusiasm for rural work. A Marxist discussion group in Cape Town – the Lenin Club – was composed of the 'left opposition': expelled CPSA members, anti-Stalinists of various hues, and avowed Trotskyists. In 1933, this grouping split into two factions. On the one hand were the Spartacists (or the Minority tendency, or the Workers Party): on the other, the Communist League (or Majority, which subsequently became the Fourth International of South Africa, FIOSA). They split on three main issues: whether there was a significant difference between British and Boer imperialism; whether a Marxist–Leninist party should remain visible or go underground; and the place of the agrarian and national questions in the liberation struggle. The Spartacists held that the agrarian question was central to the future of successful struggle; in a formulation strikingly similar to some of the passages of the 1928 Comintern resolution on South Africa, they maintained that 'The Native Problem is mainly the Agrarian Problem' – and that, given the concentration of land in white hands and the large proportion of landless peasants, the 'only solution of the Native Problem is the Agrarian Revolution'. The crucial element in any South African revolution would be the demand for land; a class alliance of revolutionary workers and the 'potentially great revolutionary reservoir' of the peasantry would lead the struggle. Again, it was asserted that 'Only the Revolution can solve this agrarian question, which is the axis, the alpha and omega of the revolution.' The Spartacists viewed even 'wage dependants' among the black population as characterised by a peasant consciousness. After a national democratic revolution they envisaged the redistribution of land on the basis of private ownership.[31]

These emphases eventually found expression in the Ten Point Programme of the NEUM: B. Kies, B. Dladla, G. and J. Gool and I. B. Tabata were members of the Spartacist/Workers Party persuasion who surfaced in the leadership of the revitalised NEUM and AAC in 1943. The Ten Point Programme called for universal suffrage, free and compulsory education, the guarantee of basic civil liberties, the reform of the criminal, tax and labour laws, and (point 7) 'revision of the land question'. This was broadly construed to mean ending 'relations of serfdom', the abolition of the Land Acts, and 'a new division of the land in conformity with the existing rural population living on the land and working the land' as the 'first task of a democratic State'. (As the NEUM/AAC policy is frequently dubbed Trotskyist it is worth briefly recapitulating the objections to this programme, and especially to the stress on the peasantry, voiced by FIOSA. It was insisted by FIOSA that the urban and rural struggles must be linked; it argued that 'reserve dwellers are, in fact, tribal proletarians, and the centre of their livelihood lies in the towns and cities . . . even their peasant outlook is steadily being changed into a proletarian one'.)

Tabata and his associates in the AAC leadership after 1943 adhered closely to the Sparticist position. In 1954 Tabata virtually restated the 'alpha and omega' thesis:

> Let me repeat once more: the agrarian problem is the fundamental problem in this country. It is the pivot and axis of the national movement. Anyone who intends to take his politics seriously must understand this fact. . . . Whoever flounders on the agrarian question is lost.

And

> All active participants in the struggle must acquaint themselves thoroughly with the land question. They must learn to know how to approach the peasant and how to link up this land problem with the national question. In order to draw the landless peasantry into the movement we must unreservedly throw in our lot with them in their struggle.[32]

Given this perspective, it is not surprising that the NEUM/AAC sought to extend its activities in the reserves in the 1940s. In practical terms, this meant that Tabata turned particularly to the

Xhosa-speaking Transkei and Ciskei. (Tabata himself had grown up in Lesseyton, Queenstown, and moved to Cape Town via Fort Hare in the 1930s.) This approach by the AAC intersected with certain political developments in the Transkei. These were: the resistance to rehabilitation and especially to its stock-culling provisions; the radicalisation of aspects of Transkeian local politics inclusing the TOB; the radicalisation of the Cape African Teachers' Association (CATA), the salience of this body in the Transkei and the impact of the political activities of its members. Each of these factors – which together are essential to an understanding of AAC tactics and advances – will be discussed more fully in turn.

Resistance to rehabilitation and stock-culling

During the 1930s, the underdevelopment and impoverishment of the Transkei intensified; so pronounced was this process that during the 1930s and 1940s different elements in the South African ruling class came to accept certain broad ideas about the 'needs of the reserves' and in favour of policies of 'betterment' or 'rehabilitation'. In the immediate post-war period, the social and political implications of urbanisation and industrialisation were debated in the party political arena. While the United and National parties differed over the competing requirements of industrial and agrarian capital, over the optimal level of African urbanisation, over the role of pass laws and influx controls and over how to obtain the political and industrial challenge of an organised working class, they were in broad agreement that the corollary to their urban platforms was a need to intervene in the reserves so as to increase and rationalise their carrying capacity. A few months before the end of the war the Smuts government announced its intention of 'dealing with the problem on a wider footing' in the reserves. A sweeping scheme of large-scale rehabilitation was unveiled, which envisaged the improvement of the methods and resources of a stratum of 'full-time peasant farmers', with residential concentration, deprivation of land and livestock and thorough proletarianisation of the majority.[33]

One of the main features of rehabilitation was stock-culling (which had been strenuously advocated by some Transkeian administrators for a decade previously) – and probably no other aspect of the policy excited such concerted and deep-rooted hostility. Surveys, fencing and the removal of families from their homesteads all met with opposition in the period under review, but fears about compulsory loss of livestock remained the most patent source of peasant discontent. As a political issue in the Transkei, stock-culling predated rehabilitation. In 1937 the Bungha (General Council) decision to carry out a mass castration of scrub bulls provoked angry popular opposition. In 1941 a Committee on Overstocking reported that in the Transkei 'at nearly every centre visited the voice of the native people was unanimous in its opposition to any suggestion of compulsory limitation' and that in many places 'the attitude adopted was definitely hostile'. Agitation on this issue adversely affected the government's recruiting efforts for labour during the war. Bungha speakers reported that some peasants 'would like to be under Germany because in this country people's stock was being taken from them'; and that at local meetings people were asking, 'Why is it that men are being called to go to war and yet at home their cattle are to be destroyed?'[34] In 1946, unprecedentedly, half the Bungha members lost their seats, and this was ascribed to the Bungha's support for stock-culling.

The first district in the Transkei to undergo a 'betterment' programme was Butterworth, and a survey of a single location here (undertaken in December 1947) provides valuable details of the scheme and its reception. Rehabilitation – the researchers found – was 'one of the most burning questions' and had met with 'spirited opposition'; cattle-culling and the coercive nature of the policy had provoked particular bitterness. Local people 'smashed fences by night and drove their cattle in'; they also broke politically with their location chief and Bungha councillors. These latter – it was felt – had misrepresented popular feeling. Opposition was voiced through a Vigilance Association (*iliso lomzi*) which had 'sprung up as a check on Bunga representatives' at 'the initiative of the people themselves.[35]

Tabata responded to these aspects of popular resistance. He toured the Transkei in 1945, and at the end of that year issued his pamphlet (in English and in Xhosa) entitled *The Rehabilitation Scheme: The new fraud*. This direct and powerful polemic opposed the call for cattle-culling thus:

> Today our people are disease-ridden because of malnutrition; they haven't the oxen to plough; the majority of the babies do not survive the first year because the mothers are too starved to be able to feed them. . . . [Africans] have far too few cattle for their requirements. It is not that the cattle are too many, but that the land is too small. There is an appalling shortage of land.[36]

The radicalisation of local politics

The second factor shaping local responses to the AAC presence was the radicalisation of politics in the Transkei. This was a complex phenomenon: it certainly involved the transmission of radical ideas and issues from urban areas through migrant workers, but the focus for this analysis is the local dimension and some of the institutional forms taken. One of the most immediate effects of the stock-culling and rehabilitation issues was a deepening of hostility towards chiefs, headmen, district councillors and Bungha spokesmen. Local popular associations explicitly opposed to councillors and chiefs sprang up in several districts between 1945 and 1948; and some of the larger of these came to be represented in the TOB. The TOB was the first political body to command support throughout the Transkei; it represented a real departure in scale and (within a few years) in militancy. Founded in 1943, it initially brought together a number of disparate organisations: Voters' Associations, the Chiefs and Peoples' Association, Vigilance Associations, an African Workers' Union, various welfare societies, a social studies club and two women's associations. Govan Mbeki played a major role in the formation of the TOB; he was elected as General Secretary in 1943 and held this post until 1948.

Up to 1945, TOB resolutions were mainly in the form of very general civil rights statements or the advocacy of specific reforms in favour of educated Transkeians. There seems to have been no TOB policy with respect to land or livestock before 1945. In 1946, however, the TOB conference took a distinctly more radical line on a number of fronts; this seems to have been partly a response to popular anti- rehabilitation protest and partly influenced by events elsewhere in South Africa in 1946. The TOB delegates in 1946 supported a cash collection for victims of the miners' strike; they pledged their support for a boycott of the Natives' Representative Council; and issued a call for 'full citizenship rights to all the people'.[37]

At this juncture the TOB was informally aligned – through Mbeki – with the ANC. Mbeki, himself a Transkeian, was a well-educated journalist-cum-political activist. He had been involved in Transkei politics in several capacities prior to the formation of the TOB: as editor of the *Territorial Magazine*, as secretary to the Transkeian African Voters Association, and at one point as a (dissident) Bungha councillor. Apart from his local efforts to involve Transkeians in national political issues, he also sought to impress on the ANC the need for the nationalist movement to give effective leadership to rural people. A number of Mbeki's letters to Dr A. B. Xuma (President- General of the ANC from 1940 to 1949) survive and they illustrate clearly both of these concerns.

In May 1941, Mbeki described the Transkei as 'to be frank, politically in midnight slumber' – but argued that much could be achieved there. He had been encouraged by an approach from younger men to invite Xuma to the region to launch the Congress there, and advised that first influential elders should be won over. By 1946, the midnight slumber was definitely broken. Mbeki wrote giving an account of the activities of the Voters' Association and the TOB, and reiterated the call for a clear lead from the ANC:

We need to prepare for a national struggle in this regard. No doubt you are aware that organisation in the Reserves is sluggish and a long softening up process is necessary if we must play our part in the national struggle. We have not tired of struggling to raise funds for the Anti-Pass Campaign. What a joy it is to be alive these days when history is being made all around us.[38]

Nine months later, this note of committed optimism was sounded again. He and his colleagues (wrote Mbeki) were very busy 'throwing everything into the fire', the Transkei was 'up and doing' (although 'remnants of the Victorian Age are still to be found'!); and again he appealed for 'the lead of a national organisation in questions of a national character'. What plans, he asked Xuma,

are you developing to clamp down on Advisory Boards, Councils, and individual chiefs? These groups have to be worked up before October next. Writing a letter like this I feel I must be frank. Our fears here are that we may work up the people only to find that the rest of the country does not attach much significance to its resolutions. Country folk have a way of being honest. We have already lost face in the Anti-Pass Campaign which was just dropped when we were working up the people, and that was immediately seized on by the gradualists as one of these 'paper fires' which do not last. . . .

He had been, he continued,

struggling all these years to reconcile different groups and to build an organisation of some sort. We are too few yet in the Reserves and the problem of organisation is by no means easy. We cannot afford to split the spearhead we have at present. To cover the need for concerted action in questions of national interest we have provision in the TOB constitution: 'to co-operate with or follow the lead of a national organisation in questions of a national character.' That is why we joined the Anti-Pass Campaign and now the boycott move. Time will soon settle this, and in the meantime we are doing all in our power to keep the Transkei abreast of the national effort.[39]

There is little evidence that Mbeki's clear-headed urging elicited any notable response from the urban leaders of the ANC before 1948. Xuma's own lack of enthusiasm for rural mobilisation was observable at several points during the 1940s.[40]

The internal history of the TOB remains to be written. By 1948, the AAC was able to make a successful bid to detach the TOB from the ANC. In 1947, Tabata and R. S. Canca (a Transkeian, and a graduate who had trained both as a teacher and a lawyer) toured extensively in the Transkei, and addressed a large number of meetings and organisations. They invited the TOB to attend the 1948 conference of the AAC in Bloemfontein – and were deft in their timing. In 1948, active opposition to rehabilitation was on the increase. In the Ciskei and Transkei there were clashes between armed police and armed peasants; militant local groups were formed in a number of districts, including Glen Grey,

Idutywa, Middledrift, Mount Ayliff, Mount Fletcher, Qumbu and Victoria East. By 1950, the TOB had swung towards the AAC. In that year, its conference voted to affiliate with the AAC; its executive already included several AAC stalwarts, with C. M. Kobus as the new General Secretary.

Cape African Teachers' Association and the Transkei

The third development which shaped the AAC's intervention in the Transkei was the radicalisation of CATA. This had been an almost ostentatiously respectable and moderate body in the 1930s, and the story of its shift to radicalism and active political involvement (paralleling that of other groups in the black petty-bourgeois intelligentsia at the time) awaits investigation. Between 1943 and 1948, CATA was riven with a prolonged internal tussle between factions identified in the body's journal *Teacher's Vision* as progressives and reactionaries. As this terminology suggests, it was the former group who controlled the publication – and from 1948 it was they who led CATA. At the CATA conference of that year the radicals won support for a statement of policy which markedly realigned the association. A preamble stated: 'Our struggle is inseparable from the general struggle of the African people', and committed the teachers' organisation to unite with other bodies to 'co-ordinate their struggles in the fight against common oppression – the fundamental oppression of the Black man'. A number of the leading militants at the 1948 conference came from the Transkei. They – L. L. Sihlali, N. Honono, C. M. Kobus, W. M. Tsotsi and others – were or became AAC activists, and CATA became the most important single constituent element within the federal structure of the AAC.

Writing in a different context, Tom Lodge has shrewdly observed that 'teachers in rural communities during the 1950s were potentially natural leaders of opposition to authority. . . . When teachers were politically motivated, they could be a very important element in rural opposition movements.'[41] In the Ciskei and Transkei, he points out, the 'dense network of mission schools long established in the region' provided a ready-made organisational base. Lodge suggests several reasons for the radicalisation of teachers at this time: their relatively high status as educated men coupled with poor pay and lack of formal power, and the threat to their security and status posed by the Bantu Authority and School Board systems. Of equal or greater importance may have been the wave of school 'strikes' (as the disturbances were usually known) which rocked some of the largest African schools and colleges between 1945 and 1947. These posed acute political questions for black teachers, either directly in the form of pressure from student organisations or indirectly in the harsh light they cast on the inadequacy of educational provision and the increasingly untenable stance of moderation and gradualism.

The role of the CATA/AAC activists in the Transkei – the meetings they held, the petitions they helped draft, the direction and shape they gave to rural grievances – strongly resembles the political position of 'intellectuals of the rural type' sketched by Gramsci. Rural intellectuals (teachers, lawyers, priests) brought peasants into contact with the local and state administration and also provided an innovatory role in moulding and formulating mass or 'subaltern' demands.[42] In less formal terminology (he was speaking, apparently impromptu) Tabata also discussed the strategic importance of politically radicalised teachers and their links with peasant movements:

> Meanwhile with the Convention [AAC] we also had the Teachers Association [CATA] . . . in every area in to the Transkei, in every village there must be a school, and if there are schools, there must be teachers. Now if there are teachers, there is a possibility of forming a teacher's branch, and indeed, in [every Transkei district] there was a branch of CATA and this branch . . . was obliged to carry the ideas of the Convention to the peasantry. They served as centres for disseminating knowledge. There were many of the teachers, naturally, who were afraid of losing their jobs, or some of them didn't want to have anything to do with politics, but the truth of the matter was, the peasants go to the teachers afterwards and say, now, look, what does this mean? This law, now, what does it mean? And if a teacher wasn't interested he found that he was forced to go and read up our literature in order to explain to the peasants. And if he didn't explain then the peasantry wanted to know what the dickens was up with the teacher. . . . So in this way, for the first time, there was a dynamic connection between the educated sector and the peasantry.[43]

Similarly, another of the AAC veterans, recalling for me in an interview his political activities in the 1940s and early 1950s, insisted on the importance of the fact that the educated men were themselves Transkeians, known locally to those whom they reached. 'We went into their huts. They knew us. We had grown up in the same conditions. . . .'

1948–58: Some aspects of resistance in the Transkei

In early 1948, Tabata's involvement in an organised movement in Mount Ayliff, his arrest and his subsequent acquittal, won him a good deal of popularity which must have reinforced the impact being made by the AAC. Resistance to stock-culling in Mount Ayliff dated from as early as

1942; in 1947 the district became the third Transkei magistracy to be designated as a rehabilitation area; the local chief who embraced the rehabilitation measures rapidly ran into organised opposition among stock-owners in the locality. The 'rebels' organised boycotts of meetings intended to promote rehabilitation measures, and police were sent in. The leaders of the opposition movement and some followers armed themselves and moved into the surrounding hills. There they formed a secret movement, the Kongo, and attracted some support from neighbouring locations. Tabata arrived in Mount Ayliff early in 1948 where he was arrested in March or April and charged with incitement to public violence. His defence, which turned on a technicality, succeeded; the case also appears to have established that the inhabitants of any location had the right to refuse to participate in rehabilitation measures. Not surprisingly, in these circumstances, Kongo affiliated with the AAC.[44]

Members of AAC and CATA were active in a number of other Transkei districts between 1948 and 1958. For the most part, the available evidence comes from sources sympathetic to the AAC and must be viewed and used accordingly. Nevertheless, the overall impression is clear. The fight against rehabilitation and cattle-culling broadened and meshed with resistance to the Bantu Authorities scheme and to the introduction of Bantu education. Members of AAC offered active political leadership in a number of local campaigns; their educational and legal skills were valued by Transkeians in their struggles against chiefs, magistrates and police. Implementation of rehabilitation was harried and delayed by boycotts and disruption of meetings; attacks on government personnel and unpopular headmen or chiefs occurred; livestock were hidden or removed, fences destroyed and so on. The annual reports of the Native (later Bantu) Affairs Department between 1948 and 1952 speak each year of 'considerable organised opposition', 'semi-secret organisation', 'alarming reverses . . . serious retardation' of policy due to 'malicious agitators'[45] – until a blanket of silence was draped over the topic by the new Minister, Verwoerd.

There is as yet scant evidence available for the internal organisation or dynamics of these peasant movements, or for the actual extent of the political work by AAC activists; but some of the available fragments make suggestive reading. *Inkundla ya Bantu* (the only African newspaper to support the NEUM) reported that the Transkei 'progressives' had

> made a definite bid to win the support of this [peasant] section of the
> population. They go into the houses and huts of the people; they sleep and eat
> and chat together with them and condition their mode of thinking in this
> intimate way.[46]

In Glen Grey district a peasant organisation called *Amadyakopu* (Jacobites) was 'formed for the purpose of coordinating resistance'. In each of the twenty-four villages in the district local committees were set up which elected members to a central committee. The latter met once a month at the law firm of W. M. Tsotsi, President of the AAC, according to whom 'This form of organisation became so effective that it was extended to the neighbouring district of Xalanga, and joint meetings were occasionally held.'[47] Hammond-Tooke conducted his fieldwork in the 1950s in Tsolo district, and consequently we have more detailed information about the Makhuluspani ('Big Team') movement than of any other. Originally a stock-theft vigilance movement, it became radicalised and acted as a militant and clandestine organisation in opposition to rehabilitation and Bantu Authorities.[48] Similar developments took place in a number of other districts; details of their activities are naturally very hard to come by.

In the later 1950s, while the influence of the AAC declined in the Transkei, the fight against rehabilitation and especially against Bantu Authorities intensified. The best-known instances of open conflict in the countryside between 1957 and 1960 took place in Zeerust, in Sekhukhuniland and in Zululand; in the Transkei the most concerted expression of this resistance was in Pondoland in 1960–61, while a more diffuse 'Thembu revolt' has been described by Lodge. In this section I have tried not to exaggerate the achievements of the AAC in the Transkei, nor to overstate the level and range of unrest in the reserve. But I have argued that the nature and intensity of resistance in the Transkei during the 1940s and 1950s was considerable; that the links established by AAC/CATA activists with local movements were important, both in what they achieved and as instances of a national movement's sensitivity to rural struggle.

The agrarian question in theory and practice after 1945

The rural unrest described in the preceding section coincided with an upsurge in urban struggle between 1945 and 1955. This decade saw the radicalisation of the ANC and its development into a mass movement based on a class alliance of urban workers and petty-bourgeois elements. The publication in 1944 of *African Claims*, the emergence of an Africanist group and particularly the new manifesto and new generation of leaders produced by the ANC Youth League are well-known milestones in that journey. By 1949, the Youth Leaguers called for a mass movement, the

use of boycotts, strikes and civil disobedience. The 1944 *African Claims*
and the 1949 manifesto both called for 'fair redistribution of land',
although the earlier document adhered to the approach of insisting on
equal *access* by Africans to land throughout the country.

Although in the late 1940s an ANC presence of sorts was established
in the Ciskei and in Rustenburg, Pietersburg and Sekhukhuniland,
Walshe concludes that until 1952 the ANC continued to encounter
'virtually insurmountable difficulties in extending its activities to the
rural areas'.[49] In 1952, however, when the Defiance Campaign was
launched, one of the six unjust laws that constituted its specific targets
was the Stock Limitation Proclamation of 1949. A page from Tabata's
book? Or perhaps more directly a reflection of the concerns of Transkeians like Mandela, Mbeki and Sisulu, now all on the National Executive? Whichever was the case, one of the most striking aspects of
the strategy and tactics of the Congress Alliance during the 1950s was
the increasing weight and emphasis that came to be given to *rural*
struggle, frequently coupled with frank criticism of the liberation
movement's prior weaknesses in this regard.

The fundamental reason for this important shift appears to have
been, simply, that the incidence and intensity of rural resistance in the
1940s and 1950s made it impossible for the urban-based movements
not to respond. From the early 1940s to 1960, country areas seethed
with discontent and erupted in open revolts. Disaffection assumed its
most dramatic forms in the Zoutpansberg and Sekhukhuniland
(1941–44), in Witzieshoek reserve (1950–51), Marico reserve (1958),
Sekhukhuniland again (1958–59), the Natal reserves (1958–59), and
Pondoland (1960). Throughout the same years 'the Ciskeian territories
were in a state of almost continual ferment'[50] – and the preceding
section sought to establish that the Transkei was also the arena of
resistance and unrest for a decade and a half prior to the Pondo revolt.

Time and again in the 1950s, elements of the ANC leadership
warned that the movement was neglecting the rural areas. In 1954 the
National Executive Committee reported that there was 'a danger of the
African National Congress becoming an urban-based and
urban-oriented organisation'; in 1955, after the Congress of the People
at Kliptown, the same committee lamented 'the great gap in our
organisation . . . on the farms and in the reserves', and asserted that
'the question of organising the peasants must be tackled with resolve
and energy'.[51] In 1956 Nelson Mandela observed that despite prolonged resistance in the Transkei the reserve was paradoxically 'the
least politically organised area in the Union'. Without co-ordination,

'isolated and sporadic outbursts' would not be sharply felt by the regime: 'The problem of organisation in the countryside poses itself as one of major importance for the liberatory movement.'[52]

Despite these urgings, the reorientation of the ANC and its allies took some time. Organisational and ideological patterns were perhaps too deeply grooved to be rechannelled easily. In 1956, the ANC Provincial Executive in Natal noted that the Peasants' Committee in that province had not yet been set up.[53] Mbeki argued that it was not until the Pondo revolt that full recognition of the potential of the rural struggle was achieved:

> The Pondo movement succeeded by example in accomplishing what discussion had failed to do in a generation – convincing the leadership of the importance of the peasants in the reserves to the entire national struggle. The leaders realised at last that a struggle based on the reserves had a much greater capacity to absorb the shocks of government repression and was therefore capable of being sustained for a much longer time than a struggle based on the urban locations. . . . The struggles of the peasants start from small beginnings, build up to a crescendo over a much longer time, are capable of pinning down large government forces, and are maintained at comparatively much lower cost.[54]

Retrospectively, and a little ruefully, another ANC leader (Moses Mabhida) has commented on the ANC involvement in the women's protests in Natal in 1959. His comments indicate that 'perhaps the leadership of the ANC did not understand very well the problems of the people'. He said: 'Unfortunately for our people, we didn't realize the extent of the organisation of the people which was at that time very high, and the women formed a very strong nucleus for a powerful organisation.'[55]

By the early 1960s the reorientation of the ANC (after 1960 a proscribed organisation, operating underground) towards a championing of rurally based struggle is plain. An early publication of the exiled wing of the ANC claimed that the movement had 'penetrated deeply into the countryside'; argued that the 'heroic struggles of the people of Peddie, Zeerust, Sekhukhuniland, Pondoland, Tembuland, Zululand and other country areas, showed immense revolutionary potential in the countryside'; and asserted that 'the ANC regards the rural population as an essential arm of the liberation movement' (although 'the urban people form the spearhead in our political struggles').[56] Similarly, in a 1963 leaflet distributed illegally in South Africa the ANC took a strongly 'rural popular' tone:

> The Government have chosen the Western Cape and Transkei as the battle fields. . . . We accept this challenge without regret. . . . The time has come for us to adopt a new attitude towards rural areas. . . . Peasant committees of

migrant workers in the cities and of people in the countryside must be formed promptly to co-ordinate activities. We must fight the culling down of stock, rehabilitation, landlessness, forced removals. . . .

A broadly similar shift in strategic emphasis took place in the South African Communist Party (SACP) – as the CPSA became after regrouping as an underground party in the early 1950s). In 1954 the veteran organiser Moses Kotane wrote a pamphlet entitled *The Way Forward* which may fairly be taken to represent the party's position at the time. It is a call for a radicalised African-led liberation movement; at one point Kotane notes that although the majority of the people of South Africa lived on the land

> as yet the democratic movement for liberation has barely begun the task of arousing and mobilising the tremendous potential forces for progress among the landless millions in the countryside. . . . The peasants are crying out for land, freedom, and a better life. It is the duty of the national liberation movement . . . centred mainly in the bigger towns, to reach out a brotherly hand of assistance to these millions of people and to help them to organize themselves. . . .

By 1962, in the new programme of the SACP, this somewhat unspecific and lofty passage (in which the fraternal and the paternal attitude to 'landless millions' are surely both present) is succeeded by a more robust enthusiasm for a rural component in the struggle against state power:

> The people of the Reserves are boldly calling the government's 'Bantustan' bluff. They are fighting bitter struggles, including armed struggles, against the Bantu Authorities. The peasant in the countryside today is not the unsophisticated tribesman of the previous century. . . . These 'new peasants' have awakened the countryside, transforming the African peasantry from a reserve of conservatism into a powerful ally of the urban working class. . . .[57]

In similar vein, in the following year the party's Central Committee wrote:

> The rural areas are no longer the placid backwaters of the country. They are becoming storm centres. . . . [Government policies] are having the effect of raising the tempo of revolutionary struggle in the countryside. . . . Some areas are close to civil war. . . . The liberation movement encourages and assists the rural people in their struggles, and helps to prepare and train their most revolutionary people for action. . . . The African National Congress itself is turning more strongly than ever to the countryside. . . . [T]hese local struggles are a starting point which can ignite the South African revolution.[58]

In the 1960s and early 1970s, the SACP continued to place great tactical stress upon revolutionary armed struggle in the shape of a rurally launched guerrilla war.[59] So closely did both the SACP and the ANC harness their strategy during these years to the concept of a rural guerrilla war that in their critique of 'the radical nationalist wing in Southern Africa' two British Trotskyists have accused the ANC and SACP of 'a flight from the towns'.[60]

Retrospect and conclusions

The available evidence suggests that from the 1920s until the late 1950s the various organs of the national liberation movement linked only fitfully and unsystematically with a wide range of localised rural movements. The foremost exceptions to this general observation are the ICU (between 1927 and 1929) and the AAC (in the decade after the Second World War. In the first of these cases, the rural alliances could not survive the collapse of the ICU into feuding factions; and in any event serious doubts have been cast as to how consistently or success-fully the ICU could have maintained a 'nationalist agrarian element . . . in its radical form' even with favourable organisational circumstances. Despite the spectacular ability of the movement to attract rural members in Natal and the Transvaal, and its entry into a series of rural struggles, the ICU leadership continued to view themselves essentially as trade unionists and they remained most assured in more con-ventionally urban-based trade-union issues. The leaders have also been criticised for 'underlying weaknesses of analysis and strategy'; for the inadequacy of 'middle class liberal understanding of the causes and solutions of oppression and exploitation'; and for a failure to translate popular support into effective political action on specific issues.[61]

In the second instance of rural involvement, the AAC's slender resources and the self-inflicted injuries sustained by the NEUM/AAC during its hostility to the Defiance Campaign were crippling handi-caps. Even more damaging may have been the AAC's signal failure to combine its efforts in the Transkei with an urban movement: as a recent student of the NEUM puts it, 'It was the failure of the AAC leadership to link the rural and urban struggles that prevented them from . . . becoming a mass organisation.'[62]

For their part, the movements of popular protest in the South African countryside between 1920 and 1960 exhibited many of the characteristics that comparative studies of rural politics would lead one to expect. Organisationally, they were small-scale, scattered and short-lived; generally spontaneous, they tended not to produce durable or powerful leadership 'from within'. Ideologically, they were frequently 'rebellious, but rebellious in defence of custom',[63] restive under exactions or injustices but without any fully developed political vision of an alternative society. Typically, they were informed and animated by an admixture of traditionalist, millenial and 'inherent' ideology, on the one hand, and traces or versions of more 'structured' ideologies, on the other. This 'complex, contradictory and discordant *ensemble*'[64] of ideologies was itself a product of the profound but uneven changes that had been wrought in the material and social realms of rural South Africa by conquest and proletarianisation. In short, both in structure and in ideology, the 'disunity, impoverishment and subordination of rural Africans'[65] were major stumbling-blocks in the way of successful mobilisation and organisation. Without political leadership from 'external' social groupings, without any class alliance, peasant unrest (in South Africa as elsewhere) was unlikely to transcend its isolated and sporadic nature and to pose an effective political threat to the state.

Yet, even when these weaknesses of rural protest have been fully acknowledged, questions of a 'what might have been' variety may still be posed. The level of rural response in the 1920s to the ICU presence, and also the measure of success attained by the AAC in the Transkei, seem to suggest that there was a good deal of scope, historically, for such linkages. The peasant committees of the Transkei were parochial and modest in size; but they also displayed a readiness to accept tactical links with and leadership from other classes and movements. The ICU 'had an astounding impact on consciousness and resistance in the countryside. It articulated popular grievances and fuelled protest to an unprecedented degree.'[66] Although class conflict in rural areas was present throughout the period surveyed in this chapter – and acutely so at different times and places – the national movements were for the most part relatively insensitive to them, until by the middle and late 1950s their intensity demanded a response. It proved difficult throughout the period to build the lessons of rural struggles into the nationally organised movements. Alan Brooks's comments on the CPSA prior to 1950 apply with equal force to the ANC: 'The failure of the party to attract peasants may have been partly a failure of the party to attempt to attract peasants. . . .'[67]

Even at those points when programmes were adopted that allotted some role to a mobilised rural population – by the CPSA in the first years of the 'Native Republic' policy, by the Cape Town Trotskyists in the 1930s, by the AAC in the 1940s and by the ANC and SACP in the late 1950s and subsequently – the level of theoretical analysis has not run particularly deeply. Programmes have not been fully articulated with the concrete demands of the various sections of the rural population, nor have they been sensitive to the social and ideological differentiation within that population. At worst, there has been a tendency to refer to the 'toiling masses' of the countryside in a general and non-specific manner: the slogans of Leninism without the detailed analysis of local situations upon which Lenin insisted.

These concluding comments are not intended to convey any tones of a retrospective *narodnik* nostalgia. They do *not* suggest that there was a readily available mass of rural militancy simply awaiting mobilisation; nor are they an easy exercise in the castigation of a wrong-headed leadership, facilitated by the benefits of hindsight. Rather, they have sought to identify the historical barriers that intervened between nationally organised movements and locally organised rural protests. These barriers stemmed partly from the nature of rural politics and partly from the class character and outlook of the leadership of the national liberation movements. Despite the realities of resistance and unrest in the countryside, the national movements – physically located in urban centres, ideologically concerned either with the vanguard role of the proletariat or with wringing political concessions for modernisers – were structurally ill equipped to respond to the inchoate and murmurous patterns of peasant resistance. They failed to lead – or to follow – them.

Notes and References

1 T. Lodge, *Black Politics in South Africa since 1945* (London 1983) p. 261.
2 *Ibid.*, pp. 261, 268.
3 On the events in Pondoland the classic account is G. Mbeki, *The Peasants' Revolt* (Harmondsworth 1964); a more recent study is by J. Copelyn, 'The Mpondo revolt', BA (Hons) dissertation (University of Witwatersrand 1974). For the 'Thembu revolt' see Lodge, *Black Politics*, pp. 283–9 and his earlier 'The rural struggle: Pogo and Transkei resistance, 1960–65', in Development Studies Group, Conference on History of Opposition in South Africa (University of Witwatersrand 1978).
4 The terminology is that of G. Rudé, *Ideology and Popular Protest* (London 1980) pp. 28–33 and *passim*.
5 For more detailed accounts of the NEUM and AAC see: T. Karis and G. M. Carter (gen. eds) *From Protest to Challenge*, vol. III ed. T. Karis and G. M. Gerhart (Stanford 1977); A. Clark, 'The Non-European Unity Movement, 1943–52', MA dissertation (University of York 1977); R. Gentle, 'The NEUM in Perspective', BA (Hons) dissertation (University of Cape Town 1978); and especially I. B. Tabata, *The Awakening of a People* (Nottingham 1974, originally published in 1950).
6 See the Introduction to W. Beinart and C. Bundy, *Hidden Struggles in Rural South Africa* (London and Johannesburg 1986).

7 This last suggestion has been made but not explored by P. Bonner, 'The Transvaal Native Congress 1917–1920: The radicalisationof the black petty bourgeoisie on the Rand' in S. Marks and R. Rathbone (eds), *Industrialisation and Social Change in South Africa* (London 1982) p. 306; also in his 'The 1920 black mine-workers strike: a preliminary account' in B. Bozzoli (ed.) *Labour, Townships and Protests. Studies in the Social History of the Witwatersrand* (Johannesburg 1978).

8 Quoted in P. L. Wickins, *The ICU of Africa* (Cape Town 1978) p. 117.

9 S. Marks, 'Natal, the Zulu Royal Family and the ideology of Segregation', *Journal of Southern African Studies*, 4, (2) 184.

10 G. Coka in M. Perham (ed.) *Ten Africans: A collection of life stories* (London 1963) pp. 293, 297. Chief Stimela Jingoes has left an equally vivid, detailed and much longer account of his experiences as an ICU organiser in the Orange Free State and Western Transvaal, in *A Chief is a Chief by The People The Autobiography of Stimela Jason Jingoes* (London 1975) pp. 99–126. The most important work on the ICU in rural areas has been carried out by Helen Bradford, including her 'The Industrial and Commercial Workers Union in the Natal Countryside', BA (Hons) dissertation (University of Cape Town 1980) and '"A taste of freedom": capitalist development and response to the ICU in the Transvaal countryside', in B. Bozzoli (ed.) *Town and Countryside in the Transvaal* (Johannesburg 1983) pp. 151–75. See also her unpublished PhD Thesis 'The African Industrial and Commercial Workers Union in the South African Countryside' (University of the Witwatersrand 1985).

11 Wickins, *The ICU of Africa*, pp. 118, 124–5; S. D. Johns, 'The ICU: trade union, political pressure group, or mass movement?' in A. A. Mazrui and R. Rotberg (eds) *Protest and Power in Black Africa* (New York 1970).

12 H. Slater, 'A fresh look at the ICU: the case of Natal', mimeo, quoted in Bradford, 'The ICU in the Natal Countryside', pp. 24–5.

13 H. Bradford, 'The ICU and the Transvaal rural popular classes in the 1920s' (paper to History Workshop, University of Witwatersrand 1981) pp. 8–9; see more generally the revised version of this paper, '"A taste of freedom"'.

14 See note 10 above.

15 See H. J. and R. E. Simons, *Class and Colour in South Africa* (Harmondsworth 1969) Ch. 17; E. Roux, *S. P. Bunting – a Political Biography* (Cape Town 1944); B. Bunting, *Moses Kotane – South African Revolutionary* (London 1975); M. Legassick, 'Class and nationalism in South African protest: the CPSA and the "Native Republic", 1928–1934' (Syracuse University 1973); B. Hirson, 'Prelude to the thirties: land, labour and the Left' paper presented to the SSRC Conference, 'South Africa in the comparative study of race, class and nationalism' (New York, September 1982). With the exception of Hirson, these accounts fail to recognise how significant was the emphasis on rural issues in the Comintern resolution embodying the new policy.

16 *South African Communists Speak: Documents from the history of the South African Communist Party 1915–1980* (London 1981) pp. 91, 95, 94.

17 *Ibid.*, p. 96.

18 *The South African Worker*, 31 Jan. 1929.

19 *Umsebenzi*, 27 March 1931.
20 *South African Communists Speak*, pp. 120–2.
21 Lodge, *Black Politics*, p. 1.
22 Bonner, 'Transvaal Native Congress'.
23 For opposing formulations, see: Bonner, 'Transvaal Native Congress', p. 305; Lodge, *Black Politics*, p. 4.
24 Bonner, 'Transvaal Native Congress', p. 275.
25 Karis and Carter (gen. eds), *From Protest to Challenge*, vol. I (ed. Karis and Geshart) p. 154; D. O'Meara, 'The 1946 African mine workers' strike and the political economy of South Africa', *Journal of Commonwealth and Comparative Politics*, XIII, 153.
26 P. Walshe, *The Rise of African Nationalism in South Africa* (London 1970) p. 48.
27 On the Independent ANC see E. Roux, *Time Longer than Rope* (Madison 1974) pp. 231–42; W. Hofmeyr, 'Rural popular organisation and its problems: struggles in the Western Cape, 1929–30', *African Perspective*, no. 22, 1983, 26–49.
28 C. Coquery-Vidrovitch, 'Peasant unrest in black Africa', in *Agrarian Unrest in British and French Africa, British India and French Indo-China* (Past & Present Society Conference, Oxford 1982) p. 34.
29 This theme is explored more fully in Beinart and Bundy, Introduction to *Hidden Struggles*.
30 B. Hirson, 'Rural revolt in South Africa, 1937–51', in *Societies of Southern Africa in the Nineteenth and Twentieth Centuries*, vol. 8 (Collected Seminar Papers, Institute of Commonwealth Studies, London 1977) p. 29.
31 See Gentle, 'NEUM in perspective', 21–34; Hirson, 'Prelude to the thirties', pp. 25–6.
32 Gentle, 'NEUM in perspective, 67; I. B. Tabata, 'The agrarian problem' ('A lecture to SOYA', mimeo, May 1954) pp. 5–6. (For a NEUM view critical of Tabata's position and more concerned to stress the proletarianised nature of the majority of the reserve dwellers, see K. A. Jordaan, 'The land question in South Africa', *Points of View*, 1, (1) (Cape Town 1959).
33 A full statement of the government's intentions is in *A New Era of Reclamation* (statement of policies made by D. L. Smit, at a special session of Ciskei General Council, Jan. 1945).
34 *Reports and Proceedings of the Transkeian General Council*, 1942, p. 117.
35 P. Tobias (ed.) *The Transkeian Survey* (NUSAS Research Journal, Johannesburg, 1951), see the chapter on Ndabakazi location.
36 I. B. Tabata, *The Rehabilitation Scheme: The new fraud* (Cape Town 1945), p. 4.
37 *Torch*, 26 Oct. 1946.
38 Xuma Papers (microfilm, University of Cape Town library), G. Mbeki to Dr A. Xuma, 7 May 1941; Mbeki to Xuma, 11 Sept. 1946.
39 Xuma Papers, Mbeki to Xuma, 27 June 1947.
40 See e.g. Xuma papers, T. R. Masethe to Xuma, 22 Nov. 1943 and Xuma's response; see also Xuma's Presidential Address to the ANC Conference, Dec. 1941, 'In all this land policy the worst and most dangerous clause is the restriction that provides that no Native may buy land from a non-Native . . .' This typifies the juridical approach to the land question.

41 Lodge, *Black Politics*, p. 119.
42 A. Gramsci, *Selections from the Prison Notebooks*, ed and transl. by Q. Hoare and G. Nowell Smith (London 1971) esp. pp. 1–16.
43 Carter-Karis Microfilms, Reel 14A (typescript of speech made by Tabata in USA: n.d., 1965).
44 See I. B. Tabata, *Awakening*, p. 70; *Torch*, 12 April, 26 April, 3 May, 10 May, 11 Oct., 1 Nov. 1948.
45 See *Report of the Department for Native Affairs*, UG 14–1948, p. 21; UG 51–1950, pp. 2, 32; UG 61–1951, p. 1 and UG 30–1953, p. 5. For examples of the AAC involvement in local movements – like the struggle in Idutywa in 1949–50 over cattle dipping – see *Torch*, 24 Oct. 1949, 7 Jan. 1950, or for the anti-rehabilitation movement in Mount Fletcher see *Torch*, 2 Feb. and 27 April 1954.
46 *Inkundla ya Bantu*, 29 Nov. 1947.
47 W. M. Tsotsi, 'Out of Court: Experiences of a black lawyer in apartheid South Africa', unpublished mss, p. 55.
48 W. D. Hammond-Tooke, *Command or Consensus* (Cape Town 1975) pp. 105–7.
49 Walshe, *Rise of African Nationalism*, p. 385.
50 Lodge, *Black Politics*, p. 268.
51 Karis and Carter (gen. eds), *From Protest to Challenge*, vol. III (ed. Karis and Gerhart) pp. 146, 235.
52 *Liberation*, Feb. 1956.
53 Carter-Karis microfilms, Reel 3B, Report of Provincial Exec., ANC, 12 May 1956.
54 Mbeki, *Peasants' Revolt*, pp. 130–1.
55 Quoted in K. Luckhardt and B. Wall, *Organize or Starve* (London 1980) pp. 305–6.
56 African National Congress of South Africa (Dar es Salaam n.d.,? 1962) p. 16.
57 'The road to South African freedom', programme of SACP adopted 1962, printed in *South African Communists Speak*, p. 304.
58 'The revolutionary way out', *The African Communist*, April/June 1963; reprinted in *South African Communists Speak*, pp. 328–9.
59 See J. Slovo, 'South Africa – no middle road', in B. Davidson, J. Slovo and A. K. Wilkinson (eds), *Southern Africa The New Politics of Revolution* (Harmondsworth 1970) esp. pp. 125, 169.
60 A. Callinicos and J. Rogers, *Southern Africa after Soweto* (London 1977) pp. 193 and *passim*.
61 P. Bonner, 'The decline and fall of the ICU – a case of self-destruction?', in E. Webster (ed.) *Essays in Southern African Labour History* (Johannesburg 1978) p. 115; Bradford, '"A taste of freedom"', p. 146.
62 Gentle, NEUM in perspective', p. 88.
63 E. P. Thompson, 'Eighteenth-century English society: class struggle without class?', *Social History*, III (2) May 1978, 154.
64 Gramsci, *Prison Notebooks*, p. 366; 'Structures and superstructures form a "historical bloc". That is to say the complex, contradictory and discordant *ensemble* of the superstructures is the reflection of the *ensemble* of the social relations of production.'

65 Bradford, '"A taste of freedom"', p. 147.
66 *Ibid.*
67 A. Brooks, 'From class struggle to national liberation: the Communist Party of South Africa, 1940–1950', MA thesis (University of Sussex 1967) p. 53.

CHAPTER NINE

Worker consciousness, ethnic particularism and nationalism: the experiences of a South African migrant, 1930–1960*

William Beinart

This chapter is based on a series of interviews conducted with one man in Bizana district, Transkei, in 1982.[1] In calling him M, it is not the intention to conjure any sense of romantic mystery about his life – although there is a quality of excitement about his memories. His lot, like that of most Africans in white-dominated South Africa, has been one of hardship. Born around 1925, perhaps a little earlier, he shared in the general experience of his generation of youths in Pondoland, migrating to work as an unskilled labourer on the Natal sugar-fields and Rand gold-mines. His description of that period of his life is similar to that recounted by other former migrants and offers striking insights into the linked worlds of compounds and rural homesteads. But neither should the designation M suggest that he was the pro- totypical Mpondo male migrant. M was sought out specifically not so much for a record of his working life but because of his significant political role in the late 1950s, a period which culminated in mass urban and rural mobilisations in Natal and Pondoland. For unlike many of his rural peers, he had by then moved to Durban, an urban environment and broader political involvements. More than most, he was able to push beyond the networks and ideas of rurally based migrants, but without completely losing his earlier identity. Indeed, it was only during the course of detailed interviews about the Pondoland revolt of 1960 that he began to recall fragments of his earlier ex- periences. These then increasingly came to dominate the discussion. And it is these, largely, that are offered here because they seemed to reveal a number of relatively unexplored strands in the consciousness of African migrant workers.

* This chapter is a product of research funded by the Social Science Research Council of the UK.

A chronicle of one man's life cannot explain or capture the totality of social change, nor can ideology and consciousness be reduced to one man's ideas. However, an exploration of an individual's experience can illuminate patterns of change and elements of broader consciousness. Biography can only be part of the raw material from which social history is constructed. But in its own right, set in context, it can suggest routes for social analysis obscured by the generality and bluntness of sociological concepts and categories. M's memories, not least because of the variety of his experience and his transition from rurally based migrant to nationalist political activist, raise issues which are important to an academic analysis of the changing patterns of African political ideas and organisation in South Africa. In particular, his memories require that such concepts as worker consciousness, ethnicity and nationalism (all of which could be said to be present and intertwined in his political thinking), their content and the connections between them, be further examined.

M was born and brought up in Bizana, the coastal Transkeian district which borders Natal.[2] (It is well known as the epicentre of the 1960 revolt and more recently as the site of a casino complex which may become second only to Sun City.) His father had no cattle of his own and, when he wished to marry around 1920, found himself a beggar for bridewealth from his male kin. He started his family with 'nothing, absolutely nothing', accumulating only a few head by purchase from his wages as a migrant labourer. M's father was also very much a traditionalist with scant respect for mission education. However, some of the members of his father's family, among whom they were settled, were both better off and, though not necessarily Christian, more 'progressive' in their attitude to schooling. Indeed, M perhaps exaggerated only slightly when he recalled that his own father was 'the only one who was a *bhungu*', member of a traditionalist youth organisation, in their cluster of homesteads. The family was also settled very near to Bizana town in the centre of the district.

In Pondoland as a whole at the time probably less than 10 per cent of children of school-going age actually attended school. But M found that his peers were being educated and there was considerable pressure on him to join them. While his mother gave him support, his father would not provide him with clothes. Being near town, however, he was able to find a way around his father's indifference. Bizana was hardly a metropolis, although it was larger than some of the other Transkeian trading and administrative centres, not least on account of its importance as a recruiting post on the routes of Pondoland to Natal.

By 1936 the village population reached 469, including 257 white and Coloured people, in a district of close on 58,000. Some of the inhabitants were no longer poor frontier traders but wealthy businessmen. They had sufficient resources, and the appropriate self-image, to sustain a golf course – thus providing a little seasonal employment for children in the vicinity. 'We used to be caddies', M remembered, 'a round of nine holes was three pennies, that was something.' Then he also 'had luck'. He 'struck friendship with the son of a lawyer here in Bizana' for whom he caddied. The lawyer's wife would give him 'a piece of job', saying, 'When you have finished I will give you a shirt.' Thus M acquired clothing for school and, achieving some economic independence from his father at an early age, pressed through rapidly to Standard V and 'became very bright'.

M's life had begun to take an unusual trajectory for the son of poor and uneducated Mpondo parents. His urge for education, and his success in proceeding further at school than the average rural youth, were to have an important influence on his later life. They helped determine what kind of rural youth association he was to join, a central social commitment, and where he would migrate to work. But M's passage to higher education was abruptly halted in 1939 when his father decided to move. Bizana still had frontiers for settlement in the 1930s; despite considerable in-migration, a coastal belt roughly ten miles wide remained sparsely inhabited. Coastal grazing was good – the area had largely been used as winter pasturage – but the sandy soil was not highly productive. Nevertheless, population pressure in some inland spots persuaded many families to migrate coastwards into the large and remote Amadiba location; general reliance on wages reduced the necessity for them to depend on rural production alone. M's father found a site in what was to become, in the next few decades, a location with a large and mixed population of increasing political importance in the district. (Areas along the main road near the casino may now become almost peri-urban.)

As most youths went away from home to a major mission institution once they reached high school, the move did not necessarily preclude further education. M had in fact spent a brief period working on the wattle plantations just across the border with Natal to raise cash. But by now his father was ill and could not migrate to work. And shortly after the move 'we got a message – by that time my brother had gone to the mines to work – that my brother had died. . . . Everything now rested on my shoulders.' Local jobs generally necessitated some post-school qualification. Though the mines sometimes took males under 18, most youths from eastern Pondoland, and more especially from Bizana district, took their first few contracts as unskilled workers on the Natal sugar estates. There was no effective age limit or medical test, and the local traders specialized in supplying youths to the estates. So that at about 15 or a little older (1939/40), M signed on with a trader in Amadiba for a six-month contract.[3]

Memories of their first few visits to the sugar-fields die hard in the minds of many older men in Bizana. They went on foot to the railhead in southern Natal, then entrained for their estate or for a clearing-house. M found himself in a compound in Durban called Thandabantu (Lover of people) where he was 'resold' to Gledhow sugar estate. As soon as they arrived on the estates, migrants were given their working clothes – a sack with holes cut for head and arms. Plantation discipline was notoriously harsh and M recalled that the compound manager was 'an aggressive chap, everybody shivered when they saw him': all this for wages of less than £2 a month and little chance to earn a bonus.

Though they may have been far from home in a harsh environment, youths from Pondoland were generally among people from home. By this time, Indian workers, apart from those in supervisory roles and in the mills, had left the sugar-fields. (Few estates still had their own mills.) And though seasonal labour from neighbouring farms supplemented that of the core migrant labour force 'there were not many Zulus there'. 'Zulus did not want to go and work in the sugar-cane fields. The compounds were manned mostly by the Pondos; the Zulus felt that to go to the sugar-cane fields was degrading.' Migrants from Pondoland to the sugar-fields were entering into one of the well-established patterns of migration from specific rural districts to particular area of employment. The importance and tenacity of these 'ethnic' patterns of migration should not be underestimated. Nor were they essentially imposed by employers, although they often provided the latter with advantages. Through such networks, workers could retain contact with home and establish defensive structures at work. The consciousness of rurally based migrants cannot be understood until these patterns of migration, and the associational forms and networks which arose, are uncovered. In this sense, 'ethnicity' was an important element in developing migrant organisation and con-sciousness. It is arguable that in the earlier phases of South African industrialisation particularist associations at work made self-protection and organisation possible, rather than constrained them.

It was at the sugar estates that M first came into close contact with the *indlavini*, the male associations established about a decade before, around 1930, which had begun to lure youths with even a smattering of education from the traditionalist *bhungu* groups.[4] He had been aware of these groups at his father's old home near Bizana town and their style and activities on the sugar-fields appealed to him. 'Although I did not join up there, I said I must line up with the *indlavini* and not with the *amabhungu*.' M joined on his return to Amadiba after working out his contract; the attachment remained a primary loyalty throughout his life. The *indlavini* groups had grown directly out of an earlier youth subculture, but not organisation, known as the *imirantiya*, which spread through the eastern Transkeian districts in the 1920s. Those who remember the term *imirantiya* – probably a vernacular rendering of 'migrant' – in Pondoland say it referred to 'people who just wander about'. Such youths wandered about in the sense that they had broken away from the highly localised *bhungu* groups which were often restricted to just one location, and to which most young men then still belonged. The *imirantiya* were impatient with the deeply rooted traditionalist character of the *bhungu* expressed in their forms of song, dance, social relationships and dress. They were social in-novators in all these respects, meshing the experience of school and compound with the older forms of rural youth organisations. At that stage they did not have a strong base in particular locations. Relatively few in number, they would gather from all over Bizana, and even beyond, at large meetings or weddings. The *indlavini* were the more localised organisations and groups which, as numbers increased, emerged from this *imirantiya* subculture.

Samuel Mazeka, a founder member of an *indlavini* group in Bizana in the late 1920s, recalled that they had formed these much tighter associations for the purposes of self-regulation, fighting strength and control over courting.[5] They had also adopted a distinctive form of dress, including baggy bell-bottom trousers apparently copied from Bhaca migrants on the Rand. *Indlavini* groups were primarily rural associations. They met every Sunday, *entabeni*, on the hills, and gov-erned themselves through a strict hierarchy of posts. They eschewed supervision by older men, drawing up a code of rules relating to courting, access to women, loyalty and discipline, fighting and weapons, as well as membership lists and lists of girlfriends, all re-corded by each group's secretary. They recruited aggressively especially among those who had been to school but dropped out early to move into contract labour. The *imirantiya* and *indlavini* subcultures extended local male networks, linking youths from different locations and districts in eastern Pondoland and providing a tight associational attachment for those leaving their blankets behind. But they remained explicitly district based and 'Mpondo' in their identity. Those who had received a little education and were migrating to work were not becoming 'detribalised', but shifting the content of what it meant to be a Mpondo youth – perhaps forging a new ethnicity.

While it is hardly surprising that M avoided the *bhungu*, he did have rather more education than the average member of the *indlavini*. His membership reflected the fact that he was clearly not in the milieu of those youths, often but not always from wealthier Christian families, who had gone as boarders to major mission institutions or who had avoided local youth groups. He was not, as in the case of Oliver Tambo or Caledon Mda (now elected MP for Bizana and leader of the minute parliamentary opposition in Transkei), one of those who joined the Bizana Students Association which was active in the late 1930s during school holidays.[6] Such youths tended quickly to escape the confines of a specifically ethnic identity and form wider networks on their way to sharing in the culture of a national élite, though that also had its regional shadings. M's membership of the *indlavini* helped to anchor him in local politics and culture. His education did, however, enable him to become secretary of an *indlavini* group in Amadiba and, later, something of an intellectual of and adviser to groups in Bizana. 'Even today they always come to me for advice and all that from *indlavini* groups all over the district.'

M went only once to the sugar fields, and then, from 1941 to 1947, on four contracts to the gold-mines which offered higher wages. This switch was by no means unusual for Mpondo migrants, although less educated youths might return to the sugar-fields on a few occasions before going north. Like many Mpondo migrants, M worked at the East Rand Proprietary Mines (ERPM) near Boksburg. While thousands of migrants went to the mines from most Transkeian and Ciskeian districts, men from the same district sometimes tried to establish themselves in particular compounds. Aside from ERPM, Randfontein on the West Rand had been popular since the first decade of the twentieth century when Mackenzies, one of the leading recruiters in Pondoland, lured many to the Robinson mines with large advances. Once there, in Angelo compound, ERPM, M worked underground.

> I wanted to work underground. You understand at one stage I was offered work as a clerk. I refused simply because clerks are paid low wages and you don't mix with your own people. I don't know why, I liked staying with my people in the compound.

'You have to belong somewhere', mused M, discussing his experience on the mines more generally.

M's sense of belonging to a group operated at different levels, but a number of these involved attachment, in different ways, to a specifically Mpondo identity. He not only encountered the *indlavini* on the sugar-fields but also, as a member, on the mines. *Indlavini* groups could on occasion be important in organising their members to go out to work. And while they were essentially rural associations, they could be strong in compounds at labour centres with large numbers of workers from Pondoland. There, because youths were removed from home and thrown very largely into the company of their male peers, the groups could be quite cohesive. M lived in a section of the compound with all workers from Pondoland but, he insisted, 'while I was in the mines, everybody knew that I was an *indlavini*'. The groups organised many of their own leisure-time activities. They were 'centred in certain places'.

> There was Bhaca *indlavinis* . . . *indlavinis* from Mount Ayliff, *indlavinis* from Lusikisiki, Flagstaff and Bizana. When we come back from work then we go out and wash, have our meal. Go out and sit there – the Bizana *indlavinis* have their own group. . . . They were the same *indlavinis* as in the rural areas. We had been recruited to work in the mines and when they were there they formed these groups. We used to have competitions with other compounds – we sing, we play and all that. From our area, Bizana, we had our *inkosi*, our *indlavini* chief. But when we are going to have competitions then we vote for one chief from the whole of Pondoland.

M was also at great pains to make it clear that the '*indlavini* are highly disciplined people' and that their structures of authority and obedience went beyond leisure activities. Such groups could be of importance in patterns both of control and of protest in the compounds; 'we are recognised by the manager there, the compound manager, he must know that there are *indlavini* there'. (Although *Bhungu*-type groups also functioned on the mines they apparently tended to lack the tight cohesion of the *indlavini* and to accept the authority of older Mpondo migrants.)

In certain contexts, however, M's identity as an *indlavini* could be subsumed in a sense of belonging to a larger Mpondo group. There were, of course, men from many other rural areas in Angelo compound, but they tended to be housed along 'ethnic' lines – as perceived by managers and many workers themselves. 'There was one wing for Pondos, one for Bhacas, one for Shangaans, one for Zulus.' Perhaps he exaggerated when he remembered that 'groups like Bhacas and Pondos, Pondos and Zulus never mixed' in their living quarters.

> If a Pondo goes to the Zulu side, the Zulus do not know him and they start abusing him and saying all sorts of things. They hit him and when he comes back to the Pondos then the Pondos start arming. . . . That was what usually sparked off faction fights.

M described the derogatory image which various groups held of one another. The 'Shangaans', perceived to be particularly uninhibited in their homosexual practices, 'were despised by the Pondos, so much so that the Pondos said "the Shangaans are not men, they are just women"'. Again, 'Xhosas speak of Pondos as boys' because Mpondo men were not circumcised. M did not like these divisions and, perhaps imposing an analysis since developed, he felt it was 'just the policy of the mines . . . that is exactly what was causing all the faction fights there'. But although he was not personally involved in a 'faction fight', he fully recognised the internal dynamic and power of the identities mobilised in such confrontations.[7] And he did have immediate experience of a conflict which directly reflected the 'ethnic' and sexual tensions in the compound. When he was still an ordinary labourer, lashing,

> a Shangaan boss boy suggested love to me. Well, I said, 'I think you have made a mistake.' He insisted, he wanted to force me. And then we fought there right on top of the shaft. His friends came to help him and I was driven down.

A white miner had to separate them.

The allocation of jobs and control of sexual relationships came within the orbit of other kinds of organisations in some compounds at the time – gangs. The Isitshozi, modelled on the lines of the Ninevites, Johannesburg's leading black criminal organisation in the early twentieth century, had become one of the strongest Rand gangs by the 1930s and 1940s.[8] Whereas migrants from Pondoland at the turn of the century were mostly new to the mines and closely locked into rural society, there were *amarumsha*, long-timers, from Pondoland, too, a few decades later. It was they who formed the core of the gangs. The Isitshozi were 'mainly Pondo, Xesibe and a few Bhacas, very few Bhacas; there were some Xhosas, hardened Xhosas, as well, but mostly Pondos'. The most powerful groups were at Randfontein and Boksburg, strongholds of migrants from the area. M fell in with a friend from home who was a member and joined himself. 'Those people are the people who killed people on the mines; I wanted to know exactly why and how they did it.' M's membership was, he claimed, fairly peripheral in that he 'did not kill anybody'. He had a scarce resource – 'fortunately I had that bit of education' – so that he could do other duties. 'These tough guys respected me because I used to write letters and read papers.'

He found 'that these people were running the business on more or less army lines'. They organised 'stealing, or burglary from white houses, stores'. They controlled the paths around the compounds and mines at night. A member was 'really free, nothing will ever harm you whereas if you know nothing you are in trouble'. The leaders ran the gangs from disused mines (*esigodaneni*) and prisons, but the organization was also strong within some compounds such as ERPM. And though migrants from Pondoland may have accused Shangaans of being women, M found that among his own people 'miners were not encouraged to go out and meet women outside but were doing homosexuality here inside the compound'. 'Although the Shangaan excelled in this even the Pondos were doing it; it was something that was open.' The pressures of massive single-sex institutions and the constraints on getting outside the compound reinforced the strength of the 'controlling body' of homosexuality, the Isitshozi. Members, including those established in the mine hierarchy, would supervise the recruitment of boy-wives from youths coming fresh from Pondoland.

> At that time, right inside the mines it was terrible. The work was very very hard. So much that a person would fall unconscious because of the hard work. It was very hot inside the mine. . . . The baas boys said: 'If you agree to be my wife then I will give you a better job.'

White managers might find that there were dangers in having strong gangs in the compounds, but some at least accepted and exploited such lines of control within the workforce. Mr McLucky, a compound manager who himself hailed from Tabankulu, Pondoland, would say: 'Hey, look here, I don't want anybody to go out courting women because you get sick. We have got enough women here inside the compound.'

Unlike the *indlavini*, the Isitshozi was not an association which itself bridged the urban and rural areas; it was not, apparently, carried back to Pondoland. But the gang as a whole, and its various branches, was associated with migrants from specific rural districts and with the compounds they favoured on the Rand. Such linkages were affirmed by the patterns of recruiting for the gang, by its leaders' sense of their own history and by the fact that individual members did go back to the countryside. Recruits were 'told about the forefathers of the whole thing . . . people like Mamsathe, Mamsathe's group at Boksburg'. Indeed, Mamsathe was from M's home location, Amadiba; 'I met him when I came back from the mines.' The hard core of the gangs was probably only 'a few hundred' in number, but very many more migrants had some experience of them.

While gangs and homosexuality, apparently operating along largely ethnic networks in the compounds, were a product of the divisions and institutions described, they could at the same time reinforce ethnic identities and associations. Women at home, according to another informant, were aware of and not necessarily opposed to such practices. They were known to warn their husbands or lovers against consorting with the opposite sex, with 'Sotho' women outside the compounds, because of the dangers of venereal disease.[9] Men without women were also less likely to form permanent liaisons in town. Such heterosexual, cross-regional relationships were no doubt of importance in the breakdown of ethnic particularism and the growth of a more generalised urban working-class culture, although this aspect of African proletarianisation has been little studied. Certainly, Hellman's portrait of a Johannesburg 'slum yard' in the early 1930s, with its mixed population, its high proportion of cross-ethnic marriages and its lack of particularist networks stands in stark contrast to compound life as described by M.[10] Yet, probably the majority of workers who came to Johannesburg, at least until the Second World War, were housed in compounds, and this had important implications for the patterns of 'worker consciousness' that emerged in South Africa.

To suggest that M's experience on the mines was predominantly one of close involvement in various groups, serving different purposes, associated with his rural background and 'ethnic' identity is not to argue that he lacked 'worker consciousness'. In the first place, these *were* the associations of workers and played a considerable part in the way that migrants responded to their position at the place of work. Secondly, although Isitshozi gangs and *indlavini* groups could be tight organisations, their members did not have to be closed to the rest of the urban world. Certainly M felt that the necessity of obtaining permits, and the dangers of *tsotsis* (urban location gangs), greatly discouraged contact with people in locations. But the compounds were not closed and it was during this period that M first started to take an interest in broader political issues. He was still 'yearning for education, although I was an *indlavini* . . . I read newspapers – that was during the war – and I was very interested in everything that was taking place'. And thirdly, he did develop contacts with migrants from other areas, particularly in the process of working underground where teams were more mixed. He learnt other languages: 'I was very good in Shangaan; I used to work mostly with Shangaans.' Even though shift bosses, and black 'boss boys' protecting their own, could divide jobs in the underground teams along ethnic lines, these groups of workers could develop solidarity as underground miners. M recalls particularly the efforts he made to incorporate into his team a Tswana youth, who had great difficulty communicating with other workers.

M does not remember that wage levels on the mines were a particular issue for him during his early contracts. Indeed, after his fight with the 'Shangaan boss boy' he became, as did most established Mpondo migrants, a 'machine boy'. A skilled driller had the opportunity to earn a better wage and bonuses. Although the machines, and the work, were heavy, 'it was worth it'. He claims to have worked up to earnings of '£7 a month and it was much better compared with the ordinary labourer'. During 1946, however, M did remember that wage issues came to the fore; 'we struck work and we refused to go underground'.

The African Mineworkers' Union had been launched in 1941 under the leadership of J. B. Marks. By 1944, it claimed 25,000 members and its conference drew '700 delegates from every mine, 1,300 rank and file members' and 'a telegram of support from the Paramount Chief of Pondoland'.[11] But it could not organise easily in the compounds. The union was 'based in Johannesburg proper and they were not allowed to enter the mines'; to M's knowledge there was 'nothing at all' in the way of union organisation among Mpondo migrants. They first heard of the action through 'pamphlets telling us about the strike', and 'papers distributed inside the compound and on our way to the mine'. Workers certainly responded 'because people were underpaid and when they say work nine months it is not ordinary months'. But for M and apparently the majority of workers in his compound, there was no real involvement in worker organisation.

O'Meara sees the strike as an important moment of transition from peasant to proletarian consciousness. The growth of the Mineworkers' Union was indeed a significant episode, but its longer-term effect is by no means so clear. Migrants had long been conscious of their wages and conditions. But in M's compound, at least, and perhaps elsewhere, it seems that the internal organization of the strike depended on networks such as those described rather than the union itself. These were associations of people being proletarianised, and through which workers could defend themselves, but they were not essentially class-conscious worker organisations. How such particularist associations operated in different compounds in the 1946 strike, the actual progress of the strike, and the position of the gangs which may have been threatened by, or may have supported union organisation, all require more investigation. The collapse of the union after 1946 may suggest its roots were insufficiently deep to withstand state repression.

M had not neglected to build up his rural base while on the mines.

Like the vast majority of migrants from Pondoland he had invested some of his wages in cattle which were 'very cheap' at the time (*c.* £2 10s. a head).[12] By 1943, after his contract on the sugar-fields, when he brought home only £10, and one contract on the mines, he was in a position to marry; he laid down five head for *lobola* (bridewealth) to which his father added four. In the next few years, taking over his father's role in Amadiba, he bought plough, planter and 'all the household implements'. Such investment of wages affirmed and cemented rural links. After completing his contract in 1947, he stayed at home for over a year, perhaps closer to two. His father was now very ill, soon to die, and his marriage was under pressure. During his final contract his 'wife had been going out with another man'; despite his long abscences he felt this to be unacceptable although he did 'forgive her'. But the family needed a wage income. A traditionalist with no education would probably have had little choice but to return to the sugar-fields or the mines. M was certainly now in a position to earn a relatively reasonable mine wage, but he was unhappy with compound conditions and underground work; he also wanted to maintain closer contact with home. Thus in 1949 he went to Durban, arranging a job through a contact from Bizana – an ex-policeman who worked as a clerk in Wispeco (the Wire Industries, Steel Products and Engineering Company). 'He said he would fix me up with a job and I had no trouble with the pass.' Starting as a labourer, M worked at the firm for the next ten years, and visited home regularly.

A move to the ports often reflected and reinforced slightly broader cultural indentifications among migrants from Pondoland, and so it was with M. He lived in a more mixed environment at the S. J. Smith hostel near the city's industrial area. Although it was for single men, there was little of the tight male organisation which he had encountered on the mines, and little homosexuality. 'Women were not allowed to go in' – but they did; access to town was also easier. It was 'quite different', 'we were just together – Zulus, Shangaans . . .'. At work he was mostly with men from Natal farms and he made sufficiently close contact to travel up to weddings and visit families as far afield as Mooi River. He also decided to continue his education and signed on with the Efficiency College. And at least one of his links with home was loosened in that his wife again formed an attachment with another man in Bizana and they were finally estranged. Now in his late twenties, he began to expand his cultural horizons and political involvements in Durban.

It was the Defiance Campaign in 1952, the protest against apartheid led by the Congress movement, which brought him into closer contact with an explicitly political organisation.[13]

> They were holding meetings and I was very interested in the spirit of the ANC at that time, people going to jail. . . . I was involved but I didn't go to jail myself although I was very keen to go to jail. . . . What the police did as the campaign got hotter, they simply didn't arrest people. Our group would walk the streets the whole night and the police would simply laugh at us.

M's entry into a nationalist political movement requires some explanation. The focus of the Defiance Campaign, after all, was essentially on urban issues such as night curfew, segregated facilities and pass raids on the streets. Certainly these were real and oppressive enough to urban dwellers, but they hardly seemed to be central questions in M's experience as a migrant before he arrived in Natal. Indeed, he does not recall that rural issues were particularly important in pushing him into broader political associations; and migrant labour itself seemed so much at the centre of his experience that he had neither the ideas nor the 'machinery to change it'. The African National Congress (ANC) programme at that moment hardly succeeded in translating rural and migrant experiences into the nationalist political platform. Initiatives taken in the 1940s to organise migrant workers on the mines, and in the sugar industry, had faded. Activists were now seeking to mobilise a mass movement through campaigns on national and race-discrimination issues rather than by taking up the demands of peasants and workers. They had only limited success among Africans in Natal. There, the ANC still had few branches and was in the throes of displacing its provincial leader, A. W. G. Champion, with Albert Luthuli. There was certainly a general politicisation as apartheid laws began to bite. But this did not, for most, involve the commitments developed by M; the ANC had not yet become a mass movement.

M responds to questions about this phase of his politicisation in a variety of ways. His shift away from compound life, which partially encapsulated the majority of migrants from Pondoland, provides the context for this important transition, a shift which was related to his early education. It is also important to stress that he did not immediately become a nationalist organiser, or even absorb all the ideas current in the Congress movement. Rather, he was now personally affected by the issues which Congress was bringing to the fore, those that most immediately affected urban residents, and the ANC therefore seemed the logical organisation to join. He had personal experience of police brutality on the streets. Contact was certainly made easier by the fact that an ANC branch had been established in the S. J.

Smith hostel – reflecting its more open character in comparison with mine and estate compounds – although M does not remember the hostel dwellers as highly politicised. And through such links he came to attend political meetings and was particularly inspired by the speeches of Bertha Mkhize, long an Industrial and Commercial Workers' Union (ICU) and ANC activist in Natal. Of course, many migrants from Pondoland and elsewhere, even hostel dwellers who shared a similar background, did not become so involved. But M points to his long interest in broader political issues and general sense of enquiry manifested in his following of news in the papers. He also maintains that he was very aware of the need to participate in organisations and associations which might answer to the pressures inherent in the specific conditions of oppression which he experienced. This is not to equate the *indlavini* with the ANC or to suggest that many *indlavini* joined the ANC in the 1950s, although there are indications that such groups shared in the general politicisation of the time, composing songs against 'Malan's laws' and the 'dompas'. However, M does see a parallel in their stress on organisation and discipline; and it was through attending Congress meetings as a rank-and-file member over the next few years that he began to develop a more generalized political analysis.

While M was broadening his involvements in town, he still kept in touch with other migrants from Pondoland in Durban, visited home and retained strong links with the *indlavini*. It was a loyalty to a particular association in Bizana, to a form of Mpondo rural identity expressed in the morality, social roots and rules of the group. M was not particularly hostile to the traditionalist *bhungu* groups although he recalled how the *indlavini* distanced themselves from them; 'we used to call them *amafilistiya*' (philistines). He could accept, even respect, them because they had values, particularly in connection with women and fighting, which *indlavini* to some extent shared. His vitriol was reserved for the so-called *amanene*, or gentlemen, who, he felt, betrayed Mpondo rural values.

By the time of M's adulthood the term *amanene*, originally used of close councillors to the chief, later of the educated Christian élite, also had ironic connotations. It referred to those youths of Christian families who were constrained neither by the traditionalism of the *bhungu*, the discipline of the *indlavini*, nor the behaviour expected in the church. M might indeed have become one of them, for they tended to stay longer at school, without becoming professionals, or to migrate to town locations rather than compounds. They were not formed into associations, but shared a wider, urban-based culture. While there had been few such youths in Pondoland in the 1930s, they had become, by the 1950s, a significant and identifiable social category, at least in the eyes of M and his fellow *indlavini*.

They were seen as particularly dangerous and unprincipled, rural *tsotsis*. Two features of their behaviour seemed to M the most unpleasant.

> Why is there that? Why the *indlavini* hate the *amanene*? The *amanene* come from more or less the same Christian families. But they differ in this way. They are not a group. And they believe in fighting with a knife. They believe in stabbing. They believe in bribing parents of the girls . . . they go straight in there and then go into the girl's house, the girl's room, and they sleep there. With the result that most of these girls who are in love with the *amanene* get pregnant and the *indlavini* do not want that.

The *indlavini* met girls away from home or at weddings; in M's view, 'the girls who are in love with the *indlavini* rarely get pregnant'. Though they were renowned for their strong-arm tactics at weddings, and their willingness to fight, *indlavini* used sticks and clubs only. It is essential to understand these elements in M's identity and morality for he was still very committed to them – so much so that in 1954 he participated in a major fight between *indlavini* and *amanene* at Amadiba.

> They had taken over our wedding. We were not invited there; the *amanene* were invited instead of us. Then we wanted to go and break that wedding. We went there and a fight took place. The *amanene* were armed with bush knives, swords, spears, hatchets. We were only armed with sticks. If you see this scar here [points to forehead] – this is a bushknife here. I was lucky I didn't die. . . . But we drove them away, we got an upper hand. The *indlavini* are skilled fighters.

He was fighting against elements of a more generalised urban location culture that was seeping into rural districts.

During the later 1950s, M drifted away from *indlavini* activities at home as he became more absorbed in politics in Durban. After nearly ten years, he had risen to a clerical position at work, and was earning 'top wages' of £5 a week. But this did not increase his security; on the contrary, he was sacked in 1958. The management, he argued, got rid of black workers who were becoming too expensive and replaced them with younger and cheaper staff. His political activities no doubt contributed to the decision. For by now he was becoming more involved in trade union activities at the place or work, reflecting the increased stress that the Congress movement began to lay on worker organisation through the South African Congress of Trades Unions (SACTU). M was now more wedded to town life and had new emotional attachments in town. He also tried to secure an income without resort to employment in a white-owned firm which rendered him so vulnerable. 'I had bought two sewing machines and I was doing a little sewing.' He continued studying so as to achieve fluency in English. And during the next two years he moved from his position as a rank-and-file follower to that of political initiator. His lines of political involvement took him back to the rural areas. There were many men who could bridge the worlds of urban Congress politics and the Transkeian élite. Many of the ANC activists came from rural Christian families and found nationalist politics through Lovedale, Fort Hare or other leading educational institutions. But there were few who could make the bridge to the ordinary peasant/migrant. M's political mentors recognised this in him, and he recognised it in himself, at a time when Congress, swept along by events, was beginning to perceive more clearly what was involved in organising an alliance of worker and peasant.

During his political work he 'became friendly' with M. P. Naicker, a radical member of the Natal Indian Congress, by this time banned from political activity but still influential in Congress circles and local editor of *New Age*. In the mid-1940s, Naicker had seen the potential for organisation on the sugar-fields at the time when the African Mine Workers' Union was reaching its peak on the Rand. A union was set up, and considerable publicity given to the atrocious conditions on many estates. But no permanent organisation was achieved. Now Naicker, together with Moses Mabhida, SACTU leader in Durban, 'sent [M] out to go and organise the sugar cane workers'. The choice was apt. Not only was it necessary for any organiser to understand the language, associations and concerns of migrants from Pondoland if he were to have success, but he had also to escape the notice of compound managers, ever vigilant for 'agitators'.

> Yes, since I was a Pondo I didn't have much trouble. I was regarded just as a visitor who had come to visit friends. Of course I did not dress like an urban African. I tried to dress like the Pondos: just an ordinary jacket, khaki shirt, khaki trousers with patches . . . looked more or less like a Pondo.

He found himself back in an environment from which he had been absent, except for occasional visits, for over a decade.

Though M might have been as good a person as was available, his efforts met with little success. He was, he felt, breaking more or less virgin territory for unionism and he saw his failure largely in terms of the highly controlled nature of the compounds. He found that even if he got into a compound with ease, the indunas and policemen would soon find out 'if you have got something to say'. And though he tried to 'strike friendship' with indunas, 'and later draw them into the discussions', many 'did not want to co-operate'. He was 'only able to meet three or four people at a time'. Moreover, the workforce was so transient that his contacts would sometimes have gone home between his visits and he would have to 'start all over again'. He also felt he had erred in starting at Tongaat. It was one of the biggest companies, employing a large number of workers and easily accessible from Durban. But Tongaat had consistently kept one step ahead of other sugar companies in the facilities it offered and was thus a relatively popular place of employment.[14] 'Although the wages leave much to be desired the living conditions are much better and even food is much better.' M and his advisers 'felt we cannot make a breakthrough here'. He switched his attention to less salubrious estates where he 'concentrated on telling the workers about low wages . . . better conditions of work and also the living quarters', which were 'very dirty and even food was no better than that of pigs'. M did feel that, despite his inability to establish any organizational base, he had made important contacts with migrants in the compounds and instilled some broader political consciousness. The sugar estates, short of workers because of industrial expansion, were beginning to make conditions more attractive, offering extra meat rations and bonuses. According to one former compound manager this helped to undercut any potential unionisation.[15]

M now began to perceive the political potential of the rural areas more clearly, and to see the need for more co-ordinated organisation. Up to this time, he had tended to accept, following the lead of most Congress leaders, that the cutting edge of politics was in town, and that it 'would take years to educate rural people'. His experience on the sugar-fields helped to make him realise that it was also urban leaders who needed to be educated in rural issues. More important was the fact that in 1958–59, rural Natal exploded in political protest and Congress, though it could hardly keep up, expanded rapidly in the rural areas and found, of necessity, that rural issues became of far greater importance in its programme. M began to travel to Pondoland more regularly. He was quite aware of the dissatisfaction and now widespread unease over rural rehabilitation schemes and Bantu Authorities. In Bizana it was rumoured that the government would establish a plantation. He made closer contact with a man he had known for some time, Theophilus Tshangela, near his home at Amadiba.

Tshangela's background was very different from M's.[16] He was born around the turn of the century into a relatively wealthy peasant family: immigrants into Bizana from the Cape, Anglicans and considerable producers of crops. Tshangela received some education and, apart from his involvement in the family farming and trading activities, became locally employed as dipping foreman. He had no experience of migrant labour, mines and sugar-fields, nor of male migrant associations. During the 1940s, when he was approaching middle age, he left the family lands nearer to town and migrated down to Amadiba location to establish a new homestead. Lack of land played its part in motivating his move as well, for he had become a large stock-owner. He was particularly keen on horses, which he had begun to keep, and even to breed and sell, on some scale. He became known as one of the most successful owners at the regular race meetings held in Transkeian districts at the time. One of the attractions of Amadiba was the expansive and relatively under-utilised communal grazing. He was known to be outspoken and independent-minded. Because of his wealth, influence and popularity, he soon became a leading councillor at the great place of the Amadiba chief, Gangatha. He also served on the district council. Tshangela hardly seemed a candidate for radical political leadership; but, unlike some men of similar background, he was not one of the élite who became strong government supporters in the political events that begun to unfold in Pondoland.

Tshangela began to move away from Chief Gangatha in the late 1950s as the state started to put pressure on the chiefs to support their rural programme. (Amadiba, with its rapidly growing population, was becoming an important part of the district.)

> There was much talk about the rehabilitation schemes, about these Bantu Authorities, fencing off and all that. So Tshangela was quite concerned about all these things. He was being paid by the Bunga for being a member, but he decided to leave the job. And he was paid handsomely by the chief for being his adviser . . . but he left that too.

Tshangela was concerned about the strength of popular feeling against the chief and the government's plans. He resented the way in which the government was going about implementing the schemes. Perhaps he was worried about the threat of stock-culling; large owners were liable to have a disproportionate number of animals confiscated. M's kraal was near Tshangela's.

> I went to see him at his house, his kraal. . . . We talked a lot and he wanted to know certain things; I had brought with me a copy of *New Age*; that was the pro-ANC paper. He was very interested and we discussed the paper. . . .

> Told him to keep every copy I sent him, because when I go back we will discuss what was said in the paper. I will say that we had great influence on Mr Tshangela.

M may exaggerate this influence. But Theophilus Tshangela became perhaps the second most important leader of the rebels in 1960.

It should not be thought that the ANC, or any other national organisation, played a major role in the disturbances of 1960.[17] The leadership of the hill committees was local and the national organisations followed rather than initiated the action except in the sense that the revolt in Pondoland took place at a time of general political turmoil. The aims of the leaders in Pondoland were still significantly particularist. They were fighting for a limited local independence from state authority and a form of local political authority which was answerable to the people. Their struggle was certainly related to the broader changes in the national political economy, and the movement increasingly imbibed some more general ideas of political liberation. But with significant exceptions, such as Govan Mbeki, Congress leaders did not fully recognise the importance and potential for organisation in Pondoland.[18] Even the Unity movement, which had a longer record of commitment to rural mobilisation, and the Pan-Africanist Congress (PAC), which attracted significant support from Transkeian migrant workers, do not appear to have made much impact.

Nevertheless, there was scope for involvement by those in national organisations who could build bridges and win trust locally. Anderson Ganyile, a protégé of Mbeki's, was dismissed from Fort Hare and returned to his home in Bizana to become secretary to the Central Committee of five elected leaders in Pondoland. And M himself came down from Durban again. Though well accepted at Amadiba, he was not automatically recognised at his first hill meeting.

> Just before I left Durban I already had wind there was going to be a mass meeting at Ndhlovu hill. . . . I went straight to the hill. . . . Of course it was my first time. There were hundreds of Pondos there. They were all talking – I mean the leaders were talking. At question time I raised a few questions. I was shouted down by the Pondos. They wanted to know where I came from. What did I know about this thing? Do I come from Durban? So in Durban you people have heard that we are making [collecting] a lot of money here so you are coming here to grab our money, steal our money. Anyway, that was nothing to me. I knew that if the people do not know you then they are sure to be hostile to you.

Nevertheless, because of his background, M was able to provide important links for the movement. He helped to arrange legal representation for Tshangela and others when they were arrested. He activated his established networks of workers from Pondoland in Durban and collected funds. He rapidly made good contact with the central leaders, played some advisory role and later put them in touch with Natal activists. He also made representations to the van Heerden Commission of Inquiry into the disturbances.

M stayed on in Durban for a decade and a half after the revolt in Pondoland. These were difficult years for former political activists and he was detained on more than one occasion. Nevertheless, he was able to purchase more sewing machines and keep his business going. After 1976, he returned to the Transkei, making a living as a tailor. Some of his custom comes from the *indlavini* for whom he makes the large bell-bottomed trousers, although they are now a fading force.

M's memories, and the character of the experiences and events he lived through, suggest that a number of important facets in the changing patterns of African consciousness in the twentieth century are still inadequately understood. It has certainly been convincingly argued that migrant workers in southern Africa could be, from the earliest phases of mass labour migration, deeply conscious of alternatives on the labour market, wages, conditions and contract terms.[19] Constrained by the restrictive and coercive environment of compounds, they were nevertheless able to resist 'in the nooks and crannies of the day-to-day situation' – resistance manifested in such acts as desertion, theft, loafing and 'impertinence'.[20] It is now also clear that migrant workers could, though not unionised, organise or participate in strike action in a wide variety of situations.[21] (Unionisation of migrants on any significant scale has, with a few exceptions, been a relatively recent and minority phenomenon.) But many migrant workers also retained deep roots in a changing rural social environment. Van Onselen reminds his readers that 'the simple act of a journey to the mines did not destroy old loyalties and obligations that belonged to a different world, neither did it automatically render obsolete beliefs and practices founded on village society'.[22] Nor did it necessarily do so even in the longer term. Indeed, to illustrate how migrants responded at the place of work is to capture only a very partial view of their diverse consciousness. The elaboration of the concept 'worker consciousness', while an important corrective to a view of migrants as passive target workers, should not obscure this fact. The importance of controls exercised on migrants within rural society, and migrants' links to their rural base, in shaping choices on the labour market and even their responses at work are only beginning to be explored.[23] One route of investigation, suggested strongly by M's experience, is the history of associations and networks among men which bridged town and countryside and perhaps took on new importance in both worlds as migrancy became more central to rural African societies.

The very nature of these groups, often associated with a particular rural area, in turn raises the question of 'ethnicity' among migrants. Ethnic and particularist associations among workers have certainly been documented in the region, especially in Central Africa, as has the potential for conflict within a workforce where uneven pro-letarianisation and the division of jobs along ethnic lines could emphasise such differentiation.[24] But in the literature on South Africa, ethnicity has tended to be seen as a product of manipulation by mine managers or the result of segregationist and apartheid policies. Certainly, industry and the state could use and intensify such divisions. However, the very unevenness of the process by which people from different areas came on to the labour market, and the rootedness of migrants in particular rural areas, suggests an internal dynamic to changing forms of ethnicity. These emerged directly out of their linked experience of town and countryside. M's narrative shows that such forms of consciousness, and networks, were the very means by which workers organised themselves and were intrinsic to the development of 'worker consciousness'. They should not be ignored in a quest for the origins of an apparently purer expression of class consciousness. The major strikes on the mines, in both 1920 and 1946, may indicate that such particularist associations in the workforce did not preclude the possibility of united working-class action. They may even have made such action possible. Clearly, far more investigation is needed of the various layers of migrant consciousness, and of the way in which these could intertwine with broader, more explicitly class-conscious ideas, or be used to divide the workforce, in specific situations.

M's shift to broader nationalist and class-conscious positions in the 1950s was clearly a response to his changing position, and geographical location, as a worker. But it was by no means a total turnabout. He took with him some of the ideas, values and networks that had been central to his previous experience; these were overlaid with, or meshed with, his newly developing political ideas. Nationalism was not an exclusive position for him, and probably for very many others like him, in the rank and file of the Congress movements. Indeed, it was the very complexity of the layers of his ideas which proved most useful to the Congress movement. If nationalist and union leaders argued against particularist consciousness and organisation, they nevertheless had to recognise that it was through people like M that they could reach the great majority of South African blacks who had not fully absorbed their generalised positions. Perhaps the advances made in mass organisation in the 1950s were in part dependent on the kind of eclecticism, and the very variety of ideas, which lower-level activists such as M carried with them into the political arena.

Finally, M's experiences give some hint as to how difficult it is to pin sociological categories on to the nature of consciousness or to grasp the totality of consciousness, individual or class, at any particular moment. Clearly, the responses of a group or class are framed by its position in the political economy of the society as a whole. But in the rapidly changing world of South Africa's industrial revolution, where people could find themselves peasants, workers, lumpenproletarians and petty entrepreneurs in close succession, and not necessarily in that order, any analysis of the development of political ideas must be able to cater for the variety of the condition of oppression. Moreover, the prevalence and institutionalisation of migrancy meant that rural social forms, always changing but in some areas deeply embedded in the pre-colonial past, exercised a continuing influence on the perceptions of very many workers. The pattern of M's earlier life, though he escaped his rural past more than most, expresses some of these complexities. Forms of consciousness, whether national, racial, ethnic or worker are not necessarily exclusive; they are neither self-evident and self-explanatory, nor mere epi-phenomena of class categories, to be 'read off' from simply abstracted relations to the means of production.[25]

Notes and references

1 All quotations are taken from the transcripts of interviews with M unless otherwise indicated. All interviews were conducted in English so that quotations, apart from some reshuffling, are in his own words. M has given permission for the article to be published but prefers to remain anonymous for the present. (Some supplementary, unrecorded discussions were held in 1984). Other interviews conducted in Bizana in 1982, including those with Samuel Mazeka, Albert Ngunze, Headman Tshangela, Mcetywa Mjomi, Petros and Phato Madikizela, George Green, Annie and Bertie Mgetyana, Anderson Ganyile, Caledon Mda and Meje Ngalonkulu, have been useful in providing background and context to M's responses. The fact that a number of interviews were focused on migrant experiences and male youth associations is reflected in the weight given to these issues in the chapter.

2 For background material on Pondoland at this time see Monica Hunter, *Reaction to Conquest* (London 1936, 1964); William Beinart, *The Political Economy of Pondoland 1860–1930* (Cambridge 1982, Johannesburg 1983).

3 More details on migrancy to the sugar estates can be found in Beinart, *Political Economy of Pondoland*, Ch. 5 and William Beinart, 'Labour

migrancy and rural production: Pondoland *c*. 1900–1950', in P. Mayer (ed.), *Black Villagers in an Industrial Society* (Cape Town 1980).

4 Discussion of the *indlavini* and other youth groups can be found in Philip and Iona Mayer, 'Self-organisation by youth among the Xhosa-speaking peoples of the Ciskei and Transkei', 2 vols, unpublished, 1972; M. C. O'Connell, 'Xesibe reds, rascals and gentlemen at home and work' in Mayer, *Black Villagers*.

5 Interview, Samuel Mazeka, Mtayiso, Bizana, 17 April 1982.

6 Interview, Caledon Mda, Bizana, 8 April 1982.

7 On urban faction fights see Ian Phimister and Charles van Onselen, 'The political economy of tribal animosity: a case study of the 1929 Bulawayo Location "faction fight"', *Journal of Southern African Studies*, 6 (1) 1979.

8 Charles van Onselen, *Studies in the Social and Economic History of the Witwatersrand, 1886–1914* (London and Johannesburg 1982) vol. 2, *New Nineveh*, 'The regiment of the hills', and 'The witches of suburbia'.

9 Discussion, Annie Mgetyana, Bizana, 1982. 'Sotho' was used as a label to describe urban women in Johannesburg because they were perceived to be in a majority there. Indeed, there had been a rapid migration of Sotho speakers to the Rand in the 1930s.

10 E. Hellmann, *Rooiyard. A sociological survey of an urban native slum yard*, Rhodes-Livingstone Papers, no. 13 (Manchester 1948); Eddie Koch, 'Without visible means of subsistence: Slumyard Culture in Johannesburg 1918–1940', in B. Bozzoli (ed.), *Town and Countryside in the Transvaal* (Johannesburg 1983).

11 Dan O'Meara, 'The 1946 African mine workers' strike and the political economy of South Africa', *Journal of Commonwealth and Comparative Politics*, 13, 1975, 158, which remains the most informed account of this central but under-researched strike.

12 Beinart, *Political Economy of Pondoland*, Ch. 3, and 'Labour migrancy and rural production'.

13 On Congress and worker organisation in Natal in the 1940s and 1950s see Albert Luthuli, *Let My People Go* (London 1962); Leo Kuper, *Passive Resistance in South Africa* (New Haven 1957), and *An African Bourgeoisie* (New Haven 1965); David Hemson, 'Dock workers, labour circulation and class struggle in Durban, 1940–1959', *Journal of Southern Africa Studies*, 4, 1977; Ken Luckhardt and Brenda Wall, *Organize or Starve!* (London 1980).

14 On Tongaat and the sugar-fields, see R. G. T. Watson, *Tongaati: An African experiment* (London 1960); Pierre L. van den Berghe (with E. Miller), *Caneville. The social structure of a South African town* (Middletown, Conn. 1964).

15 Interview, George Green, Maringo Flats, Port Shepstone, 5 June 1982.

16 Interview, Ngubake Headman Tshangela, Imizizi, Bizana, 3 June 1982.

17 Govan Mbeki, *The Peasants' Revolt* (Harmondsworth 1964); J. Copelyn, 'The Mpondo revolt of 1960–61', unpublished BA (Hons) dissertation (University of the Witwatersrand 1977); William Beinart and Colin Bundy, 'State intervention and rural resistance: The Transkei, 1900–1965' in M. Klein (ed.), *Peasants in Africa* (Beverley Hills 1980).

18 For Mbeki's background, and also the position of the Unity movement, see Ch.

8 above; for the PAC, Tom Lodge, 'The rural struggle: Poqo and Transkei resistance, 1960–1965', in Development Studies Group, *Conference on the History of Opposition in South Africa* (Johannesburg 1978).

19 Charles van Onselen, *Chibaro. African Mine Labour in Southern Rhodesia 1900–1933* (London 1976); I. R. Phimister and C. van Onselen, *Studies in the History of African Mine Labour in Colonial Zimbabwe* (Gwelo 1978).

20 van Onselen, *Chibaro*, p. 239.

21 For example, P. L. Bonner, 'The 1920 black mineworkers' strike: a preliminary account', in Belinda Bozzoli (ed.), *Labour, Townships and Protest. Studies in the Social History of the Witwatersrand* (Johannesburg 1979); William Beinart, 'Cape workers in German South West Africa: patterns of migrancy and the closing of options on the Southern African labour market', in *The Societies of Southern Africa in the Nineteenth and Twentieth Centuries* vol. *II* (Collected Seminar Papers, Institute of Commonwealth Studies, London 1980).

22 van Onselen, *Chibaro*, p. 195.

23 P. Harries, 'Kinship, ideology and the nature of pre-colonial labour migration', in Shula Marks and Richard Rathbone (eds), *Industrialization and Social Change in South Africa* (London 1982); P. Delius, *The Land Belongs to Us* (Johannesburg 1983); Beinart, *Political Economy of Pondoland*.

24 Phimister and van Onselen, 'Political economy of tribal animosity'; J. C. Mitchell, *The Kalela Dance* (Livingstone 1957); A. L. Epstein, *Politics in an Urban African Community* (Manchester 1958); H. L. Vail and L. White, *Capitalism and Colonialism in Mozambique: A study of Quelimane district* (London 1980). Papers delivered to the Conference on Ethnicity in Southern and Central Africa, (University of Virginia 1983) to be published in L. Vail (ed.), *The Political Economy of Ethnicity in Southern Africa* (forthcoming), expand further on these questions.

25 See Ch. 1, pp. 25–6.

CHAPTER TEN

Political mobilisation during the 1950s: an East London case study

Tom Lodge

The progress of popular African political opposition during the early period of apartheid, from its first dramatic assertions in the 1950 stay-at-home strikes to the destruction of radical African organisations in the early 1960s, is the subject of a considerable body of scholarship.[1] Its chronology is sufficiently well known not to require detailing here. Where there is less certainty and agreement is in the analysis of the sociology of early post-war African resistance, in the understanding of its aims and ideology and in the assessment of its extent. This chapter will address itself to these topics. It will examine them first in very general terms and secondly through the narrow lens of a local case study focused on the development of political organisations in East London's Duncan Village. The intention of this chapter is not so much to provide answers but rather to indicate the limits of existing research.

The most significant organisation, the African National Congress (ANC), grew rapidly during the 1950s, most dramatically in 1952 during the Defiance Campaign of passive resistance when its membership swelled from 7,000 to 100,000, declining thereafter but probably exceeding its 1952 peak towards the end of the decade.[2] For black South Africans this was a political movement of unprecedented size and duration, its following matched historically only by the Industrial and Commercial Workers' Union (ICU) during its much shorter life as a mass movement. Factors which contributed to popular political mobilisation during the 1950s included the doubling of the African urban population during the 1940s and the accompanying movement of Africans into secondary industry, trade-union organisation during the same period, the new threats posed to black petty-bourgeois security, status and aspirations by the Nationalist administration, the efforts to impose more stringent forms of control on African labour, the elaboration of influx control and its extension to African women and, finally, expectations generated by decolonisation and other changes in the international political environment. Most political organisation took place in towns and the ANC's following was a pre-dominantly proletarian one though its national leaders were, as in previous decades, usually men (and occasionally women) from a middle-class background. The significance of the ANC's social composition has been differently interpreted. Dan O'Meara, writing in 1975, argued that with the catalyst of the 1946 African mine-workers' strike the ANC altered from being an élitist body oriented to constitutional protest to becoming the representative of a militant class alliance whose new proletarian base was conscious 'of the need for independent class action'.[3] Thus:

> The trade union movement generated a class consciousness into which Congress could drop its roots, finally giving it a secure political base, and which reacted in turn on the growing national consciousness propagated by the Congress Youth League, raising it to a higher pitch. The 'African Nationalism' and the goals expressed in the Freedom Charter in 1955 were very different in tone from the anti-socialist individualist 'Africanism' of the original Congress Youth League manifesto . . . [they were] considerably more radical, displaying an enhanced concern with the material position of the proletariat, . . . they showed an increased awareness of the role of the capitalist mode of production in itself producing and reproducing the system of exploitation.[4]

A very different view was taken by Martin Legassick in an article published in 1974. He depicted the ANC during the 1950s as a movement 'torn between the African nationalist pressures of its mass base and the quasi-chartist ideology of its liberal or left-wing leadership'.[5] Instead of O'Meara's conception of a defensively oriented petty-bourgeois leadership discovering increasing common areas of concern with workers, here we have a leadership linked to a 'liberal bourgeoisie' in uneasy combination with proletarians aroused not so much by maturing class consciousness but rather by the 'vague populist demands' of African nationalism:

> . . . the mass appeal of African nationalism in this period of mobilised popular consciousness lay in its implicit demand for the restoration of land and resources of South Africa to the indigenous population. The quasi-chartism of the left could make no consistent allowance for such a racially based movement and indeed tended to denounce such 'racial' appeals as chauvinist – but was sufficiently vague to allow for apparently common aims.[6]

Both O'Meara and Legassick employ a Marxist conceptual framework, but either one or the other of these two opposed interpretations appear in most of the relevant literature.[7] Both views depend upon different assumptions about the history of urban African society which are seldom tested. For example, the argument that the ANC during the 1950s was in the process of being 'transformed by its new class base'[8] has as its premise that the urbanisation and concomitant growth of manufacturing which occurred in the 1940s was concurrently producing a specifically working-class-directed political culture. The wartime development of African labour organisation is cited as evidence of this. Too little attention, though, has been paid to the precise nature of the structural shift which was affecting the racial composition of the workforce. Exactly which jobs Africans were doing after entering industrial employment, the extent to which within individual industries they were growing in importance as they acquired skills or as the labour process was broken down, their regional concentration and proportional significance within urban African communities are questions which have yet to be systematically investigated. Recent research into the metal industry indicates that the introduction of new technology which heralded the takeover by Africans of most stages of production was only just beginning in the mid-1950s.[9] White workers were supplanted much earlier in textiles and food processing,[10] and not surprisingly it was here that African labour organisation proceeded most swiftly. But in the case of many townships during the 1950s the number of industrial workers would have been greatly exceeded by those working as delivery men, servants, cleaners, watchmen and in similar capacities in shops, offices, services and private households.

The level of African trade-union activity during the 1940s has been estimated by many scholars on the basis of figures produced by the trade unions themselves. Such figures need to be examined more carefully. The (African) Council for Non-European Trade Unions (CNETU), for example, in 1945 claimed a membership for its affiliates of 80,000 in Johannesburg, 15,000 in Pretoria, 5,000 in Bloemfontein, 3,600 in Kimberley, 15,000 in East London, 30,000 in Port Elizabeth, and 10,000 in Cape Town.[11] The affiliation of 40 per cent of the African urban industrial workforce was claimed by CNETU.[12] But in Port Elizabeth, for example, in 1946 the African population numbered 42,000 and the African workforce was less than 20,000[13] – CNETU's figures were obviously considerably exaggerated. Both then and later in the 1950s the strength of African trade unionism derived from organisational initiatives in three branches of light industry, food textiles and clothing, as well as in laundry and dry-cleaning establishments. When trade unions were strong they were very important in contributing to the organisational substructure of a popular political movement: this was the case in Port Elizabeth, Benoni and other East Rand townships, and Durban. In Port Elizabeth particularly, trade unionists had supplanted traders and middle-class professionals in the ANC leadership by 1950.[14] But this was by no means typical.

The squatters, the bus boycotts and other popular resistance movements of the 1940s which influenced the ANC leaders to decide upon mass-based militant forms of protest were built round a populist ideology and charismatic leadership in which class-based sentiments played no role.[15] Perhaps in recognition of this, the veteran trade unionist and Communist Party leader, J. B. Marks, announced in anticipation of his arrest just before the opening of the Defiance Campaign: 'This is the hour now. I am being crucified and I feel the weight of the cross.'[16]

But if the proletarian ethos of the ANC during the 1950s is often overestimated or misunderstood, the argument ascribing to its leadership a bourgeois dynamic is similarly questionable. At a national level in contrast to previous decades, businessmen played no role in political leadership and this was reflected in the lower echelons. In Pretoria's ANC, for example, based interestingly in the predominantly non-industrial workforce of Lady Selborne rather than among the factory workers of Vlakfontein and Atteridgeville, the organisation had a socially modest leadership during the 1950s, though it received financial assistance from the Chinese traders. Here people of professional status were absent and small-scale entrepreneurs were outnumbered by delivery men and labourers.[17] In Sophiatown's case it is possible to discern in the history of the local ANC some articulation of petty-bourgeois concerns, but even here the politicians were tending to respond to their more underprivileged constituents.[18] And when petty-bourgeois leaders evoked communal themes and values in a populist vein they were not necessarily attempting to mask class distinctions within the movement; as the autobiographical writing of African intellectuals of the time reveals[19] there was a vast area of shared experience between middle-class political notables and their proletarian neighbours. The stress on community rather than class in the discourse of African politicians during the 1950s reflected, surely, a perception of what to them was most obvious and most deeply felt. The analysis of black South African political history through class-based concepts therefore requires great caution and delicacy.

African political organisations of the period are similarly difficult to classify strategically and ideologically. Much of the existing discussion suggests that African politicians had a consistent set of strategic intentions shaped by a common ideology. So to modern sympathisers of the ANC the men and women of the 1950s were revolutionaries.

Critics on the other hand suggest that the ANC restrained popular militancy during the 1950s and was a body dominated by middle-class reformists.[20] Documents such as the Freedom Charter are quoted from selectively as evidence either of Congress radicalism or moderation. Usually very little attention is paid to the perceptions of participants of what they were trying to do or to the fashion in which political appeals were understood and received by those to whom they were directed.

The eclectic range of intellectual influences, the social complexity of both leadership and rank and file, and the regional variations in the popular impact of organisations such as the ANC or its dissident offshoot, the Pan-Africanist Congress (PAC), make any generalisation very difficult. By 1950 the ANC had been shaped by a variety of political influences and traditions of protest. The Christian liberalism of its founders remained important in determining the responses of many of those in prominent positions such as the two President-Generals of the decade, Dr James Moroka and Chief Albert Luthuli. But the reorientation of African politics in a more militant direction reflected the ascendency of two other groups: communists and nationalists. Neither group during the 1950s could be said to control the organisation and each was influenced by its association with the others. Not surprisingly long-term strategy was never clearly defined, not publicly anyway, and the ANC's actions during the decade demonstrated the full range of its intellectual heritage: days of prayer and attempts through civil disobedience and demonstrations to persuade through force of moral example alternating with the implicitly revolutionary challenge of the general stay-away strike.

Much of the direct action and popular unrest of the decade took place outside the scope of formal organisations, and the energy of local and national politicians was often absorbed by the effort to bring localised subsistence related popular movements within the ANC's orbit. In certain centres the ANC's local presence as a community organisation responding to local sources of discontent was of greater significance to local people than its national programme of activity. In Soweto, for example, where there was very little popular participation in the ANC's national campaigns, the ANC between 1954 and 1959 was deeply involved in the direction of a rent boycott. In recognition of the local salience of such struggles from 1955 Congress started energetically to contest the hitherto neglected Advisory Board elections. In these circumstances the particular ideological orientation of the ANC leadership may have mattered less to ordinary people than the organisation's performance in bread-and-butter struggles. It is interesting that the Orlando Africanists, who in 1959 were to form the PAC, never picked up much of a local following despite their advocacy of a racially motivated populism, itself inspired by what they understood to be common political perceptions. But the Orlando Africanists were not activists, they were on the whole middle class, and they were not interested in the issues arising from everyday life.

As well as functioning in different fashions on a national and a local scale the character of political movements differed between regions. In Port Elizabeth, for example, consistently the strongest centre of ANC mobilisation, trade unions had in the 1940s thrown up a political leadership and generated an organisational expertise which made the ANC a much more constant local political influence than in most centres. Trade unions and trade unionists on the other hand made a negligible contribution to the development of nationalist bodies in East London or Pretoria. In the case of the PAC during the brief period of its existence as a powerful force in black South African politics, from 1959 to 1963, its following in the Transvaal was drawn heavily from schoolchildren, teachers and clerical workers, whereas in contrast in the Western Cape it was, particularly after 1960, an organisation of migrant workers, ideologically coloured by their distinctive preoccupations.[21] In such different social contexts the purpose and strategy of the political movement would be perceived differently by different sets of participants.

Consequently, assessments of the purpose and ideology of radical African politics during this phase must be tentative and qualified. The essential ideas which motivated political activists may well have varied at different levels in the organisation, as suggested by Legassick in the passage quoted above. A comment by one of the ANC's national organisers, T. E. Tshunungwa, is suggestive. After a visit to the Western Cape, Tshunungwa warned of the 'extreme . . . confusion' that resulted when people discovered that the white 'Congress of Democrat men are taking a lead in the ANC meetings . . . a politically raw African who has been much oppressed, exploited and victimised by the European sees red whenever a white face appears'.[22] But it would be a mistake to overstress the extent of such tensions between leadership and rank and file. While the integrationist spirit central to both Luthuli's personal philosophy and the Freedom Charter would appear to negate any claims that the ANC uniformly functioned as a nationalist movement, such evidence should be evaluated within a wider context. Nelson Mandela, while subscribing to the same beliefs as Luthuli could nevertheless combine these with an acute consciousness of an African cultural identity:

> Many years ago, when I was a boy brought up in my village in the Transkei, I listened to the elders of the tribe telling stories about the good old days, before the armies of the white man. Then our people lived peacefully, under the democratic rule of their kings. . . . The names of Dingaan and Bambata among the Zulus, of Hintsa, Makana and Ndlambe of the Amaxhosa, of Sekhukhuni and others in the North, were mentioned as the pride and glory of the entire African nation. . . . The structure and organisation of early African societies in this country fascinated me very much and greatly influenced the evolution of my political outlook. . . . There were no classes, no rich or poor, and no exploitation of men by men. . . . In such a society are contained the seeds of a revolutionary democracy in which none are held in slavery. . . . This is the inspiration which, even today, inspires me and my colleagues in our political struggle.[23]

The ANC popularly helped to nurture such an identity, its visual symbols, compelling songs and iconography stressing a shared cultural identity which was felt by leaders at least at the same emotional depth as welfare socialist or integrationist ideals.

Questions of strategy tell us more about the ideology of the movement than the broad spectrum of political beliefs its members held. During the 1950s the ANC did not have a systematically conceived strategy: given the overwhelming disparity between the forces it could muster and those at the disposal of the state and considering also the absence of helpful sources of external inspiration, this was hardly startling. Rather in the fashion of the followers of Wellington Butelezi, who in the Transkei three decades before had sought their salvation through 'plane loads of black Americans',[24] so with the ANC whose leaders looked outside their own ranks for historical comfort and optimism. Some had a perception of an impending crisis, the nature of which was only vaguely grasped, but which would certainly find the state in a moment of unprecedented vulnerability to decisive opposition. Oliver Tambo expressed this understanding eloquently in 1955:

> We shall not have to wait long for the day when only one method will be left to the oppressed people in this country – precisely what that method will be is impossible to say, but it will certainly be the only method, and when that has been employed and followed up to its logical conclusion, there will be no more struggle, because the one or the other of the conflicting forces – democracy or fascism – will have been crushed.[25]

To this end the ex-Youth League leaders stressed the value of house-to-house mobilisation of membership and the virtues of a tight pyramidal organisational structure, 'The M Plan', loosely implemented in Port Elizabeth. One apparent constituent in the state's ultimate vulnerability (notwithstanding its apparent strength) was the widely held conviction that apartheid and the smooth functioning of a modern economic system were incompatible.[26] But if the more militant politicians of the 1950s recognised and to an extent welcomed the eventual likelihood of conflict this was not a general perception; for many 'non-violence' was a question of principle as much as tactics. Chief Luthuli was not atypical in his hope that a significant section of the white population might respond to reasoned Congress exhortations. As late as 1959, the Anti-Pass Planning Council was emphasising 'education' among whites 'about the evils of the pass laws' as important enough to constitute 'a second front in our anti-pass struggle'.[27]

Just why such hopes should have persisted is a difficult question. Organisational weakness and the absence of alternative sources of optimism is one element in the answer as is the pervasive influence among educated Africans of liberal ideology and institutions.[28] The small number of whites who participated in Congress activities were also important in this respect. As indicated above, the material conditions for an alternative working-class-oriented revolutionary politics were still in formation: African workers had yet to occupy a strategically advantageous position in manufacturing (indeed during the 1950s the pace of their advance in industry was considerably slower than the decade before). In such circumstances to place all one's hopes in the future possibility of ruling group demoralisation was not unreasonable. Those who rejected such a credo usually embraced instead the equally illusory millennial expectations of a violent communal uprising.

The dramatic quality of post-war African resistance has sometimes led it to being understood as posing a considerable threat and obstacle to the state's policies. Certainly this was the way the ANC and its allies were frequently pictured in government propaganda, but this should not be confused with the actual extent of opposition mobilised by nationalist organisations. The two most successful resistance movements (judged by their duration, scale and the measure to which they halted or at least delayed the implementation of state controls) were those of peasants resisting land rehabilitation and Bantu Authorities and the women's refusal to accept passes. In the case of the first, this occurred independently of any but local forms of organisation. With the women the ANC and its allies helped to co-ordinate and lead resistance, but much of the action was spontaneous and local in inception. The South African Congress of Trade Unions is sometimes credited with the upswing in black wages which happened towards the end of the decade,[29] but the upward trend was to continue into the 1960s well after the demise of the One Pound a Day Campaign and in fact the highest levels of industrial conflict during the decade were in the years preceding the campaign.[30] The most elaborate and best organised protest led by the ANC, the 1952 Defiance Campaign, drew nearly three-quarters of its participants from the townships of the Eastern Cape, in particular those of Port Elizabeth and East London.

Port Elizabeth was the setting of the most sustained ANC opposition throughout the decade and it was here, most of all, that the ANC succeeded in becoming central to the politics of everyday life.[31] Port Elizabeth, though, represented an easier environment for African political organisations than other centres. Some of the groundwork had been done by trade unions in the 1940s. These had benefited from the absence of compounds, the linguistic homogeneity of the workforce, very rapid industrial growth (in Port Elizabeth labour shortages persisted into the late 1940s) and a relatively relaxed administrative framework: there was no influx control in Port Elizabeth until 1953. Trade unionists held political office and by 1952 dominated local ANC leadership. The local ANC was advanced in other respects. A large proportion of Port Elizabeth's black population lived in New Brighton, with Orlando, an early pioneer of the new type of planned township in which many black people would be moved elsewhere in the late 1950s and early 1960s. New Brighton had existed since the 1930s and the ANC had succeeded in establishing itself in this new highly administered terrain.

In other centres the ANC was strongest in the old freehold communities – Sophiatown, Lady Selborne, Alexandra, Cato Manor – some still subject to the constraints of locally contending class interests and all, throughout the decade, with their moral and physical resources under erosion from state removal policies. Political mobilisation in Port Elizabeth was exceptional both in the quality of its achievement and in the conditions which facilitated it. In other centres popular frustration or anger, hope or despair, could suddenly well up in the momentary exhilaration of direct action, especially in reaction to the threatened or actual loss of a particular right or resource and then subside as quickly. Thereafter until the next such upheaval 'politics' would be confined to those few people with the imagination, energy, courage and resources to look beyond the daunting, exhausting and fearsome realities of normal day-to-day existence.

What follows is an account of the progress of political organisations in

East London. Each local centre had its own peculiar characteristics and East London was no exception to this. This local study does, though, serve to give substance to some of the generalisations discussed on pp. 310–18 above. Here political organisers were attempting to mobilise a community under threat. The inhabitants of the Duncan Village location had to contend with the conditions arising from a locally stagnant economy, a harsh and parsimonious administration and the social responsibilities of supporting probably the most impoverished rural region in South Africa, the Ciskeian reserves. For many of them also, this period was to represent the end of a social era: from the early 1960s the construction began outside East London of a new and differently ordered urban community, that of Mdantsane, second only in size to Soweto. As well as the helplessness and insecurity produced by these conditions, the recent rural origins of many of the villagers, together with their continuing involvement with rural society, helped to slow the development of working-class politics. Trade unions apparently flourished for a time, but their influence remained confined to the workplace while within communal politics populism reigned. The case study then is testimony to the fragility and socially inchoate character of radical African politics during the 1950s. But before looking at the nature of this politics let us first examine briefly the social and economic conditions that provided the backdrop to its development.

East London, a port city, had undergone considerable industrial expansion during the war, much of this involving African labour to replace whites recruited in the war effort. Unlike many industrial centres African labour was not accommodated in municipal compounds or hostels and equally untypically the African population displayed an even ratio between the sexes and most spoke the same language, Xhosa. While the city fathers were anxious to limit this population's expansion through various forms of influx control instituted from the 1930s, that was where they felt their responsibilities ended. The majority of workers in East London attempted to maintain their homes in the countryside, returning every weekend to the surrounding reserves to visit their families. The municipal authorities constructed no housing at all between 1926 and 1940, and when money became available after the city's proclamation under the Urban Areas Act, progress on the first subeconomic scheme of Duncan Village was so slow that in the main location four-fifths of the population lived in privately constructed wood and iron shacks. Shack owners tended to be an external group, located in the countryside.

Shortage of housing kept East London's workers oscillating between their jobs and lodgings in town, and their families and homes at weekends. Rurally derived culture remained influential during the 1950s among East London's African population with adherents of 'Red' ideology roughly equalling 'School' converts to Christianity. The 50,000 inhabitants of location tenements lived in conditions of appalling poverty: the effects of overcrowding, unemployment and low wages intensifying with each fresh wave of refugees from yet greater rural privation. East London's population was sensitive to the changing conditions in the countryside to an extent paralleled only perhaps by Durban. When, between 1945 and 1951, the Ciskei was ravaged by a terrible sequence of droughts, the iron shacks of Duncan Village multiplied to accommodate another 20,000 tenants and infant mortality peaked at 60 per cent.[32] Though conditions eased somewhat through the 1950s (by 1963 three children out of every ten died of malnutrition)[33] in essentials much remained unchanged. The local economy stagnated, African workers being concentrated in the service sector, the dockyards and unskilled jobs in labour-intensive industries,[34] with a high proportion unemployed. In 1963 administrators claimed there was a sharp increase in the number of illegal residents who had recently moved into the village. This they attributed to two causes: the post-1957 Western Cape 'endorsement-outs' and 'the existence of a certain element encouraging people in the Transkei to converge on the location in numbers with the hope that the large influx would hamper administration'.[35] If this was the case it was a symptom of the desperate conditions in the Transkei: for decades East London's African population had been subjected to the harassment of irregularly administered (and hence unpredictable) often savagely effective influx-control measures. That same year the first carefully screened tenants moved into the new houses of Mdantsane. Duncan Village was about to experience its historical twilight.[36]

Despite the absence of first-hand oral testimony one can imagine the feelings of rural people, forced out of the countryside by starvation and land shortage (or in the case of squatters and labour tenants, by white farmers), confronted with the glaring discrepancy between urban white affluence and black poverty, and bringing with them a world view in which whites were representatives of a bitterly resented officialdom. It is not altogether surprising to find that the most vigorous political group in the location throughout the 1950s was an Africanist-inspired branch of the Congress Youth League. Gerhart has argued that the intellectual evolution of Africanism was influenced by the peasant background of its original exponents. Certainly its emphasis on racial dichotomy, cultural self-sufficiency and a heroic past would have found a special resonance in the bitter antecedents of many of East London's proletarians. The East London Youth League was exceptional in the history of political groups in the town in that it brought both 'Red' and 'School' people together.[37] The Cape Youth League was unusual in that it developed first in a rural context, round Herschel (the home of A. P. Mda, a founder of the Youth League), thereafter spreading to the coastal towns. Many of its original nucleus at Fort Hare had initially been close to the All African Convention,[38] whose leadership looked to the peasantry for their political base. Accordingly, young student Youth Leaguers in the Cape had begun by organising literacy classes for farm labourers and peasants.[39]

The Youth League branch in East London was founded in 1949 and assumed an immediate importance in local communal politics. Though East London had a history of ANC and Communist Party and ICU activity at the time of the Youth League's founding none of these bodies exerted much local influence.

The ANC itself was divided into two groups, Congress A, the longer established group and by the end of the war virtually moribund, and Congress B, a branch started in 1947 by V. M. Kwinana, a secondary-school teacher at Welsh High School. The rift in local Congress politics seems to have been due to personality differences rather than over questions of ideology or strategy: Kwinana was relatively conservative though willing to co-operate with communists in the 1946 Advisory Board elections in 1946.[40] In the next few years he was to oppose the use of boycott and civil disobedience tactics.[41] The followers of Congress B were to be described by the anthropologist D. H. Reader as 'the older and more law-abiding element' of the location's inhabitants.[42]

While communists appear to have been more active in location affairs than the ANC during the mid-1940s, their ninety African members[43] being responsible for a rejuvenation of Advisory Board politics, most of their energy seems to have been devoted to building a trade-union movement in East London.[44] Notwithstanding their success in this (CNETU claimed the allegiance of 10 unions and 15,000 workers in East London in 1945)[45] they failed to produce a working-class-oriented political movement out of it. Advisory Board politicking tended to involve the better off and all the trade-union work was done outside the location. The party's local leadership was multiracial and strictly enforced curfew laws made it difficult for many of them to enter the location.[46] In the decade which followed East London was to lack that organic relationship between political organisation and trade union which was to distinguish the main centres of Congress strength.[47] In East London communists also faced competition for workers' affiliation: a local rump of the ICU presided over by an ageing Clements Kadalie had organised textile, railway and harbour workers – in 1947 textile workers came out on a wildcat strike to reinstate an ICU shop steward.[48] The ICU was scarcely militant: its leaders lived on past glories (which were remembered annually on Kadalie's birthday at beachside picnics) and otherwise concentrated on improving location amenities. One of Kadalie's final acts before his death was to start a subscription fund to build a community hall.

The small cluster of high school graduates, many of them teachers, who decided in 1949 to found a branch of the Youth League in East London were immediately to provide a more vigorous political voice than had been heard in Duncan Village for a long time. Three men formed a leadership triumvirate: C. J. Fazzie, A. S. Gwentshe and J. Lengisi. By 1949 these three men were in their mid to late twenties. Fazzie was working as a teacher and had been a member of the ANC since 1947 when he had joined Congress B at the behest of his school's vice-principal, Kwinana.[49] There is less information available on the background of the other two: Gwentshe was shortly to open a shop while Lengisi some years later would work as an attorney's clerk.[50] According to Fazzie the decision to found a branch of the Youth League in East London was inspired by developments at Fort Hare; the East Londoners were stimulated by contacts they had with such students as T. T. Letlaka, Ntsu Mokhehle and Robert Sobukwe.[51] As a result of such influences the three became 'diehard African nationalists'.[52] They set about their new role with enthusiasm, collecting food and blankets for a strike of nurses at Victoria East hospital[53] (Fazzie later married one of the nurses involved), advocating the boycott of Advisory Board elections (to the annoyance of Fazzie's original mentor, Kwinana)[54] and in June 1950 organising and leading a successful stay-away strike in concert with the ANC elsewhere. The 26 June stay-away confirmed the local Youth League's ascendancy for it was acrimoniously opposed by the older men in Congress A and B.[55]

Political ascendancy did not modify Youth Leaguer doctrine: in 1952 Fazzie was to write a sharp letter of reproof to the *Bantu World* which had employed the phrase 'Mandela/Mda' axis to describe the dominant ideological influence on the ANC's national leadership. This was, Fazzie wrote, a slur on A. P. Mda 'who had worked for years for the cause of African Nationalism'.[56] This was at the point at which the

ANC in alliance with the Indian congresses was to embark upon the Defiance Campaign, a point at which orthodox Africanists were to discern a deviation from 'clear cut' African nationalism. But whatever reservations they may have had about the ideological complexion of national ANC leadership the East London Youth League were enthusiastic and effective advocates of defiance: under their leadership nearly 1,500 local volunteers were arrested between June and November 1952, making East London after Port Elizabeth the second most important centre of the civil disobedience campaign in the country.[57] Fuelling the campaign in East London was the acute social distress which had sharpened during the 1940s as a result of the location's overcrowding as well as Youth League rhetoric which was especially well suited to the emotional needs of East London's African population, a population which, like the Youth Leaguers themselves, was of predominantly rural origin. In other centres the Youth League remained an intellectual coterie; here for a while it acquired a popular following and this, together with the proximity of the Fort Hare-based intellectuals helps to explain its adherence to Africanist dogma.

During the campaign the East London Leaguers who had been joined by T. T. Letlaka, a teacher from Fort Hare, set up the splendidly named Bureau of African Nationalism. The bureau was based at East London for there the local Youth Leaguers had access to a roneo machine, but its members were drawn from a wider group who were to include Mda, next to Lembede one of the most important early exponents of Africanism[58] and throughout the 1950s a high school teacher in Herschel, and Ellioth Mfaxa, an interpreter from near King William's Town and the ANC's organiser for the border region during the mid-1950s. The bureau was founded with high hopes. As its first newsletter proclaimed:

> The present campaign of Defiance of Unjust Laws is merely a development in detail of an aspect only of the 1949 Programme of Action. The campaign only marks the beginning of a long mass-based struggle for national emancipation. . . . Tremendous strides have been made since the emergence of a new conscious African nationalism. But much more remains undone: Firstly, the tremendous democratic forces which have been unleashed must be given a clearer direction and goal. The objectives of the struggle, both immediate and long range, must be more clearly defined and pin-pointed. The dynamic energies of the vast millions must be harnessed to the nation-building and liberatory tasks. Secondly, the people's understanding of African nationalism must be deepened, and its far-reaching implications clarified with greater vigour and zeal. Thirdly, the wiles and machinations of the enemies of African nationalism both inside and outside the general movement must be exposed and foiled and defeated. Fourthly, the struggle

must be intensified on the basis of the 1949 Programme of Action, and on the basis of African nationalism. Fifthly, a new Africanistic people's leadership must be produced, and the claims of the outlook of contemporary Renascent Africa – 'Africanism', must be established once and for all. And lastly, the African nation must be consolidated and its spiritual and material resources mobilised and harnessed to the great tasks of freeing 'Africa in our life time' on the basis of African nationalism and its higher development, AFRICANISM.[59]

In East London, though, the exhilaration produced by the local success of the Defiance Campaign was to lead to a crushing disappointment. On 9 November 1952 a police baton charge broke up a public meeting and in the shooting and rioting which followed eight people were killed, some as a result of police bullets. A white Dominican nun was killed and mutilated by rioters, many of whom, it was subsequently discovered, were young teenagers from the poorest part of the location.[60] In the aftermath of the riots, shock at the violence and fear of reprisals caused 5,000 people to leave East London, mainly shack dwellers with homes in the Ciskei. The Defiance Campaign was brought to an abrupt halt. Notwithstanding its spontaneity the riot was immediately associated with the ANC and people were no longer willing to identify themselves publicly with the Congress cause. Lengisi, Fazzie and Gwentshe had been under arrest since September and in March were tried for incitement. All three received suspended sentences as well as being restricted by banning orders. Lengisi and Gwentshe were actually banished from the Eastern Cape and removed to a remote village in the Transvaal.

In the next few years the Youth Leaguers contented themselves with private discussion groups and the issue of a few more bulletins from the bureau. These petered out in 1955. There was no alternative leadership group. Few of the former local Communist Party members were active politically after the party's dissolution in 1950. Apparently they had never, in any case, been political activists having been mainly associated with the moribund Congress A group. The trade-union base which had been built in the 1940s melted away: the only active black trade union that remained was the (Coloured) Food and Canning Workers Union and there is no record of the existence locally of its African sister union.[61] None of the former communists attempted any initiatives in African trade-union organisation, and the Africanists, teachers, interpreters, clerks, traders and messengers were usually from a background which did not provide much insight into industrial worker organisation.[62] Instead in 1955 six Youth Leaguers stood unopposed for the Advisory Board with 287 voters (1 per cent of the electorate) demonstrating their support. This action did not succeed in broadening their following; the new Advisory Board members were widely regarded as 'youngsters, elected only by youngsters' and in 1957 they withdrew in conformity with an ANC call for a national boycott of Advisory Board elections.[63] Meanwhile C. J. Fazzie, the remaining member of the original leadership triumvirate began to attend meetings in Johannesburg with the Orlando Africanists, travelling 'in disguise' because of his restriction by the authorities to East London.[64] It was Fazzie's friendship with the Orlando group which was to lead to the creation of a PAC base in East London.

Cornelius Juta Fazzie was born in Queenstown in 1924. His father, a lay preacher in the Methodist Church, was a migrant worker in Worcester in the Western Cape. He had an uncle who helped to lead the 1930 East London ICU strike. Fazzie was brought up by his mother in East London. Her family were not educated people and he only began attending school at the age of 15. By the age of 19 he entered Welsh High School which he was to attend for three years. By this stage the Second World War had awakened an interest in politics: he 'observed events very thoroughly'. He gave up his involvement in Rugby football and devoted much of his spare time to ANC activity. By 1952 he was secretary of the Provincial Executive of the Youth League and its recognised leader in East London. He led a large group of volunteers into the city centre one cold July night in defiance of curfew regulations and was imprisoned for three months, only to be rearrested on his release in September. Losing his teaching job in the aftermath of the campaign, he worked as an untrained draughtsman in an architect's office in the employ of a Mr Osmond, a city councillor and later Mayor of East London. From 1958 he ran a general dealer's store in Duncan Village, Mr Osmond apparently using his influence to obtain a site for him. Fazzie could not be described as an intellectual and he was dependent upon others for ideas and inspiration. By the late 1950s he was suffering from tuberculosis. His enthusiasm and loyalty as well as his local prominence as an Africanist earned a place on the PAC's National Executive to which he was elected at the April 1959 inaugural conference.

According to Fazzie, most of the remaining membership of the local branch of the Youth League followed him into the PAC. Fazzie claims that Lengisi and Gwentshe, recently released from their banishment, joined him in leading the local branch,[65] but is vague about the details of other office-holders and members, though they were all, apparently, socially rather similar, reasonably well educated, in modest commercial or white-collar occupations. They left a rump of the local ANC branch, about ten men who remained loyal to the ANC partly as a consequence of friendships with some of the Port Elizabeth Congress leaders (there were few defections in Port Elizabeth to the PAC). We will first follow the course of the local PAC's development before returning to examine what happened to those who stayed faithful to the ANC.

Despite the success in creating a local organisational base and notwithstanding the impression of Peter Molotsi, a visiting member of the PAC National Executive, who later claimed that East London was 'far readier than any other place in the Cape for the pass campaign',[66] in subsequent months the PAC did not appear to have succeeded in arousing much popular support locally for their 'positive action' against the pass laws. In the days which followed the opening of the anti-pass campaign on 21 March 1960 on at least four occasions Pan-Africanist supporters held public meetings in the main location of Duncan Village and urged people not to carry passes. On 28 March a small procession of a dozen or so men presented themselves without their books for arrest at the police station. It was reported that PAC leaflets were in circulation on several occasions. A man was convicted for shouting before others 'Africa belongs to the Africans'. Between 21 March and the end of April there were five attempts to burn down churches, three telephone booths were damaged and seven buses were stoned. These events were reported in a series of trials in the District Commissioner's courts in May when three groups totalling twenty-six men and women were given one-year prison sentences for incitement. Their identity was not reported in the press and this anonymity was reinforced by the status of the court: the cases were brief and not defended.[67] Neither these acts nor local ANC or PAC calls for a stay-at-home on 28 March and in mid-April[68] excited any externally discernible communal response, though in the case of the PAC strike call popular reaction to it may have been inhibited by five raids on the township by the police and army with Saracen armoured cars and in one instance a light aeroplane.[69] The 1,433 people arrested in these raids were described as 'mostly young natives with no passes – tsotsis' and the raids were expressly conducted with the motive of removing the politically volatile.[70]

Even if the police were correct in identifying a potential following for the PAC within the location, for most of East London's inhabitants it is likely that memories of the 1952 bloodshed were too recent. It is also possible that the PAC men had got too used to functioning as a small conspiratorial clique and had neglected to broaden their organisation's influence through public meetings and house-to-house canvassing in the weeks leading up to the campaign. In any case their comparative youth as well as their relatively privileged social background might have undermined their credibility in the eyes of many of the location dwellers. For some the events of 1960 signalled the virtual end of their political involvement: Fazzie, for instance came out of a one-year prison sentence to find that his shop had been ransacked. Suffering now from meningitis as well as tuberculosis, he was out of work for several months before he found a job as a timekeeper at a textile mill.[71] Though sporadically in touch with PAC leaders he felt increasingly remote from their cause. In February 1962 he visited Maseru when he heard that some of the people he had recruited into the PAC had been involved in a lorry incident. They had gone to Maseru (in obedience to directives from the Basutoland-based leadership) against Fazzie's advice. By the end of the year he had lost his influence. From December 1962 he was placed under house arrest for five years.

Despite this unpromising beginning the Pan-Africanists in East London proved to be surprisingly resilient. Three trials in 1963 involving a total of fifty-six men attested to the existence of a relatively large insurrectionary movement. The first, in February 1963, was of twenty men and boys, thirteen of whom were under the age of 20 and only one older than 30, charged with illegal meetings. They were arrested after one of these meetings was interrupted by police on 8 November. The state's case broke down because state witnesses were found to be perjuring themselves. One of these witnesses mentioned the difficulty of recruiting: 'the people were not interested'.[72] The next trial which occurred after, and resulted from, the abortive uprising was better reported. It began in East London with originally fifty-two men being charged with sabotage. A large crowd gathered outside the magistrate's court shouting slogans and giving clenched fist salutes. Slogans included 'Africa is ours, we will take it', as well as the more traditional ANC cry of 'Amandla!'.[73] To avoid a repetition of such a demonstration the trial was switched to Butterworth in the Transkei and the accused were broken down into two groups (charges were dropped against some of the men). The state's case included details of meetings held from October 1960. The participants in these, as with the majority of the accused, were young unmarried men drawn mainly from the oldest and poorest part of the location, Juliwe, or from the hostels for male migrant 'bachelors' which began to be constructed in the late

1950s as a municipal response to the overcrowding of the shacks. Nearer the time of the projected uprising meetings became more frequent and attracted larger numbers – on 8 April between 200 and 300 men assembled outside Duncan Village. The leaders were in regular communication with the Maseru headquarters and in response to instructions from John Pokela collected weapons, manufactured grenades from glass, charcoal and match heads, and organised children to fashion swords from car springs and women to hold fund-raising tea-parties. Women, incidentally, were not permitted to attend the main meetings for 'they could not keep secrets'.[74] The occupations of those men who were convicted (the majority of the accused) included car-assembly, power-plant, and timber-yard workers as well as schoolboys. Many of the state witnesses were young teenagers, though there were also indications of police infiltration of the group. Several of the principal PAC men had been identified by the police as a result of their interception of letters from Basutoland.[75] Not all state witnesses were young conscripts: a later trial in 1967 relating to the same events had several PAC office-holders testifying against C. V. Mngaza, the proprietor of a garage in the location, suggestively called Pan-African Motors. The witnesses who included an unnamed PAC regional secretary were discredited for they were found to have been in receipt of security police favours (including the provision of housing) from 1963. The court gave Mngaza the benefit of the doubt and he was released.[76]

Before attempting to draw any conclusions from the facts emerging from these cases a brief outline of the local ANC-inspired movement may be helpful. The East London 'Regional Committee' of the ANC were responsible for a series of assassination attempts, either by shooting or through Molotov cocktails tossed through windows, their intended victims being Bantu Authority urban representatives, suspected police informers and state witnesses. One young girl was killed, the niece of Chief Hoyi, one of Matanzima's supporters. Two others were badly injured. This violence was undertaken at the local leadership's initiative; this was a period when the ANC abjured bloodshed and the national leadership tried to dissuade the East Londoners from any further attempts to kill people.[77]

The East London ANC followers had been reorganised in 1960. After the departure of the Africanists in 1958–59 (the exact date of this is uncertain) a new committee was elected presided over by George Komani and Malcolmness Kondoti. It is possible that the split between ANC and PAC adherents may have been along lines of neighbourhood: apparently it followed a clash between Congress followers in two sections of Duncan Village over the use of a duplicating machine (possibly the former property of the Bureau of African Nationalism), Komani and his adherents eventually carrying it off from Mekeni section to Tsolo section where they lived. This committee was detained during the State of Emergency and was finally dissolved in October 1960 at the instigation of a visitor from Port Elizabeth, Vuyusili Mini. On his instructions a new clandestine seven-man Regional Committee was formed and began the construction (after a certain amount of external prodding) of a pyramid of seven-man cells, in certain areas consisting of three layers of cells, each linked to a superior cell through one 'contact man'. Most of the lower cells were recruited from young men – some still at school, others unemployed school-leavers. Many of the cells were formed at large meetings held in the grounds of Welsh High School and addressed by members of the Regional Committee. Other forms of recruitment included more private social functions where ANC songs would be openly sung to attract potential supporters. Aside from the assassination attempts the activities of these cells included the distribution of leaflets (the reasons for each attack were announced in stencilled leaflets), the compilation of a map of police stations in the region, the manufacture of bombs and fund-raising from location businessmen as well as through tea-parties organised by women. The attacks were carried out by various cells, and the 'youths' helped and were supervised by one of the older men on the Regional Committee. Many of the participants were arrested in mid-1963.

From the very cryptic details contained in trial records it is possible to form an impressionist picture of a movement which sociologically was not very different to the local PAC. Five members of the original seven-man nucleus were put on trial in 1964 and the two others gave evidence against them. Five of the seven were veterans of the Defiance Campaign, the most experienced ANC member joining the organisation in 1950. Two much younger men were still at school in 1960 and joined the ANC after its banning. The dominant personality in the group, Kondoti, was unusual in that he worked during the previous ten years as a casual labourer and domestic servant, changing employers on eight occasions. Of the rest there is information about four: Bongco, effectively second in command, owned and ran a photo-graphic studio in the village, the two recent school-leavers worked as clerks and typists, one for an attorney and the other at Welsh High School, and Bennet Mashiyana, an older man who turned state's evidence also worked as an attorney's clerk. The members of the lower cells were possibly a little better educated than the mass of local PAC followers and seem to have included fewer manual workers though the leadership in April 1961 did try to mobilise stevedores in the national stay-away strike in protest against the Republic celebrations.[78]

In East London there were formidable barriers to the political mobilisation of Africans. Poverty, job insecurity, and unemployment, together with a well-entrenched local tradition of authoritarian reprisals after moments of communal assertion helped to check the development of widespread involvement in radical organisations. Officially permitted channels of political participation were even less likely to evoke a popular response: this was indicated throughout the decade in the dismal voter turnout in Advisory Board elections. The decline after 1950 of trade unions meant one of the most important constituents in the organisational base of a radical black political movement was absent. Job insecurity and the population's oscillation weekly between urban and rural society probably also helped to restrict the development of proletarian class solidarity. It was consequently those who were materially and psychologically most immune to the apathy and fear arising from insecurity and repression who were most likely to participate in movements like the ANC and the PAC. At best such people represented a minority: men in middle-class occupations such as teaching or clerical work, independent businessmen and the schoolchildren and unemployed youth whose imagination had yet to be crushed by the experience of East London proletarian life. The proximity of East London to the Youth League's stronghold of Fort Hare University College helped to confirm the early ascendancy of Africanism in Congress politics; in the absence of a well-developed alternative tradition its polarised world view retained its attraction for the young inhabitants of the Duncan Village schools and hostels. For older people the realities of everyday life limited their political imagination and sapped their self-confidence. In such circumstances it is reasonable to argue that though the insurgent's insurrectionary vision was articulated by a small minority it represented wider and more popular hopes and fantasies.

The case of East London's African politics conforms in many respects with the more general pattern outlined at the beginning of the chapter. A weak petty bourgeoisie and a working class still in the process of developing an awareness of its distinct class identity produced a politics shaped not so much by sectional interests but rather the feelings of anger, fear and weakness which pervaded the whole community. At its most potent it could draw upon a strong emotional communal identity – 'Africa is ours, we will take it' – but the moments when such feelings were expressed were separated by periods of silence, fear and apathy, periods when political assertion was perceived by many to be the expression of 'youngsters, elected only by youngsters'. Of course this was not inevitable or universal: in other centres the survival during the 1950s of a trade-union tradition or the development of struggles over such matters as housing or transport helped to extend and sustain the base of local political participation. That these were not factors in the African politics of East London may have been partly attributable to the idealist predisposition of the young Africanist leaders, but it is also likely that the local environment was exceptionally problematic: an unusually stagnant economy, strong cultural distinctions between sections of the workforce, job insecurity, atrocious housing conditions, the social and geographical proximity of rural poverty and a repressive and vigilant local administration. To a greater or lesser extent these were the conditions with which African politicians had to contend throughout the country during the 1950s. Such conditions produced more often than not a politics of waiting rather than of activity. Such a politics is unusually inarticulate. Obviously the Youth Leaguers' sectarian nationalism can tell us only a limited amount about the wider society of which they formed a part. In the days before opinion polls popular political sentiments had to be read from actions, events and occasional exclamations from bystanders rather than carefully phrased ideas. Men and women shouting 'Africa!' outside a court room, the religious idiom of popularly attended political events, the sudden eruptions of violence: all these testify to a communal identity founded upon a widely shared perception of injustice expressed usually in the terminology of race and nation rather than the solidarity of class.

Notes and references

1 See especially: Leo Kuper, *Passive Resistance in South Africa*, (London 1956); Edward Feit, *African Opposition in South Africa*, (Stanford 1967); Edward Feit, *Urban Revolt in South Africa* (Evanston 1971); Thomas Karis, Gwendoline Carter and Gail Gerhart, *From Protest to Challenge*, vol. 3: *Challenge and Violence*, 1953–1964 (Stanford 1977); Gail Gerhart, *Black Power in South Africa*, (Berkeley 1978); Tom Lodge, *Black Politics in South Africa since 1945*, (London 1983).

2 For membership figures see: Cape ANC's circular letter to branches, 7 Jan. 1954, Karis and Carter microfilm collection (copy held at the University of the Witwatersrand), Reel 2b, 2 DA 1730/19: 40/13; Secretary's report to the Cape ANC Provincial Conference, 1953, Karis and Carter microfilm, Reel 2b, 2 DA

17; South African Institute of Race Relations Papers, University of the Witwatersrand, AD 1189, unsorted box, National Executive Report to the 1955 Conference of the ANC; SAIRR Papers, AD 1189, ANC 111, National Executive Report to the 46th ANC Conference, 1958.

3 Dan O'Meara, 'The 1946 African mineworkers' strike', *Journal of Commonwealth and Comparative Politics*, 12 (2) July 1975, 154.

4 *Ibid.*, p. 169.

5 Martin Legassick, 'South Africa: capital accumulation and violence', *Economy and Society*, vi (3), 1974, 284.

6 *Ibid.*, p. 285.

7 Edward Feit, for example, in the works cited above argues that the ANC was guided by 'bourgeois' preoccupations. Bernard Magubane in *The Political Economy of Race and Class in South Africa* (New York 1979), echoes O'Meara in stressing the common class interests of the ANC's leaders and followers.

8 O'Meara, 'African mineworkers' strike', p. 168.

9 See Eddie Webster, 'The colour of craft: changing forms of job protection among members of the Ironmoulders' Society, 1944–1968', Belinda Bozzoli (ed.), *Town and Countryside in the Transvaal*, (Johannesburg 1983).

10 Jill Nattrass, *The South African Economy: Its growth and change*, (Cape Town 1981) p. 173.

11 Cited in Edward Feit, *Workers without Weapons* (Hamden, Connecticut 1975) p. 38.

12 O'Meara, 'African mineworkers' strike', p. 153.

13 Union of South Africa, (Pretoria) *Population Census, 1946* UG 41, 1954.

14 See Lodge, *Black Politics*, p. 51.

15 This is especially forcefully demonstrated in Kevin French, 'James Mpanza and the Sofasonke Party in the development of local politics in Soweto', MA dissertation (Faculty of Arts, University of the Witwatersrand 1983) pp. 75–200.

16 *Bantu World*, 14 June 1952. James Mpanza used to go one stage further likening himself to Jesus and claiming to his followers to be an emissary from God. See French, 'James Mpanza', pp. 114 and 117.

17 Tom Lodge, 'Political organisations in Pretoria's African townships, 1940–1963', unpublished paper.

18 Tom Lodge, 'The destruction of Sophiatown', *Journal of Modern African Studies*, 19 (1), 1981, 107–32.

19 Outstanding in this respect is Ezekiel Mphahlele's *Down Second Avenue*, (London 1959). Mphahlele was more directly involved in political activity than most of his literary contemporaries.

20 One of the most trenchant versions of this argument was published in 1961. It remains influential. See Socialist League of Africa, 'South Africa: ten years of the stay-at-home', *International Socialism*, 5 1961.

21 See Tom Lodge, 'The Poqo insurrection, 1961–1968' (University of the Witwatersrand History Workshop paper 1984).

22 Karis, Carter and Gerhart, *From Protest to Challenge*, p. 58.

23 Nelson Mandela, *No Easy Walk to Freedom* (London 1973) p. 147. The passage quoted is from his address before sentence in his 1962 trial for incitement.

24 Bob Edgar, 'Garveyism in Africa: Dr Wellington and the "American movement" in the Transkei, 1925–1940', in *The Societies of Southern Africa in the Nineteenth and Twentieth Centuries*, vol. 6 (Collected Seminar Papers, Institute of Commonwealth Studies, London 1976).

25 Karis, Carter and Gerhart, *From Protest to Challenge*, p. 39.

26 This perception was not limited to supporters of capitalism. See Michael Harmel, 'Revolutions are not abnormal', *Africa-South* (Cape Town, Jan. – March 1959).

27 SAIRR Papers, AD 1189, ANC 111, Anti-Pass Planning Council Plan, 1959, p. 3.

28 For a suggestive discussion of the impact upon African politicians of South African liberal thought see Paul Rich, *White Power and the Liberal Conscience* (Manchester 1984) pp. 77–97, 132–33. See also Janet Robertson, *Liberalism in South Africa, 1948–1963* (1971).

29 See for example the treatment of this campaign in Ken Luckhardt and Barbara Wall, *Organise . . . or Starve* (Cape Town, London 1980).

30 See statistics in Muriel Horrell, *South African Trade Unionism* (SAIRR, Johannesburg 1961) p. 102.

31 It was in Port Elizabeth in 1954 that the use of a consumer boycott in support of workers in an industrial dispute was pioneered by the ANC.

32 *Daily Despatch* (East London) 2 May 1946.

33 *Ibid.*, 6 Sept. 1963.

34 For survey data on composition of workforce see: D. H. Reader, *The Black Man's Portion* (Cape Town 1961) p 64; B. Pauw, *The Second Generation*, (Cape Town) p. 221; H. Houghton, *Economic Development in a Plural Society* (Cape Town 1960) Table 126, Ch. 7. East London's manufacturing industry comprised mainly of textile and food-processing industries. At the end of the 1950s a car assembly plant began employing Africans.

35 *Daily Despatch*, 19 Sept. 1963.

36 For social conditions in Duncan Village during this period the richest sources are Reader, *The Black Man's Portion*, and Philip and Iona Mayer, *Townsmen and Tribesmen* (Cape Town 1974). Duncan Village still stands today, the focus still of official concern, its tenements now housing a racially heterodox population for whom no alternative housing exists. The bulk of East London's working class dwells in Mdantsane which has produced a militant political culture of its own into which myths and traditions inherited from the Eastern Cape struggles of the 1950s play a conspicuous role.

37 Mayer and Mayer, *Townsmen and Tribesmen*, p. 81.

38 *Inkundla ya Bantu*, 23 July 1949.

39 *Ibid.*, 7 May 1949.

40 *Daily Despatch*, 16 Feb. 1946.

41 Reader, *The Black Man's Portion*, pp. 25–6.

42 *Ibid.*, p. 30.

43 Clements Kadalie papers, African Studies Institute, University of the Witwatersrand, Clement Kadalie to Alexander Kadalie, 9 Nov. 1944.

44 Author's interview with Mrs Rose Schlacter (nee Behr), Johannesburg, July 1981.

45 Rheinallt-Jones papers, University of the Witwatersrand, Ja. 2. 11, 'African trade unions': minute attached to letter from CNETU, 4 May 1945.

46 Interview with Rose Schlacter.
47 See for example Port Elizabeth in Tom Lodge, *African Politics in South Africa since 1945* (London 1983) pp. 51–5.
48 Kadalie papers, Clements Kadalie to Alexander Kadalie, 22 Feb. 1943; Margaret Ballinger papers, University of the Witwatersrand, A 410: 13, 2, 14, 5, Clements Kadalie to Margaret Ballinger, 29 July 1945.
49 Interview with C. J. Fazzie, East London, 1983. I am grateful to Mr Mark Swilling for conducting this interview on my behalf.
50 Karis and Carter microfilm, Reel 10a 2X 924; Reel 11a, 2XL9.
51 Interview with C. J. Fazzie.
52 Karis and Carter microfilm, Reel 11a 2XL9.
53 Interview with C. J. Fazzie.
54 Who in 1950 complained to the Cape leadership of the Youth Leaguers' insubordination and ignorance of procedure. Karis and Carter microfilm, Reel 2b, 2 DA 16: 41/39.
55 *Eastern Province Herald* (Port Elizabeth), 27 June 1950.
56 Karis and Carter microfilm, Reel 10a, XF1.
57 Lodge, *African Politics*, p. 47.
58 Mda believed that 'the rural areas . . .' would ultimately be as important as the cities in overthrowing white rule and he urged nationalist leaders to consider the careful building of a revolutionary 'basis in the reserves', and 'careful cultivation of a leadership from the ranks of rural intellectuals' . . . defined as clergy, lawyers and teachers, 'progressive farmers and progressive traders'. Gerhart, *Black Power in South Africa*, (University of California, Berkeley 1978) p. 131.
59 Bureau of African Nationalism, Political Commentaries, no. 1, SAIRR papers, AD 1189, ANC 111, ANCYL, File 6.
60 W. B. Ngakane, 'Investigation into case histories of African juveniles involved in East London riots' (SAIRR, Johannesburg, mimeo 1953).
61 Only one African trade union and 500 unionists were located in East London by the 1949 Industrial Legislation Commission. See Union of South Africa *Report of the Industrial Legislation Commission of Enquiry* (Cape Town) UG 62, 1951 Cf. the CNETU claims of 15,000 members in ten unions cited above.
62 C. J. Fazzie, when interviewed, was fairly withering on the record of East London communists and it is possible that this passage, based on Fazzie's highly subjective account, may do the former Communist Party members less than justice.
63 The episode is described in Mayer and Mayer, *Townsmen and Tribesmen*, p. 53.
64 Karis and Carter microfilm, Reel 10a, AFI.
65 In the interview he may have been confusing their role in the CYL in 1952 with the possibility of their involvement in the PAC. According to the biographical material in the Karis and Carter microfilm collection, Gwentshe did return to East London at the end of the 1950s but Lengisi did not.
66 Mfaxa, in a better position to know, dissented from this view when interviewed. Karis and Carter microfilm, Reel 12a, 2XM 86.
67 See *Daily Despatch*, 7 May, 11 May and 16 May 1960.

68 *Daily Despatch*, 29 May and 19 April 1960.
69 *Ibid.*, 11 May 1960.
70 *Ibid.*, 19 April 1960.
71 *Daily Despatch*, 27 April 1963.
72 *Ibid.*, 14 Feb. 1963.
73 *Ibid.*, 18 Oct. 1963.
74 *Ibid.*, 31 Oct. 1963.
75 *Ibid.*, 1 Nov. 1963.
76 *State* v. *Colben Vuyani Mngaza*, part of transcript held at University of York. Also press reports of trial in *Daily Despatch*, 28 June and 30 June 1967. C. J. Fazzie in his interview claimed that he recruited Mngaza before the PAC's banning.
77 Feit, *Urban Revolt in South Africa*, p. 203.
78 All the above details drawn from *State* v. *M. J. M. Kondoti and 4 others*, Queenstown, 1964, transcript held at SAIRR.

CHAPTER ELEVEN

Batons and bare heads: the strike at Amato Textiles, February 1958

Philip Bonner and Rob Lambert

Liverpool Street, Benoni. On any Friday, passing by, you can hear the buzz of work inside the Amato Textile factory. Outside, women gabble, catching passers-by to buy steaming mealies from the sieves on the braziers. But mostly they wait for the workers to come out of the factory with their pay packets. About 3,700 men work in this factory.

But this is Friday, February 14th. Not a sound from the factory. The doors are locked . . . pay negotiations between the works committee of Amato representing the workers, and the managers have broken down. On the previous Wednesday afternoon the workers had stopped work. Urged back on Thursday morning by their union bosses, they found the doors locked, and policemen standing by to keep them out. They had been told: 'Come back on Friday morning to get your pay. You're fired.'

Now it's 1 o'clock, Friday. Standing outside the factory one can hear the songs of many people. From Daveyton, the Benoni location, and Wattville people were coming singing 'Sifuna imali' (we want money). . . . Also 'we want pound a day'.

White and black policemen were standing all round the factory. Altogether maybe 150.

Drum, April 1958, pp. 44–5

The cadets from the police training school at Benoni[1] were not standing by simply to acquire first-hand experience of crowd control. They had been assigned an actively repressive role in a carefully orchestrated plot aimed at crushing Amato's workers and the organisation of the South African Congress of Trade Unions (SACTU)-affiliated African Textile Workers' Union (ATWIU) in the plant. According to a confidential memorandum drawn up by the Amato management later in 1958, the company had already decided 'with the approval of the Department of Native Affairs, the Department of Labour and Mr Kushke, the General Manager of the Industrial Development Corporation of South Africa Ltd . . . to make a firm stand'.[2] First intimations of how firm that stand would be came when Saracen armoured cars had marshalled a 2,000-strong column of workers along the 17 kilometres between Daveyton and the plant that Friday morning, making what was perhaps their first appearance against domestic opposition.[3] It soon transpired that the police were also ready to unleash the full force at their command at the first sign of unruliness or unrest. Less visible, in the background stood the representatives of the local and central state who were preparing to bring the newly assembled armoury of repressive legislation to bear on the striking Amato workers, once they had been softened up by batons and boots.

For most of that Friday, worker discipline held firm, and it was only after two factory sections were called simultaneously to collect their pay, and were milling around in front of the gates that the police were given the opportunity to act. A solid wall of khaki charged the waiting strikers, and the workers scattered in confusion. Fleeing, they heard behind them 'the rattle of batons on bare heads'. A scattering of possessions littered the factory square in their wake – dumb testimony to the panic of their flight. 'Hats, coats, bundles and bicycles lay where they had fallen', wrote *Drum's* reporter on the scene.[4]

> 'We all ran right across a fence – we flattened it,' recalls one veteran today. 'The police were hitting us with batons and the workers were throwing stones at the police. If you lose a shoe, you can't go back and fetch it. That was the day I lost my wedding hat. It was a new hat I bought from Jay's outfitters'.[5]

The calculated ferocity of the attack can be gauged from the number of casualties sustained. According to union sources seventy-three people were hurt, a number of them seriously.[6] Organisational damage was equally severe, as the company and the state concentrated their energies on crushing organised worker opposition. By its own account the company 'eliminated about 1,000 trouble-makers and reorganised their production and European management';[7] 340 workers were blacklisted, and excluded from employment through influx-control regulations. Richard Luthi who had been at the centre of the strike was endorsed out to Nyqamakwe in the Transkei and given twenty-four hours in which to leave. He later obtained a permit from the Native Commissioner of his home district enabling him to return to Benoni where his family had remained. Upon arrival he was given thirty days by the Benoni Registering Officer to arrange for his family to depart since he was listed as an agitator.[8] A neighbour of one of our informants, Magnedi, was left unemployed for twenty years as a result of these measures. Still others fled to escape arrest. One of the key shop stewards was spirited away by the ATWIU and spent the next two months in other union centres.[9]

As a repressive response this clearly ranks as exceptional even by standards of its time. Its effect was calamitous. 'The labour trouble has not recurred', Amato's report smugly concluded.[10] Union organisation at Amato Textiles, the heart of the ATWIU had been comprehensively crushed. Organisation would not again begin to take root until 1979.[11]

The Amato strike has yet to receive serious scholarly attention, an oversight which reflects wider areas of neglect in the history of the workers' struggle in the 1940s and 1950s. Not only has there been an almost total absence of studies of factory-based struggles, but there still exists no really comprehensive analysis of a black or non-racial industrial union. Partly because of this, one of the key questions of worker and popular politics in the 1950s, remains unresolved and indeed largely unposed – and that is, why did the struggles of the new industrial proletariat, which came into existence during and after the Second World War, assume largely popular or community-based forms? And, conversely, why was factory-based organisation so fragmented, so ineffectual and small?

Edward Feit begins to address himself to these questions. Criticising *SACTU's* preoccupation with political struggle, he attributes their relative weakness as an organised industrial presence to their diffusion of energies into these populist channels. At the same time he makes virtually no effort to examine the activities of *SACTU*'s industrially based affiliates on the ground, preferring to concentrate on the co-ordinating bodies' political role. Even more startling, perhaps, he makes no single reference to the strike at Amato, which pointed unequivocally to the organised strength of the ATWIU on the factory floor, and alludes only to the Amato workers' role in the Benoni £1-a-day campaign.[12] Other writers have plugged some of these gaps. Luckhardt and Wall in their recent history of *SACTU* provide a wealth of detail on individual union activities, but present it in an unsystematic and episodic fashion, so that strikes at Amato and elsewhere are not grounded in any firm understanding of organisational imperatives, organisational constraints and organisational development.[13] In the end it is left to Betty du Toit, herself an organiser for the Textile Workers' Industrial Union (TWIU), to give some idea of the depth and durability of the union presence in Amato and of the power the workers were able to exert within the cramped confines of the factory floor.[14] Yet even here, as with the only other systematic study of a SACTU-affiliated union in the period – that by Goode on the Food and Canning Workers' Union (FCWU) – organisational gains are described but not adequately explained and are often subsidiary to wider political concerns.[15] What is still missing from all of these studies is an understanding of the trajectories of capital accumulation and proletarianisation, less so on a national level than on an industry and regionally specific basis, and of the kinds of consciousness and organisational possibilities that this evoked and made available. In this study of the Amato strike we reconnoitre that route. We would like to stress that much research – in particular interviewing – remains to be done. Here we present an interim report.

'A real strike'[16]

The Amato strike really was an exceptional event. Although strikes by African workers had reached their highest level since the mid-1940s, between the years 1955 and 1957 they were as a rule relatively small and insignificant. Thus although 113 officially recorded strikes took place in 1957, only 6,158 workers were involved, while in the following year Amato workers accounted for the bulk of the 7,128 workers who took part in 64 strikes.[17] Numerically alone, the Amato strike was unusual, but its uniqueness extends well beyond that. What marks it out as a truly significant event is the depth and durability of organisation from which the strike sprang. To anticipate our argument somewhat, it was the factory-floor strength and grass-roots militancy nurtured in a decade-long struggle at Amato, that evoked the exceptionally repressive response of the state – not simply the outbreak of the strike or the fact that 3,700 workers were involved.

The significance of sustaining an organised presence in a factory of 3,700 for over a decade can best be gauged by setting it against the record of other black worker organisations at the time. A persistent feature of black worker organisation over the decades has been organisational weakness allied to apparent numerical strength. At the apogee of African trade-union organisation in 1945 the Council of Non-European Trade Unions (CNETU) could boast a membership of 158,000. How much organisational muscle this represented is none the less open to question since this formidable total was then subdivided into 119 separate affiliated unions.[18] Even from this summary survey a picture emerges of fragmented and unstable organisation, which except under the boom conditions of a wartime economy was unlikely to maintain a position of strength. As South Africa's overheated economy cooled down under the blast of competition after the war this vulnerability was confirmed. Union membership fell off sharply, and most affiliates collapsed, so that by 1949 a full sixty-six CNETU unions had foundered. By 1955 when the rump of the organisation joined SACTU only 12,000 members remained.[19] A number of these flaws were reproduced by SACTU. Starting from a membership of 20,000 workers in 1956 it grew to 53,000 strong in 1961 but once again this was spread over 19 affiliates to begin with and 51 affiliated unions at the end. Particularly striking in this instance is the regional distribution of SACTU support. While the bulk of CNETU membership was concentrated in the Transvaal (80,000 in 1945), SACTU's membership in the economic hub of the Rand stagnated at very low levels between 1956 and 1961.[20] Thus in the fastest industrialising area of the South African economy membership stayed static at around the 15,000 mark, representing a proportional decline from 50 per cent to 30 per cent of SACTU's membership as a whole.[21]

The crushing of the Amato workers contributed significantly to this trend, but this serves only to underline that for almost a decade Amato workers represented a substantial proportion of SACTU-organised workers on the Rand, and an even greater proportion of unionised African labour. Here again the organisation in Amato displays some exceptional features, and was, as will be suggested later, a harbinger of the future.

Linda Ensor has argued that the dilemma of African trade unions in the 1950s was that they

> could only be economically effective if subordinate to the registered trade unions and that if this economic subordination (was) rejected, the only alternative (was) involvement in the political struggle.

She continues

> Given the legal non-recognition of African trade unions, the intransigence of employers against co-operating with them, and the intervention of the State when strikes are employed to demand recognition, the only way of influencing employers to win concessions is by means of the influence of registered trade unions. . . . By acting as a pressure on the registered trade union the African union can win real though limited economic gains for its members, for example, wage increases, deductions for benefit schemes, union access to factories, employers' co-operation in dealing with complaints, etc.[22]

The experience of SACTU bears out much of her claim. The major organised blocks in the Congress with their African sections were, those of the Textile Workers' Industrial Union (TWIU : ATWIU) the Food and Canning Workers' Union (FCWU : AFCWU) and the Laundry, Dyers and Cleaning Workers' Union (LDCWU : ALDCWU). Much of the explanation for the success, perhaps even for the survival of the African parallel branches of these unions, was the industrial leverage afforded by their registered 'parent'.[23] The AFCWU, for example, used the registered branch to extend agreements reached at conciliation boards to its African members, and the TWIU and LDCWU did the same.[24]

Yet here again Amato workers were in a league of their own. Practically the entire labour force in Amato was African, and it was their collective strength rather than any prior agreement negotiated by a registered union and extended to its unregistered African counterpart which was responsible for the remarkable organisational gains Amato workers made.[25] To sum up then, in the wider setting of South African labour, Amato workers were exceptional; on the Rand they were unique.

Russians, riots and spivs

How is the peculiar character of Amato to be explained? Both community and factory contexts have to be taken into account. Let us begin with the community. 'Community' is one of the most over-worked and underdefined terms in South Africa's political vocabulary. What is almost always connoted is some notion of 'community of interests', of a more or less cohesive 'people', sharing a common place of domicile and common conditions of life in a wider racially repressive system. Not only has the term gained enormous currency in recent political debate, but it has also been read back uncritically into the past. Reasonably cohesive popular communities are assumed to have existed in the townships from the time the urban population began to expand. Failure to mobilise, or more particularly to sustain mobilisation among this urban throng, is attributed either to a failure of leadership, or to state repression. Either way, 'the community's' own characteristics are not held responsible; it has been either trampled under or let down.

The same flaw is reproduced in more materialist accounts. Here, classes defined at the level of relations of production somehow naturally and inevitably engage in appropriate forms of class action. Studies of the post-Second World War African working class have yet to break free of this structuralist mould. Working-class action is reflexive, unmediated by culture, ideology or sometimes organisation. The Council of Non-European Trade Unions rises like a phoenix from the ashes of the Industrial and Commercial Workers' Union (ICU), a natural outgrowth of the new industrial working class. Its collapse elicits a deafening academic silence, only broken by faint invocations of fragile organisation or state repression. Attention immediately switches to the formation of a much reduced but still insurgent SACTU.[26] The historical account is peppered with inexplicable gaps.

Such silences can often be traced to a common source. Certain kinds of actions are read off or deduced from given relations of production. When unearthed in particular historical situations, they are then inflated out of all proportion and deemed archetypal of class action of the time. Yet as O'Meara observes 'in any conjuncture the unity of this or that class cannot simply be read off from relations of production, but needs to be constructed via the ensemble of concrete organisational and ideological forms in and through which that class exists'.[27] What is implied here is the possibility of disunity and division, more especially in moments when the working class is still in the process of being formed. At such times it is the bearer of a multiplicity of discourses, of traditions, of organisational practices and forms, some of which feed into a more cohesive working-class culture, others of which fade away. In South African history it has been the 'forerunners' of more 'authentic' class action that have generally attracted most attention. The 'blind alleys', the 'lost causes' have been ignored, or worse still, have not been noticed, even where they were the most common or the most representative forms of popular response.[28] Our understanding of the trajectory of popular or working-class action has, as a result, been radically impoverished. Organisational practices and forms are transposed unproblematically from the 1970s and 1980s to the 1940s and 1950s, or vice versa, as if in both periods we are dealing with basically the same thing.

Common sense, and a modicum of research tells us we are not. Benoni in 1938 was appreciably different from Benoni at the end of the war, and radically different from Benoni twenty years after. In 1938 Benoni's black population numbered 12,000 – the second largest on the Reef.[29] By 1945 this had doubled. Numbers continued to rise at roughly the same rate, reaching 34,000 in 1949 and then jumping by 6,000 more at the end of 1950. By 1957 it had climbed to 77,391.[30] The town's new industrial proletariat was exceptionally diverse both in terms of origin and experience. When the Daveyton location was laid out only in 1955, housing was allocated on an ethnically zoned basis. It broke down roughly as given in Table 1.

TABLE 1 THE ETHNIC BREAKDOWN OF HOUSING IN DAVEYTON, 1955

| | Over 18 | | Under 18 | | Total |
	Male	Female	Male	Female	
Xhosa	1 129	1 181	1 113	1 199	4 622
Zulu	1 699	1 858	1 753	1 878	7 193
Swazi/Ndebele	1 977	2 159	2 286	2 393	8 815
Northern Sotho	2 238	2 214	2 352	2 427	9 231
Southern Sotho	965	1 096	953	1 009	4 023
Shangane/Tonga	551	546	562	562	2 221
Venda	151	147	129	146	573
Total	8 710	9 201	9 153	9 614	36 678

Source: see reference 31.

Such categories mask as much as they reveal. At best they are linguistic groupings (e.g. Northern Sotho): at worst they group together peoples who have no common cultural or political heritage at all (e.g. the Swazi and the Ndebele). Nevertheless, for the present purposes they serve to indicate, however imperfectly, the ethnic diversity of Benoni's newly urbanised population. Experiences of proletarianisation also varied widely. Numerically preponderent among the most recent arrivals were labour tenants from white farms. Streaming in from the Transvaal, the Free State and Natal, they smuggled themselves into the urban centre by first taking work on the smallholdings round Benoni. Once familiarised with the urban job market they then vanished into the lawless anonymity of the 'Indian Bazaar', only to reappear, ethnically wrapped, in one of the new 'ethnic' units of Daveyton location.[32]

This was the path of Paulos Nkhosi, who was ultimately employed in Amato.[33] Almost as common a route was to accept a mine contract at one of the neighbouring mines, and use this as a staging post into the town. Daniel Duze first began work underground at Modder East Mine, then graduated to surface work, and then employed the skills gained in this fashion to secure employment at Burmco – a rubber factory in Benoni which was then expanding its workforce to make tyres for the war. Duze finally ended up in the highest-paying department in Amato.

In the scramble for accommodation he was equally successful. From his initial base in Modder East compound, he moved to a shack in a yard in the old location, and finally, by a ruse, secured a house in the new location at Daveyton.[34] Jackson Nomsobo took an identical path. From his home in Tsolo, Transkei, he took a contract at New Modder Mines in 1944. Two years later he moved on to Dunswart Iron and Steel, substituting the Dunswart hostel for the compound at Modder

East. The year 1948 saw Jackson employed at J & C Tools, during which time he took up residence in Benoni's old location. From there he moved job and place of residence several times ending up ultimately working in Amato and living in Daveyton.[35] Duze and Nomsobo were perhaps unusually successful. Both were clearly unusually enterprising and Nomsobo had a Standard V education. Even so, their route to the towns was followed by thousands of others, most notably mine- workers from Basutoland who came to constitute the scourge of the Reef when combined into the ubiquitous gangs of 'Russians'.[36]

Still other elements of the urban population were recruited directly from the reserves. In 1950 the influx-control officer of Benoni was complaining irritably about the large numbers of unemployed in the locations and attributing this directly to the action of employers. Firms continued to employ natives from the reserves in preference to local labour.

> They can pay them a lower salary and because of the difficulty of again being employed after discharge . . . they work harder and longer.

(The words 'they can pay them a lower salary' were later deleted by resolution of the Native Affairs Committee and substituted by 'they find such foreign natives adaptable').[37] Finally there was the resettled core of Benoni's established black urban population in whose yards many of the newer arrivals lived. Among them a Marabi-style urban culture had developed which greeted the new arrivals with certain distance and disdain.[38]

Benoni's black population was thus both layered and fragmented. While common privations and shared conditions of life in Benoni's unhealthy, congested locations gradually distilled a common working-class culture, in the early 1950s, for the majority of its population, this was still in the process of being formed.

Life in the township was also extremely unstable and insecure. Although the sex and age ratio show a slight preponderance of women and children (see Table 1) which might be read as suggesting settled family life and permanent urbanisation, many of these unions seem to have been contracted in the town. As a result for much of the 1940s and 1950s there was a significant section of the population which was rootless, unstable and had yet to settle down. Temporary unions, desertions of wives and 'unattached Basuto women', multiplied causing great concern on Benoni's town council, who feared the social problems that this would spawn.[39]

Such instability and insecurity was compounded by intense pressure on virtually every kind of urban service and resource. While population doubled during the war, virtually no new houses were constructed due to shortages of materials and the diversion of funds to other channels.[40] Only towards the end of the 1950s was this backlog wiped out. With new arrivals streaming in daily, intense competition was bred over what meagre resources existed. In a manner reminiscent of urban life all over Africa, new forms of combination were created, with the object of ensuring some measure of collective security, many of which were ethnically tinged.[41] Among the most conspicuous of these were gangs, notably the dreaded 'Russians' who were distinguished by the Sotho blanket in which their adherents were clad. As these groups began to carve up the location into separate fiefdoms socalled 'faction fights' flared up. Beginning in 1947, these had become so violent and uncontrolled that Benoni gained the reputation of being the crime centre of the Rand.[42] Much to the indignation of the *Benoni City Times* the town was described by the British newspaper the *Daily Mirror* as 'a location thirty miles from Johannesburg' where violence was endemic.[43]

To begin with conflict was located among rival factions of 'Basotho', e.g. the Matsieng and the Molapo.[44] By August 1949 it had widened to embrace conflicts between 'Xhosa' and 'Basuto', in the course of which many serious injuries were sustained.[45] Ethnic conflict flared intermittently for the rest of the next decade. In 1954 Piet Pheko recalls 'Zulus' and 'Basutos' flocking in from all over the reef to fight it out after a 'Russian' had been killed in Benoni's hostel and the 'Russians' had killed a 'Zulu' in revenge. 'The "Russians" were clever', recalls Pheko, who stood on the roof of a neighbouring Indian shop to get a grandstand view of the fight. A small band of 'Russians' lured the 'Zulus' on to waste land near the Zinchem factory, where they were surrounded by a mass of hitherto concealed 'Basutos', and then were hacked down.[46] Somewhat later, in March 1957, this more generalised 'ethnic' conflict erupted once again when a gang of Xhosa children attacked a Swazi school, killing one pupil. Children poured out on the streets and soon parents became embroiled. Because of a number of Zulu casualties Zulu parents joined the fray on the side of the Swazi, while it was rumoured that 'the Sotho' would join the 'Xhosa' camp. Schools closed and 2,000 workers stayed away from work for several days until the conflict had simmered down.[47]

Observers described these disturbances as 'faction fights' or 'tribal wars' as if by so defining them their genesis had been explained. In fact, these conflicts reflected an urgent quest to secure the barest necessities of life, like a job, or a roof over one's head, in a situation in which such resources were in desperately short supply. Jobs were, all too often, in people's gift. Jackson Nomsobo speaks of payments of up to £25 to secure a particularly prized job in Amato.[48] Piet Pheko remembers how African Malleable Factories was taken over by Basotho 'boss boys' and clerks, so that it became a 'Russian' preserve.[49] Daniel Duze recalls queueing outside Amato's gates for several weeks in 1950 waiting hopelessly for work.[50] After another riot in 1950, in which a white policeman was killed, the Location Advisory Board, representing the longer settled black population, complained bitterly that 'the unemployed of almost the whole Reef are accommodated in the Indian section'.[51] For some it was a luxury to work.

Such patterns were not immutable. In October 1954, for example, a shortage of labour had grown up on the East Rand which was so serious that influx-control regulations had to be loosened to allow workers on mine contracts and from the farms to enter heavy industry. The regulations were not reinstated until 1957, and the easing of the employment situation which was thus reflected no doubt influenced the form and phasing of popular struggles.[52]

What remained more intractable for most of the 1950s were shortages of housing. It was the need to control such resources – whether they be jobs, houses or women – that underlay much of the so-called faction fighting of the time. Following one particularly violent incident in 1949, the Township Superintendent commented:

> It is known but not proved that for some time these (gangsters) have extorted considerable sums of money from the unfortunate and gullible native people by every conceivable pretext such as the offer of physical and legal protection, housing material, representation to Council, employment, etc.
>
> The outbreak of fighting is usually an indication that a rival racketeer is trying to gain control. The prevailing conditions set out below make such lucrative business.

He went on to list the following factors:

1 Lack of proper housing.
2 Conditions in the Asiatic area.
3 Surplus of unattached Basutho women in the area.
4 Difficulty of control of entry in to the location area.
5 Lack of effective police force.[53]

While Sotho miners or ex-miners grouped themselves into ethnic factions for collective security, other layers of the town's black population escaped their common misery by resorting to other means. Citing an unnamed council official, in May 1950, the *Benoni City Times* reported:

There are also the urbanised natives who despoil the better-class natives and who are largely responsible for domestic servants and native males leaving domestic service. These natives . . . have largely emigrated to the Reef towns from the farms. Once here they take any job until they settle down – then, their imaginations are fed by other natives, they refuse to work as domestics or farm hands because the pay isn't big enough.

These natives develop into spivs and are the curse of the location. Other natives working for low wages, but quite content, have their minds poisoned by the spiv and won't work. The result is that many natives join the ranks of the dissatisfied.[54]

Despite the crude stereotyping and internal inconsistencies contained in this official's argument, at least two insights emerge: firstly the differentiation and layering of the urban population whereby one sector was relatively more advantaged in terms of houses and jobs; secondly, an introversion of competition and conflict along internal lines of fracture. What remains missing from this official characterisation is the extent to which ethnicity and layering interpenetrated or overlapped. At the present stage of research such issues remain opaque. What is apparent none the less is that some connections can be made. In the 1949 riot between 'Xhosas' and 'Basutos' 'the Xhosas approached the emergency squatter camp from the direction of Wattsville' (the squatter camp was the emergency home of the more recently arrived Basotho).[55] A similar, though not entirely analogous, context framed the fight of 1954, where the 'Zulus' dominated the hostels at Benoni, while the 'Russians' controlled the Indian section.[56]

The basic thrust of the argument so far is that the scale and rapidity of urbanisation, the lack of basic services and resources and the multiple lines of fracture in Benoni's urban population ensured that popular energies would be absorbed in communal struggles aimed at minimally meeting basic wants. Those same factors likewise inhibited sustained large-scale political mobilisation, although from the May Day march of 1950 through to the stay-at-home of 1957, Benoni witnessed some of the most militant struggles of the African National Congress (ANC) on the Rand.[57] Benoni's proletariat was in the process of being formed – no coherent popular, let alone working-class consciousness had been forged. If anything, a diffuse Africanism was the most likely and available rallying cry, not just against whites, but, in the case of Benoni, against Indians as well.[58] This was the appeal of squatter leaders like Mpanza and Mabuya, and it must be counted one of the ANC's main achievements of the period that a multiracial position was preserved. Failing larger than life revivalist/Africanist leaders, workers looked to smaller-scale patrons and factions in an attempt to improve their lot.[59] Only gradually and spasmodically did political and trade-union organisation take on these roles.

Nowhere is this more clear than in the squatter movement which began in 1945. Benoni's squatter movement closely resembles that led by James Mpanza in Orlando the previous year. Like Mpanza, its leader Harry Mabuya, was diminutive in stature, flamboyant in character, Africanist in appeal and well read in law. He also managed the same happy marriage of self-seeking opportunism and wider public concern.[60] In 1945 when congestion in the so-called Asiatic section of the location was reaching crisis point, Mabuya formed his African Housing and Rates Board. Subtenants in the area were encouraged to subscribe to the board, and to refuse to pay the inflated rentals being demanded by their landlords. Mabuya meanwhile bought tents from war surplus stores and when the subtenants were predictably evicted, he housed them on vacant council land just west of the present Wattsville. 'Tent Town' grew rapidly and the council's hand was forced. An officially sanctioned emergency camp was established and Mabuya gained the credit. Until his death his slate of candidates regularly topped the vote in the camp's Advisory Board elections.[61]

Numerous squatter communities sprang up in similar fashion mostly on smallholdings round Benoni, the most spectacular being that which in June 1950 occupied land set aside for an industrial township at Apex.[62] Again the council's hand was forced, and the new township at Daveyton was the ultimate result.[63] Ironically, it was only with the Nationalist government's 'site and service' scheme and the subeconomic housing programme that a settled urban community began to take shape and that a more coherent working-class culture began to emerge.

'Twenty years ahead of its time'[64]

If the community context of Benoni's workers inhibited working-class and even popular organisation, so too did the uneven and incomplete character of Benoni's industrialisation. Kaplan, Bloch and Webster among others have emphasised that while there was a massive proliferation of industrial establishments during the Second World War, and while the average size of establishment measured in terms of workers employed registered an appreciable expansion, the capital intensity of manufacturing actually dropped during the war. The immediate post-war period witnessed a reversal of this trend as excess profits accumulated during the war were funnelled into machinery and plant.[65] Even so, no thoroughgoing transformation of the process of production was accomplished for another decade. The implications of this pattern of arrested transformation were that the existing labour process and division of labour had yet to be fundamentally disturbed. Most factories remained small; most African workers were still consigned to relatively unskilled work. The conditions for strong factory-based organisation and for a strong workers' movement had yet to be set in place. Tables 2 and 3 illustrate the point.

TABLE 2 NUMBER OF AFRICANS EMPLOYED IN INDUSTRY IN THE BENONI AREA, 1949

African Malleable Foundries	289
Anglo-American Corporation	85
Amato Textile	1 724
Alexander and Company	6
Modder Bee Gold Mine (casual)	11
Modder Bee Gold Mine (casual)	9
Bader and Company	138
Burm Company	202
Benoni Engineering Works	358
Cape Asbestos and Insulation	113
Colonial Timbers	73
Cornthwaite and Jane	52
Delfos Ltd	91
Dunswart Iron and Steel Foundries	961
Eclipse Tube Mill Lines	76
Wright Boag and Head Wrightson	537
H. Incledon & Company	53
Industrial Iron & Steel Foundries	56
Prima Iron & Steel Foundries	136
Parrack and Till	94
Reef Timbers	120
Robert Hudson and Sons	115
Rand Milling Timbers	43
Standard Brass Iron & Steel Foundry	230
Van Ryn Estate Sand Plant	132
Aitken Engineering Works	43
Benoni Welding and Cutting Works	11
Benoni Steel Products	12
Benoni Lumber Mills	25
Benoni Stone Crushers	31
F. M. Brewis	23
J. J. Botha	23
Coronant Foundries	21
Express Fire Supply	14
Far East Crushers	31
Hume Pipes	36

Modder Bee Plantations	33
Precision Equipment	9
Pyramid Sand & Stone Supply	22
Scoop Industries	20
Stewart Raeburn	32
W. S. Thomas & Taylor	32
Thermal Welding Works	35
Vulcan Engineering Works	22
African Tile Company	23
Total	6 218
municipal employees	828
government service	600
domestic servants	2 675
trade and others	4 783
farm labourers	697
Total	9 538

Source: see reference 66.

TABLE 3 WORKERS EMPLOYED BY SECTOR, NOVEMBER 1957

Agriculture	815
Brickworks	56
Industry	11 030
Building	1 251
Government depts	149
S. A. Rand	335
Municipality	1 168
Prov. admin.	100
Commerce	3 672
Hotels	177
Domestics	1 684
Total	20 437

Source: see reference 67.

What emerges very clearly from these figures is that industrial workers still only represented about half of the urban employed, that Amato workers accounted for more than a quarter of this figure and that Amato is quite exceptional in terms of the size of workforce employed. This very disparity thus provides an early intimation of why working-class organisation at the point of production was so limited in Benoni, and why Amato was such a notable exception to this pattern. To explore the issue further a more detailed analysis of the textile industry needs to be made.

The textile industry can in many ways be regarded as the pacemaker of industrialisation in South Africa. In much the same way as the struggle of the Amato workers was a harbinger of the workers' struggle of the future, so the textile industry as a whole in some senses prefigured the path of South African secondary industrialisation. In the immediate aftermath of war the textile industry provided the blueprint for the import-substitution model of secondary industrialisation. In 1948 textile imports comprised between one-quarter and one-fifth of total imports into the Union. With a view to reducing South Africa's import bill and to promoting South African industrialisation the South African government embarked in 1947 on a programme of actively fostering the expansion of textile production. The Industrial Development Corporation (IDC) primed the pump by putting up several million pounds' worth of capital, and found ready collaborators in a number of foreign industrialists.[68] Rising wage costs among the more advanced industrialised countries were eating into the profit margins of many expatriate textile concerns. Compared with most manufacturing industries cotton production was characterised by exceptionally high wage costs as a proportion of total costs of production. The strategy that was ultimately evolved by the textile industry world-wide was therefore that of decentralising production to low-wage areas of the world.[69] Facilitating the shift was the relatively high degree of mechanisation which the industry had attained, since this allowed it to move to areas where labour, to quote the Board of Trade and Industry's (BTI) Report of 1951, was on the whole of an 'unskilled agricultural type'.[70] On this basis an alliance was struck between foreign capital and the state. The state guaranteed favourable conditions of production including contributions towards the capital costs. Foreign capital contributed capital, but above all technology and expertise.[71] As a result the first cotton textile mill in South Africa was established in 1947 (Amato). Two more were constructed by 1948 and by 1950 yet a further five had been built. Reflecting broader shifts in the character and composition of the industry, factories were large, they employed substantial complements of labour and the machinery was technologically advanced.[72]

The new textile plants that dotted the country provided a more favourable, if not more congenial, environment in which worker organisation could take root than existed elsewhere or had been present before. As a result of the mechanised nature of production the majority of workers fell into semi-skilled operative categories.

TABLE 4 SKILLED AND UNSKILLED WORKERS IN THE SOUTH AFRICAN
TEXTILE INDUSTRY, 1950

	Cotton spinning (%)	Cotton weaving (%)	Whole Industry
Unskilled	15.3	25	20.6
Semi-skilled	26.3	28.5	56.2
Skilled	8.4	46.5	23.2

Source: see reference 73.

For African labour this meant elevation out of the ranks of the un-skilled to a position which by virtue of the amount of time and money expended on training commanded a far greater measure of bargaining power. For white workers, conversely, it meant displacement, or de-valuation of skills – usually the former, which reinforced the pre-dominance of black workers in these grades.

The implications of such a radical reshaping of the customary di-vision of labour are brought into sharper focus if one considers the attributes generally accorded to this category of mill worker:

> 'Semi-skilled workers' the US Bureau of Labour Statistics observed, 'are engaged in occupations requiring the exercise of manipulative ability of a high order, but limited to a well defined work routine, or work in which lapses of performance would cause extensive damage to product or equipment.'[74]

The last phrase hints at the Achilles' heel of the new generation of factory – the need to prevent breakdowns in production when ex-pensive machinery was at work. It also pinpoints a new site of worker power. Because of

> 'The high capitalisation of the new textile industry', the BTI Report noted, '[and] an account of the modern high-productive machinery that has been installed in a period when prices were twice those in the immediate pre-war period, it is essential to reduce overheads by working the machinery for two or three shifts.'[75]

To maintain profitability, in short, machinery had to be kept in more or less continuous production. Production stoppages were costly; dislocations of production were, by implication, a vastly more significant lever of worker power.

Such characteristics were common to the textile industry as a whole. To cite the BTI Report once more 'the products are . . . to a large extent competitive . . . the basic manufacturing processes are to a very large extent similar and the type of labour required is very much the same.'[76] Accordingly, the TWIU and the ATWIU were able to organise increasingly effectively over the industry nation-wide.[77] Even so, the Amato factory did present more than usually favourable conditions. To begin with it drew its labour from the permanently urbanised population of Benoni's locations. The reason is uncertain, but the most likely explanation is that it served drastically to reduce labour turnover and absenteeism which stood up to 400 per cent in the low-wage rural areas such as King William's Town.[78] Such were the imperatives towards uninterrupted production that the personnel officer at Amato thoughtfully printed his own special pass complete with photograph and fingerprint. In a letter to an outraged Native Commissioner he explained:

> as you know we employ 3,000 natives from all over the Reef and this firm being a government subsidised operation we must depend on our labour and cover employees as far as possible as far as absenteeism is concerned. . . .
>
> These boys are residing all over the Reef and thus travel 'to and fro' daily, some on night shift. . . . [Some] must leave Springs and Johannesburg at 3.00 a.m. [so] you can imagine the loss in £. s. d. if you have a few hundred machines stopped owing to the fact that the boys may be arrested for a special pass.
>
> The special accordingly 'entitled' its bearer 'to travel to Pretoria, Heidelberg, Nigel, Randfontein, Springs and Reef locations daily until midnight'.[79]

If low labour turnover and absenteeism were important factors in siting the factory at Benoni, the decision did entail an offsetting cost. Basic wages were set at higher levels than elsewhere, while labour stability also permitted more stable worker organisation.[80]

One further weapon was also denied the Amato management, as well as the industry nation-wide, though its significance was probably much greater for Amato. According to the Factories Act 1941, and in conformity with international conventions, women workers, who might have worked for lower wages and so weakened the bargaining power of men, were debarred from working night shifts. The 1951 BTI Report approvingly quoted international moves to 'revise and render more flexible the term night' in order to overcome this problem,[81] but by the late 1950s that had not been accomplished in South Africa. The TWIU had in fact bargained away this restriction in a number of worsted factories in the Cape, although on exactly what legal basis no one was quite sure.[82] In Amato such a move was much more problematical since workers there worked twelve-hour shifts, starting at 6 a.m.[83] This once again hints at peculiar characteristics of Amato not reproduced elsewhere, which helped inject such intense militancy into the workforce it employed. It is to these that we now turn.

Tycoon capitalism

The special features of Amato Textiles owed much to the character of its progenitor, Reuben Amato. The eldest of a Spanish–Jewish family of six, he had been forced to shoulder responsibilty for his siblings after his father died while he was still only 14. Seven years later he decided to emigrate to Australia to prepare 'a new life' for his family. After gambling his money away on the boat, he was dumped penniless in the Congo. Here he started business as a petty trader before eventually moving into ground-nut plantations. Small-scale trading with Lever Brothers soon gave way to the actual production of oil once he purchased his own oil press and entered into competition with his erstwhile trading partners. From these small beginnings Reuben clawed his way up the business ladder, gradually accumulating sufficient capital to enable him to expand his operations into South Africa. In 1941 he founded his first South African company, National Feeds; in 1943 Amato Textiles was launched.[84]

Two features were stamped on Reuben Amato's character by these early experiences in the Congo. Firstly, a relentless drive to accumulate. Secondly, an authoritarian and highly personalised managerial style. Even when his enterprises had expanded massively, he remained involved directly in every aspect of their operation, in the manner reminiscent of the late-nineteenth-century business tycoons. To co-directors he

> lacked human understanding, thus riding rough-shod over people's feelings – a slave-driver in a way . . . a very very tough taskmaster. He was impatient of any interference and could not deal with board meetings. The smaller private company was better suited to his style because he was a loner, an individualist – a brilliant man but pretty unpredictable. But he had to go public to secure more capital for his expansion plans.[85]

Aggressive and impatient, Amato was in constant danger of allowing his ambitions to outstrip his financial resources. A massive loan from the IDC provided the basis for what soon became the largest textile factory in South Africa.[86] But still Amato could not rest. Ploughing back every cent of profits into further expansion, he more than doubled his company's assets between 1949 and 1956, lifting them from £4 million to £10½ million.[87] With virtually no reserve cover the company was always financially exposed. A substantial proportion of available cash resources were permanently tied up in raw material purchases. The company employed a 'roll-over' system of financing which meant that jute bought in Pakistan had to be paid in full in sixty days, the cash coming from the sale of orange pockets and grain bags made from the same jute. In addition the majority of their lines were sold under contract, requiring extremely tight production schedules. Failure to complete orders within the contract deadlines meant the imposition of penalties. Company secretary de Beer reflects

> I was in charge of finance at the time – it was hair-raising. We were on a tight-rope the whole time. There was an absolute tightness of money because of over-expansion. . . . It was a colossal affair with a turnover of about a million rand a month.[88]

Given these constraints, continuous pressure was exerted on workers to raise profitability and to keep production on schedule. When Amato Textiles was established in 1943, the shift system – that 'boundless and ruthless extension of the working day' – comprised two shifts of nine hours twenty minutes, the first from 5 a.m. until 2.20 p.m., and the second from 2.20 until 11.40 p.m. The machines then shut down until 5.00 the following morning. The working day was dramatically extended in 1950, with the introduction of three twelve-hour shifts. Two shifts, working 6 a.m. to 6 p.m. and 6 p.m. to 6 a.m., would be operative in any given week, Monday to Saturday.

> This not only increased the amount of surplus extracted, but also reduced unit costs of production.[89] To maximise the gains this extended working day was combined with an intensification of labour and to this end the company had established a differential piece rate system, founded on a low basic wage rate of £2. 2s. 6d. per week. The differential rates were ranked, starting with the highest rates, as follows: Sack sewing; Weaving and circular looms; Spinning, blowroom, winding; and the Jute section.[90]

Pressure to meet deadlines was likewise extreme, and supervisors were ruthless in disciplining workers to the sixty-day roll-over rhythm of production. It was this set of conditions – an extended working day, greater intensity of labour and necessarily despotic supervision – that underlay the volatile and refractory character of the workforce. Throughout the 1950s the company was wracked by work stoppages. The most vivid recollection of ex-workers from Amato are invariably the endless strikes that took place 'every two weeks'.[91] Daniel Duze recalls one such episode which occurred in 1952 when management tried to replace African workers with Coloureds in the sack-sewing department. Workers refused to speak to anyone except Reuben Amato. Amato duly put in an appearance and settled the matter in characteristic style.

> Mr Amato hit Mr Neville, he clubs him. He want to know why he did this thing, and he calls us inside the factory.

To restore production as quickly as possible the workers' demands for no victimisation and no replacement were fully met.[92]

Duze's account conveys some sense of the tensions that were generated by the need to meet the company's extraordinarily tight production deadlines. Amato would blame Steinhardt, the production manager, for any failure to meet deadlines and Steinhardt in turn, would pressure the supervisors.

De Beer remembers:

> Amato would come in and scream at him. Steinhardt would say, 'labour doesn't produce, there's a go slow'. There was a great deal of tension. Amato moved around the factory constantly, involving himself directly in the issues.
>
> He moved around the factory, and he always used to be in a state of massive tension and anxiety.[93]

On these conflicts, Magnedi commented:

> I still remember when we once made a strike – it was on a Monday – the director of the company came, Mr Amato, he came here and he was fighting with each and every manager and foreman because production was lost, thousands of pounds of production. He was fighting with the foremen because when his car comes in from Johannesburg, each and everybody was shouting.[94]

It was these particular conditions at Amato which provided both the incentive and the space for a strong union presence. All that was required to translate this into reality was disciplined and tactically astute worker organisation. This was supplied from both inside the factory and without. In 1951 full union recognition was conceded after a sit-in had been engineered by Coloured supervisor, Don Mateman. Mateman had first encountered the tactic when working on the coal mines at Witbank, where Shangane labourers had developed 'Tsamahantsi' to a fine art. A lunch-hour sit-in was organised on a lawned area in front of the factory offices, normally out of bounds for the African workers. It was 'a beautiful park reserved for only white girls'. Workers were told to sit on the lawn together, to do nothing and to return to work when the hooter went. The workforce of over 3,000 gathered, and it had impact.

> Workers enjoyed it. Never had they experienced such unity before. They used to look at this lush green place, but it was forbidden them. Now they broke it and sat there.

When the hooter blast signalled the end of lunch break, Mateman, Cindi and the other shop stewards led the factory back to work. Disciplined unity had been asserted. The management was impressed.

Mateman was immediately called to Steinhardt's office and the union secretary, Mike Muller, was summoned. Full recognition was granted – shop steward facilities, as well as stop orders, an unprecedented move for the 1950s. 'We know the union is responsible', Mateman was told – responsible enough, the company hoped, to prevent the endless minor stoppages.[95]

Other, more conventional strikes followed, and often served to consolidate union organisation. Factories are rarely fully organised, and constant effort is required to sustain a strong union presence. In Amato, some departments were weak – the high-bonus sections in particular[96] – and there was always a steady turnover of personnel. In these circumstances strikes could sometimes help to consolidate union organisation. Daniel Duze recalls the transformation in his own attitudes which one such confrontation occurred. Duze had no sooner secured a job at Amato in 1951 than a strike broke out. At this point Duze's awareness was at a rudimentary level, but it grew through the event. 'I didn't understand what they were doing inside', he says. He was given friendly advice by a junior foreman – leave the factory quietly, or else the people will beat you. 'I just took up my things and go outside. I didn't know if it was a strike or what. I just see the people marching.' The event led to discussion, explanation and a request that he join the union. 'There are many who were recruited after the strike. Almost all of us joined the union.' With a growing commitment over time because the union gave 'security', Duze soon found himself pushed to the forefront. He was elected a shop steward and in 1952 led the stoppage referred to above.

> I was one of the organisers. I just switched off my machine. We got a symbol when we are doing that thing. We shout, Hewowee, then all the workers rush to the door.[97]

Various means were used to co-ordinate worker action. Mateman recollects:

> There were metal containers in the factory that were used to store jute material. Workers used to beat the containers like drums. It made such a noise. Everyone knew there was a stoppage or something happening. When a woman came into the factory, workers used to joke by beating the drums. But the union taught a big lesson – the union is discipline. This helped unity. Also, textile factories are very noisy. When the machine stops, everybody wants to know what's happening.[98]

'Middle East' Cindi, so named by workers because he was the 'trouble spot of Africa', recalled the 'whispering campaigns' that were central to the planning and preparation of strike action. He said that another form of communication was 'blowing in bobbins'. This gave off a particular kind of whistle, and workers knew a strike was planned. At lunchtime they would all assemble on the green grass outside the administration office, the site of the historic recognition struggle – now spoken of as 'freedom square' by the workers – in a show of collective strength. Workers also gathered underneath tall gum-trees outside the factory where information spread between departments. The company had organised workers into football teams, 'Amato Roses' being one, with the intention, many believed, of dissipating discontent. Shop stewards hold that this rather worked to their advantage as it provided ideal cover for strategy discussions. Workers entering one shift would also meet with the new shift outside the factory, giving brief run-downs on the situation inside the plant.

Strikes were by no means uniformly successful. In May 1955 a strike over the dismissal of workers led to 163 being sentenced under the Riotous Assemblies Act.[99] Later, in December of the same year, over 300 workers in the spinning department stopped work after a supervisor dismissed two workers.

> A white guy fired them and we didn't like it. We stopped our machines and called another supervisor. We say, this white guy we don't need him here. Then they called management, and management fired him.[100]

Once more, legal action was instituted against the workers. The offenders appeared in court during 1956, charged by the labour department for participating in an 'illegal' strike and 202 were found guilty.[101]

Tension was clearly rising, fed by the workers' need for higher wages on the one side and by the company's strapped financial position on the other. By 1957 the company was in deep financial crisis. The group had expanded rapidly on the basis of extensive loan finance from the IDC and Barclays Bank. Both began to foreclose as they became increasingly unhappy with Reuben Amato's individualistic managerial style. He ignored the well-established practice of consultations over major investment decisions, and his liberal perspective on trade unions and industrial relations issues did not square with the dominant managerial practice: non-recognition and repression. It seems that Barclays and IDC with their quite considerable financial investment in the company, decided to put an end to this approach, which in their view had not succeeded in reducing the level of industrial conflict in the factory and in restoring loss of production. They therefore exerted pressure on Amato more effectively to discipline his workers. 'A strong line was what they felt to be required'.[102]

In six months of negotiations with the company, the union leadership came to realise that the company was incapable of offering a new wage deal.

> Amato had financial problems and I happened to be on the spot. I had to call the workers and say: a strike is not the way to do things, you must be disciplined. Don't demand it now. The union asked the workers to give the employers a chance to raise the money.[103]

At a crucial meeting, immediately prior to the strike, Reuben Amato pleaded for time.

> He wasn't in a position to give. He had borrowed money from many people and they were squeezing him to pay. He stood up at the negotiations and said, 'Look, fellows, I have no more money.' He stood up and emptied his pockets and said 'I'm finished.' And the workers said, 'No, how can you be finished?' He replied, 'Look I am finished, but if you give me a chance, give me just two weeks of production, while I'm trying to negotiate for money.' We understood his position.[104]

The union leadership may have understood it, but the workers in Amato were in no mood to listen, and from here the conflict began to unfold with all the inevitability of a Greek tragedy. Basic wage rates at Amato had remained stationary for the whole decade, while the cost of living had continued to climb. With the move from Apex squatter camp to Daveyton, where over half of Amato's workers now lived, rent and transport costs had soared. House rentals increased from 15s. to £3 a month, so that many tenants began to fall into arrears and evictions began.[105] Between 900 and 1,000 tenants were being interviewed by Daveyton's Location Superintendent each month of 1957 for being in arrears of rent, and ejection orders jumped from 85 in August to 412 in September of the same year.[106]

> If you are in arrears, they wake you up early in the morning – about 2 o'clock, 3 o'clock or 4 o'clock, take you to the administration board and ask lots of questions. Where are you employed? How much do you get? Why don't you pay your rent?[107]

Stop orders on pay packets were introduced at about the same time with the intention of recovering arrears, 73 being secured in August and 157 in September 1957. The practice further fed discontent.

> Workers were angry – some, the labourers, were only getting £1 19s. 3d. per week and 15 bob was deducted for rent. They've got £1 4s. at home for transport and food.[108]

Bus fares also jumped from 1s. 6d. to 2s. 6d. in the course of the year. Tension was screwing up. The Benoni branch of the ANC petitioned the council that the mounting charges 'make it explicitly impossible for people to manage their way out to a better life'.[109] 'There was a demand by the people all over for an increase in wages', Advisory Board member Sinaba advised.[110]

But Amato was in no position to pay. The post-1956 recession had hit the textile industry particularly hard. Amato's difficulties were deepened by the Suez crisis of 1956/57. With that, shipping was directed away from the South African routes and the firm's jute shipments were delayed. Production was reduced to one shift, and the company forced to seek renegotiation of credit. De Beer negotiated extensions with the shipping company Anglo-Africa, and endeavoured to persuade Barclays Bank to hold off. In addition, a good friend of the company in the IDC, Mr Carson Smit, rushed to England to raise new finance. He was the only person at the IDC who was favourably disposed towards Amato, and when he died suddenly in London, the option of additional help disappeared.[111]

Meanwhile the workers, well organised and confident after the successes of the 1957 stay-away, were now more impatient than ever with the protracted and unsatisfactory nature of the negotiations.

> We wanted the union to have the power to get the company to pay us £1 a day, to help us cope with the families, because we were really helping the company with our hands. They [the company] have to understand us. They [the union] advised us you must not bend the company, you must not fight.[112]

There were debates within the workforce over tactics when a minority argued for an alternative to strike action to win their demands – factory sabotage.

> Workers used to look at the dry hessian and say, 'It will take only one match.'[113]

In fact, a large raging fire broke out in the jute mill and two weeks prior to the strike, destroying machinery and jute and causing 'considerable damage' to a section of the building.[114] Increasingly, the majority opinion swung in favour of strike action. The shop stewards tried to hold the membership back, but by Friday they too were swept along. On 12 February the workers finally downed tools. The strike had begun.[115]

Conclusion

The defeat in the strike was a shattering disaster. Organisation in the factory was never to recover. Some shop stewards to this day are so bruised by the experience that they refuse to talk on the matter. For many a sense of bitterness will never be erased. Even this does not convey the full implications of the defeat. In 1957–58 three major confrontations were seemingly engineered by employers with the union. Each was lost by the workers and the union began a slow slide towards collapse.[116] Today it remains a faint shadow of its former self as it accepts invitations to sweetheart status from the management of Frame, the company which now dominates South Africa's textile industry.

The TWIUs were not the only casualties of this period. The FCWUs were simultaneously experiencing a similar attack, as the industry slimmed down and regrouped under the impact of the late 1950s recession.[117] Amato was a foretaste of the gathering assault that was being mounted on popular and working-class organisations. The foundations for the boom of the 1960s were being gradually set in place. A more disciplined, a more regimented, a more stable working class was being constructed, through repression on the one hand, and the provision of certain basic amenities on the other. Nevertheless, while such developments paved the way for the boom of the 1960s, the economic and social realignments that followed likewise heralded the workers' struggle of the subsequent two decades.

Notes and references

1 Interview, A. Magnedi, 7 Dec. 1980.
2 Amato Papers: document entitled 'Confidential memorandum', 2 Jan. 1959, p. 9.
3 Conversation, ex-shop steward, Amato, July 1983.
4 *Drum*, April 1958, pp. 45–6.
5 Interview, A. Magnedi, 7 Dec. 1980.
6 *Drum*, April 1958, pp. 45–6: Bettie du Toit, *Ukubamba Amadolo* (London 1978) p. 89.
7 Amato Papers, 'Confidential memorandum', p. 9.
8 *New Age* 26 Feb. 1958: carried out in terms of the 1956 amendment to the Native (Urban Areas) Act.
9 Conversation, ex-shop steward, Amato, July 1983.
10 Amato Papers, 'Confidential report', p. 9.
11 Conversations, P. Pheko, J. C. Bonner, Sept. 1983.
12 E. Feit, *Workers Without Weapons*, (Hamden, Connecticut 1975) p. 107.
13 K. Luckhardt and B. Wall, *Organize . . . or Starve!* (London 1980) especially pp. 286–8.
14 Du Toit, *Ukabamba*, pp. 63–4, 88–90.
15 R. Goode, 'For a better life. The Food and Canning Workers' Union 1941 to 1975', Hons dissertation (University of Cape Town 1983).
16 Interview, A. Magnedi, 7 Dec. 1980.
17 Luckhardt and Wall, *Organize . . . or Starve!* p. 276.

18 *Ibid.*, p. 60; D. O'Meara 'The 1946 African mine workers strike in the political economy of South Africa', *Journal of Commonwealth and Comparative Politics,* **12** (2) July 1975, 153.

19 Luckhardt and Wall, *Organize . . . or Starve,* p. 70.

20 *Ibid.*, p. 99; T. Lodge, *Black Politics in South Africa since 1945,* (London 1983) Ch. 8.

21 Luckhardt and Wall, *Organize . . . or Starve,* pp. 217–8.

22 L. Ensor, 'The Trade Union Council of South Africa and its relationship with African trade unions', Hons dissertation (University of the Witwatersrand, 1976) p. 43.

23 Luckhardt and Wall, *Organize . . . or Starve!* p. 99 (n. 4); du Toit, *Ukubamba,* pp. 67, 70–1.

24 See n. 23; Goode, 'Food and Canning Workers Union', pp. 57–8.

25 Interview, Piet Beyleveld, 11 Sept. 1983.

26 For example, Luckhardt and Wall, *Organize . . . or Starve* p. 70; O'Meara 'African mine workers strike', pp. 146–54, 166–7. Feit, *Workers Without Weapons,* also cites the Makabeni breakaway, pp. 38–9.

27 D. O'Meara, '"Muldergate" and the politics of Afrikaner nationalism', *Work in Progress,* **22,** April 1982, Supplement, 2.

28 E. P. Thompson, *The Making of the English Working Class* (Harmondsworth 1968) pp. 12–13.

29 D. Humphries and D. G. Thomas, *Benoni – Son of my Sorrow,* (Cape Town 1968) p. 107.

30 Central Archives Dept., Benoni Municipal Records (hereafter CAD:BMR) minutes of the Non-European Affairs Committee, 17 Jan. 1951, p. 62; *Ibid.*, Aug. 1957.

31 *Ibid.*, Dec. 1956.

32 *Ibid.*, Dec. 1956.

33 *Ibid.*, 10 March 1950, letter from Combined Native Advisory Boards, pp. 127–8.

34 Conversation, Paulos Nkhosi, 20 Sept. 1983.

35 Interview, Daniel Duze, 16 Aug. 1983.

36 Interview, Jackson Colbert Nomsobo, 13 Sept. 1983.

37 See, e.g. *Drum,* April 1955, pp. 29–31.

38 CAD:MBR, minutes of Native Affairs Committee, 13 June 1950, Report of Influx Control Officer for May, p. 327; Native Affairs Committee resolutions, p. 404.

39 J. Cohen '"A pledge for better times": the local state and the ghetto, Benoni, 1930–1938', Hons dissertation (University of the Witwatersrand, 1982) Ch. 5.

40 CAD: BMR, minutes of Native Affairs Committee, 13 Sept. 1949, p. 456.

41 Humphries and Thomas, *Benoni,* p. 100.

42 Among a host of examples, see M. Tamarkin 'Tribal associations, tribal solidarity and tribal chauvinism in a Kenya town', *Journal of African History,* **14** (2) 1973.

43 CAD:BMR, minutes of Native Affairs Committee, 10 March 1950, letter of combined Native Advisory Boards, 127; Humphriss and Thomas, *Benoni,* p. 115.

44 *Benoni City Times,* 14 April 1950.

45 *Ibid.*, 24 March 1950; CAD:BMR, minutes of Native Affairs Committee, 13 Sept. 1949, pp. 455, 462.
46 *Ibid.*, pp. 454–6.
47 Conversation, Piet Pheko, 13 Sept. 1983.
48 M. Horrell, *A Survey of Race Relations in South Africa 1956–57* (Johannesburg 1957) p. 88.
49 Interview, Jackson Nomsobo, 13 Sept. 1983.
50 Conversation, Piet Pheko, 13 Sept. 1983.
51 Interview, Daniel Duze, 16 Aug. 1983.
52 CAD:BMR, minutes of Native Affairs Committee, 10 March 1950, letter of Combined Native Advisory Boards, p. 127.
53 *Ibid.*, 18 March 1957, letter Chief Native Commissioner to local Native Commissioner, Benoni, pp. 148–51.
54 *Ibid.*, minutes Native Affairs Committee, 13 Sept. 1949, 456.
55 *Benoni City Times*, 12 May 1950.
56 CAD:BMR, minutes Native Affairs Committee, 13 Sept. 1949, p. 462.
57 Conversation, Piet Pheko, 13 Sept. 1981.
58 Lodge, *Black Politics*, Chs 2 and 5.
59 *Ibid.*, Ch. 2.
60 K. J. French 'James Mpanza and the Sofazonke Party in the development of local politics in Soweto', MA thesis (University of the Witwatersrand 1983); A. W. Stadler 'Birds in the cornfield: squatter movements in Johannesburg 1944–47', *Journal of Southern African Studies*, 6, 1, 1979. At the present stage of research Mabuya remains a shadowy figure. The argument suggested here is therefore based on Mpanza's character and career. Mpanza's achievement, I would argue, rested at least partly on his ability to mobilise a pan-ethnic movement – see, e.g. his adherents' chant on one occasion, 'We Xhosas, Zulus, Sesutos want a place to live' (French, 'Mpanza', p. 143). At the same time he seems to have had more specifically Zulu appeal (Stadler, 'Birds in the cornfield'). What enabled Mpanza to strike a more popular chord seems to have been his appropriation of the attributes of both Ethiopian and Zionist church leaders. His typical regalia 'was partly suggestive of a chief' (cited in French 'Mpanza', p. 78) something characteristic of Ethiopian leaders. His vocabulary was replete with biblical imagery. (The 'Israelites' being led out of Egypt, e.g. – *Ibid.*, pp. 78, 117, 162). Yet he linked this to notions of cleansing and pictured himself as a messiah figure (*Ibid.*, pp. 108, 117) – all of which seems to have struck common chords among his disparate following.
61 Stadler, 'Birds in the cornfield', pp. 31–3. Humphriss and Thomas, *Benoni*, pp. 114–15.
62 *Ibid.*, 114–15.
63 *Ibid.*, 120–2.
64 *Ibid.*, 122–34.
65 Conversation, George Bizos, Sept. 1983.
66 D. E. Kaplan 'Class conflict, capital accumulation and the state: an historical analysis of the state in twentieth century South Africa', D. Phil. thesis (University of Sussex 1977) Ch. 8, especially pp. 283–95; A. Bloch 'The development of manufacturing industry in South Africa', MA thesis

(University of Cape Town 1980) Ch. 4, especially pp. 80–1, 90–9; E. C. Webster 'The labour process and forms of workplace organisation in South African foundries', Ph.D. thesis (University of the Witwatersrand 1983) Ch. III. In the foundry sector a slight variation is encountered with rising capital intensity to 1943 and a decline thereafter – see p. 102. Webster also notes a rapid acceleration of mechanisation between 1956 and 1960 (p. 155).

67 CAD:BMR, minutes of Native Affairs Committee Meeting, 10 Jan. 1949.
68 *Ibid.*, Nov. 1957.
69 Union of South Africa, Board of Trade and Industries Report No. 323, *The Textile Manufacturing Industry*, Dec. 1950, pp. 18, 24, 46.
70 *Ibid.*, pp. 22–3.
71 *Ibid.*
72 *Ibid.*, pp. 25, 46.
73 *Ibid.*, p. 24.
74 *Ibid.*, pp. 45, 56.
75 *Ibid.*, pp. 24.
76 *Ibid.*, pp. 70–1.
77 *Ibid.*, p. 2.
78 Interview, Piet Beyleveld, 11 Sept. 1983; du Toit, *Ukubamba*, pp. 61–81.
79 Union of South Africa, BTI Report No. 323, pp. 61–2.
80 CAD:BMR, minutes of Non-European Affairs Committee Meeting, 9 Oct. 1951, encl. copy letter Personnel Officer, Amato Textiles, to Native Commissioner, Benoni, n.d., pp. 759–60. He emphasised that 70 per cent of the workforce would not need such a document, being employed in Benoni.
81 Union of South Africa, BTI Report No. 323, p. 68.
82 *Ibid.*, pp. 64–5.
83 *Ibid.*, p. 78.
84 Interview, A. Magnedi, 7 Dec. 1982; interview D. Duze, 16 Aug. 1983.
85 Interviews, Charles de Beer, 5 June 1982, Rob Amato, 15 March 1982.
86 Interview, Charles de Beer, 5 June 1982.
87 Amato Papers, 'Confidential memorandum', 2 Jan. 1959.
88 *Ibid.*
89 Interview, Charles de Beer, 5 June 1982.
90 Interview, A. Magnedi, 7 Dec. 1982. Interview, D. Duze, 16 Aug. 1983.
91 *Ibid.*, interview Jackson Nomsobo, 13 Sept. 1983
92 *Ibid.*
93 Interview, D. Duze, 16 Aug. 1983.
94 Interview, Charles de Beer, 5 June 1982.
95 Interview, A. Magnedi, 7 Dec. 1982.
96 Interview, Don Mateman, 4 June 1982: du Toit, *Ukubamba*, pp. 85–6.
97 Interview, Jackson Nomsobo, 13 Sept. 1983.
98 Interview, Daniel Duze, 16 Aug. 1983.
99 Interview, Don Mateman, 4 June 1982: Conversation, ex-shop steward, Amato, July 1983.
100 Du Toit, *Ukubamba*, p. 87.
101 Interview with shop floor leader, 24 April 1983.
102 Du Toit, *Ukubamba*, p. 87.

103 Interview, Don Mateman, 4 June 1982.
104 *Ibid.*
105 *Ibid.*
106 Interview, A. Magnedi, 17 Dec. 1958.
107 CAD:BMR, minutes Special Non-European Affairs Committee, 24 Oct. 1956, 274–5.
108 Interview, A. Magnedi, 7 Dec. 1958.
109 CAD:BMR, minutes Special Non-European Affairs Committee, 24 Oct. 1956, 274–5.
110 *Ibid.*, 15 April 1957, memorandum dated 29 March 1957.
111 *Ibid.*, 15 July 1957, extracts Joint Advisory Board's minutes 23 April 1957, 467.
112 Interview, Charles de Beer, 5 June 1982.
113 Interview, A. Magnedi, 7 Dec. 1982.
114 *Ibid.*
115 *Benoni City Times*, 31 Jan. 1958.
116 Interview, Jackson Nomsobo, 13 Sept. 1983.
117 Du Toit, *Ukubamba*.
118 Goode, 'The Food and Canning Workers Union'.

CHAPTER TWELVE

Incorporationist ideology as a response to political struggle: the Progressive Party of South Africa, 1960–1980

Brian Hackland

Introduction

The Progressive Party was formed in 1959, after a split in the official opposition United Party. Disillusioned liberals from the United Party were joined by a disaffected group from the Liberal Party which opposed its party's policies for a universal franchise. The roots of Progressive Party ideology lay deep in the liberal tradition in South Africa. The party was formed in the belief that 'race' was the most important issue and the most dangerous divide in the country. It saw as its primary objective the development of a political programme which would attract support from both the white electorate and the disenfranchised black majority.

In this chapter the Progressive Party[1] is examined during two periods of economic upheaval and intense political struggle,[2] in an attempt to show the relationship between the changed politics of the party, structural change and class struggle.

Economic instability and structural change

The 1950s in South Africa were characterised by the rapid growth of manufacturing production relative to other sectors.[3] This coincided with a period of marked urbanisation and proletarianisation of black South Africans. From 1957 to 1961, however, there was a period of economic stagnation. The average annual rate of growth of Gross Domestic Product (GDP) dropped from 5.1 to 3.2 per cent.[4] A balance of payments deficit generated by the industrial expansion of earlier years forced the state to impose fiscal and monetary constraints. These, in turn, depressed industrial production.

The crisis in international confidence which followed the Sharpeville killings in March 1960, and the subsequent declaration of a State of Emergency, led to the collapse of share prices in the Johannesburg Stock Exchange. From 1959 to 1961 there was an average net annual capital outflow of R88 million, peaking during 1960. Gold and foreign exchange reserves were cut by half to R153 million by May 1961. The government was forced to raise the bank rate, curb imports and place very severe restrictions on foreign exchange dealings to remedy the situation.[5]

Calls for political reform and accommodation of black demands came in a chorus from representatives of capitalists in virtually every sector of production.[6] In the midst of all the panic, and as share prices plummeted, Harry Oppenheimer's Anglo-American Group moved to stabilise the capital markets and restore confidence. At the same time, it acquired shares and penetrated companies and sectors which greatly enhanced its influence and strength in the South African economy.

Over ten years of boom followed, with average annual GDP increases of 6.5 per cent between 1961 and 1969.[7] Structural changes during the years of boom, including the extension of monopoly production, interpenetration of capital and especially the increased concentration of capital, contributed to rising unemployment levels. In 1960 unemployment stood at 18.3 per cent of the economically active workforce. By 1970 it had climbed to 20.4 per cent, or 1,758,000 people.[8] At the same time the contribution to GDP of the manufacturing and construction sectors increased from 24.1 per cent to 28.2 per cent (1962–70).[9]

It was the source of the boom, however, the growth of manufacturing, which contained the seeds of the slump to follow. The contradiction lay in the fact that the rapid growth of manufacturing was achieved through the importation of capital goods such as machinery and equipment. The result was that as the decade progressed, the value of South Africa's imports rose faster than that of exports, generating, once again, a substantial and growing balance of payments deficit.

During the early years of the following decade the growth of monopoly capital was accompanied by clear indications of impending problems. Although GDP growth for the first half of the decade had averaged 3.9 per cent per year, the annual rate had fluctuated between 8 per cent and 3 per cent.[10] Following the uprisings in Soweto and elsewhere, panic withdrawals of capital by foreign investors allied to work stoppages and disruptions resulted in an effect on economic activity so severe that GDP actually contracted.[11] A brief boom and the recovery of domestic demand resulted in GDP growth climbing to 8 per cent by 1980. By 1981, however, it had again dropped back to less than 5 per cent.[12] By 1982, the economy had stagnated and the country faced record inflation rates. At 16.5 per cent, inflation was at its highest level since 1920.[13]

There were other signs of economic malaise during the 1970s. The balance of payments deficit continued, averaging R838 million per year for the first half of the decade. Capital restructuring, concentration and expansion demanded an exceptionally high rate of investment, 29.2 per cent of GDP compared to 25 per cent during the period 1961–69.[14] A 5 per cent devaluation of the rand against the US dollar in 1971, and a 17.9 per cent devaluation in 1975 were necessary to improve the terms of trade.[15] In 1977, after Soweto, there was a net outflow in short-term capital of R1,086 million and a net R111 million outflow of long-term capital. For an economy which relied on foreign investors to provide 15 per cent of total investment, this was disastrous.[16]

Unprecedented increases in gold revenues, up 31 per cent in 1977–78 and 43 per cent in 1978–79, following the soaring of free market gold prices, however, led to huge current account surpluses in those years.[17] The gold boom continued into 1980 and fuelled the economic recovery. The beneficial effects of the gold price, by allowing increased domestic investment, disguised the continuing outflow of capital in pursuit of the high short-term interest rates prevalent outside the country.[18] A sharp decline in the gold price in 1981 revealed a large deficit in the balance of payments, forcing the government to turn to the International Monetary Fund (IMF) for loans of US$1,320 million in 1982.[19]

The collapse in production after 1976 affected manufacturing most severely. The GDP share of manufacturing and construction dropped from 28 per cent in 1975 to 25 per cent in 1979.[20] Unemployment continued its upward trend, climbing from 20.4 per cent in 1970 to 22.4 per cent in 1977 (2,301,000).[21] By 1980 it was probably over 2.5 million.[22]

As the above account makes clear, both periods of stagnation resulted from imbalances caused by high levels of imports attendant on increases in manufacturing production. The restructuring during the 1970s was marked by the growth of monopoly capitalist relations through centralisation, brought on by the weakness of many non-monopoly enterprises and the need for a rationalisation of production following the economic slump.[23] The Anglo-American Group was central to the processes at work. Having begun as a primarily mining organisation, by 1980 the group had diversified into every sector of the economy.[24]

Political struggle and state responses

Political events during the 1950s in South Africa were dominated by the growing nationalist struggle against white rule and against the apartheid system. While some specifically class issues were taken up, the campaigns as a whole were not overtly class based, but were based on the common oppression of black people and, especially, of African people, under white rule. The primary objective of the struggles was the winning of equal treatment for black and white under the state. Faced with a politically based struggle, the state was able to defeat the African nationalist campaign by destroying its political organisations.

By the start of the upheavals of the 1970s the disposition of class forces was different, the nature of black political organisation had changed and so had the relations of production. All combined to make the repressive option a less viable response by the state to challenges to the system. While black people were far more proletarianised, capitalists were far more dependent on black workers than they had been a decade earlier. The rapid capital intensification of production had involved increasing demands for skilled and semi-skilled factory workers. Strikes became more costly, some workers were more difficult to replace when dismissed and the existence of an organised proletariat made solidarity action more likely and reduced scabbing by unemployed workers.

Monopoly capitalist enterprises became increasingly interpenetrated with foreign multinationals, making them more susceptible to overseas pressure. Growing interpenetration and centralisation of enterprises meant that disputes tended to have wider spin-offs, affecting more than just isolated firms. As fixed capital stock increased, and the possibilities for rapid retreats from South Africa by foreign investors diminished, so the need grew for a system which guaranteed long-term stability.

The greater strength of the workers was reflected in their increased militancy. In 1973 a massive series of strikes involving 98,000 workers occurred. Between 1974 and 1979 the number of workers involved in strikes each year did not drop below 14,000.[25] In 1980, 95,000 workers went on strike,[26] and in 1981 the figure was 93,000.[27]

The response of the South African authorities to the resurgence of strikes and popular opposition, including an escalation of the armed struggle by the African National Congress (ANC), was to strengthen the armed forces and utilise and extend the repressive legislation enacted during the 1960s. As the decade progressed, however, the state came under pressure to adopt a more 'reformist' approach. With the ousting of John Vorster as Prime Minister, and following the uprisings of 1976–77, it officially began cautious moves in a 'reformist' direction. This stop–go 'reformism' will not be examined here. Suffice it to note that the response of the state, post-Soweto, was very different from its response after Sharpeville.

Changes in the policies of the Progressive Party

The two periods of instability under study coincide with the reports of constitutional commissions set up by the Progressive Party. The first, chaired by ex-Liberal Party member Donald Molteno, was set up soon after the formation of the party, to draw up its constitutional proposals. It reported in 1960 and 1962.[28] The second, which was chaired by MP Frederik van Zyl Slabbert, was set up initially in 1974, reconstituted in 1977 and reported in 1978.[29]

The Molteno Commission specifically interpreted its task as the formulation of a constitutional structure for a multiracial system, 'a frame-work within which our various racial communities may coexist and co-operate as one civilised nation'.[30] The commission understood its terms of reference as requiring the recommendation of 'safeguards for racial communities'.[31] At the same time it sought to entrench in the constitutional proposals guaranteed rights and liberties for individuals.

The majority of the commissioners interpreted their terms of reference as precluding a system of universal adult suffrage, but at the same time sought to justify the Majority Report recommendation of a qualified franchise by reference to the 'degree of civilisation' of individual voters. Such 'civilisation', they argued, was necessary for the 'effective functioning of democratic institutions'. While a minority dissented from this, the major area of disagreement was over the exact qualifications which should be demanded of voters. The majority formulated the following 'test of civilisation' according to which citizens should be judged:

> Such qualifications should embrace those elements of the population that have attained an economic level or a degree of sophistication such as to

enable them to feel sufficient identification with society as a whole – to possess sufficient 'stake in the country' – not to fall prey to totalitarian illusions.[32]

S. Cooppan, one of the black members of the commission who did not sign the Majority Report, argued that such a mere extension of privilege to a small number of black South Africans would simply substitute class for race divisions.[33] The majority commissioners ignored Cooppan's warnings, however. They regarded African nationalism as the primary threat. A provision that no past voters would be disenfranchised ensured that the qualifications would be demanded only of black South Africans, in the first instance.

Referring to possible criticisms of their report, the majority commissioners accepted that for black South Africans, 'the demand is general, among the politically conscious elements, for adult suffrage'. They did not dispute the legitimacy of this position but went on to argue:

> Whilst understanding this attitude, we are bound to point out that it bears no necessary relation to personal freedom, the rule of law, ordered progress, or any of the other values that Western democracy was conceived in order to foster. Its inspiration is rather non-White nationalism, which, like all nationalisms, is ultimately totalitarian in its logical outcome.[34]

The *Molteno Report* continued with an outline of a proposed Bill of Rights for the protection of individual freedoms. Among those 'freedoms' to be protected was the right to segregated schools, housing, transport, hospitals, prisons or 'any other service, amenity or public institution whatsoever', provided that all 'classes of the community' had equal facilities.[35]

The constitutional and franchise proposals adopted by the party in 1960 and 1962 were conservative and racist. Little notice was taken of the dissenting opinions of the black commission members,[36] and the National Executive of the party actually took a more, rather than a less, conservative position than the majority of the commission. The party was concerned with making the minimum concessions to buy off black protests and defuse the nationalist struggle while appeasing white prejudice and assuring whites of continuing power and control.

The Slabbert Committee formulated its constitutional proposals at another time of political instability in South Africa. It was a time when white parliamentary opposition was in chaos, following the final collapse and disintegration of the United Party. The Slabbert Committee, like the Molteno Commission, set out to formulate constitutional proposals which would 'remove the barriers of discrimination' without resulting in 'the domination of one group over another'. At the same time, however, it was critical of past liberal thinking which had dismissed group loyalties and group affiliations in favour of the individual. It identified the group/individual (nationalist/liberal) debate as 'largely responsible for sterile and fruitless political discussion', which had dominated white politics. Instead of the prevalent dichotomous view, a dynamic interrelationship between individual and group was the reality, the issue of overriding importance being *'that the individual should be allowed to exercise his or her right of voluntary association'* (emphasis as in original).[37] The Committee went further, however, and emphasised that one of the negative effects of the existing system was that it had 'inhibited the development of groups with cross-cutting affiliations that could counteract race and ethnic conflicts and antagonisms in our plural society'.[38]

In formulating its proposals the Slabbert Committee took specific cognisance of existing political conflict.[39] It recommended 'a structure of government where the resolution of conflict has to be achieved within the political process itself'. In adopting the committee's recommendations, the party congress of 1978 expressed its belief 'that the institution of a new political dispensation in South Africa has become a matter of urgency if we are to prevent the escalation of the present racial confrontation into violent conflict'.[40]

Slabbert's *Report* differed from the *Molteno Report* in that it stressed the party's commitment to 'an equal right to full citizenship' for all South Africans. The qualified franchise was abandoned, together with notions of 'Western civilisation', and a universal adult suffrage was proposed. Its terms of reference called for a sharing of political rights by all citizens and equal economic opportunity. They precluded 'all inevitable forms of statutory or administrative discrimination on the grounds of race, colour, religion or sex' as 'unacceptable in the ideal society for which the party will strive'.[41] In elaborating these principles, the party leader, Colin Eglin, made it clear that he recognised that such equal political representation was essential:

> The Party believes that the possession of full citizenship rights is the basis of loyalty towards our country. Without this we will not be able to maintain an orderly society or effectively defend our country against external or internal attacks.[42]

The Slabbert *Report* was critical of the Molteno Commission, by implication, for confusing the issue of domination with that of the franchise: 'the threat of domination is incidental to and not a consequence of the system of franchise in operation. *It all depends what*

the structure of government is within which the franchise is exercised.'
(Emphasis as in original.)[43] Accordingly, the committee rejected a
Westminster-style system and opted instead for a system including
proportional representation, decentralised executive, legislative and
judicial systems and a minority veto. While this system, combined
with a bill of rights, was designed to guarantee the impossibility of
majority domination, the committee, like the Molteno Commission
before it, was at pains to deny any racist motivation:

> it would be a complete misrepresentation of the recommendations in rela-
> tion to domination if the minority veto is presented as a measure to preserve
> the privileged position of a minority at the expense of other groups in
> society.[44]

Harry Oppenheimer, chairman of the Anglo-American Corporation,
welcomed the *Report* as a valuable contribution to the debate on the
direction in which the country should move. He said,

> I'm actually rather pleased with this. I've read the thing through ... and I
> feel that at long last there is a real basis for sensible discussion, and I think
> this is about all one needs – or really can give. I was very pleased with this.[45]

The Slabbert Committee perceived the need for a break with the
ideologies of the past, both liberal individualist and racist, and the
adoption of new ideological forms. In a conscious effort to accommodate black disillusionment with capitalism in South Africa, Van Zyl
Slabbert dropped the notion of a 'free enterprise economy' from the
recommendations. He was of the view that 'free enterprise' would not
be an issue within five or six years. 'It is an ideological concept which
will become the target of aggression for a whole range of black political
organisations.'[46] Slabbert sought to re-create an ideology of state
neutrality and separation from capital. He held that the role of government should be to distribute wealth, not to create it, wealth creation
being the role of business: 'The wealth generators are the economic
entrepreneurs; the wealth distributors are the political entrepreneurs.'[47]

It is not coincidence that the production of major constitutional
reports by the Progressive Party occurred in periods of intense
economic upheaval and class struggle. The party was responding to
political change and pressures in South Africa, and also to the needs of
its class constituency. Both studies were set up at the height of these
periods of unrest and upheaval. Both were attempts to provide answers
to problems requiring immediate resolution. From the point of view of
the party, they reassured its class constituency that something dynamic

was being offered as an alternative to chaos. To liberal voters and conservative black South Africans, they provided models for continued hopes of peaceful reconciliation in the future. They also bolstered the image of the party as a viable political alternative to the National Party. This was particularly important after 1977, when for the first time the Progressive Federal Party (PFP) became the official parliamentary opposition to the government.

Relations with black groups

During both periods under consideration, the Progressive Party attempted to establish working alliances with black groups or individuals sympathetic to its objectives. Initially, the ANC cautiously welcomed the formation of the Progressive Party. The ANC leaders were even prepared to take some credit for the emergence of the party, seeing it as a response by liberal whites to the demands of the Congress movement. Vigorous opposition by the Progressive Party to the state of emergency, the banning of the ANC and the Pan-Africanist Congress (PAC) and detentions without trial, further improved relations with the Congress movement.

The publication of the first volume of the *Molteno Report*, however, and the decision to pursue a qualified franchise, crystallised the differences between the organisations and brought into the open the party's antagonism to African nationalism. According to Dr Jan Steytler, the first leader of the Progressive Party, 'Extremism and Black nationalism would have to be broken', before black people would subscribe to the party's policies.[48]

Despite this, co-operation between the organisations continued. In March 1961 Progressive Party representatives participated in an 'All-In' African Conference called by forty leaders of the ANC, PAC, Liberal and Progressive parties.[49] Before the 1961 general election, Albert Luthuli, President of the banned ANC, issued a statement supporting the Progressive candidates. After the election Lutuli announced that while he deeply regretted the increased support for the National Party (NP), the support received by the Progressive Party was an encouraging sign.[50] Similar messages of congratulation on the results of the general election were sent to the Progressives by Joe Daniels, Secretary of the Coloured National Convention Movement, and Monty Naiker, President of the South African Indian Congress.[51] The year ended with relations between the Progressive Party and many black leaders and groups on a cordial footing, despite continuing condemnation by the party of 'non-white nationalism'.

Early in 1962, however, a watershed in party policy was reached with the presentation to the National Executive of a memorandum on relations with extra-parliamentary groups. The paper, written by Donald Molteno and Peggy Roberts, argued for co-operation with black political groups (by definition extra-parliamentary) on the grounds that demonstrating black support would be the only way of winning white votes. Black protests, they wrote, were essential to persuade voters that there was a need for change and, therefore, for the Progressive Party.[52] The memorandum proved too radical for the National Executive Committee of the party, however, and was rejected. At the same time an active campaign was launched to recruit African members directly to party ranks, something which had been dismissed by Molteno and Roberts as doomed from the start.[53] There were two main reasons for the rejection of the memorandum. The first derived from worries about the effects on white electoral support of a close association with groups which were seen by most whites as dangerously subversive. The second was related to the party's franchise proposals. Organisations like the ANC enjoyed mass support among exactly those black South Africans whom the Progressives proposed to exclude from the franchise as insufficiently 'civilised' to vote. The party leadership felt unable to collaborate with the organisations of people it believed to be unfit to vote.

Once the party had decided against co-operation with black political organisations, it soon became commonplace for its spokespersons to condemn in the same breath African nationalism, the sabotage campaign and the independent black countries in the rest of Africa. This was combined with optimistic reports of the 'encouraging' increases in African membership of the party and of the establishment of African branches.[54] In fact very few black members joined the party until the launching of its campaign among Coloured voters two years later.

In January 1964 the party began a campaign to win the four seats representing Coloured voters in Parliament. Many of the Coloured people registered as voters by the Progressives joined the party. The Progressives claimed this, and the success of the Democratic Party in the Transkei Assembly elections in 1963, as evidence of widespread black support for their policies. In fact the overwhelming support for the Democratic Party in the Transkei, like Coloured votes for Progressive Party candidates, was more probably a demonstration by black voters of their opposition to apartheid, rather than an endorsement of the specific policies of the parties.

Progressive Party attitudes to black South Africans were very different during the 1970s. The party had ceased to be a multiracial party in 1968 with the passage of the Prohibition of Political Interference Act. The government might well have done the party a service with this legislation, by releasing the Progressives from the embarrassment of claiming extensive black support in the absence of any significant black membership. After the passage of the Act, party efforts were devoted to establishing contact with black 'leaders' and political organisations instead of competing with such organisations for membership. Soon after the election of Colin Eglin as the new leader, in February 1971, the party was involved in high-profile publicity exercises to demonstrate the acceptability of its policies among black people. In October 1971, Eglin and Helen Suzman made an extensively publicised tour of independent African countries. They were received by Leopold Senghor of Senegal, Gambian President Dauda Jawara, Kofie Busia in Ghana, Kenyan Vice-President Daniel Arap Moi, Julius Nyerere of Tanzania and Kamuzu Banda of Malawi.[55] A year later a similar high-profile 'consultation exercise' with Bantustan leaders, and some opposition politicians, in the Transkei, Ciskei, Kwa Zulu, Lebowa, Gazankulu, Venda and Bophuthatswana was held by Eglin, Suzman and Ray Swart, NEC (National Executive Committee) chairperson.[56] The party was apparently quite unembarrassed by its consultation with Bantustan leaders who were the linchpins of NP plans to foist 'independence' on the inhabitants of these areas.

While there were some contacts with more radical black leaders,[57] it was with more conservative organisations that the party had its strongest links. Relations with the anti-apartheid Coloured Labour Party were cordial, for instance, with several ex-Progressive Party members prominent in the leadership of the party. The most important link, however, was with M. G. Buthelezi's Inkatha YeNkululeko YeSizwe. Contact was formalised in an 'on-going liaison committee with the PFP and Inkatha', according to the architect of the links, Ray Swart.[58] After a meeting between Eglin, Swart, Buthelezi and S. M. Bhengu (Secretary-General of Inkatha) in 1978, a joint statement was issued. It said that much common ground had been discovered and that there was a basis for agreement on a new constitutional framework for South Africa. Buthelezi expressed support for the structure proposed by the PFP's Slabbert Committee.[59] Close co-operation continued. A commission set up by Buthelezi to formulate a new constitutional structure integrating white Natal with KwaZulu was chaired by Professor Denys Schreiner, a long-time member of the Progressive Party. After the Buthelezi Commission reported, Slabbert and Buthelezi met, on 5 April 1982, and issued a joint statement reaffirming their commitment to full citizenship rights for all South Africans and to 'equality of opportunity in the economy'.[60]

In a very revealing document tabled by Buthelezi for discussion at the meeting, he argued that the PFP could not survive as a political force without the support of Inkatha. He wrote:

> The PFP has no future whatsoever outside a Black partnership, nor do whites in general have any future outside a Black partnership. The PFP seeks a new dispensation and the voice in the wilderness which it now constitutes can only become the voice of authority when its roots extend into Black soil.
>
> In the reality of the South African situation, PFP continuity into the future and its survival as a political force in fact depends on Inkatha. Inkatha is the only mass organisation of the people. It has the only Black leadership which is structured. It is the only Black political organisation which has tackled the game of constituency politics. It is only in this constituency politics that Black and White can establish co-operation.[61]

Perhaps Buthelezi was correct that from the point of view of the PFP there was only one significant potential ally among existing black organisations. Slabbert identified the difficulties he faced:

> it's easier to talk to the moderate political organisations. If it's a black consciousness kind of movement then part of its rationale is not to have contact or seek contact with whites. . . .
>
> There is no alliance or any formal structure of an alliance between us and black organisations. I think also one reason being that the diversity of opinion and attitude in blacks makes it very difficult. You can't get an alliance going between say the Committee of Ten, Inkatha and ourselves. It's simply not on.[62]

The independent trade unions, apart from legal bars on association between trade unions and political parties, were not interested in a political alliance with 'the party of the bosses'. Links with exile movements were out of the question.

As long as the African nationalist organisations posed a significant threat to the system, during the early 1960s, the Progressive Party sought to preserve its potential as an organisation of compromise in the event of an extension of the conflict. Once the organisations had been destroyed by the state and forced underground, the party made the sudden discovery that links with them would be a major electoral liability. It proceeded to condemn African nationalism as a danger on a par with 'communism', and as totalitarian. It then sought to compete against such organisations for membership, and interpreted votes by black people against apartheid as votes for its policies and for 'moderation' rather than confrontation.

By the start of the second period, having lost its black members, the party rediscovered the need to demonstrate its 'consultation' with internal black leaders, and in the absence of 'moderate' leaders recognised by black South Africans, was forced to turn to those appointed by the South African government. As political confrontation grew, the party attempted to make contact with leaders of more radical currents, but found itself either rejected by these groups or talking to 'opinion makers', people like Nthato Motlana of the Committee of Ten, who declined to be termed 'leaders' and refused to become involved in anything other than informal contact.[63] Instead the party was forced to rely almost exclusively on its contact with Inkatha to demonstrate the compatibility of its policies with black aspirations: a fact Buthelezi was not slow to point out.

Party ideology and relations with active capitalists

At its Inaugural Congress in November 1959, the Progressive Party adopted basic statements on economic and social policy. Harry Oppenheimer was closely consulted on these, alterations being made to accommodate most of his criticisms.[64] The policy adopted on African trade union rights by the congress, for instance, called for the 'restoration of the freedom of the trade unions', but qualified the call with a recommendation that unskilled workers be organised into separate unions under the control of the Department of Labour.[65] This formulation catered for the worries expressed by Oppenheimer about the maintenance of 'a proper standard' of unionism.[66] Thus the party avoided one of the major political drawbacks of an unequivocal commitment to free trade unions – the objections of mining capitalists, and especially the gold-mine owners, to the unionisation of mine-workers.

Such discrimination was justified by reference to the freedom of individual black South Africans to improve their situation. The Progressive Party did not object in principle to discrimination or inequality. Its objection was to the fact that the discrimination and inequalities were imposed only on people of colour, and on all people of colour. If the colour bar was lifted, in its view, the inequalities would no longer be offensive to the critical outside world or to liberal sensibilities inside South Africa. Allowing an equal bite at the cake to a minority of black people would satisfy the moral scruples expressed by liberal opponents of apartheid. This fitted well with the needs and demands of capitalists at that time. They wanted the political challenges to the state bought off by political concessions. They wanted more skilled workers and supervisors who could only come from the ranks of black South Africans. They did not want a redistribution of wealth or a destruction of the cheap labour system. An ideology of individualism was admirably suited to those needs. As the Natal leader of the party, Leo Boyd, expressed it in a confidential memo to Steytler, the party's policies

> seek to break down the group complex, focusing attention upon the individual so that ultimately we become a nations [*sic*] of individuals and not members of majority or minority groups. SECURITY for the individual must also be prominently featured in our programmes.[67]

Speaking at a dinner for business people in 1963, Harry Oppenheimer warned of the consequences of continued suppression of the rights of individuals because of their colour.

> It is a terrible mistake, because revolutions are not made by the masses of the people. Revolutions anywhere are made by disgruntled individuals of ability who find no room for the exercise of their talents and if you attempt to keep them back by reference to some assumed level of the group to which they belong, then you are simply taking steps to provide the leaders who can eventually . . . change the affairs of this country, and change them by violence.[68]

On the macro-level, therefore, the Progressive appeal for support from the capitalist class was based on the danger of a revolutionary overthrow of the system. On the micro-level the Progressive Party attacked the government for limiting economic growth through the restrictions it imposed on production. The general argument was contained in an early recruiting pamphlet entitled *The Progressive Answer*. It read:

> In South Africa we are all poorer than we should be because we do not make the best use of our human resources. Job reservation, aimed at protecting the White workers, actually harms both White and Black. . . . Government restrictions are at present limiting our potential out-put and wealth.[69]

After the State of Emergency which followed Sharpeville, the party had a far stronger case to argue and did so in an election pamphlet called *Into a New World*. Referring directly to the aftermath of Sharpeville the pamphlet read:

> Nationalist legislation has resulted in the deterioration of our economy and our way of life. Money has poured out of the country at an unprecedented

rate and the prospect of sustained recovery is unlikely unless reforms are instituted soon. World opinion is against us. We embarrass our friends and our enemies make capital out of our mistakes.[70]

The party believed that overseas investors would respond most favourably to the introduction of policies designed specifically to ameliorate the causes of the conflicts. The argument ran thus:

> The obstacle to investment today is purely and simply political. In order to regain a flow of capital, we need to convince the outside world – or rather, the capital-exporting nations – that, to put it bluntly, there is not going to be a revolution in South Africa.[71]

Although the party did make appeals to the capitalist class for financial and electoral support the main thrust of its propaganda during the first half of the 1960s was directed at issues of concern to the white electorate as a whole. After its humiliating performance in the 1966 general election, however, a thorough reassessment of the party's approach was made. The new strategy evolved included a decision to direct its efforts and propaganda specifically at 'business'. The new, specific orientation to the capitalist class after 1966 meant that by the start of the second period of political upheaval the party was far more closely allied to the sympathetic sections of that class.

After Soweto, certain sections of the capitalist class, disillusioned with the state as a vehicle for reform, decided to set up their own organisation. Its task was to engage in exemplary reformist activities to encourage similar action by the state, but also to buy off some of the black resentment and frustration which had exploded in Soweto. This organisation, the Urban Foundation, was set up in 1977. Irene Menell, a PFP representative in the Transvaal Provincial Council, who was instrumental in setting up the Urban Foundation, contrasted the attitudes of capitalists with whom she had contact, before and after Soweto. At first, opposition to apartheid was ritualised and formalistic, confined to annual meetings and reports:

> It happened once a year. The rest of the year one went on getting permits or an exemption to put a plant there, or an exemption to employ more people there, and it kind of worked and your company grew. . . . And your profits were fine.[72]

After Soweto, however, attitudes changed:

> It's still a bit patchy and a bit confused but there is an evergrowing awareness that you can't hope to survive as a flourishing business in the long term in South Africa against this political climate, and the economic and socio-economic climate. So, therefore, you'd better get out and use your resources to try and make some corrections, hopefully in time.[73]

This new attitude by capitalists was reflected in their relationships with the Progressive Party. At about the same time as its electoral breakthrough in 1974, the Progressive Party achieved a similar breakthrough in attracting vastly increased support from its 'natural' constituency in the capitalist class. From 1973 to 1977 the party National Treasurer and chief fund-raiser was Gordon Waddell, an executive director of the Anglo-American Corporation and ex-son-in-law of Harry Oppenheimer. As Irene Menell expressed it in an interview in 1978, 'There are few big Johannesburg companies who have not been approached and given.'[74] With Gordon Waddell going around soliciting donations it was very hard for fellow capitalists to say no. So successful was Waddell's fund-raising, that in January 1974 the party's newspaper, *Progress*, reported a 100 per cent increase in funds and a 200 per cent increase in large donations.[75]

This increase in financial support from the capitalist class coincided with the development of an economic analysis which took account of the structural changes which had occurred in the economy. Noting the tendency towards greater concentration of capital, Gordon Waddell argued that the use of low-wage, unskilled labour slowed growth and reduced living standards for all the country's inhabitants. Arguing that the potential of the country's whole population should be harnessed, he said:

> we cannot continue to move forward as we should by simply employing larger and larger numbers of unskilled workers in industry or on mines at low wages. That phase is over and the realisation of our potential for further rapid growth depends on the development of greater skills by the mass of workers who are already in industry or who will join it in the future so that their productivity and their earnings can be steadily increased.[76]

The Progressive Reform Party, as it became, extended the argument beyond the contention that a new deal for black people was necessary for economic growth. In an article published in May 1976, the new chairperson of the party's Federal Executive, Harry Schwarz, argued that a new form of capitalism was called for in South Africa, to combat the threat of socialism. 'Old-time capitalism', he said, was dead:

> The test of free enterprise is not how good it is for the capitalist and how much profit can be made out of it. The true test is what it does for the man who has no capital, what it does for the worker and for the individual. Is he better off in a free enterprise system than he would be under socialism? . . .
>
> The problem in South Africa is not only colour; it is a potential conflict between capital and labour. This is why one has to convince the people who represent labour, who are the Black consumers, that there is a place for them in the free enterprise system.

Unless the free enterprise system got on to the offensive and attacked socialism, he concluded, it was doomed.[77]

The arguments of the party leadership had changed markedly since the 1960s, in line with changed realities. The question of colour was no longer seen as fundamental, but as a divide which disguised far more dangerous class divisions. The threat of revolution was no longer primarily a threat to white power, or to 'Western civilisation', but to capitalism itself.

The experience of the Soweto uprisings sharpened party anxieties. In a speech to the Graduate School of Business at the University of Cape Town in September 1976, Colin Eglin urged business people to play a more active part in the politics of the country. Race conflict, he warned, was becoming class conflict:

> The sharpening of class conflict has been accelerated by events outside as well as the very real and wide gap between the 'haves' and the 'have nots' within South Africa. It is seen, felt and increasingly resented by millions of South African citizens.
>
> The free enterprise system, in spite of its many positive achievements, runs the risk of being seen not as an instrument for eliminating one of the causes of conflict but as one of the ingredients of conflict. . . .
>
> Those who believe in the free enterprise system and who want to eliminate conflict will have to find ways and means of enabling black South Africans to share significantly in economic progress, not merely as workers but as share-holders and partners and participants in the ownership of business in South Africa.[78]

In October 1979, the leadership of the PFP set up an Economic Commission chaired by Harry Schwarz to formulate a programme of economic reform for South Africa. Schwarz described one of the most important roles of the Commission as developing 'effective answers to be given to Marxism as an economic doctrine'.[79] When the *Charter for Social and Economic Progress* formulated by the commission was published, in November 1981, however, it proved to be a generalised restatement of party calls for an extension of economic benefits to all South Africans, rather than a radical programme for a new economic order. Among its provisions were the establishment of a corporatist relationship between 'capital, management and labour based upon the recognition that each have an interest in the welfare of others'. Industrial democracy, profit-sharing and common decision-making were to be encouraged. All workers were to be accorded the right 'to organise in trade unions of their choice', in contrast to the policy adopted in 1959. Nationalisation was to be avoided, and the state's role in planning was to be 'indicative not compulsive'.[80]

Such redistribution of wealth as was entailed in the proposals was not to be allowed to affect the wealthy:

> The wide gaps in income and wealth in South Africa require special action to enable those in a disadvantaged position to better their situation. This aim can be achieved only by uplifting the under-privileged rather than by impairing the standards enjoyed by the more fortunate.[81]

The new economic policy of the party reflected the needs of the now dominant group within the capitalist class, monopoly capitalists, for an educated, skilled and incorporated workforce with a high level of commitment to the system. It also reflected the need to expand domestic demand through increased consumption, to provide a larger market for the goods of the new capital-intensive, highly productive, industrial enterprises. Most of all, however, it reflected the need for a stable, peaceful country in which capital accumulation could continue unhampered by threats of disruption or revolution. In exchange for that, the PFP and its supporters within the capitalist class were prepared to extend political rights to all black South Africans, and to open up economic opportunities to them.

Conclusions

Two periods of intense class struggle and economic change in South Africa were marked by structural differences in capitalist production as well as differences in the nature of political challenges to the apartheid system. The period 1960–80 saw the rapid monopolisation of capitalist production with attendant concentration, centralisation and interpenetration of capital, leading to the emergence of a more united, dominant, monopoly group within the capitalist class. It saw the continuing proletarianisation of black South Africans as a result, coupled with the emergence of strong and militant workers' organisations. After state action had destroyed the nationalist opposition in the early 1960s, the 1970s were associated with the emergence of a combination of populist and overt class struggle. The African nationalist organisations had mobilised opposition to apartheid on the basis of the historical and moral rights of all South Africans, including Africans, to political equality. The Black Consciousness movement stressed the common interests of all *black* people against white domination, while the independent trade unions pursued the specific interests of workers in a capitalist society. By the end of the 1970s workers' organisations had taken an overtly class view of their society and even black consciousness organisations had introduced the concept of class into their analyses. The militancy of young black people, the increased effectiveness of the liberation struggle and the strength and resilience of workers' organisations forced the state into a confused process of 'reform' and accommodation.

In the context of the shift to a more proletarianised society and to overt class struggle, equivalent adjustments occurred in the ideology of the Progressive Party. As political struggles against the state changed from nationalist opposition to class opposition, so the emphasis of Progressive ideology shifted from race to class. At a time when the African nationalist struggle challenged white privilege, the party proposed answers designed to buy off a black élite and satisfy the aspirations of an influential black minority. When the struggle developed into a wider opposition to the whole system of exploitation, it proposed an extension of political rights and economic opportunity to all, in an attempt to persuade black South Africans that their interests were best served by a capitalist, rather than a socialist, system. At the same time, the traditional liberal image of the party changed into that of a party representing the views of 'progressive' capitalists. As a coherent group of monopoly capitalists emerged and became politicised, the party became more closely associated with them.

The dramatic shifts in direction by the party reflected its role as a politically innovative organisation formulating alternatives to government policies. While it sought to reflect the day-to-day needs of its constituency, as an opposition party without control of the state its major role was to identify long-term dangers and offer alternative solutions to these.

Notes and references

1 In 1975 the Progressive Party merged with the Reform Party to become the South African Progressive Reform Party. In 1977 this party merged with the Committee for a United Opposition to become the Progressive Federal Party of South Africa. Where reference is made to the party over periods when it has borne more than one name, it is called the Progressive Party. Otherwise the different names are applied according to the period under discussion.

2 These periods are roughly 1959–62 and 1973–78.

3 Sheila van der Horst, 'The changing face of the economy', in Ellen Hellman and Henry Lever (eds), *Race Relations in South Africa, 1929–79*, (London 1980) pp. 97–130; Dan O'Meara, 'Afrikaner capitalism and the South African state', D. Phil. thesis (University of Sussex 1979) p. 278.

4 Aubrey Dickman, 'Investment – the implications for economic growth and living standards', *Optima*, 27 (1) no. 3, 1977, 42–3.

5 D. Hobart Houghton, *The South African Economy*, 2nd ed. (Cape Town 1967) pp. 172–9; Duncan Innes, 'Monopoly capitalism and imperialism in Southern Africa: the role of the Anglo-American Group', D. Phil. thesis (University of Sussex 1980).

6 Muriel Horrell, *A Survey of Race Relations in South Africa, 1959–60*, (South African Institute of Race Relations (SAIRR) Johannesburg 1961) pp. 90–3.

7 Dickman, 'Investment', pp. 42–3.

8 Figures calculated by Charles Simkins and cited in Norman Bromberger, 'South African unemployment: a survey of research', in Charles Simkins and Cosmas Desmond (eds), *South African Unemployment: a Black Picture* (Development Studies Research Group, Pietermaritzburg 1978) pp. 3–25 (p. 15).

9 Innes, 'Monopoly capitalism', p. 391.

10 Dickman, 'Investment', p. 45; Muriel Horrell, *A Survey of Race Relations in South Africa, 1970*, (SAIRR, Johannesburg 1971) pp. 79–80; Muriel Horrell and Tony Hodgson, *A Survey of Race Relations in South Africa, 1975* (SAIRR, Johannesburg 1976) p. 150; Muriel Horrell *et al.*, *A Survey of Race Relations in South Africa 1976* (SAIRR, Johannesburg 1977) p. 266.

11 Loraine Gordon *et al.*, *A Survey of Race Relations in South Africa, 1977* (SAIRR, Johannesburg 1978) p. 183; Michael Williams, *South Africa: The crisis of world capitalism and the apartheid economy* (London 1977) p. 4; Loraine Gordon *et al.*, *Survey of Race Relations in South Africa, 1981* (SAIRR, Johannesburg 1982) p. 102.

12 Loraine Gordon (ed.) *Survey of Race Relations in South Africa, 1979* (SAIRR, Johannesburg 1980) p. 174; Loraine Gordon (ed.) *Survey of Race Relations in South Africa, 1980* (SAIRR, Johannesburg 1981) p. 73; Muriel Horrell (ed.) *Survey of Race Relations in South Africa 1981* (SAIRR, Johannesburg 1982) p. 102.

13 'Pretoria inflation UP', *Morning Star* (London), 26 May 1982.

14 Dickman, 'Investment', pp. 43–5.

15 *Ibid.*, p. 45; Horrell and Hodgson, *Survey, 1975*, p. 151.

16 *Financial Times* (London), 21 June 1978; Dickman, 'Investment', pp. 43–5.

17 Gordon, *Survey, 1979*, p. 174.

18 Gordon, *Survey, 1980*, pp. 73, 124.

19 Horrell, *Survey, 1981*, pp. 102–3; 'Labour fights SA loan' *Guardian* (London), 11 Oct. 1982; 'UN moves to stop loan to Pretoria', *Guardian*, 22 Oct. 1982.

20 Van der Horst, 'The changing face of the economy', p. 98.

21 Bromberger, 'South African unemployment', p. 15.

22 Government figures indicated a further increase between 1977 and 1980 of 8.6 per cent. Total calculated from figures in Gordon *et al.*, *Survey, 1978*, p. 170, and Gordon, *Survey, 1981*, p. 88.

23 See Innes, 'Monopoly capitalism', pp. 417–31 for an intriguing description of the processes involved.

24 In 1976 it owned South Africa's top five mining houses, controlled or had substantial interests in five of the top ten industrial concerns, owned two of

the top ten property companies and the largest township developer. It had interests in seven of the top ten banks and owned one of the top three life assurers. Overall it controlled the three market leaders in the country and ten of the top fifteen. (Innes, 'Monopoly capitalism', p. 439).

25 Muriel Horrell and Dudley Horner, *A Survey of Race Relations in South Africa, 1973* (SAIRR, Johannesburg 1974) p. 268; Gordon, *Survey, 1980*, p. 187.

26 Comment in *South African Labour Bulletin* 6 (5) 1980, 1.

27 'Second worst strike year for S. Africa', *Guardian*, 26 May 1982.

28 Donald Molteno (Chairman), *Molteno Report*, vol. I: *Franchise Proposals and Constitutional Safeguards*, (Progressive Party, Johannesburg 1960) and *Molteno Report*, vol. II: *Rigid Constitution, the Decentralization of Government and the Administration of Justice*, (Progressive Party, Johannesburg 1962).

29 F. van Zyl Slabbert (Chairman), *Report of the Constitutional Committee of the Progressive Federal Party and Policy Decisions Made by the Federal Congress of the P.F.P.*, (Progressive Federal Party, Cape Town 1979).

30 Molteno, *Molteno Report*, vol. I, p. 7.

31 *Ibid.*

32 *Ibid.*, p. 10.

33 *Ibid.*, p. 38.

34 *Ibid.*, pp. 12–13.

35 *Ibid.*, p. 67.

36 Similar dismissal of the minority reports of black commissioners was apparent in press reports. An article in the *Star* of 14 Nov. 1960, 'The vote: who should get it?', made repeated reference to the minority reports of Suzman, and Oppenheimer and de Beer but made only one reference to the existence of reports by Cooppan and van der Ross, and gave no indication of the nature of their objections to a qualified franchise.

37 Van Zyl Slabbert, *Report of the Constitutional Committee*, p. 11.

38 *Ibid.*, p. 12.

39 *Ibid.*, pp. 7–8.

40 *Ibid.*, p. 15.

41 *Ibid.*, pp. 4–5.

42 *Ibid.*, p. 6.

43 *Ibid.*, p. 12.

44 *Ibid.*, p. 14.

45 Harry Oppenheimer interviewed by B. Hackland, 30 Oct. 1978, p. 6 of transcript.

46 F. van Zyl Slabbert interviewed by B. Hackland, 17 Oct. 1978, p. 7 of transcript.

47 *Ibid.*, p. 9.

48 'Steytler: "We must stay in U.N."', *Rand Daily Mail*, 18 Nov. 1960.

49 Muriel Horrell, *Action, Reaction and Counter-Action: A brief review of non-white political movements in South Africa* (SAIRR, Johannesburg 1971) pp. 48–51.

50 'Progs light an eternal flame – Lawrence', *Rand Daily Mail*, 26 Oct. 1961.

51 'Non-white leaders are backing Progs', *Rand Daily Mail*, 28 Oct. 1961.

52 Donald Molteno and Peggy Roberts, 'Memorandum on extra-

parliamentary activities', 1 March 1962 (University of the Witwatersrand Library (UWL), A883 PFP Records, III/1 1962) p. 2.

53 'Minutes of a meeting of the Leader's Committee held in the Progressive Party Office, Cape Town, on Saturday the 9th June, 1962, at 9.30 a.m.' (UWL, A883 PFP Records, III/1 1962), p. 5; 'Minutes of National Executive Meeting held on Saturday, the 19th January, and Sunday morning, the 20th January, 1963, held in the Protea Room Langham Hotel, Johannesburg, at 9.30 a.m.' (UWL, A883 PFP Records, III/2 1963).

54 'Our African membership is growing fast', *Progress*, Nov. 1962, p. 3.

55 Joanna Strangwayes-Booth, *A Cricket in the Thorn Tree: Helen Suzman and the Progressive Party*, (London 1976) pp. 241–3; 'Message of hope for S.A.', *Progress*, Nov. 1971, p. 1.

56 'Progs mount internal S.A. dialogue campaign', *Progress*, Sept. 1972, pp. 1 and 12.

57 Helen Suzman, for instance, had an appointment to meet Steve Biko, at the time of his death. She also visited Nelson Mandela on Robben Island once a year for several years when fellow political detainees nominated him as their representative.

58 Ray Swart interviewed by B. Hackland, 25 Oct. 1978, p. 3 of transcript.

59 Gordon *et al.*, *Survey, 1978*, p. 30.

60 'Slabbert and Buthelezi issue joint statement', *Deurbraak*, April, 1982, p. 1.

61 'Consequences of a confederation will be terrible – Buthelezi', *ibid.*, p. 1.

62 *Ibid.*, p. 4.

63 Van Zyl Slabbert interviewed by B. Hackland, pp. 5–6.

64 Harry Oppenheimer, 'Notes for: Mr H. G. Lawrence', 12 Nov. 1959, (University of Cape Town Library (UCTL), BC 640 H. G. Lawrence Papers, H1.136) p. 1.

65 Progressive Party, 'Main principles and policies adopted at Inaugural Congress, November 13th and 14th, 1959, Johannesburg' (UWL, A883 PFP Records, 1/3 Oct.–Dec. 1959) p. 6, para. 12.

66 Oppenheimer, 'Notes', p. 1.

67 Leo Boyd, 'Plan of campaign for 1963', Nov. 1962 (UWL, A883 PFP Records, III/1 1962) pp. 6–7.

68 Harry Oppenheimer, 'Text of address by Mr Harry F. Oppenheimer to Cape Town businessmen at dinner given by the Progressive Party (Cape Western Region) in Constantia Room, Grand Hotel, Cape Town on Tuesday, 24th September, 1963' (UCTL, BC 640 H. G. Lawrence Papers, H3.37) pp. 5–6.

69 Progressive Party, *The Progressive Answer* (Progressive Party of South Africa, Johannesburg, undated – probably 1959).

70 Progressive Party, *Into a New World* (M. K. Mitchell, Progressive Party election agent, Johannesburg, undated – probably 1961).

71 Progressive Party, *Policy Directive 17*, 19 July 1962, 'Progressive economics and economic progress – II', p. 2, (Progressive Federal Party Head Office Library, 1 I 8 Progressive Party Notes).

72 Irene Menell interviewed by B. Hackland, 21 Aug. 1980, pp. 1–5 of transcript. Irene Menell's husband, Clive, was Chairman of Anglo-Vaal Holdings and Deputy Chairman of Anglo-Transvaal Consolidated In-

vestment Company, among the largest mining and industrial groups in South Africa.

73 *Ibid.*
74 *Ibid.*, p. 18 of transcript.
75 'Boost in party funds', *Progress*, Jan. 1974, p. 11.
76 Gordon Waddell, text of address published in *Progress*, July 1974, p. 4, 'Gordon Waddell on inflation and price escalation'.
77 Harry Schwarz, speech in Parliament reported in *Progress*, May 1976, p. 1, '"Old capitalism is dead"'.
78 Colin Eglin, speech reproduced in *Progress*, Oct. 1976, pp. 7 and 12.
79 'A system that cares', *Impact*, Feb. 1980, p. 4.
80 Harry Schwarz (Chairman), *Report of the Economic Commission of the Progressive Federal Party*, (Progressive Federal Party, Cape Town, 20 Nov. 1981).
81 *Ibid.*, p. 6.

CHAPTER THIRTEEN

Ideological struggles within the South African state

Stanley B. Greenberg

Introduction

In June 1979, P. J. Koornhof, Minister for Co-operation and Development, proclaimed before the National Press Club in Washington that 'apartheid is dead'. He may have been addressing an international audience, of course, but Koornhof's words also resonated at home where doubts about ideological orthodoxy were being expressed both within and outside the state. The Bureau for Economic Policy and Analysis at the University of Pretoria, with well-developed contacts within the government and the Afrikaner business community, reported in July 1980 that the 'failure of socio-economic growth in the territories of the Black national states . . . is becoming embarrassing'.[1] The head of the bureau, Jan Lombard, referred to 'separate development' as a 'sinking philosophy'.[2] The perception has spread to yet more official 'think tanks': the Bureau for Economic Research, Co-operation and Development (BENSO) has published articles that now refer to the failure of the 'development paradigm'.[3] Little wonder, then, that outside observers have written about an 'organic crisis' or a 'crisis of hegemony'.[4]

The observations are curious, however, as just a few years earlier, in the late 1960s, apartheid seemed an ascendant political ideology, hegemonic within the white community and within the state. It had enshrined racial–national groups as privileged social categories, and secured and mystified the political and material privileges of the white section. As the state apparatus was elaborated during the first two decades of Nationalist rule, this ideology successfully placed the political moment at the centre: national groups achieved realisation only when fully associated with their own states; the state itself was placed over civil society, subordinating the will of individuals, classes and markets – forces in society that, if left to develop, would threaten the integrity of racial-national groups. The inequalities that characterised society were not obscured or rationalised; they were elevated and inscribed in the state.

By the early 1960s, this newly constructed state ideology had come to enjoy broad acceptance at all levels within the state, from party functionaries and ideologues, to department secretaries, and local control officials administering the affairs of Africans: they all now gave voice to state control and apartheid's national contrivances.[5] The Chief Bantu Affairs Commissioner for the Witwatersrand, for example, applauded the essential firmness of the state in the face of employer and African efforts to circumvent government policy: the labour bureaucracy must deal with 'the ruses, dodges and trickery of very determined people, comprising the illegal Bantu entrants themselves, their agents or representatives and some of their employers, whether real or feigned'.[6] In 1965, the President of the Institute of Administrators of Non-European Affairs warned that the future welfare of the African depends upon influx control and the identification of the African with 'his tribesmen . . . [in] an independent, self-governing nation'.[7]

This coherent state ideology rationalised the privilege and seemed to guarantee the future status of vital class elements party to the dominant political alignment. The ideology, however, had almost nothing to say to the growing African working class. Apartheid ideology spoke of the integrity of national aspirations and of the essential equality in separation. Such tenets resonated in white politics and helped rationalise a narrowly co-optive and patronage strategy centred on 'tribal chiefs'. But for African workers, who were a growing and dominant presence in South Africa's capitalist order, such tenets must have seemed archaic and irrelevant. More important was what apartheid had to say about the central state and the future role of African workers. Africans faced a state, an ideological edifice, that was racially exclusive, ever-present, monolithic and coherent.

By the mid-1970s, the lack of coherence and effective control were becoming inescapably evident. The two decades of escalating state repression – the suppression of African trade unions and political organisations on the one hand and the massive application of pass and influx-control laws on the other – brought no respite, just growing contradictions. Increasing labour control necessitated yet more control, as rising labour surpluses in the Bantustans threatened to overrun the institutions of labour control.[8] The African working class, stuck in an ideological limbo, a full-fledged proletariat that had been given no normative basis for participation in this order, began to strike out: uncontrolled strikes spread across the major industrial centres and urban revolts swept the African townships, attacking whatever state institutions – police stations, schools and pass offices – that were in reach; Africans formed unions that confronted the entire social order but organised locally, at the workplace, where worker power was concentrated and more secure.

In this context, some state officials, Afrikaner intellectuals and businessmen in particular began to question the ideological orthodoxy and to construct a new, more incorporative ideology, in effect, to universalise the scope of hegemony. The obvious starting-point was the racial exclusions that symbolised the partiality of the state and the inequities of the economic order. Changing the racial exclusiveness of the state was no small task, yet this was not the most demanding aspect of the ideological project: How could the state become national in the broad sense, universal and impartial, able to mediate and temporise conflict? How could the bourgeoisie, after emerging as an integral part of the racial order, become a progressive force in society, engaged in private activity, but contributing to the public good? How could the African working class, after growing up in this racial and repressive system, come to view the economic and political orders as legitimate?

The burden of the new ideological project was, in effect, the philosophic project that has always confronted developing market and capitalist societies, though it had been put off in the South African case: how to separate the political and economic spheres. How can one depoliticise the social order, constricting the terrain and lowering the stakes for social conflict? How can the political order appear universal, even as inequalities characterise the world of property and markets? How can the economic order, although a realm of private accumulation, gain prestige as the source of broad opportunity and material welfare?

In the contemporary South African context, this ideological project includes negating the racial character of the state, diminishing the direct and visible role of the state in the labour market and workplace and shifting the locus of prestige to the private sector. With this ideological construction, the social foundations of the economic and political orders may be broadened.

The move from an hegemonic racial-statist to a fragmentary market-oriented ideology has occasioned widespread struggle both within and outside the state. To reconstruct the state, even ideologically, is to reconstruct the role of an officialdom whose lives and identities are caught up in the traditional racial and state presence; such a reconstruction advantages certain class actors, like businessmen in monopoly sectors who employ few migrant workers, do not require a state-managed labour market and who value a more stable order; yet the effects are uneven, disadvantaging businessmen in other sectors who have demanded and come to depend upon the state management of African labour supplies; reconstruction threatens the position of marginal middle- and working-class elements in the Afrikaner community who value their dominant political position and state support.

The abandonment of conventional ideology represents the abandonment of a narrow, but very real hegemony, under which important elements in white society had found material well-being and a sense of order. The fate of the alternative, an encompassing bourgeois hegemony, is genuinely problematic. Those who advance it, even in fragmentary form, confront a social order built on vast racial inequalities, a massive state presence and growing African disaffection.

The search for hegemony

The first concrete ideological stirrings in dominant politics came from Afrikaner intellectuals and businessmen, many of whom had come face to face with the essential problem: the visible and sanctioned entanglement of politics and economics. Though the intellectuals and businessmen were cautious about relaxing controls in practice, they began to confront the ascendant state ideology and to fashion a new one that would give greater prominence to the market.

Other actors, particularly those within the state apparatus, would take up ill-formed fragments of such a new ideology, but inconsistently and sometimes without evident conviction, sometimes to serve expedient purposes that had little to do with the developing ideological discourse. Only the intellectuals and businessmen seemed able to articulate a comprehensive statement, and only they seemed able to point the way to a reconstructed and expanded hegemony.

This new ideological thinking, fashioned largely outside the state apparatus, confronted the ascendant ideology at each essential tenet: it diminished the evident partiality of the state by denying the state's racial character; it sought to contain political conflict by diminishing the visible role of the state, by depoliticising what had become a deeply political social order; it shifted the centre of gravity to private actors in economic life, businessmen, whose enterprises would prove a source of wealth and opportunity. By taking these ideological initiatives, these intellectuals and businessmen hoped to reach out to Africans, to lay the basis for a broader identification with the capitalist order and a loyalty to a more universal state.[9]

Intellectuals: diminishing the state

During the late 1970s, a range of prominent intellectuals, many of them participants in state commissions or advisory boards, began to offer sceptical observations about what had passed for conventional ideology. They questioned the economic viability of the Bantustans; they wondered aloud about the future of urban Africans; they asked whether any system built centrally around racial discrimination could prove legitimate internally or externally. More broadly, and perhaps more importantly, Afrikaner intellectuals wondered whether emotive and symbolic notions, like 'separate development' or 'apartheid', could any longer offer some hope for an orderly future. As Hermann Giliomee has observed, apartheid had lost its hegemonic character and emerged as purely instrumental.[10] The consequent formalism, Jan Lombard writes, has left white South Africa 'dissatisfied with itself' and without 'faith in its future'. South Africa, consequently, has had no choice but to 'fall back on the abilities of its defence and police forces to protect the order against external attack and domestic lawlessness'.[11]

The first task before the intellectuals was the diminution of the political, the narrowing of a realm, central to conventional ideology, that now seemed to leave the social order exposed. The intellectuals now denied the appropriateness and efficacy of state intervention in the economic realm; they opposed the centrality of the state, counterposing it to a decentralised, depoliticised, non-racial and limited political order.[12]

There was a strong emphasis in this developing body of thought on limiting the state's scope of activity and control over society – thus removing the state as the object of social conflict. Under the present entanglement of politics and economics, politics is 'explosive, a trap', Lombard writes. The 'more the functions and power of decision are delegated to government, the more important it becomes to BE the government, or at least to CONTROL the government and its administration'.[13] Following on this argument, a Pretoria economist closely associated with the business community advocates stripping the state of its historic functions:

It is therefore clearly of crucial importance for constitutional reform that no major decisions about welfare matters such as income re-distribution, development assistance, education, health, housing and the like are taken by the central authority. Any such link would immediately re-establish the need for individual and/or group representation in the central authority.[14]

The denial of the political has even spawned a revisionist understanding of history that denies the historic importance of the state. The most eloquent of the revisionist formulations is found in the introduction to the Wiehahn (labour reform) Commission, presumably authored by its chairman, formerly an academic in Pretoria.

The Republic of South Africa subscribes to the principles of a free market economy based on individual freedom in the market place. This freedom relates to freedom of choice either as consumer or as producer, and freedom of competition within a political democracy. This ideology has been practised by successive governments of South Africa since the dawn of the industrial and commercial history of the country and the Commission has no reason to believe that this philosophy will be abandoned.[15]

Though Lombard is more sensitive to the laws and administrative practices that limit the workings of the free economy, he too indulges in selective minimisation of the political reality. After reviewing major pieces of legislation, including the Marketing Act which fostered European co-operative control of commercial agriculture and the Industrial Conciliation Act which excluded African workers from the statutory collective-bargaining framework, he concludes that 'the control functions of state agencies' were not very important. They amount to little more than the 'keeping of registers, issuing of licences and the proclamation of agreements'. Discrimination was 'purely functional'. The state 'was mainly to act as an umpire in and a protector of this process'. Lombard also denies, against an impressive body of evidence to the contrary, that Afrikaners used their control of the state to realise economic gains: 'Between 1900 and 1950 the Afrikaner people regarded politics as a means to freedom, not as a vehicle for economic advancement.'[16]

A more developed and theoretically interesting form of mystification is the notion of 'market failure' – a term that has surfaced in the Riekert Commission and the works of P. J. van der Merwe and Jan Lombard. The term is unassuming, as it suggests a principle for limited state activity rooted in the logic of the market. All capitalist societies, after all, are permissive of state meddling where individual, rational market decisions produce in the aggregate 'undesirable' results 'from the standpoint of the community or society'.

In this instance, however, the intellectuals turn a presumed market principle into a defence of massive state abrogation of labour markets. Van der Merwe offers, as a prime example of 'market failure', 'the social costs as opposed to the strictly private cost which results from the large scale importation of workers from the subsistence sector in the black states in and around South Africa and which leads to over-crowding, slum conditions, high unemployment rates, etc. in urban areas'. Both van der Merwe and Lombard observe that Africans may not have acquired the degree of 'rationality' necessary for the effective use of markets, producing suboptimum allocation decisions, and, therefore, encouraging state interventions. Lombard suggests that a 'liberal system of influx control or group areas would be based on the symptoms of civilised behaviour (i.e. as demanded by a sophisticated market economy) rather than on colour as such'.[17] A system, con-structed around and rationalised by the notion of 'market failure' allows an elaborate state penetration of markets and, at the same time, an affirmation of the primacy of market principles.

Closely related to the first of the intellectuals' tasks, the diminution of the political, is a second which elevates the economy over the political as a source of wealth, employment and public welfare gener-ally. Sometimes this task emerges as an assertion and a hope. By leaving greater room for economic forces, the state is in fact opening the way for new forms of job creation. It 'is therefore up to the business sector', van der Merwe writes, 'to take advantage of this climate, to create employment opportunities for Blacks in metropolitan and decentralised areas and to move Blacks up the occupational ladder'.[18] For others, this task requires something more strictly classical: market processes bring an elaborated division of labour, specialisation and a flowering of productive forces, often stifled by state-directed systems. 'Once every adult participating in the pro-cess of production and exchange is able, willing and free to explore the most profitable application of his talents, whether intellectual or physical,' Lombard writes, 'no alternative system of organisation can measure up to the productive performance of the market system.'[19]

Drawing profoundly on the first two tasks, the market theorists have confronted a third – the necessity of finding common principles in social organisation. Clearly, a race stratified society based on labour-repressive policies offers few such principles, as the state is profoundly partial. In emphasising the individual, equality, freedom and material advantage, all universal concepts, market theorists hope to enlist the black population in a broader identification with the society and state. Market society, Lombard believes, makes possible a 'consistent set of basic political principles which will be acceptable to all the people of South Africa'.[20]

For many of the theorists, these universal notions – the market, freedom and equality – are a potential counter-idiom to that of socialism and Marxism. The Free Market Foundation, for one, has conducted surveys among Africans and uncovered a partiality to 'Marxist rhetoric'. It has proposed, in response, a market-based idiom calling for 'economic liberation'.[21]

Afrikaner business: shifting the locus of prestige

Afrikaner businessmen in the middle and late 1970s began questioning the framework that had sustained state policy over two decades, although Afrikaner business in particular had played a formative role in the framework's construction. The Afrikaanse Handelsinstituut (AHI) – the principal Afrikaner business association, representing medium and large firms, as well as some co-operatives and quasi-state enterprises – questioned the efficacy and plausibility of Bantustan policies, state control measures and efforts to deny African proletarianisation: 'The black stream to the cities will thus become stronger and exert pressure, despite all our laudable efforts and incentives to decentralisation and homeland development. . . . Economic integration of the Blacks is inevitable and unstoppable if work and welfare is to be created and maintained.'[22] In the next twenty years, the AHI predicted, there will be 20 million more urbanised Africans and, remarkably, seven more Sowetos.[23] The Urban Foundation (supported by English and Afrikaner businessmen) has tried, through repetition, to legitimise the premise that urbanisation is 'inevitable', 'natural' and 'desirable'. It has even tried to associate urban communities symbolically with the emerging economic order: 'Urban communities are, by and large, free enterprise communities; and thus free enterprise links at every level with the complexities of urban life.'[24]

Afrikaner business in the 1970s also expressed growing concern about the poverty and discontent of some Africans and the problems raised by an illegitimate social order. While the Prime Minister at the first of two historic meetings with the business community spoke of a 'constellation of states', business participants spoke repeatedly of poor living conditions or unemployment among urban Africans. These concerns were reiterated at the second meeting in 1981 where businessmen concentrated, in particular, on the housing and training needs of the industrialised and stabilised portion of the African population.[25] In the absence of a policy responsive to this new reality, the AHI wrote, whites would face a growing vulnerability in the face of black discontent:

> The danger must be avoided that unemployment, particularly in white areas, creates a breeding ground for communism. The small top layer of whites at the pinnacle of the labour pyramid is continually getting relatively smaller as against the base with a broad Black foundation.[26]

This new reality demanded a new ideological initiative that would end the evident partiality of the state, open up opportunities for 'stable' and 'middle- class' elements, and, most importantly, diminish the role of the state. The first step in this ideological process was deracialisation – a repudiation of the historic enshrinement of social privilege within the state and economy. Even this limited exercise in incorporation demanded at the ideological level a shift towards more universal principles. For businessmen, deracialisation has come to mean simply removing visibly discriminatory measures, particularly those that hamper the position of the emerging educated middle class. For others, the notion involves black collaboration in the labour-control bureaucracy, above all, in influx control, to remove the racial stigma from such state activity. In 1976, the AHI thought that a black take-over of the labour-control administration would end the 'incitement of hate against the whites since in present circumstances the Whites have to enforce their laws . . .'. The Director of the Urban Foundation, while not wholly supportive of influx control, could envision its retention, 'if there was bigger black participation in it'.[27]

The AHI and other business organisations urged the government to remove impediments and expand opportunities for a segment of the African population. Any new dispensation must make room for 'stabilised elements', an 'African middle class', and the 'black entrepreneur'. The African must be given a 'stake' in the system, some form of ownership, such as housing, which can be a 'stabilising influence on black urban communities'.[28] By allowing black workers to participate in 'responsible collective bargaining' and the enterprising to 'engage in business', it becomes possible to establish 'the trust and loyalty of the blacks in the system of free enterprise'.[29] A former President of AHI observed, ruefully, the African 'has participated as a worker, but he has not shared the sweet fruits of the system'.[30] Those who 'can enjoy the fruits of hard work, knowledge and capital amid stiff competition' can ultimately become 'supporters of capitalism'.[31]

The AHI has also proved willing to extend this concern with incorporation to the political level. While the government was speaking publicly and cautiously about a qualified participation by the Coloured and Asian minorities in a segregated parliamentary framework, the AHI was thinking more expansively, extending the 'new dispensation' to Africans in white areas. More theoretically and in the longer run, the AHI suggested that 'consociationalism will need to be replaced by non-discriminatory criteria', perhaps including a 'qualified franchise' or a 'meritocracy of proportional ethnic bloc votes'. South Africa must move towards 'multi-ethnic co-operation', as 'the white minority cannot fight alone on the borders and in the interior and at the same time retain all responsibility for administration and the operation of the private sector'.[32]

The most important and consistent element in the Afrikaner business response was the attempt to shift the locus of prestige and power within Afrikanerdom from the state to the private sector. Andreas Wassenaar's polemical attack on the Vorster government was, above all, an attempt by the leading Afrikaner business magnate to denigrate the value of the political and assert the supremacy of the economic. He called on the public to 'retard or stop the slide towards ever-increasing state absorption of the private sector, bit by bit, piece by piece'. He countered this trend by elevating the position of the economic: the 'full economy of a country' cannot be 'sound unless the private sector, as a whole, is sound'; the private economy represents the 'material life of a people'.[33]

The elevation of the economic suggests, from this perspective, two policy- related conclusions: first, the strategic importance of the private sector in coping with problems of employment and African living standards; and second, the necessity of curtailing state involvement in the economy. In the middle 1970s, the AHI came increasingly to justify profits and free enterprise as a 'system that can solve the problem of poverty'. By allowing the private sector room to operate, the country receives the 'best guarantee for growth and prosperity', in effect, the capacity to deal with its immense political problems.[34] Simultaneously, the AHI launched an attack on the public corporations, particularly the Industrial Development Corporation and the Iron and Steel Corporation. In 1972–73, the AHI suggested, tentatively and privately, that these public entities 'had gone beyond their terms of reference'. By 1976, the AHI was attacking directly the growing fixed capital of public corporations and the tendency to destroy the 'goose which lays the golden egg', the private sector.[35]

The Afrikaner business community has in practice proved unwilling to relinquish fully state-control measures. The AHI, when defending the labour- control framework, criticised the 'self-seeking' type of capitalist who recruits black labour, regardless of the social consequences 'arising from an uncontrolled influx'. They also warned against 'socialistic labour policies' that might follow if the state was too dependent on 'popular support to stay in power'.[36] Those strong cautionary remarks combine, however, with a strong generalised attack on the state's inclination to restrict and hold back the private sector:

> It is time to reflect seriously on the slow subversion of our free enterprise system on which South Africa's growth and prosperity is based, and to stimulate private initiative and the profit motive instead of restricting it. We will have to scrap the many unnecessary regulatory measures and laws, decrease and consolidate the unnecessary [government] departments and councils, make public services more efficient and better remunerated, better utilise and decrees the number of officials. . . . We make too many laws to protect and regulate with the result that we are increasingly enslaved to our bureaucracy which controls and regulates us.[37]

Here, in the realm of Afrikaner business, the state must yield to the prestige and force of civil society.

Officials, the state and ideological conflict

While Afrikaner businessmen and intellectuals were reconstructing the ideological foundations of the social order, state officialdom has remained, in essential terms, unreconstructed. While actors with productive or intellectual roles outside the state apparatus sought to detract from the partiality and centrality of the state, these actors, whose function and identity are situated within the conventional statist ideology, have held tightly to core tenets. Above all, they have refused to relinquish the state's visible control of civil society and to put their faith instead in market mechanisms.

The continuing prominence of the state no doubt complicates attempts to reconstruct ideology and fashion something that achieves hegemony. None the less, within this limiting condition, actors within the state apparatus have increasingly clashed over how to maintain control, how to come to terms with a growing and assertive Afrikaner bourgeoisie and how to respond to the spreading expressions of African disaffection. Where officials stand in this contradictory ideological discourse would seem to depend on their role in the bureaucracy and their connection to elements outside the state apparatus.[38]

In defence of statist ideology
Officials refuse to relinquish the core tenet in state ideology – the state's essential control over markets. This commitment has survived the Soweto disorders and the Biko murder; it has survived the ideological discourses surrounding the Wiehahn and Riekert Commissions; and it has survived the apparent coming together of business and political leaders at the

Carlton Centre and at Cape Town's Civic Centre. Adherence has not simply lingered in the rural backwaters or at the bottom-most parts of the bureaucracy. The centrality of politics and the subordination of the economic remain central to ideological thinking at all levels within the state.

Officials describe their functions in formal and in service terms – 'to bring the employer and labourer together' (Labour Bureau [LB], Johannesburg); 'to place people in employment and to correlate the demand and supply' (LB, Krugersdorp); 'the main purpose is to supply labour according to the demand' (Central Transvaal Administration Board [AB]).[39]

But the formal responses are nearly always overshadowed by a constant attention to maintaining 'control'. 'True,' one labour official observes,

> we bring the employer and employee together, but influx control is just as important. It is our job to see that blacks coming to the urban areas are on an organised basis, to see that blacks won't flow to an area where there aren't facilities (LB, Carletonville).

Few officials, whether simple operatives at the bottom or policy-makers at the top, can imagine life in the absence of controls:

> If you allow everybody to come in without the necessary documents, you will have a flooding (East Rand AB).

> You'll have them in the bushes around Cape Town. . . . We are a developing country and with the political situation around us, if everything is abolished, the whole of South Africa would be overrun by the blacks. Then it would be impossible out of the chaos to maintain an economically sound basis (Western Cape AB).

> The influx from the rural areas into the urban areas, as elsewhere in the world, will be controlled. If you don't do that, you will create social problems that we will not be able to handle (Manpower Commission).

The enduring commitment to control translates into two streams of thought that are difficult to reconcile with the new ideology: first, officials evidence almost no sympathy or understanding of market principles; and second, officials envision a growing, rather than a diminished role for the state in the regulation of economic life, particularly over the movements of African labour.

Hostility to market principles
Labour officials who have been tutored in an administered system find it very difficult to comprehend the market. In the absence of state

administration, one official remarks quizzically, 'the employer would have to get his own labour; he would not end up with the best type of employee'. As for the employee, 'there is no control over there; you will have uncontrolled entry of blacks' (Port Natal AB). A process that would certainly seem dear and appropriate to adherents of free enterprise, in official eyes, appears unseemly:

> [Without] any inducement for an employer or an employee to abide by legislation for registered employment, there would be no canalisation whatsoever; with the result that you would have undesirable social circumstances. People would flock in by the thousands. Employers would hire and fire them. There would be squatting conditions and crime (West Rand AB).

> [If the labour bureaux were abolished], how would you regulate the employee? You would throw the whole labour market open to whomever wanted to work wherever. What are you going to have then? It would be chaotic (Chief Commissioner [CC], Northern Transvaal).

One official finally asks, 'Isn't supply and demand the same as influx control?' (CC, Natal).

In any event, officials argue, 'the African' is in many respects unprepared for market arrangements. When he cannot find a job in the city, the African does not return home. 'Even with these new penalties', and the high unemployment, 'they are streaming into the urban areas. . . . They have a different mentality. You can't always understand these people' (LB, Kempton Park). That mentality apparently includes a continued attachment to traditional culture, 'even in the industrial situation', and a certain market impracticality compared with the white man: 'These people just get on the train and they create the problem, like we have at Crossroads' (Employment Services Committee, Manpower Commission; Deputy Minister). 'A majority of the blacks, the unskilled labourers, have not yet learned to think for themselves, that there is no sense going to a place where there is no job' (Orange-Vaal, AB).

The African's lack of understanding for labour markets leads him, almost inexorably, to the labour bureaucracy. 'It is in their culture', one official observes. 'They want somebody to lead them in a direction' (Employment Services Committee, Manpower Commission). With respect to the labour market, the 'blacks need help' (Boksburg, LB). 'They are so used to the system now', one official observes, 'they expect us to find a job for them' (Johannesburg, LB).

Elaborating the state
The ideological discourse among businessmen and intellectuals takes as axiomatic the diminished role of the state. Within the bureaucracy, at every

level, the opposite is the case. In these offices, there is a very strong belief that markets bring a corresponding increase in state efforts to regulate them. Politics, consequently, continues to subordinate the economic.

This theme is propagated right from the top. A principal adviser to the Minister for Co-operation and Development, member of legislative drafting committees, and formerly a Chief Commissioner, speaks eloquently of the process:

> Hopefully, it [expanding markets] should bring less [state regulation], but I know as a fact that it will bring more. How can you avoid that, because there are bound to be employers who will take the chance? They will find a loophole somewhere. You fill the loophole and that means another regulation.

He joins this general observation with a range of specific recommendations suggestive of an overarching state structure: 'What I would like to see is a system in this country whereby the faulting employee, as well as the faulting employer, are tried in the same forum, simultaneously, and punished in that same forum. We should have new courts – labour-control tribunals.' With regard to labour supplies, he notes, 'there is a flaw, a weakness in our system of distribution. . . . If we could have a reservoir at a strategic point, then we could insist that nobody take a shortcut.'

For officials at lower levels of the labour bureaucracy, the state role is simply a common-sense extension of their generalised commitment to control. 'Personally,' a Kempton Park LB official observes,

> I think control will be more needed. You will have more people looking for work so you will need a proper system to canalise people, so that you can maintain proper health conditions.

A Klerksdorp official underlines the presumption with a simple definitiveness:

> There should always be control. Control is a very good thing. Without control, we don't have much of a chance of surviving – not just in South Africa but all over the world. . . . Maybe less regulation, but control must always be there.

The conclusion presupposes an expanded role for the bureaucracy itself. 'Because these are the people who are handling the labour, who have the experience with the labour', an official at Carletonville observes, 'they must have more to say in the flow of labour.' Across a broad range of administration boards, there is a feeling that growing industrialisation and urbanisation, even with recent 'reforms', would bring more labour bureaux, more inspectors, and more state regulation (East Rand, Western Transvaal, Central Transvaal LBs).

Narrow legitimacy: protecting the locals

The pervasive concern with control is combined, throughout the bureaucratic structure, with an apparent desire to protect the local or urban African population. This concern may seem paradoxical or, at least, disingenuous; it is none the less central to the rationalisation of this area of state practice.

As apartheid ideology has lost its hold on important elements in the dominant coalition, as its tenets fail to make sense of a dangerous reality, officials hold tightly to this narrow justificatory belief. The Bantustans, the traditional basis for moral order, now seem slightly implausible, even for these unreconstructed adherents of the conventional faith. Indeed, at the lower levels, the Bantustans are hardly mentioned, except as places where certain categories of workers live.[40] At the policy-making levels, there is a great deal of self-congratulation on this 'concession', on the 'acceptance' of a proletarianised African population. 'It is now recognised', the chairman of the Manpower Commission declares, 'that the black labour force is there to stay.' It is accepted 'at the senior level', the economic adviser to the Prime Minister observes, 'that increasing numbers of blacks are in the urban areas; and provision is already being made in the plan for the PWV (Witwatersrand) region.'

The recognition of African permanence is not confined to 'reform circles' at the top. The tenet has equal or greater currency among the outgoing officials and at the lower reaches of the bureaucracy. A Department Secretary, for example, is eloquent on the point:

> There isn't any doubt in anybody's head that there will be a permanent black population in the cities. We can't wish them away. We can't dream them away. You can't carry on with the factories without these people.
> In the old days, some said they were here only as long as they sold their labour, but that is the old days. Not any more.

The former Chief Commissioner for the Western Cape observes that he and the local authorities have had a 'soft spot' for 'their locals' – 'their coloureds and for their local blacks who have been here 20 years and have qualified'.

At the level of the administration boards and labour bureaux, the protection of urban Africans emerges, ideologically, as the primary preoccupation of the labour-control officialdom. The purpose of influx control is not so much to protect the standards of the white community as to ensure the stability of the local black community; it 'is to protect the local boy, specifically, without any doubt, that is the main reason' (East Rand, LB). Another official notes, 'the main thing to remember is that the local labour supply must not be exploited. It must be utilised first. They are the local residents as far as employment is concerned' (Carletonville, LB).

If influx control were to be relaxed, if the state were to leave the labour market to its own dynamic, the local labour would be the first hurt. They would be thrown out of work and their wages undercut, as cheap labour from outside became available. 'The locals would starve', a Durban LB official concludes. A Transvaal official describes dire consequences:

> If you do away with the labour bureau, abolish influx control, everybody will be running in the street, even the Europeans. . . . We'd have crowding again. . . . The employer, he wants the outside people; he's not so fussy. . . . You would frustrate the local people and you will get riots (Northern Transvaal, AB).

It is not difficult to understand how such a posture would fit within the official's general ideological stance. The concern for the welfare of local Africans is, in fact, a justification for influx control, for continued state control over the developing labour market. Officials can advance this argument, with good conscience, in a period when politicians and actors outside the state have questioned the old order and cast about for new ideas, in a period when the conventional ideology has lost its sense of purpose and order.

The uneven path to legitimation

The continuing reverence for the state and caution about markets set the stage for intense political struggles within the state apparatus itself. For some officials, particularly at the lower reaches of the bureaucracy, these beliefs combine with a more encompassing commitment to traditional ideology, isolating them within the state structure and from the emergent discourse outside. They express little concern about legitimacy, African support or the partiality of the state; they describe existing structures as non-discriminatory and non-problematic. Indeed, reminiscent of more traditional ideologues, these officials pinpoint employers as the personification of the market, as an exploitative force destructive of social order.

Officials at the top find themselves in a peculiar position, for they, as much as the intellectuals and businessmen, want to minimise social conflict and broaden compliance. These beliefs place them in a contradictory position: while they share the concern of officials generally with continued state control, they recognise at the same time that a disaffected African proletariat promises future troubles; while they are comfortable with the new ideological thinking about legitimation, they seem loath to substitute the market for state directive. They find themselves, consequently, in an ambiguous position, pulled by conflicting affinities and by a contradictory ideological posture requiring both an elaborated and depoliticised South African state.

Upper-level officials: depoliticising the state
While officials at the policy-making level will not easily relinquish control over the market, they are anxious to put a different face on the process. 'The influx control side is still there', one official observes and then proceeds to a frank account of depoliticisation.

> The impact of influx control will be phased out. In the future, it will not be a political issue but a practical issue. In the future, it will be a question of accommodation and jobs.
> In the 1950s, when we started with the labour bureaus, the main issue was to keep the numbers down. At that time, the government of the day made that determination. But at this time, it has been turned around, to get everybody in a job, to protect them, to give them a service. But the political sting of influx control is no longer so important (Employment Services Committee).

Control based on availability of employment and housing, the chairman of the Manpower Commission concludes, is 'more morally defensible also more economically defensible'. The economic adviser to the Prime Minister generalises the problem and the government's intent: 'The idea of managing the economy through indirect means still is hard to sell.'

The emphasis on 'indirect means' carries over into a range of policy areas, particularly the removal of racially discriminatory appearances. Control measures are now applied to Africans, not as Africans, but as rural dwellers in a situation of labour surplus. The Manpower Commission chairman observes:

> It is not a question of race discrimination. It just so happens that blacks are the people in the rural areas. At one time, there was a political basis for it, but not anymore.

Franz Du Randt, principal drafter of new labour-control legislation, told the Institute of Administrators of Non-European (now, Community) Affairs to eschew the term, 'influx control', which 'will soon disappear from our vocabulary as it is really a misnomer and to my way of thinking very offensive'; instead, he suggested that officials speak of a 'mechanism "to regulate the rate of immigration to urban areas"'.[41]

Nicholas Wiehahn, chairman of the Commission of Inquiry into Labour Legislation and later of the Industrial Court, adopts a more active posture towards deracialisation, though framed by the same ideological context. 'The problem' with influx control 'so far' is 'that it has been discriminatory', he observes. 'If one retains influx control, it must be made applicable to all citizens', or at least all citizens whose entry into urban employment would tax water, housing and transportation facilities. The key, he points out, is 'imagery', the imagery of 'removing discrimination'.

The attempt at ideological mystification is reflected in the disassociation of employers from the market critique.[42] Employers are no longer seen as the 'magnets' creating social problems by attracting black labour; instead, social problems derive from processes that have been stripped of their class character. Influx control is necessitated by 'development problems' – the 'uneven' location of industrial sites and employment opportunities.

Officials at this level view employers as the principal pressure group that has forced the state to face the problem of legitimation. The disorders in Soweto and elsewhere were important, as were the economic boom between 1969 and 1972 and the appearance of skilled labour shortages; but direct action by employers provided the main impetus. 'It was an overwhelming pressure from private thinking', the chairman of the Employment Services Committee observes. Wiehahn agrees: 'Business pressed hard for such a commission.' The coolness that historically separated the state and business community has now 'changed completely', the economic adviser to the Prime Minister notes. 'With the breakthrough of Afrikaner businessmen into mining and industry, there is a more complete coalition with business. When Afrikaner businessmen pressed for the same things as English businessmen, the government began to listen.'

Lower-level officials: holding on
Administration Board and Labour Bureau officials operate outside the networks that have brought greater identification with employer perspectives on legitimation and the state. Though groups of intellectuals, Afrikaner businessmen and high officials have begun to cast the employer in a public-spirited role, these officials remain committed to the traditional ideological depiction. In the halls of the labour-control bureaucracy, employers are still the villains of the piece, putting their immediate labour requirements ahead of the larger community's interest in limiting the influx of labour.

Wherever you turn in the officials' depiction of the labour market, employers are a disruptive force. At the point of recruitment in the Bantustans, only the officials stand between the African and exploitation. 'If you allow it [direct employer recruiting], with all respect to my fellow white man, it lends itself to so much irregularity, bribery and corruption, to the detriment of the black man', one official notes (Northern Transvaal, CC). In the labour market generally, officials restrain the employers' exploitative impulses. A Natal official describes his mediating role.

> I don't need to tell you that labour is a commodity like any other commodity. The employer will go for an illegal worker who will be cheaper. . . . It is our responsibility to protect the permanent resident. . . . There is exploitation. In our own way, we are trying to use the legal system to fight this exploitation.

The officials dealing directly with the African worker on a daily basis and removed from the heady discourses at the top, are uniformly hostile to the role of business. Indeed, they seem to define their role in direct opposition to the employer:

> You simply have to protect these local blacks. These employers want a black from the outside. He is normally illegally in the area and he will give a higher standard of work; he will take more from an employer before getting fed up. But as soon as they get the right to be in the area, they are the same as the local ones. But the employer is always seeking the outsider (Carletonville, LB).

> Though I'm a white man, as far as I'm concerned, a lot of white employers will take advantage of the black man (Klerksdorp, LB).

> Employers – some employers – prefer contract workers. If we get a slack of employment and we want to place the local people, they moan. They say we always used these people. Some of these employers are very clever; they are only interested in their pockets. The outside man is prepared to work for a lower wage (Boksburg, LB).

In their isolation from the mainstream of the ideological discourse, officials at this level have remained reasonably indifferent to the broader legitimation problem. There is almost no mention here of depoliticising labour control, that is, removing the visible state presence in the market. They seem little concerned with changing the racial character of state institutions. Indeed, most of these officials deny that these institutions in their present form have a racial character. 'It is not discriminatory', a Boksburg official declares.

> We are there to help them. When I took one of the boys to Umtata to recruit labour, I had to show my book, just like him. It didn't bother me. Why should it bother them?

An official at Kempton Park is equally adamant in his denials:

> I can't accept that we have any [discrimination] here at all, except that we only deal with blacks. Our machinery is not set to handle whites. We mainly cater to the ordinary labourer.

Officials in the Administration Boards are willing to entertain recent proposals that would consolidate departments and bring blacks and whites under a uniform administration. But, like the Labour Bureau officials below them in the hierarchy, they deny that existing structures are tainted by a racial character – and are, therefore, partial and illegitimate. 'As far as I am concerned, it is not discrimination', a Transvaal official says. 'In the case of the Bantu, you have the numbers that count; so you have to control to avert chaos' (Central Transvaal, AB). The Chief Commissioner for the Witwatersrand adopts a similar stance: 'influx control would have been necessary even if all rural blacks were poor white. We would have to have the same control.' An official at the East Rand Administration Board concludes with a definiteness that seems to negate the problem:

> There is no racial discrimination in a labour bureau. There is no race in this. This is labour, even though the labourer is a black man and the employer a white man.

The bureaucratic tangle

The differing perspectives within the state apparatus, and the differing relations to class actors outside it, have produced enormous acrimony among officials and between state institutions. Andreas Wassenaar, chairman of one of South Africa's largest financial enterprises, initiated the public encounter by declaring that the government, particularly the bureaucracy, is the 'foe'.[43]

That challenge has reverberated within the bureaucracy. Officials, with close ties to the business community and the present political leadership, have subsequently come into direct conflict with the labour-control bureaucracy. The chairman of the Manpower Commission observes that officials in the Department of Co-operation and Development are 'a real problem. . . . They wear blinkers.' (By contrast, officials at Manpower Utilisation, 'much more closely associated with business', are seen as able to implement policy.) A principal adviser on the Riekert Commission, and now an official, observes that 'the bureaucrats in the various sections are now as cold as ice to me'. His experience was shared by a chairman of one of the labour reform commissions who observes that, when visiting the Minister of Co- operation and Development, 'the people don't talk to me – the upper level of civil servants. Those that aided in the preparation of the report are deeply opposed to the policy recommendations.' He declares, with remarkable boldness, that we have 'to break the mafia that could think of no other way of dealing with the black man' and con- cludes, with some confidence, that 'the private sector will not allow the mafia to kill these proposals.'

Within the state bureaucracy there are upper-level officials, many with close relations to the business community, who hold the labour-control officialdom in contempt. Their estrangement has in some cases proved so profound that these officials now applaud the overrunning of control efforts. The massive African illegal flight to the cities, one policy-level official observes, 'is good . . . just as well':

> People are bypassing the red tape. The market works where the state system doesn't. In spite of all the regulations, the free market functions. I'm very glad of it.

There are, at the same time, upper-level officials, including an immediate past Director-General of the Department of Co-operation and Development, who reject the government's shift to regulation at the workplace and residence, favouring, instead, broader police functions that control idle and disorderly persons.[44] There are lower-level control officials who speak of the impending 'massive urbanisation' of the Bantustans and yet tighter control of labour markets: '. . . influx control and labour bureaux in the relevant black states' should be employed as much as possible to assure that black workers in white cities all 'should be of the same ethnic group'.[45]

These contrasting perspectives within the bureaucracy itself constitute a remarkable tangle – a far cry from the ascendant unity that characterised the control bureaucracy in apartheid's heyday. Then, officials at all levels seemed extravagant in their elaboration of the state and their receptivity to the lead of politicians.[46] Today, the politicians themselves seem uncertain of their purpose and beliefs, though embarked on a new path to hegemony.

The political use of ideas

Some factions of the National Party, now organised in the opposition, ritualistically affirm conventional tenets about the Bantustans and the reversal of African urbanisation; new political cultural organisations, like the Afrikaner Volkswag, want to reinvigorate the *volk*, to confront 'our soft elements'.[47] Within the government, there are important centres of traditional thought. The Deputy Minister for Co-operation and Development still talks about 'keeping the numbers down' and the need for more 'regulation with a greater influx of people'. And some state agencies, like the South African Broadcasting Corporation (SABC) as late as 1983, were reaffirming core philosophic notions: 'the black man will be stunted and frustrated if he is isolated from the mainstream of his people and is culturally alienated'; the black man 'cannot survive, let alone fulfil himself, as a fragmented, isolated individual'; 'the greater and the greatest must be attained by him within his own nation'. The evolving framework of the 1980s, the SABC declares, recognises the 'existence of the black nations that have a primary allegiance to their own people, language, culture and political aspirations'.[48]

But these ideological currents have been subordinated within the media and within the state. The dominant political leadership begins with two premises: one, articulated by the Minister of Co-operation and Development, that 'apartheid is dead'; the other, articulated by the Prime Minister himself and every major commission in recent years, that the 'maintenance of free enterprise' is 'the basis of our economic and financial policy'.

But what do political leaders intend when they advance these new ideological principles? Are they constructing a new state ideology? Have they come to a common understanding with intellectuals and businessmen that markets and private actors should play a larger role, that the state should shed its racial character in favour of a more universal posture?

Political leaders offer what probably should be characterised as a formal affirmation of free market tenets. The Prime Minister now supports market-oriented financial policies favoured by the business community: floating exchange rates, reduced marginal tax rates and limits on capital investment by parastatal enterprises.[49] He, and other members of the government, speak freely of the economic bounty in free enterprise. His Finance Minister, drawing directly on Adam Smith, states that free enterprise makes possible an 'unprecedented rise in real wealth and income'.[50] The SABC lauds the free enterprise system as the 'most efficient – and ultimately the most equitable – wealth-creating machine devised by man'.[51] Finally, the political leadership has adopted the prevailing rhetoric of businessmen and intellectuals that demeans the conventional state role in economic affairs: '. . . private enterprise must be considered the norm and state interference with private enterprise must be regarded as a deviation from the general principle, to be justified in each instance by reference to the special circumstances of the case'.[52]

These affirmations, however, lack internal consistency and conviction. As the adviser to the Prime Minister points out, free enterprise principles are not well understood in the bureaucracy, even in the economic departments, and 'there is not much clarity' at the 'cabinet level'.[53] 'Quite honestly', the head of one of South Africa's largest business associations exclaims, not many of these people know what free enterprise means. . . . They are sublimely disinterested [sic] in the philosophy of enterprise. South African politicians take a pretty pragmatic view. They are looking for an economic machine that is efficient and effective, employment creation above all.[54]

For the political leadership, 'free enterprise' is largely a strategic political resource. It provides a loose set of principles, and some emotive terms, upon which the state can organise opposition to external forces, broaden support for the regime among Africans, and enlist the economic resources of business in new state initiatives.

Countering Marxism and enlisting Africans

Free enterprise is, above all, a counterpoint to the Marxist, 'total onslaught' – both external and domestic. On the external front, the Prime Minister has associated free enterprise with South Africa and counterposed it to the tyranny and subversion that comes with Marxist regimes: 'the order which Marxism creates leaves no room for freedom'.[55] The Minister of Defence, General Magnus Malan, believes South Africa is caught up in a 'communist-inspired onslaught' which intends the 'overthrow of the present constitutional order and its replacement by a subject communist-oriented black government'. South Africa's association with free enterprise is part of a broader association with 'free' nations opposed to such an international onslaught.[56]

Because a direct assault from outside seems implausible in the short term, the main focus is on domestic subversion, thus the concern with legitimation. By associating free enterprise with the regime, political leaders apparently hope to broaden opportunities for a shared identification with the existing social and political order and reduce the likelihood of political conflict. Koornhof views this association as the primary task before the government – how to prevent lingering dissatisfaction from becoming an anti-regime ideology and how to form a new ideology that enlists black co-operation.[57]

Support for 'free enterprise' as a counter-ideology is strong across the dominant political leadership. The Defence White Paper in 1977, organised by General Malan, sets the stage by asserting the need to enlist the 'entire population, the nation and every population group' in the 'national strategy'.[58] The Human Sciences Research Council plan for the early 1980s places a considerable emphasis on 'the susceptibility of the various cultural groups to ideologies'.[59] To counter the 'liberation ideologies' and make attractive an alternative rooted in 'free enterprise', Africans, white political leaders believe, will have to be provided with concrete reasons for becoming adherents. The Prime Minister told the Carlton Centre conclave that the 'benefits [in free enterprise] must be made apparent'; the Finance Minister told a gathering on free enterprise that 'the man on the shop floor must have the feeling that for him or his children there are no insurmountable barriers . . .'.[60] Indeed, the Governor of the Reserve Bank points to the close linkage of economic stability, political stability and development: economic development and the welfare of all groups depend, ultimately, on the 'increasing participation of all race groups'.[61]

Political leaders have not moved easily from rhetorical support for free enterprise to a lessened state role in the labour market. They none the less have expressed a keen interest in a less visible state and in depoliticisation – in a reduction and dispersal of political conflict. This interest is evident in the SABC's new-found interest in African local government, that is, the 'optimum devolution of power, or the shifting of authority from the highest to the lowest level of government'.[62] It is at this level, rather than the level of the central state 'that the most complex issues of South African politics have grown and will have to be resolved'.[63] Disputes between capital and labour need to be resolved in an institutional context in which the central state is absent. In South Africa's industrial relations system, guided by 'the principle of free enterprise', 'labour issues were deracialised and depoliticised in that the state, after providing the institutional framework, was taken out of the arena'.[64] The black majority, African workers in particular, therefore, have little reason to raise its concerns to the level of the state which remains outside this arena of potential conflict.

Enlisting business support

The real thrust is coming from economic forces. Once they accepted that 5 percent growth rate goal, they had to talk about our world. That is why [our business organisation] is able to have so much more influence.[65]

Free enterprise also represents an idiom and bargaining resource that, political leaders hope, will bring closer business–state co-operation and broaden support for the state in society. Such a trade-off was evident at the outset of the Carlton Centre meeting with business leaders, when the Prime Minister outlined 'free enterprise' concessions to business: restrictions on government investment and the 'release of resources to the private sector', lower tax rates and the 'general deregularisation of the economy as evidenced by the re-examination of price, rent and exchange control'. Moreover, he drew a clear line between the proper role of government and the proper role of business:

I believe we in government must understand that economic growth as such is mostly the responsibility of private enterprise. Of course, governments have a key role to play in areas such as the creation of physical and social infrastructure. Essentially, however, it is private enterprise which combines all the elements of production to produce wealth. . . . No government can successfully prescribe to private enterprise what to produce, how to produce, for whom to produce, and where to invest.

In exchange, the Prime Minister appealed to business leaders for greater co-operation in the implementation of government policy; specifically, for business leaders to invest in the Bantustans and deconcentration points:

In the extension of co-operation the Government can, however, only create a framework; the greatest real contribution to the extension of those relationships lies in the domain of the business sector. If you as business leaders extend your activities within our region in an innovative and energetic manner, you will be making a significant contribution to the happiness and well-being of all those peoples who make a living under the Southern Cross.[66]

While Botha posed this exchange at a high level, other observers and political leaders have focused on the more directly political aspects of the bargaining process. An Afrikaner businessman who served on the Wiehahn Commission suggests that a loose free enterprise ideology is part of an accommodation between the government and business, at the expense of white workers. The state could only address the question of legitimation, if it 'could break the power structure of the whites'. For that, the government would have to enlist the prestige and position of Afrikaner businessmen. At the cabinet level, the accommodation around free enterprise concepts may represent nothing more than a straightforward political bargain. 'For most cabinet members', the economic adviser to the Prime Minister observes,

[free enterprise] means forming a coalition of government and big business. It brings the Latin American model to mind. There is a belief, if only leading business people and leading government officials can get together, they can work out the country's problems.[67]

Ideological dissolution

It should be apparent from this extended discussion that the racial-state ideology, forged during the 1950s and 1960s, had yielded by the mid-1970s to widespread disunity. The ideology that had placed the state at the centre, that had inscribed racial privilege on the state and

that had offered a certain thematic unity and moral order, had fallen on
difficult times: its integrating element, the Bantustans, now seemed
implausible; its central themes, the state and race, now seemed to
compromise support for the political and economic orders; its appeal
to the white community now seemed to preclude a larger hegemony
including the growing African working class; its ascendancy had now
yielded to political turmoil and conflicting ideological perspectives
within the state.

The developing contradiction of an entangled political–economic
order has spun off groups of diverse position and perspective. Officials
at the bottom of the labour-control bureaucracy, very much isolated
from the growing association with business and weakened politically
by the general isolation of white workers, have sought to defend their
control functions, identity and the traditional role of the state. They
have expressed little interest in efforts to deracialise and depoliticise
labour-control activities or build support among Africans; they have
continued to view employers and the market as threats to the white
community. Officials at the policy level, while insisting on the maintenance of market control, have struggled with the implications of a
politicised market, partial state and growing black disaffection.

Political leaders have seized on the idiom in free enterprise to build a
closer alignment with business, though they have not yet faced up to
the contradictions of depoliticising and universalising a state that, in
practice, remains deeply mired in the market and that continues to
represent racial and class privilege. While political leaders have now
repudiated the narrow hegemony represented by apartheid ideology,
they have left themselves exposed – dependent on the fragments of a
new ideology they barely understand and caught up in a struggle
within the state for coherence and with the African majority for its
loyalty.

Notes and references

1 Bureau for Economic Policy and Analysis, *Focus on Key Issues: Political
  stability*, No. 26 (University of Pretoria, July 1980).
2 Jan Lombard, *On Economic Liberalism in South Africa* (Bureau for
  Economic Policy and Analysis, University of Pretoria) p. 25.
3 For an example, see R. J. W. van der Kooy, 'In search of a new economic
  development paradigm for Southern Africa: an introduction', *Development Studies Southern Africa*, 2, 22.
4 John S. Saul and Stephen Gelb, *The Crisis in South Africa: Class defense,*

class revolution. (Monthly Review Press, New York 1981) pp. 1–8; Stanley B. Greenberg, *Race and State in Capitalist Development: Comparative perspectives*. (New Haven 1980) pp. 398–403.

5 The lack of enthusiasm of officials for apartheid ideology and new state practices in the 1950s is detailed in Stanley B. Greenberg, 'State against the market', unpublished paper, 1984.

6 M. Smuts, 'The "farm" labour scheme', in *Bantu*, July 1959, p. 31.

7 Institute of Administrators of Non-European Affairs, *Fourteenth Annual Conference*, 1965, p. 127.

8 See Greenberg, 'State against the market'.

9 By beginning with intellectuals and businessmen, I do not mean to imply that the initiative for this discourse originated outside the state. There is credible evidence suggesting an interactive process, with political leadership inviting the questioning and initiatives of businessmen and intellectuals.

10 Hermann Giliomee, *Parting of the Ways: South African politics 1976–82* (Cape Town 1982) pp. x–xi, nn. 1–3; also Robert T. Tusenius, 'Prosperity Southern Africa', *Proceedings of the South African Economic Convention*, 27–28 June 1979, p. 28.

11 Jan Lombard, 'Cause of the black welfare economy', in *Volkshandel*, March 1978; Lombard, *On Economic Liberalism*, p. 54.

12 P. J. van der Merwe, 'An analysis of the report of the Commission of Inquiry into legislation affecting the utilisation of manpower', *Finance and Trade Review*, 13 June 1979, p. 34.

13 Lombard, *On Economic Liberalism*, pp. 16, 34.

14 I was asked by this individual not to attribute this document to him or any organisation.

15 Republic of South Africa, *Report of Commission of Inquiry into Labour Legislation* (Wiehahn), p. 181.

16 Lombard, *On Economic Liberalism*, pp. 12–13, 30–31. See Heribert Adam and Hermann Giliomee, *Ethnic Power Mobilized* (Yale University Press, New Haven 1979) for a discussion of the Afrikaner economic advance.

17 Van der Merwe, 'An analysis', pp. 34–6; Lombard, *On Economic Liberalism*, pp. 8, 23, 39.

18 Van der Merwe, 'An analysis', p. 56; also see Willie Breytenbach, 'The Botha strategy and the "Eighties"', *South Africa Foundation, Briefing Papers*, No. 5, July 1980.

19 Lombard, *On Economic Liberalism*, pp. 17–18, 34–5.

20 *Ibid.*, pp. 33, 51.

21 Interview, General Secretary, Free Market Foundation. Also see *Free Market*, 1, 1980, 26; and Jan Lombard, 'Socio-economic prospect for the eighties', speech before Institute of Personnel Management, Pretoria, 23 Sept. 1981, p. 5.

22 *Volkshandel*, April 1976, trans. Maretha du Toit. In October 1981, *Volkshandel* published a strong editorial reiterating these themes.

23 *Volkshandel*, May 1982, trans. by Neil Lazarus.

24 J. H. Steyn, 'The quality of life in our future towns – services hold the key', speech to South Africa Institute of Civil Engineers, 1980, pp. 3–4, and 'Free enterprise and urban communities', speech to National Conference of the 1820 Settlers' National Monument Foundation, Nov. 1979, p. 1.

25 'Towards a constellation of states', meeting between the Prime Minister and

business leaders, Carlton Centre, 22 Nov. 1979, pp. 24, 29; 'A regional development strategy for Southern Africa', meeting between the Prime Minister and business and community leaders (Good Hope), Civic Centre, Cape Town, 12 Nov. 1981, pp. 32–6.

26 *Volkshandel*, April 1976, trans. M. T.

27 *Volkshandel*, April 1976; interview, Urban Foundation.

28 J. G. van der Horst, 'Old mutual', speech at Good Hope Conference, p. 37.

29 *Volkshandel*, June and Dec. 1979, trans. M.T.

30 Interview, former President, AHI; F. J. C. Cronje, Nedbank, Good Hope Conference, p. 40; also AHI memorandum to the Wiehahn Commission, *Volkshandel* Feb. 1978.

31 *Volkshandel*, Aug. 1979, trans. M.T.

32 *Volkshandel*, July and Aug. 1982, trans. N.L.

33 A. D. Wassenaar, *Assault on Private Enterprise: Freeway to Communism* (Tafelberg 1977) pp. 65, 67.

34 Interview, former President, Afrikaanse Handelsinstituut; also *Volkshandel*, May 1976, trans. M.T.

35 *Volkshandel*, May 1976; also March 1977, trans. M.T.

36 *Volkshandel*, Oct. 1981 (trans. N.L.), Aug. 1979 (trans. M.T.), and July 1982 (trans. N.L.).

37 Interview, former President, AHI; *Volkshandel*, March 1977, May 1976, trans. M.T.

38 This report on the interview material concentrates on the main lines of thought. It does not include, for lack of space, a discussion of the exceptional views that pepper the bureaucracy.

39 During the period, Feb. 1979 to Aug. 1983, I conducted interviews with individuals holding positions at various levels within the labour-control framework and with individuals in strategic positions outside. A list of the state interviews is presented below:

Policy-makers
Chairman, Manpower Commission
Director, Manpower Commission
Chairman, Employment Services Committee, Manpower Commission
Special Assistant to the Minister for Co-operation and Development
Deputy Minister, Department of Co-operation and Development
Economic Adviser to the Prime Minister
Senior Deputy Governor of the Reserve Bank
Chairman, Commission of Inquiry into Labour Legislation
Chairman, Commission of Inquiry into Legislation Affecting the Utilisation of Manpower
Deputy Secretary for Labour, Department of Co-operation and Development

Middle level
Chief Commissioners (CC) – Witwatersrand, Western Cape, Natal, Northern Transvaal
Chairman or Director of Administration Boards (AB) – Central Transvaal, Western Cape, Western Transvaal, West Rand, Port Natal, East Rand
Directors of Labour, Administration Boards (AB) – Central Transvaal,

Western Transvaal, East Rand, Orange-Vaal, West Rand, Western Cape, Eastern Cape, Port Natal, Northern Transvaal
Lower level
Directors of Labour Bureaux (LB) – Carletonville, Johannesburg, Krugersdorp, Klerksdorp, Lichtenburg, Germiston, Boksburg, Kempton Park, Langa, Grahamstown, Durban, Empangeni, Pretoria, Mabopane, Pietersburg

40 It is interesting that the strongest affirmation of the Bantustan connection came from two officials who had lost their positions. A former Department Secretary spoke of Bantustans in genuine national terms: '. . . if a chap just gets on a train, he is breaking the laws of his country and my country'. A former Chief Commissioner in the Western Cape used a similar idiom: 'Every government has the right to have its borders protected.'

41 F. B. Du Randt, comments before the Institute of Administrators of Community Affairs, Southern Africa, 22nd Biennial Congress, Durban, 29 Oct. 1981, p. 50.

42 The former officials at this level, unlike the present officials, continue to view employers as associated with the problem. The former chief commissioner for the Western Cape describes the squatter problem after the war as an 'employer's paradise'.

43 Wassenaar, *Assault*, pp. 85–7.

44 J. H. T. Mills, dissenting observations, Komitee Insake Wetgewing Betreffende Swart Gemeeskaps-ontwikkeling (Groskopf).

45 *Fidelitas*, Dec. 1982 and March 1983.

46 See Stanley B. Greenberg, 'Constructing state ideology', unpublished.

47 See *Washington Post*, 6 May 1984.

48 SABC, *Current Affairs*, 17 July 1974, 3 Dec. 1975, 11 June 1976, 7 Sept. 1983.

49 See Nigel Bruce, 'Monetary Policy on the Mend', *Energos* (1980).

50 Owen Horwood, opening address to the National Conference of the 1829 Settlers' Monument Foundation, 19 Nov. 1979, pp. 24–5.

51 SABC, March 23, 1984.

52 Horwood, Opening address, p. 3. One should contrast this quotation with the ideological position discussed on pp. 379.

53 The Director of the Urban Foundation made a similar observation.

54 P. W. Botha, opening address, Carlton Centre Conference, p. 10.

55 P. W. Botha, opening address, Carlton Centre Conference, p. 10.

56 Magnus Malan, quoted in Deon Geldenhuys, 'Some foreign policy implications of South Africa's "Total National Strategy", with particular reference to the "12 Point Plan"', The South African Institute for International Affairs, Johannesburg, March, 1981, p. 3.

57 *Rand Daily Mail*, 12 Oct. 1979.

58 Republic of South Africa, *White Paper on Defence* (1977).

59 Human Sciences Research Council, 'Possible national research programmes'. Unpublished Document.

60 P. W. Botha, opening address, p. 11; Horwood, opening address, pp. 19–20.

61 SABC, October 20, 1983.

62 SABC, February 1, 1984.
63 SABC, October 14, 1983.
64 SABC, May 2, 1984.
65 Interview with executive director, business association (anonymous).
66 Botha, opening address, pp. 11–12, 21; see also comments at the Good Hope Conference, pp. 20–1.
67 See the discussion of 'technocratic ideology' in Giliomee, *The Parting of the Ways*, pp. 35–40.

CHAPTER FOURTEEN

The language of domination, 1978–1983*

Deborah Posel

The language of the present South African state[1] has shifted away from
Verwoerdian ideological orthodoxy in some noteworthy ways, some
more sensationalist than others. In 1978 the Prime Minister warned
white South Africans to 'adapt or die'. The Minister of Co-operation
and Development assured an American audience that 'apartheid is
dead' and declared 'war on the dompas'. Since apartheid and influx
control remain conspicuously alive, such rhetoric has little impact on
attempts to legitimise the South African state, except perhaps in some
overseas circles where the pulse of apartheid is faint. The more
significant shifts in legitimatory rationale concern criteria for 'effective
government' which establish new political and ideological priorities.
'Pragmatism' now trumps 'ideological principles'; uncompromising
racial separatism must yield to 'rational reform', including the extension of 'free enterprise'. 'Effective government' entails a 'total
strategy' in defence of 'civilised values', rather than a moral crusade
upholding white supremacy for its own sake.

These catchphrases are not altogether new. Each has its own history
of meaning and usage. What is novel from about 1978 onwards is their
repetition, emphasis and interrelated definition. Previously discrete,
they now exhibit systematic connections in their meaning and
application. To this extent, they can be seen as the rudiments of a new
language[2] in terms of which current state practices are depicted and
defended – or in other words, a new *language of legitimation*. However, the result is not a complete or uncontested ideological shift.
Orthodox ideological symbols coexist with the new, as symptoms of

* This version was written in 1983, which explains why it is written in the present tense
  despite the fact that certain aspects of the discussion are limited to the period being
  examined. Since 1983, there have been further adjustments in some of the ideological
  patterns and political alliances discussed in this chapter.

419

an unresolved struggle within the state over the terms of its legitimation.

This chapter examines the content and role of the new legitimatory language as a form of state control, and its contradictory coexistence with Verwoerdian ideology of old. The argument thus divides into two parts. The first is an analysis of the new language of 'effective government', which looks at why a new legitimatory rationale emerged, and the conditions proscribing its content. The second discusses the relationship between the state's new and old languages of legitimation, and its possible effects on the ideological efficacy of the new legitimatory discourse.

The new language of legitimation

According to the state's proponents of 'reform', it is more important that state policies be 'effective' than that they conform to rigid 'ideological' standards as ends in themselves. The dimensions of such 'effectiveness' are elaborated in three related themes which feature prominently in the state's new legitimatory discourse: technocratic rationality, 'total strategy' and 'free enterprise'. The full meanings of each of these themes is established by its interrelations with the others. This is not to suggest that the users of this language either perceive or manipulate the production of meaning in this fashion. The communication of meaning is rooted in, but supersedes, subjective intention and control. The following discussion therefore focuses on the content of each theme in relation to the others, rather than the discernible intentions of state ideologues.

Habermas[3] alleges that the ideology of late capitalism typically deviates from that of earlier *laissez-faire* variants. While still relatively competitive, capitalism could be legitimated by a liberal individualist ethic. Late capitalist ideology, however, replaces this avowedly normative yardstick of legitimacy with a technocratic, allegedly apolitical one: 'technological rationality'. State practices are depicted as merely technical, instrumentally rational strategies, devoid of substantive political or ideological doctrine.

The new 'reformist' language currently prominent within the South African state upholds such a standard of technocratic rationality, recognisable in two guises: in the call for 'realistic' and 'pragmatic' government, and in the powers assigned to 'experts' in administering 'objective' solutions to 'national' problems.

In terms of the first, the 'effectiveness' of the state is said to derive from its pragmatic response to the *facts* of the country's local and international situation. In the words of the Prime Minister, for example,

> The acceptance of multinationalism, the recognition of minorities, the existence of various cultures, ideas and traditions *is not an ideology, it is a reality. We did not create it, we experience it.* It is a reality we have to take into account.[4]

Apparently therefore, 'multinationalism' (ethnic, political, social segregation) is not a result imposed by National Party (NP) policy; it is asserted as an objective fact. And the logical, self-evident response to this fact is allegedly a policy of segregation. Apartheid thus acquires the full weight of 'reality' behind it, being neither chosen for, nor subject to, 'ideological' (value-laden) considerations.

The process of 'reform' is similarly depicted, as 'necessitated' by the 'economic realities' of the time.[5] Being thus independent of any particular 'ideology', reform is presented as rationally incontestable.

This commitment to 'policies of reality' goes hand in hand with technocratic standards of legitimate decision-making. For, the 'reality' confronting the state is said to be complex, spawning many difficult 'problems' needing 'expert' attention. 'Effective government' involves objective problem-solving, requiring the participation of 'experts' able to contribute the necessary expertise devoid of 'ideological' bias.

Problems of industrial decentralisation and homeland 'development', influx control and urban African housing, for example, are often cast in these terms, as engendered by the 'facts' of economic growth and industrialisation, rather than as the creations and pivots of NP policy. Properly problems of *political* control, they are presented as if merely *technical* ones, the solutions to which can and should be non-'ideological' and therefore non-contestable. Such solutions depend on the findings of economic, academic or military 'experts', rather than on the outcome of partisan[6] and inexpert 'political' debate.[7]

Overall, the effect of this technical discourse is a redefinition of the state's political agenda. Large areas of state control are depoliticised by being depicted in technical terms which disclaim their political contestability. The legitimation of such policies then devolves upon 'proving' their effectiveness, rather than demonstrating their 'democratic' basis.

Another facet of the state's 'effectiveness' is said to be its 'total strategy' against a 'total onslaught' on the country. The notion of a 'total onslaught' seems to have entered the political arena during the early 1970s, propagated by the military, as the rather diffusely conceived threat of 'international communism and its cohorts – leftist activists, exaggerated humanism, permissiveness, materialism and related ideologies'.[8] This theme of a 'total onslaught' against South Africa and its 'civilised values' came to dominate most, if not all quarters of the state after 1978 (although talk of a 'total onslaught' has lessened recently, following the commitment to 'peaceful co-operation' with neighbouring states via agreements such as the Nkomati Accord). Described in the terms of the state's new discourse itself, 'total strategy' is seen as

> the comprehensive plan to utilise all the means available to a state according to an integrated pattern in order to achieve the national aims within the framework of specific policies. A total national strategy is, therefore, not confined to a particular sphere, but is applicable at all levels and to all functions of the state structure.[9]

In short, this 'total strategy' is seen to encompass the whole process of 'effective government'. Not surprisingly therefore, the full meaning of the 'total strategy' theme is constituted partly in relation to the preceding legitimatory theme concerning the technocratic, pragmatic character of 'effective government'. The 'total onslaught' on the country is declared to be a 'fact', and the state's 'total strategy' therefore a rational necessity.[10] Furthermore, the only proper constraints on the scale and content of this 'total strategy' are purported to be 'realism' in the face of the 'facts'. Otherwise the state is said to need a free hand, unfettered by matters of 'ideological' principle, to pursue whichever strategies are deemed 'necessary' by the appropriate 'experts'.

A large part of this 'total strategy' is military. On this front, the two themes of technocratic rationality and 'total strategy' interweave in such a way as to approve a much-enlarged role for senior military personnel in civil government, in their capacity as 'experts' in matters of the 'onslaught', who can be relied upon to deal objectively with the 'necessities' of the strategy in response to it. Indeed, since the idea of a 'total strategy' covers the full range of government policy, civil and military, the symbol can be used to represent any issue as one affecting 'national security' and therefore best dealt with by appealing to military expertise.

The 'total strategy' required for 'effective government' is not wholly military, however. It also encompasses a commitment to 'free enterprise', seen as a means of deflating the appeal of the communist 'onslaught' to South Africa's black population. The meaning of 'free enterprise' in state discourse after 1978 is thus integrally bound up with the idea of 'total strategy', and in turn, with the technocratic standards of 'effective government'. For this reason, the legitimatory theme of 'free enterprise' now espoused by the South African state differs significantly from traditional liberal variants. The latter defended capitalism on ethical grounds, an appeal to individual economic rights and liberties concealing economic and political control of the working class. In the South African case, however, it is the language of technocratic rationality and 'total strategy' that defines and legitimates 'free enterprise': capitalism is depicted and upheld *explicitly as a system of co-optation and control.* 'Free enterprise' is defended on pragmatic, rather than principled grounds, and as an 'effective' part of the state's 'total strategy' against the ubiquitous 'onslaught'. In the words of P. W. Botha,

> We hope to create a middle class among the nations of South Africa. Because, if a man has possessions and is able to build his family life around these possessions, then one has already laid the foundation for resisting Communism. If anyone has something to protect, to keep as his own, then he fights Communism more readily.[11]

The interlocking of the themes of technocratic rationality, 'total onslaught' and 'free enterprise' also serves to justify extensive state intervention in the market, together with explicit business participation in the political arena. Casting 'free enterprise' as part of the state's 'total strategy' allows the state to claim a legitimate vested interest in the regulation of the market according to the said 'realities' and 'problems' of the moment.[12] Likewise, the public political role of capital can be construed as a series of objective, 'expert' interventions in the 'technical' problems surrounding economic growth and industrialisation. These are exactly the grounds on which P. W. Botha has urged the business community to 'play a more active role in helping to solve the development problems in Southern Africa'.[13]

While distinctive in its links with the language of 'effective government' and 'total strategy', the South African state's vocabulary of 'free enterprise' also now reproduces the characteristically liberal confidence in the rationality of the capitalist market, in eroding its political fetters. Once discarded as the language of the liberal opposition, this view is now incorporated into the state's discourse of 'free enterprise' by way of its newly 'pragmatic' and 'realistic' appraisal of the country's problems and needs. Thus state actors allege that it is the 'realities' of capitalist development that have engendered the 'necessity' for political and economic reform.

> Economic forces, more than anything, are increasingly eroding Apartheid.[14]

Why should there have been such marked changes in the legitimatory rationale promulgated within the state from about 1978 onwards?

This question is partly answered[15] by investigating the structural problems confronting the state during the 1970s, which exposed the need for reforms of the sort which would undermine the legitimatory credibility of orthodox Verwoerdian ideology, at the very time when the *process* of legitimating state practice to wider black and white audiences acquired a newly heightened salience in efforts to bolster state control. A new language of legitimation was not simply the ideological reflex of changing structural conditions and ensuing reforms; it became an instrument of control in itself, with alleged strategic priority.

During the 1970s, existing economic and political arrangements were widely perceived to be inadequate for the effective renewal of state control on the one hand, and economic growth on the other.[16] Developments during the decade exposed to the business community and state actors alike that failure to boost the state's capacity to deter militant opposition and address the problems of unemployment and shortage of skills, would jeopardise continued economic growth and political stability. In particular, 'reformist' sectors of the state had begun to concur with industrialists in favouring the so-called 'stabilisation of labour'. For, the interests of each would be served simultaneously by measures which acknowledged and protected the existence of permanent urban African communities, and allotted them relatively privileged residential, educational and employment opportunities, distinct from those of temporary urban residents (allegedly) based in homelands or rural areas. Such measures, it was claimed, would improve urban Africans' access to skills, while simultaneously buttressing economic and political stability by the creation of a relatively affluent urban African population with a 'stake in the system'.

Such strategies of 'reform' however, violated the Verwoerdian blueprint, in terms of which all Africans were to remain 'temporary sojourners' in South Africa, being thus denied permanent residential status, opportunities for higher education and accumulation of capital in the country. The 1970s thus laid the structural ground for the kind of reforms which would discredit the orthodox ideology in terms of which the apartheid state had asserted its legitimacy until then. The credibility of a 'reform' initiative would depend instead on the concomitant promulgation of a new language of legitimation within the state, and this at a time when prominent members of government, business and military circles had come to stress the increased importance of establishing the credibility and legitimacy of the state, among Africans in particular. For, the mounting limitations of the state's near-total reliance on coercion and repression as methods of control over black people had been exposed. In the words of General Malan, then Defence Chief of Staff,

> the lesson (of black 'unrest') is clear . . . we must take into account the aspirations of our population groups. We must gain and keep their trust.[17]

Businessman and then the Prime Minister's economic adviser, Jan Lombard, for example, recognised explicitly that such attempts to renew and diversify state control over the black population would require a new form of state discourse:

> South Africa must 'normalise' the character of its socio-economic regime. . . . If. . . . the maintenance of order requires discriminatory provisions in our legal system, these provisions must be defined in terms of other characteristics correlated to the maintenance of order. To declare or imply that racial differences as such are, in themselves, a threat to political order or socio-economic stability is simply no longer accepted.[18]

While the economic and political conditions of the 1970s account for the structural roots and perceived strategic priority of a new legitimatory rationale for the state, it was the so-called 'Muldergate' scandal of 1978 which facilitated the onset of such a change (albeit incomplete and contradictory). The exposure of corruption in the Department of Information, among others, discredited some (although not all) of the *verkrampte* elements within the state, and sponsored the ascendancy of the 'reformists' under the leadership of the then Minister of Defence, P. W. Botha. More responsive than its predecessor, the Vorster regime, to the pressures for reform from organs of capital and the military, it was this newly aligned state which undertook to address the problems which it had inherited, with a series of 'reforms', and which announced and defended this intention in a new language of legitimation.[19]

Having thus considered how and why a new language of legitimation for the South African state emerged after 1978, it remains for us to assess why these changes in legitimatory rationale took the *particular form* of a discourse of technocratic, pragmatic government, dedicated to the extension of 'free enterprise' as part of its 'total strategy' to bolster its defences.

An answer to this question lies, at least in part, in the functions which the new legitimatory language can play as an instrument of control over the political agenda, and as a means of simultaneously addressing different audiences with discrepant interests. Of course, it is unlikely that this functional potential is fully intended or designed by any individuals or groups. Nor has it been uniformly or consistently utilised. My aim is simply to show how the instrumental political roles which this discourse can play, can account for its relatively sudden and widespread prominence within the state after 1978.

Control over the political agenda

The new language of legitimation defines the agenda of party politics in a way which facilitates and supports the dominant alliance of interests within the South African state after 1978, as well as the manner in which state control has been exercised in this period.

The 1978 realignments within the government allowed for significant changes in the *form* of state control. Thus, power has been highly centralised in select areas of the executive, reducing its answerability to Parliament on the one hand, and the NP rank and file on the other. Executive power has been concentrated in a series of cabinet committees, appointed by and answerable to the Prime Minister alone. As Dan O'Meara points out (and analyses in greater detail),

> the entire principle of Cabinet responsibility has been shifted into the office of the Head of government, dramatically increasing his power.[20]

Furthermore, the Prime Minister's power as leader of the NP has greatly expanded. The role of the party's provincial congresses, once (at least allegedly) policy-making sessions, has been reduced expressly to the evaluation of party 'principle' only.[21]

This noteworthy degree of independence enjoyed by the executive core is bound up with its openly close collaboration with the military. For Botha's reorganisation of the executive and style of government has advanced greatly the interests and role of the military in the arena of civil government. Members of cabinet committees need not be Members of Parliament. Thus many senior military officials have been incorporated into these committees, in their capacity as non-aligned 'experts'. This has led Dan O'Meara, for one, to assert that 'for the first time ... the military [has] a vitally important institutionalised role within the executive'.[22] An article in the South African *Financial Mail* too, reports a claim that 'SADF representatives now take part in all interdepartmental meetings, regardless of whether direct SADF interests are involved'.[23] This interpenetration of civil and military spheres of government has been furthered too, by the enlarged powers of the Department of Military Intelligence, purported to have ousted the Department of National Security.[24] Finally, the National Security Council, established in 1977 to spearhead the state's 'total strategy', is now the main advisory and planning body in the extended propagation of this strategy.[25]

At the same time, the Vorster government's attempt to keep businessmen at arm's length, at least publicly, has been reversed. After 1978, the state and business community consulted openly, having been declared by the Prime Minister to be a 'team'.[26] Public overtures to businessmen to engage in 'continuous consultation'[27] were made through the Carlton Conference of 1979 and the Good Hope Conference of 1981, attended by leading representatives of government and the business community. More significantly, leading business people have been incorporated into cabinet committees as experts on such matters as economic development, industrial decentralisation, labour relations, inflation, etc. Also 'teams' of business and government representatives have been set up to handle such problems as urban African housing, promotion of African business, industrial decentralisation. Businessmen sat on the Viljoen and Steyn Commissions on Housing, many of whose recommendations on ways of easing the urban African housing crisis have been incorporated into state housing policy. Many large corporations have put up substantial sums of money to finance this policy.[28] The Small Business Development Corporation was set up after the Carlton Conference to promote similar 'teamwork' in respect of aid to small businesses, among Africans in particular. The extent of real power exercised by the business community has not yet been researched fully. However, it has (at least) acquired a legitimate public political platform from which to advance its interests.

The state's new language of legitimation affords a control over the political agenda which contributes to and justifies these facets of current state practice in various ways. The present Nationalist government's 'reform' initiative has included strategies which orthodox Verwoerdian policy had forbidden, for example, the registration of African trade unions, declared acceptance of permanent urban African communities and a plan for so-called 'power-sharing' with Coloureds and Indians. Especially in view of the long-standing dissension between Nationalist *verligtes* and *verkramptes*, the Botha regime could not have expected unqualified support for its 'reformist' moves, either within the National Party or the state.[29] It is not surprising, then, that the commitment to 'reform' should have been accompanied by the increased centralisation of decision-making and withdrawal from the arena of party and parliamentary discussion. The terms in which the state's new legitimatory rationale define the scope of popular politics aid and abet this concentration of power in the executive.

All of the reforms instituted or planned are profoundly political, being part of the state's attempt to reorganise the workings of apartheid in ways which reduce its economic and political liabilities. Yet, as we have seen, many of these reforms have been depicted as the objectively inescapable, expert solutions to merely technical problems. This way of *naming* their policies helps the country's leaders to defuse parliamentary or party opposition. Declaring a problem a complex, technical one legitimises handing it over to administrative and planning experts in the sorts of ways mentioned above. Such discourse tacitly disclaims the *relevance* of popular or parliamentary scrutiny or approval, as solutions to such problems become the proper task of technocrats. Furthermore, this discourse can constrict the agenda of NP congresses in particular. We have seen that the powers of these provincial congresses have been cut to the appraisal of matters of 'ideological principle' only, while the state's current technocratic language stresses the 'non-ideological' character of its 'reforms', as being 'policies of reality' rather than principle. This turn of phrase can thus automatically define such issues as beyond the proper preserve of party debate.

In some cases this pre-emption of opposition by way of a depoliti-cised, technicist discourse, was a deliberate strategy on the part of leading reformists within the state. The reform of South Africa's trade-union legislation is an important example. During an interview, Nic Wiehahn (who chaired the government commission which re-commended this reform) stressed that the commissioners had been acutely aware of the importance of the language in which their discussion was cast. Technical, non-emotive terms were expressly used.

> You can't recommend multi-racial unions. It's too emotive . . . so you say 'keep membership open'. . . . You can't speak about freedom, so you call it labour mobility; that's a technical term. When you tell the man in the street about horizontal labour mobility, he won't react.[30]

The legitimation of an elected government as democratic requires at least some measure of demonstrable support for its political principles. In the current South African case, the new language of legitimation prominent in state circles protects the degree of legitimacy which the state enjoys among the (predominantly white) electorate simply by narrowing the arena of its avowed politics.

The state's new legitimatory discourse has also been instrumental in promoting the recent forms of collaboration between the government executive and the military. For, as we have seen, the scope of the state's 'total strategy' is defined sufficiently widely to cover anything which the government or military experts deem a matter of 'national security', thereby allowing the boundary between civil and military issues to blur. The language of 'total strategy' and technocratic 'effectiveness' thus promotes the inclusion of military personnel into civil decision-making processes on the grounds of their ideological neutrality and indispensable expertise in such matters. And the nominal depoliticisation of this involvement exempts such 'experts' from answerability to Parliament or party rank and file.

The language of technocratic rationality has likewise contributed to the political incorporation of leading business people. This language allows the collaboration between the state and organs of capital to be depicted as politically neutral and ideologically indifferent 'teamwork'. Neither the state nor non-Nationalist business could have afforded to enter a public relationship which was not depoliticised in this way. English-speaking business leaders who actively support the opposition political party, the Progressive Federal Party (PFP), would surely have risked their party political credibility by being seen to engage in an openly *political* alliance with the leaders of the NP. The language of technocratic neutrality forestalled this threat; it enabled businessmen to offer spoken and financial support of the state's urban African housing and industrial decentralisation policies, for example, without it appearing to be public support of NP principles. As far as the government is concerned, open political collaboration with English 'big business' has always jeopardised its ideological and political credibility in Afrikaner Nationalist circles which still remember 'Hoggenheimer' (a caricature of the Oppenheimers of the Anglo–American Corporation) as the symbol of the liberal capitalist threat to Afrikaner interests. A purportedly non-ideological language of mutual address has thus been a necessary condition of and instrument in the development of this public relationship.

While the power to label an issue 'technical' enables state actors to *open* it to capitalist intervention, the state also possesses the ideological instrument to *close* or narrow this opening. By declaring a proposal 'political', state actors can thus remove it from the scope of legitimate capitalist participation, and retrieve it for the domain of governmental decision-making alone. Indeed, the language of 'effective government' as a whole ensures that strategies to legitimise the state within capitalist circles need not devolve upon the consistent and unfaltering promotion of capitalist interests. For, this discourse legitimates *whatever* is required for 'effective government' and in whatever measure. Had the alliance between state and capital been defended on ethical/principled grounds instead, then vacillations by the state, in sometimes promoting and sometimes subordinating particular interests of capital, would have appeared as flagrant violations of newly affirmed principles, thereby detracting from these attempts to sustain legitimacy within local and foreign business communities.

Strategies for enlarging consent

Traditionally, acceptance of the South African apartheid system has been confined largely to the exclusively white, predominantly Afrikaans supporters of the NP.[31] The escalation of black militancy during the 1970s, however, had once again exposed the price of a narrow base of popular support. It was shown to have sustained the increasingly vociferous and determined opposition from many quarters: African, Coloured and Indian workers, students and community groups, local and foreign capital, overseas governments. At the same time, existing support from the right wing of the NP could not be guaranteed once the process of 'reform' was initiated.

The 'reform' initiative inaugurated by the state after 1978 seems, therefore, to have included an attempt both to renew and to extend its base of popular consent, by promoting its legitimacy anew and to a wider range of 'audiences' than previously. The Broederbond for example, using the language of 'total strategy', noted that

> in the strategic planning of South Africa, it is accepted that in the defence of the country, only 20% can be achieved by military preparedness; the other 80% depends on spiritual preparedness.[32]

State actors saw that the required legitimation drive should be one which would placate whites, Afrikaners in particular, in the face of changes which would erode certain existing white privileges (e.g. job reservation), and would persuade such audiences that their own interests were still being served. Simultaneously, however, the *same* language of legitimation was to address new audiences, among the African, Coloured and Indian population. The terms of the state's reassurance to whites would have to be suitable for its attempts to win approval from these other groups too. Botha's rhetorical question makes the point bluntly:

> Must I estrange these people, or must I take them with me so that the country's security can be maintained?[33]

The state could never exact such support from among these groups as long as the language used by state actors smacked remotely of racism or betrayed a lingering adherence to Verwoerdian standards of old.

The minimum condition for effectively securing their consent has been a promise of 'reform' which could advance their interests and prospects.

A further audience to which the state's new legitimatory discourse has been directed is 'big business'. Its interests and priorities thus account for a further set of constraints upon the forms which this language, in order to be effective, could have taken. Most representatives of the business community have favoured the sorts of reforms which violate the Verwoerdian orthodoxy, for example, the registration of African trade unions, recognition of a permanent urban African population and the extension of its economic and educational opportunities. Industrial and commercial organisations have urged vociferously that the state pursue what they consider to be the more 'rational' ways of organising the country's economy and polity. For them too, therefore, it was a language of 'rational' and 'pragmatic reform' which could best make the state's case for its legitimacy. In addition, in order for the public collaboration between organs of the state and capital in pursuit of these reforms, to remain publicly legitimate, state actors required a language which could address this audience *qua* the business community alone. As we have seen, unless the terms of their mutual address sidestepped or disclaimed issues of party politics and ideological principle, the party political standing of both Nationalist and many capitalist 'team' members would have suffered, and their public relationship would have been exposed as a sign of political collaboration.

Clearly, therefore, the prospective legitimation of the state's reforms to all of these audiences simultaneously (the white electorate; African, Coloured and Indian; capitalist) presupposed a language which *spoke of 'reform' at the same time as avoiding or repressing 'ideological' issues altogether*. References to recognisably political and ideological norms would become embarrassing to each. Also, any language of 'ideological' principle, *irrespective* of its particular content, would inevitably have failed to achieve legitimatory success among Nationalists, and African, Coloured and Indian audiences simultaneously. For, if the principles in question were clearly congruent with the Verwoerdian legacy, so as to appease Nationalists, the newly courted African, Coloured and Indian audiences would have been alienated once more. To win their support on grounds of ideological principle would have required the endorsement of an altogether non-discriminatory ethic, at least, which is guaranteed to provoke widespread Nationalist disaffection. In short, therefore, a key factor affecting the state's pursuit of enhanced support has been the ability to promise 'reform' without pinning it to a particular ethical or 'ideological' stance.

We saw how and why, during the 1970s, the extended legitimation of the state was perceived increasingly as a strategic priority. We can now recognise the ways in which the language of technocratic rationality, 'total strategy' and 'free enterprise', is well suited to the task. For, its overall effect is precisely to *repress* issues of 'ideological' principle, by declaring them extraneous to the 'business of purposive reform'.[34] The extension of 'free enterprise' is defended on grounds of expediency rather than principle, and likewise, the yardstick of successful 'reform' is pragmatic rather than ethical. In so far as Africans, Coloureds, Indians and whites all confront the same 'realities', state actors can claim that 'reformist policies of reality' serve all their interests simultaneously.

The language of 'pragmatic reform' has thus given many Coloured and Indian leaders a vocabulary in terms of which to announce their participation in the new tricameral Parliament, for example. They have accepted the constitutional changes on pragmatic grounds, as the best available under present circumstances, so that participation is held to be the most rational course available to their communities at present. As far as the business community is concerned, the state has wooed its support by speaking the same language as liberal industrialists, in terms of which 'economic realities' ineluctably erode racial restrictions and necessitate 'rational' reform.

So far, we have seen that the specific content of the new legitimatory rationale prominent in the South African state after 1978 can be accounted for in part by its contribution to present state practice. On the one hand, the new discourse facilitates and protects the dominant alliance of interests within the state after 1978, and on the other hand, its aprincipled vocabulary is the minimum condition for attempts to legitimise 'reform' to different audiences with conflicting interests, simultaneously.

The production and use of this new discourse was not simply a well-devised and carefully orchestrated conspiracy on the part of shrewd state ideologues, however. Adam and Giliomee point out correctly that

> to conceive of an ideology as being consciously invented by a braintrust or some other conspiracy would be misleading. A legitimating rationale gradually emerges through repetition and refinement by opinionmakers. A new formula 'catches on' while older interpretations fade out because it better reflects the changing needs of its adherents.[35]

My argument imputes neither complete control nor conspiratorial intent to the proponents of the new legitimatory language (although there is clearly a degree of deliberation and calculation in evidence, on the part of some state actors at least). Rather, certain themes and sets of symbols, each present within state discourse before 1978, came together as a single 'formula' after 1978, a formula which 'caught on' because it reflected some of the changing needs and interests of the dominant alliance within the state.

The contradictions in state discourse

On its own, the picture gained so far, of apparently efficacious legitimatory discourse used within the South African state after 1978, would be misleading. It should be completed by a look at some of the ambiguities and contradictions which have pervaded state discourse as a whole during this period. Spotlighted by recent stormy conflicts within Afrikaner ranks, these ambiguities and contradictions have precipitated intra-Afrikaner struggles which have been drawn on to an unmistakably *ideological* terrain. As we shall see, this has affected significantly the role and impact of the state's new reformist language in various quarters.

The Verwoerdian ideology of apartheid[36] had embodied an *ethical* defence of separate development, as the inviolable right of each ethnic group. Whites, led politically by Afrikaners, were said to bear a moral obligation to bestow and preserve this right on the part of Indians, Coloureds and the various African ethnic groupings. Apartheid was thus vaunted as the only moral Christian course for South African politics. The right of whites to national self-determination (manifest historically as white economic and political supremacy) was God-given, and any move towards political or social integration with other ethnic groups was morally indefensible.

The ideology of apartheid was historically and conceptually bound up with that of Afrikaner nationalism. Afrikaners were depicted as the rightful purveyors of the white man's moral and political mission. In claiming this moral prerogative of undiluted power, the Afrikaner *volk* legitimated its drive towards national unity and ascendancy which would enable it to win and exercise such power. Thus Afrikaner nationalism was made a political issue, and the politics of apartheid an Afrikaner nationalist crusade.[37]

The legitimatory rationale which emerged within the state and the NP after 1978 contravenes this ideological orthodoxy in many ways, as we have seen. Yet, throughout this period, strands of the old discourse of apartheid have run alongside the new. Especially in front of Afrikaans and National Party audiences, stress is still laid on the Nationalists' 'ideological' integrity, measured by allegiance to sacrosanct principles inherited from Hertzog in the 1930s, and upheld by Verwoerd and Vorster. The lack-lustre standards of pragmatic realism and 'purposive reform' recede when the present government is praised for keeping to

> the golden road of General Hertzog, Dr Malan, Mr Strijdom, Dr Verwoerd, Dr Vorster.[38]

Here, the state claims legitimacy on the grounds of the continuity with the past, rather than its preparedness to change, and by adherence to principles valued for their own sake, rather than to standards of pragmatism and adaptability.

Considered in its entirety therefore, the discourse of the South African state currently upholds contradictory standards of legitimacy. On the one hand, 'fundamental change is what it's all about',[39] since the NP has finally looked 'reality' in the face. Yet, on the other hand, 'the National Party's Programme of Principles has remained unchanged, in essence, since 1935'.[40]

The status of the Afrikaner *volk* in this discourse is likewise contradictory. In the language of pragmatic rather than principled government, the *volk* warrants no special privilege or rank over and above that of the white population generally. No longer the sacred preserve of the Afrikaners, government is now said to involve 'teamwork' with both English- and Afrikaans-speaking 'experts'. Hence P. W. Botha's warning that

> people should not become so emotional about 'Afrikaner unity' that they lost touch with reality.[41]

Yet, placed on the defensive by attacks from the Afrikaner right wing, NP and state ideologues have become intensely 'emotional' about just this issue, being intent on reaffirming their Afrikaner nationalist credentials.[42]

The persistence of these contradictions seems to be explained by certain inherent characteristics of the new legitimatory discourse itself, together with the present political conjuncture which brings the ideological limitations of this discourse to the fore.

The first section of this chapter discussed how the conditions of the legitimatory functions of the language of 'reform' account for its silence on matters of 'ideology'. Indeed, the state's reforms were upheld expressly for their immunity from 'ideological' bias enabling the 'objectivity' appropriate to 'policies of reality'. The state's language of 'reform' then, has *nothing to say* about matters of 'ideological' principle if and when they *do* arise. For this reason, therefore, the state's new legitimatory rationale could never completely *substitute* for the old ideology of apartheid and Afrikaner nationalism; the two address different sorts of issues. At best, the language of 'reform' could gain a greater currency and audience than the pre-existing ideology, edging it off the centre stage of state discourse. But still, the latter would persist, because the suppression of 'ideological' debate by the new discourse involuntarily renews the role of the old ideology. For, as long as issues concerning the ethics of apartheid and status of the *volk are* raised and debated, Verwoerdian ideology will retain its currency, since new reformist discourse cannot substitute new answers to these questions.

Conflicts within Afrikaner ranks after 1978 have revolved around *exactly* such ethical and 'ideological' issues, the status of Afrikaner nationalism in particular. For example, the Conservative Party, formed in March 1982 and commanding a significant degree of electoral support among Afrikaners, has strenuously defined the issue dividing it from the NP in 'ideological' terms: the Nationalists are accused of betraying the principles of apartheid and the integrity of the *volk*.

> A party once described by Dr Malan as the 'political national front of the Afrikaner' is now visibly associating with the traditional enemy of the Afrikaner, namely Hoggenheimer, to form a relationship against fellow Afrikaners. Such a relationship can destroy the ways of the Afrikaner *volk*.[43]

At its public meetings, the Conservative Party keeps 'ideological' issues at the top of the agenda, and traditional symbols of Afrikaner nationalism (raising the flag of the old Afrikaner republic, for example) feature prominently.

Similar conflicts have swept through a range of Afrikaner institutions, with rare public virulence and openness. The Afrikaans newspaper *Rapport* called 1982 'the year of the Afrikaner ... and especially at conference time when the Afrikaner's identity [was] ... laid out on the dissection table'.[44] During this year, the Federasie van Afrikaanse Kultuurvereenigings, the Afrikaanse Student Bond (ASB) and the Broederbond were preoccupied with questions concerning Afrikaner identity.[45] The Dutch Reformed Church faced dissension in its ranks over the ethical status of apartheid. Afrikaans teachers clashed over the question of mixed sport in schools – an issue about the proper limits of segregation.[46]

Despite the fact that its new legitimatory rationale dismisses issues of moral and 'ideological' principle as irrelevant to the 'business of purposive reform', the vehemence and spread of this *broedertwis* has forced the state's 'reformists' to enter such debates. For, the maintenance of Afrikaner electoral support has required that government leaders declare their stand on such issues as the ethical foundations of apartheid and the place of Afrikaner nationalism within the polity. On such occasions, state discourse has thus re-entered the 'ideological' terrain which the language of 'reform' had circumvented. And the position taken on such occasions coincides with the ideology of old. For, refusing to jettison the support of more conservative Nationalists, government leaders have refused to adopt a more liberal ethic, reiterating instead the principles of separate development as the only 'right' and 'just' ones.

The issue of constitutional reform is a clear and important illustration of this process. Government leaders mooted their plans for the 'sharing of power' between whites, Indians and Coloureds, in the language of pragmatic reform, as part of the 'national strategy for stability and survival'.[47] (It is in similar terms too, that many Indian and Coloured leaders have explained and justified their incorporation into the new tricameral Parliament.) But the issue of 'power-sharing' was thrust to the top of the 'ideological' agenda of white politics by immediate virulent right-wing opposition to the proposals, on grounds of principle. Indeed, it was this issue which provided the final trigger for the split within the NP and which has continued to fuel its conflict with the Conservative Party. During such debates, National Party (and therefore government) leaders engage the issue as an 'ideological' one, and reaffirm their ongoing allegiance to the principles, as opposed to the methods, of the past.[48]

Arguably, this contradictory return to a defence of constitutional reform on grounds of 'ideological' continuity, functions well to protect the technocratic, 'non-ideological' language of reform in other areas. The vehement politicisation of this constitutional issue has moved it to the centre-stage of white political and ideological debate in the country. White public opinion has been concentrated on this one issue, as if it embodies the very crux of 'reform' as a whole. This depiction of, and preoccupation with, the 'power-sharing' proposals as *the* fundamental reform, promotes the depoliticisation of other 're-forms' which are arguably of equal or greater political import (for example, those concerning African trade unions, or African housing policy).

The dynamics of white politics during the recent period have thus reproduced the contradictions within the state's legitimatory discourse. Power struggles within Afrikaner ranks have taken on an intensely 'ideological' form; the battle-lines have been drawn in such a way as to force the reformist bloc on to old ideological ground. If the new discourse of 'effective government' fulfils certain 'needs' on the part of the state, so too do the persistent remnants of the Verwoerdian ideology violated by the practice of some of these reforms. At the same time, the prominence of these conflicts concerning constitutional 're-form' helps deflect the 'ideological' spotlight from other areas of state practice in which the new discourse of 'effective government' can maintain its hold.

However, the persistence of old ideological symbols and themes which contradict the new, cannot be fully accounted for in this in-strumentalist fashion. Certainly, ideologies acquire a complex momentum of their own, so that they are not readily replaceable or changeable simply according to economic or political 'need'. Thus, for example, the resistance on the part of many white South Africans to moves to scrap the Immorality and Mixed Marriages Acts testifies to the way in which racist ideology has been internalised and reproduced in whites' perceptions of their personal and sexual identities.[49]

This is the measure of truth in the state's new language of political 'realism' (albeit for different reasons from those proferred by the discourse itself): for most white South Africans, having internalised an ideology of apartheid, 'multinationalism', segregation, etc. *do* have the status of 'realities'. For it is these ideological categories which have contributed to the meaning of their experience – social, political, economic and cultural.

This leads finally to the structural factor which accounts for the persistence of the contradictions in state discourse, namely, the in-herent *ideological* limitations of the state's new discourse of 'effective government', which seem to mitigate against the possibility of it ever being able to develop into a fully-fledged, wide-ranging ideology on its own. Thus, even if Afrikaner political conflicts were to abate, the language of technocratic reform could not *of itself* constitute an effective ideology.

In order to make this point, the concept of 'ideology' should be defined and discussed in brief, so that the difference between an ideology and a mere language of legitimation can be made clear, together with the pertinence of the distinction for the present dis-cussion.

According to Max Weber,

> organized domination requires that human conduct be conditioned to obedience towards those masters who claim to be the bearers of legitimate power.[50]

Weber ascribed too little to the role of coercion in 'organised domination' – an omission especially conspicuous in the South African case. But his comment is useful in enabling us to locate 'ideology' as one of the means whereby this 'conditioning of conduct' occurs, which Goran Therborn has called the 'constitution of subjectivity'.[51] This approach leads us into a two-part conception of the nature of 'ideology'. Firstly, an ideology embodies a set of ideas, symbols and practices, which depict the social/economic/political order as legitimate and thus worthy of popular consent.[52] Secondly, an ideology must be effectively persuasive, to some degree and among one audience at least. There seems to be little point in calling, say, a set of ideas offering some newfangled defence of monetarism which no one believes, an ideology; it is simply a set of ideas. In order to discard such cases from the scope of the concept, let us therefore stipulate that a set of ideas, symbols, etc. qualifies as an 'ideology' when it persuades members of at least one audience that the system depicted best promotes their interests, as individuals or groups, and that it is right and justified in doing so.

This persuasive capacity depends upon the degree to which the ideas, images, symbols in question are internalised and reproduced as part of these individuals' own way of thinking and experience. In other words, ideologies are vehicles for the constitution of subjectivity, albeit to varying degrees (depending on the form and content of the ideas and images in question). Ideologies furnish a vocabulary in terms of which an individual construes his or her identity and place in society, its meaning and order. The identity of the subject is thus addressed in (some or all of) its manifold dimensions – social, psychological, political, cultural, economic – so as to depict and 'create' a meaningful world of subjectivity and intersubjectivity.[53]

An ideology and language of legitimation thus differ in the following way. An ideology includes, but is not exhausted by, a language of legitimation. The latter becomes an ideology once it is effectively persuasive, and internalised into the experience and subjectivity of at least one audience. Studies which fail to make this conceptual distinction take for granted, and gloss over, the conditions whereby a legitimatory language can come to contribute to the constitution of subjectivity. Ideologies are thus treated as if uniformly and wholly effective. This chapter, on the other hand, has left this process open to question. It has referred thus far to the South African state's new legitimatory rationale as a language of legitimation only, since the extent to which it can fulfil an ideological function has not yet been considered in the course of the argument.

The Verwoerdian discourse of apartheid can be conceived as an ideology (as I have done throughout this chapter) since it embodies a set of (Christian Nationalist) principles and standards according to which the moral and social meaning of apartheid policies was interpreted and justified, and the identity of white subjects was constituted. Political, economic, social, cultural and sexual segregation were cast as divinely ordained, historically vindicated and the foundation of a just and harmonious society. 'Being white' meant being socially and culturally distinct, politically and economically privileged and physically segregated from all those who were not. Apartheid ideology has thus had the resources to function as a vehicle for the constitution of subjectivity, producing (in part, of course) 'white' individual subjects who interpreted their world and their place in it according to this ethic of segregation.

The state's new language of legitimation makes a narrow and secondary contribution, if any, to subjectivity itself. The ideas and symbols of 'total strategy', 'total onslaught', 'free enterprise' and 'reform' can inform individuals' constructions of the political and economic 'realities' in which they are implicated, and offer new definitions of 'goodies' and 'baddies'. But this conceptual grid remains parasitic upon the more pervasive and wide-ranging categories of Verwoerdian ideology. The new language of legitimation does not displace or substitute new ideological categories which define 'being white' or 'being black', 'being Afrikaans' or 'being English'. On the contrary, as we have seen, the new legitimato-y discourse works to banish issues of moral, social, religious identity and 'ideological' principle, and thus to a large extent sets itself *apart* from the systems of significance in terms of which individuals (black and white, Afrikaans- and English-speaking) interpret their subjective and intersubjective 'reality'. It thus fails to reshape or reconstitute the identity of those individuals who have internalised Verwoerdian values and meaning, and it has little to offer to the constitution of subjectivity among its new black audiences. To this extent therefore, the ideological potential of the state's new legitimatory discourse seems inherently limited. Hence, too, the limits of the alternatives to coercive or repressive control in the maintenance of 'organised domination' by the present 'reformist' state.

One or all of three basic questions have oriented those social scientists and theorists who have undertaken studies of ideology and legitimation in general terms: the relationship between an ideology (including a language of legitimation) and dominant sectional interests within the state, class interests in particular; the extent to which an ideology can be knowingly and deliberately produced or changed by social actors, and correlatively, the extent to which it is itself an objective structural phenomenon which precedes and shapes social action; and finally, the effects which an ideology (and language of legitimation) has on its audiences.

This discussion of state discourse and legitimation in South Africa after 1978, contains implicit answers to each of these general questions, in a way which also illustrates the limits of any wholly general, all-embracing theory on the subject. Thus, the paper suggests a close, but not exhaustive connection between the content and function of the state's new legitimatory discourse, and the sectional interests dominant within it (namely, those of the 'reformist' Nationalists, the military and sections of the business community, notably 'big business'). The relationship has taken the form of an explicit 'strategic' alliance, which has given industrialists and other businessmen a political platform but without necessarily reducing the state's degree of autonomy in this relationship. While the technocratic language of reform legitimates and furthers the state's active and open promotion of capitalist interests, it also functions as an instrument of control in the hands of state actors in this alliance. This degree of independence on the part of the state both allows for and reflects the role of other forces and interests in shaping state discourse and its effects. The dominant alliance between *verligtes*, military and various organs of capital, has not altogether supplanted government pursuit of Afrikaner support mobilised on ethnic grounds. The current language of state discourse thus also evidences attempts to sustain legitimacy in these quarters.

The explanation given in this chapter of the emergence and operation of the new legitimatory language has exposed a significant degree of instrumentalism in its production and use, this language having been perceived and pursued as a means of co-option and control. We have been dealing with a period which thus shows a high degree of deliberate and instrumental legitimatory 'work' on the part of state actors and ideologues.

The chapter has also exposed the objective limits of this legitimatory strategy and thus, too, the limits of an analysis of it in instrumentalist terms. Structural problems which had deepened considerably during the 1970s and which the present state inherited, set the conditions which any effective legitimation strategy would have had to take account of and address. Immediate political factors, too, set constraints upon the process of legitimation, and shaped the content of state discourse as a whole. Dialogue with its Afrikaner audiences took state discourse onto an expressly 'ideological' terrain in a way which both contributed to and underlined its internal contradictions. That old and new legitimatory themes and symbols persist, in this contradictory fashion, attests to both the structural and situational limits on the production and revision of the state's terms of legitimation.

The mutually contradictory strands of state discourse are likely to have different effects on their audience. Indeed, the persistence of the state's earlier ideological vocabulary seems allied to the limited capacity of the new legitimatory language to 'produce' a meaningful world of subjectivity and intersubjectivity. Being unable wholly to substitute for the old ideology in the performance of this function, it coexists with the old.

The explanations in answer to each of the three broad questions addressed by general theories of ideology have drawn on factors pertaining to the specific historic juncture in question. These have affected the process of legitimation in integral ways, which could not have been simply read off from any supposedly complete general theory. A general theoretical perspective and set of categories is necessary to locate and define the object of our inquiry, and informs the analysis of it. But the explanations thus produced will also be inescapably concrete.

Notes and references

1 I take the concept of 'the state' to refer to the locus of political power, which we can identify empirically as a set of administrative, judicial, military and repressive institutions. This is a minimal definition which is readily operationalised. It leaves important questions about the relationship between the state and dominant class/class alliance *open* to inquiry, as opposed to fixing it *a priori* as part of the very definition of the concept. For it is a bad definition which substitutes for the work of explanation.

2 Semioticians have argued that the basis of any first- or second-order language is a grammar, i.e. a system of rules of signification which define the meaning of individual signs (units of meaning) according to their relation to other signs in the same system. Note that the signs in the new legitimatory language under discussion are second-order, i.e. they are words which have a pre-existing ordinary language (first-order) meaning,

but which acquire an additional second-order meaning by virtue of their relations to others in the same second-order system.

3 J. Habermas, *Towards a Rational Society* (London 1972) Ch. 6.

4 *Nat '80s*, a National Party Publication, April 1981 (my emphasis).

5 See for example, the *1981 National Party Election Manifesto*.

6 The Nationalist government thus supports what it calls 'consensual politics', the meaning of which derives from this sort of constriction of the range of popular politics. The merit of 'consensual politics' is said to be its bypassing of debate about principles, sterile because different parties to such debate would take conflicting 'political' stances. Public attention is urged to focus on 'practical' questions of how best to implement government policies accepted as 'necessary' (*Sunday Express*, 1 Aug. 1982).

7 *Rapport* 29 May 1983; reported in *South African Digest*, 3 June 1983.

8 *White Paper on Defence and Armaments Production* (Pretoria 1973) p. 1.

9 *White Paper on Defence* (Pretoria 1977) p. 5.

10 See for example, *South African Digest*, 27 May 1985, p. 4.

11 *Nat '80s*, April 1981, p. 8.

12 *Dynamic Change in South Africa* (Dept. of Foreign Affairs and Information, Pretoria 1980) p. 20. Also, *South African Digest*, 2 April 1982.

13 *The Good Hope Plan for Southern Africa*, p. 28.

14 *South Africa: Target or opportunity?* (Dept. of Foreign Affairs and Information, Pretoria 1980)

15 A structural analysis exposes necessary but not sufficient conditions of a legitimatory practice (in this case). A full explanation would include an account of conjunctural factors too, and the intentions and actions of particular actors.

16 Economic and political features of this decade are discussed in chapters 1 and 7 in this volume, which I have taken as read for the purposes of this paper. Otherwise see D. Posel, 'Language, legitimation and control: the South African state after 1978', presented to the XIth International Congress of Anthropological and Ethnological Sciences, Vancouver, Aug. 1983, pp. 8 and 24.

17 *Rand Daily Mail*, 13 June 1979.

18 J. Lombard, 'The economic aspects of security', in M. H. H. Louw (ed.), *National Security: A modern approach* (Institute of Strategic Studies, Pretoria, 1978) p. 19.

19 D. O'Meara, *Volkskapitalisme. Class, capital and ideology in the development of Afrikaner nationalism* (Cambridge 1983) last chapter.

20 D. O'Meara, 'From "Muldergate" to total strategy. The politics of Afrikaner nationalism and the crisis of the capitalist state in South Africa', unpublished paper, Maputo, 1983, p. 37. An earlier draft under a different title was published in *Work in Progress*, 22, 1983.

21 *Ibid.*, p. 37.

22 *Ibid.*, p. 39.

23 Quoted in *Facts and Reports* (press cuttings on Southern Africa) vol. 12, 14 May 1982, edited by the Holland Committee on Southern Africa.

24 G. Moss, 'Total strategy', *Work in Progress*, 11, 1980, p. 9.

25 *Ibid.*, p. 10.

26 *The Good Hope Plan*, p. 24.

27 *Ibid.*, p. 14.
28 For example, Sanlam Insurance Company provided R15 million towards Coloured housing in the Western Cape (*Sunday Times*, 3 Oct. 1982); the Anglo-American Corporation has contributed substantially towards urban African housing. Standard Building Society has put up R1.5 million for Africna housing in Mamelodi near Pretoria (*South African Digest* 4 March 1983, p. 8).
29 See O'Meara, *Volkskapitalisme*, for more detail on the *verligte – verkrampte* conflicts.
30 Interview with Nic Wiehahn, 1 Aug. 1984.
31 Note that popular consent to the capitalist system but *not* apartheid is a separate question and is not explored in this chapter.
32 'Masterplan for a white country: the strategy', a Broederbond secret document quoted in I. Wilkins and H. Strydom, *The Superafrikaners* (London 1980) p. 280.
33 *South African Digest*, 21 May 1982.
34 *Rand Daily Mail*, 27 March 1982, quoting Prof. Gerrit Olivier's address to the Conference of the Manpower and Management Foundation of South Africa.
35 H. Adam and H. Giliomee, *Ethnic Power Mobilized* (New Haven 1979) p. 133.
36 This discussion of Verwoerdian philosophy is cursory and does not take into account its historical mutations and gradations. The focus is on its general features which have persisted. See Adam and Giliomee, *Ethnic Power Mobilized*, ch. 4 for more detail.
37 *Ibid.*, Ch. 4.
38 *Die Beeld*, 16 March 1982.
41 *South African Digest*, 19 March 1982.
42 See editorial of *Die Transvaaler*, 6 June 1982.
43 *Die Patriot*, 23 July 1982.
44 *Rapport*, 18 July 1982.
45 *Daily News* 19 July 1982.
46 *Ibid.*
47 *Dynamic Change in South Africa*, p. 14.
48 *Rapport*, 22 Aug. 1982.
49 When Botha became Prime Minister he announced a 'Twelve Point Plan' for reform, which included the 'abolition of unnecessary and hurtful discrimination', including these two Acts. However, a right-wing outcry followed and the matter was dropped. It has now surfaced again and Botha has offered to appoint a commission of enquiry into the matter.
50 M. Weber, 'Politics as a Vocation', quoted in H. H. Gerth and C. Wright Mills (eds.) *From Max Weber* (London 1977) p. 80.
51 G. Therborn, *The Power of Ideology and the Ideology of Power* (London 1971) p. 2.
52 This applies to both ideologies of the status quo and ideologies of change, such as revolutionary ideologies. In the latter case, the social order legitimated is a future one, to be striven for.
53 For a more detailed, general discussion of such processes, see, for example, Therborn, *Power of Ideology*.

Notes on contributors

William Beinart: Lecturer in African History at the University of Bristol, William Beinart's major publications have been on rural history in South Africa: *The Political Economy of Pondoland 1860–1930* (1982); *Putting a Plough to the Ground* (1986) with Peter Delius and Stanley Trapido; and *Hidden Struggles in Rural South Africa* (1986) with Colin Bundy.

Iris Berger: Dr Berger teaches History and African and Afro-American Studies at the State University of New York at Albany. Her publications include *Religion and Resistance: East African Kingdoms in the Pre-colonial Period* and *Women and Class in Africa* (co-edited with Claire Robertson). She is currently at work on a book on women industrial workers and trade unionists in South Africa.

Philip Bonner: Associate Professor at the Department of History, University of the Witwatersrand, Philip Bonner has written on nineteenth-century Swaziland and the Transvaal, including *Kings, Commoners and Concessionaires* (Cambridge University Press 1982). He has also worked on labour history and current labour relations and is an editor of the *South African Labour Bulletin* and *African Studies*.

Colin Bundy: Professor of History at the University of Cape Town, Colin Bundy studied at Pietermaritzburg, Johannesburg and Oxford. He has taught history and politics in South Africa, Britain and the United States, and his publications include *Rise and Fall of the South African Peasantry* and (with William Beinart) *Hidden Struggles in Rural South Africa*.

Saul Dubow: A graduate in History of the University of Cape Town, Saul Dubow is currently a doctoral student at St Antony's College, Oxford. His thesis analyses the development of segregationist ideology and 'native administration' in South Africa during the inter-war years.

Ian Goldin: Since completion of his doctorate at Oxford University, Ian Goldin has worked as a development economist. Whilst at Oxford he was an economics tutor at St Peter's College and worked as an economic consultant to various international organisations. Among his forthcoming publications is a book to be published by Longman on coloured identity, race and class in South Africa.

Stanley Greenberg: Associate Director of the Southern African Research Programme at Yale University, Stanley Greenberg's principal works include *Politics and Poverty* (1974) on racial politics in America's poor communities, *Race and State in Capitalist Development* (1980) on the impact of industrial development on patterns of racial domination, and *Legitimating the Illegitimate* (forthcoming) on the breakdown of state control in South Africa.

Brian Hackland: After completing his thesis, Dr Hackland organised an international conference on 100 years of colonialism in Namibia before taking up his present post in the House of Commons as a researcher on Northern Ireland. He has written on Namibia and South Africa and is currently co-authoring a dictionary of contemporary southern African politics.

Robert A. Hill: A Jamaican, Robert Hill is currently Associate Professor in the Department of History, University of California, Los Angeles. He is also the Editor-in-Chief of the Marcus Garvey Papers Project, which forms part of UCLA's African Studies Center. To date, five of the projected ten volumes have been published.

Isabel Hofmeyr: A graduate of the University of the Witwatersrand where she lectures in African Literature, Isabel Hofmeyr's article comes from work undertaken at the School of Oriental and African Studies. She has published on South African literature and culture.

Bob Lambert: Robert Lambert is Senior Lecturer in the Department of Sociology at the University of Natal, Durban. His doctoral thesis is on the South African Congress of Trade Unions.

Tom Lodge: Senior Lecturer in Politics at the University of the Witwatersrand, Dr Lodge has researched and written extensively on the history of black South African political organisations. His book, *Black Politics in South Africa since 1945*, was published by Longman in 1983. He is currently working on a history of the South African Communist Party.

Gregory A. Pirio: Currently director of the Portugese-to-African Service of the Voice of America, Dr Pirio was for several years Senior Editor of the African Series of the Marcus Garvey Papers at the University of California, Los Angeles. He has written on black seamen in the British merchant marine, black American settlement in Brazil and pan-africanism in Portugese-speaking Africa.

Deborah Posel: Currently a Junior Research Fellow at Nuffield College, Oxford, Deborah Posel's doctoral thesis examines state policy on African urbanisation during the 1950s. She has lectured in political science at the University of the Witwatersrand and has written on race, class and the state in South Africa, and on power, semiotics and structualism.

Maureen Swan: A lecturer in Economic History at the University of Cape Town, Maureen Swan is author of *Ghandi: the South African Experience*, based on her Oxford D. Phil.. She has been a research fellow at the University of the Witwatersrand, and has lectured at the University of Calgary.

Index

448